RANDOM HOUSE

LARGE PRINT

The End and the Beginning

John Paul II in Częstochowa, June 1983.
(L'Osservatore Romano)

The END *and the* BEGINNING

Pope John Paul II —
The Victory of Freedom,
the Last Years, the Legacy

George Weigel

RANDOM HOUSE
LARGE PRINT

Published in the United States of America by
Random House Large Print in association with
Doubleday, New York.
Distributed by Random House, Inc., New York.

Jacket design: Laura Duffy
Jacket photograph: associated press

The Library of Congress has established a
Cataloging-in-Publication record for this title.

ISBN: 978-0-7393-7761-1

www.randomhouse.com/largeprint

FIRST LARGE PRINT EDITION

Printed in the United States of America

10 9 8 7 6 5 4 3 2 1

This Large Print edition published in accord with
the standards of the N.A.V.H.

In Memoriam

Robert Charles Susil
1974–2010

CONTENTS

PART TWO

KENOSIS
The Last Years of Pope John Paul II
2000–2005

Chapter Eleven
The Measure of a Pontificate

A surprising preparation • An unprecedented
record • Ten enduring accomplishments • Questions of
context • What didn't go right • The Christian radical
and the new humanism

745

A BRIEF NOTE ON PRONUNCIATION

Polish pronunciation, which can seem daunting, is in fact far more regular than English. The native English speaker, having learned the invariable rules of Polish pronunciation, will have an easier time of it with Białystok, Jasna Góra, and Wadowice than a native Polish speaker—or "American" speaker—trying to figure out Gloucester, Leicester, Slough, Worcester, and so forth.

The following rules and examples should be helpful.

The letters ą and ę are pronounced as a nasal **aw** and **en** in English.

C is pronounced as **ts** in English.

Ch is pronounced as a hard **h** in the Scottish "loch."

Cz is pronounced as **ch** in "church."

Dz is pronounced as **j** in "jeans."

I is pronounced as **ee** in English.

J is pronounced as **Y** in English.

Ł and **ł** are pronounced as **W** in English.

Ó and **ó** are pronounced as "oo" in the English "cool."

Ś is pronounced as **s** in the English "sure."

Sz is pronounced as the English **sh.**

W is pronounced as **V** in English.

Y is pronounced as a **y** in the English "myth."

The accent in Polish is almost always on the second-to-last syllable.

Thus . . .

Częstochowa is pronounced **Chens-toe-HOE-vah.**

Dziwisz is pronounced **JEE-vish.**

Kraków is pronounced **KRA-koov.**

Malecki is pronounced **Mah-LETS-kee.**

Rybicki is pronounced **Rih-BEETS-kee.**

Stanisław is pronounced **Stan-IS-wahv**.

Środowisko is pronounced **Shroe-doe-VEES-koe.**

Wałęsa is pronounced **Vah-WHEN-sah.**

Wawel is pronounced **VAH-vel.**

Wojtyła is pronounced **Voy-TEE-wah.**

Wujek is pronounced **VOO-yek.**

Wyszyński is pronounced **Vih-SHIN-skee**.

The surnames of married men and women are masculine and feminine, thus "Piotr Malecki" and "Teresa Malecka." These have been retained, but for the sake of simplicity the masculine plural form ("the Maleckis") is used when referring to couples together rather than the Polish plural, which in this instance would be "the Maleccy."

The Millennial Pope

As March gave way to April in the spring of 2005 and the world kept vigil outside the apostolic palace in Rome, the pontificate of Pope John Paul II, then drawing to a poignant end, was already being described as one of the most consequential in two millennia of Christian history.

Eight months after his election to the papacy on October 16, 1978, John Paul had ignited a revolution of conscience in his native Poland—a moral challenge to the Cold War status quo that helped set in motion the international drama that would culminate in the collapse of European communism in 1989 and the demise of the Soviet Union in 1991. The Millennial Pope's impact on the world was not limited to his native region, however. Over the first two decades of the pontificate, John Paul also played important roles in democratic transitions in venues ranging from Central and South America to East Asia, even as he established himself as a universal moral witness to the dignity of the human person and the world's principal exponent of the universality of human rights. As he neared the end of his earthly pilgrimage, John Paul II—of whom the world knew very little at the beginning of his papacy— had become the singular embodiment of the trials, tragedies, and triumphs of the second half of the twentieth century for billions of human beings.

His impact on the Catholic Church had been just as dramatic as his influence on world affairs. Over two and a half decades, he had reinvigorated the Church spiritually and intellectually, restoring a sense of the adventure of discipleship for many Catholics and constantly reminding the entire Church that it did not exist for its own sake, but for its evangelical mission: to proclaim the Gospel of God's saving love for humanity throughout the world. Vigorously deploying the tools of the modern communications and transportation revolutions, John Paul II had given new meaning to the papal title "Universal Pastor of the Church," bringing the ministry of the Bishop of Rome to the Church in a series of papal pilgrimages inside Italy and around the globe that was unprecedented in history. One of the signature events of those travels, itself an astonishment to many, were World Youth Days in which the Pope confounded the expectations of both secure secularists and insecure churchmen by demonstrating that young people from the developed world, the formerly communist world, and the developing world all responded enthusiastically to his forthright challenge to live lives of heroic virtue.

Equally surprising to some had been John Paul II's robust commitment to the quest for Christian unity, his determination to forge a new relationship between Catholicism and Judaism, his investment in interreligious dialogue with the increasingly restive worlds of Islam, and his interest in building bridges between religious faith and science. At the same time as he was giving new meaning to the traditional papal title of "pontiff"—which derives from the Latin word for "bridge"—and even as he was reinventing the papacy as an office of evangelical witness rather than bureaucratic management, John Paul II was creating the most intellectually consequential body of papal teaching in centuries, calling the Catholic Church to deepen its commitment to its doctrinal and moral traditions while engaging modernity's critique of revealed religion and classic morality. Perhaps most strikingly, John Paul had proposed a fresh reading of Catholicism's sexual ethic in which faithful and fruitful marital love was understood as an icon of the interior life of the Holy Trinity.

In his intellectual method—putting classic truths of faith and morals into rigorous dialogue with contemporary understandings of the human person—as in other facets of his pontificate, John Paul II had been a sign of contradiction as well as a "witness to hope," as he described himself at the United Nations in 1995.

Revered by hundreds of millions of people, many of them neither Catholic nor Christian, he had been sharply criticized by many Catholic intellectuals and activists throughout his papacy, which his critics (who included priests, religious sisters, and bishops) deemed one of "restoration"—an abandonment of the commitments the Catholic Church had undertaken at the Second Vatican Council, held from 1962 through 1965.

A champion of freedom who had done as much as anyone to liberate his Slavic brethren from the totalitarian yoke, he was resented by some for his insistence that freedom is not a neutral faculty of "choice," and that freedom rightly lived is always freedom tethered to moral truth and ordered to goodness.

A genuine intellectual with a profound reverence for the life of the mind, he was accused by some of being an opponent of academic freedom; a pastor with more than five decades of experience in helping men and women grapple with the ambiguities and temptations of the human condition, he was not infrequently charged with being insensitive and authoritarian. Yet even his critics had to concede that he had become a global moral reference point—a man whose thought mattered, even to those who opposed it and opposed the Church he led.

How had he come to this point? What were the influences that had formed this unique and striking personality—a man who, while thoroughly grounded in a particular faith, had come to exercise a kind of universal fatherhood that touched hearts, minds, and souls across the spectrum of human experience and conviction?

The story of the pre-papal life of Karol Wojtyła and the first twenty-two years of his papacy is told in Witness to Hope: The Biography of Pope John Paul II, to which this volume is both complement and sequel.[1] In the years since that book's publication, information has become available that sheds new light on the drama of Karol Wojtyła's forty-year struggle against communism—and communism's forty-year effort to impede Wojtyła's work and destroy his reputation. It is a striking tale, for Poland's communist authorities, their masters in Moscow, and their allies throughout the Soviet bloc long regarded Karol Wojtyła as a mortal enemy—and, after his election as pope, as a mortal threat to the communist position in central and eastern Europe, to the communist project throughout the Third World, and indeed to the very survival of communism itself. In these judgments they were not mistaken, although they were often wrong in their conception of Wojtyła's strategy and in their reading of his mind.

Vast human and financial resources were expended in the communist war against Karol Wojtyła and, after his election as pope, against the Church he led. Those efforts ultimately proved futile, for the weapons Wojtyła deployed were weapons whose impact communist tactics could not blunt. Yet the communists tried, hard, to destroy his work and his authority, first in Kraków, later when he came to Rome. Many remain convinced that these efforts included the assassination attempt of May 13, 1981; in any event, the war against Wojtyła included an extensive campaign to suborn, blackmail, and recruit as informants his associates in Poland and in Rome. These clandestine enterprises were frequently coordinated by the intelligence agencies of the Soviet bloc, with all information gathered by Warsaw Pact intelligence services shared with the KGB in Moscow, where copied records of these operations likely remain (and remain closed to scholars).

Many records of the communist war against Karol Wojtyła and against Pope John Paul II were destroyed during and immediately after the communist crack-up in 1989, but a vast archive that had only begun to be explored in the first half decade after John Paul's death remained. Careful analysis of even a modest selection of these primary source materials—all of which were originally classified, and some of which were considered so sensitive that they were only available to the most senior communist party and communist secret police officials—yields a much richer and more detailed portrait of how and why communism went to war against Karol Wojtyła, when he was archbishop of Kraków and after he became Bishop of Rome. These materials also illustrate how communist governments and secret intelligence services penetrated the Vatican and sought to use diplomatic contacts with the Holy See as means to advance their interests (which could have been expected) and to strengthen their efforts to penetrate the highest levels of Catholic leadership, particularly in the Vatican itself (a process to which many senior Vatican officials seemed largely oblivious). The records of the KGB, the Polish Służba Bezpieczeństwa (or SB), and the East German Stasi also offer a window into the mind-set of Vatican diplomacy, even as they confirm the intuition that John Paul II and his diplomats often had dramatically different views of the strategy and tactics appropriate for meeting the communist challenge.

Before telling that previously untold story (which is Part One of the present volume), before accounting for the last six years of the life of John Paul II (which follows in Part Two), and before attempting to assess the man and his accomplishments in detail (Part Three), a brief synopsis of Wojtyła's pre-papal life, and of the accomplishments of the first two decades of John Paul's pontificate, is in order.

SON OF POLAND

Karol Józef Wojtyła was born on May 18, 1920, a member of the first generation of Poles to be born in a free country since the late eighteenth century. Wojtyła's mother, the former Emilia Kaczorowska, died one month before her second son's ninth birthday; his older brother, Edmund, a doctor, died in 1932 after contracting scarlet fever from a patient he was treating. Thus the principal figure in the childhood and adolescence of the boy known as Lolek to his family and friends was his father, the elder Karol Wojtyła: "the Captain," as he was known to everyone in Lolek's hometown of Wadowice (located several dozen kilometers southwest of Kraków), for he was a retired army officer. He was also a man of profound Catholic faith and granitelike integrity, whose example of manly piety left a lasting impression on his son.

The Poland in which young Karol Wojtyła grew to early manhood was an ethnically, linguistically, and religiously plural country with substantial Jewish, Ukrainian, and German minorities. In the struggle to define the meaning of Polish national identity and patriotism in the immediate aftermath of Poland's recovery of its independence in 1918, the elder Karol Wojtyła stood firmly on the side of the pluralists and against the narrow nationalists for whom "Poland" meant an exclusively Catholic-ethnic enclave. His father's convictions on this question, as well as the experience of growing up with numerous Jewish friends in a town that was 20 percent Jewish and that prided itself on living out the tolerance preached by the local Catholic clergy, set the foundations for the future pope's polyglot abilities (his father taught him German as a boy), his deep respect for the religious convictions of others, and his distinctive sensitivity to the pain and anguish of European Jewry in the mid-twentieth century and thereafter.

After a sterling high school career in Wadowice, during which he read deeply in the literature of Polish Romanticism and began to nurture a lifelong fascination with the theater, young Karol Wojtyła and his father moved to Kraków in 1938 so that Lolek could begin his studies in Polish philology at the venerable Jagiellonian University. Founded in 1364, the Jagiellonian, home to Copernicus from 1491 until 1495, had been a crossroads of Christian and humanistic culture for centuries; one of its early fifteenth-century professors, Paweł Włodkowic, would make occasional appearances in late-twentieth-century papal documents as a critic of coercion in matters of religious conviction. Yet because of the lethal ambitions of Europe's two great totalitarian powers, Nazi Germany and the Soviet Union, Karol Wojtyła's promising university career lasted only a year. After the Nazi invasion of Poland on September 1, 1939, and the partition of the country following the September 17, 1939, Soviet invasion from the east, the Jagiellonian University was shut down by the Nazi occupation, with distinguished members of its faculty deported to the Sachsenhausen concentration camp.

Poland under Nazi occupation was a brutal and deadly place in which the rule of law was superseded by the rule of arbitrary terror. The occupiers believed the Poles to be a low-level race of **untermenschen** who were to be minimally educated, and just as minimally fed, in order to provide a workforce for the greater glory of the Thousand Year Reich; those who resisted, and were caught, were condemned to concentration camps or summarily executed. Young Karol Wojtyła spent the war years as a manual laborer: first, at the Zakrzówek quarry in Kraków; later, at the Solvay chemical factory on the southern periphery of the city, near the convent where a then-obscure Polish nun, Sister Mary Faustyna Kowalska, had died in 1938. Wojtyła was also engaged in clandestine studies—the Jagiellonian University had quickly reestablished itself as an underground institution—and in the Polish resistance, joining a movement called UNIA which, in addition to its wartime activities (which ranged from paramilitary actions to protecting Jews to sponsoring underground networks of Polish culture), worked to set the foundations for a postwar Poland governed by Christian democratic principles. UNIA sponsored the Rhapsodic Theater, founded by Mieczysław Kotlarczyk and young Wojtyła in August 1941—an experiment in avant-garde minimalism in which the five-member troupe, without costumes or props, practiced a "theater of the living word," where the classics of the Polish dramatic and poetic repertoire were performed clandestinely in order to keep alive the Polish culture the Nazis were determined to exterminate. During the war years, Karol Wojtyła also took his first steps in Carmelite spirituality under the tutelage of Jan Tyranowski, a lay mystic and autodidact specialist in the works of St. John of the Cross and St. Teresa of Ávila. In addition, Tyranowski, whom Wojtyła later memorialized as an unexpected "apostle," recruited Lolek as a leader for the "Living Rosary" groups of young men he was forming in Wojtyła's parish of St. Stanisław Kostka, in the working-class Dębniki district of Kraków.

Wojtyła's work with the Rhapsodic Theater, and with Tyranowski in the Living Rosary, was undertaken at risk of his life, for such activities were strictly forbidden by the occupation. Wojtyła had one or two close scrapes with the Gestapo and, in an incident unrelated to his resistance work, suffered a broken shoulder and a concussion when he was hit at night by a German army truck and left in a road-side ditch—from which he was rescued by a local woman and a German officer who had him taken to a hospital. The death of his father on February 18, 1941, accelerated the vocational struggle that the experiences of the war had also influenced: was he destined for the theater (and, perhaps later, for a university career) as a Catholic layman, or was he being called to another form of the dramatic life, as a Catholic priest?

After resolving that question over months of prayer, Wojtyła presented himself to the archbishop of Kraków, Adam Stefan Sapieha, who accepted him as a candidate for the priesthood and, in the fall of 1942, gave him a place in the seminary Sapieha was conducting clandestinely, the Nazis having closed the archdiocesan seminary. For two years, Wojtyła lived a triple life—as underground theatrical performer, manual laborer, and clandestine seminarian—taking his first steps in philosophy and theology during the night shift at Solvay and being examined on what he had learned by professors who (like their students) came surreptitiously to Sapieha's residence. There, he also received spiritual direction and occasionally served the archbishop's Mass; during this period, one of his fellow seminarians, Jerzy Zachuta, was discovered by the Gestapo and shot. On August 6, 1944, the Gestapo swept Kraków, seeking to arrest all the city's young men in order to forestall a repetition of the Warsaw Uprising, which had broken out on August 1. Archbishop Sapieha called in his clandestine seminarians and hid them in his residence, where the seminary was reconstituted underground for the last six months of World War II. During those months, Wojtyła had daily contact with the "prince-archbishop" who would become his model of heroic episcopal leadership.[2]

After the Soviet "liberation" of Kraków on January 18, 1945, the archdiocese reclaimed the Kraków seminary (which had been used as a German prison), such that Karol Wojtyła had his one year of relatively normal seminary experience in 1945–46. Yet even that period was marked by drama, for Wojtyła was a leader in a student organization that organized a pro-democracy demonstration on May 3, 1946, a traditional day to celebrate Polish independence; the demonstration was brutally suppressed by the Polish secret police and their comrades of the Soviet NKVD. Sapieha, who was created cardinal in 1946, had formed the highest impression of Karol Wojtyła, and decided to send him to Rome for graduate studies in theology, ordaining him a priest in the chapel of the archiepiscopal residence at Franciszkańska, 3, on November 1, 1946. Father Karol Wojtyła said his first three Masses the next day, All Souls' Day, in the St. Leonard's Crypt of Wawel Cathedral, hard by the tombs of such Polish national heroes as King Jan III

Sobieski and Tadeusz Kościuszko; it was, he wrote a half century later, a way to express his solidarity with, and gratitude for, those who had formed him as a Polish patriot dedicated to the universal cause of freedom.

It was a commitment he would later apply, with considerable effect, on a global stage.

SON OF VATICAN II

While completing his doctorate at Rome's Angelicum with a dissertation on the idea of faith in the thought of St. John of the Cross, Father Karol Wojtyła traveled in Europe, exploring the French worker-priest movement, doing pastoral work among Polish miners in Belgium, and finding the Paris Metro a splendid place for contemplation. He returned to the archdiocese of Kraków in the summer of 1948; Cardinal Sapieha sent him briefly to a rural parish in Niegowić, outside the city. Eight months later, however, Sapieha reassigned Father Wojtyła to the Kraków parish of St. Florian, where he developed a pastoral method that would change the face of the Catholic Church in ways that no one could imagine in Stalinist Poland.

Sapieha—by this time a man of immense moral authority—was convinced that one key battle in the

Church's war with communism for the future of Poland would be fought in the hearts and minds of
young Poles. With Father Jan Pietraszko leading a
highly successful student ministry at the collegiate
church of St. Anne near the Jagiellonian University,
Sapieha sent Wojtyła to St. Florian's to start a second center of student chaplaincy. In addition to fulfilling this assignment successfully, Wojtyła became
the center of several networks of students whom he
eventually came to call his **Środowisko** [Milieu];
for the rest of his life, they called him **Wujek**
[Uncle], a Stalin-era nom de guerre invented for a
time when priests were not supposed to work with
groups of young people.[3] In outings and vacations
with **Środowisko**, Wojtyła developed the talents for
hiking and skiing with which he had grown up in
Wadowice, while adding kayaking to his repertoire
as an outdoorsman. In mastering the kayak, Wojtyła
formed a close friendship with a layman and an engineer, Jerzy Ciesielski, with whom he wrote essays
defending a radical innovation in Polish pastoral
ministry: a priest spending weeks in the mountains
and on the lakes and rivers of the country with young
laypeople, both men and women.

As Father Wojtyła helped form his young friends
into mature Christian adults and helped them prepare for the responsibilities of marriage and parent-
ing, they were helping form him into one of the most
dynamic young priests of his generation. For in addition to his work at St. Florian's, Wojtyła was estab-

lishing a reputation as an essayist in the independent Catholic newspaper, **Tygodnik Powszechny** [**Universal Weekly**], the only serious organ of journalism in Poland, even as he continued to write poetry (published pseudonymously) and plays (whose publication would have to await his election as pope). Cardinal Sapieha's successor, Archbishop Eugeniusz Baziak, decided that Wojtyła should further hone his intellect with a second doctoral dissertation, the habilitation, that would qualify him to teach at the university level. Thus in September 1951, Wojtyła moved from St. Florian's to an archdiocesan house on Kanonicza Street, near Wawel Castle and Cathedral, in order to write his habilitation thesis on the philosophical ethics of the German phenomenologist Max Scheler, which he completed in 1953. Concurrently, Wojtyła maintained his contacts with **Środowisko** while embarking on new experiments in pastoral ministry to health care workers.

The Jagiellonian University's faculty of theology was shut down by the communist regime in 1953—an act of cultural vandalism that Karol Wojtyła never forgot—and thus it was that the newly minted Dr. hab. Wojtyła complemented his pastoral work in Kraków with a commuter professorship at the Catholic University of Lublin [KUL], where he taught philosophical ethics at the undergraduate and graduate levels. In addition to forming another network of young friends and colleagues at KUL, Wojtyła's conversations with his Lublin students helped refine his thinking on sexual morality, which led to his first book, **Love and Responsibility**. At Lublin, Wojtyła also engaged in a searching conversation with, and critique of, modern philosophy. That encounter led him to a conviction that would remain with him for the rest of his life: that Enlightenment theories of ethics, which locked moral obligation inside human consciousness, were one source of the cultural, and ultimately political, crises of the late twentieth century. At the same time that he was teaching at KUL, Wojtyła taught courses in social ethics and other subjects to seminarians in Kraków, developing a familiarity with modern Catholic social doctrine.

On July 4, 1958, Pope Pius XII, in one of the last acts of his nineteen-year-long pontificate, appointed Father Karol Wojtyła titular bishop of Ombi and auxiliary bishop of Kraków, to work under Archbishop Baziak. Baziak consecrated Wojtyła a bishop at Wawel Cathedral on September 28, 1958, after which the youngest bishop in Poland embarked on a new set of pastoral commitments while continuing to teach at Lublin. Fourteen months after his episcopal ordination, on December 24, 1959, Bishop Karol Wojtyła began an annual tradition of celebrating Christmas Midnight Mass in an open field in Nowa Huta, the model socialist new town outside Kraków—and the first settlement in Polish history deliberately built without a church. Shortly after that dramatic event, the young bishop received a request by the Vatican commission preparing the agenda for the recently summoned Second Vatican Council. He responded with a letter, in which he outlined the crisis in Western humanism—a crisis in the very idea of the human person—that he believed to be central to the mid-twentieth century's bloody turmoil. The letter further proposed that the Council called by the new pope, John XXIII, should put the revitalization of Christian humanism, the humanism that finds the truth about the human person in the person of Jesus Christ, at the center of its work.

Archbishop Eugeniusz Baziak died in June 1962, four months before Vatican II opened; his temporary successor as apostolic administrator of Kraków was Bishop Karol Wojtyła, elected to that post by the Metropolitan Chapter, a committee of senior priests. Wojtyła would eventually be named archbishop of Kraków in his own right by Pope Paul VI, in an appointment signed on December 30, 1963, and announced the following month.

If the Second World War was the chief formative experience of Karol Wojtyła's life—the experience in which "humiliation at the hands of evil," as he once put it, compelled him to spend out his own life in defense of the dignity of the human person through the priesthood of the Catholic Church—then the Second Vatican Council was the decisive experience of Wojtyła's ministerial life. For the next forty years, he would consider himself a son of Vatican II—the Council that introduced him to the world church and its unity in diversity; the Council that ratified his own explorations in liturgical reform with his students in Kraków; the Council that gave him an accelerated, postdoctoral course in contemporary Catholic and ecumenical theology; the Council at which he helped define the Catholic Church's commitment to the first of human rights, religious freedom. Wojtyła was an active participant throughout the four years, or periods, of Vatican II—which met for extended working sessions in the autumn months of 1962, 1963, 1964, and 1965—and in the "intersession" between Vatican II's third and fourth periods, during which he helped refine the draft of the Council's Pastoral Constitution on the Church in the Modern World. In addition to his work at Vatican II on liturgy, the theology of the laity, religious freedom, and the Church's encounter with social, cultural, political, and economic modernity, the Council years were the beginning of Wojtyła's fascination with, and devotion to, the new churches of Africa. He also used the Council as a foil for his literary and intellectual work, writing several poems during Vatican II and thinking through what would become his unfinished philosophical masterwork, **Osoba i czyn** [Person and Act], which was eventually published in 1969.[4]

At the conclusion of Vatican II on December 8, 1965, Archbishop Karol Wojtyła returned to Kraków, where he led the archdiocese's participation in the 1966 celebrations of the Millennium of Polish Christianity, wrote a vade mecum of the Council's documents that was published under the title **Sources of Renewal**, launched a synod to plan the implementation of Vatican II in the archdiocese, and fought tenaciously with the communist regime for free space for the Church—including a church in Nowa Huta. Wojtyła's dynamic leadership in Kraków was built on six pastoral priorities: the defense of religious freedom; the strengthening of the seminary and the local faculty of theology (which had been cast adrift by the Jagiellonian University and was operating independently); youth ministry; marriage preparation and ministry to families; dialogue with leaders of culture and Polish intellectual life; and the works of charity, including outreach to the sick, the psychologically disturbed, and the homebound. Archbishop Wojtyła maintained a rigorous and extensive program of parish visitations, sometimes staying in a parish for as long as a week, and maintained his affiliation with the Catholic University of Lublin—although now his doctoral seminar students and the students whose doctoral dissertations he was directing came and worked with him in Kraków. He continued to write poetry and plays, deepened his already close relations with his **Środowisko** (including annual summer kayaking vacations), and led a group of Kraków theologians in the preparation of a lengthy memorandum to Pope Paul VI on the moral issues involved in family planning, as the Pope was struggling with the encyclical that would be known as **Humanae Vitae** at its publication in 1968.

After being created cardinal by Paul VI on June 28, 1967, Karol Wojtyła became a significant figure in Vatican affairs, participating in international Synods of Bishops in 1969, 1971, 1974, and 1977, and serving on several Vatican congregations (the equivalent of U.S. cabinet departments). Cardinal Wojtyła traveled to the United States and Canada in 1969, represented the Polish Church at the International Eucharistic Congress in Melbourne, Australia, in 1973, and returned to the United States for the International Eucharistic Congress of 1976, at which he gave a major address. In 1974, Wojtyła made a deep impression on an international conference of Catholic philosophers, gathered in Fossanuova to mark the seventh centenary of the death of St. Thomas Aquinas; the German Thomist, Josef Pieper, was so taken with Wojtyła's paper on "The Personal Structure of Self-Determination," and with the Polish cardinal's homiletic skills and personal charm, that he urged his friend, Professor Joseph Ratzinger, to begin a correspondence and an exchange of books with Wojtyła. Both in Kraków and abroad, Wojtyła was given indispensable support by his priest-secretary, Father Stanisław Dziwisz.

Pope Paul VI died on August 6, 1978, after a pontificate riven with strife—one that raised the question of whether any man could fill the shoes of the fisherman in the late twentieth century. Some evidently thought Karol Wojtyła could, for he seems to have received a scattering of votes at the conclave that elected Albino Luciani, patriarch of Venice, as Pope John Paul I on August 26. Still, a Polish pope was beyond the imagination of most of the cardinal-electors—until the profound shock of John Paul I's death after a thirty-three-day pontificate reshaped the psychological dynamics of the second conclave of 1978, creating the human conditions for the possibility of doing the previously unimaginable. Thus on October 16, 1978, the archbishop of Kraków, Cardinal Karol Józef Wojtyła, was elected the successor of St. Peter, taking the name John Paul II: the first non-Italian pontiff in four and a half centuries and the first Slavic pope ever.

THE EVANGELICAL PAPACY AND THE UNIVERSAL CALL TO HOLINESS

If the Holy Spirit had seen fit to call the archbishop of Kraków to be Bishop of Rome, John Paul II once said, then that must mean that there was something in the experience of Kraków that was of value for the universal Church.[5] Thus the new pope did not await instruction from the traditional managers of popes on how to conduct his office, but seized the papacy in his capable hands and bent its functioning to his understanding of what it meant to be a bishop in the post–Vatican II Church. He quickly broke out of the gilded cage of the Vatican, visiting Italian shrines and introducing himself to his new flock. He immediately took up the cause of the "Church of Silence" behind the communist Iron Curtain. He insisted on maintaining direct, personal contact with friends and colleagues all over the world by telephone and letter, and turned the **sala da pranzo** of the papal apartment into a seminar room, where he hosted guests for meals twice or more each day, probing them for information and analysis of the world situation and their local churches. He even left the Vatican surreptitiously to go skiing, knowing that he needed a certain amount of exercise to keep himself psychologically and spiritually, as well as physically, fit.

His inaugural encyclical, **Redemptor Hominis** [The Redeemer of Man], issued on March 4, 1979, was the first extensive papal exposition of Christian anthropology and provided the program notes for the next two decades of the pontificate. **Redemptor Hominis** was later complemented by two other encyclicals in a Trinitarian triptych: **Dives in Misericordia** [Rich in Mercy], a 1980 meditation on God the Father as the Father of mercies; and **Dominum et Vivificantem** [Lord and Giver of Life], a 1986 letter to the world Church on the Holy Spirit. Over the next twenty years, John Paul II also wrote a triptych of encyclicals on Catholic social doctrine:

Laborem Exercens [On Human Work], a 1981 exposition of work as man's participation in God's ongoing creativity of the world; **Sollicitudo Rei Socialis** [The Church's Social Concern], a 1987 letter that defined a human "right of economic initiative" and warned against the dangers of a consumerism that confused having more with being more; and **Centesimus Annus** [The Hundredth Year], which recast the Church's social doctrine for the twenty-first century while commemorating the social doctrine's magna carta, Leo XIII's **Rerum Novarum.** John Paul also wrote encyclicals on the evangelization of the Slavic lands (**Slavorum Apostoli** [The Apostles of the Slavs], issued in 1985); on the Blessed Virgin Mary (the 1987 letter, **Redemptoris Mater** [The Mother of the Redeemer]); on Christian mission (the 1990 letter, **Redemptoris Missio** [The Mission of the Redeemer]); on the renewal of Catholic moral theology (the 1993 letter, **Veritatis Splendor** [The Splendor of Truth]); on the Church's commitment to Christian unity (the 1995 letter, **Ut Unum Sint** [That They May Be One]); on the defense of life from conception until natural death (the 1995 letter, **Evangelium Vitae** [The Gospel of Life]); and on the complementarity of faith and reason (the 1998 letter, **Fides et Ratio**).

In addition to his encyclicals, John Paul II wrote apostolic letters on a wide range of issues and questions: the nature and meaning of suffering; modern feminism; priestly celibacy; and the importance of

Sunday in both human and Christian terms. The apostolic exhortations by which he completed the work of various international Synods of Bishops proposed a vision of authentic Catholic higher education, defended the family as the first unit of society, called the Church back to the practice of sacramental confession, lifted up the lay mission in the world, and called for sweeping reforms in both priestly formation and consecrated religious life. Over the first two decades of his pontificate, John Paul II also became one of history's premier papal legislators, issuing a new code of canon law for the Latin-rite Church in 1983 with the apostolic constitution **Sacrae Disciplinae Leges** [The Laws of Its Sacred Discipline], and promulgating history's first code of canons for the Eastern Catholic Churches in 1990 with the apostolic constitution **Sacri Canones** [The Sacred Canons]. In three other apostolic constitutions, John Paul revamped the process by which the Church recognizes someone as a saint, restructured the Roman Curia, and refined the rules for papal elections.

In addition to all this, the Pope turned his weekly general audiences from 1979 through 1984 into catechetical moments that were eventually collected into what became known as the Theology of the Body—perhaps John Paul's boldest proposal in the field of Christian thought. Subsequent weekly audience catecheses in the 1980s and 1990s yielded a four-volume papal reflection on the Creed, in which the Pope explored the theology of the Trinitarian persons and the nature of the Church, and a fifth volume on the Virgin Mary's roles as Theotokos [God-Bearer] and model of Christian discipleship. And in 1994, John Paul did something that no pope had ever done before, publishing an international bestseller, **Crossing the Threshold of Hope**, that eventually appeared in more than five dozen languages.

Thus, throughout the first twenty years of his papacy, John Paul II was creating a body of papal teaching with which the Catholic Church—and indeed the entire world of human culture—would be grappling for centuries. He understood his teaching to flow from the teaching of the Second Vatican Council, which he took to be a development of the Church's tradition, not a rupture with that tradition. Toward the end of securing that understanding of Vatican II, he summoned an Extraordinary Assembly of the Synod of Bishops, which met in Rome in November and December 1985 to consider both the Council's accomplishments and the Church's failures to implement it properly—an exercise that accelerated the process of interpreting the Council as an extension of 2,000 years of Catholic doctrine and that led to the 1992 promulgation of the **Catechism of the Catholic Church.**

John Paul II's determination to implement the Second Vatican Council faithfully and fully, which he had said at his election would be one of the principal tasks of his pontificate, was not merely, or even primarily, a matter of winning an argument over what had transpired in Rome between October 1962 and December 1965, however; it was a matter of reigniting in the Church the experience of Vatican II as a "new Pentecost," a preparation for a third millennium of ever more energetic evangelization. And the most effective form of evangelization, the Pope believed, was not argument, but sanctity: the witness of lives lived as a gift to others, as our lives are a gift to each of us. The Holy Spirit, John Paul II believed, had not exhausted his charismatic and sanctifying gifts to the Church at the first Pentecost, recorded in Acts 2. The Holy Spirit had been active throughout history and was still active in the modern world, calling forth new witnesses to the love of God, manifest in new experiences of the love of Christ. Those convictions about the energetic presence of the Holy Spirit in the Church were the source of two more distinctive attributes of the pontificate in its first two decades: unprecedented numbers of beatifications and canonizations, and John Paul's forthright support of new renewal movements and new Christian communities.

His **beati** and his new saints were a remarkable panorama of human personalities, including such extraordinary figures as Maximilian Kolbe and Edith Stein, both martyred at Auschwitz; Mary Faustyna Kowalska, the apostle of divine mercy; 103 Korean martyrs of the nineteenth century; 110 Vietnamese martyrs of the eighteenth and nineteenth centuries;

Albert Chmielowski, the Polish avant-garde painter turned advocate for the destitute; Kateri Tekakwitha, the seventeenth-century "Lily of the Mohawks"; Brother André Bessette, the twentieth-century Thaumaturge at Montréal's Oratory of St. Joseph; Fra Angelico, the master of the early Renaissance fresco; Miguel Pro, shot during the Cristero uprising in Mexico in 1927 (and quite possibly the first person whose martyrdom was photographed); Pier Giorgio Frassati, "the man of the Beatitudes" who was also a Milanese bon vivant in the Roaring Twenties; Mary MacKillop, an Australian nun once excommunicated by an irate bishop; and Father Damien of Molokai, who gave his life for lepers.

The renewal movements and new Christian communities that had been founded, or had flourished, after the Second Vatican Council were a "charismatic" fruit of the Council, the Pope was convinced. Moreover, John Paul knew that virtually all true reform in the Church had been initiated outside the bureaucratic structures of Catholic life, even if such "charismatic" reforms eventually had to be incorporated into the regular rhythms and structures of the Church's life in order to be completely fruitful spiritually. Nonetheless, the Pope was also determined to protect what was new, and often seemed strange, to more cautious churchmen, and thus demonstrated on numerous occasions an intense, personal interest in such movements and communities as the worldwide charismatic renewal, Communion and Liberation, the Emmanuel Community, Focolare, the L' Arche community, the Neocatechumenal Way, Regnum Christi, and the Sant'Egidio Community, while granting the status of a personal prelature (a kind of global diocese) to Opus Dei.

All of this, John Paul II believed, was a matter of the Bishop of Rome supporting what Vatican II, in its Dogmatic Constitution on the Church, **Lumen Gentium** [Light of the Nations] had described as the "universal call to holiness." He had learned all about that in Kraków, from his **Środowisko** and others, long before anyone had dreamed of a new ecumenical council. And in the first two decades of his pontificate, in fidelity to that experience and in obedience to the teaching of Vatican II, he challenged the Church throughout the world to recognize that sanctity is every baptized person's human and Christian destiny.

APOSTLE ON THE MOVE

John Paul II's living redefinition of the papal office as one of evangelical witness in and for the world seized the public imagination from October 1978 on. That redefinition was embodied in the Pope's extensive travels, which he insisted were "pilgrimages"—the successor of St. Peter fulfilling the mission given to Peter by the Risen Christ, to "strengthen your brethren" (Luke 22.32). From the beginning of his pontificate, the Pope set about to re-evangelize Italy, making more than ninety pastoral visits to Italian cities, towns, dioceses, and regions between 1978 and 1999, while personally visiting hundreds of Roman parishes; there, the Polish-born Bishop of Rome celebrated Sunday Mass and preached in his sonorous Italian. John Paul II thus lived his title of "Primate of Italy" far more intensely than had any Italian pope in centuries, and perhaps ever.

Then there was the world beyond the Alps. Among more than ninety papal pilgrimages outside Italy between 1979 and 1999, several were of decisive importance for the Church and the world.

In Mexico in January 1979, John Paul II challenged the Church in Latin America to be an effective force for social, economic, and political reform while rejecting Marxist distortions in the theologies of liberation. His very presence in Mexico, and the reception he received, altered the anticlerical attitudes in parts of the Mexican establishment, allowing the Catholic Church in Mexico to be itself openly for the first time in decades.

John Paul's first pilgrimage to Poland, the "Nine Days" of June 1979, created a hinge point in the history of the twentieth century and will be discussed in detail in Chapter Three, and Poland II (in 1983) and Poland III (in 1987) in Chapter Four.

In the United States in October 1979, John Paul II demonstrated his ability to communicate his message of evangelical adventure through (and occasionally around) a skeptical media, and forcefully defended religious freedom as the first of human rights in his first address to the General Assembly of the United Nations.

A month later, in December 1979, the Pope underscored his commitment to ecumenism during a visit to the Ecumenical Patriarchate of Constantinople, where he told Patriarch Dimitrios I that he hoped the day when they could concelebrate the Eucharist together would come very soon.

In June 1980, John Paul gave what was one of his favorite public addresses, a dense analysis of the centrality of culture in the human experience, which he delivered in Paris before the 109th meeting of UNESCO's executive council. On that same pilgrimage to France, the Pope forthrightly asked the "eldest daughter of the Church" whether she had forgotten the vows of her baptism.

In May and June 1982, John Paul II refused to let the Falklands War impede a planned pilgrimage to Great Britain, inviting the bishops of Britain and Argentina to concelebrate Mass together in St. Peter's before he went to Britain and then adding Argentina to the immediate post-U.K. papal travel schedule.

In March 1983, John Paul II stared down Sandinista demonstrators at his Mass in Managua, Nicaragua, pleaded for reconciliation in El Salvador, and began the process by which Marxist revolution was rolled back throughout Central America.

From January 31 through February 11, 1986, the Pope visited India to lift up the work of a great friend, Mother Teresa of Calcutta, whose living embodiment of the Gospel of love he deemed the best method of advancing the Christian proposal in a culture deeply resistant to it.

In April 1987, John Paul went to Chile and Argentina, where his teaching and example accelerated transitions to democracy in two countries long held under the boot of military dictatorship.

June 1–10, 1989, saw history's first papal pilgrimage to Scandinavia, where the Pope demonstrated the possibilities of personal evangelical witness in thawing the chill of centuries of embittered ecumenical relations.

On January 15, 1995, John Paul II gathered the largest crowd in human history on the world's least-Christian continent, when he celebrated the closing Mass of World Youth Day in Manila, capital of a country whose People Power revolution he had supported a decade earlier.

Back at the United Nations on October 5, 1995, John Paul II defended the universality of human rights as a moral truth of the human condition that could be known by reason, proposed the natural moral law as a universal public "grammar" by which humanity could turn cacophony into conversation, and challenged the world to turn a "century of tears" into a "springtime of the human spirit."

In January 1998, John Paul took his message of Christian humanism and freedom to Cuba, where, as in Poland in June 1979, he tried to give back to an oppressed people their authentic history and culture.

And then there was Africa—a continent beset by Cold War tensions before the collapse of European communism and ignored after the fall of the Berlin Wall. Alone among the world statesmen of the late twentieth century, Pope John Paul II refused to consider Africa either a political pawn or a hopeless case, devoting eleven pilgrimages to every part of the continent between 1980 and 1995.

Pope John Paul II had thus become not only the most visible human being in history but the most consequential pope in five centuries. From the mid-1990s on, as his health began to deteriorate in various ways, his best days were often said to be behind him, at least by those watching from the outside. Those who knew Karol Józef Wojtyła better, however, sensed that the trajectory of his life pointed through the Holy Door of St. Peter's—which he would open on Christmas Eve 1999 to inaugurate the jubilee year—toward

something more. The drama of that "something more" would match the drama of his epic struggle with communism, to which we now turn, before rejoining John Paul II during the Great Jubilee of 2000.

PART ONE

NEMESIS

Karol Wojtyła vs. Communism

1945—1989

CHAPTER ONE

Opening Gambits

May 18, 1920	Karol Józef Wojtyła is born in Wadowice and baptized on June 20.
August 16–17, 1920	Red Army invasion of Europe is repelled at the "Miracle on the Vistula."
August 1938	Wojtyła moves to Kraków to begin undergraduate studies in Polish philology at the Jagiellonian University.
September 1, 1939	Germany invades Poland, launching World War II in Europe.
September 17, 1939	The Red Army invades Poland, which is subsequently divided between two totalitarian powers.
November 1939	Karol Wojtyła, now a manual laborer, begins underground academic life and resistance activities.

Fall 1942	Wojtyła is accepted into Kraków's clandestine seminary program.
Fall 1945	Wojtyła's name first appears in communist secret police records.
May 3, 1946	Wojtyła participates in a student demonstration that is attacked by communist secret police and internal security forces.
June 30, 1946	Kraków returns largest anticommunist vote in Poland during falsified "people's referendum."
November 1, 1946	Karol Wojtyła is ordained a priest and leaves Poland two weeks later for graduate studies in Rome.
January 17, 1947	Parliamentary "election" confirms communist control of Poland.
November 12, 1948	Stefan Wyszyński is named archbishop of Gniezno and Warsaw and Primate of Poland.
March 17, 1949	Father Karol Wojtyła begins academic chaplaincy at St. Florian's Church in Kraków.
March 5, 1953	Stalin dies.
September 25, 1953	Cardinal Wyszyński begins three years of house arrest.
October 12, 1954	Dr. hab. Karol Wojtyła begins teaching in the philosophy department of the Catholic University of Lublin.

February 25, 1956	Nikita Khrushchev denounces Stalin's cult of personality at twentieth Soviet Communist Party Congress.
June 28, 1956	General strike in Poznań leads to armed repression and deaths of Polish workers.
October 23, 1956	Hungarian Revolution breaks out.
October 28, 1956	Cardinal Wyszyński is released from house arrest and returns to Warsaw.

The truth of Witold Pilecki's life would beggar the imaginations of the great tragedians.

He was born in Russia, in 1901, of a Polish family forcibly resettled after the failed anti-czarist insurrection of 1863–64. After fighting with Polish partisans in the last days of World War I, he served with Polish forces in the Polish-Soviet War of 1919–20: a largely unknown affair that saved newly resurrected Poland from Bolshevik conquest and prevented the Red Army from blazing its way across war-exhausted Europe. Decorated twice for heroism in the struggle to defend Poland's new independence, Pilecki was mustered out and spent the interwar years as a farmer; he married and fathered two children.

Less than a week before the outbreak of World War II, Pilecki took command of a cavalry platoon in the 19th Polish Infantry Division. After two weeks of fighting against the German invaders, the division was demobilized in the wake of the Soviet invasion of Poland; Pilecki and his commander, Jan Włodarkiewicz, went to Warsaw and launched the **Tajna Armia Polska** [Secret Polish Army] as an underground resistance movement. In 1940, its 8,000 members were incorporated into the **Armia Krajowa** [Home Army, or AK]: successor to the Polish military in occupied and partitioned Poland, and the fighting arm of the London-based Polish government-in-exile.

Later that year, Pilecki brought his AK superiors a daring plan: he would get himself arrested and sent to **Konzentrationslager Auschwitz,** located in that portion of Poland that had been incorporated into the Third Reich. There, he proposed to organize prisoner resistance, collect intelligence, and get it out to the AK, which had ways of transmitting such information to London. The superiors agreed. So, under the nom de guerre "Tomasz Serafiński," Pilecki deliberately got himself caught in a Gestapo sweep of civilians; he was arrested, tortured, and then dispatched to the labor camp at Auschwitz, where he became prisoner 4859. At Auschwitz, Pilecki got busy organizing the **Związek Organizacji Wojskowej,** or Union of Military Organizations [ZOW], which worked to improve prisoner morale, distribute smuggled clothing, food, and medical supplies, and train a resistance movement capable of taking over the camp in the event of an Allied attack. Contacts were maintained with local Polish patriots, and intelligence on camp operations was gathered. By 1941, ZOW had managed to build a radio, and Pilecki's intelligence reports on life, death, and torture at Auschwitz I got out to Polish resistance and thence to London. The prisoners' hope was that these reports would lead to a joint attack on the camp by the Home Army and the Western Allies, perhaps using the Polish Parachute Brigade that had been formed in exile.

After two years, however, Pilecki decided to escape and make his way to AK headquarters; he wanted to make the case in person for a relief attack on the Auschwitz complex, which had now been expanded to include the gas chambers and crematoria at Birkenau (sometimes known as Auschwitz II). With the help of local patriots, he made good his escape in April 1943 and eventually worked his way to Warsaw. His reports on Auschwitz were considered exaggerated by the British, who seemed incapable of imagining mass murder on an industrial scale; and without Allied air support, the Home Army leadership concluded, an attack on the concentration and extermination camps was impossible.

Pilecki then joined a unit within the AK that, in addition to its anti-Nazi activities, was dedicated to resisting a postwar Soviet takeover of Poland—a possibility not unlikely in light of evolving Allied strategy. After the Warsaw Uprising broke out on August

1, 1944, Pilecki initially fought anonymously as a private. Later, on revealing his true rank, he took command of an important sector that held out for two weeks against fierce German assault. When the AK authorities surrendered after sixty-three days of epic struggle, Pilecki was captured and spent the rest of the war in two German POW compounds. After these camps were liberated, he joined the famous Polish II Corps, victors at Monte Cassino and in Normandy's Falaise Pocket. The commander of the Polish II Corps, General Władysław Anders, had another mission for the intrepid officer who had demonstrated such remarkable courage and ingenuity for five years. Pilecki was asked to return to a Poland being strangled by the Red Army and the NKVD (predecessor to the KGB); there, he was to reestablish his intelligence network and report to the government-in-exile in London, which still claimed legal authority over Polish affairs. It seemed another futile mission, but Pilecki agreed to go, and in addition to performing his assigned intelligence duties wrote a study of Auschwitz. When the government-in-exile decided that its situation was hopeless and ordered the remaining resistance fighters to return to civilian life or try to escape to the West, Witold Pilecki dismantled his intelligence networks but remained in Poland. In 1947, he began collecting information about NKVD and Red Army atrocities against Polish patriots, often former members of the AK or Polish II Corps.

Arrested by the Polish communist secret police in May 1947, Pilecki was brutally tortured prior to his trial, but revealed nothing that would compromise others. The suborned "evidence" used against him at his March 1948 show trial came from, among others, a fellow Auschwitz survivor, Józef Cyrankiewicz, who would later become one of communist Poland's prime ministers. Pilecki freely admitted that he had passed information to Polish II Corps headquarters, which he believed to be his duty as an officer. Falsely charged with plotting assassinations, which he denied, Witold Pilecki was given a capital sentence and shot on May 25, 1948, at the Mokotów prison in Warsaw. His grave was never found; it is thought that the body may have been disposed of at a garbage dump near a local cemetery.

This was the Poland in which Karol Wojtyła, whom the world would come to know as Pope John Paul II, was ordained a Catholic priest in 1946: a country in which men of unblemished honor and extraordinary heroism could be convicted as traitors and murdered by communist thugs, their bodies tossed onto garbage heaps. The forces that created, and brutally maintained, this particular heart of darkness were the nemesis—the seemingly invincible opponent—against which Karol Wojtyła contended for more than three decades.[1]

THE TIME AND THE PLACE

By most historical accounts, Poland was something of a bit player on the twentieth-century global stage: rarely a protagonist, often a victim, a country whose heroic virtues seemed to go hand in glove with a striking incapacity for governance and diplomacy. Yet if we define the "twentieth century" not by conventional chronology but by its central drama, the truth of the matter is that Poland played a pivotal role at several crucial moments between 1914 and 1991: those seventy-seven years of Western civilizational crisis that began when the guns of August launched World War I and ended when one of the greatest effects of the Great War, the Soviet Union, disappeared.

By Lenin's own admission, the "Miracle on the Vistula" in 1920—in which the Polish forces of Marshal Józef Piłsudski repulsed the Red Army cavalry and thrust Trotsky's forces back into Russia proper—was a "gigantic, unheard-of defeat" for communist world revolution.[2] Nineteen years later, Poland was the first European state to offer armed resistance to Adolf Hitler, demonstrating the imperative of defending freedom against totalitarianism rather than attempting to appease its appetites. Fifty years after that, in 1989, Poland once again asserted its right to freedom against seemingly insuperable odds, and became the fulcrum of a nonviolent revolution that swept European communism into the dustbin of history while giving birth to a new, democratic European order.[3]

The Poland in which Father Karol Wojtyła would spend the first years of his priesthood was a Poland that had been dramatically—some would say, "completely"—changed by the Second World War, and by the postwar arrangements agreed to by the Soviet Union, the United Kingdom, and the United States.[4] It had been picked up and moved several hundred kilometers to the west, losing territories that had been Polish for centuries and gaining lands that would be a bone of contention with postwar Germany (and an excuse for Soviet hegemony) for decades. Politically, the Poland that emerged from World War II was a wholly owned subsidiary of the USSR, a central piece in the postwar Soviet imperial puzzle and the land bridge to communist East Germany. Postwar Poland was ethnically more Polish than Poland had ever been, its Jews having been destroyed in the Holocaust and its Ukrainians incorporated into the Ukrainian Soviet Socialist Republic. Culturally, postwar Poland was arguably the most intensely Catholic country on the planet, not only because of genocides and population transfers, but because the Catholic Church, which suffered terribly during World War II, had emerged with its honor intact and its historic role as the repository of Polish national identity and memory confirmed. Economically, the country was a ruin, having been one of the battlegrounds on which two totalitarian powers had fought an armed struggle to the death. Psychologically, Poland was dazed and depressed; fear stalked the land even after the country's putative liberation. One-fifth of Poland's prewar population had died between 1939 and 1945. The survivors sensed that the flower of the nation had been sacrificed in the war Poland lost twice, even as the new postwar communist order was imposed with a ruthlessness matching that of the previous, Nazi occupying power.

Yet Poland had somehow survived World War II— as Poland had, somehow, been reborn in the waning days of World War I, after 123 years of exile from the political map of Europe. It was a close-run thing. Crushed in September 1939 between the totalitarian pincers of the Wehrmacht and the Red Army, the Second Polish Republic was in mortal peril. As one historian puts it, by October 1939 "the Polish state . . . faced the threat of not only total military defeat, but also the loss of legal and constitutional continuity. Almost its entire territory was controlled by an enemy alliance, and its constitutional authorities had been incapacitated by an erstwhile ally."[5] That ally, Great Britain, would continue to regard Poland as a diplomatic headache throughout the war, despite the heroic contributions of Polish squadrons to British victory in the Battle of Britain, and of Polish infantry and armor to Allied victories in Italy and Normandy.

Poland's postwar fate was sealed by one event and

one decision. The event was the Battle of Kursk, the greatest armored battle in history, which, in August 1943, effectively ended the German invasion of the Soviet Union and set in motion the long, bloody process by which the Red Army fought its way to Berlin. The decision was the strategic choice made by Winston Churchill and Franklin Roosevelt at QUADRANT, their Québec City conference that same month. By agreeing to the American plan to invade Hitler's **Festung Europa** from the west, across the English Channel (rather than from the south, through the Balkans), the Western Allies ensured that Poland would be overrun by the Soviet army rather than liberated by Anglo-American forces. During the latter part of the war, the incapacities and internal quarrels of the Polish government-in-exile were not inconsiderable. Yet those Polish failures were, in a sense, as irrelevant to the great power Realpolitik game being played at the "Big Three" conferences in Tehran and Yalta as were the heroics of Polish RAF pilots during the Battle of Britain and of Polish soldiers at Monte Cassino: cursed by the geographical reality of being a broad, flat plain between Germany and Russia, Poland was now a pawn in the emerging, bipolar, and deadly chess match between the Soviet Union and the West.

In 1945, few could have imagined that Poland would eventually provide the key to the ultimate victory of the forces of freedom in that contest. Yet some of the elements of such an outcome could be discerned in the Polish experience of the Second World War, if one looked keenly enough and below the surface of events. The Warsaw Uprising of August and September 1944, for example, is not infrequently regarded as a suicidal exercise with virtually no political effect.[6] Yet, in the retrospect of late-twentieth-century history, one can perhaps see that Poland's refusal to concede its sovereignty to the German occupation sowed seeds of resistance that would flower, albeit in a very different form, in the 1980s.[7] The brutalities of Poland's Soviet masters—including the 1940 Katyń Forest massacres of at least 22,000 Polish officers by the NKVD—could not be discussed publicly in Poland in the decades after the war. But families knew that husbands, fathers, uncles, and brothers had disappeared, and those bitter memories were a living, inextinguishable reminder that the communist regime, which claimed a unique legitimacy as Poland's liberator, was in fact built on a foundation of homicidal falsehoods. The self-sacrifice of a man like Father Maximilian Kolbe, who gave his life in the Auschwitz starvation bunker to save the life of a prisoner who was the father of a family, belied the communist claim that the Catholic Church was the historic oppressor of the working class—as did the sacrifices of thousands of other Polish priests, nuns, and laity who went to their deaths under the crooked Nazi cross, for the sake of the cross of Christ.

True, Poland looked like, felt like, and in many respects was a different country in 1945 and 1946 than it had been in its brief twenty-one years of modern independence. There were different people, a different economy, and a different government denouncing different enemies. Yet there was a cultural and spiritual continuity to Polish life that would eventually falsify the communist claim to be building a new Poland. The presence of Red Army troops, the links between the Polish internal security services and the NKVD/KGB, and the Western policy of "containment" might mean that, by conventional reckoning, Polish sovereignty was a pious fiction. Yet, as Poland would demonstrate between 1939 and 1989, there are powerful forms of cultural and spiritual sovereignty that can resist, and eventually defeat, the harshest political regimes.

FITTING THE COW WITH A SADDLE

Ioseb Besarionis dze Jughashvili, more widely known by his Bolshevik nom de guerre of "Stalin," was an ethnic Georgian who adopted certain classic Russian attitudes toward Poles and Poland: which is to say, he hated both. His August 1939 pact with Hitler, intended to buy time to prepare his defense against the Nazi assault he knew was coming, involved gobbling up large chunks of traditionally Polish territory and deporting thousands of Polish families to the steppes of central Asia. When the Western Allies summoned up the spine to insist that some form of "Poland" be reconstituted after Hitler's defeat, Stalin made sure that the new Poland would be a Soviet vassal state. As the Red Army moved across Poland in 1944, its divisions were followed by the agents, assassins, and executioners of the Soviet secret police, who made it their business to ensure that no political resistance could be mounted against the Soviet-sponsored Lublin Committee (which claimed to be the true government of liberated Poland), rather than the Polish government-in-exile in London.

A vast secret police apparatus of repression was thus born along with what eventually became the Third Polish Republic. At the time of V-E Day, the so-called ministry of "public security" had 11,000 employees, a number that would more than double in a few months' time, while the numbers of agents, informers, and provocateurs also grew. The Polish army, now controlled by communists or their pawns, conducted propaganda campaigns with the civilian population even as it indoctrinated its own forces and conducted expulsions of German ethnics in the "recovered territories" in the west.[8] Stalin would later say, memorably, that trying to make Poland a communist country was like fitting a saddle to a cow. In the early days of communist Poland, the man Churchill and Roosevelt referred to as "Uncle Joe" was taking no chances with the cow.

The brutality by which the NKVD and its post-war allies in the Polish internal security services liquidated thousands of Poles whose only "crime" had been their patriotic defense of Polish independence through the AK or other resistance movements reflected the paranoid style that was a long-standing feature of Soviet communism. It was neither a Western cold warrior nor a Polish critic of Russia, but the great Russian novelist and poet Boris Pasternak who once described Lenin as "vengeance incarnate" and Stalin as a "pockmarked Caligula."[9] Soviet communist paranoia expressed itself in many forms, ideological, political, cultural, and economic; its most lethal expression was that series of secret police agencies that eventually came to be known as the KGB. Ironically, its founder, in the days when it was known as the Cheka, was a Polish communist, Feliks Dzerzhínskii. Its subsequent leadership, according to British intelligence historian Christopher Andrew, included men "more suited to a chamber of horrors than to a hall of fame," a truth perhaps unconsciously recognized by the fact that the officers' club at the Lubyanka, the KGB's Moscow headquarters, did not display photographs of former KGB chairmen (three of whom had been shot in various purges, one of whom had killed himself, and several of whom were clinical psychopaths).

Among the enemies of Soviet communism, real and imagined, none was more feared by the KGB and its predecessors than the Catholic Church, which was regarded as a prime ideological enemy even before the Bolsheviks seized power in a crumbling Russia in 1917. That fear was subsequently transmitted to allied internal security and intelligence services in the Soviet bloc (many of which, to be sure, did not require excessive instruction on this point). Vatican diplomats and others who imagined that Soviet intelligence and the intelligence services of its Warsaw Pact allies acted more or less like their Western counterparts were sorely mistaken. There was a ruthlessness about the communist persecution of Catholicism that was fed by a deeply ingrained paranoia—which in turn may have reflected the fact that Marxism-Leninism was itself a quasi-religious system (if of an ultramundane sort), complete with a doctrine, a theory of morality, an idea of salvation, a concept of the "last things," and a martyrology.[10] Communism and Catholicism could not peacefully coexist. In a confrontation extending over the medium and long haul of history, someone was going to win and someone was going to lose. That, in any event, was how real communists saw the matter.

Thus from the communist point of view, the difficult business of fitting the Polish cow with the saddle of Marxism-Leninism was made far more difficult by Poland's intense Catholic faith and Catholicism's links to Polish national identity and Polish patriotism. But there were further complications, involving recent history. The Soviet suzerains had made a deal with Hitler to divide Poland; their Polish com-

munist vassals had not been deeply involved in anti-
Nazi resistance in World War II Poland. The Catholic
Church had been, however, and had acquired a substantial moral credit by its sacrifices. That heroism,
which the communists could not match (despite relentless propaganda to the contrary), posed one set
of challenges to the communization of Poland. So
did ideology. And so did postwar geopolitics. For,
given their assumptions and their fears, Soviet and
Polish communist leaders in the immediate postwar
period took the intensity of Poland's Catholic faith
to be, not so much the natural cultural and historical
phenomenon that it was, but the local expression of
the pro-Western, anticommunist polemics and policies of Pope Pius XII and the worldwide Catholic
Church—in Bolshevik eyes, a global conspiracy bent
on undoing the achievements of Lenin's revolution.

In the months immediately following World
War II—the months in which Polish Catholicism
could come out from the catacombs—public Catholicism in Poland was divided. Some Catholic intellectuals tried to maintain a certain distance from
politics, even as the communist regime and the
Polish primate, Cardinal August Hlond, came into
conflict. Other lay activists tried to find an accommodation with communism that would allow them
to play a political role. Still others invested fruitless
efforts at forming Catholic political parties. Adam
Stefan Sapieha, the heroic archbishop of Kraków
who had defied the Nazi gauleiter Hans Frank, was

allowed to go to Rome and receive his cardinal's red hat in 1946. Still, the enthusiasm with which the old prelate was received on his return to Poland—students picked up his car at the main train station and carried it (and the seventy-nine-year-old cardinal) to his residence—must have reinforced the communist sense that the heroism of Cracovian Catholicism during the war, and the general disdain for communism in Poland's cultural capital, were going to pose a particularly difficult set of cow-saddling problems.

It was in these years—1945, 1946, 1947—that a young churchman named Karol Józef Wojtyła first came to the attention of the Polish communist secret police.

A YOUNG MAN OF CONSIDERABLE PROMISE

Karol Wojtyła's vocational discernment was profoundly shaped by his experiences of the Second World War, in that part of Poland that historian Norman Davies described as "Gestapoland": his daily life amidst brutality and random death; his resistance activities; his first experience of manual labor and his first steps in Carmelite spirituality; the death of his father and the murder of his friends. As he would put it later in a memoir of those hard days, the combination of "humiliation at the hands of evil" and the heroism he had encountered in the face of such mortal danger gradually led to "a detachment from my earlier plans": the priesthood, he came to understand, was a way of life in which he could resist the degradation of human dignity with spiritual and cultural weapons. As he pondered his situation, Karol Wojtyła's conviction that there are no mere coincidences in the world—that what appears to us as "coincidence" is in fact an aspect of God's providence we don't yet grasp—grew, and began to bend his discernment in the direction of the altar. As he would write a half century later, it was not so much a choosing as a being chosen, to which there could only be one answer.[11]

After six months in Archbishop Sapieha's underground seminary, the "house arrest" period of Karol Wojtyła's extraordinary preparation for the Catholic priesthood ended in mid-January 1945, when advancing Red Army troops forced the Germans to abandon Kraków. The 1945–46 academic year was thus the only reasonably normal period that Karol Wojtyła spent in the seminary. Those were also the years in which his name first appeared in Polish communist secret police files, along with those of fellow seminarians Andrzej Deskur and Stanisław Starowieyski, both of whom had lived underground in the archiepiscopal residence at Franciszkańska, 3. Why the attention? Sapieha's headquarters, to which evidence had been brought during the war of NKVD complicity in the Katyń Forest massacres, was under regular surveillance, and the seminarians would have been seen coming and going in the weeks after the Red Army "liberation" of the city. Wojtyła may also have become an object of suspicion because of his work as vice president of a Jagiellonian University student organization called **Bratniej Pomocy** [Fraternal Aid], which helped get Western relief aid to needy students. Perhaps of even greater interest to communist internal security ferrets was the patriotic demonstration mounted by **Bratniej Pomocy** on May 3, 1946, a traditional national holiday the communists were intent on stamping out. A riot ensued when student marchers were attacked by the police (aided by the Soviet NKVD); many were beaten, some were shot when the regime used live ammunition, and there were arrests. As one historian of the city of Kraków puts it, "it was on this occasion that the new powers revealed their true intentions, and took the opportunity to incite an anti-intelligentsia witch hunt."[12]

A month after that melee, Karol Wojtyła passed the examinations required to complete his preordination theological training. Cardinal Sapieha decided to ordain Wojtyła a priest on an accelerated schedule so that he could begin graduate theological studies in Rome in the fall of 1946; the cardinal, who had an acute sense of the local political situation, may also have been concerned that his prize student, a brilliant young man and a natural leader, was drawing too much attention from the secret police because of his **Bratniej Pomocy** activities. Thus Sapieha ordained Wojtyła on November 1, 1946, the Solemnity of All Saints; two weeks later, Father Karol Wojtyła left for Rome and two years of graduate study in theology. When this young man in whom Cardinal Sapieha saw considerable promise returned to Poland in the summer of 1948, he came back to a country struggling to breathe in the thick fog of Stalinist repression.[13]

HARD TIMES

In Rome, Karol Wojtyła missed Poland's rigged parliamentary "election" on January 19, 1947: a charade in which "some people voted, but other people counted," as acerbic Poles put it. By some estimates, the principal anticommunist party, the Polish Peasants Party [PSL], received almost 70 percent of the vote. According to the official tally, the PSL garnered 10.3 percent of the suffrage, with the communist bloc gaining 80 percent of the vote.[14] Kraków returned an especially heavy anticommunist vote, which led the regime to brand the city as a "bastion of reaction"; in their distinctive style of deprecation, the communists pledged an "uncompromising fight against Kraków's narrow-mindedness, its reactionary clergy, Krakow's backward bourgeoisie, Kraków

speculators, and [the] pre-war epigones of a bureaucratic world."[15]

The first years of Polish communism were not
without their farcical elements. The traditional Polish taste for mordant humor, honed during more
than a century of resistance against the loss of independence, flourished in the sometimes-madcap
atmosphere of Polish communism's early Stalinist period: wits noted that among one hundred so-
called Bolsheviks you'd likely find one committed
Bolshevik, thirty-nine criminals, and sixty idiots.[16]
Yet for all the farce, the regime's principal characteristic in its early days was its brutality, which reflected
both the pathologies of its Soviet master, Stalin, and
the regime's own fears of illegitimacy. Thus former
members of the AK paid for their patriotism by becoming special targets of a fierce persecution, the first
victims of which were Poles like Witold Pilecki—
patriots whose wartime heroism might have given
them a claim to a voice in the nation's future, and
who therefore, in the logic of Stalinism, had to be,
and were, liquidated.

A vast bureaucracy was quickly built to manage, or
mismanage, a command economy; according to one
historian, it was noteworthy for "a strictly observed
hierarchy" and "a total lack of competence." Virtually every form of independent social activity—from
unions to sports clubs to youth groups to patriotic
associations—was sucked into the insatiable maw of
the party-state, which was determined to substitute

itself for civil society in a "progressive sovietization of all of public life."[17] The rule of law, in any meaningful sense of the term, ceased to exist. Courts were corrupted; the "degree of social harmfulness" of an alleged crime was taken into account in sentencing, especially with political prisoners; politically acceptable judges with only secondary educations were given a fifteen-month cram course before joining the bench and meting out such sentences.[18]

Needing an enemy, communists throughout the new Soviet bloc tried to foment popular hysteria against alleged Western warmongering—and in Poland, against German revanchism in Poland's western "recovered territories" (which had been German during the interwar period). This external process had its domestic parallels: decrees on "official secrets" and "state secrets" helped ensure a permanent dragnet for putative spies, foreign and Polish.[19] In less than a decade, communist organs of internal security recruited or suborned some 75,000 "pairs of eyes," men and women who would keep their controllers informed of any untoward comment or activity by a neighbor or coworker. The net result was that, by 1954, six million Poles—one in every three Polish adults—were listed on the "register of criminal and suspicious elements."[20]

Despite having gained control of the machinery of governance while murdering or interning tens of thousands of political prisoners, Poland's communist masters nonetheless remained worried about the Catholic Church. Secret police memoranda of the time stressed the need to counteract the bad influence of "reactionary" clergy, and divided Poland's priests into three categories: enemies, neutrals, and "positives." Perhaps not surprisingly, given the strong leadership of Cardinal Sapieha and their resistance to the prior totalitarian regime, the Cracovian clergy were almost uniformly slotted as "enemies."[21]

By the end of 1947, the Polish communist regime had destroyed virtually "all institutions capable of crystallizing and articulating anti-communist sentiments," according to historian Andrzej Paczkowski.[22] Yet those sentiments were real, and, in the vacuum, the Catholic Church increasingly came to embody them. Church leaders wisely declined to take a direct political role. But their criticism of the bogus election of January 1947, their proposals for constitutional reform, their defense of civil liberties, their protests against the elimination of religious education from the schools, and their complaints against arbitrary police power and unnecessary nationalization of Church property (including several Catholic printing presses) turned the Catholic bishops of Poland into a de facto opposition. Having eliminated every other form of anticommunist political activity, both overt and covert, Polish communism could turn its attention to battling the Church for the hearts, minds, and souls of the Polish people.

The secret police maintained a file on every parish in the country, with "pairs of eyes" identifying the most active parishioners and describing their plans. From the day he entered the minor seminary, every young Pole studying for the priesthood had a secret police file and watcher, as did every priest. Children were warned not to discuss what they had heard in catechism class, even if the man questioning them wore a cassock and a Roman collar.[23] The Catholic press, including such intellectually assertive vehicles as the Kraków-based **Tygodnik Powszechny** [**Universal Weekly**] and its allied monthly **Znak** [**Sign**], were closely scrutinized and subjected to constant censorship.

The Polish Church's position was sometimes made more difficult by the Vatican. A 1948 letter from Pope Pius XII to the bishops of Germany, in which the Pope expressed concern for the twelve million Germans who had been expelled from Poland's "recovered territories," was used as a club against Polish Catholicism by Polish communism. A year later, Pius XII threatened those who joined communist parties with excommunication. The threat was aimed primarily at Italy, where the practice was not uncommon, but it was eagerly seized upon by Polish communists as an excuse to ratchet up pressure on Polish Catholics—5,500 priests were called in for "explanatory and cautionary talks."[24]

Yet for all the pressure and the intense surveillance (which involved a vast expenditure of state resources, and thus constituted a form of theft from civil society), Stalin-era Polish communism never quite "got" the Catholic Church. Raw intelligence is only as good as the analysis that filters and explains the data. And throughout the extended Soviet empire, the insistence by communist spymasters on reading the Church through their own experience—that is, as another political mafia bent on power—proved a serious impediment to grasping the internal dynamics of communism's principal ideological enemy.

So would the exceptional political skills and unshakable courage of the man who would lead Polish Catholicism through these hard times: Stefan Wyszyński.

THE PRIMATE

Wyszyński kept one step ahead of the Gestapo throughout World War II, serving as a kind of roving chaplain after the occupation closed down the seminary in which he was teaching. At the end of the war, the man known by the underground name of "Sister Cecilia" returned to Włocławek to reopen the seminary as its rector, but was quickly plucked from that post in order to become the bishop of Lublin in March 1946; he left the seminary on the day five of his prewar colleagues returned from the Dachau concentration camp. The young bishop's days in Lublin would be brief, however, for two and a half years later, on November 12, 1948, Pope Pius XII appointed the forty-seven-year-old Wyszyński as archbishop of Gniezno and Warsaw and successor to Cardinal August Hlond as Primate of Poland.

Throughout Polish history, the primate had been the "Interrex," the "king between kings," during those periods when the nobility was deciding who should be Poland's next elected monarch. There were no more kings, of course. But Stefan Wyszyński, a strong personality whom an admirer once described as a "fantastic, almost medieval character," took to the role of Interrex with conviction.[25] Just as important, Primate Wyszyński brought to his unchallenged leadership of Polish Catholicism a carefully considered view of the postwar situation, which he regarded as dire in the extreme. The Church had suffered terribly during the war—and had shown, in venues ranging from Dachau to the Warsaw Uprising, that it knew how to suffer, to sacrifice, and to die if necessary. Now, Wyszyński believed, the Church had to show that it knew how to live, even in a Stalinist environment. As a thinker, he stood well to the left of the conservative Polish clerical establishment and was an acknowledged expert in Catholic social doctrine, with its emphasis on workers' rights; yet he was also an ardent anticommunist. At the same time, however, he believed the Church had to find some sort of modus vivendi with the new regime, gaining breathing room in which to rebuild its pastoral strength.

Wyszyński held firmly to three other convictions that would shape his governance of Polish Catholicism and his political strategy for three decades. He was convinced that Polish popular piety—especially Polish devotion to Mary, Mother of God—was far stronger than communist propaganda and could be drawn upon as a font of cultural resistance. He believed that he understood the Polish ecclesiastical and political situation far better than anyone in the Vatican. And, as a Polish patriot, he was determined to prevent Poland's extinction by the Soviet Union, if the cost were at all morally bearable. These convictions did not always sit well with Church authorities in Rome, who tended in the late 1940s to prefer a directly confrontational approach to communism. Wyszyński was not afraid of confrontation, but he wanted to be the one who defined the terms and terrain on which battles would be fought; indeed, during the long struggle that lay ahead, he would sometimes deliberately provoke a confrontation, when he thought that things had gotten a bit slack and that the moral tension of Catholic life under communism had to be recharged. His initial instincts on becoming successor to St. Adalbert and primate in 1948, however, were to try to work out some sort of deal by which the Church could gain time.

Thus in 1950 the Church and the Polish government agreed on a set of ground rules for a tense coexistence. The regime recognized the Church's internal autonomy, its religious links to the papacy, its liturgical and ceremonial life (including public manifestations of faith, such as pilgrimages), its independent publications, and its pastoral ministries in schools, hospitals, and prisons; the communists also agreed that monastic orders (always a Bolshevik bugaboo) would be permitted, as would the Catholic University of Lublin, the only Catholic institution of higher learning behind what Churchill had begun to call the Iron Curtain. The Church, for its part, recognized the communist regime as the legal government of Poland, acknowledged the western "recovered territories" as legitimately Polish, committed itself to work for national reconstruction, and pledged to avoid "activities hostile to the Polish People's Republic."[26] Some in Rome thought that Wyszyński had conceded too much. The Primate, no fool, knew that the communist authorities would bend, twist, and, if necessary, ignore their agreements, such that constant vigilance would be required; but he also believed that the ground rules for an ongoing struggle had been set, and that he had defined the ground he could successfully defend. Rome eventually came around to the Pole's point of view and Wyszyński was created cardinal in 1952.

By that time, however, he was neck-deep in confrontation with a regime that had already begun violating the 1950 agreement. Parents were threatened with loss of employment if they didn't send their children to communist schools and youth groups. Catholic publications, already censored, were frequently harassed by "paper shortages," and some were eventually closed. Large numbers of priests were arrested, and the bishop of Kielce, Czesław Kaczmarek, was sentenced to twelve years' imprisonment after a classic 1951 show trial. Bolesław Piasecki, leader of a communist-friendly pseudo-Catholic association, "PAX," was a regular propaganda mouthpiece for the regime, accusing the Vatican (and, by implication, the Polish Catholic hierarchy) of collaboration with "German revanchists"—a favorite NKVD/KGB slander. The direct confrontation Wyszyński had sought to avoid became inevitable when, in May 1953, the regime ordered the implementation of a law by which it, not the Church, would appoint and remove pastors, vicars, and bishops. The Church would become, de facto, a subsidiary of the Polish communist state.

Wyszyński threw down the gauntlet in a historic sermon at Warsaw's St. John's Cathedral: "We teach that it is proper to render unto Caesar the things that are Caesar's and to God that which is God's. But when Caesar sits himself on the altar, we respond curtly: he may not." The Polish bishops then met in Kraków under Wyszyński's chairmanship and told the Polish communist Caesar that "he may not" in no uncertain terms: the peace of Poland, the bishops declared, depended solely on "the government's forsaking its radical, destructive hatred towards Catholicism, and abandoning its aim of subjugating the Church and turning it into an instrument of the

State . . . We are not allowed to place the things of God on the altar of Caesar. **Non possumus!** [We cannot!]"[27] The communist government charged the bishops with treason or, in the communist euphemism, "an attack on the constitution." On the night of September 25–26, 1953, Cardinal Wyszyński was arrested and began three years of internment, first in a former monastery in the northwest of the country, later in a convent in the south. By the end of the year, eight bishops and 900 priests were in prison for the faith. Their numbers would increase to 2,000 over the next two years, while theological faculties were closed, parents threatened, religious education stopped in the schools, and onerous taxes laid on the Church.[28]

CREATING ZONES OF FREEDOM

On his return from Rome in the summer of 1948, Father Karol Wojtyła was assigned by Cardinal Sapieha to the Church of the Assumption of Our Lady in Niegowić, which was then a rural village in the Carpathian foothills, some fifteen miles east of Kraków. The young curate's primary responsibilities involved the religious education of the local children, who were spread over five villages, which he visited regularly by horse cart. Back at the Church of the Assumption, the young curate spent hours in the confessional and began a lifelong immersion in youth ministry, starting a theatrical group and a Living Rosary circle; both activities gave him expanded opportunities for forming young souls, who were being regularly exposed to communist propaganda, even in a relative backwater like Niegowić. Told by one of his youngsters that communist ferrets had been seeking information on the parish youth ministry, Wojtyła brushed the young man's concerns aside with the reassurance that "they'll finish themselves off." Showing early that he was a man of no small ambitions, at least where the life of the Church was concerned, Father Wojtyła convinced the parishioners to build a new brick church in honor of their pastor's golden jubilee of ordination.[29]

Cardinal Sapieha did not intend that his most promising young priest should spend much time in a rural ministry, however, and after eight months in Niegowić, Wojtyła was transferred to a much different assignment: curate at St. Florian's parish near the Kraków Old Town, a center of the city's Catholic intellectual and cultural life. There, Wojtyła was to initiate a new student chaplaincy for the young men and women attending the Kraków Polytechnic and the Kraków Academy of Fine Arts, both of which were within a good stone's throw of St. Florian's.

Wojtyła did so, and in the process defined a new style of ministry to university students. He taught his young charges Gregorian chant and gave them missals so that they could participate actively in the Mass—a radical innovation in the early 1950s. He organized off-campus seminars where students could read Thomas Aquinas and the other greats of Catholic intellectual life as an antidote to the Marxist intellectual rubbish to which they were subjected at school. He used the drama as a means of catechesis at St. Florian's, where he also launched the first marriage-preparation program in the history of the archdiocese. He led retreats and days of recollection for students, often timed to help them prepare for their exams. And in another startling innovation for the time—one that challenged both traditional Polish clerical culture and the communist regime's restrictions on youth ministry by priests—he traveled with groups of young men and women, sharing their enthusiasm for hiking, skiing, and kayaking in the brilliant Polish countryside, beyond the dour, gray, soot-filled environs of the city.

Young people were attracted to Father Karol Wojtyła for many reasons: his intelligence, his friendliness, his human sympathy—his "permanent openness," as one member of the network that came to call itself **Środowisko** put it: "While he was among us, we felt that everything was all right. . . . We felt that we could discuss any problem with him; we could talk about absolutely anything." Those conversations were serious, sometimes funny, and often pointed. Wojtyła, who was already a master of the art of listening, would pose sharp questions; but, at the end, he would always tell his young friends, both in campfire conversation and in the confessional, "**You** must decide." As these young people moved from their undergraduate studies into graduate work, they occasionally ran into political difficulties and conundra; rather than arguing grand political theory, Wojtyła and his students would discuss the quotidian moral challenges of life in the communist culture of the lie. Yet **Środowisko** was not the kind of "conspiracy" feared by Poland's communist masters—it was something far more dangerous. Father Karol Wojtyła's sharp mind, spiritual depth, openness to others, and insistence on personal moral responsibility—"**You** must decide"—created zones of freedom in which the students who became his friends could forge their own decisions to live as serious Christians. And that meant, de facto, to live in opposition to the alternative construction of society and the alternative idea of human goods being relentlessly promoted by communist propaganda.[30]

At the same time as the first threads of the rich tapestry of **Środowisko** were being woven, Father Wojtyła was taking his initial steps as a public personality: preaching intellectually demanding sermons at St. Florian's, meeting regularly for discussion of religion and science with a group of young physicists, getting to know the habitues of some of Kraków's Catholic intellectual salons, and contributing essays to Poland's most important newspaper, **Tygodnik Powszechny**—the Kraków-based weekly to which serious Poles turned for truth amidst Stalinist lies. Poland's communist regime denied posts in state-run universities to rising young Catholic scholars; **Tygodnik Powszechny** eagerly hired such academic exiles for its staff. The young writers, in turn, were guided by the firm, competent hand of editor Jerzy Turowicz, who quickly recognized in Karol Wojtyła a rare clerical talent—an essayist, poet, and playwright who could speak effectively outside the sanctuary and the pulpit.

From the perspective of Wojtyła's early wrestling with the challenge of communism, perhaps the most intriguing of his literary works during his first years as a priest was the play **Our God's Brother**, which he completed in 1950. Its main character is the Polish artist-turned-monk Adam Chmielowski, who left the world of avant-garde painting to become an advocate for the poor and the founder of a small religious community. A partisan in the 1863 Polish insurrection against czarist rule, Chmielowski lost a leg in battle and, after recovering, moved to Munich and Paris, where he established a reputation as a serious modernist painter. Returning to Poland, he grew increasingly dissatisfied with the artist's life and increasingly angry at the municipality of Kraków's neglect of the downtrodden and homeless. Adopting a sackcloth habit and styling himself "Brother Albert," Chmielowski began a personal ministry to the poor that eventually grew into two religious communities, the Albertine Brothers and the Albertine Sisters.

His funeral, in 1916, was attended by thousands of people from every stratum of Cracovian society.

Wojtyła had become intrigued by the figure of Brother Albert while he was a student, and used Chmielowski's vocational struggles as the dramatic device for working out his own thinking about the challenge of Marxist theory and practice. In the play, the Chmielowski character, "Adam," debates the cause of the poor with a character called "the Stranger"—"crypto-Lenin," as the playwright himself once called him, for Wojtyła had adopted, for his dramatic purposes, the local legend that Chmielowski had met Lenin in Zakopane, in the south of Poland, during the latter's pre–World War I exile from Russia. Wojtyła's dramatic art was subtle: the Stranger/crypto-Lenin is not an unattractive character, and he debates Adam/Chmielowski over both strategy and tactics—which is the more effective program for the poor: the work of Christian charity and social reform or the work of revolutionary violence? Yet where Adam sees real human beings, the Stranger can see only categories: the impossible lumpenproletariat, workers ripe for revolution, and so forth. At an even deeper level, **Our God's Brother** explores the meaning of freedom. Adam, fully aware of the injustices in the social order, nonetheless comes to believe that the only true freedom is the Christian freedom that passes through the redemptive suffering of the cross, transforming evil into good and liberating men and women for genuine social transformation. Politics, by itself, could not liberate. Converted hearts and minds, giving birth to a truly humanistic culture, would eventually transform politics in a more humane direction.[31]

PRESSURES INCREASE, AND PLANS CHANGE

The political masters of the moment were not unaware of this dynamic young priest with a penchant for attracting students, intellectuals, artists, scientists, and young professionals. In 1948, Wojtyła's connections to the Rhapsodic Theater were noted in secret police records, as was his friendship with Tadeusz Kudliński, a fellow actor who had once tried to talk Lolek out of entering the underground seminary and who had been arrested because of his membership in UNIA (from which Wojtyła had had to resign on entering the seminary).[32] A November 1949 report from ŻAGIELOWSKI, a secret police informer who was a Cracovian priest, noted that, in the Kraków archdiocesan headquarters, "Wojdyła" (as he misspelled the name) was regarded with esteem as a comer, a man to watch.

The Polish communist authorities were intensely interested in the goings-on in the Kraków curia for several reasons. They feared that Cardinal Sapieha had documentation that identified the Soviet NKVD as the perpetrators of the Katyń Forest massacres (which the Soviets insisted for decades was the work of the Nazis). They knew that Sapieha was doing everything he could to maintain the rudiments of civil society, by creating, for example, a Catholic charitable organization, Caritas Poland, which the communists had subsequently shut down. And they wanted any information they could get on who might succeed the aging cardinal.

Sapieha had no immediate successor as archbishop—at least formally. The cardinal died on July 23, 1951. According to the 1950 agreement Primate Wyszyński had hammered out, when a bishop died, the Polish Church (which, in practice, meant Wyszyński) would consult with Rome and then propose a name to the government to fill the vacancy; the government could veto a candidate but could not impose its own substitute. On the death of Cardinal Sapieha, the Church proposed that his successor be Archbishop Eugeniusz Baziak, the Latin-rite archbishop of L'viv in Ukraine, who had lived in Kraków since he had been expelled from Ukraine by the Soviets. The Polish government would not accept Baziak (who would have been anathema in Moscow because of his post in Ukraine); the Church would not back down; so, technically, the archbishopric of Kraków remained empty for the next twelve years, although the Church in Kraków considered Baziak its archbishop, as did the Church throughout Poland.

Eugeniusz Baziak was a reserved, formal man who took the view that his task, at the apogee of Stalin-era repression, was to stand firm, rocklike, without ever lowering the mask of severity he thought essential to keeping the communists at bay. Because of that severity, Baziak never became the popular figure that Sapieha had been. But he protected the Church as best he could under the most difficult circumstances—and at no small personal cost, as he was a man of warm affections on those rare occasions when he could take off the mask, behind closed doors with old friends from L'viv.

An open and determined attack on the Church in Kraków began in earnest in 1952 with the arrest of two local priests, Msgr. Tadeusz Kurowski and Father Mieczysław Noworyta. A year later, in 1953, Archbishop Baziak was put under house arrest outside the archdiocese, and his auxiliary bishop was also expelled from the city. When Stalin died in March 1953, **Tygodnik Powszechny** refused to run the required, laudatory obituary and was closed down, to be reopened months later under a new editorial board linked to the PAX association, committed to collaboration with the regime. That same year also saw the demise of Karol Wojtyła's beloved Rhapsodic Theater, banned by the regime as too independent-minded.[33]

By this time, the local Ministry of Public Security section dealing with religious affairs had expanded considerably, to include separate offices dealing with virtually every aspect of Catholic life. Section One spied on and attempted to penetrate the Kraków archdiocesan curia and the curia in the neighboring diocese of Tarnów. Section Two dealt with Catholic religious orders, with subsections for male monasteries and convents of nuns. Section Three's target was the diocesan Catholic clergy, while Section Four worked on other religious communities, including Jehovah's Witnesses (whose minuscule numbers throughout the Soviet bloc were in inverse proportion to the viciousness with which they were persecuted). Tactics during this period tended to be brutal: clergy (like ŻAGIELOWSKI) were blackmailed with threats of sexual scandal or charges (true or false) of collaboration with the Nazi occupation during the war. Arrests and interrogations were also tools by which the secret police attempted to recruit in-house Catholic sources. The yield was not much, in terms of either intelligence or agents. But the effort was relentless and intensified in 1953 as the struggle against the Church took on a new urgency in light of the bishops' **Non possumus!**

Cardinal Sapieha and Archbishop Baziak were agreed that the battle with communism had to be fought on every front, including intellectual life. Thus, six weeks after taking over from the deceased Sapieha, Baziak (who must have discussed the plan with his predecessor) removed Father Karol Wojtyła from his work at St. Florian's and gave him a two-year academic leave during which he was to prepare his habilitation, the second doctoral thesis that would qualify him as a university professor. Wojtyła moved into the Dean's House, a Church property in Kanonicza Street near Wawel's Royal Castle, and settled down to analyze the ethical theory of the German philosopher Max Scheler and Scheler's possible utility as a philosophical basis for contemporary Christian moral theology.

It was a bold question to ask at this moment in Catholic intellectual life, for Scheler's phenomenological approach to ethics was far removed from the abstract scholastic categories of philosophical and theological analysis in which Wojtyła had been trained in the seminary and during his graduate studies in Rome. Scheler was also a philosophical world removed from the Kantian formalism that tended to dominate the field of philosophical ethics at the time. In the end, Wojtyła decided that Scheler's account of the moral life, while illuminating certain aspects of our decision-making, was incomplete, inadequate, and too focused on the emotions. Yet he also argued that Scheler had things to teach Catholic thinkers, for his emphasis on the subjective states of persons making moral decisions was an important complement to the traditional Catholic insistence that there was an objective truth of things that we can know by moral reason. This both/and strategy—subjectivity and objective truth; passion and reason—would be the hallmark of Karol Wojtyła's intellectual work for the next half century, and would give him powerful conceptual tools with which to continue the battle against a communist tyranny that claimed, as its ultimate legitimation, a firm grasp on the scientific truth of things.[34]

In November and December 1953, the theology faculty of the Jagiellonian University accepted Karol Wojtyła's dissertation and awarded him the habilitation doctorate early the following year. But before he could take up a position as a docent, the lowest rung on the Polish academic ladder, the communists shut down the Jagiellonian faculty of theology. This act of cultural vandalism, which was yet another facet of the regime's war against the Church, nevertheless made it possible for Wojtyła to accept a position at the Catholic University of Lublin—"the only place between Berlin and Seoul where philosophy was free," as his colleague, Stefan Swieżawski, neatly put it.[35]

The survival of the Catholic University of Lublin—"KUL" as it was usually called—was one of the achievements of Cardinal Wyszyński's 1950 modus vivendi with the Polish communist government. There was irony here, for the 1944–45 "Lublin Committee," the Soviet-manipulated and indeed Soviet-manufactured alternative to the legitimate Polish government-in-exile in London, embodied everything that was false and despicable about Poland's geopolitical situation. Fully aware of this, the communist regime substituted July 22, the day the

Lublin Committee published its political manifesto in 1944, for the traditional May 3 national holiday in honor of Poland's 1791 Constitution, the first written, democratic constitution in Europe.[36] As for KUL, the regime tried its best to marginalize it by building another, larger institution, the Marie Curie–Skłodowska University, virtually next door. Stefan Swieżawski believed that the communists did not openly persecute KUL because "they couldn't believe that something new could happen in such a medieval place," which the regime imagined to be the Catholic version of "a Hasidic ghetto."[37] Yet while the university maintained its independence, it was also subject to relentless surveillance and penetration efforts by the secret police, some of which were successful at the highest levels of university administration.

Father Wojtyła—now Dr. hab. Wojtyła—commuted to Lublin by train from Kraków, beginning with the 1954–55 academic year. In addition to his introductory undergraduate course in philosophical ethics, where he played to standing-room-only crowds in crammed lecture halls, he gave graduate-level lectures and directed doctoral students in their research and dissertation work. Wojtyła's graduate or "monographic" lectures were an exercise in the ecumenism of time, as the young professor engaged in a conversation over the centuries with Plato, Aristotle, Augustine, Thomas Aquinas, Immanuel Kant,

David Hume, Jeremy Bentham, and Max Scheler. In those lectures, he honed a set of convictions that he would deploy in his battle against communism.

Human beings, he insisted, had a natural instinct for the truth of things, a built-in inclination to the true, the good, and the beautiful. Yet men and women were free to make real choices, choices that we can know by reason to be decisions between what is objectively good and what is objectively evil, between what is noble and what is base. To reduce those choices, as communism did, to expressions of class interest or other economic forces was to dehumanize the human person. And if communism misunderstood human dignity and human freedom, it also misunderstood human community and society. The communist culture of the lie and the toxic social relations it created were nicely captured in a famous joke of the period: "Communist Party boss: 'How much is 2 + 2?' Polish worker: 'How much would you like it to be?'" Communism was not just wrong; it was unnatural. It taught a false humanism, for men and women could only be free when they lived in the truth about themselves, their communities, and their destiny. The truth about the human person was thus the most powerful weapon of resistance that could be deployed—particularly in a situation in which the proponents of the lie had a monopoly on other forms of power.[38]

Karol Wojtyła's work as a philosopher intersected with his vocation as a priest. He continued to be a magnet for the young, and his experience of helping his students and friends prepare for the responsibilities of marriage and family soon led him into a serious reflection on another aspect of human freedom: the freedom to love. Thousands of hours in the confessional and in spiritual direction had convinced him that the quest for love built into our natures as sexual beings is also a quest for a pure love, a love that expresses itself as the gift of oneself to another and the reception of that other as gift. Giving or using: that was the fundamental option in sexual love (and, indeed, in every other form of human relationship). Thus Wojtyła's philosophical reflections on ethics, his pastoral experience, and his convictions about God's ways with the world came together in what he would term the "Law of the Gift": the truth of human freedom is found in the free gift of oneself to others, and, in marriage, the free reception of the spouse's gift of self.[39] This conviction, which he brought to a more complete expression in his first book, **Love and Responsibility**, cast a new light on classic Christian sexual ethics, giving the Church's teaching on sexuality, marriage, and responsible family planning a new, richly humanistic texture.[40]

And here, too, Wojtyła's thought and work was a form of countercultural resistance against the communist culture of the lie. Permissive abortion laws, communist youth camps that encouraged sexual experimentation, work schedules that separated husbands and wives, parents and children—all of these were tools in the communist campaigns against traditional Polish culture and against the Church and its moral teaching. Wojtyła's work in the sphere of marriage and the family challenged the regime to battle on the question "Whose is the more humane understanding of freedom? Who takes more seriously the moral capacities of our people? Who treats them like adults, capable of mature decisions, and who treats them like children, mere packages of desires?"[41]

Karol Wojtyła's KUL period, during which he maintained an intense program of pastoral work in Kraków, was a time of intellectual and pastoral maturation. The young man who had once imagined his adult life as a combination of theatrical work and academic life found a happy equilibrium in a combination of priestly ministry and intellectual activity, both of which fed his continued literary work in poetry and drama. As he approached forty, the pattern of his life seemed set. Yet there were changes in the offing, not least because of changes in the dynamics of the constant, relentless struggle between the Catholic Church and the Polish communist regime.

A THAW OF SORTS

The death of Stalin in March 1953 set loose a power struggle within the USSR; one of its first casualties was the loathsome KGB chairman, Lavrenti Beria, a sadistic sexual predator executed in December 1953. Nikita Khrushchev's denunciation of Stalin's atrocities and cult of personality at the February 1956 Congress of the Soviet Communist Party sent shock waves throughout the Soviet bloc. The Polish Communist Party chieftain, Bolesław Bierut, a hard-core Stalinist, was sufficiently shocked by Khrushchev's speech that he died of a heart attack a few weeks later. Hungarian resentments began to build toward the boiling point that would be reached in the Hungarian Revolution of October–November 1956—a premature effort at self-liberation ultimately crushed by Soviet tanks, but one that left a permanent scar of anti-Western and anti-Catholic paranoia on the Budapest KGB **rezident**, Yuri Andropov, shocked by the workers' revolt against the workers' state. Even before the abortive Hungarian revolt gripped the world's attention, the unrest had taken hold in Poland; demonstrations in Poznań during a June 1956 general strike were crushed by tanks under the command of Marshal Konstantin Rokossovsky of the Red Army, Poland's defense minister. With Moscow demanding repression, the Soviet Army poised to invade, and Soviet warships sailing menacingly off Poland's Baltic Coast, the new communist leader, Władysław Gomułka (who had himself been rehabilitated in the post-Stalin turmoil) decided that only one man could calm the situation—short of the Soviet invasion that Gomułka, a thoroughgoing communist but also a Polish patriot, desperately wanted to avoid—Cardinal Stefan Wyszyński.

So Gomułka invited the Primate to return to Warsaw from his internment and take up his duties publicly. Wyszyński drove a hard bargain: the 1953 decree that had triggered the **Non possumus!** had to be rescinded; an ongoing mixed commission of governmental and Church representatives would have to be created; Bishop Kaczmarek was to be released from prison and other bishops allowed to return to their dioceses; the choke hold was to be taken off the Catholic press; and the normal patterns of Church governance were to be reinstated. Gomułka agreed, and by the end of 1956 Wyszyński's requirements had been met: thus Archbishop Baziak returned to Kraków, and **Tygodnik Powszechny** was once again led by Jerzy Turowicz rather than by an editorial board of collaborators.[42] In addition, optional religious education was permitted in the schools, the Church's prison and hospital ministries were reestablished, Catholic intellectuals' clubs were approved, and a small Catholic parliamentary group was permitted.

Things became better, but hardly normal. The regime persistently denied building permits for new churches; parishioners hid materials in their homes, prefabricated them in sections there, and then assembled the churches overnight, creating faits accomplis for the state. The deal on religious education in the state schools (which were the only schools there) was broken; the Church created thousands of catechetical centers. Taxes were raised on priests; bishops instructed their priests not to pay. Members of religious orders were ordered not to teach catechism; the instructions were ignored.

While these quotidian struggles were being played out across Poland, communist efforts to penetrate and disrupt the Church intensified. By 1956, the party leadership was exceedingly nervous about the power of the internal security apparatus, the secret police. It was too independent and might turn on its putative political masters; moreover, one of its senior officers, Józef Światło, had defected to the West in late September 1954 and become a commentator on the Polish service of Radio Free Europe, from which platform he was providing unprecedented details about secret police brutality and the character of his former colleagues, whom he described as a depraved, divisive, and power-grabbing clique.[43] So the whole operation was brought under much stricter party control, the Committee on Public Security was rebranded as the **Służba Bezpieczeństwa**, or Security Service (universally referred to as the SB), and a thorough review of methods and operations, including operations against the Church, was conducted. This review, undertaken at the outset of what seemed, on the surface, to be the Gomułka "thaw," led to the conclusion that the brutal methods of the past had not been successful; even those clerics who had signed agreements to cooperate with the secret police were providing unreliable information, more fluff than substance. Thus it would be better, the SB decided, to try more subtle methods: playing on clerical and lay resentments against Cardinal Wyszyński's strict style of ecclesiastical governance; using passports for study abroad or publishing possibilities as bait to catch intellectually curious clergy; bolstering the meager salaries of Church employees by putting them on secret police retainers.

These new methods of recruitment had some success. ARES, a longtime lay employee of **Tygodnik Powszechny**, worked for the SB for almost a quarter century, reporting on the financial situation of the Kraków curia, the antigovernment comments of curial employees, and the local ecclesiastical gossip. ERSKI, another lay mole who earned a regular salary from the SB, bugged the offices of **Tygodnik Powszechny** and gave the office keys to his SB handlers so they could conduct clandestine searches of the premises.[44]

And then there was the usual harassment. In 1956, Father Karol Wojtyła was invited by the authorities to what turned out to be a rather boring, even banal, conversation about his academic activities in Kraków (where he was teaching in the seminary) and Lublin.

Attempts to drag the young professor into a discussion of politics were unsuccessful, according to the file on the conversation kept by the SB.[45]

The Gomułka "thaw" led to a period of what historians describe as "maturity" for Polish communism. The mass murders of 1945–47 were a decade in the past. The "brutal, open, and mass coercion that had characterized the period of 'full Stalinism'" was over.[46] Marshal Rokossovsky and most of the other Red Army officers serving in the Polish military were back in the USSR; Cardinal Wyszyński was restored to authority as primate; and Gomułka had shown sufficient political skills and flexibility to forestall a Polish repeat of the Hungarian revolt that had led to draconian repression in that unhappy country. The stifling world of "socialist realist" culture cracked and then shattered; once-forbidden books could be printed, Western films could be shown, avant-garde art was tolerated, and Poland became "the liveliest barracks in the camp."[47] Yet it was still a camp, and the regime remained determined to bring the Church to heel while weaning the Polish people from their traditional religious loyalties. The opening gambits had been played. The war had entered a different, more subtle, and in some respects more dangerous, phase.

CHAPTER TWO

Defensor Civitatis

July 4, 1958	Father Karol Wojtyła is named auxiliary bishop of Kraków.
October 28, 1958	Cardinal Angelo Roncalli is elected pope.
January 25, 1959	Pope John XXIII announces the Second Vatican Council.
December 24, 1959	Bishop Wojtyła begins celebrating Christmas Midnight Mass in Nowa Huta.
June 1962	Department IV is formed within the Polish secret police to combat the Church.
July 16, 1962	Bishop Wojtyła elected temporary administrator of the Archdiocese of Kraków.

October 11, 1962	The Second Vatican Council opens.
October 22, 1962	World learns of Cuban Missile Crisis.
Spring 1963	Msgr. Agostino Casaroli visits Budapest and Prague; John XXIII issues **Pacem in Terris**, encyclical on world peace.
December 30, 1963	Karol Wojtyła is named archbishop of Kraków by Pope Paul VI.
November 18, 1965	Polish bishops' letter to the German hierarchy, forgiving and asking forgiveness, is published.
December 8, 1965	Solemn closing of the Second Vatican Council.
June 28, 1967	Karol Wojtyła is created cardinal.
July 4, 1967	Archbishop Agostino Casaroli becomes Vatican foreign minister.
August 1968	Prague Spring is crushed by Soviet tanks.
December 14, 1970	Strike at Lenin Shipyard in Gdańsk leads to widespread social unrest throughout Poland and many worker deaths.
November 19, 1973	"Independent Group D" of the SB's Department IV is formed with the aim of "disintegrating" the Catholic Church in Poland.
April 16, 1974	Cardinal Wojtyła defies Czechoslo-

	vak communist regime at funeral Mass of Cardinal Stefan Trochta.
July 1974	"Permanent Working Contacts Group" established by the Holy See and the Polish People's Republic.
December 1, 1977	Polish Communist Party leader Edward Gierek is received in private audience by Pope Paul VI.
May 15, 1977	Consecration of the Ark Church in Nowa Huta.
March 3, 1978	Paul VI agrees to defer resolution of the question of a permanent Vatican diplomatic representative in Warsaw until October.
May 25, 1978	Cardinal Wojtyła defends human rights of all Poles, believers and unbelievers, at annual Corpus Christi procession in Kraków.
August 6, 1978	Pope Paul VI dies.

The weather could have been more cooperative on May 15, 1977.

All morning long, rain poured down on Nowa Huta, the new town built outside Kraków as a model communist city—a city without God. Yet it would have taken nothing less than a Category V hurricane, and perhaps not even that, to keep the people of Nowa Huta from walking through the downpour to the Bienczyce neighborhood to participate in something that was never supposed to happen: the consecration of a Catholic church in Nowa Huta.

As the hour for the consecration ceremony approached, the local people were joined by fellow Catholics from all over Poland, and indeed from all over Europe. For one day, it seemed, the Iron Curtain had fallen. Delegations came from Yugoslavia, Czechoslovakia, Hungary, and the oxymoronic German Democratic Republic. A flock of West Germans came. Pilgrims came from the Austrian diocese of Sankt Pölten, which had donated the new church's tabernacle, sculpted to evoke the cosmos; in its center was a piece of moon rock given to Pope Paul VI by an American astronaut. The Dutch came to hear the bells they had donated. There were delegations from France, Belgium, Portugal, Great Britain, the United States, Finland, and Italy—there was even a guest from Japan.

It was a striking building, this Church of Our Lady, Queen of Poland, and the rain that attended its consecration was strangely fitting: for the church had been built along modernist architectural lines to evoke the sense of an ark, within which the Queen of Poland, Mary, Mother of God, was protecting her children from the storms outside. In addition to a large replica of the Black Madonna of Częstochowa, its chief interior decoration was a gigantic figure of

Christ crucified, forged by the steelworkers of the Lenin Steelworks. The church had taken ten years to build, with volunteer labor coming to Nowa Huta from all over Europe. Its cylindrical exterior, covered with two million stones polished in the riverbeds of Poland, was now being baptized from the skies, even as Cardinal Karol Wojtyła, the metropolitan archbishop of Kraków, proceeded with the lengthy ceremonies of consecration inside.

The fight for the Ark Church had been the symbolic centerpiece of Wojtyła's personal war with communism for almost two decades, from the time he was first named auxiliary bishop of Kraków in 1958. He had tenaciously and skillfully defended the rights of the workers of Nowa Huta to have a church in their new city, celebrating Christmas Midnight Mass in a freezing, open Nowa Huta field during the years in which the Polish communist regime refused a building permit. Then, on October 13, 1967, the authorities finally budged, and permission was given for construction. The very next day, October 14, Cardinal Wojtyła drove to Nowa Huta and turned the symbolic first spade of earth, preparing the ground for the cornerstone, which was donated by Paul VI and taken from a fragment of Constantine's ancient basilica of St. Peter in Rome.

Now, after a decade, the Ark Church was ready to receive its pilgrim people. And Cardinal Wojtyła was ready to speak his mind, in cadences long honed in public defense of the rights of those people:

We want this temple, which has a Mother as its patroness, to be our mother. We also want this temple, whose patroness is the Queen of Poland, to reign over us. Most of all, however, we long for the Mother. We feel such a strong need for her presence at this turn of history where mankind now finds itself, where Europe and our homeland find themselves. . . .

This city is not a city of people who belong to no one. Of people, to whom one may do whatever one wants, who may be manipulated according to the laws or rules of production and consumption. This is a city of the children of God [and] this temple was needed so that this could be expressed, [so] that it could be emphasized. . . .

We still have among us those who . . . began to build [this church] with their suffering. We pay them the highest respect. . . . Was it not possible— is it still not possible—to take another path as we continue to struggle to build other houses of God which are so necessary in Poland?

. . . Let us hope that, in this our homeland, which has a Christian and humanitarian past, these two orders—light and the Gospel, and respect for human rights—come together more effectively in the future.[1]

Nine days later, Cardinal Wojtyła gave a sermon at a reunion of priests whom he had ordained three years earlier, in 1974. He told these young men of his experience with others like them over the past two decades, especially when he asked each seminarian why he had come to the seminary:

> And often . . . I hear the answer that it was these times, times of great struggle between good and evil, times of the great struggle between Mary and Satan, that draw many . . . into the priesthood, so that they might participate in this great battle fully, decisively, in a defined manner. . . .
>
> I will say even more: this battle runs through the heart of each of us. A priestly ordination, a priestly vocation, does not free us from the battle.[2]

During his twenty years as a bishop in Kraków, first as auxiliary to Archbishop Eugeniusz Baziak and later as archbishop in his own right, Karol Wojtyła turned himself into an extremely effective combatant in that battle. Doing so was something of a stretch for a man with a rich and complex interior life, a mystic who found it easiest to express his deepest intuitions about the human condition in poetry—a man not naturally given to raising his voice. Yet he learned to do precisely that, and to do it eloquently, because that was what his bishop's vocation, his conscience, and his convictions about human rights required of him.

Wojtyła's twenty years as a bishop in Kraków saw significant changes in the dynamics of the Catholic Church's struggle against Polish communism, in-

cluding the entry onto the stage of Vatican diplomats determined to play a role in the ongoing drama.
Throughout those two decades, and in the face of
growing communist opposition, Karol Wojtyła grew
into the traditional Cracovian bishop's role as **Defensor Civitatis** [Defender of the City]. At the end
of those two decades, in October 1978, Poland's
communist rulers were terrified at the thought of
Wojtyła, the articulate, charismatic, indefatigable
defender of the rights of his people, as Primate of
Poland. His twenty years' experience as a bishop in
Kraków, however, were preparing the way for a new,
unexpected twist in the story of Karol Wojtyła and
communism.

THE YOUNGEST BISHOP IN POLAND

Cardinal Stefan Wyszyński was not a man to waste
time during his three years of internment, between
1953 and 1956. Rather, he used those years to think
through a bold initiative aimed at maintaining a
healthy moral tension between the Catholic Church
and the communist masters of Polish politics. The
year 1966 would mark the Polish Millennium—the
one thousandth anniversary of the beginnings of
what we now know as "Poland," a country that took
such anniversaries with great seriousness. Wyszyński

knew his adversary's mind well, and he anticipated that the communist regime would use the millennium celebration to rewrite Poland's history to its ideological tastes, and to serve its future political purposes. Something had to be done.

That something would be the Great Novena—a nine-year program of preparation for the millennium of Poland's baptism that would effectively recatechize the entire country. Its symbolic centerpiece would be a pilgrimage. Polish Catholicism had a great pilgrimage tradition, with hundreds of thousands of Catholics going by foot to such shrines as Kalwaria Zebrzydowska, which evoked the Holy Land in the hills outside Kraków, or to the Marian shrine at Piekary Śląskie, which drew Silesian miners and industrial workers to a vast annual outpouring of male piety, or to the greatest of all Polish shrines, that of the Black Madonna on Jasna Góra, Częstochowa's Bright Mountain. Wyszyński's Great Novena pilgrimage would adopt the pilgrimage tradition but give it a dramatic new form: the Black Madonna, that most treasured of national icons, would herself go on pilgrimage throughout Poland, visiting every parish in the country.

Westerners inured to this dimension of religious experience might dismiss the Great Novena and the pilgrimage of the Black Madonna as a bizarre if grandiose exercise in folk piety, something rather out of place in the second half of the twentieth century. Poland's communist masters knew that it was a grave threat. For, if successful, Wyszyński's cat-echetical program could undo whatever effects more than a decade of communist propaganda and indoc-trination had had. As for the Black Madonna pil-grimage, it threatened to underscore, from city to town to village to farm, that real authority in Poland lay elsewhere than in the Polish Communist Party. (Eventually, the communists put the icon under a kind of house arrest at Jasna Góra and forbade its peregrination throughout the country; Wyszyński, undeterred, sent the icon's frame instead.)[3]

Thus it was no surprise that the beginning of the Great Novena in 1957 should have been the pre-lude to a ratcheting up of communist pressure on the Church. The 1956 shake-up in the Polish in-ternal security apparatus, aimed at giving the party stricter control of the secret police, had led to a new division of labor, in which Department III of the Ministry of Internal Affairs took the leading role in carrying out operations against the Catholic clergy. From June 1962 on, counter-Church surveillance, intelligence analysis, and operations were concen-trated in Department IV of the Ministry of Internal Affairs, usually known as the fourth division of the SB. Department IV had provincial branches all over Poland, all of which had one purpose: to intensify SB surveillance of the Church and to increase secret police penetration of Catholic institutions.[4]

The security services took a much greater inter-est in Father Karol Wojtyła when, on July 4, 1958,

Pope Pius XII named the thirty-eight-year-old priest-professor auxiliary bishop of Kraków. It was an unusual appointment, given Wojtyła's youth and background; Cardinal Wyszyński had a well-developed nervousness about intellectuals, whom he feared would be unreliable in crises. Yet the appointment would not have been made without Wyszyński's approval—and would not have been approved if the SB had suspected that it was about to gain a formidable new enemy. Indeed, SB files from the time of Wojtyła's nomination as bishop suggest just how poor some of the intelligence coming to the secret police was: one informant reported, and the local SB passed on to headquarters, that Wojtyła's nomination had been poorly received by the Kraków clergy, which was the precise opposite of the truth (although it was certainly true of the clerical agent ŻAGIELOWSKI, whom the files suggest nursed a bitter grudge against Wojtyła for years).[5]

Wojtyła was ordained a bishop on September 28, 1958, in ancient Wawel Cathedral, hard by the tomb of St. Stanisław, the martyr-bishop who set the pattern of the Cracovian bishop as **Defensor Civitatis**. Bishop Wojtyła began to be referred to in SB internal communications as PEDAGOG and was kept under constant surveillance; for the next twenty years, his every move was followed and his residences were bugged; his friends and associates among the Kraków clergy became special targets for SB recruitment efforts. Most resisted; some did not. These efforts represented an intensified form of the TEOK [Technical Operational Evidence on Priests] effort, the building of files on every Catholic priest in Poland. In those files, the regime sought to record not simply such basic biographical data as the priest's date and place of birth, parentage, education, and visits abroad, but also information on his character traits, hobbies, friendships, recreational activities, political views, medical history, drug and alcohol use, and criminal record. The Wojtyła files from this period stress the young bishop's work with university students; the regime's hatred for a Church that was poaching what communism regarded as its future is evident between, and within, the lines.[6]

An SB profile of Bishop Wojtyła from 1960, developed by the source WŁODEK, is instructive in that it demonstrates that the SB could, sometimes, get it (mostly) right. According to the more insightful parts of the report, Wojtyła displayed an "unusual combination of intellectual qualities with those of an active, practical, and organized man." He had, according to the source, "a very active analytic-synthetic intelligence, astute at grasping the essence of a problem and being able to formulate it clearly and accurately, particularly in writing." The young bishop was "sometimes less well formulated orally—much depends on his level of tiredness, the need to adapt material to a given audience, etc." As for personality, Wojtyła was "very approachable, obliging, and responsible"; he was "not overly ambitious" and had "a very level-headed opinion of himself and his abilities." He was "very unlikely to do anything rash," being a "well-balanced individual" with "strong beliefs" and a strong will. In his interactions with others, WŁODEK reported, Wojtyła was "not easily influenced" but was "willing to take advice." He "can be obstinate," but "he knows people well, can see their shortcomings, is serious but can see the funny side in events and people and has a sense of humor." Above all, Bishop Wojtyła was "a man of integrity" who could "see his own mistakes and admit them to himself, at least." An acute observer of men and events, "he is not at all superficial," a "devout man in a more rational and 'metaphysical' way rather than an emotional one."[7]

The SB's intensified attempts to gather information about and to suborn the Polish clergy followed what the security service hoped would be a new and improved strategy of penetrating the Church, by seeking informants from within Catholic ranks who would exchange information for various favors, ranging from consumer goods to money to passports for foreign study and travel. Through its agents and provocateurs, the SB also attempted to foster divisions and factions within the ranks of Polish priests, especially in a tightly knit priestly fraternity like that of Kraków, with its history of resistance against oppression. In the early years of Wojtyła's episcopate, the sources ŻAGIELOWSKI and TORANO (who may in fact have been the same person) kept a close watch on the new bishop's activities with young people, which were of particular concern to the SB. But it was Nowa Huta, and Wojtyła's determination to support the townspeople in their quest for a church, that was a particular thorn in the SB's toe.

Thus a few months after Bishop Wojtyła began celebrating Christmas Midnight Mass in an open field in Nowa Huta in December 1959, a new clerical recruit, a source called MARECKI, began reporting to the SB on Wojtyła's intense interest in the "godless" new town. MARECKI, ironically, was transferred by the archdiocese from pastoral work in Nowa Huta to an assignment in the Kraków curia, from which he stole documents for the SB, photographed the inside of the curia, and made duplicate imprints of the archdiocesan seal. On April 27, 1960, there was a riot in Nowa Huta, following the removal of a cross erected by the townspeople as a reminder of their missing church. The authorities asked Wojtyła to write a letter to the townspeople, instructing them to keep the peace and renounce violent protests. Wojtyła complied, but with a twist, beginning his letter by noting that, as the cross would not be removed in the future, there would be no reason for protest. When the local authorities, shown the letter, refused to accept Wojtyła's condition, he raised the stakes by proposing to add to the letter the statement that the only way to keep peace in Nowa Huta would be to build the church that had long been denied to the people. The cross was restored, as was peace in Nowa Huta.[8]

SB Department IV's new approach—seduction rather than threat—had a degree of success in penetrating Cracovian Catholicism; by 1967, some 270 active informants had been recruited from among the local clergy and active laity. One of the latter, ARES, was the administrative director of the weekly newspaper **Tygodnik Powszechny** and an archdiocesan bureaucrat; his self-congratulatory reports touched on a number of matters, including a battle between the archdiocese and the local government over use of the archdiocesan seminary building—a battle Wojtyła won by an adroit compromise that maintained the Church's position while giving the government a reasonably graceful exit from the confrontation.[9]

The formation of Department IV of the SB and the intensification of its efforts to penetrate Polish Catholicism coincided with, and may have reflected, a new and vicious bout of religious persecution in the Soviet Union under Nikita Khrushchev. Many churches, monasteries, and seminaries that had been reopened in the wake of the post-Stalin "thaw" were shut down again; at the same time, according to Vasili Mitrokhin and Christopher Andrew, the Soviet regime's "ferocious anti-religious campaign" saw the dismantling of "half the [Russian] Orthodox parishes" in the USSR.[10] This persecution coincided with another KGB initiative aimed at global Christianity: the Russian Orthodox Church was permitted to join the World Council of Churches [WCC], whose operations and pronouncements the Soviet secret police believed it possible to influence. Russian Orthodox representatives at the Geneva headquarters of the WCC duly denied for decades that there was any repression of their community in the Soviet Union. A leading Orthodox figure in these ecumenical affairs, both within the Orthodox-Protestant world of the WCC and between Russian Orthodoxy and Catholicism, was Metropolitan Nikodim of Leningrad (known to his KGB controllers as ADAMANT), whose ordination in 1960 at age thirty-one as the youngest bishop in the Christian world "was in itself unmistakable evidence of KGB approval," according to Andrew and Mitrokhin.[11] ADAMANT/Nikodim would eventually rise in WCC ranks to become one of the organization's six presidents.

Ironically, the renewed persecution of Christian churches and communities within the USSR in the early 1960s took place at precisely the same time that Pope John XXIII and the diplomats of the Roman Curia decided to initiate a new approach of their own to the problem of communism—the so-called **Ostpolitik**.

Vatican II and the Early Years
of the *Ostpolitik*

When seventy-seven-year-old Cardinal Angelo Giuseppe Roncalli, patriarch of Venice and veteran
Vatican diplomat, was elected pope on October 28,
1958, he was expected to be a transitional figure,
bridging the gap between the nineteen-year reign of
Pius XII and an indeterminate papal future. Roncalli had other ideas. Less than three months after
his election he announced his intention to summon the Second Vatican Council, which would
become the most important event in Catholic history since the sixteenth-century Reformation and
Counter-Reformation.

After more than three years of preparation, Vatican II opened on October 11, 1962, with all the
bishops of the Catholic Church present in St. Peter's
Basilica—save for those forbidden by communist
mandarins to come to Rome. Five days later, on October 16, McGeorge Bundy, national security adviser
to the president of the United States, showed John
F. Kennedy reconnaissance photographs of offensive
Soviet missiles being installed in Cuba. On October
22, after six days of deliberations with his advisers,
President Kennedy announced to the nation and
the world that the United States would implement a
naval quarantine of Cuba in order to compel the removal of Soviet missiles from the island. For a week,

as the Council got itself organized, the world stood on the brink of nuclear war.

This largely unremarked historical coincidence—the opening of Vatican II and the Cuban Missile Crisis—had a profound effect on John XXIII and an even more profound effect on Vatican diplomacy. From the time of his election, Pope John, an old-fashioned diplomat who believed that human contacts could change seemingly intractable situations, had tried to defrost the Vatican's relations with the communist world. Thus he invited Russian Orthodox representatives to attend Vatican II as observers, while bending every effort to see that Catholic bishops from behind the Iron Curtain could attend the Council. After the nuclear showdown in the Caribbean abated, the shaken Pope determined to write an encyclical on world peace, which was published six months later, in April 1963, as **Pacem in Terris** [Peace on Earth]. He also intensified his personal diplomacy, welcoming Khrushchev's son-in-law, Alexei Adzhubei, to the Vatican in March 1963; this contact may have helped the Pope arrange for the subsequent release from the Gulag of the leader of the Greek Catholic Church in Ukraine, Metropolitan Iosyf Slipyi.

The principal agent of John XXIII's new **Ostpolitik,** which would continue under Pope Paul VI when John died in June 1963, was the Italian curialist and diplomat Agostino Casaroli. His early career in the papal diplomatic service had been spent on Latin American issues, but in March 1961, after being named vice-secretary of the Congregation for Extraordinary Ecclesiastical Affairs (as the Vatican foreign ministry was then called), his portfolio was broadened to include European questions, and he began to lead Holy See delegations to various UN negotiations being conducted in Vienna. From there, in 1963, he began to probe behind the Iron Curtain, making quiet trips to Budapest and Prague in order to test the diplomatic waters.

In his memoirs, Casaroli described the Soviet bloc in 1963 as a "vast, immobile swamp" that had "finally begun to ripple, though only lightly, under the wind of history."[12] In Casaroli's view, the immobility was not simply the communists' fault; it was also caused, at least insofar as the Catholic Church was concerned, by the confrontational policies of Pius XII, whose polemics were such that any contacts with the Holy See by citizens of the Soviet bloc—such as bishops and cardinals—were considered acts of espionage by communist authorities. Moreover, Casaroli believed, the 1949 Vatican condemnation of Catholic participation in communist parties, which remained in force, was regarded by the communists as an ongoing "declaration of war."[13]

Yet with the election of John XXIII, Casaroli thought, things had begun to change, if slightly; thus it was taken as a sign of a new openness to serious dialogue that Nikita Khrushchev sent greetings to the Pope on his eightieth birthday in November 1961.[14]

Casaroli was clear, in his own mind, on communist intentions: "squeezed and suffocated by the coils of a hostile power . . . religious life and the Church would have had to succumb to a 'natural' death."[15] As there seemed no possibility of a dramatic or even significant change in the division of Europe into two contending blocs, Vatican diplomacy's task was to prevent that "natural death" by a counterstrategy of **salvare il salvabile**, or saving what could be saved—which meant, in practice, ensuring the ongoing sacramental life of the Church by giving the Church behind the Iron Curtain bishops, who in turn could ordain priests.

In addition, John XXIII's **Ostpolitik** had several immediate, practical goals. The Pope wanted to make it possible for Catholic bishops from Soviet-bloc countries to attend Vatican II. He also wanted to see if there was any possibility of resolving the situations of two senior churchmen: the Hungarian primate, Cardinal József Mindszenty, who had been living in the American Embassy in Budapest since the abortive Hungarian Revolution in 1956; and the Czechoslovakian primate, Josef Beran, a hero of the Catholic resistance in World War II who had survived three Nazi concentration camps only to be jailed in communist prisons or detained under house arrest since 1949. Thus it was no accident that Casaroli's first two sallies behind the Iron Curtain were to Budapest and Prague.

And then there was the Pope's desire to position

the Holy See as a potential interlocutor in a super-power crisis threatening nuclear war, a strategic goal that seemed ever more urgent in light of the nuclear showdown of October 1962. It was an ambitious agenda, in which the Pope's concern for the Church under communism intersected with John XXIII's commitment to peace. The initial accomplishments of John's **Ostpolitik** were modest. Yet according to one of Casaroli's chief deputies, Achille Silvestrini, the dying pontiff was satisfied, because he believed that "nothing would be able to re-seal the crack that he had managed to open in the iron curtain." Thus when Casaroli briefed the Pope on his quiet visits to Budapest and Prague in the spring of 1963, John, who would die three weeks later, said, at the end of the audience, "Let us go forward with goodwill and trust, but without rushing."[16]

Giovanni Battista Montini, who took the name Paul VI at his election on June 21, 1963, was another papal veteran of the Vatican diplomatic service, although he had had little experience in the field, having spent most of his career as a senior Vatican bureaucrat prior to becoming archbishop of Milan in 1954. One of his admirers (and another agent of the **Ostpolitik**), the Viennese cardinal Franz König, appreciated Paul's intellectual and spiritual gifts while acknowledging his weaknesses: he was "often uncertain," König once conceded, but that was "because he was so intelligent and wanted to make the best of everything."[17] At the beginning of a difficult, fifteen-year pontificate, Paul, who brought what Casaroli once described as a "more pessimistic" cast of mind to the **Ostpolitik**, nonetheless agreed that the policy John XXIII and Casaroli had begun must continue, in order to achieve a **modus non moriendi**, a "way of not dying," for the Catholic Church in central and eastern Europe. In practical terms, this meant that Paul VI deferred to Casaroli and the team he had begun to assemble, which included fellow Italian curial diplomats such as Achille Silvestrini and Luigi Poggi, on the steps to be taken—including a ratcheting down of papal anticommunist rhetoric. That the Vatican's new geniality would not be met by a comparable geniality on the part of Soviet-bloc communist authorities created a situation that was "a torment" for Paul VI; years later, Casaroli would remember having to "restrain" the pope when Paul VI was determined to speak out against some communist act of perfidy.[18]

Casaroli and his colleagues brought diplomatic skill, a gift for languages, and patience to their work. What they did not bring was experience—experience of life in what the Czech playwright Václav Havel would later describe as the communist "culture of the lie," and experience in dealing with Soviet-bloc intelligence agencies. They were afraid, as was Paul VI, that an underground Catholic Church, detached from Rome and left to its own devices behind the Iron Curtain, would produce various aberrations even as it slowly suffocated. But they did not seem willing to take seriously the counsel of completely loyal churchmen in east central Europe who insisted that normal diplomatic methods would only work to the disadvantage of local Catholic Churches.[19]

And indeed to the Vatican's disadvantage—for the Holy See had virtually no developed counterintelligence capability with which to resist the penetration, disinformation, and destabilization efforts that the **Ostpolitik** unintentionally, but inevitably, made possible. Pope John's determination to bring bishops from behind the Iron Curtain to Vatican II was matched by aggressive and extensive efforts on the part of Soviet-bloc intelligence agencies to use the Council as an opportunity to penetrate the Vatican and influence the diplomacy of the Holy See. Thus the Hungarian delegation that came to Rome for the Council's opening in 1962 included several informants and operational agents, while a year later nine of the fifteen Hungarian bishops, theologians, and journalists at the Council's second session were working for Hungarian intelligence. The Hungarians, in fact, already had an intelligence asset in place in Rome: Fritz Kusen, an employee of Vatican Radio and a friend of the conservative curial theologian Sebastian Tromp, S.J.; Kusen worked under the code name MOZART and may have been a double agent. When the **Ostpolitik** ripened to the point at which serious discussions could begin between Vatican representatives and the Hungarian communist authorities, MOZART and two fellow moles in Rome helped prepare the Hungarian side of the negotiation, explained that there was a split in the Vatican between those determined to support the intransigent Cardinal Mindszenty and those who were seeking a way around the embattled Hungarian primate and were working with their Vatican contacts to support the anti-Mindszenty party in Rome. By contrast, the Holy See's representatives to the talks that began in Budapest in May 1963 were not so well briefed on the local situation. And in any event, the day before Casaroli arrived to begin the negotiation, Hungarian intelligence laid out an operational plan by which seventeen secret police agents were to track his every move throughout the country.

Things would go from bad to worse in Hungary in the years ahead, even as the **Ostpolitik** seemed, on the surface, to be working well there. An agreement, including provisions for the nomination of bishops, was signed between the Vatican and the Hungarian regime of János Kádár on September 15, 1964, the first such agreement between the Holy See and a communist government. Yet within the next five years, many of the Hungarian bishops nominated under this accord would cooperate with both Hungary's internal security and foreign intelligence agencies, to the point that, in 1969, the Hungarian bishops' conference was in large measure controlled by the Hungarian state. As this was unfolding in Hungary, the Hungarian College in Rome became a subsidiary of Hungarian intelligence. The emigrant clergy who had lived there since the 1956 revolution were expelled. Every rector of the College between 1965 and 1987 would be a trained and skillful agent, with expertise in both disinformation operations and bugging. Over half the visiting students and scholars who came to the College were agents; the College's leadership had ready access to Archbishop Casaroli, Archbishop Giovanni Cheli (Casaroli's point man on Hungary), and others in charge of the **Ostpolitik**, in which capacity they became important instruments of the Hungarian communist government's Vatican policy.[20]

While their Hungarian colleagues were exploiting the **Ostpolitik** with considerable success, the Polish SB also tried to turn the Second Vatican Council into a moment of opportunity in its war against the Church. It had the advantage of a well-placed clerical collaborator, code-named JANKOWSKI—Father Michał Czajkowski, a biblical scholar devoted to advancing the Jewish-Catholic dialogue, who seems to have been lured into working for the SB in the conviction that cooperation with the government would undermine the influence in Poland of Cardinal Wyszyński, whom Father Czajkowski regarded as far too conservative; here, as in Hungary, Soviet-bloc intelligence exploited the widening ideological divisions in the Catholic Church for its own purposes. JANKOWSKI reported to the Polish intelligence services on the activities of the Polish bishops at Vatican II (where he was working as a journalist) and on Roman curial affairs, maintaining contacts with both the Roman SB chief and a controller in Poland from Department IV.

Cardinal Wyszyński's concerns about the relentlessness of the SB's efforts to penetrate and then divide the Catholic Church in Poland shaped his thinking about certain issues at the Council. Thus, under Wyszyński's leadership, the Polish bishops were not enthusiastic about proposals from western European bishops and theologians to restore the diaconate as a permanent office in the Catholic Church and to ordain married men as deacons. To Wyszyński and other Polish Church leaders, a corps of married deacons would provide the SB with a rich new menu of targets for its penetration and recruitment efforts.[21] For its part, disempowering Wyszyński seems to have been the primary strategic goal of the SB during Vatican II. Throughout the four sessions of the Council, Polish intelligence worked to erode Wyszyński's authority with both the Polish bishops and the Vatican, while sowing seeds of discord about the proper interpretation of the Council's documents among the Polish bishops and undercutting Wyszyński's efforts to maintain his position as the sole contact between the Vatican and the Polish government; the Vatican architects of the **Ostpolitik** were, for example, eager to explore the possibility of diplomatic relations between the Vatican and Poland, which the

Polish cardinal regarded (and not without reason) as but another opportunity for the communists to play divide-and-conquer.

The SB was not above attempting to pervert the Council's discussion of some of the more specialized points of Catholic theology. Throughout the first two sessions of the Council, the question of whether Vatican II should issue a separate document on the Virgin Mary, or incorporate its reflection on Mary's role in the history of salvation into its major document on the Church, was a point of some controversy. The SB saw an opportunity here to use Cardinal Wyszyński's well-known Marian piety against him. Thus the director of Department IV, Colonel Stanisław Morawski, worked with a dozen or so clerical collaborators who were theological experts in Mariology to prepare a memorandum for the bishops of the Council, suggesting that the Polish primate's views on Mary were excessive and even heterodox. The final form of this memorandum was prepared by a collaborator, STOLARSKI, who was a biblical scholar and a priest. The "Memorandum on Certain Aspects of the Cult of the Virgin Mary in Poland" was distributed to all the bishops at Vatican II, was widely disseminated in Europe, and was regarded as authentic by many journalists covering the Council. It cannot be doubted that it had an effect, if a temporary one, on Wyszyński's reputation among his brother bishops, while weakening his position vis-à-vis the curialists working to establish Vatican diplomatic relations with Warsaw.[22]

"A Very Dangerous Ideological Opponent"

When Vatican II began in October 1962, Karol Wojtyła was one of the youngest bishops in the world and was seated, as befit his junior status, some 500 feet from the high altar, near the door of St. Peter's. By October 1965, when the Council's final session opened, Wojtyła had become a significant figure in the Council's deliberations, playing important roles in developing Vatican II's texts on religious freedom and the vocation of the laity; he also helped draft one of the Council's most controversial documents, the Pastoral Constitution on the Church in the Modern World.[23] Wojtyła's increasing prominence guaranteed that he would receive closer attention from the SB.

SB activities during Vatican II, including the campaign against Cardinal Wyszyński, were run out of the Polish Embassy in Rome, where agents of Department I (foreign intelligence) used diplomatic assignments as cover for their activities, and the consular section (which handled passports) was another venue for intelligence work. Polish priests working in Rome had to renew their passports annually, and the conversations initiated during routine consular activities were used as an opportunity to identify potential recruits or to elicit information that could be useful to SB analysts. Blackmail, using compromising materials gathered (or fabricated) in Poland, played a large role in these recruitment efforts; if recruitment was rebuffed, the blackmail material could be used back home to damage a man's reputation.

SB activities extended far beyond the Polish Embassy, of course. One particularly valuable Department I agent during the Vatican II years was Ignacy Krasicki, who was in Rome under the auspices of Polish Radio. The son of an aristocratic family, he had ready access to Church circles, which he used to gather information for his controllers in Warsaw. In all of this work, Department IV agents, contacts, and collaborators worked closely with Department I; as one student of these affairs put it, "close contacts between Department I and [Department IV] constituted a routine operational practice at the stage of recruiting a new collaborator by intelligence services [and] these practices were constantly used in [assigning] further tasks and [in the] evaluations [of operations]." During the Council years and beyond, SB activities in Rome, and particularly those directed at the Roman Curia, were aimed at determining whether the Council's **aggiornamento** or "updating" of the Catholic Church, of which the new **Ostpolitik** was a part, could be used to advance the interests of local communist parties and of Soviet foreign policy.[24]

The SB's intense interest in Catholic affairs during the Council years did not always lead to keener communist insight into certain prominent Catholic personalities, however, as the story of Karol Wojtyła's nomination as archbishop of Kraków neatly illustrates.

Archbishop Eugeniusz Baziak died on the night of June 14–15, 1962. On July 16, the Metropolitan Chapter of the archdiocese, a group of senior priests, elected Karol Wojtyła, the younger of Kraków's two auxiliary bishops, as vicar capitular, that is, temporary administrator of the archdiocese, until a successor to Baziak could be agreed upon according to the procedures established in 1950—Cardinal Wyszyński would clear a name with Rome and then submit it to the government for review; the government could veto any candidate, but it could not impose its own. A deadlock quickly ensued and lasted for eighteen months. Wyszyński would secure approval from the Vatican for a nominee; the name would be sent to Zenon Kliszko, the second-ranking member and chief ideologist of the Polish Communist Party, and the Speaker of Poland's rubber-stamp parliament, the Sejm; Kliszko would reject the name. This went on for a year and a half, through seven rounds. Then, in the fall of 1963, Stanisław Stomma, head of the miniature Catholic party permitted in the Sejm, had a talk about the Kraków situation with Kliszko, who told Stomma that "I'm waiting for Wojtyła and I'll continue to veto names until I get him." Stomma thanked the keeper of Polish communist ideological orthodoxy for sharing this confidence, all the while trying to keep a straight face; Wojtyła was precisely the nominee he, other activist Catholic laity, and the most engaged of Kraków's priests wanted. Wyszyński, who had his doubts about Wojtyła, finally agreed, and the appointment was made by Pope Paul VI on December 30, 1963.

The SB had not been inactive during the eighteen-month-long struggle to find a successor to Archbishop Baziak. Its files were full of warning flags about Wojtyła's recent activities, which would have been shared with Kliszko: the young bishop's skill in keeping the Kraków seminary under the control of the archdiocese; his bold gesture of defiance in saving the Silesian seminary building in Kraków from a planned communist takeover (he had threatened to stand publicly with the faculty and students if they were evicted); his ongoing association with the suspect Rhapsodic Theater; his Christmas Midnight Masses in Nowa Huta; his January 1963 sermon in Wawel Cathedral, when he praised two fighters of the anti-czarist 1863 rebellion, Adam Chmielowski (who became "Brother Albert") and Rafał Kalinowski (who became a Carmelite monk), and reminded Poles how often they had had to "break through to freedom from underground." There was ample reason behind the judgment in one of Wojtyła's SB files: "Despite his seemingly conciliatory and flexible nature, Wojtyła is a very dangerous ideological opponent."[25]

In the calculus of Zenon Kliszko and other Polish communist authorities, these storm signals and that judgment may have been offset by Wojtyła's youth, his relative inexperience in political hardball, and his "theoretical" nature (after all, the man wrote poetry and taught philosophy)—all of which may have suggested that he could be manipulated into a compromising (or at least helpful) position in the government's relentless game of divide-and-conquer with Cardinal Wyszyński. Wyszyński may also have feared this, not because of any doubts about Wojtyła's loyalties but because of concerns about his shrewdness. Asked in Rome in 1964 about the new archbishop of Kraków, the Primate rather brusquely dismissed the query with a single sentence: "He is a poet." That, in turn, suggests that Wyszyński may have been under at least some pressure from the Holy See to resolve the long-festering question of the Kraków succession (which from a canonical point of view had dragged on since 1951) by accepting Wojtyła, who had made a strong impression at Vatican II.

Then there is the possibility that the men at the higher altitudes of Polish communism actually believed their own ideology, according to which ideas were ephemera, the exhaust fumes of economic processes, and intellectuals were by definition incapable of coping with the "real world." True, there was that side of Wojtyła referred to in his 1960 SB profile—he could be a skillful administrator and tenacious defender of the Church when circumstances demanded. Yet, at bottom, he was a man of ideas, not a man of power as they understood power. Kliszko and the comrades may even have believed that Wojtyła's intellectual interests and contacts could be turned to their advantage, by helping keep the always restive Kraków Catholic intelligentsia under control. Communist party and SB rivalries may also have played a role, if a minor one, in Kliszko's decision: yes, the SB was worried that Wojtyła was "a very dangerous ideological opponent," but the party chieftains would manage him nonetheless.

While the question can never be resolved with certainty, it seems most likely that the communist leadership's determination to play divide-and-conquer against the main ideological opponent, Cardinal Wyszyński, trumped the concerns the SB raised about Karol Wojtyła. Kliszko and the comrades seem to have been convinced that Wojtyła could be manipulated; fissures would open up in the solid front the Catholic Church in Poland had long maintained; those fissures could then be exploited in the war against the Church. As Father Andrzej Bardecki, an old friend of Wojtyła's, put it years later, it was a perfect example of how "the Holy Spirit can work his will by darkening as well as enlightening people's minds."[26]

The War Over the Millennium

Karol Wojtyła was solemnly enthroned as metropolitan archbishop of Kraków on March 8, 1964. Two
months later, an updated profile of the new archbishop was prepared by Department IV of the SB
for the Polish Communist Party Politburo and described Wojtyła in these terms: "He . . . has a sense
of realism and is willing to compromise in certain
situations . . . Modest and direct. Reads a great deal
and works at perfecting himself . . . Material things
are of little importance to him. He specializes in
socio-philosophical problems."[27] It was an interesting report, in that other SB profiles of Polish bishops
from this period tend to focus on putative or actual
negative qualities such as cupidity, financial greed,
allegations of alcoholism, and so forth—aspects of
a personality that, accurate or not, could be used
against a man.[28] There is none of that here, which
suggests a certain degree of respect for Wojtyła, but
also a lack of dirt to be used against him. Wojtyła's
virtues would soon enough prove a major threat to
Polish communism; at about the same time Department IV was revising its profile of the man Zenon
Kliszko had been determined to get as archbishop
of Kraków, the exasperated warden of a prison in
Gdańsk told one of his more distinguished inmates,
a Camaldolese monk, that "Wojtyła has swindled us!"[29]

The "swindle" would get worse as Archbishop Wojtyła settled into his new responsibilities. Kliszko and the comrades may have imagined him something of a political naif, unable to play the game the way the tough men played it. They were soon disabused of any such fantasy. Determined not to let a millimeter of separation appear between himself and Cardinal Wyszyński, Archbishop Wojtyła became a stalwart support to the Primate in two Wyszyński initiatives that drove the Polish communist leadership into virtual apoplexy.

The first took place in late 1965, toward the end of the fourth session of Vatican II. Poland's relocation westward as a result of the Yalta agreement had never been recognized formally by the West German government, and so was not recognized formally by the Vatican, which defers to governments in matters of defining territorial sovereignty. Thus the situation of the Catholic Church in Poland's "recovered territories" was canonically irregular, the appointment of residential bishops was impeded, and the Church in western Poland would remain in a kind of canonical limbo until a formal Polish-German agreement on borders was reached. Wyszyński and the Vatican were both determined to resolve the matter after twenty years; but both the Primate and the Holy See understood that the ground would have to be prepared. So as the Council was drawing to a close, the Polish bishops, under Wyszyński's leadership and with the strong encouragement of Pope Paul VI, prepared a bold gesture: two decades after a war in which Germany had devastated Poland, the Poles would take the initiative in forgiving and asking forgiveness. Thus, as the Poles were sending letters to other episcopal conferences around the world, inviting their brother bishops to the celebrations of the Polish Millennium in 1966, the letter to the German hierarchy would include a plea for reconciliation. Word of this plan, which Wojtyła strongly supported, inevitably leaked, and the SB bent every effort to monitor the drafting of the letter and derail it if possible. SB reports indicated that Wojtyła had been assigned the delicate work of negotiating the drafts of the letter through the Vatican bureaucracy, working with Paul VI's close associate, Giovanni Benelli.[30]

The letter was published on November 18, 1965. After a lengthy evocation of the difficult history of relations between the two countries, the Polish bishops recalled the immense suffering of their people during World War II, while acknowledging that Germans had also suffered at Polish hands. It was the letter's conclusion—"We forgive, and we ask your forgiveness"—that sent the Polish Communist Party into a rage. A campaign of vilification against the Church was immediately launched, under the rubric "We shall not forgive, we shall not forget," and the bishops were accused of betraying the national interest, which amounted to a charge of treason.[31]

It was a bizarre reaction in a way, in that securing legal sovereignty over the "recovered territories" was

certainly in the interest of the Polish People's Republic—and the letter, as any astute observer would have
understood, was a step toward that end. But the Polish communist leadership, in whose minds "forgiveness" was not a term with much meaning, saw an
opportunity to drive a wedge between the bishops
and their people and seized it. By stressing that Poles
had no reason to ask forgiveness of Germans for anything, the communist campaign against the Church
appealed both to patriotic sentiment and to the scars
many Poles still carried from the days of the Nazi occupation. Even some of the members of Archbishop
Wojtyła's **Środowisko** were puzzled, even disturbed,
by the bishops' initiative and **Wujek**'s role in it.

The SB immediately went into action against
Wojtyła, using popular resentments at the bishops'
initiative to fabricate an open letter to the archbishop
from the workers at the Solvay chemical plant, where
Wojtyła had once been a **robotnik**. After excoriating
Wojtyła and the other bishops for suggesting that
there was something for which Poles should seek
forgiveness from Germans, the letter (which was
published in **Gazeta Krakowska** on December 22,
1965) made its ideological pedigree and geopolitical purpose unmistakably clear by claiming that "the
direct guilt for bringing on the Second World War
and its bestial course falls exclusively on German imperialism and fascism, and its successor, the Federal
Republic of Germany."

Archbishop Wojtyła responded calmly but forcefully in a letter dated December 24 and read in Kraków's churches, as it was initially refused publication in the press. The archbishop recalled with affection his days at Solvay and what they had taught him about life, and then noted that the text and spirit of the bishops' appeal to the German bishops had been a key moment of preparation for the Polish Millennium, rooted in the "deepest principles of Christian ethics contained in the Gospel." Wojtyła also told the workers that the bishops' letter was clearly in the national interest, in that it would help pave the way for a conclusion of the legal controversy over the "recovered territories," a point which the German bishops had acknowledged in their response. (The German acknowledgment had, of course, been ignored in the SB-concocted open letter.) Finally, Wojtyła wrote,

> I respond to this letter, above all, as an individual who has been wronged. . . . When we worked together during the occupation, a lot of things united us—and among these, the first and foremost was a respect for the human being, for conscience, individuality, and social dignity. This is what I learned in large measure from the workers at Solvay—but I am unable to find this fundamental principle in your open letter. . . . Not only do I have a right to my good name, but all of the people whom I represent and for whom I am a shepherd as the archbishop of Kraków have a right to my good name.[32]

The SB's clumsy attempt at intimidation thus gave Wojtyła an opportunity to define the line of battle on which he would fight communism for as long as he was archbishop of Kraków: the defense of the dignity of the human person. As the celebration of Poland's Millennium unfolded—the second Wyszyński initiative the communists were determined to undermine—there would be further skirmishing along that line.

The Millennium commemorated the baptism of the Piast prince, Mieszko I, in 966—the event from which the history of what the world knows as "Poland" is dated. Cardinal Wyszyński intended the Millennium celebrations to be both a reminder to the nation of its Christian origins and a moment of consecration for the future—for the celebrations would conclude with a great act of national rededication to the Virgin Mary, Queen of Poland, on the feast of Our Lady of Częstochowa, August 26. Wyszy ski's plan thus challenged Poland's communist rulers to a battle over the nation's future as well as its past, a battle that also involved questions of national identity and regime legitimacy. The gauntlet was picked up by the authorities, with the SB playing a crucial role.

In February 1966, a special "party-state commission" to deal with Wyszyński's Millennium was established; its membership included representatives of the security services as well as officials from the ministries dealing with transport, culture, education, radio, television, tourism, and sports. Efforts to penetrate and subvert the Church were increased. A counter-program was developed so that various sports and cultural events would compete with the Church's Millennium program. A "Parade of the Millennium" was scheduled for July 22, the anniversary of the Lublin Committee Manifesto. When Wyszyński came to Gniezno and Poznań to lead religious commemorations of the Millennium, "patriotic" events featuring the party chieftain, Gomułka, and the defense minister were mounted. Józef Cyrankiewicz, the prime minister (and the man who had betrayed Witold Pilecki), was intended to be the alternative to the Primate during the Millennium celebration in Kraków. The closing Mass in Warsaw ended with crowds clashing with the armed militia, the ZOMO, which blocked the streets leading to communist party headquarters. The most serious disturbances were in Lublin, where 290 people were arrested. As historian Andrzej Paczkowski writes, "in all these disturbances, organized groups of 'worker activists' took part alongside regular security forces; some of them were actually SB officers, whose behavior toward the public was aggressive and on occasion simply provocative."[33]

Pope Paul VI became a player in the Millennium drama. He had a great personal affection for Poland, where he had spent a few months as junior diplomat, and he was eager to accept Wyszyński's invitation, tendered in 1965, to come to Poland and receive the nation's Millennium vows of consecration at Częstochowa. The communist authorities might have been expected to be open to such a papal pilgrimage, for part of their strategy, during and immediately after Vatican II, was to set the man they imagined to be the "progressive" (Paul VI) against the well-known enemy reactionary (Wyszyński), as a means of splitting the Polish hierarchy and the Polish laity while creating a separate line of communication between the Vatican and the Polish communist authorities. The Polish government's rage over the bishops' letter to the German episcopate, and Paul VI's strong support for the Polish initiative at reconciliation, overrode these strategic considerations, however. Despite a secret negotiating mission to Poland by Agostino Casaroli (dressed in suit and tie), the regime set conditions for the visit that the Pope was certain to reject: the pontiff could come for only a day; he would visit Wrocław, the former German Breslau, rather than Warsaw (thus tacitly ratifying Polish sovereignty over the "recovered territories"); Cardinal Wyszyński would play no significant role in the papal visit.[34] The conditions were clearly impossible, and the Pope reluctantly had to decline Wyszyński's invitation. At the Mass of national reconsecration in Częstochowa on August 26, the hundreds of thousands of Poles who managed to attend, despite the regime's efforts to keep them away, saw the Pope's framed portrait on an empty chair. The chair was decorated with red and white roses—the Polish national colors.[35]

Paul VI would not undercut Wyszyński by visiting Poland under circumstances bound to diminish the Primate's authority. But Wyszyński was not without highly placed critics in the Roman Curia, especially among some of the diplomats charged with devising and executing the **Ostpolitik**. In part, this reflected the typical curial resentment against "little popes," local churchmen who controlled local Catholic affairs closely and were not afraid to rebuff curial initiatives; in the case of Wyszyński, this touched directly on the Primate's determination that he, and he alone, would be the Catholic interlocutor with the Polish government. The resentments against Wyszyński also reflected the tensions of the late 1940s, when the Primate, now thought inflexible and intransigent, had been too flexible for the tastes of some of Pius XII's diplomats. Roman officials were aware of Wyszyński's skills; Casaroli, who battled him for years, once described him as a "real prince" and a man with an admirable and acute political sense of just where the edge of the cliff was located.[36] On the other hand, those same officials quite understood that Wyszyński thought them ill prepared for dealing with communists, whom he believed he understood far better than they did. From the SB's point of view, curial resentments against Wyszyński, and the well-propagated charge that the Primate was out of sympathy with the reforms of Vatican II, proved to be quite useful in recruiting clerical collaborators who resented what they regarded as Wyszyński's authoritarian style, or who had a different theological view of the Catholic future. A senior member of the philosophy department at the Catholic University of Lublin, Father Mieczysław Albert Krąpiec, O.P., was an SB collaborator of the first sort; Father Mieczysław Maliński, a seminary classmate of Karol Wojtyła whom the SB knew as DELTA, was a collaborator of the second sort, as was Father Michał Czajkowski, whose work with the SB at Vatican II has already been noted.[37]

Paul VI, who had a great respect for Karol Wojtyła's work at Vatican II, wanted to create the young Polish archbishop a cardinal in his first post–Vatican II consistory, in June 1967. The Polish government likely acquiesced to the nomination in order to advance its divide-and-conquer strategy against the Church: two cardinals might well lead to two factions in the hierarchy and—who knew?—two camps in the Polish Church, one "progressive" and one "conservative," in a split that could be exploited to the regime's advantage. The newly created Cardinal Wojtyła, for his part, refused to play according to the comrades' script. He bent every effort to defer to Primate Wyszyński when the two were at public functions together, while defending the older prelate with both restless Catholic intellectuals and resentful Roman officials. Even behind the closed doors of the Polish bishops' meetings, Wojtyła deferred to the older man, waiting to express his opinions until the Primate noted that "we have not yet heard from Cardinal Wojtyła on this question."

The SB further intensified its surveillance of Wojtyła from the time he was created cardinal. A detailed questionnaire dispatched to SB informants, collaborators, and agents, including ARES and ERSKI, suggests just how obsessed the security services were with dredging up every potentially useful detail on the new cardinal. The four-page-long "character profile" was divided into seven sections. The section on "daily routines" queried everything from Wojtyła's shaving habits to the questions of who bought his underwear and who polished his shoes, while not ignoring how often, with whom, and what the cardinal drank, and whether he smoked cigarettes (the precise brand being also of interest). The second section, on "audio-visual equipment," asked, among many other things, his opinion of current radio and television programs, with particular attention to whether he listened to Radio Free Europe. The third section, on the cardinal's health, posed a number of expected questions while also inquiring as to how often Wojtyła went to the dentist. Section four, on "interest in technology and collectibles," asked whether Wojtyła collected stamps or coins, and how well he typed. Section five was on "sports, travel, and leisure," perhaps not surprisingly since the cardinal was a well-known hiker, kayaker, and skier;

here, the SB was interested in knowing about the quality of his skis and the extent of his recreational apparel, both winter and summer. The sixth section of the questionnaire, on his "family situation," would have brought a meager haul, as the cardinal had few second cousins and all his direct relatives were long dead; nonetheless, the security services wanted to know if he was involved in any family conflicts and, if so, what were the causes and present circumstances. The final section, the seventh, was an attempt to build a roster of the cardinal's "personal contacts," including his "closest professional contacts" and his "closest friends."[38]

Despite this intense surveillance, which included the thorough bugging of Wojtyła's residence as well as increased spying on those friends and contacts identified in the character profile, the SB continued to misread their man with regularity. In 1967, French president Charles de Gaulle, pursuing his own **Ostpolitik**, made a state visit to Poland and, under pressure from the communist authorities, decided not to meet with Primate Wyszyński. When he came to Kraków and wished to visit the cathedral, he was guided by the sacristan, having been informed that Cardinal Wojtyła was otherwise engaged. SB documents reported this snub as an expression of Wojtyła's poor judgment and fear of Wyszyński, when in fact it was a clear indication of Wojtyła's loyalty and of his determination not to be used, even by **Le Grand Charles**, against the Primate.

EVENTS OF CONSEQUENCE

Karol Wojtyła's first year as a prince of the Church coincided with two events that would bear profoundly on his personal future, and on the dynamics of the Polish Church's war with communism.

On July 4, 1967, Agostino Casaroli, who had succeeded in maneuvering the Czechoslovak primate Josef Beran out of house arrest and into a Roman exile and had arranged for the Vatican's first exchange of diplomatic envoys with a communist state (Yugoslavia), was appointed Vatican "foreign minister" by Paul VI and ordained a bishop. From this point on, Archbishop Casaroli had the formal authority to develop the Vatican **Ostpolitik**, of which he had long been the driving force. No one, least of all Cardinal Wyszyński, doubted that this would mean ever more energetic efforts by Casaroli to maneuver the Holy See into a position as intermediary between hardpressed local Catholic Churches behind the Iron Curtain and local communist governments.[39] The complications attendant upon such efforts would be great—in part because they would coincide with a new, bloc-wide assault on the Church, led by the KGB. For within three weeks of Casaroli's appointment, Moscow's spymasters brought together in Budapest intelligence services from throughout the Soviet bloc in order to "discuss work against the Vatican," "measures to discredit the Vatican and its backers," and "measures to exacerbate the differences within the Vatican and between the Vatican and the capitalist countries." Senior KGB officials addressed the conference, describing "hostile activity" by the Vatican and the Catholic Church in the USSR and the work of the KGB in countering these alleged aggressions. Attention was also paid to "agent operational work against Vatican institutions." Work against the Vatican was to be intensified, "in close relation with the work against the Main Adversary [the United States]."[40]

The second event, which would have a marked bearing on the future of the struggle between Catholicism and communism, was the Prague Spring of 1968, crushed by Soviet tanks in August of that year. This act of brutal repression caused some in the employ of communist governments, appalled at the violence, to reconsider. It was after the tanks rolled into Prague that Vasili Mitrokhin began copying a vast archive of KGB records he would eventually exfiltrate to the West.[41] The assault on the Prague Spring was also a crucial factor in persuading a Polish army officer, Ryszard Kukliński, to find contacts with U.S. intelligence through which he could inform the Western alliance of future Warsaw Pact military plans.[42] Furthermore, the liquidation of the Prague Spring was a crisis for intellectuals chafing under Marxism, for it seemed to underscore the impossibility of any "reform communism." Polish philosopher Leszek Kołakowski began a revisionist account of the history of Marxism, eventually going into exile and concluding in his masterwork, **Main Currents of Marxism**, that Stalinism was Marxism's natural outgrowth, not the aberration described by Nikita Khrushchev at the twentieth Soviet Communist Party Congress.[43] Bronisław Geremek, a medieval historian of Jewish heritage who had received a Catholic elementary education in postwar Poland, resigned from the communist party and began seeking contacts among other dissident intellectuals.

The events in Czechoslovakia were mirrored, if in a less dramatic way, by considerable unrest in Poland in 1968. The excessive response to that unrest—which included thousands of detentions and arrests and large-scale student expulsions from the universities, which were in an uproar throughout the country—reflected a rising level of paranoia in the communist leadership throughout central and eastern Europe. It was relatively easy for Władysław Gomułka and others to blame Geremek's dissent on "Zionism" and to try to deflect attention from the country's real problems by an official campaign of anti-Semitic agitation. But it was a clear sign that the longtime Polish party leader was losing his grip when he told the Politburo that Leszek Kołakowski, a thoroughly secular philosopher, was "one of Wyszyński's clients."[44]

That was not plausible. But something in fact had shifted in the Polish Catholic hierarchy's address to these waves of unrest and repression, perhaps under the influence of the newly created Cardinal Wojtyła.

The Church had long taken up the cudgels to defend its people and its priests. Now, the Polish bishops defended the human rights of those intellectuals and artists who had not only been irreligious, but who had previously shown antagonism toward the Church.

The most extreme form of paranoia during the upheavals of 1968, however, came from the KGB. Yuri Andropov, still bearing the psychological scars of having been surprised by the Hungarian Revolution of 1956, had become KGB chairman in 1967— just in time for the surprise of the Prague Spring. The juxtaposition was evidently too much and reinforced Andropov's long-standing fear of anti-Soviet conspiracies emanating from the Vatican, which he was convinced was bent on the ideological subversion of the USSR (which was, of course, true, if not in the sense that Andropov understood "ideological subversion"). Thus, at precisely the time that the Casaroli **Ostpolitik** was entering its most energetic phase, the KGB was working on an assumption that would have boggled the curial diplomat's mind, had he known about it: Andropov and his comrades were persuaded that the Vatican Secretariat of State had worked out a master plan to splinter the unity of the Soviet Union and that the plan was under the direction of Paul VI's closest aide, Archbishop Giovanni Benelli.[45]

TO "DISINTEGRATE" THE CHURCH

Karol Wojtyła came into his own as a bishop and a human rights advocate in the late sixties. In the thirteen years left to him in Kraków after the conclusion of the Second Vatican Council, he sustained a tremendous pace of pastoral activity that marked him as one of the most creative, dynamic bishops in the post-conciliar Catholic Church. At the same time, his work at several international Synods of Bishops and in the Roman curial congregations to which he was assigned as a cardinal, and his occasional forays into international intellectual life, drew the respect of senior churchmen around the world. Those who came to visit him in Kraków could see for themselves that the **Defensor Civitatis** was not only a happy warrior, but an effective one.[46]

His effectiveness was all the more impressive because of the complex political and ecclesiastical circumstances he faced. The political situation was, in one sense, simple—"we" and "they," "the society" and "the power," all the time. In other respects, however, the politics were far more complex than they had been in the classic period of Polish Catholic anticommunist resistance, from 1953 to 1956.

In December 1970, protests broke out in Gdańsk, quickly spread throughout Poland's Baltic region, and then spilled over into much of the country, leading to dozens of deaths, a thousand injuries, thousands of detentions (often followed by harsh beatings)—and the resignation of Władysław Gomułka as head of the Polish Communist Party, fourteen years after he had taken power in response to the unrest of 1956. Gomułka's replacement was Edward Gierek, whose political base was industrial Silesia and who could, it was hoped, appeal to workers who remained on a high boil of unrest after Gomułka's demise. In a dramatic move, Gierek went to Gdańsk and, after listening to a long litany of complaints about incompetence, brutality, harsh working conditions, poor wages, and food prices, challenged the shipyard workers to be part of the solution: "So what do you say? Will you help?" He got the answer he wanted, if unenthusiastically: "We will help!" As Andrzej Paczkowski puts it, "That fragment of dialogue"—that simulacrum of a democratic conversation—was "seized on and repeated endlessly by official propaganda," becoming the "first slogan" of the Polish 1970s. The fundamental question about the system, which was raised by one of the workers who met with Gierek, remained unanswered: "Why must the workers pay for every change with their blood?"[47]

The "change" was a parody of real economics: "consumer socialism," to be paid for by extensive foreign borrowing. Some aspects of everyday life improved, at least temporarily; but the gap between life behind the Iron Curtain and life in western Europe became more and more of a chasm, a fact known by every Pole with access to a radio. Yet the regime persisted in mounting a crude "propaganda of success," trumpeting its accomplishments in providing a variety of cultural and sporting events even as the first economic accomplishments of the "change" soon dissipated and the promised cornucopia of consumer goods never materialized. The propaganda barrage and the regime's relentless boasting simply served to alienate ordinary Poles even more and to depress the public spirit.[48]

This unhappy situation helped create the political and economic context for Wojtyła's work as archbishop; other factors added to the complexity of his situation. There were new dynamics in Polish dissent: the first probes at rapprochement were under way between restive workers (almost universally Catholic) and dissident intellectuals (often secular, and sometimes anticlerical). Ironically, the regime, while using the SB to penetrate and suborn these efforts, helped make this new, coalitional opposition activism possible, as the government's need to service Poland's foreign debt provided a measure of protection for the new dissidents against too public a display of regime brutality.[49] Another complicating factor for Wojtyła was the Vatican **Ostpolitik**, which was becoming ever more energetic even as Cardinal Wyszyński's skepticism about it increased. Wojtyła was devoted to Paul VI, who was ultimately responsible for the **Ostpolitik**; yet he had to maintain a common front with Wyszyński against the government, and his own experience led him to the conviction that a vocal, public defense of the human rights of all was a moral imperative, whatever Archbishop Casaroli and his negotiators were doing with Poland's communist leaders behind closed doors. And in the midst of these tensions and complexities, he had the tremendous task of leading the implementation of Vatican II in his archdiocese.

Whatever other superficial changes there were in the Gierek years, one fact of Polish ecclesiastical and political life did not change: the regime's war against the Church took on a new, harder edge in November 1973 with the formation of "Independent Group D" of Department IV of the SB. Led by a veteran SB anti-Church operative, Konrad Straszewski, Group D was charged with "disintegrating" Catholic activities through a coordinated assault on the integrity of the Church.[50] Working with four other officers, Straszewski led a program whose mission statement identified four objectives: to discover and impede the "inimical ideologies" as well as the "social activities" of the Catholic Church, focusing on the diocesan clergy, the religious orders, and lay organizations; to identify and combat those Catholic priests and bishops deemed especially dangerous; to uncover and sever the Polish Church's contacts with other Catholic entities and organizations outside of Poland; and to enhance the loyalty of Polish Catholic clergy and laity to the Polish People's Republic.[51] Thus all of Wojtyła's initiatives as archbishop came under close scrutiny by the SB, which did everything in its power to undermine and "distintegrate" his plans using collaborators in the Kraków archdiocesan curia. They were unsuccessful, but it was not for lack of effort.

Soviet-bloc intelligence operatives were also hard at work in Rome. In the years immediately following Vatican II, the KGB received reports from sources in the office of Paul VI's secretary of state, the French cardinal Jean Villot, and in the Holy See's "foreign ministry," the Council for the Public Affairs of the Church—including virtually verbatim reports on Pope Paul's conversations with West German chancellor Willy Brandt and South Vietnamese foreign minister Tran Van Lam, and an outline of the Pope's 1970 discussion with U.S. president Richard M. Nixon. Electronic eavesdropping devices were placed in the apartment of the **Ostpolitik**'s principal architect, Archbishop Casaroli, while Vatican counterintelligence measures ranged from primitive to nonexistent: stenographic transcripts of delicate negotiating sessions were archived in the Vatican Secretariat of State with evidently little concern that copies might find their way to Warsaw, East Berlin, and Moscow.[52]

Given all of this, and the new intensity of the Polish communist regime's assault on the Church through the SB, there is no little irony in the fact that, in precisely this same period, the architects of the Vatican **Ostpolitik** achieved what seemed to them a major breakthrough: in 1974, "permanent working contacts" were established between the Holy See and the Polish communist government, with Kazimierz Szablewski, who worked out of the Polish Embassy in Rome, and Archbishop Luigi Poggi as cochairmen.

The Vatican's diplomats thought this arrangement a useful first step toward establishing formal diplomatic relations between the Holy See and the Polish People's Republic. From the SB's point of view, however, the permanent working contacts group created new opportunities to undercut Cardinal Wyszyński's position, another strategic goal of the "disintegration" campaign. Thus Archbishop Poggi's Polish interlocutors would stress to their Vatican contacts, and particularly to Archbishop Casaroli, their difficulties with the Polish primate. Meanwhile, the SB used its operational contacts in Rome, which included both Department I (foreign intelligence) and Department IV (anti-Church activity) collaborators and informants, to uncover the diplomatic strategies and tactics of the Poggi team; the information gathered was passed along to Szablewski and the other Polish members of the contacts group. Concurrently, the Szablewski/Poggi meetings and the informal contacts that necessarily accompanied the formal sessions created occasions for Department IV to conduct disinformation campaigns against Polish bishops it particularly wished to "disintegrate"—actions approved, it should be noted, by the Central Committee of the Polish Communist Party. Konrad Straszewski's Independent Group D also had its piece of the Roman SB action, and was responsible for "distintegration" activities against the Polish service of Vatican Radio; in these operations, Group D utilized a number of secret collaborators among Rome-based members of religious orders, including Jesuits and Franciscans. In aid of these and other efforts, Group D maintained both official and informal contacts with the KGB.[53]

AN ARCHBISHOP IN FULL

The years of the SB's relentless effort to "distintegrate" the Catholic Church in Poland were a period of growing charisma for Cardinal Karol Wojtyła—the years in which he became a magnetic public personality. His pastoral plans required a shrewd sense of how to maneuver around regime-imposed restrictions on the Church. If Catholic youth groups were banned, then the Church would utilize other settings—altar boys' picnics, for example—as moments for catechesis and Christian formation as well as recreation. If the "Oasis" summer camps of the Light and Life renewal movement were harassed by the local police and the SB, the cardinal-archbishop would provide what protection he could by arranging to visit the camps and the families who were fined for letting Light and Life use their property as campsites.[54] These stratagems by the **Defensor Civitatis** were undoubtedly an aggravation to the communist regime. What truly frightened them, however, was Wojtyła's emergence as a dynamic public speaker, who increasingly used great religious events as moments to challenge the regime on human rights.

Kraków's annual Corpus Christi procession, a springtime ritual, was one such event. The communists, determined to eradicate such public displays of Catholic piety, first forbade the procession from leaving Wawel hill; the procession could circumnavigate the courtyard of the Royal Castle, period. After years of agitation, Wojtyła won permission for the Corpus Christi procession to leave Wawel hill and enter Kraków's Old Town, although along a route much shorter than had been customary in the 1930s. At the four altar stations set up along the path of the truncated procession, Karol Wojtyła came into his own as a dramatic public speaker, as year by year he ratcheted up the pressure on the regime before crowds that gathered in the hundreds of thousands. In 1971, the cardinal-archbishop rejected the communist notion that Polish Catholicism and Polish patriotism could be separated: "We are the citizens of our country, the citizens of our city, but we are also a people of God which has its own Christian sensibility. . . . We will continue to demand our rights. . . . We will demand!" Three years later, the cardinal insisted before the vast crowds that "We are not from the periphery!" In 1975, Wojtyła, whose sense of humor inclined toward the ironic, indulged in a rare moment of public sarcasm; noting that the procession was still forbidden from entering Kraków's great market square, he caustically commented, "I am inclined to think that such actions do not favor the processes of normalization between the Church and the state"—which could also have been taken, for those with ears to hear, as a subtle reminder to the Vatican champions of the **Ostpolitik** that "permanent working contacts" were not satisfactory substitutes for basic human rights such as religious freedom and freedom of association and assembly.[55]

The great Marian shrine at Piekary Śląskie, in the heart of Silesia, was another venue at which Cardinal Wojtyła displayed his new skills as a public human rights advocate. Every May, a pilgrimage of Silesian workers, principally miners, came to the shrine in the hundreds of thousands—grandfathers, fathers, and sons, the elders wearing the colorful uniforms that distinguished their ranks in the miners' fraternity. Karol Wojtyła had first learned about manly piety from his father; the Captain's lessons were embodied in the Silesian miners who walked across fields and down roads to pay homage to the Mother of God. Preaching in front of these men, their sons, and their teenage grandsons, Karol Wojtyła became an ever more assertive proponent of their dignity, as human beings and as men who earned their living by the sweat of their brows. In 1973, the cardinal challenged the government and its claims to represent the interests of workers on the always tense question of building permits for churches: "We have a right to have more space in this homeland where we are the majority! We have a right to have more roofs over our heads when we pray! We have the right . . . to more room for teaching religion, for catechesis in the parishes! And this right is not aimed against anybody; it is for the good of all! It is for peace!"[56] In 1974, he blasted the "tremendous threat to family life" represented by the regime's pro-abortion policies: "We are afraid that it may so happen in our country that more lives are terminated than propagated. That would lead to incalculable and disastrous consequences."[57]

In 1975, he took on the regime's promotion of atheism, which included both propaganda and the manipulation of family life and workers' schedules:

The Church of the People of God in Silesia has a . . . specific religious profile . . . one which is the union of prayer and work. . . . When we are in Piekary, we come to realize that one cannot fight with religion in the name of the working class, or in the name of its interests and needs! One cannot undertake a program of propagating atheism in the name of the truth of the Silesian coal miner. . . . It is necessary to keep demanding . . . that the principle of religious freedom be respected; that parents should have complete liberty, without any outside pressure, to raise their children and their youth in the truths of the faith that have accomplished so much here . . . that no one should suffer because of their religious beliefs, that you not be threatened with dismissal from work, regardless of whether you are a miner or a manager . . . that you not be forced to work on Sundays.[58]

In 1976, he chose two key themes of Vatican II, defending the apostolic vocations of laypeople in the name of a Christian humanism more truly humane than the ersatz humanism the regime propagated in the name of workers:

If people are being degraded because they are believers and profess Christ, and attend church; if people are barred from academic promotion, that is a scandal! Because science must serve the truth! And we have a right to demand, from this place, that the Constitution be observed! That the bill of human rights, signed by the government of our country, be respected! . . . [This] hardworking, generous society . . . [must not be] handicapped because it does not embrace atheism, because human dignity and conscience do not allow it.[59]

And in his last appearance at Piekary Śląskie as archbishop of Kraków, he reminded his listeners, many of whom were compelled to work sometimes on Sundays, that God had mandated the Sabbath for a reason: so that men and women could rest and rediscover within themselves the image of the God who had rested on the seventh day. To lose touch with that image was to waste the gift of life: "[So] let us ask—are there not too many lives being wasted in our Homeland? Let us ask—are the new generations of Poles not threatened . . . by the feeling of the absurdity of life and work?"[60]

The Piekary Śląskie pilgrimage was a particular aggravation for the regime during the 1970s, Silesia being party chieftain Gierek's political base. Surveillance of the pilgrimage by local communist officials and the SB was extensive; buses bringing pilgrims had their license plates photographed; work schedules were arranged by coal mine and steel mill managers to drive down the numbers of pilgrims. And still they came by the tens and hundreds of thousands, spilling down the wooded hillside below the Marian shrine, as far as the eye could see.[61] They knew they were performing an act of resistance; but it was resistance of a different sort. Or, as one coal miner answered, when asked why he had come to a similar event a few years later, "To praise the Mother of God and to spite those bastards."

The Kraków Corpus Christi procession and the pilgrimage to Piekary Śląskie were similar in that they were struggles for space: space for the Church to be itself, space for Poland to be itself, in a country where the regime tried to occupy all public space. The battle for the church in Nowa Huta was another struggle for space, at once both similar and in certain respects different. Nowa Huta was deliberately created to be a godless space; it was located hard by Kraków in order to punish the recalcitrant Cracovians for returning the highest anticommunist vote in the fake "people's referendum" in 1946 and in the equally bogus 1947 parliamentary "election." Nowa Huta was also a sociological experiment in rapid communist-style urbanization; thousands of men and women from rural areas were enticed to the new city by the promise of higher-paying industrial jobs and better recreational facilities; failures on both these fronts, as well as all the tensions attendant on people being uprooted from a settled way of rural life and transplanted into a completely different social environment, made for innumerable social problems. Then there was the public imagery of the place, for Nowa Huta was, in part, an attempt to re-create Poland's national mythology. The nineteenth-century rebuilding of Kraków's magnificent Old Town embodied the romantic myth of Polish nationalism in stone and brick and decoration at a time when "Poland" did not exist. The functionalist design of Nowa Huta, with its vast apartment blocks and its heavy industry, was intended by at least some communist planners to kill the Polish national myth found in the living stones of the Kraków Old Town and to supplant it with the new mythology of the workers' state.[62] No one was fooled, least of all the workers. But a response was required.

Cardinal Wojtyła gave that response, by winning the battle for a church in Nowa Huta and building a striking modern building, one that lifted rather than depressed the spirits of the people who would use it. As his longtime secretary, Stanisław Dziwisz, would write, decades after the battle had been won, "The Nowa Huta experience permanently shaped Wojtyła's pastoral program as an archbishop, just as it permanently shaped [his] personality as an unyielding defender of human rights, of the rights of freedom of conscience and religion." Wojtyła's battle "on behalf of the dignity of the human person began right there at Nowa Huta."[63]

There was a notable symmetry, or perhaps better, congruence, between Wojtyła's increasingly vocal human rights advocacy—with its evocations of Poland's Christian roots and contemporary identity—and the evolving mood in the country, especially among dissidents. The 1970 Gdańsk massacres were a historic turning point in the four decades of Polish communism. As the 1970s unfolded, the old symbols of national self-consciousness that had kept the idea of "Poland" alive after the final 1795 partition were rediscovered and reappropriated: Poland began to reimagine itself in categories pioneered by the nineteenth-century Polish Romantics: as a suffering community, its suffering given meaning by a profound religious conviction that such suffering had a purpose. Here, as one keen observer put it, was a nationalism with a universal horizon.[64] Nurtured by the country's real leaders, such as Cardinal Karol Wojtyła (who was himself steeped in the literary traditions of nineteenth-century Polish Romanticism), this recovery of the past would eventually prove to be a potent instrument for creating a different future.

"The Only Real Ideological Threat in Poland"

By the mid-1970s, the communist government of Poland and its secret police apparatus had come to loathe and fear Cardinal Wojtyła more than they feared Cardinal Wyszyński. It was not as if the Primate had lost his toughness; it was just that, after thirty years of confrontation, both sides knew the steps in this particular dance. Moreover, the communists understood, as did Archbishop Casaroli, that Wyszyński was a man with a keen sense of where the edge of the abyss was located and a settled determination not to go beyond that edge. It was different with Wojtyła. He had "swindled" the party, as the prison warden in Gdańsk had complained a decade before. He had refused to be drawn into divide-and-conquer politics, remaining steadfastly loyal to Wyszyński. And yet this poet, this philosopher, this mystic had become a man of action, deploying words as weapons in a way that struck at communism on its own home ground—its claims to be the true humanism, the true bearer of the truth about man, and the true champion of human freedom. Worse yet, Wojtyła had become a point of contact between various clusters of dissidents, both Catholic and secular. If Wyszyński were to die, who knew what Wojtyła would do, were he to become Primate of Poland.

SB reports sent to KGB headquarters in Moscow suggest that Polish prosecutors, on three occasions in 1973–74, had considered arresting Wojtyła and charging him with sedition under article 194 of the criminal code.[65] But 1973 and 1974 were not 1953, and Gierek did not dare do what his predecessors had done to Stefan Wyszyński. So the surveillance on Wojtyła and the attempts to suborn his associates were increased, and so was the threat of brutality. On one occasion, Father Andrzej Bardecki was beaten senseless by thugs, either SB or SB-inspired, while walking home from a **Tygodnik Powszechny** editors' meeting with Wojtyła; the cardinal came to see the priest in the hospital the next day and said, "You replaced me; you were beaten instead of me."[66]

Meanwhile, while the authorities ground their teeth in frustration over their inability to silence the man party ideologist Andrzej Werblan had declared "the only real ideological threat in Poland," the cardinal and his friends adopted their own methods of frustrating the comrades ever more.[67] One such method involved the archiepiscopal car, an Opel Admiral driven by the cardinal's chauffeur, Józef

Mucha, a legendary character in Cracovian Catholic circles. One July, as they were leaving Warsaw for the drive into the countryside where the archbishop's annual kayaking trip would begin, Mr. Mucha (as he was always called) pointed out to the cardinal and his friend, Stanisław Rybicki, a veteran member of Wojtyła's **Środowisko**, the spies on the side of the road, keeping the car under surveillance. Mr. Mucha then looked into his rearview mirror, where he noticed a car following them. As Dr. Rybicki recalled with relish years later, Mr. Mucha "smiled with ironic tolerance" as he sped up the far more powerful Opel and watched the SB tail getting smaller and smaller in the mirror. On entering the forest that was their destination, they slowed down, just missing a gigantic elk that had sauntered across a dirt road, and finally eluded the SB.

On what turned out to be Wojtyła's last kayaking-and-camping excursion, in 1978, a different tactic was adopted, reflecting the kayakers' experience with the local police and militia the year before. Mr. Mucha drove the cardinal to a prearranged, isolated place, off the main roads but near the initial campground; then, while the SB tails labored to catch up with the Opel, Wojtyła's modest luggage and the cardinal were spirited into Stanisław Rybicki's car for transport to **Środowisko**'s gathering point. Mr. Mucha then turned around, reentered the main highway, drove back toward Kraków, and watched, perhaps with more "ironic tolerance," as the tails sailed by on the other side of the road, still trying to catch up.[68]

It was not all camping trips and shaking SB surveillance, of course. In April 1974, Cardinal Wojtyła defied the exceptionally hard-line communist leadership of Czechoslovakia by attending the funeral of Cardinal Stefan Trochta, who had died of a heart attack after a severe interrogation by the Czechoslovak secret police. The authorities refused permission for Wojtyła and the other senior churchmen present to concelebrate the funeral Mass in Litom ice. At the end of the service, Wojtyła walked from his pew and stood beside the casket of the late cardinal, who had survived the Theresienstadt concentration camp only to be murdered by communists, and began his commendation of Trochta (which the communists had also forbidden) with the words, "I am not worthy to celebrate the Mass on the steps of the altar where the martyr stood."[69]

Ten months after Cardinal Trochta's funeral, the KGB hosted yet another all-Soviet-bloc conference of intelligence services to coordinate anti-Vatican activities; during the conference, the Poles, the Czechoslovaks, and the Hungarians all reported "significant agent positions in the Vatican." The Mitrokhin records do not note a similar claim by the KGB, despite a now eight-year-old effort to cultivate senior Vatican officials, including Archbishop Casaroli and Archbishop Poggi, the two key figures in the Vatican **Ostpolitik** toward Poland. The same KGB active

measures campaign included placing agents masquerading as Lithuanian seminarians (ANTANAS
and VIDMANATAS) at Rome's Gregorian University and using ADAMANT (Russian Orthodox
Metropolitan Nikodim) as an ecumenical disinformation conduit.[70] Andrew and Mitrokhin note that
none of this seems to have had "a discernible effect
on Vatican policy"; it is also true, if surprisingly, that
none of it seems to have raised questions or serious
concerns in the minds of Casaroli and his key aides
about increased Soviet-bloc penetration of the Holy
See at the height of the Vatican **Ostpolitik**.[71]

The Mitrokhin records do not indicate, but it is
not difficult to surmise, that during the exchange
of information at this conference, the Hungarians
shared with their comrades their judgment that
Wojtyła would be an especially dangerous man as
pope.[72] Whether or not that possibility had occurred
to the SB, Department IV was keeping a close watch
on Cardinal Wojtyła, with a 1976 analysis emphasizing his intellectual ability and his stress on the
difference between society and the state.[73] During
this period, however, the SB evidently did not discover Wojtyła's clandestine ordinations of priests for
Czechoslovakia, which were carried out in the chapel of the archbishop's residence, after the candidate
had been smuggled across the Czechoslovak-Polish
border and the proper authorization had been received from the candidate's superior; the clandestine
courier (who, in one authorization system, had half

a torn card sent by a legitimate religious superior) did not travel to Kraków with the ordinand (who had the matching, other half of the torn card).

In 1976, the SB undertook further active measures to "distintegrate" the Kraków intelligentsia and Wojtyła's work with them, by trying to exacerbate and exaggerate divisions within various groups (intellectuals being notoriously fractious), by mounting disinformation campaigns about alleged liturgical aberrations, and by trying to foment jealousies between Kraków's Catholic theologians and philosophers and their colleagues at the Catholic University of Lublin.[74] Wojtyła, undeterred, intensified his contacts with the Catholic dissident movement, including such important new figures as Bohdan Cywiński, and then used those contacts to initiate conversations with secular dissident intellectuals such as Jacek Kuroń—gestures particularly appreciated as the regime stepped up its pressure on new dissident groups such as KOR, the Workers' Defense Committee.[75] In the wake of the 1976 strikes at the Ursus tractor factory (a showpiece of Gierek's new economic model and a colossal failure) and in Radom, Wojtyła supported a strike fund to assist workers.

The struggle for "space" continued, and even as the Ark Church began to rise in Nowa Huta, there were losses: Father Józef Kurzeja, who was working to build a second Nowa Huta church in the Miestrzejowice neighborhood of the city and was constantly harassed and interrogated by the SB, died of a heart attack at age forty on August 15, 1976—the date in 1941 on which the remains of Maximilian Kolbe had been cremated at Auschwitz. Andrzej Paczkowski sums up the Polish Church-state situation in the mid- and late 1970s in these terms:

Relations with the Church assumed increasing importance for the Gierek leadership as economic problems worsened. Nevertheless, extremely strong barriers of both an ideological and political kind caused official policy toward the [Church] to be characterized by about-faces and duplicity. The communists, too, had their **non possumus**: fulfilling the demands of the Church and the recommendations set out in bishops' homilies or official documents would have required a fundamental change in the entire system. Thus, while trying to preserve appearances . . . the party leadership did not actually budge an inch: it took no steps toward granting the Church legal status; the return of religious instruction to the schools was out of the question; atheistic propaganda continued; publishing was strictly controlled and circulation restricted; and building permits were issued grudgingly and sparingly.[76]

Nor would things change significantly after what was regarded as another triumph for the **Ostpolitik**: the meeting at the Vatican on December 1, 1977, between Edward Gierek and Pope Paul VI.

In the months after that audience, the Casaroli team worked hard to persuade the ailing Pope that some form of diplomatic relations should be concluded with the Polish communist government: perhaps first, an apostolic delegate accredited to the Polish hierarchy but resident in the old Vatican Embassy in Warsaw; then a full-fledged exchange of diplomatic representation at the ambassadorial level—which would, among other things, have cut Cardinal Wyszyński out of the serious conversations, despite Paul VI's assurances to the contrary. In March 1978, five months before Paul died, the Primate sent a trusted aide, Bishop Bronisław Dąbrowski, to Rome to try to slow the process down. The Pope asked the Polish prelate whether the Primate didn't understand that the Holy See had the Polish Church's best interests in mind; Dąbrowski asked for time. The Pope agreed to let the situation develop a little further, although it seems clear that Archbishop Casaroli was eager to close the deal and even had a candidate chosen for the post in Warsaw—Archbishop Poggi, whose appointment Wyszyński would likely have regarded as making a bad deal even worse.[77] According to Stanisław Dziwisz, there was no disagreement between the Primate and the archbishop of Kraków on the inadvisability of a Vatican Embassy in Warsaw at this juncture.[78]

While this drama was being played out in Rome, Cardinal Karol Wojtyła was looking forward to his annual kayaking expedition with his **Środowisko** friends and their families. It was one of the curiosities of the SB's obsession with Wojtyła that it never seems to have occurred to Department IV or Independent Group D to try to suborn the cardinal's lay friends. Somewhat in the manner of some pre–Vatican II clergy, the Polish secret police seemed to think that the only serious people in the Catholic Church were priests, bishops, monks, nuns, and other religious professionals. That a cardinal could be having serious conversations with laypeople was simply not within the realm of the ferrets' imagination.[79] In yet another irony, the communists were infinitely more clericalist in their obsession with ordained churchmen than was the dangerous clergyman whose work they were so eager to distintegrate.

That the SB and the Polish communist leadership regarded Karol Wojtyła as an enemy, however, was obvious from the vast resources expended on watching him and attempting to impede his pastoral activity. They would shortly discover just how great a threat the **Defensor Civitatis** could be.

CHAPTER THREE

Confrontation

September 28–29, 1978	Pope John Paul I dies during the night.
October 16, 1978	Cardinal Karol Wojtyła is elected pope and takes the name John Paul II.
October 17, 1978	Warsaw KGB **rezident** sends report on Wojtyła to Moscow Center.
October 22, 1978	Pope John Paul II solemnly inaugurates his ministry as Bishop of Rome and challenges the world to "open the doors for Christ!"
November 5, 1978	John Paul II visits Assisi and defends "Church of Silence."
November 16, 1978	First Stasi analysis of the impact of John Paul II's election.

November 20, 1978	Pope John Paul II meets with Cardinal Iosyf Slipyi, major-archbishop of the illegal Greek Catholic Church in Ukraine.
November 22, 1978	Lithuanian Catholic Committee for the Defense of Believers' Rights is formed.
January 24, 1979	Soviet foreign minister Andrei Gromyko meets with John Paul II at the Vatican.
January 26–February 1, 1979	John Paul II, in Mexico, challenges "anthropological error" of Marxism.
March 26, 1979	Stasi analysis of Vatican operations under John Paul II.
April 3, 1979	Colonel Zenon Płatek, head of SB Department IV, goes to Vienna in aid of Operation TRIANGOLO.
April 12, 1979	Stasi analysis of Vatican **Ostpolitik** under John Paul II.
May 18, 1979	Further Stasi analysis of **Ostpolitik** under John Paul II.
June 2–10, 1979	John Paul II in Poland.
October 2, 1979	John Paul II defends religious freedom and other basic human rights at the United Nations.
November 13, 1979	Central Committee of the Communist Party of the Soviet Union issues decree outlining operational

initiatives for dealing with the threat posed by John Paul II.

August 14–31, 1980 • Shipyard strike in Gdańsk gives birth to Solidarity trade union and movement.

October 24– November 10, 1980 • Solidarity registration crisis.

December 5, 1980 • Soviet government cancels planned Warsaw Pact invasion of Poland.

December 16, 1980 • Pope John Paul II writes Leonid Brezhnev in defense of Polish sovereignty.

January 15–18, 1981 • John Paul II receives Solidarity delegation at the Vatican.

March 1981 • Bydgoszcz crisis leads to unrest throughout Poland.

April 2, 1981 • Fears of losing control in Poland expressed at Soviet Politburo meeting.

May 13, 1981 • John Paul II is shot in St. Peter's Square.

May 28, 1981 • Cardinal Stefan Wyszyński, Primate of Poland, dies.

September 5, 1981 • First Solidarity National Congress opens in Gdańsk.

October 18, 1981 • General Wojciech Jaruzelski is named First Secretary of Polish Communist Party.

December 12– 13, 1981 • General Jaruzelski declares "state of emergency," imposes martial law

	throughout Poland, and orders arrests of thousands of Solidarity activists.
December 15, 1981	Cardinal Agostino Casaroli discusses martial law crisis with President Ronald Reagan and senior American officials.
December 17, 1981	Cardinal Casaroli discusses Polish crisis with Eugeniusz Wyzner, Poland's ambassador to the United Nations.

John Paul II was keenly aware of being the first non-Italian pope in 455 years. So from the very beginning of his pontificate, he bent every effort to introduce himself to his new local flock in terms they could understand and appreciate.

Within an hour of his election on October 16, 1978, he stood on the loggia of the patriarchal Vatican basilica, St. Peter's, gently brushed aside a fussy master of ceremonies, and, in a break with precedent, began to address the crowd in the square—most of whom were wondering who this "Voy-TEE-wah" was. Tepid in their response at the beginning, the throng began to warm to their new bishop as he told of his fear in accepting his election, and how he had overcome that fear by invoking the protection of the Virgin Mary, dear to both Italians and Poles. Then he won their hearts by asking for their help: "I don't know if I can make myself clear in your . . . in **our** Italian language. **Se mi sbaglio, mi correggerete!** [If I make a mistake, you will correct me!]" A tremendous burst of applause rang throughout the square and echoed down the Via della Conciliazione toward the Tiber and the Castel Sant'Angelo, onetime refuge of popes. A moment before, he had been **lo straniero**, the foreigner. Now, he was a Roman among the Romans, even if he was, as he had put it in introducing himself, a "man from a far country"—a phrase intended as a subtle reference to the persecuted Church behind the Iron Curtain.

Continuing his campaign of introducing himself to his adopted home—for one of Karol Wojtyła's new titles was "Primate of Italy"—he went on a brief pilgrimage to the Marian shrine at Mentorella on October 29, just a week after he had solemnly inaugurated his papal ministry by challenging the Church to fearlessness and asking the world to open its doors to Christ. It was a place he had visited often, for it was steeped in the history of both Poland and Italy: the priests who cared for the shrine, the Resurrectionist Fathers, had been inspired by the greatest literary figure of nineteenth-century Polish Romanticism, Adam Mickiewicz. When word of the Pope's visit spread, a large crowd gathered and John Paul II apologized to the local officials for causing such a fuss; but he had often come to Mentorella to pray as a visiting Polish cardinal, and now he had to come and pray as Italy's Polish primate.

A week after his visit to Mentorella, John Paul II went to the heart of Italian Catholic piety by going on a brief pilgrimage to Assisi, the home of one of Italy's patrons, St. Francis. He was there, he told the vast throng, because he felt the need for a "spiritual birth" in his new home. And so he had come to the town of Francis, the man who had written "Christ's Gospel in incisive characters in the hearts of the men of his time," to ask for the prayers of **Il Poverello**. Assisi draws pilgrims from all over the world, so it was not surprising that there were emigrés from behind the Iron Curtain present that day, eager to greet the new pope. One of them shouted out, "Don't forget the Church of Silence!" evoking the persecuted local Catholic Churches of central and eastern Europe. "It's not a Church of Silence anymore," replied John Paul II, "because it speaks with my voice."

The KGB was not happy with any of this. It had already been aggravated by several of John Paul II's gestures that it regarded as "anti-Soviet" in character. The new pope had sent his red cardinal's zuchetto to the Marian shrine of Ostrabrama in Vilnius, Lithuania (a city once located in Poland). He seemed likely to give a significant Vatican post to Msgr. Audrys Bačkis, the Paris-born son of the last ambassador of free Lithuania to France. He was known to be sympathetic to the Greek Catholic Church of Ukraine, the largest underground Church in the world and the repository of Ukrainian national identity. And then there was that business about "opening the doors to Christ"—could that be anything other than a direct challenge to the Marxist-Leninist order? Moreover, there were the Poles to worry about: some members of the Polish Communist Party seemed quite happy about the election of their fellow Pole as pope. Black humor was making its way back from the SB in Warsaw to Moscow Center, the KGB headquarters in the Lubyanka: right after his election, the story went, the Pope had contacted the Polish interior minister (the SB's overseer) and said, "Comrade Minister, your important instructions have been carried out!"[1]

There would be nothing humorous about the reaction of the KGB, the SB, other Warsaw Pact intelligence agencies, and indeed the entire communist apparatus in central and eastern Europe in the months immediately ahead. The election of John Paul II, the more astute communist leaders recognized, posed a mortal threat to the post-Yalta European order, and perhaps even to the Soviet Union itself. These, after all, were men who could bring themselves to believe that the Vatican during the **Ostpolitik** of Paul VI was in fact plotting to dismember the USSR—a risible thought, but one that fit without too much difficulty into the paranoid cast of mind that had long characterized communist analysis of the Catholic Church.

Karol Wojtyła had always understood himself as

a priest and a bishop, not a politician; that sense of his vocation did not change when he assumed the Chair of Peter as pope. As priest and bishop, however, he had frequently spoken in defense of the dignity of the human person and in defense of religious freedom. He would not—could not—change those convictions as pope. Moreover, if he took his election as an act of Divine Providence rather than as simply the result of papal electoral arithmetic, he had to conclude that his distinctive life experience had brought him to the papacy at this moment in history for a reason.

There are no coincidences, he used to tell his **Środowisko** friends; what seems coincidence is actually a facet of God's providence that we don't understand yet. That a man from behind the Iron Curtain was now pope must mean something, not just for the man but for the Church and the world. He now had a global megaphone with which to teach the truth about freedom. So he would not hesitate to use it.

A determined pope, who would neither seek nor avoid confrontation; an equally determined enemy, which sought confrontation precisely in order to prevail. The stage was set for one of the epic struggles of modern history—made all the more compelling because, despite its surface appearances and what might seem its similarities to other contests for power, it was ultimately a struggle in the realm of the human spirit.

"BETTER SOLZHENITSYN AS UN SECRETARY-
GENERAL THAN A POLISH POPE . . ."

At the death of Paul VI on August 6, 1978, the Vatican's **Ostpolitik** was fifteen years old and could count a number of accomplishments, as diplomatic achievement is normally calculated. Agreements of various sorts had been reached with several communist governments, including those of Hungary, Czechoslovakia, and Yugoslavia; the Yugoslavs had even reestablished full diplomatic relations with the Holy See. Cardinal Mindszenty had been coaxed out of his self-imposed internment in the U.S. Embassy in Budapest and a successor appointed. Archbishop Beran had agreed to leave Czechoslovakia for Roman exile and a cardinal's red hat; the government had agreed to his being replaced by an apostolic administrator. Archbishop Agostino Casaroli, architect of the strategy of **salvare il salvabile**—saving what could be saved—had traveled several times to Poland for official discussions and had secured the first formal Vatican diplomatic contacts with the Soviet Union in half a century. In 1975, Casaroli had signed the Helsinki Final Act, with its "Basket Three" guarantees of human rights, on behalf of the Holy See. The winds of history seemed to be blowing a bit more freely across what Casaroli had perceived in the early 1960s as the "vast immobile swamp" behind the Iron Curtain.

Some of the cardinal-electors who gathered in

Rome to choose a successor to Paul VI were not enthusiastic about the **Ostpolitik**, however.[2] Various cardinals knew that the four new bishops Casaroli had ordained in Czechoslovakia in 1973 were of dubious loyalty and were openly acquiescent to the most hard-line regime in the Soviet bloc; at the same time, the underground Catholic Churches in Bohemia, Moravia, and Slovakia flourished, suffered, and—as Paul VI had feared—produced aberrations such as a married bishop. Yes, what some regarded as the Mindszenty logjam had been broken in Hungary; but the Church there was now completely under the thumb of the Kádár regime and was withering away as a result. Stefan Wyszyński believed that the Holy See was on the verge of making a catastrophic mistake by putting an apostolic delegate or nuncio into Warsaw, who would function as a kind of on-site Vatican overseer for central and eastern European affairs while undercutting the Polish primate's position with the Polish government. Cardinals who were directly affected by the **Ostpolitik** (such as Wyszyński) or who were indirectly affected by it (such as the Germans) believed that, while Casaroli was a man of great diplomatic skill, he had been far too accommodating in his negotiations. The issue of the **Ostpolitik** must have been rather broadly discussed in Rome during the interregnum; bits of the conversation eventually found their way back to the Stasi, the East German secret intelligence service.[3]

These worries—which, for a man like Wyszyński, were matters of ecclesiastical life and death—were one facet of the broader concern that quickly surfaced during the post–Paul VI interregnum: the fear that the Catholic Church was losing its edge and that the Church's higher leadership was losing its grip. That fear was not confined to what the international media always called the "conservative" party in the College of Cardinals; cardinals such as Vienna's Franz König, a major progressive force at Vatican II and an early agent of the **Ostpolitik**, were also worried.[4] Thus the **Ostpolitik** came in for more criticism than it had likely ever received before, during the daily meetings of cardinals after Pope Paul's death and in the **prattiche**, the "exercises" or informal discussions among the electors about papal candidates, in late August 1978.

To what degree Albino Luciani, who was elected pope on August 26, 1978, would have stiffened the **Ostpolitik** will never be known; the man who took the unprecedented papal double name of John Paul I died after only thirty-three days in office. But it seems unlikely, given the criticisms during the interregnum, that there would have been no changes. In any event, John Paul I's brief pontificate was marked by one moment of high drama in the Catholic contest with communism. On September 5, 1978, the new pope received Metropolitan Nikodim of Leningrad, one of the six presidents of the World Council of Churches and a man who struck many Westerners

as deeply pious. The KGB knew Nikodim as ADA-
MANT, as it knew his secretary, Nikolai Lvovich
Tserpitsky (code name VLADIMIR). At the end of
his private audience with John Paul, ADAMANT
suffered a massive heart attack and died in the Pope's
arms. John Paul I later remarked that Nikodim had
spoken "the most beautiful words about the Church
I have ever heard" during their meeting; his last
words, as the Pope held the fallen bishop, were said
to have been "I am not a KGB agent." But he was.[5]

Three weeks after losing the services of ADA-
MANT, KGB headquarters issued a secret order,
#00122: "Measures to Strengthen Agent Operational
Work in the Struggle with the Subversive Activity
of Foreign Clerical Centers and Hostile Elements
among Church People and Sectarians." That glori-
ously Stalinist title notwithstanding, the order offers
a window into the mind-set of Moscow Center the
day before John Paul I died; according to Vasili Mitrokhin's notes, it included the following analysis in
which concerns about the Vatican certainly played a
role:

Under the pretense of concern for the freedom of
belief and the rights of believers in the USSR, imperialist intelligence services and foreign anti-Soviet
centers are organizing ideological sabotage, aimed at
undermining the moral and political unity of Soviet
society and undermining the basis of the Socialist
system; they sought to discredit the Soviet state and

social order, incite religious organizations towards confrontations with the state and stimulate the emergence of an anti-Soviet underground among sectarians. With encouragement from abroad, hostile elements have launched active organizational and provocational activity aimed at forming illegal groups and organizations within the sectarian milieu, setting up printing presses and establishing contacts with foreign clerical centers.[6]

In the context of that analysis, historian Andrzej Paczkowski's characterization of Karol Wojtyła's election on October 16, 1978, is not exaggerated: the election of a Pole as pope was "an event . . . whose consequences [were] difficult to overestimate"—for Poland, for the future of the Catholic contest with communism, and for the Cold War.[7] The KGB had targeted Wojtyła for surveillance under its PROGRESS operation since 1971; PROGRESS used the infiltration of "illegals"—foreigners often masquerading as businessmen—to monitor the activities of those suspected of subversion. On October 17, the day after Wojtyła's election, the KGB **rezident** in Warsaw, Vadim Pavlov, sent Moscow Center an SB assessment of the man who had just become Pope John Paul II. The assessment suggests that the SB's agents and informers at the Kraków Corpus Christi processions and the Marian pilgrimages to Piekary Śląskie had been taking careful notes:

Wojtyła holds extreme anti-communist views. Without openly opposing the Socialist system, he has criticized the way in which the state agencies of the Polish People's Republic have functioned, making the following accusations: that the basic human rights of Polish citizens are restricted; that there is an unacceptable exploitation of the workers, whom "the Catholic Church must protect against the workers' government;" that the activities of the Catholic Church are restricted and Catholics treated as second-class citizens; that an extensive campaign is being conducted to convert society to atheism and impose an alien ideology on the people; that the Catholic Church is denied its proper cultural role, thereby depriving Polish culture of its national treasures.[8]

Jerzy Turowicz, Wojtyła's longtime friend and editor at **Tygodnik Powszechny**, got a pithier reaction to John Paul II's election from a distinguished Italian journalist who, Turowicz knew, had good Soviet connections: Moscow, the journalist told Turowicz, "would prefer Aleksandr Solzhenitsyn as Secretary-General of the United Nations than a Pole as pope."[9] Solzhenitsyn himself was convinced that something important had happened. When the news of Wojtyła's election reached the Nobel laureate in his exile in Cavendish, Vermont, he threw out his arms and exclaimed, "It's a miracle! It's the first positive event since World War I and it's going to change the face of the world!"[10] Solzhenitsyn, who admired Stefan Wyszyński, did not know Karol Wojtyła personally, but he knew what his election meant: the Catholic resistance to communism would be rooted in religious conviction and expressed through the instruments and symbols of culture, which Solzhenitsyn believed were the strongest and most effective weapons available.[11]

The tremendous outpouring of joy in Poland when Wojtyła's election was announced was described to the East German Stasi in some detail by CLEMENS, an agent who happened to be in Kraków on October 16, 1978, and who padded his report with speculations on a new axis of power involving Wojtyła as pope and the Polish-born Zbigniew Brzeziński as U.S. national security adviser.[12] Whatever it may have thought of CLEMENS's geopolitical analysis, its own acute sense of self-preservation made it advisable for the Polish communist government to observe the proprieties and send an official delegation to Rome for the great outdoor Mass in St. Peter's Square on October 22, 1978, which marked the solemn inauguration of John Paul II's service as pope. During the course of the lengthy service, the Soviet ambassador to Italy leaned over to Henryk Jabłoński, the Polish president, and acidly remarked that "the greatest achievement of the Polish People's Republic was to give the world a Polish pope."[13] Whatever modest hopes the Soviets may have entertained of controlling this new menace through pressures on the Polish Church were quickly dispelled during the ceremony. The masters of the Kremlin may have missed the significance of a typical gesture of loyalty and gratitude from Karol Wojtyła: John Paul II rearranged the normal order of precedence among the cardinals paying him homage in order to give pride of place to communism's old enemy, Stefan Wyszyński, whom the new pope stepped down from the papal throne to embrace. But they would have had to have been completely deaf to miss the challenge contained in the Pope's homiletic appeal to fearlessness and openness:

Be not afraid to welcome Christ and accept his power. Help the Pope and all who wish to serve Christ and with Christ's power to serve the human person and the whole of mankind.

Be not afraid. Open the doors for Christ. To his saving power open the boundaries of states, economic and political systems, the vast fields of culture, civilization, and development.

Be not afraid. Christ knows "what is in man." He alone knows it. . . .

I ask you . . . I beg you, let Christ speak to [you]. He alone has words of life, yes, of eternal life.[14]

The architects of the Vatican **Ostpolitik** had had some experience of the new pope and knew him for a "great personality" who was well respected throughout the leadership of the world Church.[15] Perhaps they imagined that this pope could be managed, as the Curia had managed popes for centuries. Yet John Paul immediately made clear that he was prepared to make symbolic gestures that were bound to aggravate communist sensibilities (such as sending his cardinal's zuchetto to Lithuania) and to meet with prominent Catholic personalities whom Moscow considered untouchables (such as Ukrainian Greek Catholic major-archbishop Iosyf Slipyi, whose persecuted Church the Soviet Union did not recognize legally). But the changes being rung were not just symbolic: on several occasions within his first weeks in office, John Paul II went out of his way publicly to defend religious freedom as the first of human rights.[16]

The KGB did not waste time in taking countermeasures. Shortly after John Paul II's election, several "illegals" were sent into Poland, among them Oleg Petrovich Buryen (DEREVLYOV), whose cover was to act as the representative of a Canadian publishing company interested in Polish missionaries in Asia. DEREVLYOV was told that, were he to be arrested by the police or the SB, he was to hold fast to his cover; in an emergency, however, he could contact Colonel Jan Slovikowski of the SB, who seems to have helped previous KGB agents who had gotten into difficulties in Poland. Buryen/DEREVLYOV worked hard to build a relationship with Father

Józef Tischner, a philosopher who was close to John Paul II.[17]

The Polish SB already had a considerable intelligence asset in Rome: Edward Kotowski, or PIETRO, an able and intelligent art historian who for the past three years had been given Italian language training and instructed to learn everything he could about the Vatican and its ways. Deployed to Rome from Warsaw in October 1978, PIETRO worked undercover as a diplomat at the Polish Embassy in Rome, cultivating contacts—as diplomats would—with Vatican counterparts. Decades later, Kotowski told the Polish historian Andrzej Grajewski that the "majority" of Polish diplomats in Rome in the first five years of John Paul's pontificate were in fact working for the SB; the primary task of these SB assets was to try to influence the work of the Poggi/Szablewski working contacts group. Other SB assets in Rome in the first years of the pontificate included employees of LOT Polish Airlines and the Polish state travel agency, Orbis; members of the Polish trade mission to Italy; representatives of Polish companies involved in international business; and various "illegals," who communicated directly with SB headquarters in Warsaw, rather than with Kotowski. It was an extensive network, on which considerable resources were being expended; it would grow; and the damage it attempted would become more severe over time.[18]

On the analytic side, an early Soviet-bloc interpretation of the likely implications of John Paul II's election was done by the KGB and shared with allied intelligence services. The translation of the document by the East German Stasi, which is dated November 16, 1978, is marked STRENG GEHEIM [STRICTLY CONFIDENTIAL]; its distribution list was limited to Stasi spymaster Markus Wolf and two others. From internal evidence in the document, the principal sources for the analysis seem to be the Polish secret police and the Polish internal security services. The biographical details are accurate and reflect previous SB analyses of Wojtyła's abilities and character. The analysts miss John Paul II's morally driven view of politics and underestimate his political savvy; their claim that he likes and seeks applause is laughable. Interestingly, however, the Polish sources do report accurately on the roots of Wojtyła's critique of communism in his major (and very difficult) philosophical masterwork, **Person and Act**: that totalitarianism's denial of basic human rights is ultimately an antihumanism because it diminishes personal moral responsibility. Wojtyła's most recent contacts with dissidents such as Jacek Kuroń are duly noted, as is the enthusiasm with which his election was received by "anti-socialist groups in Poland." As for the future of the **Ostpolitik**, "opinions are widely divided," with some expecting a continuation of the Casaroli approach; the "predominant opinion," though, was that John Paul II's "hands-on experience" of life under communism would lead to a "tough Vatican position" in matters of human rights.[19]

The architects of the Vatican **Ostpolitik** may not have been overly concerned about efforts by Soviet-bloc security services to penetrate the Vatican. It seems that John Paul II was, however. In any case, he was taking no chances and changed the papal routine accordingly. Unlike previous popes, he did not dictate memoranda of conversations with prominent personalities or political figures (for the duration of his pontificate, such memoranda would have been filed for ready reference in the Vatican's Secretariat of State, whose counterintelligence capabilities were not overly developed). Rather, in the evening, John Paul II would go over each day's meetings and conversations, both those on the official schedule and those of an unofficial or private nature, with his long-time secretary, Stanisław Dziwisz. Dziwisz recorded all of this in a series of diaries that were kept in the papal apartment, where those who had no business seeing the thematic record of these papal conversations would have no possibility of access to them.[20]

Thus there was no aide-mémoire of the Pope's conversation on January 24, 1979, with Soviet foreign minister Andrei Gromyko, who came to Rome with an eye to sizing up the new menace for himself. He informed the Pope and Archbishop Casaroli that "rumors" of religious persecution or discrimination against believers in the USSR were the result of

Western disinformation campaigns. John Paul, for his part, later described the meeting to a group of reporters as the "most tiresome" he had had thus far as pontiff.[21]

Two days after Andrei Gromyko had reinforced his reputation as a formidable liar, John Paul II landed in Mexico to address the decennial conference of CELAM [the Council of Latin American Bishops' Conferences]. The first of John Paul's papal pilgrimages outside Italy had several strategic goals. The Pope wanted to support the bishops of Latin America in their work to build authentic societies of freedom. He was also determined to urge them to do so without embracing the "Marxist analysis" that underwrote many of the new theologies of liberation. Thus his critique of Marxism's "anthropological error" in his address to the bishops on January 28 added another item to the KGB's list of grievances against the Pope, for the liberation movements prominent in several Latin American countries, especially in Central America, were crucial to Moscow Center's strategy of winning the Cold War in the Third World.[22]

In addition to his concerns about the future of the Church in the most Catholic continent on the planet, John Paul II presciently saw the links between a Mexican pilgrimage and Poland. Despite the intense Catholic piety of its people, Mexico was, officially, an aggressively secular state in which priests and nuns were forbidden to wear religious habits in public. John Paul, showing himself shrewder than some of his cautious diplomats, knew that if he were permitted to come to Mexico, the calculus regarding any future Polish visit would change: "If they receive me in an anticlerical country like Mexico, how can they refuse to allow me to return to Poland later?" he asked his aides.[23]

Two months after the Pope's Mexican trip, on March 26, 1979, another Stasi analysis of the Vatican under John Paul II was completed. "Diverse Information on the Vatican" was based on information from "an IM" [**Inoffizielen Mitarbeiter**, Unofficial Employee] who lived in Rome, had "professional relations in the Vatican," and was reporting on John Paul II's new order based on his conversations with "various . . . dignitaries of the Curia." John Paul II had been well received by both Church bureaucrats and people, the IM's sources reported. The Stasi analysis also included speculations on impending changes in senior curial positions, noted that some Vatican officials saw "special significance" in the Pope's meeting with Soviet foreign minister Gromyko, and suggested that a "formal understanding about the continuation of the so-called Vatican **Ostpolitik** was reached." The IM reported that the Pope's Mexican trip was regarded as a considerable success, briefly described John Paul's disinclination to micromanage the Vatican, and noted that the new pope had upset those who thought they knew how to manage popes: John Paul violated "protocol traditions cultivated for years," and had instructed his collaborators that "letters addressed directly to the Pope are to be [delivered] to him unopened." The analysis concluded with remarks on the likely future of Vatican relations with the German Democratic Republic and complaints about the ways in which the Catholic Church in West Germany provided material and financial support to the Church in East Germany.[24]

The Stasi analysis was a striking combination of insight and misapprehension. The IM, who was clearly proud of his access to prominent Catholic personalities, nicely captured curial resentments over John Paul II's insistence on maintaining his own lines of communication to the world outside the Vatican, and curial worries about the Pope's distinctive management style. On the other hand, there is little in this document that couldn't have been cobbled together by anyone with an ear closely attuned to the Roman rumor mill, and there are some striking misunderstandings and misreadings of situations. The analysis of the Pope's first encyclical, **Redemptor Hominis** [The Redeemer of Man] as a kind of papal thank-you note to those who elected Wojtyła is bizarre; the encyclical was in fact a clear statement of the Pope's distinct Christian anthropology, the theoretical basis of his defense of human rights. The IM reported that an exceptionally large number of cardinals were present at the funeral of the secretary of state John Paul II had inherited from Paul VI, the French cardinal Jean Villot; yet there was nothing surprising about such a show of respect for the Church's second-ranking figure; and the IM's speculations on possible successors to Villot (the Genoese cardinal Giuseppe Siri and Paul VI's former chief of staff, Giovanni Benelli) were, to put it gently, strange.[25] The IM (who may, of course, have been telling his masters what he thought they wanted to hear) dramatically overstated the meaning of the Gromyko audience—although the notion of its "special significance" may also reflect what the Vatican architects of the **Ostpolitik** wanted to believe about that encounter. Moreover, and perhaps most strikingly, the IM missed the single most important personnel move that John Paul II had made: installing as his principal secretary Stanisław Dziwisz, the man who would see to the execution of the Pope's orders and who would make sure that John Paul saw and talked with those whom he wanted to meet, formally or informally.

A month later, another Stasi analysis—"Information on Some Essential Questions of Vatican Politics after the Election of Wojtyła as Pope"—took up in greater detail the question of the future of the Vatican **Ostpolitik**. According to this April 12 analysis, Vatican sources were reporting that the **Ostpolitik** would continue in "general" terms, but that the Pope's personal experience with "Marxist praxis" will lead to a "more determined approach" to problems than was evident under Paul VI: "Thus it is not to be excluded that this could lead to a temporary worsening of Vatican relations with the governments of the socialist states." On the other hand, the analysis affirmed, John Paul II would insist that the Church throughout the world not be a political institution; his personal task would be that of defending the Catholic Church's evangelical activities against "state atheism." In this regard, the analysis warned of future papal statements in defense of human rights and religious freedom, even as the Pope urged Catholics to contribute to the welfare of the societies in which they lived. According to the Stasi, the Vatican (meaning the Vatican's diplomats) "is not inclined to burden its politics with the socialist states and its relations to them by supporting 'dissidents' who live abroad," nor did the Vatican bureaucracy favor open support for "opposition forces in the socialist states, even though it is thoroughly informed about such forces or movements." Yet the analysis also warned that John Paul's approach to these issues "over the long haul is not . . . clear." The analysis correctly noted that John Paul "considers the Polish episcopate far more combative . . . than the Hungarian [episcopate]," and that the Pope believes "the Hungarian episcopate should do more for the religious education of the people." The analysis concluded with a lengthy speculation on the Pope's likely approach to German affairs, including the familiar complaints about the Church in West Germany and its alleged interference both in East Germany and with the Vatican.[26]

Like its March 1979 predecessor, this Stasi analysis combined both insight and ignorance. The analysts clearly grasped the tactical purposes of John Paul II's insistence that the Church does not do politics; but they missed his larger strategic goal, which was to redefine the battlefield in the Church's contest with communism, moving the contest from the realm of politics to the realm of conscience and culture. The analysts' Roman sources seem to have figured out that there would be tensions between the initiatives emanating from the papal apartment and the diplomatic instincts of the Secretariat of State. Moreover, there is a striking similarity between what the Stasi reported as Soviet concerns about "many incalculables" with John Paul II and the concerns of the Vatican's diplomats: both in Moscow (that is, in the minds of Brezhnev and Andropov) and among some in Rome (that is, in the minds of Casaroli and his associates), stability was a paramount value, if for different reasons. In the same way, if also for different reasons, this analysis suggests that both Moscow and the Vatican's diplomats shared a concern that the Poles could begin to pose major problems, during and after any future papal visit to Poland: a suggestion confirmed by a subsequent directive to all

Stasi IMs with Catholic contacts to intensify their reporting on "any planned hostile action" during John Paul's expected pilgrimage to his homeland.[27]

On April 30, 1979, John Paul II confounded the Stasi's Roman sources by appointing Archbishop Agostino Casaroli as the new secretary of state of the Holy See (technically, the pro-secretary of state, until Casaroli could be elevated to the cardinalate in June). Four days after Casaroli's appointment, John Paul named Casaroli's deputy, Achille Silvestrini, as Vatican "foreign minister" in place of Casaroli. Both men were thoroughly committed to the **Ostpolitik** of Paul VI, about which John Paul II manifestly had his doubts. Their appointments to the two key diplomatic positions in the Holy See meant that the Pope would henceforth pursue a dual-track approach to the Catholic contest with communism. The old diplomacy of the **Ostpolitik** would continue, and perhaps something could be achieved along those lines; in any event, no one could accuse the Church of reneging on previous agreements, what with Casaroli and Silvestrini in charge. Meanwhile, John Paul would pursue his personal campaign on behalf of human rights and religious freedom, appealing to consciences and cultures over the heads of communist rulers.[28]

The Stasi refined its analysis of the future of the **Ostpolitik** in the wake of the new Vatican appointments in a May 18, 1979, analysis, "Information on Several Aspects of the Further **Ostpolitik** of the

Vatican during the Pontificate of Pope John Paul II."
The analysis correctly notes that intellectuals and
young people would be primary concerns of a pontificate determined to strengthen Catholic doctrinal identity. Seven months into the papacy of John
Paul II, it now seemed clear to the Stasi that, while
"no basic changes of principle are to be expected"
with respect to the **Ostpolitik**, "one should nevertheless expect to deal, in part, with a more aggressive
and offensive Vatican course." Part of this shift was
attributed to John Paul II himself, but the Pope was
said to be following decisions reached by the College of Cardinals during the 1978 conclaves, which
stressed that religious freedom should be the "exclusive" goal of the Vatican's diplomacy behind the
Iron Curtain. The primary resistance to this shift,
the Stasi suggested, came from "the right wing of
the Curia," which was said to prefer a more aggressive posture toward international communism than
was characteristic of either John XXIII or Paul VI.
"According to present estimates" from Stasi sources
in Rome, local bishops and their bishops' conferences would play an increasing role in the Vatican's
Ostpolitik, such that these conferences, and not
Vatican diplomats, would frame much of the "diplomatic dialogue" in Czechoslovakia, Poland, and
Hungary, while the curial diplomats would take
the lead role in dealing with Albania, Bulgaria, and
the German Democratic Republic. The purpose of
strengthening the local bishops' hands was to com-

pel the "recognition of the institutional Church" as a genuine actor in society. The Stasi analysts suggested that John Paul had taken the side of the curial diplomats against Cardinal Wyszyński in the question of a Vatican nunciature in Warsaw, and that the appointments of Casaroli and Silvestrini to the Holy See's key diplomatic posts were made against the "wishes of the West German bishops, who have had strong reservations about Casaroli and his course until now." The document concluded with the admonition not to use the information it contains for propaganda purposes, "in the interest of the security of the sources."[29]

As before, this Stasi analysis displayed a keen grasp of some matters: John Paul II's outreach to young people and intellectuals; his conviction that doctrinal laxness and confusion had diminished the Church's capacity to shape society, culture, and politics, including world politics; the fact that things were going to be different, diplomatically, with the new pope. Yet the analysts continued to miss crucial aspects of John Paul II's program: his conviction that effective pastoral work and witness has political consequences, under certain circumstances, and his dual-track approach to the **Ostpolitik**. Stasi sources in Rome may have been reflecting certain curialists' sentiments (or hopes) in reporting a rift between John Paul II and Cardinal Wyszyński on the question of a Vatican Embassy in Warsaw; but no such rift existed, ever.[30]

If these Stasi documents, which reflect the analyses of one of the communist world's most professionally accomplished intelligence services, may be taken as reflecting at least something of a consensus among communist leadership, it would seem that, while the comrades knew that John Paul II posed a grave threat to their interests, they were unsure, half a year into his papacy, as to the strategy he would follow and the tactics he would deploy. Answers to those questions would not be long in coming.

THE NINE DAYS OF JOHN PAUL II

Edward Gierek's economics may not have made much sense, but the Polish Communist Party leader was not a fool when it came to reading the sentiments of his countrymen. Thus, advised by Leonid Brezhnev in early 1979 to refuse permission for the Pope to return to his homeland, Gierek explained that it was simply impossible, "for political reasons." "Well," Brezhnev responded, "do as you wish. But be careful you don't regret it later."[31]

John Paul's original idea was to return to Poland in May 1979 so that he could celebrate the annual day in honor of St. Stanisław, his predecessor, in Kraków, while simultaneously presiding at the solemn conclusion of the Synod of Kraków he had convened to implement Vatican II. The communists, sensitive to the symbolic power of the feast day (Stanisław had been martyred while defending the Church's liberty), dug in their heels and said no to a May pilgrimage. But they agreed to a papal visit the following month. After some serious and effective negotiating, John Paul II happily accepted nine days in June in place of two days in May, and a program that included Gniezno and Częstochowa as well as Warsaw and Kraków. (The Church, for its part, simply shifted the celebration of St. Stanisław to June.)

Despite this strategic error, the Polish communist regime did everything it could to impede the Pope's visit and diminish its impact, in what the SB and its party masters regarded as a "gigantic 'damage limitation' operation" code-named LATA '79 [SUMMER '79]. Informants in the Catholic clergy and laity were mobilized and divided into eight categories. The first group, an elite that had had access to Cardinal Wojtyła in the past, included seven moles: DELTA, KAROL, MAREK, JUREK, TUKAN, TRYBUN, and LESZEK; JUREK, a clergyman, was a member of the Church's organizing committee for the papal pilgrimage. These informants and those in other categories were not simply to provide information to the SB on plans for the papal visit. They were also ordered to infiltrate various Catholic groups and organizing committees to influence their decisions on how to participate in the papal pilgrimage (e.g., to limit the number of participants by raising concerns about safety). This massive anti-papal operation continued during the papal events themselves; 480 SB agents were assigned to monitor events and cause what difficulties they could while the Pope was in Kraków (June 6–10).[32]

The SB coordinated its anti-papal activities in this period with the Stasi, which deployed several hundred agents to monitor foreign visitors during the papal visit.[33] A special Stasi working group was established in Frankfurt an der Oder; the SB arranged for dedicated telephone numbers in Warsaw and Kraków so that Stasi agents could be connected directly to Stasi headquarters in East Berlin; and it was agreed that the two services would share information on the papal visit, especially any that came from circles close to John Paul II. One Stasi agent with access to the Pope, JUNGE, was a Polish priest who worked for East German rather than Polish intelligence. The entire operation was coordinated by Joachim Wiegand, the head of Stasi Department XX/4, which was charged with counter-Catholic activities. Meanwhile, the Stasi chieftain, Markus Wolf, had his own personal source in the Vatican, of whose identity Wiegand was unaware: LICHTBLICK, the German Benedictine Eugen Brammertz, who was registered by the Stasi in 1960 but had Stasi connections long anteceding that date. Brammertz worked in Rome for the German edition of **L'Osservatore**

Romano, the Vatican daily, did occasional work in the Secretariat of State, and would have had access to at least some of its files.[34]

John Paul II and his closest associates were unaware of the details of LATA '79 and parallel activities by other communist intelligence services, although they certainly assumed that their old enemies would be at work. Years later the Pope's secretary would recall their concerns:

> The authorities in Warsaw were not acting like Poles; that much is certain. Their determination to give the papal visit the lowest possible profile, their manipulation of the television coverage, their effort to throw up a bunch of ridiculous obstacles in the way of the people, especially by making it hard for the buses to shuttle the pilgrims around— all of that . . . had nothing to do with Poland or its traditions of hospitality. . . . I've no doubt that the authorities were bowing to pressures from Moscow as well as Prague. They were terrified of how Big Brother might react.[35]

In the event, none of it made any real difference. June 2–10, 1979, became the dramatic pivot of Karol Wojtyła's thirty-year-long struggle with communism—nine days during which the history of the twentieth century turned in a fundamental way, thanks to the largest religious gatherings ever seen in the communist-controlled world.[36] As a nervous

Edward Gierek watched from a hotel window high above Warsaw's Victory Square, John Paul II celebrated Mass before an enormous crowd and invoked the power of the Holy Spirit to "renew the face of the earth—of **this** land!" From that moment until he wiped a tear from his eye and left for Rome from Kraków's Balice airport on June 10, Karol Wojtyła showed himself the true master of Polish hearts and minds, by giving back to his people their authentic history and culture—their true identity. He never mentioned politics or economics; beyond the necessary courtesies during the arrival and departure ceremonies, he went about his business as if the authorities of the Polish People's Republic simply did not exist, at least not in any meaningful sense.[37] But by restoring their authentic identity to a people who had been oppressed for forty years—by giving Poland back to the Poles, and giving the Poles back to themselves—he created new tools of resistance that communism simply could not match. Igniting a moral revolution between June 2 and June 10, 1979, John Paul II gave his people the key to their own liberation: the key of aroused consciences.

He could do this because he had grasped the essence of Poland's modern drama, which he knew from the inside. Thus in his Victory Square homily he reminded his fellow countrymen of the epic heroism and the unshakable faith that had sustained the Warsaw Uprising in 1944, when Poland was abandoned by its Western allies and the Red Army sat across the river, doing nothing. Yet beneath the rubble that was Warsaw after the Uprising, Poles found the figure of Christ carrying the cross, fallen from the shattered Holy Cross Church. And that figure reminded Poland of what John Paul called the "one criterion"—Jesus Christ, the true measure of man, of freedom, and of history.

During his Nine Days, John Paul could give one of the greatest performances by a public figure in the twentieth century because of his unique personal gifts, including his uncanny ability to make it seem, in the largest crowds imaginable, that he was talking to each one present personally. In Częstochowa, he addressed a crowd that may have numbered a million, including tens of thousands of Silesian coal miners who had made the trek to Jasna Góra because Edward Gierek wasn't about to have a pope, even (or perhaps especially) a Polish pope, in his political backyard.[38] At one point during John Paul's sermon, one miner began to make a remark to another, only to be cut off: "**Pieronię** [Damn it, or Thunderation], don't talk when the Pope's speaking to me!" It was an experience replicated all over the country.

What struck observers was not simply the size of the crowds—estimates were that one-third of the country, some eleven million people, saw John Paul II in person—but their orderliness. The Church organized cadres of "papal guards" to help with crowd control (and to assert the Church's right to conduct its own events). The crowds needed very little control, though, for the Pope's call to conscience created a new atmosphere, unlike the normal rhythms of life under totalitarianism. As the secular dissident Adam Michnik would put it afterward, "those very people who are ordinarily frustrated and aggressive in shop lines were metamorphosed into a cheerful and happy collectivity, a people filled with dignity."[39] In a country where trust had broken down because of SB provocations and manipulations, Poles could look at one another, see how many "we" were and how many "they" were, and begin to trust one another again. Civil society was on the mend, breathed back into existence by the pope who had called out to God "from the depths of this millennium" to renew the face of Poland and give it a new birth of freedom.

As the people of Poland "saw others who believed the same things and were now willing to say them publicly," they "rediscovered their own strength"— and, at the same time, "discovered the regime's weakness."[40] The regime, whose "entire propaganda machine was precisely calibrated to downplay the significance of the visit and, above all, to conceal the size of the enthusiastic crowds," was hardly unaware of this. Every evening during the papal visit, Stanisław Kania, then a member of the Polish Communist Party Politburo, complained to Archbishop Casaroli, who was accompanying the Pope in his new role as pro-secretary of state, about what the Pope had said that day or might say the next day. Casaroli, for his part, was at least mildly sympathetic to Kania's complaints, believing as he did that the Polish leadership was constantly looking over its shoulder at Moscow; and he conveyed their concerns to John Paul, who received the information politely and continued on the path he had chosen.[41] According to the Stasi's reports and analysis, Casaroli himself believed that the papal pilgrimage was "the crowning of the Vatican **Ostpolitik.**" But it is not easy to see how that could have been the case, as getting the Pope into Poland was the personal accomplishment of a Polish pontiff and the terms in which he spoke during those nine days were not the terms of the papal diplomats.[42]

Whatever its causal relationship to the prior Vatican **Ostpolitik**, the June 1979 papal pilgrimage to Poland was a turning point, the ramifications of which soon began to make themselves clear. What historian Andrzej Paczkowski once called, in reference to artists, "the exodus from the censored world" now began in earnest, all over Poland.[43] Links between the Church and the dissidents of the secular Left accelerated. The Workers' Defense Committee [KOR] reconstituted itself as the Committee for Social Self-Defense [KSS KOR] and focused its energies on building an "alternative society" while "living in the truth" and preparing the way for evolutionary change in Poland.[44]

None of this was lost on Moscow Center. The KGB, reporting that the visit had confirmed its worst expectations, charged the Pope with "ideological subversion"; evidently, during the papal visit, the KGB even feared a political uprising by Polish dissidents and made plans to evacuate the Soviet trade mission (which was led by a KGB officer) from Katowice to Czechoslovakia. The Moscow spymasters were also upset because John Paul had called himself, not just a Polish pope, but a "Slav pope"—which led the Politburo of the Soviet Communist Party to conclude that the Pope and the Church had begun "an ideological struggle against the Socialist countries."[45]

That analysis could only have been confirmed (if not in the precise terms the KGB understood by "ideological subversion") by John Paul II's address to the United Nations General Assembly on October 2, 1979, four months after his Victory Square homily. Cardinal Casaroli tried to edit out of the Pope's speaking text the lines he thought might be offensive to Soviet and other communist ears; John Paul II restored them, and gave a speech in defense of basic human rights that left the delegates from communist countries worried, and not a little angry.[46] The Pope began by reminding the world of power that any politics, including world politics, had to begin from a proper understanding of the dignity of the human person; that was why the 1948 Universal Declaration of Human Rights was both a "milestone on the long and difficult path of the human race" and the "fundamental document" of the United Nations. Respect for human rights, the Pope continued, was the prerequisite to true peace, for those who committed "injustices in the realm of the human spirit" made peace within and among nations impossible. Then, as if to underscore precisely who the perpetrators of those particular injustices were, John Paul II borrowed from Karol Wojtyła's sermons at Kraków's Corpus Christi processions and at Piekary Śląskie and chided those countries in which believers were treated as second- or third-class citizens, their professional careers impeded, their right to educate their children denied. The search for truth was essential to man, the Pope concluded. Believers and nonbelievers ought to be able to agree on this as a common matter of humanistic conviction.

The Central Committee of the Soviet Communist Party might not agree on that. It did agree, however, that something had to be done about John Paul II. Six weeks after the Pope spoke at the UN, the Central Committee Secretariat issued an "absolutely secret" decree, entitled "On Measures of Opposition to the Politics of the Vatican in Relation to Socialist Countries." This was a political document, assigning tasks to different organs of Soviet state power: the various propaganda, radio, television, and press organs; the Soviet Communist Party's international department; the Soviet foreign ministry; the KGB; the Soviet Academy of Sciences; the Soviet Council on Religious Affairs; and the Central Committee's Academy of Social Sciences. Each of these instruments of the Soviet state was to do its own distinct work in combating the "perilous tendencies in the teaching of Pope John Paul II," which were to be "condemned in proper form." The decree was signed by the party's chief ideologist, Mikhail Suslov, and was accompanied by several analyses of the situation, including a memorandum, "On the Socio-Political and Ideological Activities of the Vatican on the Contemporary Stage," that was prepared by the KGB, although nominally authored under the auspices of the Council on Religious Affairs.[47] There is no mention in this Central Committee decree of "active measures" against John Paul II; but according to Vasili Mitrokhin's archive, at the same time as the decree was issued, the "KGB was instructed . . . to embark on active measures in the West" aimed at frustrating the designs of John Paul II and demonstrating that his efforts were a danger to the Catholic Church. "Active measures" in this context would have included propaganda, disinformation campaigns, blackmail, and other tactics as required, with special focus on persuading the world media that John Paul II was a threat to peace. Contrary to some reports, the Central Committee decree did not order the assassination of John Paul II, for the Central Committee Secretariat was an administrative body that lacked the competence to order such measures. But, according to historian Andrzej Grajewski, the very existence of the decree, as well as what seems to have been a parallel set of secret operational instructions to the KGB on active measures, strongly suggests that, within a year after John Paul II's election, the Soviet political leadership and the Soviet intelligence considered the Pope the single greatest threat to their position.[48]

Four months later, in March 1980, John Paul II met in the Vatican with Jan Szczepański, a distinguished sociologist, a member of the Polish Council of State, and a Protestant from the western "recovered territories." While Szczepański made clear that his was an unofficial visit, in that he was not officially representing the Polish government, his report to the Polish ministry of foreign affairs sheds some light on John Paul's thinking, and Cardinal Casaroli's, nine months after the Pope's triumphant visit to his homeland. John Paul, Szczepański reported to the foreign ministry, was "very aware" of the "contradictions" between Marxism and Catholicism, and rejected any form of dialogue aimed at the creation of a hybrid combining "elements from both worldviews," which, the Pope was convinced, was impossible and would result in something "artificial." So if the communist side of the equation wished the Church's assistance in addressing the very real social, political, and economic problems that both sides recognized, it would have to do so on the basis of the Church being allowed to be the Church. At the same time, John Paul II was quite aware that his primary task lay not in being a "player" in solving these problems, but in strengthening Catholic identity and maintaining the continuity of Catholic doctrine and tradition, which he believed had been seriously eroded in western Europe. In that respect, the Pope's position "regarding the conflict between atheism and religion" was similar to his concerns about the attenuated religious sensibility in affluent societies: both denied, albeit in very different ways, the instinct toward religious belief that was an integral part of human personhood.

John Paul suggested that Professor Szczepański meet with Cardinal Casaroli, and their discussions were joined by Kazimierz Szablewski, the Polish co-chairman of the Polish-Vatican permanent working contacts group. Casaroli's conversation, as reported by Szczepański, was on a different plane than that of John Paul II, focusing on the sociology of the Christian communities behind the Iron Curtain and the dynamics of politics, stressing the "importance of realism" and the Church's long history of riding out waves of anticlericalism. There would always be a kind of Thermidor in any revolutionary situation, the cardinal suggested, after which "relations between the Church and socialist countries will become more normalized—and for that, the Church is prepared to wait indefinitely."[49]

Some in the Vatican may have indeed been prepared to wait indefinitely. As events would soon demonstrate, however, the wait would not be indefinite nor would the breakthrough come from some Polish communist Thermidor.

The Carnival

The rise of Solidarity, the trade union that was also a social movement and a de facto political opposition, intensified the communist war against John Paul II, even as it challenged the diplomatic conventions of the Vatican **Ostpolitik** and set Poland on a social and emotional roller-coaster ride that would be known later as "the Carnival."

There had been nationwide waves of dissent in communist Poland before: in 1956, 1968, 1970, and 1976. 1980 was different, because dissent in Poland had matured—not least because of the revolution of conscience ignited by John Paul II in June 1979. To be sure, Polish dissidents were better organized in 1980, more sophisticated in their communications strategies, and more clever politically than they had been in the past. The dissident coalition was more comprehensive, involving both workers and intellectuals; that diversity gave it a tensile strength that proved far more resilient against communist provocation, deception, disinformation, and pressure than in previous eruptions of mass protest. Yet the character of the opposition had also matured. Living in the truth, the theme that John Paul II had hammered on throughout the Nine Days of June 1979, had become both a watchword and a program for human rights organizations throughout central and eastern Europe, as both religiously based dissidents and secular dissidents recognized that this form of morally grounded, culturally focused resistance struck at the heart of the communist enterprise, which was constructed on a foundation of falsehoods and maintained through an official strategy of lies.

What began in the Gdańsk shipyard in August 1980 represented a coming together of several strands of national experience, some reaching back into the nineteenth century, others of more recent vintage. The Polish insurrectionary tradition, which had been fed by the poems, novels, and plays of Polish Romanticism, met a new Catholic maturity, forged in Wyszyński's Great Novena and refined in John Paul II's Nine Days, to produce a unique movement of social renewal and antitotalitarian resistance that was politically sophisticated and determinedly nonviolent. There were more prosaic factors at work, of course. The economy was a wreck, which had a drastic effect on what one historian neatly described as the "Achilles' heel of a socialist economy," food prices and supplies.[50] The Gierek regime's dependence on Western credits limited the government's scope for brutality, which was also tempered by memories of the 1970 crisis and the fall of Gomułka. Still, the "1980 difference" that made the most difference was a moral difference, which displayed itself in the character and program of those who, as John Paul II later put it, took "the risk of freedom."[51]

That moral difference showed itself almost immediately as the Gdańsk shipyard strike broke out on August 14, 1980. It was an occupation strike, in which the workers took over the entire shipyard complex, thus creating an oasis of free space in the totalitarian system. Rigorous discipline was maintained, aided by an absolute ban on alcohol in the yards. Religious seriousness was manifest, publicly evident in open-air Masses and confessions. Perhaps most crucially from the point of view of what followed, the workers, having been tutored by John Paul II in the larger meaning of their dignity as men and women, refused to settle for the economic concessions the regime quickly offered. Thus on the night of August 16–17, the **Międzyzakładowy Komitet Strajkolwy** [Inter-Factory Strike Committee, or MKS] was established to press a broader set of demands, including the establishment of independent, self-governing trade unions, and to coordinate strike activities throughout the Baltic region. The famous "21 Points" agreed upon by the MKS presidium (in which the key actors were Lech Wałęsa, Joanna and Andrzej Gwiazda, Bogdan Lis, and Andrzej Kolodziej) emphasized economic change while including a full menu of basic human rights, specifically mentioning, among others, freedom of speech, freedom of the press, and an end to discrimination against religious believers "of all faiths" in terms of access to the media. The goals of dissent had been enlarged and deepened; as one worker-poet would put it a few months later,

The times are past
when they closed our mouths
with sausage.[52]

A few days after the strike broke out, the MKS leaders' negotiating position was strengthened when a seven-member experts' commission, which included the Catholic intellectuals Tadeusz Mazowiecki and Bohdan Cywiński and the secular historian Bronisław Geremek, arrived in Gdańsk. This unprecedented coalition of workers with meager educations and activist intellectuals had been prepared, throughout the mid-1970s, in the experience of KOR and similar groups; it also reflected the sense of national solidarity across traditional class barriers that had been created in the Nine Days of John Paul II. Thus, facing government negotiators who were themselves nervous about a local situation that had rapidly become a national movement, the striking workers were in a far stronger position than ever before.

The results proved the point, as the government agreed to the principle of free trade unions and signed an agreement with the MKS on August 31. It was not an accident, as Poland's remaining Marxists might have said, that Wałęsa signed for the strikers using a giant pen topped by a portrait of John Paul II—a souvenir from the Nine Days of June 1979 that underscored the linkage between that epic journey and the path embarked upon by what quickly became a vast and unprecedented national social movement.[53]

On September 17, a national meeting of strike committees from across the country was held in Gdańsk, and Karol Modzelewski's suggestion for a name by which the new union would be known was adopted: the Independent Self-Governing Trade Union Solidarity [**NSZZ Solidarność**]. "Solidarity" had been the name editor Krzysztof Wyszkowski had given to the strikers' bulletin published in the Gdańsk shipyard in August.[54] "Solidarity" was also, and perhaps not altogether coincidentally, the title of one of the concluding sections of Karol Wojtyła's 1969 philosophical magnum opus, **Person and Act;** there, the future pope described "solidarity"—a condition in which personal freedom serves the common good and the community supports individuals as they grow into true maturity—as the most humanistically authentic attitude toward society.[55] The first words of the organization's title were, of course, as important as the last, soon to become world-famous in the jumbly-letter logo that had been invented for the strikers' bulletin by artist Jerzy Janiszewski: "independent" meant "not under the control of the communist party or the state," and "self-governing" meant that its members were taking responsibility for their own decisions and actions. Both themes echoed lessons taught in the Nine Days of June 1979. Solidarity also took care to reappropriate parts of the Polish past that the regime had long tried to ignore or deny. Solidarity buttons often featured the crowned Polish eagle, an emblem banned by the communist regime because it evoked memories of Mary, Queen of Poland. Moreover, the workers' demands in Gdańsk had included the building of a memorial to those workers killed by the regime in 1970—the dramatic Three Crosses Monument was finished in a few months and dedicated in December 1980.

The growth of Solidarity, the independent self-governing trade union that was also a social movement, was phenomenal. Within sixteen months, the union/movement had some ten million members— more than one-fourth and almost one-third of the country—brought together in a cascade in which Poles from every class and sector of society (including farmers, peasants, and students) participated. Moscow's reaction to all of this was predictable and ominous. Both the Politburo and the KGB agreed that "the Gdańsk Agreement represented the greatest potential threat to the 'Socialist Commonwealth' . . . since the Prague Spring of 1968." Two weeks before Solidarity was officially formed and named, the Politburo adopted "theses for discussion with representatives of the Polish leadership," a not-too-subtle way of describing the demands that the Soviets intended to make of the Polish comrades, among which was to "prepare a counterattack" that would give "overriding significance to the consolidation of the leading role of the Party in society." Always aware of the danger from the east, Polish black humor asserted itself again: referring to Gomułka's ouster in 1970, one joke queried the difference between Gomułka and Edward Gierek, to which the answer was, "None, only Gierek doesn't know it yet!" Leonid Brezhnev was not, however, in a joking mood, telling the Politburo on October 29 that "the counterrevolution in Poland is in full flood," and broaching the possible "necessity" of martial law. The next month, KGB chairman Andropov warned the new Polish interior minister, General Mirosław Milewski, that Solidarity and the Church were a lethal, and linked, threat:

> Even if you left Wyszyński and Wałęsa in peace, Wyszyński and Wałęsa would not leave you in peace until they had achieved their aim or they had been actively crushed by the Party and the responsible part of the workers. If you wait passively . . . the situation slips out of your control. I saw how this happened in Hungary [in 1956]. . . . There is every reason to fear that the same may happen in Poland also, if the most active and decisive measures are not now taken [against] . . . Wałęsa and his fascist confederates.[56]

Among the "measures" Andropov immediately took was a new infiltration of "illegals" into Poland, aimed at penetrating Solidarity, through the Church if necessary. One such illegal, FILOSOV (Ivan Bunyk), posed as a French poet and made contact with an old friend and colleague of John Paul II, Father Andrzej Bardecki. Bardecki (who, as Andrew and Mitrokhin note, had "no possible means of identifying" Bunyk, one of his many foreign visitors, "as a KGB 'illegal'") introduced FILOSOV to Tadeusz Mazowiecki, then editing the Solidarity weekly newspaper, **Tygodnik Solidarność** (and equally unaware of the true identity of his visitor).[57]

Mazowiecki, for his part, had gone to Rome in early October, after the formation of **NSZZ Solidarność**. He was received by John Paul II, eager for news from Poland from sources in whom he had confidence. The Pope had one overriding question: "Will it last? Does this movement have a future?" Mazowiecki assured John Paul that it did.[58] But if the Pope received this news with satisfaction, tempered by concern over what the Polish communists or the Soviet Union might do to strangle the infant Solidarity in its cradle, the **Ostpolitik** managers of the Roman Curia took a somewhat different view, which began with concern rather than satisfaction. "Stability" was the diplomats' watchword, and it was clear to both Cardinal Casaroli and Archbishop Silvestrini that Solidarity had the capacity to be a deeply destabilizing force throughout central and eastern Europe: not in and of itself, but because of the Soviet reaction it might provoke. True, Primate Wyszyński had given Solidarity his blessing; but according to Silvestrini, Wyszyński was also worried that a Soviet intervention would trigger the collapse of the Polish communist regime, thus effectively partitioning Poland a fourth time by turning it into a de facto province of the USSR. As for the curial diplomats, while they could see Solidarity as a "natural effect" of the Nine Days of June 1979, they also worried that Wałęsa and the other Solidarity leaders might not have Wyszyński's well-honed sense of where the edge of the cliff was. Moreover, information was sketchy; direct telephonic communication between John Paul II and the Primate, or between the Vatican diplomats and the Primate, was impossible because of bugging.[59]

The curialists' concerns about Wałęsa were misplaced. Throughout September and October, when the Polish regime set numerous obstacles in the way of Solidarity's legal registration, the Gdańsk electrician consistently played a moderating role, giving Solidarity radicals a chance to speak their minds but always guiding decisions toward a resolution that did not back the regime into a corner from which it could extricate itself only with massive repression— its own, or the Soviets'. Given the intoxicating, first experience of democracy, this was no easy task, but Wałęsa's own political skills, as well as what one suspects was his intuition that John Paul II would have wanted things played the way he was playing them, kept the movement on course, even if it cost Wałęsa some support within the Solidarity rank and file and among the more radical union leaders.[60] That rank and file, for its part, was still growing rapidly, drawing members from previously dormant rural areas and student groups; both Rural Solidarity and the students' group were refused registration, which only led to greater demands from **NSZZ Solidarność** on their behalf. Then, on October 27, "the [democratic] plague invaded the citadel" (as Andrzej Paczkowski neatly put it) when a group of communist party members met in Toruń to form a "Consultative-Coordinating Commission of Party Organizations" that directly challenged the "democratic centralism" of the Polish Communist Party and thus the party's capacity to mount a coordinated response to the Solidarity challenge.[61] Yet this crack in the party walls itself mirrored the public mood toward the regime, aptly characterized by KOR founder Jacek Kuroń: "If the government had actually produced a golden egg, people would say that it was not golden; second, that it was not an egg; and third, that the government had stolen it."[62]

ON THE BRINK OF THE ABYSS

The dispute with the regime over Solidarity's legal registration, which unfolded over three weeks in late October and early November 1980 and was resolved on November 10, was quickly followed by an even graver confrontation, this time international in scope, in late November and early December. As early as October 30, East Germany ended free movement across its Polish border, a step replicated by the equally hard-line Czechoslovak regime on November 18. Polish-Soviet military exercises on Polish territory began on November 9. Party newspapers in Berlin and Prague attacked Stanisław Kania (the new Polish party chieftain, who had replaced Edward Gierek on September 6) as a weakling and drew ominous comparisons between the fall of 1980 and the Prague Spring of 1968—rhetorical attacks that would have been unlikely absent prior Soviet approval. Kania's Central Committee responded on December 4 by making an unprecedented appeal to its "fellow-countrymen," while the Central Committee's press spokesman warned on December 5 that "if power slips from the hands of democracy . . . Poland's communists will have the right and duty to call for assistance"—a formulation both ironic (what democracy?) and ominous ("assistance" could only mean the Red Army).

The crucial meeting took place that same day, with Vasili Mitrokhin providing details from the KGB files:

On December 5 an extraordinary meeting of Warsaw Pact leaders assembled in Moscow to discuss the Polish crisis. Kania heard one speaker after another castigate the weakness of his policies and demand an immediate crackdown on Solidarity and the Church. Otherwise, he was told, Warsaw Pact forces would intervene. Eighteen divisions were already on the Polish borders and Kania was shown plans for the occupation of Polish cities and towns. The meeting was followed by a private discussion between Kania and Brezhnev. Military intervention, Kania insisted, would be a disaster for the Soviet Union as well as for Poland. "OK, we don't march into Poland now," Brezhnev replied, "but if the situation gets any worse we will come."[63]

Christopher Andrew and Vasili Mitrokhin argue that Brezhnev's threat was a bluff.[64] Andrzej Paczkowski suggests that a complicated game was being played: that a decision on Warsaw Pact military intervention had only been deferred, with the Poles being urged to take tougher anti-Solidarity measures and the Soviet comrades assuring a Polish communist party that "plainly did not feel strong enough to engage in a once-and-for-all showdown" that military "assistance" was available if needed. "Somehow or other," Paczkowski concludes, "crisis was averted."[65]

The game was complicated indeed. Thanks to the brave work of Colonel Ryszard Kukliński, the Polish officer who had been providing the United States with Warsaw Pact operational plans, the U.S. government (then in the last days of the Carter administration) had a very clear idea of how the invasion would proceed—perhaps a clearer idea than General Wojciech Jaruzelski, the Polish defense minister. The Soviet plan, it should be noted, included the complete elimination of the Solidarity leadership by summary courts-martial and firing squads. Kukliński's materials were amplified by ongoing satellite reconnaissance, and by information being fed to the West by a Red Army general in Moscow. President Carter's national security adviser, Zbigniew Brzeziński, was sharing information with President-elect Ronald Reagan's national security adviser, Richard V. Allen, and the two men had agreed to coordinate their principals' public statements. Allen was also sympathetic to a plan by Lane Kirkland, the president of the AFL-CIO, the American trade union federation, to threaten a global blockade of Soviet international commerce by coordinated union action throughout the world; Brzeziński made sure that news of this initiative leaked to the **Wall Street Journal**. At the same time, Brzeziński took advantage of the sievelike U.S. State Department by sending it a memo on possible U.S. military sales to China, knowing that the memo, like the AFL-CIO plan, would leak to the papers and thus get quickly to Moscow. With Reagan's agreement, President Carter sent a "hotline" message to the Kremlin, warning of "grave consequences" should the Warsaw Pact invade Poland.[66]

On December 7, when it was still unclear what moves, if any, the Soviet Union and its clients would make toward Poland, Brzeziński called Pope John

Paul II to brief him on what the United States knew (from Kukliński and other intelligence sources) and on the steps the Carter administration had taken to signal Moscow in every way possible that invading Poland would be a very bad idea. John Paul II then prepared his own direct appeal to Soviet leader Brezhnev, which took the form of an unprecedented personal letter dated December 16 (when, of course, no one in the West knew that the invasion had been either scuttled or deferred).[67] Although written in a formal diplomatic style, it was a tough letter: it described events in Poland as that country's internal affair, citing the Helsinki Final Act; it defended Solidarity by a deft reference to the "solidarity" necessary if societies were to move forward economically and socially; and, by referring to Poland's martyrdom in 1939, John Paul subtly suggested that he was prepared to use all the moral power at his command to identify Brezhnev and any new invasion of Poland with the "fascists" who remained a principal boogeyman of the Soviet propaganda machine. The letter, according to then-Vatican foreign minister Silvestrini, was John Paul's "personal initiative"; its language suggests that the Vatican's senior diplomats were at least consulted about the text, which they were responsible for getting to Moscow.[68]

Whatever effect John Paul's letter had on the Soviet Union continuing to stay its hand in December 1980, it undoubtedly underscored to the Soviet leadership the mortal threat posed by this Polish pope who commanded the world's attention, who was determined to support Solidarity, and who would almost certainly be in sympathy with the vigorous anticommunist stance that would be taken by the incoming Reagan administration in the United States. Their response to that threat would not be long in coming.

A ROMAN MEETING, AND A NEW AMERICAN PRESIDENT

The SB's efforts to suborn those close to John Paul II into cooperating with the Polish secret intelligence service were enlarged in the months after Solidarity's founding. Among the targets were men and women long known to be close to Karol Wojtyła: Fathers Stanisław Dziwisz, Tadeusz Rakoczy, and Andrzej Bardecki; the philosopher Stanisław Grygiel; the poet and journalist Marek Skwarnicki; and Wanda Półtawska, a survivor of Nazi "medical experiments" at the Ravensbruck concentration camp who had helped Wojtyła launch his family ministry program as archbishop of Kraków. None of these efforts succeeded; nor did an exceptionally energetic campaign aimed at Father Adam Boniecki, M.I.C., the chronicler of Wojtyła's life who had been brought to Rome in April 1980 to launch a Polish monthly edition of the Vatican newspaper, **L'Osservatore Romano**. In Boniecki's case, when direct efforts at seduction were unavailing, the SB fabricated "compromising" material about him aimed at discrediting him with the Pope. None of it worked.[69]

As the SB was bending every effort to penetrate the Pope's closest circle of Polish friends and advisers, Vatican diplomats were being approached by some of their official Polish interlocutors in an attempt to minimize the impact of a visit that a Solidarity delegation was going to make to the Vatican in mid-January 1981. During the first week of that month, Kazimierz Szablewski, the Polish head of the permanent working contacts group established by the **Ostpolitik**, met with Archbishop Achille Silvestrini, the Vatican "foreign minister" (formally, the head of the Holy See's Council for the Public Affairs of the Church). According to a secret, coded cable sent to Polish deputy foreign minister Józef Czyrek on January 9 (and shared with party leader Kania and defense minister Jaruzelski), Silvestrini told Szablewski that he counted on him for reliable information about events in Poland, evincing aggravation at the "Poles surrounding the Pope, who do not see fit to act in accordance with the rules and customs prevailing in the Curia," as Szablewski put it. In the Curia's view, Szablewski reported, the most urgent requirement in Poland was to "achieve a stable situation as soon as possible," because a "prolonged unstable situation in Poland" was "potentially dangerous for everyone," including the Vatican. Evidently piqued that the planning for the Solidarity delegation's visit was being done by the papal apartment and the Solidarity leadership, rather than through the Secretariat of State, Silvestrini was, according to Szablewski, astonished when the Polish official told him some of the details of the plan, which Szablewski had seen in Warsaw.* Silvestrini then told Szablewski that he would do everything possible to make the Solidarity visit "as reasonable and ordinary as possible," while also assuring the Pole that he and Cardinal Casaroli would try to ensure that the visit did not have "dangerous consequences." Szablewski, who concluded the cable by telling Czyrek that he would meet with Cardinal Casaroli in a few days, noted that Archbishop Silvestrini seemed "particularly troubled" by plans for a press conference by the Solidarity delegation, as "there were bound to be questions about the talks between Wałęsa and the Pope."[70]

Even considering the possibility that Archbishop Silvestrini was dissembling a bit with his Polish interlocutor in order to provide some maneuvering room for the Pope in a situation in which the Polish government was clearly unhappy, the Szablewski cable suggests that there was tension between senior papal diplomats, such as Casaroli and Silvestrini, and the

---

*In the cable, the Polish phrase for the archbishop's astonishment is virtually untranslatable, suggesting as it does that Silvestrini "grabbed his head" or "clapped his hands to his head"; a colloquial English equivalent would be "his jaw dropped."

Pope on the question of how to handle the Solidarity movement. John Paul's insistence that his involvement in Polish affairs would be run out of the papal apartment with assistance from the papal Secretariat of State, rather than run through the Secretariat of State, clearly rankled. The Pope was determined that the Solidarity delegation's visit should strengthen the union's hand in Poland, so he wanted it to have the highest possible character; the diplomats, for their part, wanted it downgraded as much as possible, so as not to complicate their ongoing work with the Polish government through the permanent working contacts group. That Casaroli should have agreed to see Szablewski on short notice suggests how urgently the secretary of state wanted to communicate to Warsaw his continuing commitment to "normalization" and his concern that things not get out of hand in the wake of the Pope's meeting with Wałęsa and his delegation. At one point in the conversation, when Silvestrini was assuring Szablewski that he and Casaroli knew that the situation was volatile and "potentially dangerous for everyone," he added (according to Szablewski) "especially since the Pope himself is Polish"—which could have meant two things: that any unraveling could become an international incident, or that the Pope, being Polish, was unpredictable and thus perhaps uncontrollable.[71]

John Paul met with the Solidarity delegation in several formats and venues between January 15 and January 18, 1981.[72] At one meeting, Tadeusz

Mazowiecki remembered, the Pope "began by speaking about solidarity to Solidarity," emphasizing that "Solidarity was not **against** something or somebody but **for** something." It was important, the Pope stressed, to "fight **for** something," not simply against something. This was a new and different kind of revolution, a revolution of conscience "directed **toward**—toward the common good" of national reform. It was a theme to which the Pope returned in a Mass he celebrated for the delegation in the papal apartment chapel before hosting them to breakfast on January 18. Concluding his homily, the Pope asked his fellow Poles and indeed all Poles to "let your work serve human dignity, let it elevate man, let it elevate families, let it elevate the whole people." Solidarity, the movement, would serve freedom's cause if it were guided by a familiar biblical antiphon: "I come, Lord, I come, Lord, to do thy will."[73]

If the Pope's views on Solidarity caused concern among his professional diplomats committed to stability and "normalization," they were enthusiastically shared by the new president of the United States, Ronald Reagan, who was inaugurated two days after the Solidarity delegation's closing Mass and breakfast with John Paul II. Reagan brought to the White House long-standing interests in communism (having fought communists for control of the Screen Actors' Guild) and in John Paul II; the incoming national security adviser, Richard V. Allen, remembered how impressed and indeed moved Reagan had been by John Paul's Nine Days, about which the former California governor had spoken in a national radio address. A month after Reagan's inauguration, as John Paul was returning from a grueling first pilgrimage to Asia and the papal plane briefly touched down in Alaska for refueling, the president sent his old friend William Wilson as his personal emissary to greet the Pope during his minutes on American soil, having rammed Wilson's clearance through the sclerotic State Department in record time.[74]

Journalists would later speculate about a "holy alliance" between Ronald Reagan and John Paul II.[75] No such "alliance" ever existed. There were, however, interesting parallels between the two men. Both were orphans, at least of a sort; Wojtyła was a genuine orphan before he was twenty-one, while Reagan's difficult experiences with an alcoholic father had given him something of an orphan's sensibility. Both were men of the theater, with shared convictions about the power of words. Both took unconventional routes to positions of eminence that the conventional wisdom assumed they would never hold. Both were what might be called **positive** anticommunists, in that the cause of freedom and the promotion of human rights set the context for their respective critiques of communist theory and practice. As the two men considered the world, neither was locked into the conceptual categories of Realpolitik, as were old-school American conservatives, liberal American arms controllers, and more than a few senior Vatican diplomats. And because of this, both were unafraid of challenging the conventional wisdom and their own bureaucracies. That challenge would come both in terms of policy (Reagan's commitment to disarmament rather than arms "control," and his determination to launch the Strategic Defense Initiative; John Paul's open support for Solidarity, and for the persecuted Church behind the Iron Curtain) and in terms of personal initiative (as John Paul had done in December 1980, Reagan wrote a personal appeal to Leonid Brezhnev in April 1981; in both instances, the principals' diplomats were unhappy). Reagan, of course, had ways of signaling his policy that were unavailable to John Paul, for instance, arranging for the booby-trapping of American technology the USSR was stealing through Canada. The bottom line was the same for both men, however: communism, being false, was to be defeated, not simply contained or managed.[76]

They would soon share another common experience: surviving an assassination attempt, which in Reagan's case deepened his conviction that the quest for a new, peaceful world order was his vocation, which he ought to pursue in concert with men like John Paul II.[77]

EVIL TAKES A HAND

Throughout the spring of 1981, Poland lived through a war of nerves between Solidarity and the Polish regime.[78] The economy was crumbling. Solidarity was trying to formulate its platform, with Wałęsa struggling to keep the rambunctious movement together and directed on a course of "self-limiting revolution." A major crisis erupted over brutality against Solidarity activists in Bydgoszcz in March 1981; by keeping its collective head, maintaining nonviolence, gaining some regime concessions through the threat of a general strike, and mounting a major international media offensive, Solidarity managed to pry a major public relations victory out of the jaws of a very ugly situation.[79] When the Soviet Union wasn't spreading disinformation about an alleged meeting between John Paul and the Soviet ambassador to Italy in March 1981 (i.e., behind the backs of a beset Solidarity leadership), its satellites were up to more deadly forms of mischief. Moscow's client intelligence service, the Afghanistani KHAD, plotted to disrupt a public event John Paul II held in Pakistan in February 1981 by detonating a bomb during the Pope's homily in a Karachi stadium filled with 100,000 worshipers; the bomb exploded prematurely at the stadium entrance, killing the agent who was to detonate it, along with a local police officer.[80]

Meanwhile the Polish political scene was changing, with General Wojciech Jaruzelski installed as prime minister on February 9, 1981, not least because he was known as "a sincere friend of the Soviet Union."[81] That friendship would quickly be tested when Jaruzelski and Stanisław Kania, still clinging to his post as head of the Polish Communist Party, were verbally assaulted on March 4 by Leonid Brezhnev and other members of the Soviet Politburo at a Moscow meeting to which they had been peremptorily summoned. Kania, for his part, had made it known to a Polish comrade that "I don't want to go down in history as the butcher of the Polish people"—a sentiment immediately relayed to the KGB, which presumably read it as a sign of fatal weakness. Nonetheless, on March 27, Kania and Jaruzelski signed a document, "The Central Concept of Introducing Martial Law in the Territory of the Polish People's Republic," which set the theoretical and "legal" framework for a massive state intervention to "liquidate Solidarity."[82] A month later, on April 2, Dmitri Ustinov, the Soviet defense minister, told the Politburo that "bloodshed is unavoidable" if communism were to survive in Poland, while KGB chairman Andropov railed against Solidarity as the unthinkable—a political opposition.

The Soviet Politburo clearly recognized that, in the wake of Bydgoszcz, it was losing the game, both in Poland and in the battle for world opinion. Thus on April 3, Jaruzelski and Kania were ordered to come to Brest-Litovsk (scene of the Bolsheviks' surrender to Wilhelmine Germany in World War I) to be given what amounted to an ultimatum: they were to declare martial law and crush Solidarity, or the Soviet Union would intervene militarily. Jaruzelski and Kania asked for more time. Three weeks later, the Soviet Politburo approved a political analysis of the Polish situation which stated that Solidarity had "been transformed into an organized political force, which has the capacity to . . . take de facto power into its own hands." In order to forestall this, and "as a deterrent to counterrevolution," the Politburo agreed to "exploit to the utmost the fears of international reactionaries and international imperialism that the Soviet Union might send its troops into Poland." At the same time, the Soviet leadership agreed to "support Comrades Kania and Jaruzelski, who despite their well-known waffling, are in favor of defending Socialism." On the other hand, the two Poles must be "put under constant pressure to pursue more significant and decisive actions to overcome the crisis and preserve Poland as a Socialist country friendly to the Soviet Union."[83]

These fears were exaggerated, however, for things did not unravel for the communist authorities in Poland in late March, April, or early May 1981; they began to unravel for Solidarity. The Bydgoszcz crisis, and the dramatic debate within the movement over whether to use the weapon of a general strike, turned out to have been the high point of the first phase of the Solidarity revolution. Afterward, as one Solidarity historian put it, "it was Solidarity that began to gradually lose the support of a society increasingly weary of the economic crisis and the propaganda noise of the government."[84] Veteran dissident Jacek Kuroń detected the change, after Solidarity had won concessions to conclude the Bydgoszcz crisis: "A wave of relief has swept the country. Once people hoisted Wałęsa's car shoulder high. A short while later they were happy they wouldn't have to go to war. Then came the disappointment that nothing had changed."[85]

That Solidarity had passed its first apogee was not, of course, understood at the time, in either Rome or Moscow. Indeed, Moscow's campaign to "exploit to the utmost the fears" of the West about a Soviet military intervention in Poland had a pronounced effect in the Roman Curia. In a secret, coded cable of April 3, 1981, Kazimierz Szablewski reported to deputy foreign minister Józef Czyrek on his meeting the day before with Archbishop Achille Silvestrini. The Holy See, Silvestrini indicated, was very, very worried, and Poland had become the chief preoccupation of its international diplomacy. He then reiterated his conviction, and Casaroli's, that "stability" in Poland was in the interests of the Vatican—and then spelled out what this meant. As Szablewski reconstructed the conversation,

[Stability] means . . . maintaining and developing everything that lies in the interest of the nation, and rejecting everything that threatens independence and internal peace or could cause grave international upheavals. With this in mind, [Silvestrini] re-iterated Casaroli's well-known arguments about the need to reconcile internal reform and change with basic principles of the political system and inter-national conditions. Poland is viewed very sympa-thetically in the world for its efforts to reform, but no major world power is interested in developments in Poland that could seriously upset the balance of power—a balance achieved with such effort.[86]

Silvestrini also worried that what he perceived as saber-rattling by the new American administration was making matters worse, and bringing "some des-perate acts closer rather than distancing them from us." The Vatican's role in this very grim situation was "obvious: to preserve détente, encourage dialogue, to appease conflicts and strengthen peace."[87]

A month later, on May 6, Kazimierz Szablewski met with Cardinal Casaroli and had what he de-scribed to deputy foreign minister Czyrek in another enciphered and secret cable as a "lengthy conversa-tion." According to Szablewski, Casaroli told him that, while there is "great potential for change in the system," the blunt fact of the matter was that, for Poland, "there is no alternative to socialism"—meaning communism. Casaroli then urged party leader Kania to "persevere" on his "chosen path"; at the same time, the Vatican secretary of state said, "If I could, I would . . . wish [Polish] society to be more patient." Casaroli was full of admiration for Wyszyński's handling of the March crisis, in which the Primate had supported Wałęsa's moderating line, but he worried aloud to Szablewski that Wyszyński's declining health would create a bad situation in that his replacement "is unlikely to have the same authority in society." The senior Vatican diplomat then promised to try to urge moderation on the Reagan administration when he visited the United States in mid-May, and asked that Szablewski keep him fully informed of the Polish government's views on the Polish situation.[88]

Cardinal Casaroli thus remained confident that the course of prudence was to stabilize the Yalta system, the balance of power, and the European status quo that, as Silvestrini noted in April, had been achieved with such great effort. The secretary of state's admonitions to patience on the part of Poles also reflect the veteran diplomat's sense, which was not shared by John Paul II, that rowdy social movements tended to make a mess of things and in any event vastly complicated the work of the professionals, who ought to be allowed to arrange things according to the dictates of prudence.

That this commitment to stability and playing by the rules of the game was not universally shared was unmistakably demonstrated seven days after the Casaroli/Szablewski meeting, when, on May 13, 1981, Pope John Paul II was shot in St. Peter's Square and gravely wounded by a Turkish gunman and trained assassin, Mehmet Ali Agca.[89] It was a very close-run business: according to Gabriel Turowski, a physician and a longtime member of Karol Wojtyła's **Środowisko** who came to Rome to help the convalescent pontiff, the bullet that cut through the Pope's abdomen missed the main abdominal vein by five or six millimeters; had that vital vein been severed, John Paul would have bled to death in five minutes. Moreover, when another bullet hit the Pope's finger, its trajectory was deflected so that it missed damaging the Pope's spinal cord and paralyzing him from the waist down.[90]

It seemed, to many, a brazen attempt to liquidate someone whose continued witness on behalf of freedom could not be tolerated; that certainly was the consensus opinion among the vast throng that gathered in a "White March" in Kraków's Old Town market square to express their solidarity with their fellow Cracovian in Rome. President Ronald Reagan, who still bore the scars of a gunshot wound inflicted six weeks before, called Cardinal Terence Cooke of New York to express his sympathy and concern, while issuing a statement deploring this "terrible act of violence" and sending a telegram of concern to the Pope himself, promising his prayers.[91] Reagan's CIA, however, was loathe to consider, much less investigate, what seemed evident to most Poles and to many close friends of John Paul II: that the Soviet Union was not an innocent in this affair, no matter that the actual gunman had been a Turk with Bulgarian connections.[92]*

Two weeks after the assassination attempt on the Pope, Cardinal Stefan Wyszyński died in Warsaw—another hard blow to Polish morale and to the Church's capacity to give a measure of protection to Solidarity. Whether the assassination attempt on John Paul II was timed to coincide with Wyszyński's demise cannot be proven, but that the Primate was in grave condition at the time when the Pope was shot

---

*Other intelligence agencies were not so reluctant to play in this lethal game (although the SB seems not to have been involved, at any stage—perhaps because it was not fully trusted in Moscow). In August 1982, under the personal direction of Markus Wolf, the Stasi would initiate "Operation **Papst**" [Operation Pope] in response to requests from its sister secret intelligence service in Bulgaria to cover any tracks that might lead to a Bulgarian link to Mehmet Ali Agca. Operation **Papst** worked to reinforce a bit of Soviet-bloc disinformation that had previously gotten into international media circulation, to the effect that Agca's connection to the Grey Wolves, a murky "right-wing" Turkish terrorist outfit, proved that he was motivated by Islamist passions—a curious suggestion, given Agca's striking lack of religious sensibility. The full details of Operation **Papst** are unknown, but it is inconceivable that an operation of this sort would have been mounted without the approval, and even the supervision, of the KGB. As was typical of such efforts on the part of Soviet-bloc intelligence services, the work of Operation **Papst** was described as a response to anticommunist campaigns by the West—which in this case was a particularly ludicrous suggestion, given that no Western intelligence agency wanted to touch the idea of a Soviet connection to Agca and the assassination attempt on John Paul II.[93]

was certainly known to Soviet-bloc intelligence. The Pope was thus faced with the difficult task of choosing a replacement for the irreplaceable Wyszyński, while he was himself recovering from Agca's bullets and from the effects of a virulent cytomegalovirus he had contracted from a tainted blood transfusion; gravely weakened, the Pope had had to return to the Policlinico Gemelli, where a proper diagnosis of his condition was finally made in late June.[94] Time was of the essence, as Solidarity's first National Congress was scheduled for September and the ever-present threat of a Warsaw Pact attempt to crush Solidarity by armed force was never far from the Pope's mind, or Cardinal Casaroli's. The choice eventually fell on Bishop Józef Glemp, whom Wyszyński may have recommended to John Paul as the kind of man needed for what the Primate saw as the next phase of the struggle: a lawyer, with degrees in both canon and civil law, who could read the fine print in any proposed deal.[95]

On the Way to a Coup d'Etat

For their parts, Polish Communist Party first secretary Stanisław Kania and prime minister/defense minister Wojciech Jaruzelski were more interested in surviving than in deal-making with the new archbishop of Gniezno and Warsaw. In the late spring of 1981, the KGB's Moscow Center told the Warsaw KGB that it was time for Kania to go and that Poland needed both a new party leader and a new prime minister; the Soviet candidates were two hard-liners, Tadeusz Grabski and Stefan Olszowski, who, according to the KGB, were "imbued with a firm Marxist-Leninist outlook and are prepared to act decisively and consistently in defense of Socialist interests and of friendship with the Soviet Union."[96] Meanwhile, several Polish generals approached the KGB with a proposed plot to replace Jaruzelski because of his unwillingness, thus far, to impose martial law.[97] Nonetheless, Moscow decided that it was best to keep Jaruzelski, so he and Kania remained in power for the moment, although they brought into prominent positions two hard-liners: General Czesław Kiszczak as minister of internal affairs and Jerzy Urban as party spokesman. Kiszczak's appointment suggested that the plans for martial law, which had been under development since the fall of 1980, were maturing, as Kiszczak would brook no internal party opposition to a crackdown when the time came.[98] Underscoring the urgency of the situation from the communists' point of view, the party's membership continued to crumble, even as Solidarity's continued to increase.[99]

By August, the month before the Solidarity Congress was to open, General Jaruzelski had decided

that martial law would have to be imposed; the
prime minister/defense minister cleared his detailed
plan with the Warsaw Pact commander in chief,
Soviet Marshal Viktor Kulikov, while interior minister Kiszczak informed KGB chairman Andropov
that the SB had deeply penetrated the Church and
that the new primate, Glemp, would be far easier
to deal with than Wyszyński. The remaining problems, Kiszczak concluded, were the Pope and the
moral authority of the Polish Church. Andropov
seemed impressed and did not badger Kiszczak as
he had the Pole's immediate predecessors. But the
KGB chairman was still very worried: "The class
enemy has repeatedly tried to challenge the people's
power in the Socialist countries. . . . But the Polish
crisis is the most long drawn out, and perhaps the
most dangerous. The adversary's creeping counter-
revolution has long been preparing for the struggle
with Socialism."[100]

The first Solidarity National Congress embodied
what the Polish Communist Party claimed to be and
manifestly wasn't: an assembly representative of Polish society. The Congress opened on September 5 in
Oliwa, near Gdańsk. Its chaplain was John Paul II's
old friend Father Józef Tischner, who preached several brilliant sermons on the reform of Polish labor.
One of them concluded in these lyrical terms, far
removed from the world and the words of Yuri Andropov and Czesław Kiszczak:

We must look at the issue [of work] from above, like looking from the peaks of the Tatras, where the waters of the Vistula have their beginning. The very liturgy of the Mass encourages us to do this. . . . This bread and this wine shall become in a moment the body and blood of the Son of God. This has a deep meaning. . . . Were it not for human work, there would be no bread and wine. Without bread and wine, there would not be among us the Son of God. God does not come to us through a creation of nature alone, holy trees, water, or fire. God comes to us through the first creation of culture—bread and wine. Work that creates bread and wine paves the way toward God. But every work has a part in this work. Our work, too. In this way our work, the work of each one of us, paves the way to God. . . .

Our concern is with the independence of Polish work. The word **independence** must be understood properly. It does not aim at breaking away from others. Work is reciprocity, it is agreement, it is a multifaceted dependence. Work creates a communion. . . .

We are living history. A living history means one that bears fruit. Christ has said, "Let the dead bury their dead" [Matthew 8.22]. Thus, let us do the same. Let us become occupied with bearing fruit.[101]

While Father Tischner was preaching (and the Congress was adopting a resolution to include his words in its official records), Soviet and other Warsaw Pact warships were cruising off the Baltic Coast, visible on the horizon beyond the famous cranes of the Gdańsk shipyard. The Soviet Politburo was beside itself, accusing Solidarity of having become a "political opposition that conflicts with the vital interests of the nation and the state."[102] The Soviet press agency TASS ranted on about an "anti-socialist and anti-Soviet orgy."[103] In the aftermath of the Congress, the Polish Communist Party, while flatly rejecting Solidarity's call for free elections, made a pro forma attempt at co-optation, proposing a new kind of "national front" in which Solidarity would play a role; the trade union, which took the word "independent" in its formal title seriously, declined.[104]

The sands were running out on Stanisław Kania, the man who didn't want to be the butcher of the Polish people, and on October 18, 1981, he was replaced as party first secretary by General Jaruzelski, who now held all the levers of power: party chief, prime minister, and defense minister. Nine days later, Leonid Brezhnev phoned Jaruzelski to congratulate him:

"Hello, Wojciech," Brezhnev began. "Hello, my dear, deeply esteemed Leonid Ilyich!" Jaruzelski replied. He maintained the same sycophantic tone throughout the conversation: "Thank you very much, dear Leonid Ilyich, for the greeting and above all for the confidence you have in me. I want to tell you frankly that I had some inner misgivings about accepting this post and agreed to do so only because I knew that you support me and that you were in favor of this decision. If this had not been so, I would not have agreed to it."[105]

Brezhnev's mental faculties might not have been at their most acute in late 1981, but he knew his man in General Jaruzelski. Even as the SB continued its efforts to penetrate and disrupt Solidarity and the rubber-stamp Polish parliament considered draft legislation with the ominous title "Extraordinary Measures to Defend the Interests of Citizens and the State," Jaruzelski agreed to a "Big Three" meeting on November 4 with Primate Glemp and Solidarity chairman Wałęsa, which achieved nothing. While the facade of legality and "dialogue" was being re-furbished, plans for the imposition of martial law were refined and Kiszczak's interior ministry gave a preview of what was to come by using a helicopter assault to break up a student strike.[106]

The decision to declare a "state of emergency" and impose martial law was taken by the Polish Party Politburo on December 5.[107] The cast of mind of the hard-liners was neatly summed up by Józef Czyrek, recipient of those encoded cables reporting on Vati-can attitudes: "Major historical crises have never been resolved by expanding democracy but by giv-ing extraordinary powers to rulers, by introducing dictatorship."[108] This attempt to cast General Jaru-zelski in the role of Cincinnatus may have been of some comfort to those Polish comrades who believed they were being forced into this position by the imperative of acting themselves, lest Soviet tanks crush Poland. But it ill fit the facts. Unlike the situation a year before, when Soviet and Warsaw Pact forces were poised on Poland's borders, no such imminent threat of invasion was being mounted at this juncture.

On December 11, Solidarity's radicals won a debate at a meeting of the union's National Commission in Gdańsk, and adopted a resolution calling for a referendum—either nationwide or within Solidarity—on whether Poland's future should be communist. Official regime propaganda later cited this as the casus belli for the imposition of martial law—which was a lie, as that course had been irrevocably adopted a week earlier. Indeed, if there was a note of classic historical drama in Poland in December 1981, it did not have to do with Jaruzelski-as-Cincinnatus but with the fact that the impasse toward which Poland had been heading at least since August 1980, and more likely since the Nine Days of John Paul II in June 1979, had finally been reached: as Jan Olszewski, a Warsaw lawyer and Solidarity leader put it with admirable concision, "People are determined not to reconcile themselves to the system and the government is not prepared to change it."[109]

On the night of December 12–13, 1981, the Polish Communist Party and government staged what amounted to a coup d'etat against the Polish state and Polish society. General Jaruzelski spoke to the country at 6 A.M. on December 13, long after the first arrests had been made and telephone communication cut off within the country and between Poland and the world. "Our homeland was on the edge of a precipice," Jaruzelski declared, and therefore he was assuming absolute authority as chairman of a Military Council of National Salvation [WRON]— a title rich with irony, as it was the nation against which war was being waged and the party that was to be saved.[110] Three days earlier, Jaruzelski had warned the KGB that Primate Glemp could become "a second Khomeini," declaring a holy war; it was as unlikely a casting as Jaruzelski-as-Cincinnatus, for Glemp urged calm in two December 13 sermons, begging, "Do not begin a fight of Pole against Pole. Do not lose your heads, brother workers . . . every head and every pair of hands will be invaluable in rebuilding the Poland that will exist, and will have to exist, after martial law has ended."[111] Five thousand Poles were arrested in December 1981; between then and the end of martial law in July 1983, that number would more than double, with many spending months in internment camps. The worst violence took place outside Katowice, at the **Wujek** mine, where a Polish Special Forces platoon opened fire on striking miners, killing nine.[112] The SB behaved with its accustomed "casual brutality," subjecting Lech Wałęsa's wife and daughters to strip searches and inflicting similar humiliations and beatings on other Solidarity activists, while doing everything in its power to dismantle Solidarity's organizational and communications machinery.[113] The WRON controlled the entire media and used it for mindless propaganda, adding yet another joke to the thick catalogue of Polish anticommunist humor: "What is the lowest rank in the army? Television commentator."[114]

John Paul II was informed of the imposition of martial law at 1 A.M. on December 13, in a phone call from the Polish ambassador to Italy. Unable to reach anyone in Poland by phone, the Pope spent a difficult Sunday, using the word "solidarity" six times during his Angelus address and repeating the invocation of the word now banned in Poland during the weekly general audience the following Wednesday—during which he also began the custom of invoking Our Lady of Częstochowa at the end of his remarks. The day after the massacre at the **Wujek** mine, John Paul wrote General Jaruzelski an "urgent and heartfelt appeal . . . a prayer for an end to the shedding of Polish blood," ending with "an appeal to your conscience, General."[115] While the Pope had been warned by a phone call from Zbigniew Brzeziński that something seemed to be afoot in Poland, Stanisław Dziwisz remembers the Pope as being "anguished and surprised" that martial law had been imposed. It was, Dziwisz later said, "a profound humiliation for Poland. After all that it had suffered throughout its history, Poland didn't deserve this new martyrdom. It didn't deserve to be punished so severely."[116] The humiliation, of course, came from the fact that the latest martyrdom was inflicted on Poles by Poles.

President Reagan called the Pope on the evening of December 14, beginning by saying that he wanted John Paul to know "how deeply we feel about the situation in your country" and assuring the Pope that "our sympathies are with the people, not with the government."[117] That same day, the Pope met in Rome with Solidarity leader Bohdan Cywiński, who had been out of the country when martial law was imposed; they met on three other occasions during the following week, to exchange what information they had and to consider the future. It was, Cywiński recalled, a time for serious reflection, after the initial shock had been absorbed. Solidarity had clearly underestimated the staying power of the communists, as some in the Church had previously underestimated Solidarity's possibilities. John Paul regularly expressed concern for the suffering families of interned Solidarity activists; but neither he nor Cywiński engaged in any "conspiracy" to assist those families using Vatican funds or recycled funds from Western intelligence sources, reports to the contrary notwithstanding.[118] Throughout the initial period of martial law, according to both Cywiński and former Radio Free Europe Polish service head Jan Nowak, John Paul II was cautious, careful not to say or do anything that would make matters worse, and doubtless concerned that serious and detailed information was hard to come by.[119]

On December 15, Cardinal Agostino Casaroli had a working lunch with President Ronald Reagan in the White House Map Room. Casaroli was accompanied by Archbishop Pio Laghi, the apostolic delegate in Washington, and by Archbishop Silvestrini's deputy, Msgr. Audrys Bačkis; in addition to Reagan, the Americans present included Vice President George Bush; Secretary of State Alexander Haig; presidential chief of staff James Baker; acting chief special assistant for national security affairs James Nance; William Wilson, the president's personal envoy to the Vatican; principal deputy assistant secretary for European and Canadian affairs, H. Allen Holmes; and Dennis Blair, a member of the National Security Council staff. The burden of the ninety-minute conversation was carried by President Reagan and Cardinal Casaroli.

At the outset of the discussion, and according to the classified memorandum of the conversation that summarized each point in it, Casaroli said that he believed Jaruzelski had acted "both because of Soviet pressure and to prevent the Soviets themselves from intervening." Based on "his personal knowledge of Jaruzelski," the cardinal "felt that he was nationalist enough not to want the Soviet Union to intervene directly." The discussion (which took place the day before the **Wujek** mine massacre) then turned to reports, unconfirmed, that striking workers had been fired upon, with Cardinal Casaroli saying that he "could understand harsh punishments for sabotage, but could hardly see them applying to workers who failed to come to work."

President Reagan, operating on the assumption (which turned out to be false) that it was Solidarity's call for a referendum on Poland's communist future that had triggered martial law, said that the West should take "full propaganda advantage" of that response to a call for free elections, because it was "a clear comment on the lack of popular support for the government." Casaroli responded that "this was a telling point," but then argued that "it was unrealistic to think that one east European country could be extensively liberated on its own," as "the Soviets would simply not tolerate such a situation." Casaroli also suggested that, while "it was important to support movements for liberalization in Eastern Europe," it was also his settled view that "no country could be far ahead of the others." The Vatican secretary of state also told the Americans that John Paul II was convinced that "change in Eastern Europe would come only gradually and at the same rate in all Eastern European countries."

Later in the conversation, Casaroli suggested that "the events in Poland were unfortunate but predictable," as he had been told by a visiting Polish government official that the "economic deterioration in Poland" was due to a "lack of worker discipline." This, in addition to the continuing pressure from the Soviet Union, made it almost inevitable that "the Polish government would be forced to intervene openly."

Reagan argued that "the Vatican and the Pope had a key role to play in events in Poland and elsewhere in Eastern Europe," for the Pope's June 1979 visit "had showed the 'terrible hunger' for God in Eastern Europe." Casaroli responded, that, yes, "there was a hunger for God in specific groups in Eastern Europe," but that "in general, youth was 'insensible' to God," which reflected what Casaroli judged to be a general apathy among young people. Thus, Casaroli concluded, "the time is not ripe yet for real change in Eastern Europe," a judgment he subsequently repeated.

The conversation then turned to Reagan's determination to reduce the danger of nuclear war by reaching real disarmament agreements with the Soviet Union. Casaroli, who had suggested to Secretary Haig a U.S. strategy of "minimum deterrence" by which the United States would "accept an imbalance so along as the United States and NATO had a small but significant" nuclear force of their own, talked at some length of the arms race as an action-reaction cycle; Reagan responded by saying that he thought it more likely that the Soviets would consider real arms reductions when the United States had made clear to them that it would not lose any arms race. Casaroli responded, some minutes later, that "it was important that a major power be able to 'save face,' and for that reason some discreet diplomacy might be valuable"—diplomacy that the Holy See was prepared to provide, if asked. The conversation ended with Casaroli arguing in favor of "quiet diplomacy" rather than a "public campaign" in the matter of human rights in communist countries.[120]

This striking conversation strongly suggests that President Reagan was rather more attuned to John Paul II's way of reading and conducting world politics than Cardinal Casaroli. Throughout the ninety-minute conversation, it was Reagan who spoke in terms of moral witness and the power of moral conviction, and Casaroli who spoke in terms of Realpolitik. Whatever the elements of truth in Casaroli's analysis of General Jaruzelski's situation, it is noteworthy that it was the American president who was clearly outraged by the imposition of martial law, while the Vatican secretary of state took the measured, diplomatic view. The divergent views between Reagan and Casaroli on the prospects for change in central and eastern Europe are similarly striking; and it is not easy to see that Casaroli was accurately reflecting the Pope's true view when he suggested that John Paul II shared the cardinal's conviction that the time was not ripe for serious change because of apathetic young people who were "insensible" to God—a judgment that contradicted thirty years of Karol Wojtyła's pastoral experience and had been most recently invalidated by the Nine Days of June

1979, which Casaroli had witnessed but seemed not to have understood very well. In the group's discussion of arms control and disarmament, it was, again, Reagan who was the visionary and Casaroli the exponent of Realpolitik. Moreover, a close reading of these exchanges suggests (as did Archbishop Silvestrini's conversations with Kazimierz Szablewski) that Casaroli and Silvestrini tended to accept the general European view that Reagan's arms policies were irresponsible and provocative. The closing exchange, in which Casaroli gently warned the president against too vociferous an approach to human rights, is also instructive.

Cardinal Casaroli went from Washington to New York, where he asked to meet with Eugeniusz Wyzner, the Polish ambassador to the United Nations. The meeting took place on December 17, and Wyzner's secret report was encoded and sent by cable to deputy foreign minister Józef Czyrek on December 18. According to Wyzner's report, Casaroli began the conversation by reporting on his recent lunch with President Reagan, Vice President Bush, Secretary Haig, and others, during which, according to Casaroli, he had tried to nudge the Americans away from thinking about the imposition of martial law as the intervention of a "foreign empire," but rather as a Polish initiative taken "to avoid placing the country in a more dangerous situation." Casaroli then repeated what he had told the Americans: that, on meeting General Jaruzelski in June 1981, he had formed the impression of a man who would "behave patriotically for the good of the country."

Wyzner, for his part, complained about American condemnation of martial law and the Reagan administration's speculations about its origins, while also criticizing "statements by the [Polish] Episcopate [that were being] used to inflame and incite the public." Wyzner then reported that Casaroli, rather than fighting back, "accepted our position and the information given him," which he promised to give to John Paul II the next day. Casaroli then assured the Pole that he "would act in a spirit of understanding and willingness to help." The most important thing, Casaroli suggested, was to avoid a civil war; the Polish government might take into account that the Polish bishops sometimes had to say things for "fear of taking an opposing view to that of the nation," and that this sometimes happened "contrary to their own convictions." The cardinal then told the Polish ambassador that he had been unable to persuade the Americans to give serious economic assistance to Poland, suggesting that while he welcomed American assurances of humanitarian assistance, he thought the refusal of American aid to stabilize the collapsing Polish economy was shortsighted. Wyzner concluded his report by stating that Casaroli "understands the context and the necessity of our decision."[121]

Four days after the imposition of martial law and the day after the **Wujek** mine massacre, Cardinal Casaroli was still defending stability as the guiding norm for all right-thinking statesmen. John Paul II, Casaroli told Wyzner, had instructed Archbishop Silvestrini to tell Kazimierz Szablewski that, as there was no outside intervention under way in Poland, the Polish government had a special responsibility to maintain national unity and dignity. Yet Casaroli, in his conversation with Wyzner, seemed to accept the view that the WRON had acted in the face of an imminent Soviet threat, which in fact did not exist. The American administration was working under this misapprehension, too; but it seems odd that the Pope's secretary of state would side with the Polish government's preferred interpretation of recent events rather than with the Polish pope's. As for Casaroli's remarks on the Polish episcopate (which in fact had been urging moderation since December 13), it is possible that Casaroli was trying to give the Polish bishops some protection by suggesting that they were acting contrary to their true convictions; but this was, under any circumstances, a curious suggestion to make. Wyzner, for his part, may have been interpreting Casaroli's remarks in a way that would be most agreeable to Warsaw. Yet the direct citation of Casaroli's promise that he would "act in a spirit of understanding and willingness to help" suggests that, for the cardinal, preserving permanent working contacts with the Polish government took clear precedence over even a minimal expression of moral outrage on the day after workers were gunned down near Katowice. Here, as elsewhere, it does seem that John Paul II and Cardinal Casaroli had dramatically different sensibilities, which led to very different readings of situations and personalities.

A KGB report on the immediate post–martial law situation in Poland, which seems to have originated with the Hungarian intelligence service and its Roman contacts, was circulated to Soviet-bloc intelligence agencies in late December. The analysis noted "much anxiety" among "Vatican officials" over a possible Polish civil war, which would lead to Warsaw Pact intervention and enormous casualties[122]— a rather obvious expression of the settled views of the veterans of the pre–John Paul II **Ostpolitik**, and a confirmation of Ambassador Wyzner's report that Cardinal Casaroli understood the "context and necessity" of the martial law decision. For his part, John Paul II came to the view (which his cardinal secretary of state almost certainly did not share) that the imposition of martial law by the WRON was the desperate act of a crumbling regime. That judgment, like the Pope's words and actions during the Nine Days of June 1979, rested on a set of assumptions that clearly distinguished the Pope's view from that of his most senior diplomats, some of whom seemed to look with favor on what a Stasi informant described in January 1982 as an "Argentine solution" to the problems of Poland—rule by a military junta and a return to "normality."[123] For John Paul II, however, "normalization," meaning recognition of and respect for basic human rights, was an interim goal to be sought on the way to transformation. For Cardinal Casaroli, "normalization" was a goal in itself, a way of living normally under communism. Or as Zbigniew Brzeziński once put it, "for Casaroli, the status quo was something that could not be changed but could be made more palatable; for John Paul II, making the status quo more palatable was a tool for undermining it." That difference in strategic vision reflected a prior difference in moral and political judgment: "For Casaroli, communism was a system of power with which one had to live. For John Paul II, communism was an evil that could not be avoided but could be undermined."[124]

On Christmas Eve, 1981, at 6 P.M., a lit candle was placed on the windowsill of the papal apartment, overlooking St. Peter's Square. Lit candles in windows had become an international symbol of solidarity with Solidarity and with Poland, an initiative begun by two Swiss clergymen, one Protestant and one Catholic. The papal message for the World Day of Peace on January 1, 1982, condemned the "false peace of totalitarian regimes," such as that which reigned in Poland during the Christmas holidays. Yet because the human quest for freedom was "inscribed in human conscience" (as John Paul II put it to the diplomatic corps accredited to the Holy See on January 16), the freedom tide was rising and what the diplomats recognized as "normality" would, one day, be overcome.

CHAPTER FOUR

Victory

June 7, 1982	Pope John Paul II and President Ronald Reagan meet at the Vatican.
November 12, 1982	Yuri Andropov succeeds Leonid Brezhnev as general secretary of the Communist Party of the Soviet Union.
February 1983	Operation TRIANGOLO attempts smear of Pope John Paul II.
March 1983	John Paul II challenges Marxist governments and guerrilla movements in Central America.
April 25, 1983	Jerzy Kuberski meets Archbishop Achille Silvestrini to discuss John Paul II's impending visit to Poland.
June 16–23, 1983	John Paul II's second pastoral pilgrimage to Poland.

July 22, 1983	Martial law in Poland ends.
October 5, 1983	Norwegian Nobel Committee announces awarding of Nobel Peace Prize to Lech Wałęsa.
October 19, 1984	Father Jerzy Popiełuszko is murdered.
March 11, 1985	Mikhail Gorbachev succeeds Konstantin Chernenko as general secretary of the Communist Party of the Soviet Union.
December 1985	John Paul II meets Elena Bonner, wife of Soviet dissident Andrei Sakharov.
January 13, 1987	John Paul II receives General Wojciech Jaruzelski in the Vatican.
June 6, 1987	John Paul II and President Reagan meet in the Vatican.
June 8–14, 1987	John Paul II's third pastoral pilgrimage to Poland.
June 1988	John Paul II sends Vatican delegation led by Cardinal Agostino Casaroli to Moscow celebration of millennium of Christianity among eastern Slavs.
February 6– April 5, 1989	Polish Round Table negotiations; Operation TRIANGOLO documents disappear.
June 4, 1989	Polish elections return overwhelming Solidarity victory.

September 12, 1989 • Tadeusz Mazowiecki becomes post-war Poland's first noncommunist prime minister.

November 24, 1989 • Cardinal František Tomášek aligns Catholic Church with Czechoslovakia's "Velvet Revolution."

December 1, 1989 • Pope John Paul II receives Mikhail Gorbachev at the Vatican.

Cardinal Franciszek Macharski, John Paul II's successor as archbishop of Kraków, had learned about the archbishop's role as **Defensor Civitatis** early in life. On the morning of September 1, 1939, as the Luftwaffe bombed the city, the twelve-year-old Macharski heard his father call the prince-archbishop, Adam Stefan Sapieha, to ask what should be done. "I stay!" replied Sapieha. The elder Macharski turned to his family and announced, "We stay, too." Some four decades later, in that same spirit, Cardinal Macharski defended his people against the depredations of the self-inflicted wound of martial law—which, on the evening of June 22, 1983, had been in force for more than a year and a half.

On that night, the last of John Paul II's second pilgrimage to his homeland, Cardinal Macharski expected to host the papal party and several distinguished guests at dinner in the archiepiscopal residence at Franciszkańska, 3. The residence was on the edge of the Planty, the great greenbelt the Austrians had created around Kraków's Old Town along the line once occupied by the city's fortifications. The papal party, including Cardinal Agostino Casaroli, the secretary of state, had arrived, as had other guests, including Cardinal Jean-Marie Lustiger of Paris, the son of Polish Jews who had moved to France; Lustiger's mother had perished in the gas chambers at Auschwitz. Everything was ready except for one thing: the guest of honor, Pope John Paul II, was not present.

General Wojciech Jaruzelski had decided that he must have a last, one-on-one meeting with the Pope, who had insisted on seeing the still interned Lech Wałęsa the day before, much to the regime's displeasure. John Paul agreed to the change of schedule and the meeting with Jaruzelski was set for late afternoon in a room in Wawel Castle. It may be assumed that the conversation involved a "frank exchange of views," as the diplomats say.

Cardinal Macharski told his guests to start eating, as the soup was getting cold. While the first course was being consumed, John Paul II came in, sat down, ate a bit of soup, and then heard a boisterous crowd of young people who were gathered on the Planty, calling for him to come to the window. So the Pope got up, went to the window, and bantered back and forth with the crowd for fifteen minutes or so. At which point, as Cardinal Lustiger later recalled, Car-

dinal Casaroli burst out to a startled dinner company, "What does he want? Does he want bloodshed?
Does he want war? Does he want to overthrow the
government? Every day I have to explain to the authorities that there is nothing to this!"[1]

But there was something to it—something that
would bend the course of world history in a new
and better direction.

John Paul II had always taken quite literally
Christ's injunction to Peter to "strengthen your
brethren" (Luke 22.32). That strengthening took
different forms, given diverse circumstances. Poland
I, the Nine Days of John Paul II in June 1979, ignited the revolution of conscience that gave birth to
the Solidarity revolution. Poland II, the papal pilgrimage in June 1983, was intended to lift the spirits
of a people who had been crushed yet again so that
they might be strong enough to return to the path
that martial law was supposed to have blocked—the
path to responsibility and freedom. Poland III, in
June 1987, would set in place the moral foundations
for the successful completion of that remarkable
journey, which would come two years later with the
election of a Solidarity-led government: something
that seemed beyond imagining on the night of June
22, 1983—at least to those for whom the preservation of stability was the prime moral and political
imperative.

BACK TO THE UNDERGROUND

Time magazine named Lech Wałęsa "Man of the
Year" in its January 4, 1982, issue, which included
a lengthy story that introduced many Americans to
the details of the drama that had been unfolding in
Poland since 1979. The more consequential Polish-
American conversation of the moment, however,
did not involve magazines but letters: a dozen or so
letters exchanged by President Ronald Reagan and
Pope John Paul II during Reagan's first year in office. In this classified correspondence, the two men
explored issues of mutual concern, including martial law in the Pope's homeland and the president's
determination to propose genuine disarmament,
not just arms "control," to the Soviet Union when
the two sides began negotiations over intermediate-
range nuclear missiles in Geneva later in 1982.[2]

President Reagan clearly understood that John
Paul would continue to play a crucial role in Poland,
and perhaps beyond. Thus, on Reagan's instructions, General Vernon Walters and CIA director
William Casey briefed the Pope in Rome on U.S.
intelligence findings and policy directions. According to former Radio Free Europe Polish service director Jan Nowak, then a consultant on Polish affairs
to the U.S. National Security Council, the president
insisted that the Pope be informed about sources as
well as given information; thus John Paul knew of

the work of Polish colonel Ryszard Kukliński, whose reports had been invaluable in the December 1980 crisis and who had been keeping his U.S. contacts informed of martial law plans before he and his family were exfiltrated in November 1981.[3] The Reagan administration provided substantial funding for underground Solidarity in the years after martial law was imposed, with much of the money being managed through the AFL-CIO. John Paul II would have been informed of this, and doubtless appreciated it—especially as it helped relieve the suffering of the families of interned Solidarity activists.

In Poland itself, post–martial law politics gave new meaning to Václav Havel's memorable description of communism as a culture of lies.[4] Prior to the imposition of martial law, the "Front of National Unity," the political facade behind which and through which the communist party controlled the Sejm, the rubber-stamp Polish parliament, was dissolved; a new entity that would maintain the fiction of a political coalition in charge of Poland's affairs was needed. Thus the Patriotic Movement for National Renewal [PRON] was born; slightly more pluralistic than its predecessor, it nonetheless shared the old Front's task of being a "platform on which various groups that supported the status quo could rally to the side of the party."[5] Its further purpose, in addition to providing cover for martial law, was to create a regime-controlled alternative to underground Solidarity.[6]

Martial law inevitably led to political divisions within Solidarity. Some Solidarity leaders proposed organizing for a general strike, while others preferred what came to be known as the "long road" approach, which focused on rebuilding civil society. After the imposition of martial law, these options were debated in a clandestine press despite the regime's efforts to crush Solidarity's publishing capabilities; historian Andrzej Paczkowski estimates that "during the course of 1982 at least eight hundred illegal periodicals appeared, most of them associated with Solidarity groups and organizations."[7] An Interim Coordinating Commission [TKK], which came to be recognized as the de facto leadership of underground Solidarity, was established on April 22, 1982. The TKK subsequently spun off affiliated organizations, including a Foreign Coordinating Bureau in Brussels. Clandestine educational, cultural, scientific, and farmers' organizations were also organized, all parts of a complex network of "underground society." The Church in Poland played a key role in providing free space for independent, non-regime-controlled educational and cultural activities. Churches opened themselves to "evening poetry readings, theater performances, exhibitions, and even popular scientific sessions."[8] St. Brigid's Church in Warsaw (Wałęsa's parish), St. Maximilian Kolbe Church in Nowa Huta, and the Church of St. Stanisław Kostka in Warsaw were among the leaders in this kind of work; at the latter, a young priest named Jerzy Popiełuszko began to make a name for himself as a popular preacher at a regular "Mass for the Fatherland." Such Masses, and the cultural and educational activities surrounding them, "played a major role in maintaining the will to resist among the broad ranks of believers."[9] Like John Paul II, the Polish episcopate had been cautious in its public statements after the imposition of martial law. Still, the sanction given by the Catholic hierarchy to these church-based exercises in "free space" (or, perhaps better, "moral extraterritoriality") cannot be gainsaid as a significant factor in maintaining a civil society alternative to totalitarianism in Poland.[10]

The debate over direct action or the "long road" did not last more than a few months. Despite the wealth of clandestine enterprises under way, it was clear to most activists that the regime's political and economic control of the country was such that only the path charted by John Paul II during the Nine Days of June 1979—the reconstitution of civil society and public moral culture—held any hope of success over time. Meanwhile, the Pope himself was being as supportive as he could of Poland's underground society. One of his contacts was Jacek Woźniakowski, whom Karol Wojtyła had first met in his early days as a curate at St. Florian's parish. Woźniakowski had since become a distinguished art historian, but his anticommunist views had consistently impeded his academic career, so he made part of his living working at **Tygodnik Powszechny**. Woźniakowski managed to get to Rome in January 1982 and was quickly invited to the Vatican, where he spent all morning, lunch, dinner, and the bulk of the evening in the papal apartment, briefing John Paul II on the situation at home; evidently unhappy with the information he was getting through his Secretariat of State, John Paul told his old friend that his was "the first decent report on what's happening in Poland" that he'd received.[11] Some time later, after the Solidarity foreign bureau had been set up in Brussels, its head, Jerzy Milewski, asked Woźniakowski to act as an intermediary with the Pope. Woźniakowski, back in Rome from a teaching position in Toulouse, asked John Paul whether he thought the Brussels operation was a good idea. "Yes," the Pope replied, "you can tell him I think it's a good idea."[12]

Tadeusz Mazowiecki had a harder time of it, having been jailed on December 13, 1981, and then put into an internment camp, formerly a military base. When families were permitted to visit, letters were smuggled in and out. Cardinal Franciszek Macharski also came to visit the former editor of **Tygodnik Solidarność;** he and Mazowiecki's son smuggled out of the camp letters written by the imprisoned Solidarity leader to John Paul II and got them to Rome. In one of these letters, Mazowiecki asked the Pope not to abstract the "idea of solidarity" from its specific expression in the trade union/mass movement that had been created, and then crushed: the legalization of Solidarity, Mazowiecki suggested, had to be the minimal baseline for any agreement with the regime—"there were some things that could not be given back." After some time, Mazowiecki recalled, he received a brief, handwritten letter from John Paul II, which had been smuggled into Poland; "I've read your letter," the Pope wrote Mazowiecki, "and I've been thinking carefully about the situation. I have read your letter three or four times." Mazowiecki immediately understood the code: he and John Paul II "understood each other" on the matter of a legal restoration of Solidarity.[13]

On June 7, 1982, John Paul received Ronald Reagan at the Vatican. In his remarks after their meeting, the president went out of his way to highlight "the martyred nation of Poland—your homeland," noting that Poland had for centuries been "a brave bastion of faith and freedom in the hearts of her courageous people, if not in [the hearts of] those who rule her."[14] That rhetorical shot across General Jaruzelski's bow had little effect on the situation on the ground, however, as the martial law regime rejected all TKK proposals for a settlement. These proposals included an amnesty for those arrested, the release of political prisoners, reinstatement in their jobs for those fired for having supported Solidarity—and, ultimately, restoration of the legal status of **NSZZ Solidarność;** the TKK had previously proposed that the principles of Catholic social doctrine be the basis for a national dialogue.[15] The authorities rejected all of this, and Jaruzelski viciously attacked the union in the Sejm on July 21, 1982. That same month, negotiations between the Holy See and the martial law regime on a previously planned 1982 papal pilgrimage to Poland broke down, and the Vatican announced that the visit would be held at a later date.

The TKK leadership then called for peaceful public protests on August 31, the anniversary of the 1980 Gdańsk Accords. Large, if not overwhelming, numbers of protesters turned out that day and were met with aggressive countermeasures by the SB, the police, and the paramilitary militia, the ZOMO; four were killed and eight wounded in the worst incident, in Lublin, "where the ZOMO opened fire on demonstrators and literally went hunting."[16] These demonstrations were the high-water mark of public support for underground Solidarity, which subsequently began to decline as the passions of the previous nine months abated.[17] The regime, for its part, was sufficiently confident of its control that it released Lech Wałęsa on November 14, announcing that "the former leader of the former Solidarity trade union is currently a private citizen."[18]

Whether that would remain true would have no little to do with another government announcement, made at the same time: an agreement with the Church had been reached, and an invitation extended to John Paul II to return to Poland in June 1983.[19]

"ONE GREAT CONCENTRATION CAMP"

The months leading up to Poland II, John Paul II's second pilgrimage to his homeland, coincided with a period of maximum paranoia in the Soviet leadership. For the first time in Soviet history, the KGB gave the party its new leader; former spymaster Yuri Andropov succeeded Leonid Brezhnev as general secretary of the Communist Party of the Soviet Union on November 12, 1982. Some Western reporters fawned over Andropov as a sophisticate whose tastes in Scotch, jazz, and popular American novels suggested a new kind of Soviet leader, which was correct, if not in the way the Western press intended: Andropov was pathologically suspicious about the West in general, and the United States and the Catholic Church in particular. Now, his paranoia focused on fears of an American nuclear first strike that would obliterate the USSR.

Eighteen months before, as Mehmet Ali Agca stalked John Paul II, Brezhnev and Andropov had denounced Reagan's alleged warmongering to a KGB conference, with Andropov asserting that "not since the Second World War . . . has the international situation been as explosive as it is now." At the end of the conference, Andropov announced an unprecedented initiative: a joint operation, RYAN, to be conducted collaboratively by the KGB and Soviet military intelligence (the GRU), to discover the Americans' first-strike plans. Nothing was discovered, there being nothing to discover. But among Andropov's first priorities as general secretary was to intensify RYAN activities, as the former KGB chieftain remained convinced that Reagan was determined on a nuclear first strike. Christopher Andrew and Vasili Mitrokhin note that, during his brief tenure as Soviet leader, Andropov's most frequent visitors were his old KGB associates, while RYAN remained the primary operational priority of the KGB's First Chief Directorate [Foreign Intelligence].[20]

In this atmosphere—which longtime Soviet ambassador to the United States Anatoli Dobrynin frankly described as "paranoid"—it was hardly surprising that planning for Poland II was extremely difficult, or that the SB did everything possible to impede the pilgrim's progress of John Paul II.[21] The most dastardly of these SB efforts involved what was known as Operation TRIANGOLO.

The full range of TRIANGOLO activities remains a mystery. One early reference to an SB operation with that code name comes from a note dated April 3, 1979, two months before the Nine Days of John Paul II: in it, Colonel Zenon Płatek, head of the SB's Department IV, remarked that he was going to Vienna for six days to meet a secret coworker, TOM, who has not been identified. Some sources suggest that Agca was in Vienna at this time, but that suspicion runs counter to the assumption that the SB would have been left out of whatever complicated network of deceit was being spun around (and with) Agca. In any event, the fact that Płatek, the head of one of the SB's most important departments, would be gone for such a length of time clearly indicates that something important was afoot—as does Płatek's SB history, which featured work with the Ukrainian KGB to organize sophisticated provocations against Bishop Ignacy Tokarczuk of the Diocese of Przemyśl, including the forging of Vatican documents.[22]

If TRIANGOLO was in fact the code name for an ongoing SB project of "disintegration" against John Paul II, then the SB officer (or, on May 13, 1981, officers) who regularly monitored John Paul's general audiences may have been working under this operational rubric. Zenon Płatek attended meetings of intelligence agencies in Moscow and other communist capitals on a regular basis, where the agencies' battle against the Vatican was often discussed. While there is no presently available documentary evidence to suggest that TRIANGOLO operations were discussed in these sessions (there is no reference to TRIANGOLO in the Mitrokhin archive, for example), it does seem unlikely that an active measures campaign aimed at the man whom these very intelligence services regarded as a prime enemy would not have been bruited with the senior officials of those services.

Whatever other TRIANGOLO provocations may have been conducted between 1979 and 1982 remain unknown. The single most bold attempt to "disintegrate" John Paul II's second pilgrimage to Poland, however, was a TRIANGOLO operation in early 1983. The SB created a personal journal, said to have been the work of Irina Kinaszewska, an employee of **Tygodnik Powszechny** who had died some years before; abandoned by her husband, she would have likely drawn the sympathy of Cardinal Wojtyła. The SB intended to suggest that there was far more to the relationship, and forged a diary in which Kinaszewska claimed to have been Wojtyła's lover.

The plan was to plant (and hide) the diary in the apartment of Father Andrzej Bardecki, where it would then be "discovered" in a police raid. So one night in February 1983, four SB operatives from Independent Group D, knowing that Bardecki was out, went to the priest's apartment on Sikorski Place and planted the forged diary; the leader of the operation was Captain Grzegorz Piotrowski. After hiding the forgery, Piotrowski went out with one of his Group D colleagues and got roaring drunk. Driving away from the bar, he crashed his car and was arrested by the police. Unable to control himself, or perhaps trying to get himself out of an embarrassing scrape, he bragged of being a member of Independent Group D and revealed what he had been up to prior to his alcoholic binge. Then word of the operation began to leak out of the police. Meanwhile, Father Bardecki found the not very well hidden "diary" and took it to the Kraków curia, where it was quickly recognized for the forgery it was. Word of the provocation soon spread from that source, as well, and for a brief period this crude attempt at "disintegration" became notorious in circles alert to such matters.

What did the SB hope to accomplish through this TRIANGOLO operation in February 1983? The "diary" was doubtless intended as an instrument with which to blackmail John Paul II and the Church in Poland. To what ends? With the terms and program of the June 1983 papal pilgrimage still being negotiated between the martial law regime and the Vatican, any number of possibilities suggest themselves. A pope fearful of blackmail, they likely thought, would be less determined to press for certain events in June that the regime was eager to avoid: such as a papal meeting with Lech Wałęsa. A blackmailed pope might moderate his public statements while in Poland. A Church fearful of scandal might be more accommodating to the WRON's plans to hand over post–martial law authority to the PRON, while ignoring Solidarity as if it did not exist. And there was always the possibility that a scandal would further demoralize the Polish people, thus rendering them more malleable and acquiescent. None of this made a great deal of sense; even if Piotrowski's "disintegration" operation had not been disintegrated in turn by his own drunken chatter about the forgery and the plant, how many Poles (familiar with these tactics for thirty years) would have believed that John Paul II was as duplicitous as the "diary" suggested? None-theless, the February 1983 TRIANGOLO diary af-fair does suggest just how frightened the martial law regime remained of its papal countryman, even as it illustrates graphically the lengths of prevarication to which it was prepared to go in order to destroy his reputation, and thus his moral authority.[23]

As for Captain Grzegorz Piotrowski, he would reenter the drama the following year, in an even more brutal context.

Meanwhile, in Rome, the able SB agent Edward Kotowski was using the contacts he had cultivated since 1978 to provide information to his superi-ors (and, ultimately, to Moscow Center) on John Paul II's plans for Poland II.[24] After five years in Rome, Kotowski, or PIETRO, who had a tremen-dous memory and exceptional skills as an interlocu-tor, had developed three levels of contacts. Each of these sets of contacts would have helped Kotowski and his superiors try to get inside the mind of John Paul II and his closest associates; some were far more dangerous than others.

The first level of PIETRO's contacts involved those with whom he would have met in the normal course of his diplomatic work—for as far as Vatican dip-lomats were concerned, Kotowski was not an agent of Polish intelligence but their diplomatic counter-part, with whom a certain openness, albeit matched by a certain discretion, was expected. Prominent among these contacts were the head of the Polish section of the Vatican's Secretariat of State, Msgr. Józef Kowalczyk; another Vatican diplomat, Msgr. Janusz Bolonek, a priest of the Łódź diocese who worked closely with Cardinal Casaroli; and Father Adam Boniecki, M.I.C., the editor of the Polish edition of **L'Osservatore Romano**. These were, in the jargon of the trade, "official contacts"; none of them was clandestine; all took place in an appropriate setting; and there is no suggestion that they produced anything other than what might be expected from normal diplomatic conversations. At the same time, however, PIETRO used these contacts to convey to Vatican officials both accurate information about the Jaruzelski government's thinking and plans, and disinformation aimed at muddying the waters.[25]

The second level of PIETRO's contacts included informants who thought they were talking to a diplomat, not a skillful intelligence agent, but whose openness was not combined with discretion or caution. These "informal" contacts included some seventeen Polish priests, most of them working in Rome, others just visiting. Those who worked in Rome were in low-level agencies such as Vatican Radio. The hundreds of cyphergrams sent back to Warsaw reporting on what they had said suggest that, as historian Andrzej Grajewski put it, there was "much stupidity and vanity involved," but nothing particularly revealing or damaging.

The third, and by far the most dangerous, of PIETRO's three levels of Vatican contacts were SB agents who found themselves in Rome, permanently or occasionally, and whom PIETRO contacted knowing that they were already part of the SB apparatus. One of these, HEJNAŁ, was a Polish Dominican, Konrad Hejmo, who worked with Polish pilgrimage groups. HEJNAŁ was not in a position to get the SB deeply inside the Pope's mind or plans, although he sent back, directly or through PIETRO, a stream of information for which he was well paid. Far more dangerous was POTENZA, whose identity was not known as of 2009. A Kraków archdiocesan priest, his contacts with the papal apartment fed the SB's insatiable interest in John Paul II's views about martial law, other Polish bishops, plans for Poland II, themes to be developed in the Pope's addresses, and Lech Wałęsa's political future. POTENZA also provided his SB spymasters with analyses of the Polish Church situation as he knew it. POTENZA was not "operational" in the sense that he was not an agent deployed to try to impede Poland II by various forms of skulduggery; rather, he was an expression of the SB's determination to get inside John Paul II's view of Solidarity's prospects by digging as deeply into the Vatican as possible for information. Needless to say, the most important news was immediately shared with the KGB's Moscow Center.[26]

The month after the TRIANGOLO diary affair, John Paul II added another item to the KGB's bill of complaints against him with a seven-day pilgrimage to Central America. By standing firm against Sandinista attempts to drown out his sermon in the Nicaraguan capital, Managua—a provocation televised all over Central America, thanks to some adept advance work by Father Roberto Tucci, S.J., the Pope's travel planner—John Paul helped strengthen the local pro-democracy forces then contending with Marxists such as the Sandinistas and the Farabundo Martí National Liberation Front [FMLN] in El Salvador for the future of the region. At the same time, he buttressed the position of Church reformers who had stood against both oligarchic brutality and Marxist revolution. None of this was received with satisfaction in the KGB's Moscow Center, which had high hopes for winning the Cold War in the Third World and had invested considerable resources in promoting the Sandinistas and the FMLN in North America, not least among religious activists affiliated with fronts like CISPES [Committee in Solidarity with the People of El Salvador].[27] Throughout this period, Moscow Center used Cuban intelligence assets at the Cuban diplomatic mission to the Holy See (with which Fidel Castro had never broken diplomatic relations) to try to advance the communist cause in Latin America and to impede John Paul II's effective countermeasures.[28]

Eight days after the Pope left Central America, Polish foreign minister Stefan Olszowski met in Warsaw with Archbishop Luigi Poggi, still head of the Polish-Vatican permanent working contacts group, to discuss the impending papal pilgrimage to Poland. In an "Urgent Note" that served as a memorandum of conversation for the Polish foreign ministry, Olszowski painted a detailed picture of the conversation, in which he stressed to Poggi that "stability was returning in politics and society" and that "stability had the upper hand." An example of this was the formation of PRON, "which was very much in favor of upholding the constitution" and was being led by a notable Catholic writer, Jan Dobraczyński. The remaining difficulties in Poland were the result of Western policies, especially the "sanctions imposed by the United States and other NATO countries" and the rise of "neo-revisionism in the Federal Republic of Germany." Olszowski then argued that the impending papal visit was "evidence of our openness in our politics and [our] commitment to the principles embodied in the constitution." He then averred that the "government is cooperating fully in all preparations for the visit" but that there were "forces abroad and in a few places in our country that want to sabotage the visit and stir up opposition." Thus it was important that "religious gatherings" during the Pope's visit not "be used to spread anti-government propaganda, for example by the use of banners, or for demonstrations intended to cause disturbances."

In Poggi's reply as recounted by Olszowski, the veteran Vatican diplomat agreed that the acts of "Western empires" had had "negative effects on Polish society." Poggi then mentioned the Pope's January 1, 1983, World Day of Peace message and its stress on "dialogue" in "maintaining peace." The visit concluded with a discussion of the government's recent suspension of the distribution of the Polish edition of **L'Osservatore Romano**, which contained the text of a speech given by Msgr. Francesco Canalini of the Holy See at the Madrid Conference on Security and Cooperation in Europe. There, the Vatican representative had spoken sharply about human rights violations and the suppression of Solidarity. Olszowski argued that the publication of this text violated an agreement that the Polish monthly edition of the Vatican newspaper "should not include material that does not promote understanding and good relations between Poland and the Apostolic See." Poggi, Olszowski concluded, promised to "convey our point of view," but also asked that the Vatican's request that the next edition be distributed be "considered in a positive light," as it would help prepare for the papal visit.[29]

Olszowski's initial approach, with its stress on "stability," demonstrated that the Polish government well understood the imperatives as understood by Cardinal Casaroli, Archbishop Silvestrini, and Archbishop Poggi. The foreign minister's description of PRON was risible, of course, as was his emphasis on the "principles embodied in the constitution"— which did not provide for martial law, hence the de facto coup d'etat of WRON on December 13, 1981. Olszowski's concern for the Pope's safety was rather ironic, in light of May 13, 1981, and his fretting about those, even inside Poland, who were trying to "sabotage" the visit obviously did not include the SB, which had just failed, in the TRIANGOLO diary affair, to blackmail the Pope and the Church. There was something a bit pathetic in the foreign minister's plea that religious events not turn "political": would a regime as "stable" as Olszowski claimed the Polish regime was be afraid of banners? The Holy See intervention at the Madrid Conference on Security and Cooperation in Europe clearly rankled, as the sparring over the Polish **L'Osservatore Romano** indicated. It is instructive that Archbishop Poggi did not defend the Canalini speech, nor did he mention, to a foreign minister representing a government steeped in mendacity, that the 1983 World Day of Peace message had stressed that truth was essential to genuine dialogue. That a government confident of "political and social stability" would not be engaged in the most crude forms of censorship also seems to have gone unremarked from the Vatican side of the table. Poggi's generally accommodating—and certainly nonconfrontational—line with Olszowski, the representative of a regime still holding thousands of political prisoners under martial law, may, in the Vatican diplomat's mind, have been necessary in order not to exacerbate tensions prior to the papal visit. But with Olszowski eager for a visit that would redound well on the Polish government, some might argue that a bit more push-back was in order from the Holy See's diplomats, particularly over the censorship of texts that had been cleared by Poggi's associates in the Secretariat of State and that reflected the concerns of the Pope.[30]

The issue of **L'Osservatore Romano** and its Polish distribution came up again the following day, when Archbishop Poggi met with four other Polish officials, led by the minister for religious affairs, Adam Łopatka. According to a classified aide-mémoire prepared afterward, the meeting began with some preliminary joshing about how Poggi's Polish would improve if the nunciature that Casaroli and the Polish government had long wanted were established. Poggi replied with some ice-breaking of his own, expressing his pleasure at talking to "a minister who is also a professor of constitutional law." The two delegations then discussed numerous practical issues, including church building permits, that ought to be cleared up before the Pope arrived in June. Poggi rather apologized for pressing so many questions at once, noting that "too much meat has been put on a fire that is not hot enough," but pressed harder on the resumption of distribution of **L'Osservatore Romano** than he had the day before with Stefan Olszowski. Łopatka took particular umbrage at the charge, made at Madrid, that there are "flagrant and permanent violations of human rights on a massive scale" in Poland, which he flatly (and brazenly) denied. Poggi did not challenge this, perhaps assuming that the battle over the distribution of the next Polish issue of **L'Osservatore Romano** had been won. The

meeting concluded with Polish governmental complaints about the Roman activities of Cardinal Slipyi,
the Ukrainian Greek Catholic major-archbishop, in
the course of discussion of whether a Greek Catholic
diocese could be restored in southeastern Poland.[31]

Minister Łopatka's continued carping about the
Canalini intervention at Madrid suggests two things:
that the "stable" Polish regime was extremely sensitive to international criticism on its human rights
record, and that it was even more nervous that John
Paul II would take a similar line in June, openly
challenging the regime. The Polish delegation's self-
evident lack of interest in doing anything to help the
Ukrainian Greek Catholics of southeastern Poland,
and the deprecatory references to Cardinal Slipyi,
also suggest that Polish policy on Ukrainian Catholics in Poland was driven by Soviet fears that Catholicism was the repository of Ukrainian nationalism,
which the Soviets had attempted to stamp out in
1946 by "dissolving" the Greek Catholic Church in
Ukraine and having it merged into the local Russian
Orthodox Church.

On April 25, 1983, five weeks after Poggi's meetings in Warsaw, Jerzy Kuberski (who had replaced
Kazimierz Szablewski as Archbishop Poggi's coun-
terpart in the Polish-Vatican permanent working
contacts group) met with Archbishop Achille Silvestrini, the Vatican foreign minister. In a secret, coded
cable, Kuberski reported on the meeting to foreign
minister Stefan Olszowski. The short report con-

tained excerpts from the Pope's official response to the official invitation to come to Poland that had been extended by the chairman of the People's State Council, Professor Henryk Jabłoński. Kuberski also reported that, while a general release of political prisoners was not, according to Silvestrini, an absolute precondition of the papal pilgrimage from the Vatican's point of view, such a gesture would certainly help prepare the "conditions" for a successful visit.[32]

Less than two months before the Pope was scheduled to arrive in Poland, the Polish government was under severe pressure from East German communist leader Erich Honecker and Czechoslovak party boss Gustav Husak to take the hardest possible line on an amnesty for political prisoners and on lifting martial law. The tacit agreement seems to have been that a full amnesty would follow Poland II—so there was, in fact, and despite regime denials, a link between the visit and the end of martial law. At the same time, however, the regime seems to have been flexing its own muscles, hinting that it was strong enough to do both—manage a papal visit and a postvisit amnesty. The Kuberski cable contained two other noteworthy points. In his letter to Henryk Jabłoński, John Paul II asserted his right to be a Polish patriot—or, as he put it, he still had "the sacred right and responsibility to feel at one with the nation."[33] John Paul was not, in other words, ceding to the Polish government a monopoly on the definition of what constituted Polish patriotism, no matter how much the regime might complain about Holy See interventions in defense of human rights at international conferences. The second noteworthy thing about the cable was that the name of "Comrade Jabłoński" (the nominal head of state) appeared below that of "Comrade Jaruzelski" on the decoded cable's distribution list. Whatever line Polish diplomats were spinning to their Vatican interlocutors about PRON, it was clear to everyone involved, in Poland, that real power remained with Jaruzelski.

As the June papal visit drew closer, the Polish regime's nervousness about it, and attempts to impede it, grew more grave and more comic. On April 5, the new KGB chairman, Viktor Chebrikov, received a request from Polish interior minister Czesław Kiszczak for " 'material and technical assistance in connection with the Pope's visit': 150 rifles of the kind used for firing rubber bullets, 20 armored personnel carriers, 300 cars for transporting plainclothes personnel and surveillance equipment, 200 army tents and various medical supplies."[34] According to Vadim Pavlov, KGB **rezident** in Warsaw, Kiszczak was almost panicking, fearful that the Pope would frontally assault the martial law that Kiszczak, as interior minister, had so brutally imposed. "At the present time," Kiszczak was reported to have said, "we can only dream of the possibility that God will recall him to his bosom as soon as possible." Grasping at whatever straws were available, Kiszczak shared with the KGB a bizarre SB report that John Paul had leukemia and masked its effects with cosmetics. The KGB's worries that the Polish comrades were losing their grip in anticipation of Poland II were intensified when the Polish government agreed to large, open-air Masses in Kraków and Katowice, thus opening the dread possibility of "inflaming religious fanaticism among the working class."[35]

Moscow Center had reason to worry, at least about the competence of parts of the SB, which had mounted a particularly silly and futile effort to keep the Pope out of Katowice and the country's Silesian industrial core. In this instance, the effort involved a regime-generated letter-writing campaign, by which ordinary Polish citizens would write the bishop of Katowice, stating, simply, "We don't want the Pope." When the people refused to participate, the SB forged both the letters and the signatures and delivered them in large postal bags to the bishop's residence. One day, the sister who answered the door looked at yet another bag and asked, "How many more of these will there be?" The dim apparatchik delivering them answered, "I don't know; we haven't finished yet."[36]

The battle over the Pope's itinerary continued; John Paul II won on Kraków and Katowice, but the regime, led by Kiszczak and his deputy, veteran SB hard-liner Konrad Straszewski, told papal-trip planner Father Roberto Tucci, S.J., that Gdańsk was out of the question. The regime was also adamant that the Pope not meet with Wałęsa; the Pope insisted that he would not come unless he could do so. As Stanisław Dziwisz recalled latter, "to get beyond the impasse, they worked out a compromise. It was a pretty flimsy one, though. A lot was still up in the air, or was left implicit, and many of the details were still vague."[37] Kiszczak, for his part, refused to even use Wałęsa's name in his negotiations with Tucci, referring to him as "that guy" or "the man with the big family" and demanding to know why the Pope "wants to meet with a man who doesn't represent anybody in this country."[38]

Kiszczak and his comrades were not the only ones who were nervous about what Poland II would bring. According to Bohdan Cywiński, the underground Solidarity leadership was worried that the "political message" of any papal visit under martial law wouldn't be the right one—that, contrary to the Pope's intention, Jaruzelski would use the visit to bolster his position by demonstrating that John Paul was coming to Poland at the general's behest. The Pope, for his part, thought that direct contact with the people of Poland was of such importance that it was worth the risk—and, as Cywiński put it, fifteen years later, "he was right."[39]

It didn't begin with the explosion of emotion that had greeted John Paul II on his arrival in Warsaw on June 2, 1979. Yet, as was so often the case, Karol Wojtyła's sense of how to play a particular scene won out. During the welcoming ceremonies on June 16, he stood with a bowed head and a somber expression on his face. The country immediately got it. As one older woman said, "He is sad. You see, he understands." From that welcome, at which Henryk Jabłoński prattled on about "the gradual normalization of life in our country," John Paul went to St. John's Cathedral, where he said he had come to Poland to stand alongside those "who are most acutely tasting the bitterness of disappointment, humiliation, suffering, of being deprived of their freedom, of being wronged, of having their dignity trampled on." The censors cut his statement about "the painful events connected with the date December 13, 1981" from both the secular and Catholic press, but it didn't make any difference. The tens of thousands of Poles who marched from the cathedral past communist party headquarters chanting "So-li-dar-ność, So-li-dar-ność," "Lech Wa-łę-sa, Lech Wa-łę-sa," and "De-mo-kra-cja, De-mo-kra-cja" knew that the Pope knew what they had borne.[40]

As for General Jaruzelski, reporters noted that he looked shaken, even agitated, after his meeting with the Pope at Warsaw's Belvedere Palace. Well he might, for John Paul had opened their private session by telling the general that Poland was "one great concentration camp."[41] But the Pope wasn't through with making it clear to his "hosts" that he would do what he thought he had to do. The "compromise" on his seeing Wałęsa was indeed flimsy, and no agreement had been reached about a meeting. The Pope then told his aides, "If I can't see him,

then I'm going back to Rome." "Some of his entou-
rage" raised objections, Stanisław Dziwisz recalled; it
can only have been Cardinal Casaroli. But the Pope
was not to be deflected from the course of what he
regarded as a moral responsibility, stating flatly, "I
have to be consistent in the eyes of the people."[42]
The diplomats got to work, and a deal was reached:
the Pope could see the interned Solidarity leader at a
cabin in the south of the country, in what the regime
insisted would be a "strictly private meeting." Father
Józef Tischner blew that euphemism away with a
single statement of fact: "There are no private meetings with the pope."

Despite the exceptional efforts of the SB and other
Warsaw Pact intelligence agencies to impede or even
implode it, Poland II accomplished what John Paul II
had hoped for his pilgrimage, both as a pastor and
as a patriot: it restored hope to a people who had
begun to lose hope. In so doing, Stanisław Dziwisz
contended, it "decided the future of Poland."[43] No
one imagined that the path ahead would be simple
or easy; maintaining morale in a virtual police state
suffering serious economic deprivation is never an
easy business. But by drawing on Poland's long history of resistance to tyranny backed by overwhelming material force—in Kraków on June 22, John
Paul II beatified two monks, Rafał Kalinowski and
"Brother Albert" Chmielowski, both of whom had
been rebels in the 1863 insurrection against czarist

Russia—John Paul II reminded his people that tools of resistance can be forged from holiness and courage. He even managed to restore a sense of humor in the resistance: an underground Solidarity cartoon had SB agents disguised as sheep and goats carrying boom microphones as they tried to eavesdrop on the Pope's conversation with Wałęsa in that cabin in the Tatras.[44] The only person who didn't seem to get the message was the deputy editor of **L'Osservatore Romano**, who wrote an odd editorial suggesting that Poland II had been a papal farewell to Solidarity, which the editor described as a spent force. It remains unclear whether this editorial was planted by someone in the Secretariat of State, but in any event it certainly did not represent the Pope's judgment.[45] As Stanisław Dziwisz put it years later, the entire point of the pilgrimage, from a public point of view, was to demonstrate "that the movement for freedom and solidarity hadn't died." That was why the meeting with Wałęsa was "a very decisive moment."[46]

On July 22, 1983, a month after the papal pilgrimage, martial law was formally ended and the WRON was dissolved. The Polish authorities may have seen this tactic as a means of defusing underground Solidarity; a restoration of a measure of constitutional normality was likely regarded as a necessity for getting Western sanctions lifted as well. However the communist logic ran, something else had changed:

Poland II created the spiritual and psychological conditions for the possibility of a revival of civil society in the aftermath of martial law.

THE MARTYRS' ROAD TO FREEDOM

The sixteen months after John Paul II's second Polish pilgrimage were, by the testimony of Solidarity historians, a very difficult period for the underground trade union and the broader social movement it represented. The awarding of the Nobel Peace Prize to Lech Wałęsa in October 1983 sent Yuri Andropov into a rage, and reignited his paranoia about the Catholic Church. In a letter to General Jaruzelski sent from his sickbed, the Soviet party chief charged that "the Church is reawakening the cult of Wałęsa. . . . This means that the Church is creating a new kind of confrontation with the Party. In this situation, the most important thing is not to make concessions."[47] Jaruzelski and his comrades refused to let Wałęsa receive his Peace Prize in person (his wife and son accepted for him). But in the wake of the papal visit, Jaruzelski was also concerned to put a favorable interpretation on what had been some forthright, even confrontational, conversations with John Paul II in June. Thus he wrote the Pope a letter in November, stating that he was still thinking about their discussions because, "regardless of understandable differences of assessment, they were full of heartfelt concern for the fate of our motherland and the well-being of man."[48] That "heartfelt concern" was not evident, however, in the stepped-up repression pursued by the regime Jaruzelski led. Solidarity historian Henryk Głębocki describes the situation in early 1984 in these stark terms:

> The turn of 1984 was marked by an offensive of police reprisals. There were beatings and mysterious deaths. Piotr Bartoszcze, the leader of Farmers' Solidarity, died in mysterious circumstances. Especially brutal was the intimidation campaign against Solidarity members conducted by the SB in Toruń which abducted people in broad daylight, tortured them, and forced them to collaborate. Beaten and stripped down to their underwear, they were dumped in nearby forests. . . . In February and March 1984, the SB launched a broad campaign not only against political activists but also against charitable-aid committees operating under the protection of the Church. The campaign involved several thousand people, of whom some 200 were arrested.[49]

The increased pressure in Poland mirrored, and may have reflected, continuing fears in Moscow that John Paul II's defense of human rights threatened to unravel the entire "socialist order." At a June 1984 conference called by the KGB, Warsaw Pact and Cuban intelligence operatives met to consider "joint measures for combating the subversive activities of the Vatican." Among the issues discussed was the ongoing struggle in Poland, the demise of liberation theology's influence in Latin America (blamed largely on the Roman Curia in concert with the Reagan administration), the beginnings of what John Paul II would call the "new evangelization" in Africa and Asia, and what was thought to be the de facto alignment of the Vatican with NATO and the People's Republic of China. In addition to intensifying the use of informants and electronic eavesdropping equipment, the conferees agreed to do whatever they could to exploit the internal Vatican tensions they perceived between the Pope's hard line and the tendencies of the veterans of the pre–John Paul II **Ostpolitik**. They also agreed to use "malleable publishers in capitalist and developing countries" to intensify campaigns aimed at destroying the Catholic Church's international image by explorations of the Inquisition, the Church's alleged affinities with mid-twentieth-century fascism, its wealth, and so forth. These efforts were to be complemented by blackmail campaigns against Vatican personnel, especially at Vatican Radio.[50] Later that same year, in September 1984, LICHTBLICK (the German Benedictine Eugen Brammertz), using his Vatican sources, reported to his masters in East Berlin (and thence to the KGB) on the alleged cooperation of conservative U.S. Catholics with the Reagan administration, and the alleged effects of this cooperation on the U.S. bishops.[51]

The amnesty proposed by the Jaruzelski regime and adopted by the rubber-stamp Sejm on July 21, 1984, did not mark any easing of the authorities' determination to crush the opposition; quite the contrary, it was aimed at burying underground Solidarity once and for all while providing a reason for the West to lift sanctions and for Poland to rejoin the international economy.[52] Continuing disputes between the TKK (which wanted stronger action against the government) and the Wałęsa-led Solidarity leadership (which kept calling for dialogue with the regime), coupled with increasing public apathy and demoralization, resulted in the emergence of radical organizations such as Fighting Solidarity, which attracted young activists. The government seemed on the verge of achieving its goal of so demoralizing the populace and so fracturing the opposition that it could have its way without excessive difficulty.

The homicidal brutality of the SB then changed the moral and political calculus, decisively.

Father Jerzy Popiełuszko had long been an aggravation to the SB and the interior ministry, not least because the young priest kept alive the message of John Paul II in his monthly "Mass for the Fatherland," celebrated before a packed Church of St. Stanisław Kostka in Warsaw's Żoliborz neighborhood, with thousands of congregants standing

outside and listening on loudspeakers. During Poland II, John Paul II had challenged his people to
"vanquish evil with good." The thirty-five-year-old
Father Popiełuszko used his sermons to spell out
what that might mean. He urged his listeners to respect the human rights of all, and to live Christian
charity. At the same time, he demanded resistance—
people should live "as if" they were free, refusing
to participate in the continuing culture of lies that
was communism. Next to the altar at which Father
Jerzy celebrated each Mass for the Fatherland was
a banner of St. Maximilian Kolbe, the martyr of
the Auschwitz starvation bunker and the "Patron of
Long-suffering Poland" (as the banner read). With
that icon of spiritual resistance to evil before them,
Popiełuszko challenged his congregants to choose:
"Which side will you take? The side of good or the
side of evil? Truth or falsehood? Hatred or love?"[53]

This was unprecedented. As **New York Times**
correspondent Michael Kaufman would write later,
"Nowhere else from East Berlin to Vladivostok could
anyone stand before ten or fifteen thousand people
and use a microphone to condemn the errors of state
and party. Nowhere, in that vast stretch encompassing some four hundred million people, was anyone
else openly telling a crowd that defiance of authority
was an obligation of the heart, of religion, manhood,
and nationhood."[54]

Unprecedented, to be sure, but also intolerable,
from the SB's point of view: this meddlesome priest

would have to be eliminated. Thus, on the night of October 19, 1984, Father Popiełuszko's car was stopped on the road between Bydgoszcz and Warsaw by an SB detachment led by Grzegorz Piotrowski, the man who had bungled the TRIANGOLO diary affair the year before. Piotrowski was taking no chances this time. He and his comrades beat Father Jerzy to death, then dumped his trussed corpse into the Vistula River near the city of Włocławek.

The next day, state radio announced that Popiełuszko was missing and was presumed kidnapped by parties unknown. Thousands upon thousands of people began to converge on the church in Żoliborz, where Masses for the missing priest's deliverance were said hourly. Lech Wałęsa came on October 21 and begged for peaceful resistance: "Dear countrymen: There is a great danger hanging over our Fatherland. I appeal to you, please, do not let anyone provoke you to bloodshed. I beg you to maintain peace and to pray constantly for Father Jerzy."

The Masses went on for nine more days. Then, on October 30, came the news all had been fearing: the body of Father Jerzy Popiełuszko had been dredged from the Vistula. A friend of Father Jerzy's, Father Antonin Lewek, asked the stunned crowd to remember Christ weeping at the tomb of Lazarus. And then, as Father Lewek recalled, something remarkable happened. Three times, the throng repeated the invocation of the Lord's Prayer: "And forgive us our trespasses as we forgive those who trespass against us. And forgive us our trespasses . . ."

There were no riots then, nor were there any on the day of the funeral Mass, November 3, when hundreds of thousands of Warsavians, and Poles from all over the country, came to the church of St. Stanisław Kostka for the funeral Mass and burial of Solidarity's martyr-priest. Father Jerzy Popiełuszko's grave in the Żoliborz churchyard quickly became a "Solidarity sanctuary, a little piece of free Poland," as activist Janusz Onyszkiewicz put it. The murder of the man who had fearlessly preached that "one cannot murder hopes," and the massive demonstration of support for Solidarity that his funeral Mass evoked, reenergized a demoralized people. These events also demonstrated, irrefutably, that Jaruzelski's vaunted "normalization" was a fiction, and would remain so until the regime began a serious conversation with its opponents about the country's future.[55]

Father Jerzy Popiełuszko was, in a sense, the voice of John Paul II in Poland in the aftermath of Poland II.[56] The themes of his preaching—the demands of conscience, the imperative of resisting evil, the obligation to remain nonviolent, the challenge of "living in the truth"—somehow extended the Nine Days of June 1979 and the Poland II pilgrimage into a period when both the activist resistance and the general populace of Poland were flagging, morally, spiritually, psychologically—and politically. Being the voice of John Paul II cost Jerzy Popiełuszko his life. Like Karol Wojtyła, the man whose fearlessness inspired him, Father Jerzy lived—and died—in the mystery of Jesus Christ, priest and victim.[57]

Four months after Father Popiełuszko's funeral, on March 10, 1985, Konstantin Chernenko (who had succeeded Yuri Andropov as leader of the Soviet Communist Party on Andropov's death in February 1984) died, and Mikhail Gorbachev was chosen to succeed him. Gorbachev had been a protégé of both Andropov and Andrei Gromyko, and the latter assured his Politburo comrades that, while the younger and more stylish Gorbachev "has a nice smile," he also "has iron teeth."[58] John Paul II, however, thought that there might be something a bit different here. Brezhnev, Andropov, Chernenko: these were men whose formative political experience had been Stalin's purge trials in the late 1930s. As young men, they had seen their friends disappear, only to reappear, be charged with treason, and then be shot in the back of the head in the Lubyanka basement. Experiences like that did something to a man, as the subsequent careers of Brezhnev, Andropov, and Chernenko illustrated. Whatever else Mikhail Gorbachev was or was not, he was "of a new generation," as the Pope put it years later, and would likely take a different approach: "he wanted to save communism 'with a human face.'"[59]

That, of course, would prove impossible, as John Paul II knew it would: the fundamental errors in communism's understanding of the human person, human community, and human destiny were not reparable by the patchwork fix of perestroika and glasnost. The system itself would have to go; the human yearning for freedom would have to be realized, politically and economically, in central and eastern Europe; the artificial Yalta division of Europe into two competing, hostile camps would have to be repaired. But with Gorbachev as leader of the USSR, perhaps the path to a different future would no longer be marked by the graves of so many martyrs.

ENDGAME

On April 11, 1985, a month after Mikhail Gorbachev's accession to power in the Soviet Union, over 1,000 priests—one-third of the Catholic clergy of Czechoslovakia—came to the shrine at Velehrad in Moravia to concelebrate Mass together. During the liturgy, eighty-six-year-old Cardinal František Tomášek of Prague read a letter from John Paul II, who urged the priests to "continue intrepidly on the path of evangelization and testimony, even if the present situation makes it arduous, difficult, and even bitter." Three months after that, more than 150,000 Catholic pilgrims came to Velehrad on July 5 to mark the 1,100th anniversary of the death of St. Methodius, whom John Paul had named a co-patron of Europe with his brother, St. Cyril (creator of the alphabet used in eastern Slavic languages). The regime of Gustav Husak, one of the most bitterly anticlerical leaders in the Warsaw Pact, refused permission for John Paul II to attend, while trying to co-opt the Methodius anniversary and turn the event into a "peace festival." When officials welcomed the pilgrims to Velehrad in those terms, the people of Bohemia, Moravia, and Slovakia shouted them down with cries of "This is a pilgrimage! We want the Pope! We want Mass!"[60]

The radical change in the public character of Catholicism in Czechoslovakia was another result of John Paul II's strategy of moral revolution in central and eastern Europe. At the time of Karol Wojtyła's election as pope in 1978, the Czechoslovak Catholic situation was desperate and getting worse, thanks in part to the failures of the **Ostpolitik**, which had succeeded in getting bishops ordained in Czechoslovakia but had gutted the Church's capacity for effective resistance in the process. The nominal head of the Church, Tomášek, was quiet and deferential to the regime. The activist clergy and laity were demoralized, believing that their counsel had been ignored by Agostino Casaroli and other agents of the **Ostpolitik**. There was even concern that Vatican investigations of the extensive network of underground clergy in the country had been useful to the regime in identifying and harassing underground priests.[61]

This all began to change when the newly elected

John Paul II drew the shy František Tomášek into an embrace in the Sistine Chapel at the end of the second conclave of 1978 and told the aging prelate that "we are standing very close to one another and will stand closer still, because the responsibility for you is being transferred to me." John Paul was as good as his word, underscoring his "special feeling of nearness" to Tomášek and his people in a Christmas 1978 message; three months later, in a March 1979 letter marking the anniversary of the canonization of the Bohemian martyr St. John Nepomucene, the Pope challenged priests and people alike to be "fearless in avowal and practice" of Catholic faith. With the aging Tomášek now assured of papal support for a more assertive line, the entire country watched what human rights activist Pavel Bratinka would later call "this singular spectacle of the cardinal getting older **and tougher** at the same time."[62]

John Paul II's emphasis on respect for human rights as the public meaning of the inalienable dignity of the human person meshed neatly with themes that were being developed by such secular human rights activists as Václav Havel in Czechoslovakia. As in Poland, the Church's defense of human rights had to be universal: a defense of the rights of all, not a matter of seeking institutional breathing space from the totalitarian state. This political ecumenism, as it were, opened up the possibility for resistance coalitions in which Catholic dissidents and secular dissidents joined in a common effort. Institutionally, the Polish Church was a model of assertive, effective witness under totalitarianism; with the election of John Paul II, the Czechoslovakian Church was given permission to emulate that model, which the **Ostpolitik** had discouraged. And at a personal level, both the secular activists and the Catholic activists believed that they now had a pope who "understood their situation," "who was an example of deep faith, who understood the communists, who wasn't naive," and who defended the resistance Church in Czechoslovakia.[63] The first, dramatic, public demonstration of this new Czech and Slovak Catholicism, a fighting faith that would no longer shelter behind acquiescence, came at Velehrad in July 1985: an event John Paul II was not permitted to attend, but for whose success he could take considerable credit.[64]

As the previously moribund Catholic Church in Czechoslovakia was being reborn in resistance, John Paul II was looking toward something few had dared to imagine at the beginning of the 1980s: a post-totalitarian future for central and eastern Europe. He remained a point of reference for dissidents and human rights activists from throughout the region, believers and unbelievers alike. In December 1985, through the good work of one of his informal diplomatic agents, Irina Ilovayskaya Alberti, he met in the Vatican with Elena Bonner, wife of the leading Soviet dissident Andrei Sakharov. The Pope spent two hours with Bonner, a very tough lady, who came out of their meeting saying, "He's the most remarkable man I've ever met. He is all light, he is a source of light."[65] Shortly thereafter, East German Communist Party leader Erich Honecker, who had visited the Pope in Rome in April 1985, received a classified Stasi report speculating on continued tensions between Cardinal Casaroli and his diplomats, on the one hand, and John Paul II, on the other. The Pope, it was suggested, might "modify his present course of relatively uncompromising behavior" in order to facilitate relations with Mikhail Gorbachev, thus paving the way for a proposed papal visit to Lithuania and clearing the atmosphere for his third Polish pilgrimage in 1987.[66] Seven years into the pontificate, the most astute of the Soviet-bloc intelligence agencies still didn't understand their target.

The first two summits between Ronald Reagan and Mikhail Gorbachev, held in Geneva in November 1985 and in Reykjavik, Iceland, in October 1986, produced little in the way of specific agreements, but signaled a marked improvement over the state of affairs a mere three years before, when Yuri Andropov was convinced that the American administration was plotting a nuclear first strike against the Soviet Union to end the Cold War by force. John Paul II was briefed by U.S. officials after each summit, at Reagan's order. The briefer in 1986 was General Edward Rowny, an American of Polish descent, who, while hurrying toward the Pope along a marble corridor, tripped over a step he hadn't seen and had his fall broken by a senior cleric in a red zuchetto. As

John Paul stepped forward to help the presidential
envoy, the Pope couldn't resist a joke: "Nice catch,
for a cardinal." The Pope was also aware that Rowny
had been critical of the U.S. bishops' pastoral letter
on nuclear weapons, which had been issued in 1983.
During their meeting, John Paul, with a twinkle in
his eye, said, "Tell me, General, how are you getting along with your bishops in the United States?"
Rowny replied, "Holy Father, I didn't know they
were my bishops. I thought they were your bishops."
John Paul smiled and conceded, "**Bardzo dobrze**
[Very good]."[67]

General Wojciech Jaruzelski was not likely in a
bantering mood when he came to the Vatican for an
official visit on January 13, 1987; indeed, as a Swiss
Guard assigned to the Polish leader's escort recalled,
the general was "visibly nervous."[68] That was not,
however, the impression of his performance Jaruzelski tried to convey in a lengthy, classified report to
the Polish Communist Party Politburo, which seems
to have been written to convince Jaruzelski's Polish
comrades, and perhaps the comrades in Moscow as
well, that he still had a firm grip on affairs. His rather
clumsy attempt to propose a future of Polish church-
state relations characterized by "ideological/philo-
sophical competition, political coexistence, [and]
social cooperation" could not have made much of an
impression on John Paul II. The Pope, for his part,
stressed Poland's traditions of religious tolerance,
citing the Reformation-era king Zygmunt August,

who had famously said to his religiously contentious subjects, "I am not the king of your consciences."

Some elements of Jaruzelski's report were almost comical; he stressed that he had been given special treatment, which "set a precedent as far as visits of heads of state are concerned," and seemed particularly struck that he had been accompanied by the Swiss Guard throughout the three-and-a-half-hour visit; in fact, he received the same welcome and escort as any other similarly situated leader. He made one of his clerical escorts, the prefect of the papal household, Dino Monduzzi, a cardinal more than a decade before John Paul II did. Yet there was also something almost plaintive about Jaruzelski's conversation that day, at least as conveyed (probably unintentionally) by his report—his reference to his "dialogue" with John Paul II in 1983 (which had begun with the Pope suggesting that the general was running "one great concentration camp") hints at a man reaching for a political lifeline.

Jaruzelski suggested that, since the Pope had last been in Poland, "society views the authorities with greater credibility," and defended martial law as a necessity in creating the conditions for the possibility of reform. John Paul II, for his part, knew that both assertions were as untrue as Jaruzelski's claim that "the healing process has . . . started in the very foundations of the economy"—which was, in fact, falling apart. Jaruzelski congratulated the Pope for suggesting, in the 1987 papal message for the Janu-

ary 1 World Day of Peace, that nonbelievers and her-
etics were "not excluded from the human family"—a
strange, even bizarre, compliment, as it suggested
that the opposite was once settled Catholic doctrine,
changed by papal fiat. The general expressed a desire that the Polish episcopate speak more frequently
on "the militarization of the world"—meaning, of
course, the policies of the Reagan administration.
Yet Jaruzelski also urged the Pope to keep those
same Polish bishops in check, lest they "ruin opportunities" for the forthcoming third papal pilgrimage,
scheduled for June, to result in more "positive relations between Church and State." As if to underscore yet again that he had been the man driving
the conversation and setting the terms of "dialogue,"
General Jaruzelski ended his report to the Politburo
by noting that "the talks were conducted in an atmosphere of deep mutual concern for the future of our
country," and that the "Pope's conversations with
the Chairman of the State Council [i.e., Jaruzelski]
were sincere, courteous, and very respectful."[69]

Wojciech Jaruzelski, whose views as reflected in
this report suggest that he held to a kind of modified Brezhnev doctrine in terms of Poland's future
("the state is ours, what's yours we can discuss"),
may have been sincere in his hope for a June 1987
papal visit that would lead to more positive church-
state relations within the political status quo. John
Paul II had something rather different in mind: he
was going to Poland to lay the moral, spiritual, and

conceptual foundations for his country's transition to freedom, which he now seemed to believe could come far sooner than had once been thought possible.

Whatever Jaruzelski's real intentions, however, getting Poland III done the way John Paul II wanted it done was not an easy business.

Barred from Gdańsk during Poland II, John Paul was determined to go to the birthplace of Solidarity in 1987. Gdańsk's bishop, Tadeusz Gocłowski, a tenacious defender of Solidarity, was equally determined to get the Pope there. Some months before the visit, Gocłowski was in Rome to discuss plans, and had brought with him to dinner a personal letter, inviting the Pope to his city. Prior to the meal, the Pope's secretary, Stanisław Dziwisz (who knew what Gocłowski wanted), said, with reference to the letter, "Wait until the right moment; I'll tell you." The fourth party to the dinner conversation was Bishop Bronisław Dąbrowski, the secretary of the Polish bishops conference; he was a man loyal to his early patron, Cardinal Wyszyński, but he was also of a diplomatic temperament, and as one of the Polish episcopate's chief interlocutors with the Jaruzelski regime, he tried to avoid confrontations.

As the discussion unfolded, Dziwisz gave Gocłowski the signal, and the bishop of Gdańsk handed the letter across the dining room table to John Paul II, who said, "I know what's in it; thank you." Gocłowski replied, "We'll be glad to welcome you." But then

Dąbrowski interjected, "It's still impossible," meaning the regime would never allow it. Silence ensued, for perhaps a minute, with the Pope looking down at the table. Then John Paul said, "If I can't go to Gdańsk, I can't go to Poland. If I don't go to Gdańsk, I'll just be an instrument of the communists."[70]

So Gdańsk made it onto the program. But there were still arguments about what the Pope was to do there. Gocłowski's plan was for the Pope to have four events: a meeting with workers; a meeting with the sick and their doctors; a meeting with young people (at Westerplattte, where World War II began); and a public event at the Three Crosses Monument to workers killed in 1970, built at the Lenin Shipyard in response to one of Solidarity's August 1980 demands. The Polish bishops were nervous about this program, Gocłowski knew, and some were opposed to it, thinking it too provocative. So the bishop wrote another private letter to the Pope, reiterating the four points on the program; the letter came back, with "Yes—JPII" handwritten beside each point.[71]

Poland III, which began on June 8, 1987, took the Pope to Warsaw, Lublin, Tarnów, Kraków, Szczecin, Gdynia, Sopot, Częstochowa, and Łódź, in addition to Gdańsk. Throughout the country, for the first time since martial law, large numbers of white-and-red banners with the famous jumbly-letter **Solidarność** logo rose above the crowds, giving the papal events a festive and yet decidedly pointed visual framework. In Warsaw, John Paul II went to Żoliborz, where he knelt, prayed, and kissed the tomb of Father Jerzy Popiełuszko in the churchyard at St. Stanisław Kostka. In Gdańsk, as throughout the country, he used the once forbidden word "solidarity" time and again, telling hundreds of thousands in the banned union's birthplace that "this word has been pronounced in a new way, and in a new context, here, and the world cannot forget it."

The visit opened briskly, with the Pope reminding Wojciech Jaruzelski and his government of "the following pertinent words of the Second Vatican Council: 'One must pay tribute to those nations whose systems **permit the largest possible number of citizens to take part in public life** in a climate of genuine freedom.'"[72] Then, having said what he had to say publicly to the representatives of Poland's morally bankrupt regime, the Pope turned his attention for the next six days to the Polish people and nation, with whom any real hope of reform, reconciliation, and national renewal lay. The visit was conducted in the context of a National Eucharistic Congress, which the Pope opened in Warsaw on June 8 and closed on June 14. The redemption wrought by Christ, John Paul preached, was a redemption "of the history of man and of the world." Christ, present in the Holy Eucharist, made that redemption available to the men and women of today, and empowered them to build genuine human community out of liberated consciences, freed "from the inheritance of hatred and egoism." Poles had something to conquer, but it was not the communist state, which John Paul sensed was collapsing of its own implausibility. No, what had to be conquered was a "way of seeing the world" in which God is a pious myth, and love, compassion, and tolerance are equated with impotence. Having broken free of those restraints on their humanity, the Polish people could reclaim Poland in true freedom. Ordaining fifty new priests in Lublin on June 9, John Paul sketched a vision of a new Poland in which these newly ordained men would "collaborate with lay people aware of their responsibility for the Church, and for a Christian form of life [in society]." By liberating within their people a new awareness of their inalienable human dignity, Poland's new priests would be servants of "the truth that liberates every man."

Living in the truth; living responsibly, living in solidarity, living "a more mature way of life"—John Paul relentlessly drove home the message that the change for which so many Poles longed had to be built on the revolution of conscience that had given birth to Solidarity seven years before. The Pope knew that, even when its external forms were gone, communism would leave a deadening residue in its wake: the conviction that men and women were not responsible for history, that what we call "history" is simply the exhaust fumes of impersonal economic and political processes. That attitude constituted another form of slavery, and the Pope was determined to challenge it.[73]

Wojciech Jaruzelski, whose minions had complained to Vatican officials about the Pope's "tone" throughout the visit, was not happy with all this. He demanded an extra fifty-minute meeting with John Paul, and then crudely suggested (with the international press present) that, while the Pope would return to Rome with the country's "image" in his heart, "you will not take with you the homeland's real problems."[74] It was a startling performance, and to those with ears to hear, Jaruzelski sounded like a man who knew that the endgame had begun, that a "national compromise" was impossible, and that this was a game that would end when someone won, and someone else lost.

There were still a few moves left on the board before the endgame was completed. In November of 1987, after a large reorganization of ministries in the central government, Jaruzelski tried to hold a plebiscite on the country's future; the opposition urged a boycott of the voting or a "no" vote on the government's proposals, which duly failed to be ratified by a no longer cowed populace. Meanwhile, the resurrection of Solidarity continued, with Wałęsa in control and a new National Executive Commission established in October 1987. With the economy collapsing in late 1987 and the first half of 1988, things were unraveling at such a pace that even the regime realized that the end was at hand. Prodded by the Polish episcopate, which on August 26, 1988, urged "union pluralism," the government conceded that talks with "representatives of a variety of social and occupational groups" were required. Thus on August 31, 1988, the eighth anniversary of the Gdańsk agreements that launched Solidarity, interior minister Czesław Kiszczak met with "that man," the winner of the "so-called Peace Prize," at the beginning of a process that led to the Round Table negotiations on Poland's political future, which were conducted between February 6 and April 5, 1989. In the midst of these maneuvers, Edward Kotowski—PIETRO, perhaps the SB's most effective Vatican operative, who had been back in Warsaw since 1983 and working at the government's office for religious affairs—was used by Jaruzelski as a contact point with the Polish bishops; Kotowski, by his own account, pushed Jaruzelski to complete a deal by which the government would issue a decree recognizing the legal personality of the Church.[75]

(For his part, John Paul II was already, and typically, thinking ahead. When two old friends, Piotr and Teresa Malecki, visited the Pope at Castel Gandolfo in the late summer of 1988, **Wujek** posed a question: "What do you think will happen if Wałęsa wins?" The Maleckis, surprised, replied, "**Wujek**, that's science fiction for us." But John Paul pressed on: "Are you ready? Is Poland ready for a break?" and then talked at length about Poland's postcommunist future.)[76]

The Round Table was no easy affair, for while the Solidarity side was united, the communist negotiators were fractured, with various factions seeking to get what they could out of the proceedings. Some were clearly taking advantage of this interim period to clear up the historical record—or, better, obliterate it; thus the TRIANGOLO records disappeared from the files of the SB while the Round Table was in progress.[77] Nevertheless, after two months of work, an agreement was reached; it provided for "union pluralism," for partially free elections to the Sejm, and for an open election to a newly created Senate.[78]

After a brisk campaign, in which Wałęsa did not run but was photographed with every Solidarity-backed candidate for his or her campaign materials—thus making unmistakably clear who was "one of ours"—the June 4 election was an unambiguous and overwhelming victory for Solidarity. Finally given a choice, Poland had said no to communism. That this "no" had much to do with the "yes" to solidarity and Solidarity preached and taught by John Paul II, no one doubted.

When a new government led by Catholic intellectual and veteran Solidarity adviser Tadeusz Mazowiecki took office in September, the SB was abolished. Nemesis had been defeated, in Poland.

Surrender

The wave that first crested in Poland in June 1989 soon swept over the rest of central and eastern Europe, with nonviolent transitions to various forms of democracy taking place throughout the fall of 1989, and one violent overthrow of communism in Romania. The last domino to fall in the Soviet external empire was Czechoslovakia, where a priest inspired by John Paul II, Father Václav Malý, served as a kind of master of ceremonies at the great public pro-democracy demonstrations in Wenceslas Square in November 1989. The nonagenarian cardinal, František Tomášek, cagily declined the government's offer to serve as a mediator between the regime and the democratic opposition, firmly aligned the Church with the movement whose most visible leader was Václav Havel, and became the third great symbol of what history would know as the Velvet Revolution, along with Havel and the deposed leader of the 1968 Prague Spring, Alexander Dubček. The remarkable transformation of the cardinal and the Catholic Church in Czechoslovakia, which began in earnest when John Paul II greeted Tomášek in the Sistine Chapel on October 16, 1978, was complete.[79]

Then there was Russia, and the Baltics, and Ukraine—and the Soviet Union.

Karol Wojtyła had a deep appreciation of Russian theology and Orthodox culture. He had read

the modern Russian theological masters seriously—
Nikolai Berdyaev, Sergii Bulgakov, Simon Frank,
Pavel Florensky, Georges Florovsky, and Vladimir
Soloviev, among others.[80] His pan-European view
of the continent's cultural history led him to speak
frequently of Europe as a body with "two lungs"—
Catholicism and Orthodoxy. The health of both was
essential if Europe was to recover from the disasters
of the twentieth century.

Thus the Pope did everything in his power to lift
up Russian Orthodoxy, as Gorbachev's glasnost created new opportunities for open religious expression
in the USSR. It was a delicate business. Throughout the 1980s, the Russian Orthodox leadership remained firmly in the control of the KGB.[81] With
rare exceptions such as Aleksandr Menn, the dissident Russian Orthodox clergy was anti-ecumenical,
identifying "ecumenism" with the work of KGB-
manipulated and KGB-owned Orthodox clergy at
the World Council of Churches. Then there was
the underground Greek Catholic Church in the
Ukrainian SSR; it had been "dissolved" and forcibly
merged into Orthodoxy at the illegal L'viv "Sobor"
[Council] of 1946, thus creating the world's largest illegal religious community and underground
Church. Wojtyła had long been sympathetic to the
Ukrainian Greek Catholic cause, which was an un-
touchable issue for Russian Orthodoxy for both ecclesiastical and political reasons; keeping faith with
that long-standing commitment while seeking a

bridge to Orthodoxy created endless difficulties.[82] The Pope was also aware of Orthodox depredations and Soviet persecution of Catholics in Lithuania, where the resistance Church played a role similar to that of the Greek Catholics in Ukraine, serving as the repository of national identity in a situation in which the central political authority was determined to obliterate that identity.

Many of these issues came to a head in the planning for the celebration of the Millennium of Christianity among the eastern Slavs in 1988. The Ukrainians claimed the anniversary as their own, given that it was the baptism of Prince Vladimir and Princess Olga of Kievan 'Rus that was being commemorated. Russian Orthodoxy, for its part, was determined to claim the Millennium for itself, even as it held stubbornly to the position that the Greek Catholic Church of Ukraine did not exist. Had John Paul II's wish to come to the Soviet Union for the Millennium celebrations been granted, he would have had to traverse an ecumenical and political minefield perhaps unprecedented in world Christianity. Patriarch Pimen, head of the Moscow Patriarchate and a man completely under the KGB's thumb, refused to have John Paul in Russia for the occasion.[83] So the Pope sent an exceptionally prestigious Vatican delegation, led by Cardinal Agostino Casaroli, the secretary of state, and including the papal spokesman Joaquín Navarro-Valls.[84] The delegation met with Mikhail Gorbachev and delivered a personal letter from John

Paul II. Gorbachev, for his part, sought to put Casaroli at ease by telling him that both he and foreign minister Eduard Shevardnadze had been baptized and that his parents had kept an icon hidden behind the obligatory photo of Lenin in his childhood home.[85]

John Paul II could not come to Moscow, but Gorbachev could come to Rome and did so on December 1, 1989. Seemingly nervous at the beginning of his day at the Vatican, he was sufficiently relaxed at the end of his ninety-minute private conversation with John Paul II that he could introduce his wife to the Pope in glowing terms: "Raisa Maximovna, I have the honor to introduce the highest moral authority on earth . . . and he's Slavic, like us!"[86]

It was not Canossa, with a repentant Holy Roman Emperor standing in the snow, craving a papal absolution. But it was, symbolically, a moment of surrender. The communist war against Karol Wojtyła, which had been prosecuted with an array of weapons for more than four decades, was over. Wojtyła had won, not only by playing an effective defense but by deploying an offense whose power communism simply could not match. For the power of Wojtyła's resistance was a moral power—and this was, at bottom, a war over the truth about man and the truth about the good.

John Paul II would never think of his triumph as a personal victory. Nor would he have regarded his struggle against communism as essentially political

in character. Zbigniew Brzeziński understood that
John Paul's authority derived from the depth of
his faith, and from the intelligence with which he
had brought that faith to maturity and used it as
an optic through which to understand the world.
Yet Brzeziński could write in his memoirs of being
impressed, after a 1980 Vatican conversation, with
"how political the Pope's thinking was."[87] Henry
Kissinger had a different recollection of a conversation with John Paul II, which perhaps gets closer to
the mark in grasping the essence of the Pope's politics, such as they were.

Shortly after the first papal pilgrimage to the United
States in October 1979, Kissinger was in Rome and
met with the Pope. John Paul asked how the former
secretary of state thought the American visit had
gone. Kissinger replied that it was not for him, a
non-Catholic, to analyze or comment on the visit,
but that, as a political man, he couldn't help notic-
ing that the Pope had chosen themes for his homilies
that were guaranteed to create some friction with his
primary constituency, the Catholics of the United
States. The Pope replied by saying that he was deeply
concerned about the degree to which the Church
had become politicized, with the lines blurred in
Latin America between Catholicism and Marxism.
"The Church is in the business of truth," John Paul
concluded, and if he adapted his message to please
every different audience, Catholicism would end up
as just another social service agency. Kissinger was

impressed, and later remembered thinking that "no politician would ever say such a thing."[88]

Perhaps, however, there was an exception to that rule: a politician who grasped the moral core of John Paul II's approach to the affairs of the world, the moral passion that shaped his strategy throughout his long battle against communism, and the convictions that forged the unique weapons he deployed to such effect in the last decade of that battle. If so, that politician was Václav Havel, suddenly the president of a free and democratic Czechoslovakia, who welcomed John Paul II to Prague on April 21, 1990:

> I am not sure that I know what a miracle is. In spite of this, I dare say that, at this moment, I am participating in a miracle: the man who six months ago was arrested as an enemy of the State stands here today as the President of that State, and bids welcome to the first Pontiff in the history of the Catholic Church to set foot in this land.

> I am not sure that I know what a miracle is. In spite of this, I dare say that this afternoon I shall participate in a miracle: in the same place where, five months ago, on the day in which we rejoiced over the canonization of Agnes of Bohemia, when the future of our Country was decided, today the head of the Catholic Church will celebrate Mass and probably thank our saint for her intercession before him who holds in his hand the inscrutable course of all things.

I am not sure that I know what a miracle is. In spite of this I dare say that at this moment I am participating in a miracle: in a country devastated by the ideology of hatred, the messenger of love has arrived; in a country devastated by the government of the ignorant, the living symbol of culture has arrived; in a country which until a short time ago was devastated by the idea of confrontation and division in the world, the messenger of peace, dialogue, mutual tolerance, esteem and calm understanding, the messenger of fraternal unity in diversity has arrived.

During these long decades, the Spirit was banished from our country. I have the honor of witnessing the moment in which its soil is kissed by the apostle of spirituality.[89]

THE DIFFERENCE THE *OSTPOLITIK* DID, AND DID NOT, MAKE

Cardinal Agostino Casaroli once said, rather wistfully, "I would like to help this pope but I find him so different."[90] As John Paul's spokesman, Joaquín Navarro-Valls, noted afterward, the "difference" was the difference between a man who had been a Church bureaucrat and diplomat for fifty years (albeit an exceedingly competent one) and a man from the front lines.[91] The man from the front lines, however, recognized the skills that Casaroli brought to the Holy See's diplomacy, even if Casaroli could never quite bring himself to acknowledge that this "different" pope had a deeper, more penetrating, and, ultimately, more realistic view of the European communist project than he did. John Paul II took full advantage of Casaroli's skills; promoting the author of the **Ostpolitik** of Paul VI to the second-highest position in the central bureaucratic leadership of the Catholic Church also gave needed cover to a more assertive papal stance on human rights and religious freedom. That did not mean, however, that the difference Casaroli felt was not real. It was. John Paul II believed himself to be the voice of the voiceless, as he made clear at Assisi shortly after his election, when he said that the Church of Silence was no longer silent because it spoke with his voice. Cardinal Casaroli sympathized with the plight of the voices that had previously had no voice; yet, until the end, he remained convinced that their plight could be quietly resolved with governments, without much reference to the voices that had been silenced.

The **Ostpolitik** and Agostino Casaroli created diplomatic openings and contacts that were useful during the last decade of Karol Wojtyła's struggle against communism; they added, as it were, another string to his bow. But it is not easy to see that the old **Ostpolitik** was successful beyond that—beyond being an accompaniment, and a minor one at that, to John Paul II's moral revolution and its effects in central and eastern Europe.

Cardinal Miloslav Vlk, a former underground priest in Czechoslovakia compelled to work as a window washer in order to avoid arrest as a vagrant, believed that the old **Ostpolitik** was designed and executed by men who didn't understand communism because they hadn't lived it. And because they didn't understand it, they made serious strategic and tactical errors. As Vlk once put it, speaking of Czechoslovakia, Pope Paul VI "saw a Church without bishops" and tried to make deals with the government to rectify that; "he ended up with bishops who were puppets."[92] The same could be said for Hungary.

Jan Nowak, who also knew communism from the inside and who played a major role in supporting the Solidarity revolution from abroad (as he had in keeping Poles informed by his prior work at Radio Free Europe), liked Cardinal Casaroli personally while disagreeing with his analysis of the situation in east central Europe. Casaroli, according to Nowak, believed that the martyrdoms in the region in the immediate postwar period, the inability of Cardinal Mindszenty to function while living as a refugee in the American Embassy in Budapest, and the similar disempowerment of the interned Archbishop Josef Beran in Czechoslovakia all meant that the underground Church, the resistance Church, was wrong, both tactically and, over the long haul, strategically. Casaroli also shared Paul VI's concern that an underground Catholicism cut off from Rome would lead to sectarianism, deviations, and various ecclesial corruptions. Nowak disagreed and once discussed the question with John Paul II, who took the view that Nowak was right and Casaroli mistaken.[93]

Not infrequently (and not surprisingly), the most bitter criticisms of the old **Ostpolitik** came from advocates of the Greek Catholic Church in Ukraine, who often believed that the Curia and its diplomats were hopelessly naive about the Soviet Union and about the Russian Orthodox Church. Fiercely loyal Greek Catholics charged that the Vatican's efforts at a "dialogue of love" with Russian Orthodoxy meant, in practice, a "dialogue of love" with the KGB, which was clearly impossible, and just as clearly counterproductive. As one of those passionate Ukrainians, a distinguished historian, once said, "Imagine Christians being torn to pieces by wild beasts while St. Peter conducts a 'dialogue of love' with Nero"—a dramatic, and perhaps exaggerated, image, but one that came easily to the minds of many in the world's largest illegal Church, most of whose leaders had perished in the Gulag. As for the more sophisticated analysts, they were no less critical of what they thought was the tactical ineptness of the old **Ostpolitik**: thus when Paul VI agreed that Ukrainian Greek Catholics without churches of their own could take holy communion in Russian Orthodox churches, he seemed unaware that the Orthodox would take this as an admission that the Greek Catholics (whose existence they continued to deny as a legal matter) didn't really need their own churches, didn't really need to celebrate Mass in the forests clandestinely, didn't really need their own (clandestinely educated and ordained) clergy. Given the intransigence of Russian Orthodoxy on a full array of ecumenical issues during the pontificate of John Paul II, this is not an easy critique to rebut.[94]

Even as they miscalculated the degree to which ecumenical accommodation and a distancing of the Vatican from underground Catholic Churches could eviscerate morale and witness among Catholics determined to hold fast to their faith against communist persecution, the practitioners of the Casaroli **Ostpolitik** seem to have badly overestimated both the staying power of communism and the **Ostpolitik**'s role in preparing the ground for the Revolution of 1989 in central and eastern Europe and the collapse of the Soviet Union in 1991. Thus Cardinal Casaroli's claim that Poland was "ripe" in 1978 and 1979 was true; but that ripening had virtually nothing to do with the **Ostpolitik**, for Poland was the country least affected by Casaroli's initiatives and most resistant to some of them.[95]

The extraordinary efforts made by Soviet and Warsaw Pact intelligence agencies to penetrate the Vatican, suborn and recruit Vatican officials, and thereby impede Church initiatives coincided precisely with the high point of Casaroli's **Ostpolitik;** of this there can be no question. The more accommodating the Holy See was, the more aggressive the KGB, the SB, the Stasi, Hungarian intelligence, Bulgarian intelligence, and the rest of the sordid lot became. Both the Italianate institutional culture of the Roman Curia and the innate aversion of diplomats to confrontation led to a situation in which those responsible for the **Ostpolitik** never grasped what Karol Wojtyła understood in Kraków: that it was "us" and "them," all the time; that it was, in fact, all war, all the time.[96] This was not an adjudicable struggle of the sort to which diplomats were accustomed. Somebody was going to win, and somebody was going to lose. On being elected pope, John Paul II did not believe that the day was close at hand when communism would lose. But he did understand the nature of the confrontation, and he was convinced that a forthright moral challenge to the communist culture of the lie was the most effective response to it—because it was the truest response to it.

There is no evidence that the penetration of the Vatican by Warsaw Pact intelligence services led to any alterations in John Paul II's strategy or tactics. The Pope's "Polish policy" between his election and the completion of the Solidarity Revolution in 1989 was run out of the papal apartment, not out of the Vatican's Secretariat of State—in part because John Paul thought he understood the situation better, and in part, it seems likely, because of concerns that the Secretariat of State was not adept at counterintelligence. The vast expenditure of communist intelligence resources and personnel on espionage in the Vatican of John Paul II did nothing to impede the Pope; it did much to underscore the naïveté of the architects of the **Ostpolitik**, and to highlight the venality of more than a handful of second-, third-, and fourth-tier clerics in the employ of the Holy See.

One more point about the **Ostpolitik** should be noted. In the immediate postwar period, communist strategy aimed to separate local Catholic Churches from Rome. This was, for example, the ploy in Yugoslavia, and the refusal of Archbishop Alojzije Stepinac to go along with "secession" and create a Yugoslav Catholic Church "independent" from Rome led to his show trial, imprisonment, internment, and ultimately his death. Perhaps the most unfortunate effect of the **Ostpolitik** was that it created a situation in which the Soviet Union and its satellites could cleverly reverse this strategy, using Rome— and pressure from Vatican diplomacy—against local Catholic Churches (like those in Czechoslovakia and Hungary) that had resisted the "secession" approach.

The **Ostpolitik** of Agostino Casaroli and Pope Paul VI was the Vatican's version of détente: a strategy of engagement and dialogue with communism that promised much and delivered little, primarily because the proposed dialogue partner was not interested in dialogue. The **Ostpolitik** did not even manage to "save what was savable" in Czechoslovakia and Hungary; indeed, in those situations, it inadvertently made matters worse, just as détente did little to strengthen the hand of dissidents and human rights activists behind the Iron Curtain. Détente did help make possible the 1975 Helsinki Final Act of the Conference on Security and Cooperation in Europe, which then Archbishop Casaroli signed for the Holy See. And the CSCE's "Basket Three" human rights provisions did help keep Western public opinion focused on the plight of human rights activists in communist countries who appealed to the Helsinki Accords for legitimation and protection.[97] But it took leaders like President Ronald Reagan and Pope John Paul II—the men who deliberately moved beyond détente and beyond the **Ostpolitik**—to give those voices and those appeals for freedom global reach, and global effect.

Thus Henry Kissinger's verdict on the negotiations that produced the Helsinki Accords might well be applied to the diplomacy of the Vatican **Ostpolitik** between 1963 and 1978: "Rarely has a diplomatic process so illuminated the limitations of human foresight."[98]

THE INDISPENSABLE MAN?

The notion that John Paul II played a pivotal role in the collapse of European communism was largely missed during and immediately after the Revolution of 1989 and the demise of the Soviet Union—a myopia presaged in the **New York Times** editorial of June 5, 1979, which declared that, while John Paul's Nine Days (then under way) would "reinvigorate and inspire the Roman Catholic Church in Poland," the Pope's pilgrimage certainly did not "threaten the political order of the nation or of Eastern Europe."[99]

Twenty-five years later, the true picture was coming into sharper focus. John Lewis Gaddis of Yale, America's premier historian of the Cold War and a man with no Catholic agenda to advance, was unambiguous in his judgment on the matter: "When John Paul II kissed the ground at the Warsaw airport on June 2, 1979, he began the process by which communism in Poland—and ultimately everywhere—would come to an end."[100] Gaddis was not, of course, suggesting that John Paul was alone in bringing communism to its knees; rather, John Paul II was one of a number of leaders with the insight and courage to see a new situation and seize the opportunities inherent in it. For it was not until the early 1980s, Gaddis wrote,

that the **material** forms of power upon which the United States, the Soviet Union, and their allies had lavished so much attention for so long—the nuclear weapons and missiles, the conventional military forces, the intelligence establishments, the military-industrial complexes, the propaganda machines—began to lose their potency. Real power rested, during the final decade of the Cold War, with leaders like John Paul II whose mastery of **intangibles**—of such qualities as courage, eloquence, imagination, determination, and faith—allowed them to expose disparities between what people believed and the systems under which the Cold War obliged them to live. The gaps were most glaring in the Marxist-Leninist world: so much so that when fully revealed there was no way to close them other than to dismantle communism itself, and thereby end the Cold War.[101]

Gaddis's conclusion—that "it took visionaries—saboteurs of the status quo—to widen the range of historical possibility"[102]—is neatly put, and applies to any number of figures during the 1980s, among whom he lists, in addition to the Pope, Lech Wałęsa, Margaret Thatcher, Deng Xiaoping, Ronald Reagan, and Mikhail Gorbachev. The latter two bear a moment's reflection, in their relationship to John Paul II.

Ronald Reagan was smitten with Poland, with Polish courage, and with the Polish pope. He clearly understood that he and John Paul II had their separate and independent spheres of authority and influence, different sets of instruments at their disposal, and differing degrees of room for maneuvering. Yet Reagan also saw his work and the Pope's during the 1980s as proceeding along parallel tracks toward a common goal: the defeat of communism and the victory of freedom. Both Reagan and John Paul II were regularly dismissed as "conservative" by commentators for whom that description was not meant as a compliment, but as a polite placeholder for "reactionary." The truth of the matter was that both men were radicals, and in two important senses: they both had a clear vision of the roots of the problem—that is, the communist lie about the human person and human aspirations—and they both disdained liberal shibboleths about "stability," "détente," and arms "control," preferring change, liberation, and real disarmament.[103]

John Paul II respected Mikhail Gorbachev as a man of principle, who was prepared to risk his power and his position for the sake of what he believed to be true—which was Karol Wojtyła's acid test in measuring politicians.[104] Yet, while Gorbachev was undoubtedly a key actor in the drama of the collapse of communism, his role was rather different from that played by John Paul II and Ronald Reagan, who truly were architects of the end of the Cold War. The Polish pope and the American president had "destinations in mind and maps for reaching them," as John Lewis Gaddis points out.[105] Gorbachev had no such map, and it seems likely that, until the end came in 1991, he still held firm to the possibility of reform communism, a hybrid that Reagan and John Paul deemed impossible. Gorbachev was not prepared to hold the "Socialist Commonwealth" together by armed force, a point he made to a Comecon leadership meeting in Moscow in November 1986. Yet as Christopher Andrew and Vasili Mitrokhin put it, "though the east European regimes were, predictably, unwilling to share the secret with their subjects, it was only a matter of time before they discovered it"—and acted on it. Moreover, Gorbachev's miscalculation of the possibilities of reform communism in the USSR seems to have been presaged by a similar misapprehension about what would likely unfold in the late 1980s in the Soviet external empire; as Andrew and Mitrokhin note, "It did not occur to Gorbachev . . . that he might be opening the way to the end of the communist era in eastern Europe. He expected the hardliners, when they could hold out no longer, to be succeeded by a generation of little Gorbachevs anxious to emulate the reforms being introduced in Moscow. Few peacetime miscalculations have had such momentous consequences."[106]

It may have surprised a Polish audience that Cardinal Agostino Casaroli would put it in such terms, but it should have been no surprise to those who knew his mind and his understanding of the way the world worked that in a lecture in Kraków on June 2, 1990, the Vatican secretary of state described Mikhail Gorbachev as "someone who ran to the rescue to repair by democratic means the mortal wounds on the socio-political, moral, and economic levels inflicted on peoples during the long dictatorship."[107] But there was no rescue, and no rescuer.

What difference, then, did John Paul II make, in the last phases of the Cold War? And what were the differences in John Paul II that made the John Paul II difference in the world?

In retrospect, it now seems likely that communism would have collapsed at some point because of its inability to compete in an international economic environment increasingly dominated by information technology. But why did communism collapse in 1989, rather than in 1999, or 2009, or 2019, and why did it collapse in the way it did—in the main, without mass bloodshed, which was the twentieth century's normal procedure for achieving great social change? No account of the largely nonviolent collapse of communism in 1989 (rather than in 1999, or 2009, or 2019) will be complete or satisfactory unless it takes full account of the revolution of conscience that the Pope ignited in June 1979. The Nine Days of John Paul II were the trigger for all the rest. And, of course: no John Paul II, no Nine Days.

As for the differences inside John Paul II that account for the difference he made in the world, perhaps the crucial difference was that the Pope knew communism from the inside: he had taken the full measure of its theoretical flaws and practical failures; he had successfully resisted both its seductions and its brutalities; he was battle tested as a leader, in both strategy and tactics. He was an intellectual with deep convictions about the integrity and power of popular piety and the traditions of Polish culture. His nationalism, however, was not narrow, but rather of the sort that led him to appreciate other nations and their cultures. Thus he was a patriotic Pole who appreciated and could see possibilities for change inherent in the struggles to preserve national identity in Lithuania and Ukraine (which many Poles disdained), and who had a deep appreciation for the long-repressed spiritual culture of Russia (which many Poles loathed). He was a man who took decisions after much thought and even more prayer; still, he was willing to trust his own instincts and experience, even when those instincts collided with the caution of Vatican diplomats. He was shrewd, deploying those diplomats and taking advantage of an **Ostpolitik** with which he disagreed for whatever bits of tactical advantage those deployments might yield. Yet he insisted on continuing his own ministry of moral witness far beyond what the diplomats thought appropriate, or even prudent, even as he could be cautious when caution was required. He brought to the papacy a unique and formidable combination of insight, experience, and courage. Those qualities made him the pivotal figure in the defeat of European communism.

Similar qualities of intellect and spirit would, over the remaining decade and a half of his pontificate, allow him to offer the world a singularly powerful witness to the human truths he believed were most fully captured in the faith of the Catholic Church: truths about living and, finally, truths about dying— truths about beginnings and ends, and about ends and beginnings.

PART TWO

KENOSIS

The Last Years of Pope John Paul II

2000–2005

CHAPTER FIVE

The Great Jubilee of 2000

Up to Jerusalem

November 10, 1994	Pope John Paul II issues apostolic letter, **Tertio Millennio Adveniente**, "On Preparation for the Jubilee of the Year 2000."
November 29, 1998	John Paul II issues **Mysterium Incarnationis**, Bull of Indiction of the Great Jubilee of 2000.
June 29, 1999	John Paul II publishes **Letter Concerning Pilgrimage to the Places Linked to the History of Salvation.**
December 24, 1999	Pope John Paul II opens the Holy Door of St. Peter's Basilica and solemnly inaugurates the Great Jubilee of 2000.

December 25, 1999	Opening of the Holy Door at the Basilica of St. John Lateran.
December 31, 1999	**Te Deum** celebrated in St. Peter's; papal midnight blessing at the turn into the new year.
January 1, 2000	Opening of the Holy Door at the Basilica of St. Mary Major.
January 2, 2000	**Jubilee of Children.**
January 18, 2000	Ecumenical opening of the Holy Door at the Basilica of St. Paul Outside the Walls.
February 2, 2000	**Jubilee of Consecrated Life.**
February 11, 2000	**Jubilee of the Sick and of Health Care Workers.**
February 18, 2000	**Jubilee of Artists.**
February 19, 2000	**Jubilee of Permanent Deacons.**
February 23, 2000	John Paul II's jubilee pilgrimage to the holy places begins in Rome with the Commemoration of Abraham, Our Father in Faith; **Jubilee of the Roman Curia.**
February 24–26, 2000	John Paul II's jubilee pilgrimage continues at Mount Sinai in Egypt.
February 25–27, 2000	Jubilee Convocation to Study the Implementation of Vatican II.

March 12, 2000	• Jubilee "Day of Pardon" in St. Peter's Basilica on the First Sunday of Lent.
March 19, 2000	• **Jubilee of Artisans.**
March 20, 2000	• John Paul II looks into the Holy Land from the Memorial of Moses on Mount Nebo.
March 21, 2000	• John Paul visits one of the traditional sites of Jesus's baptism in the River Jordan, then flies to Israel.
March 22, 2000	• John Paul II in Bethlehem.
March 23, 2000	• John Paul II, in Jerusalem, celebrates Mass in the Cenacle, visits the Yad Vashem Holocaust memorial, and addresses an interreligious meeting.
March 24, 2000	• In Galilee, John Paul II celebrates Mass on the Mount of Beatitudes, visits Tabgha, and prays at Peter's house in Capernaum.
March 25, 2000	• John Paul celebrates Mass in the Basilica of the Annunciation in Nazareth, prays at the Garden of Gethsemane in Jerusalem, and visits the Greek Orthodox patriarch of Jerusalem.
March 26, 2000	• John Paul II's Holy Land pilgrimage concludes with prayer at the Western Wall of the Temple, Mass at the

Holy Sepulcher, and prayer at the
Twelfth Station of the Cross.

On the afternoon of March 26, 2000, Pope John
Paul II had a favor to ask of his Israeli hosts.

It was his last day in Jerusalem, the conclusion
of a pilgrimage that had riveted the world's attention and fulfilled a spiritual and pastoral ambition
the Pope had nursed for a quarter century—to walk
where Jesus had walked. The universal pastor of
the Church, he believed, should embody the truth
about the Church: that it is always a Church **in via**,
a Church "on the way" to the New Jerusalem and the
fulfillment of God's saving purposes. How better to
embody the pilgrim Church than for the chief shepherd to go himself to "the places where God chose to
pitch his 'tent' among us," as John Paul once put it?[1]

The Pope had begun that brilliant spring Sunday
morning in Jerusalem by praying at the Western
Wall, the sole surviving part of Herod's Temple, after
which he celebrated Mass at what tradition regards
as the tomb of Jesus. It had already been a full day,
especially for a man two months shy of his eightieth birthday who walked with difficulty because of a
form of Parkinson's disease and a not altogether successful hip replacement. But the cup was not yet full
for John Paul II. So he asked his Israeli hosts, whose
security forces had code-named him OLD FRIEND,

if they would allow him to return privately to the Basilica of the Holy Sepulcher, so that he could pray at the place where Jesus had died, which he had not had an opportunity to visit earlier in the day.

Having regathered their wits after the shock of the Pope's request, the security forces did the best they could to clear the warren of streets around the basilica so that OLD FRIEND could do what he believed he must do. The traditional site of the crucifixion, the Twelfth Station of the Cross, is on the second floor of the basilica. So seventy-nine-year-old Karol Wojtyła, Pope John Paul II, returned to Christianity's holiest site, and then, slowly and in pain, walked up the narrow spiral of a stone staircase so that he could spend a half hour in prayer at the place where the Lord he had served throughout his life had laid down his life.

John Paul II had been Bishop of Rome and universal pastor of the Catholic Church for twenty-one years, five months, and ten days when he walked the last steps of the **Via Crucis,** the Way of the Cross, to the Twelfth Station in Jerusalem. On October 16, 1978, the day of his election as pope, the Primate of Poland, Cardinal Stefan Wyszyński, had told Karol Wojtyła that he had been chosen by the Holy Spirit to lead the Church into the third millennium. Since 1994, John Paul had led a sometimes reluctant and sometimes uncomprehending Church in an extensive preparation for celebrating the two thousandth anniversary of the Incarnation—the moment when, according to Christian conviction, "God chose to pitch his 'tent' among us" in a definitive way. The Pope had come to think of the Great Jubilee of 2000 and the turn into the new millennium as the "key" to his pontificate, which was already one of the most consequential in history. But what kind of key was this?

John Paul II had become the most visible man in human history, having been seen live by more people than anyone who ever lived. Yet he had always tried to make his visibility into a transparency: for in his mind, his task was not to point to himself but to make himself a pointer, directing the people of the Church and the world to Jesus Christ. "Don't look at me, look at Christ; don't look to me, look to Christ"—that had been his message in an extraordinarily diverse array of settings throughout the world.

And why look to Jesus Christ? Because, as the Pope had said in many variations on the same great theme, Jesus Christ is the answer to the question that is every human life.

That was why he had to go to the Twelfth Station. Karol Wojtyła's rich and complex spiritual life had been formed in part by more than a half century of reflection on the great sixteenth-century Spanish Carmelite mystics, St. John of the Cross and St. Teresa of Ávila. For these Spanish Carmelite reformers, as for so many other saints, **kenosis**, the outpouring of self in conformity to the self-sacrifice of the crucified Christ, was the key to the spiritual life—and thus the key to the world and its story. So Karol Wojtyła had to go to the Twelfth Station to fulfill a desire of his heart and soul. Yet his slow walk up those stone stairs to Calvary was more than a personal matter, for he had long since ceased to belong to himself. It was a matter of his vocation, for a Catholic priest is ordained to bring his people ever more closely into the paschal mystery of Jesus Christ, crucified and risen.

Karol Wojtyła, Pope John Paul II, lived in the conviction that Christ had taken the world's fear upon himself at Calvary and, in a perfect act of obedience to the will of God the Father, had offered himself and the world's fear in a perfect sacrifice—to which God had given the perfect answer on Easter Sunday, by raising Jesus from the dead. At Calvary, John Paul II believed, Christ had conquered fear and the world had been empowered to live, not without fear, but **beyond** fear.

"Be not afraid!" had been the antiphon of his pontificate since that glorious autumn morning of October 22, 1978, when he had challenged the Church to fearlessness and the world to a new openness to the person and message of Jesus Christ. "Be not afraid!" could be a compelling challenge rather than a trite slogan because Christ had taken all the world's fear upon himself on the cross. That was why Pope John Paul II had to go to Calvary: for the fearlessness he preached and embodied in a world-changing pontificate all began there.

THE YEAR 2000

Viewed conventionally, the pontificate of John Paul II divides roughly into two parts. From October 1978 through August 1991, the pontificate's focal point was John Paul's challenge to communism, vindicated by the Revolution of 1989 in east central Europe and the collapse of the Soviet Union in August 1991. After the May 1991 encyclical **Centesimus Annus**, in which John Paul reflected on the epic events of the recent past and scouted the social, political, economic, and cultural terrain of the postcommunist future, the pontificate pivots so that from 1992 until the end of the story in 2005, the focal point is the Great Jubilee of 2000. There is something to be said for this neat periodization, but the deeper truth of the matter is that John Paul II was acutely aware of the coming new millennium from the day of his election—a point not readily grasped by some of the Catholic Church's bishops and cardinals.[2]

To more than a few senior churchmen, as to much of the world, the year 2000 was a calendrical happenstance of no particular significance. No one really knew when Jesus had become incarnate of the Virgin Mary (as the Creed put it) and born in Bethlehem (as Scripture and tradition held). Many scholars believed that, thanks to medieval dating errors, Jesus of Nazareth was likely born in what we call 7 B.C. So why bother celebrating 2000? Then there were the mathematicians, who reminded everyone that, as there had been no year "0" between what the conventions called "B.C." and "A.D.," the year 2000 was the last year of the second millennium, not the first year of the third. Indeed, the people who seemed most interested in "2000" were the world's apocalyptics, among whom ancient millenarian expectations were given a new, technological twist: fear of a "Y2K" computer glitch that would shut down the world.

The dubieties of the churchmen and the apocalypticism of the millenarians made little sense, and no difference, to Karol Wojtyła. His immersion in Polish culture and its reverence for anniversaries had taught him something about the spiritual rhythms of time and the perennial human need to acknowledge those rhythms—which was an important way of acknowledging that the human story could not be reduced to a sequence of random accidents with no inherent meaning or direction. Moreover, his life as a philosopher had convinced him that the post-Enlightenment Western intellectual world's disdain for any notion of purpose in nature could, and did, have dramatic effects on the way human beings think about themselves, their historical responsibilities, and their possibilities in shaping the future. In some corners of the popular imagination, a random world led to random human beings who were, at best, congealed stardust. That self-image, John Paul II thought, had a lot to do with the twentieth century's moral confusions, which had had horrific consequences: they had turned the twentieth century into an abattoir. Restoring a sense of historic trajectory and historic possibility to the human story was essential, he was convinced, to the rescue of civilization itself.

As archbishop of Kraków, Karol Wojtyła had seen how Cardinal Wyszyński's Great Novena and the celebration of the Polish Millennium in 1966 had helped preserve the country's cultural identity and historical memory after two decades during which Poland had been ground between the totalitarian millstones of Nazism and communism. He also knew that the Polish Millennium in 1966 had not been merely a recovery of the past: to remember the nation's origins was to give the nation a firm foundation from which to build the future. Thus 1966 was, for Poland, less about the baptism of the Piast prince Mieszko I than about celebrating a vision of the Polish future in continuity with the culture that had been born from Mieszko's embrace of Christianity.

Immersion in anniversaries—the reclamation of the past as a platform from which to launch out into the future—was an integral part of Karol Wojtyła's experience as a Pole. And if, as he sometimes said, the Holy Spirit had seen fit to bring the archbishop of Kraków to Rome as universal pastor of the Catholic Church, then there was something of importance in the Polish and Cracovian experience for the world Church, and just perhaps for the world.

So he would not regard "2000" as a calendrical oddity, but as an evangelical opportunity.

In early 1994, John Paul sent the cardinals of the Church a lengthy memorandum, "Reflections on the Great Jubilee of the Year 2000," and requested written responses. The memorandum laid out an ambitious jubilee program: preparatory continental synods of bishops; new ecumenical and interreligious initiatives; a revision of the Church's official martyrology to take account of the vast outpouring of Christian blood in the twentieth century; and an examination of conscience by which the Church would come to grips with its infidelities over twenty centuries. The Pope then summoned the cardinals to a special consistory, held in the Vatican on June 13, 1994, to consider the memorandum and the responses.

John Paul II must have sensed a certain lack of enthusiasm about the jubilee among the men who were supposed to be his senior counselors, for he began the consistory with a major address in which he reread the Second Vatican Council as a providential initiative intended to prepare the Church for its third millennium. He also stressed the millennial imperative of accelerating the quest for Christian unity: **"We cannot come before Christ, the Lord of History,"** he underscored, **"as divided as we unfortunately have been during the second millennium."** In addition, the Pope emphasized the importance of a new martyrology and defended his generosity in giving the Church new saints, a practice which some had criticized: to ignore or minimize the gifts of the Holy Spirit in more recent centuries, he suggested, was to undercut the Council's "universal call to holiness" in future centuries. The Church constantly needed conversion, he reminded the cardinals. And that, not some kind of ecclesiastical political correctness, was why the Church also had to prepare for the new millennium by seeking God's forgiveness for the errors and betrayals of the sons and daughters of the Church over the previous 2,000 years.[3]

The cardinals concluded their two days of discussions by adopting two resolutions: one deplored the slaughters then under way in Rwanda; the other supported the Pope's efforts to prevent the forthcoming Cairo World Conference on Population and Development from declaring an internationally recognized right to abortion. About the Great Jubilee of 2000, the College of Cardinals, among whom there was no little skepticism about the possibility of organizing (much less carrying out) a program as ambitious as the Pope had outlined, had nothing formal to say.

Having tried collaboration, an undaunted John Paul II now took the reins of the Great Jubilee into his own hands through an apostolic letter, **Tertio Millennio Adveniente** [The Coming Third Millennium], which was signed on November 10, 1994, and issued four days later.

It was a document of great substance and deep lyricism, in which the Pope began by reminding the Church that biblical religion was not a matter of our search for God, but of God's coming into history in search of us, and of our learning to take the same road through history that God is taking. Thus, as John Paul wrote, in God's covenant-making with the chosen people of Israel and in the Incarnation of the Son of God, "it is not simply a case of man seeking God, but of God who comes in Person to speak to man of himself and to show him the path by which he may be reached." In the God of Abraham, Isaac, and Jacob, and above all in Jesus, "religion is no longer a 'blind search for God' (cf. Acts 17.27) but the **response of faith** to God who reveals himself."[4]

That was why, in a biblical view of the world, time was of utmost importance. Time had been sanctified, because "eternity entered into time":

In Christianity, time has a fundamental importance. Within the dimension of time, the world was created; within it the history of salvation unfolds, finding its culmination in the "fullness of time" of the Incarnation, and its goal in the glorious return of the Son of God at the end of time. **In Jesus Christ, the Word made flesh, time becomes a dimension**

of God, who is himself eternal . . . [and] from this relationship of God with time there arises **the duty to sanctify time.**[5]

People of biblical faith had fulfilled this duty to sanctify time in various ways: sabbath observance, recurring feasts in the liturgical calendar, and jubilees. The jubilee tradition among the people of Israel was permeated by themes of liberation, reconciliation, and the restoration of justice, all of which were reminders that the human path through history had been illuminated by the divine presence. Those themes carried over into Christian jubilees, to which was added the conviction that history had reached its axial moment in Jesus Christ: for in the Incarnation of the Son of God, we are shown both the face of the merciful Father and the truth about our own humanity.[6] So the Great Jubilee of 2000, John Paul wrote, would be both an act of thanksgiving for the past and an act of consecration for the future, in which the Church would commit itself to a "**new springtime of Christian life.**"[7] Throughout the letter, the Pope underscored the linkage between the Great Jubilee and Vatican II, citing the four principal documents of the Council in order to describe a jubilee focused on the worship of God (**Sacrosanctum Concilium**, the Constitution on the Sacred Liturgy), the word of God (**Dei Verbum**, the Dogmatic Constitution on Divine Revelation), the mystery of the Church (**Lumen Gentium**, the Dogmatic Constitution on the Church), and the Church's encounter with the world (**Gaudium et Spes**, the Pastoral Constitution on the Church in the Modern World).[8]

John Paul then laid out the program for the Great Jubilee of 2000. There would be three years of preparation, each focused on one of the divine Persons and one of the theological virtues: thus 1997 would be the Year of Jesus Christ and a period of reflection on faith; 1998 would be the Year of the Holy Spirit and a time of reflection on hope; 1999 would be the Year of the Father and a year of reflection on love. The Pope would continue his own pilgrim journeys throughout the world, while planning for a jubilee pilgrimage to the central places of salvation history—those associated with God's call of the people of Israel; those associated with the life, death, and resurrection of Christ; and those first touched by the Christian mission to the world. He also challenged the Church to a deeper cleansing of historical conscience, and to intensified action on behalf of both Christian unity and interreligious dialogue.[9]

All of this required a considerable amount of organization, so a Central Committee for the Great Jubilee of the Year 2000 was appointed. The president, French cardinal Roger Etchegaray, was joined by a presidential council consisting of Cardinal Camillo Ruini, the papal vicar for the Diocese of Rome; Nigerian cardinal Francis Arinze, head of the Pontifical Council for Interreligious Dialogue; Australian cardinal Edward Cassidy, head of the Pontifical Council for Promoting Christian Unity; and Cardinal Virgilio Noë, the archpriest of St. Peter's Basilica. The membership of the Central Committee included prelates from throughout the world Church: the theologian of the papal household, Father Georges Cottier, O.P. (who also served as president of the jubilee's critical theological-historical commission); several curial figures; and three laypeople, including Harvard law professor Mary Ann Glendon.[10]

The Central Committee's general secretary would be the man responsible for coordinating the planning for the Great Jubilee of 2000 and then overseeing the jubilee events. This crucial position went first to an Italian curial diplomat, Archbishop Sergio Sebastiani, who was replaced in November 1997 by a more efficient Italian curialist, Archbishop Crescenzio Sepe.[11] A jubilee logo was commissioned, as was a jubilee hymn; the logo's design and the hymn's tune reflected the conviction, widespread in some Italian Catholic circles, that the Church made itself more attractive by appealing to tastes formed by contemporary popular culture.[12] A glossy journal, **Tertium Millennium**, was created to keep those interested informed of the work of the Central Committee's commissions and committees: the commission for the new martyrs, charged with preparing the updated martyrology; the pastoral commission; the artistic-cultural commission; the social commission; the mass-media committee; the Rome committee; the Jerusalem committee; the technical committee; and the theological-historical commission, formed to address the delicate questions raised by the Pope's insistence that the Church cleanse its conscience in preparation for a new springtime of evangelization in the third millennium of its history. In addition to this preparatory work, the Central Committee (and the relevant Roman curial offices) were responsible for organizing the jubilee year in terms of vocational groups, such that virtually every state of life in the Church would have its own particular jubilee celebration during the year 2000—another innovation of John Paul II's jubilee.

As the Holy See organized itself for the Great Jubilee, the city of Rome prepared for a tidal wave of jubilee pilgrims, and the facade of St. Peter's was given a cleaning that papal spokesman Joaquín Navarro-Valls called "the restoration of the century."[13] Concurrently, the continental Synods of Bishops in preparation for the Great Jubilee were held over two busy years so that the Church could reflect on the distinctive accomplishments of the past two millennia, and the unique challenges of the twenty-first century, in each region of the world.[14]

Mysterium Incarnationis [The Mystery of the Incarnation], the Bull of Indiction or papal decree formally convoking the Great Jubilee of 2000, was issued on November 29, 1998, the First Sunday of Advent. Its title, taken from the first words of its Latin text, summed up John Paul II's answer to the question, "Why 2000?" The answer, John Paul wrote, had been given by St. Paul in his letter to the Ephesians and its great hymn to the mystery of the Incarnation:

> Blessed be the God and Father of our Lord Jesus Christ, who has blessed us in Christ with every spiritual gift in the heavenly places, even as he chose us in him before the foundation of the world that we should be holy and blameless before him. He destined us in love to be his sons through Jesus Christ, according to the purpose of his will. . . . For he has made known to us in all wisdom and insight the mystery of his will, according to the purpose which he set forth in Christ as a plan for the fulness of time, to unite all things in him, things in heaven and on earth [Ephesians 1.3–5, 9–10].

Here, John Paul wrote, was the poetic heart of Paul's proclamation that "in Jesus Christ, the history of salvation finds its culmination and ultimate meaning." The Apostle's hymn also taught us that "the birth of Jesus in Bethlehem is not an event that can be consigned to the past," for "the whole of human history in fact stands in reference to him: our own time and the future of the world are illumined by his presence." Thus "in the encounter with Christ," who is "the genuine newness which surpasses all human expectations," every human being, in every time and place, "discovers the mystery of his own life" and learns that "no one can be separated from the love of

God, except through their own fault," for "the grace of mercy is offered to everyone."[15]

The Pope then reviewed several aspects of the jubilee tradition as it had evolved in the Catholic Church: the tradition of pilgrimage, "which is linked to the situation of man who readily describes his life as a journey"; the tradition of the Holy Door, which "evokes the passage from sin to grace which every Christian is called to accomplish"; and the tradition of the jubilee indulgence, which is an "expression of the total gift of the mercy of God." Indulgences— pious acts leading to the remission of "temporal punishment due to sin" in that experience of purification Catholics traditionally called Purgatory—had been a point of bitter controversy during the Reformation. In **Mysterium Incarnationis**, John Paul presented the indulgence tradition as one that recognizes the "surfeit of love" left to the Church by the saints, on which the men and women of today can draw through a "spiritual communion," which itself testifies to the truth that "no one lives for himself alone."[16]

To these traditional "signs" of a jubilee, John Paul then decreed a cleansing of the Church's conscience for the past sins of her children, an intensification of charity (particularly with reference to international debt), and a renewed focus on the memory of the Church's martyrs, especially its modern martyrs— three facets of the Great Jubilee he had been stressing since 1994.[17] The Bull of Indiction concluded with an explanation of the conditions for gaining the jubilee indulgence, which were expanded to include acts of penance and generosity, such as work for, or contributions to the support of, homeless children, troubled teenagers, or the needy elderly.

In late 1999, with the preparatory process under the control of Archbishop Sepe, Bishop James M. Harvey, the prefect of the papal household, and Bishop Stanisław Dziwisz, the Pope's longtime secretary, John Paul II agreed to make some adjustments in his own schedule for the jubilee year.[18] **Ad limina** visits—the quinquennial visit that every Catholic bishop in the world makes to Rome, and on which John Paul had previously expended as much as 40 percent of his time—were suspended for the year 2000; the last national group of prelates the Pope received were the bishops of the Dominican Republic, whom he met as a group on December 11, 1999. (Previously, that fall, John Paul had received the bishops of Zambia, Malawi, Chad, Burundi, Puerto Rico, Lithuania, Latvia, Canada, the Central African Republic, Germany, and Portugal.) Given that he would preside over each of the vocational days that would be celebrated almost weekly throughout the jubilee year, in addition to an International Eucharistic Congress in June and World Youth Day in August, the Pope also agreed to reserve each Tuesday during 2000 as a day of recreation: a day in the hills outside Rome, when weather permitted, was particularly welcome.

AN OPEN DOOR

While the Catholic jubilee tradition traces its deepest roots to the Hebrew Bible, the origins of "holy years" celebrated at St. Peter's in Rome can be dated with some precision: on February 22, 1300, Pope Boniface VIII published the Bull **Antiquorum habet fida relatio** convoking the first holy year, which Boniface intended to be repeated every hundredth year thereafter. The jubilee proved so popular that it was repeated in 1350, 1390, and 1423, before returning to mid-century in 1450 and then continuing in a rhythm of every quarter century, beginning in 1475. In 1423, Pope Martin V opened the first jubilee Holy Door at the papal cathedral, the Basilica of St. John Lateran. The first recorded opening of the Holy Door at St. Peter's took place at Christmas 1499, to inaugurate the jubilee year of 1500; the tradition of opening holy doors at the three other major Roman basilicas (St. John Lateran, St. Mary Major, and St. Paul Outside the Walls) also began in 1499–1500. The ritual for opening the Holy Door of St. Peter's was codified by John Burckhard, master of papal ceremonies, for the ceremony on Christmas Eve 1499 and remained essentially the same for five centuries. The principal changes in the rite took place in 1975, when the exterior of the bronze holy door was no longer bricked up; only the interior was closed with masonry.

In **Tertio Millennio Adveniente**, John Paul II had written that "the Holy Door of the Jubilee of the Year 2000 should be symbolically wider than those of previous Jubilees, because humanity, upon reaching this goal, will leave behind not just a century but a millennium."[19] That fact, as well as the Pope's desire that the Great Jubilee emphasize God's mercy, led to a further development in the symbolism of the rite on Christmas Eve 1999: the Pope would not knock on the interior wall blocking the Holy Door with a hammer, as in the past; rather, the interior masonry, which at the end of the previous jubilee had sealed off the Holy Door from the inside of the basilica, would be removed beforehand so that the Pope could open the two great bronze doors by gently pushing on them. The Great Jubilee of 2000 would begin, not with knocking down a wall, but with opening a door: Christ, the door through which the sheep of his flock enter in order to meet the Father of mercies in a land of good pasture (John 10.9).

And so, at 11 P.M. on Christmas Eve 1999, John Paul II came to the Holy Door of St. Peter's, vested in a shimmering, ultramodern red, blue, and gold cope, the patterns of which were replicated in the decoration of the chasubles and miters of the prelates who would concelebrate Christmas Midnight Mass with him. He began the rite of opening the door, and the Great Jubilee of 2000, by invoking the Holy Trinity and thanking the Father, the Son, and the Holy Spirit for the gifts of grace that had been poured out upon the Church during the previous three years of preparation. A deacon proclaimed that passage of Luke's Gospel in which Jesus, in the synagogue of Nazareth, takes the scroll of the prophet Isaiah, reads the passage proclaiming a year of favor in which prisoners are freed, the blind see, and the oppressed are given freedom, and then announces that "Today, this scripture has been fulfilled in your hearing" (Luke 4.21). John Paul then walked to the Holy Door and prayed antiphonally with those present:

> This is the door of the Lord. The just will enter through it.
> I shall go up to your house, O Lord. I shall prostrate myself in adoration in your holy temple.
> Open to me the gates of justice. I shall enter them and give thanks to the Lord.

Finally, in silence, with the interior lights of the vast basilica dimmed, John Paul II placed both his hands on the two panels of the Holy Door and gently pushed them open, before kneeling in silent prayer in the portal, his head bowed and his hands grasping the silver pastoral staff of the crucified Christ with which he had once greeted the crowds at the Mass inaugurating his pontificate, waving it back and forth as if it were a great sword of faith. It took a hardened heart not to recognize that here was a man living the supreme moment of his life, the moment toward which the previous seventy-nine years had been directed—and doing so in such a way that he pointed beyond himself to Christ, the door.

Five and a half years before, more than one senior churchman believed that arranging something as massive as the Great Jubilee in the form that John Paul II imagined it was simply impossible. Yet now, with the world's attention focused on the man kneeling in the portal of the Holy Door of St. Peter's, what had seemed impossible had become reality—in large part because of the indomitable will of John Paul II himself. But that may be to put the matter too psychologically, as a question of willfulness or stubbornness. It was the indomitable faith of John Paul II—his conviction that the Incarnation was indeed the axial moment in human history—that brought him to the Holy Door on Christmas Eve 1999 and to the axial moment of his own pontificate.

As the choir sang "Christ yesterday and today/ the end and the beginning/Christ the Alpha and the Omega/to him be glory forever," the Pope rose from his knees and returned to the portable cathedra in the narthex of the basilica while Catholics from Asia, Australia, and Oceania decorated the Holy Door with flowers and perfumes, and African Catholics sounded traditional horns; these innovations, designed by the papal master of ceremonies, Bishop Piero Marini, were intended to highlight the new churches of the second millennium, as the entire

Catholic Church symbolically crossed the threshold of the third millennium through the Holy Door. The Pope then returned to the now garlanded door, stood in the portal showing the Book of the Gospels to the thousands gathered inside, and led the procession up the basilica's center aisle for the celebration of Christmas Midnight Mass.

When the procession reached the high altar, the Book of the Gospels was enthroned and incensed, after which the deacon and the choir, in an antiphonal chant, sang the proclamation of the Great Jubilee of 2000, which led immediately into the singing of the **Gloria**, the liturgical hymn derived from the angelic salutation to the shepherds on the first Christmas night. Then, after the proclamation of Luke's Christmas narrative in both Latin and Greek, John Paul II (now vested in a less dramatic white chasuble) blessed the congregation with the Book of the Gospels and preached his first homily of the new millennium.[20]

Typically, he began with a reminder that, for the faithful there is nothing to fear: "On this holy night, the angel repeats to us, the men and women living at the end of a millennium: 'Be not afraid; for behold, I bring you good news of great joy . . . to you is born this day in the city of David a Saviour'" (Luke 2.10–11). In these words, John Paul said, "the 'today' of our redemption becomes a reality," for today "we are spiritually linked to that unique moment in history when God became man." That moment forever changed history—for now, "the incomparable 'today' of God has become present in every human life." This was the truth that had sustained the Church for two millennia; this was the truth the Church "wants to pass on to the third millennium"—that "ever since the night of Bethlehem, humanity knows that God became Man . . . in order to give man a share in his divine nature." And so on this night, above all other nights, the Church confesses its faith and prays, "You, O Christ, the Son of the living God, be for us the Door! Be for us the true Door, symbolized by the door which on this night we have solemnly opened! Be for us the Door which leads us into the mystery of the Father! Grant that no one may remain outside his embrace of mercy and peace!"[21]

John Paul returned to the theme of Christ the Door in his message for the traditional Christmas blessing **Urbi et Orbi** [To the City and the World], which he delivered from the central loggia of St. Peter's at noon on Christmas Day, calling humanity to turn to Christ the " 'Door of our salvation,' the 'Door of Life,' and the 'Door of Peace,' and pleading that legislators and political leaders, men and women of goodwill . . . be committed to welcoming human life as a precious gift."[22] Later that afternoon, the Pope opened the Holy Door at his cathedral, the Basilica of St. John Lateran, and preached at the celebration of Christmas Second Vespers. There, the Pope prayed that his Roman diocese would embrace the Christmas "mystery of holiness and hope" so that the "special dimension of the history of salvation which is linked to the graces of the jubilees and the historical memory of the Church of Rome" might "grow in faith and missionary zeal," for these were "the principal legacy of the Apostles Peter and Paul."[23]

The first week of the Great Jubilee of 2000 concluded with the traditional **Te Deum** for the conclusion of the year and the celebration of First Vespers of the Solemnity of Mary, Mother of God, on the evening of December 31, 1999. The **Sediarii** (who had once carried pontiffs on the **sedia gestatoria**, a kind of papal sedan chair) slowly wheeled the Pope up the center aisle of St. Peter's on a rolling platform, with John Paul stopping at various moments to touch hands or caress a baby. His Vespers homily, a meditation on time and the human immersion in time and history, stressed the universal call to holiness and thanked God for all "the saints of this millennium: those raised to the honors of the altar and, even more numerous, those unknown to us who sanctified time by their faithful adherence to God's will." For the saints remind us that Christ is the Lord of time, Christ who is "the same yesterday, today, and forever," Christ who is "the goal of human history" and the "focal point of the expectations of every human being."[24] That night, moments after midnight, the Pope came to the window of the papal apartment in the Apostolic Palace and blessed the tremendous crowd that filled every inch of available space in St. Peter's Square. "In crossing the threshold of the new year," he said, "I should like to knock on the door of your homes to give each of you my cordial greetings for a happy new year in the light that, from Bethlehem, radiates throughout the entire universe! . . . Thank you! Happy new year to everyone! May Jesus Christ be praised!"[25]

In another break with jubilee precedent, John Paul opened each of the holy doors of the four patriarchal Roman basilicas; so on January 1, 2000, the Solemnity of Mary, Mother of God, and the annual papal World Day of Peace, the Pope opened the Holy Door at the Liberian basilica, St. Mary Major; there, he invoked the intercession of Mary, Queen of Peace, to whom he entrusted "the days of the new year, the future of the Church, the future of humanity, the future of the entire universe."[26] In his message for the 2000 World Day of Peace, John Paul had stressed characteristic themes: that respect for human rights and for the dignity of every human person was the essential foundation for peace; that crimes against humanity cannot be considered any country's internal affair and that humanitarian intervention is an obligation in cases of real or impending genocide; that true international community can only be built on the foundation of a "culture of solidarity" in which the poor become "the agents of their own development" and all are empowered to "exercise the creativity which is characteristic of the human person and on which the wealth of nations is dependent." Returning to a theme from his 1995 Address to the General Assembly of the United Nations, the Pope also described the natural moral law that can be known by reason as a " 'grammar' of the spirit" that can turn cacophony into genuine dialogue about the "problems posed by the future of humanity."[27]

John Paul II maintained a vigorous pace as the second week of the Great Jubilee opened, meeting with tens of thousands of children in St. Peter's Square at the **Jubilee of Children** on January 2, and greeting individually more than 200 graduates, faculty, and friends of a joint American-European seminar on Catholic social doctrine in the Sala Clementina the next day. The Pope hosted the seminar faculty to lunch on January 4, joked about the Goodyear blimp hovering above St. Peter's Square ("You see? **Buon Anno!**"), and showed his guests the Kazanskaya, the priceless and historic Russian icon he hoped to return personally to Moscow at some point.[28] On January 18, he completed the opening of the four holy doors of the patriarchal Roman basilicas, inviting Anglican primate George Carey and Metropolitan Athanasius of the Ecumenical Patriarchate of Constantinople to join him in opening the jubilee door at St. Paul Outside the Walls—a unique ecumenical gesture that initiated the annual Octave of Prayer for Christian Unity. The Liturgy of the Word celebrated at the basilica on the Ostian Way was the largest ecumenical assembly in Rome since the Second Vatican

Council, with representatives of twenty-two Christian communities participating.[29] In his homily, John Paul urged all present to "give new impetus to the ecumenical commitment" as an "imperative of Christian conscience," for "the future of evangelization and the proclamation of the Gospel to the men and women of our time" depended "in great part" on healing the breaches in the one Church of Christ that had opened up during the previous two millennia. The Pope, who had bent every possible effort to unite his separated brethren as they crossed the threshold of the third millennium, completed the opening phase of the Great Jubilee of 2000 with an eloquent plea and a heartfelt prayer:

From this basilica, which sees us gathered together with hope-filled hearts, I look ahead to the new millennium. The wish that flows from my heart and becomes a fervent entreaty before the throne of the eternal Father is that, in the not too distant future, Christians will at last be reconciled and be able to walk together again as one people obedient to the Father's plan, a people that can repeat with one voice and in the joy of renewed brotherhood, "Blessed be God, the Father of our Lord Jesus Christ, who has blessed us in Christ with all the spiritual blessings in the heavens" [Ephesians 1.3].

May the Lord Jesus hear our prayers and our ardent plea. Amen![30]

On January 23, John Paul II took a cinematic break from the public events of the Great Jubilee, hosting the distinguished Polish filmmaker Andrzej Wajda and the cast of Wajda's new film, **Pan Tadeusz**, to Mass and a private screening of the movie in the Vatican. For Karol Wojtyła, who had taken part in a 1942 Rhapsodic Theater production of Adam Mickiewicz's classic during the Nazi occupation of Poland, it was an emotionally charged moment. Afterward, the Pope stunned both director and cast by reciting large chunks of Mickiewicz's epic poem from memory.[31]

Walking with Abraham and Moses

The **ad limina** visits of the world's bishops may have been suspended for the Great Jubilee, and the Pope may have agreed to a weekly day off, but the papal schedule remained formidable. On January 6, the Solemnity of the Epiphany, John Paul ordained twelve new bishops at St. Peter's. In the Sistine Chapel on January 9, the Feast of the Baptism of the Lord, he baptized eighteen infants from Italy, Brazil, Spain, the United States, and Switzerland. On January 10, he gave his annual address to the diplomatic corps accredited to the Holy See. Speaking from the experience of the twentieth century to the political leaders of the twenty-first, he made an impassioned plea for solidarity, for religious freedom, and for a new awareness of the divine presence in human affairs:

> I speak to you as one who has himself been a fellow-traveler of several generations of the century just ended. I shared the harsh ordeals of my native people [in] the darkest hours experienced by Europe. Twenty-one years ago, when I became the Successor of the Apostle Peter, I felt myself charged with a universal fatherhood which embraces all the men and women of our time without exception. Today, in addressing you who represent practically all the peoples of the earth, I would like to share with each one something personal: at the opening of the doors of a new millennium, the Pope began to think that people might finally learn to draw lessons from the past. . . .
>
> The words which Deuteronomy puts on the lips of God himself come to mind: "See, I have set before you this day life and good, death and evil . . . therefore choose life, that you may live" [Deuteronomy 30.15–19].[32]

The vocational jubilee days continued in February with the **Jubilee of Consecrated Life** (February 2, the Feast of the Presentation of the Lord), the **Jubilee of the Sick** (February 11, the liturgical commemoration of Our Lady of Lourdes), the **Jubilee of Artists** (February 18, the day before the liturgical commemoration of Fra Angelico, whom John Paul had beatified in 1982), and the **Jubilee of Permanent Deacons** (February 19). The **Jubilee of the Sick** included a festival of sound and light in St. Peter's Square, with thousands of pilgrims participating in a Marian procession **aux flambeaux**, as at the shrine of Lourdes in the Pyrenees.[33]

John Paul had intended to begin his personal jubilee pilgrimage to the places most closely linked to the history of salvation by going to the home of Abraham: "If it be God's will, I would like to go to Ur of the Chaldees, the present-day Tell el-Muqayyar in southern Iraq, the city where, according to the biblical account, Abraham heard the word of the Lord which took him away from his own land, from his people, from himself in a sense, to make him the instrument of a plan of salvation which embraced the future people of the Covenant and indeed all the peoples of the world."[34] Whatever God's will in the matter may have been, it was the will of Saddam Hussein, the Iraqi dictator, that eventually made it impossible for John Paul to begin his jubilee pilgrimage as he wished.

In his June 1999 **Letter Concerning Pilgrimage to the Places Linked to the History of Salvation**, John Paul had emphasized that his would be "an exclusively religious pilgrimage in its nature and purpose," for "to go in a spirit of prayer from one place to another, from one city to another, in the area marked especially by God's intervention, helps us not only to live our life as a journey, but also gives us a vivid sense of a God who has gone before us and leads us on, who himself set out on man's path, a God who does not look down on us from on high, but who has become our traveling companion." He then added that he would be "saddened if anyone were to attach other meaning to this plan of mine." Saddam Hussein, for his part, saw nothing but political possibility in the desire of John Paul's heart, and demanded that the Pope defy the UN's ban on direct flights to Iraq. The Pope, following traditional Vatican policy, had long opposed sanctions against Iraq; but he would not allow himself or his pilgrimage to become a pawn in Saddam's chess match with the United Nations, and at the end of 1999, he reluctantly concluded that the Iraqi dictator had made it impossible for the first step on his jubilee pilgrimage to be the kind of step it had to be. On December 10, 1999, Joaquín Navarro-Valls told the press that the Vatican had been informed by Iraq that the "abnormal conditions" created by the postwar international embargo and the no-fly zones in the north and south of the country did not "allow for an adequate organization of a visit by the Holy Father." There was no need for further comment on the Iraqi regime's crude effort to twist the story for its own propaganda purposes.[35]

If John Paul II could not go to Ur, then the Ur

of his religious imagination could come to Rome, such that John Paul would make a "spiritual pilgrimage" to the home of Abraham. Thus on February 23, 2000, the Paul VI Audience Hall in the Vatican was transformed into an evocative setting for a Celebration of the Word in Commemoration of Abraham, Our Father in Faith. The platform in the rear of the audience hall was decorated with oak trees, to commemorate the terebinths of Mamre beneath which Abraham had pitched his tent and offered sacrifice to God. To the right of three copper pots containing burning candles was an uncarved and rough stone, reminiscent of the stone of Isaac's sacrifice and the altars built by Abraham during his sojourns. Next to the stone was the focal point of the platform: a reproduction of perhaps the greatest of icons, Andrei Rublev's portrayal of the three angels visiting Abraham, a scene that Christians have long regarded as a proto-expression of God the Holy Trinity. John Paul was seated on a small, red throne beside the iconic display; the audience hall was filled with thousands of pilgrims, and an even larger crowd watched the Commemoration on giant television screens in St. Peter's Square. After a video showing the ruins of Ur and the rivers of Canaan, the land of promise, there were readings from the book of Genesis, recounting the call of Abraham, God's covenant with him, and the drama of the sacrifice of Isaac; from Paul's Letter to the Romans and the Letter to the Hebrews, extolling Abraham as the father of all believers; and from John's Gospel, recounting Jesus's dramatic proclamation that "Abraham rejoiced that he was to see my day" (John 8.56). In his homily, John Paul stressed that it was Abraham's radical obedience to the will of God for his life that had made him not only the father of a great nation, but the father of all believers in the one, true God. Abraham's faith, John Paul said, posed a continuing challenge, down the centuries, to grasp the remarkable breadth and depth of the divine promises: for "the land to which human beings are moving, guided by the voice of God, does not belong exclusively to the geography of this world." Abraham's life and the fulfillment of God's promise to him points to the truth that man is ultimately destined for "a promised land that is not of this world," which is a destination we only reach in "the obedience of faith." The Commemoration concluded with the burning of incense atop the stone, recalling the worship of the one, true God that Abraham had inaugurated.[36]

The following day, February 24, John Paul flew to Cairo on the first leg of his pilgrimage to Mount Sinai, where Moses had met "the God of your father, the God of Abraham, the God of Isaac, and the God of Jacob" (Exodus 3.6). At the airport exchange of greetings with Egyptian president Hosni Mubarak and local religious leaders, the Pope set the theme of this phase of his jubilee pilgrimage, thanking the Egyptian leader for making it possible "for me to go where God . . . gave his Law as a sign of his great mercy and kindness toward his creatures." John Paul then went to visit the residence of the Coptic Orthodox patriarch, Pope Shenouda III, noting that the successor of Peter felt at home in the house of the successor of Mark, traditional founder of the Church of Alexandria and Peter's longtime companion. Later that same day John Paul went to the intellectual center of Sunni Islam, Cairo's Al-Azhar University, where he met the Sunni spiritual leader Sheikh Muhammad Sayyid Tantawi and was greeted enthusiastically by other Muslim scholars and religious leaders, who seemed eager to get as near the Pope as possible.[37]

At Mass in a Cairo stadium on February 25, John Paul returned to the theme of the law that liberates in a homily before some 15,000 worshipers from the local Armenian, Chaldean, Coptic, Greek, Latin-rite, Maronite, Melkite, and Syrian communities. The Ten Commandments, the Pope said, were a gift from God, given to a recently enslaved people so that they would not revert to the habits of slaves. The same gift was available to those who did not wish to be slaves to the various false gods on offer in the twenty-first century; here, in the Ten Commandments, the men and women of the new millennium would find a moral code that "frees us from idols and makes every life infinitely beautiful and infinitely precious." Speaking extemporaneously at the end of the Mass, John Paul praised the persecuted Sudanese Christians who had made the trek to

Cairo to be with him and sent his greetings to their hard-pressed brethren at home.[38]

The Christian unity for which the Pope had pleaded at St. Paul Outside the Walls on January 18 was dealt a few new blows on February 26, when John Paul went by helicopter to the monastery of St. Catherine on Mount Sinai. The Greek Orthodox monastic community there offered him a warm welcome, as did its leader, Archbishop Damianos; but the Orthodox declined to pray with the Pope in a Liturgy of the Word celebrated outside the monastic enclosure in a garden. To do so, Damianos suggested, would be inappropriate while Rome and Orthodoxy were not in full communion. It was a position John Paul II did not share, but there was nothing he could do about such principled recalcitrance.

The Orthodox monks thus missed being present at one of the great homilies of the Great Jubilee, and indeed of the pontificate. In it, John Paul preached on the mystery of "liberating obedience," which, he said, had been enshrined "at the heart of our religion" by God's encounter with Moses in this very place. The Ten Commandments, he insisted, "are not the arbitrary imposition of a tyrannical Lord." Rather, the Ten Commandments reflect the fact that the God who created us is also our redeemer, who inscribes an instinct for moral truth inside every man and woman. The Ten Commandments "were written in stone; but before that they were written on the human heart as the universal moral law." There was still a wind blowing from Sinai, John Paul continued, a wind that reminded the men and women of the twenty-first century that the Ten Commandments are "the law of freedom: not the freedom to follow our blind passions, but the **freedom to love, to choose what is good in every situation**, even when to do so is a burden." The law liberates; the law reveals, and unveils, and clarifies: for "in revealing himself on the Mountain and giving his Law, God revealed man to himself. **Sinai stands at the very heart of the truth about man and his destiny**."[39]

Tradition marks a spot on the mountain where God spoke to Moses from the burning bush. On coming to that spot, John Paul II went down on his knees and was lost in prayer.

MEMORY, CONFESSION, PARDON, RECONCILIATION

Of all John Paul II's plans for the Great Jubilee of 2000, the most controversial was his insistence that the Church cleanse its historical conscience at the end of the second millennium, in preparation for a new springtime of evangelization in the third.[40] He had put the case succinctly, and sharply, in **Tertio Millennio Adveniente**:

[I]t is appropriate that, as the second millennium of Christianity draws to a close, the Church should become ever more fully conscious of the sinfulness of her children, recalling all those times in history when they departed from the spirit of Christ and his Gospel and, instead of offering to the world the witness of a life inspired by the values of faith, indulged in ways of thinking and acting that were truly **forms of counter-witness and scandal**. Although she is holy because of her incorporation into Christ, the Church does not tire of doing penance. Before God and man, she always **acknowledges as her own her sinful sons and daughters**.[41]

The Pope's proposal raised many questions. From a communications standpoint, how could the Church's confession of the sins of her children be done in such a way that these acts of confession did not become confused with various exercises in political correctness in which politicians groveled before groups claiming victim status? From a historical point of view, was it even possible to pass a serious historical judgment on events that had taken place centuries before, events shaped by many unknown facts, motivations, and pressures? Then there was the problem of the Church's long entanglement with coercive state power: where was the Church responsible for certain injustices, and where was injustice to be tallied to the account of the state? The gravest questions were theological. As **Tertio Millennio**

Adveniente indicated, there were two facets of the Church's life to be reconciled: the Church's belief that she was preserved in truth and holiness by the power of the Holy Spirit, and the Church's constant practice of (and need for) purification, confession, and penance.

All of these questions were examined by the International Theological Commission [ITC] at the request of its president, Cardinal Joseph Ratzinger, prefect of the Congregation for the Doctrine of the Faith and himself a distinguished theologian. In December 1999, the Commission issued "Memory and Reconciliation: The Church and the Faults of the Past," a thirty-five-page study that examined several key aspects of the relationship between the holiness of the Church and the sinfulness of Christians: the biblical approach to the problem; the theological foundations of a solution; the relationship of historical judgment to theological judgment; the question of ethical discernment, both in the present and over time; and the importance of the issue for pastoral and missionary work, ecumenical relations, and interreligious dialogue.[42] The ITC study did not take up particular cases, but rather sought to establish a coherent intellectual framework for the Church's reckoning with the shadow side of its past. The conclusion of "Memory and Reconciliation," which cited both Irenaeus of Lyons and John Paul II, took the entire discussion far beyond the shallows of political correctness and offered a moving testimony to the conviction that truth, however painful, is in the final analysis liberating:

[I]n every form of repentance for the wrongs of the past, and in each specific gesture connected with it, the Church addresses herself in the first place to God and seeks to give glory to him and to his mercy. Precisely in this way she is able to celebrate the dignity of the human person called to the fullness of life in faithful covenant with the living God: "The glory of God is man fully alive; but the life of Man is the vision of God." By such actions, the Church also gives witness to her trust in the power of the truth that makes us free [cf. John 8.32]. Her "request for pardon must not be understood as an expression of false humility or a denial of her 2,000-year history, which is certainly rich in merit in the areas of charity, culture, and holiness. Instead, she responds to a necessary requirement of the truth, which, in addition to the positive aspects, recognizes the human limitations and weaknesses of the various generations of Christ's disciples." Recognition of the Truth is a source of reconciliation and peace because, as the Holy Father also states, "Love of the truth, sought with humility, is one of the great values capable of reuniting the men of today through the various cultures." Because of her responsibility to Truth, the Church "cannot cross the threshold of the new millennium without encouraging her children to purify themselves, through repentance, of past errors and instances of infidelity, inconsistency, and slowness to act. Acknowledging the weaknesses of the past is an act of honesty and courage. . . ." It opens a new tomorrow for everyone.[43]

In the course of eighty-nine pastoral pilgrimages outside Italy over the two decades between his election and the opening of the Great Jubilee, John Paul II had discussed the Church's need for forgiveness for the failures of its sons and daughters in a variety of settings; many of the papal requests for God's forgiveness touched on sins against the unity of the Church, although others involved what the world media insisted were the more salient issues, such as the Inquisition, the Galileo case, and the European wars of religion. This entire, unprecedented process of a corporate, ecclesiastical examination of conscience reached its apogee in St. Peter's on March 12, 2000, the First Sunday of Lent in the Great Jubilee, which had been designated the Day of Pardon.

It began with John Paul, vested in Lenten penitential purple, kneeling in prayer before Michelangelo's statue of the **Pietà:** just as the Mother of the Church had embraced the crucified Lord of the Church, so the Church, John Paul said, must embrace the one who had died for the sins of the world and ask the merciful Father's forgiveness. As the procession moved slowly up the basilica's center aisle, the choir sang the Litany of the Saints, asking the Church in glory to intercede with the Father for both the

Church in the world and the Church being purified in Purgatory. Next to Bernini's great bronze balda-chino and the basilica's high altar, a giant seven-foot fifteenth-century crucifix, taken from the Church of St. Marcellus, had been erected, along with seven candles, which remained unlit; the St. Marcellus cross had been venerated during holy years in Rome for centuries. John Paul's homily asked the entire Church to place itself "before Christ, who out of love, took our guilt upon himself," to make a "**profound examination of conscience**," and to "**forgive and ask forgiveness!** " Throughout the years of preparation for the Great Jubilee, the Church had examined its conscience about the past; now it must examine its conscience about the present, asking itself "what our responsibilities are regarding atheism, religious indifference, secularism, ethical relativism, the violations of the right to life, disregard for the poor in many countries."[44] There was, no doubt, apostasy and infidelity in the world; what had Christian apostasies and failures done to create a modernity that seemed to have forgotten God?

The general intercessions of the Mass then took the form of seven confessions of sin and requests for God's pardon, after each of which the senior churchman making the petition lit one of the seven candles beside the St. Marcellus crucifix. Cardinal Bernardin Gantin, the dean of the College of Cardinals, made a general confession of Christian sinfulness in history; the Pope prayed God's forgiveness for these sins; the entire congregation chanted **Kyrie eleison** [Lord, have mercy] three times. The same pattern was replicated as Cardinal Joseph Ratzinger asked God's pardon for the times when Christians have "used methods not in keeping with the Gospel in the solemn duty of defending the truth." Cardinal Roger Etchegaray confessed the sins that had broken Christian unity. Cardinal Edward Cassidy asked God's forgiveness for Christian sins against the Jewish people. Archbishop Stephen Fumio Hamao invoked Christian sins "against love, peace, the rights of peoples, and respect for cultures and religions," and Cardinal Francis Arinze remembered those sins that had been committed against the dignity of women and the unity of humanity. Archbishop Francis Xavier Nguyên Van Thuân concluded the confession by asking God's pardon for the sins Christians had committed against human rights, including a disregard for the dignity of those unborn. With all seven candles now lit, John Paul II walked slowly to the St. Marcellus crucifix and, as a sign of penance and a request for God's pardon, embraced and venerated it.

It was, perhaps, not surprising that the **New York Times** missed the point, suggesting editorially that the "Pope's apology" (as it mistakenly described the Day of Pardon) had not gone far enough, for John Paul had not retracted the Church's discriminatory teaching on artificial means of family planning, on abortion, and on the inadmissability of women to holy orders.[45] More surprising was the continuing skepticism that was exhibited by senior churchmen. Cardinal Giacomo Biffi of Bologna (usually a supporter of John Paul) had once challenged the formulation in the Pope's 1994 letter to the cardinals on the impending jubilee year, which had stated that "the Church acknowledges as her own the sins of her children." Biffi thought that statement theologically ambiguous, at best; the Pope, during a lunch with the cardinal in July 1997, asked whether Biffi had noticed that the formulation of this in **Tertio Millennio Adveniente** was different so that it now read, "The Church always acknowledges as her own her sinful children." Biffi was gratified that the Pope had taken his counsel and told John Paul that the new formulation was unexceptionable. But he then said that "the unheard-of initiative of asking pardon for the errors and inconsistencies of past centuries would . . . scandalize the 'little ones' . . . because the faithful, who do not know how to make theological distinctions, would see these self-accusations as a threat against their serene adhesion to the ecclesial mystery, which . . . is essentially a mystery of sanctity." John Paul agreed that "that will require some thought." In 2007, in his memoirs, Cardinal Biffi said that "unfortunately, he did not reflect on it sufficiently."[46]

But he had. He had been reflecting on such matters for a long time, beginning with the Polish bishops' letter to their German colleagues in 1965, and he was convinced that the iconography of confession and repentance carried the Gospel message forward in ways that scholarly historical analysis of the past could not. It would be difficult to find examples of those "faithful" whose "serene adhesion" to the Church was threatened by the Great Jubilee's Day of Pardon. On the contrary, John Paul II's humility before the fact of Christian failure reinforced the themes he was determined to emphasize throughout the jubilee year: that all are called to holiness, and that, as he had long put it to those who came to him for confession, a man's dignity is increased by the very act of his getting down on his knees to acknowledge before God that he has failed.

The holiness of the Church had been celebrated the week before, on March 5, 2000, when John Paul II beatified forty-four martyrs—lay catechists, priests, religious women—who had given their lives for the truth in venues ranging from seventeenth-century Vietnam and Brazil to twentieth-century Thailand and Belarus. Now, on the Day of Pardon, the Church had confessed before God the times when her sons and daughters had not lived up to the universal call to holiness. The dialectic of penitence and grace, the rhythm of all genuine pilgrimages, had been embodied in two ceremonies at St. Peter's on succeeding Sundays: a fitting preparation for the papal pilgrim who, eight days after the Day of Pardon, left for the holy lands of biblical tradition and his own vivid religious imagination.

The Pope's preparation continued immediately after the Day of Pardon, when John Paul began the annual papal and curial Lenten retreat. The retreat master for the jubilee year, by the Pope's invitation, was the Vietnamese archbishop, Francis Xavier Nguyên Van Thuân, who wore a pectoral cross made from barbed wire and electrical wire, souvenirs of his fourteen years of imprisonment in a communist prison camp. Choosing as his theme "Witnesses to Hope," the diminutive archbishop made a deep impression on the retreatants by meditating aloud on what his time behind bars had taught him about faith and fidelity, forgiveness and integrity.

To Touch the History of Salvation

"Be not afraid!" was John Paul II's signature antiphon in the world. With respect to the Holy Land, **"Quando me permetterete di andare?"** [When will you let me go?] was the papal antiphon within the Roman Curia. Weeks after his election in October 1978, John Paul had floated the idea of spending his first Christmas as pope in Bethlehem. His curial diplomats were aghast: the Holy See had no diplomatic relations with any of the states involved; there was no time to arrange things properly; the security would be a nightmare; popes simply didn't pack up and go places, especially places that were political minefields. For once, John Paul II conceded to the ingrained caution of the traditional managers of popes and didn't follow his own pastoral and spiritual instincts; the pattern was thus set for more than twenty years of frustration, during which the Pope asked, time and again, **"Quando me permetterete di andare?"**[47]

He was a patient man but his patience had limits. Moreover, the diplomatic situation had been clarified by the Holy See's 1993 Fundamental Agreement with Israel, the 1994 establishment of diplomatic relations with the Hashemite Kingdom of Jordan, and the ongoing exchange of diplomatic contacts with the Palestinian Authority.[48] Enough was enough. So John Paul finally announced that he was going, period, in the June 1999 **Letter Concerning Pilgrimage to the Places Linked to the History of Salvation.** In addition to the places of pilgrimage identified in **Tertio Millennio Adveniente** (Ur, Sinai, Bethlehem, Nazareth, Jerusalem, and Damascus), the pilgrimage letter added Athens to the jubilee itinerary, in honor of St. Paul's famous sermon on the Areopagus about the "unknown God" (Acts 17.16–34)—a New Testament vignette John Paul frequently cited as a metaphor for the Church's situation in the modern world. The spiritual and emotional centerpiece of the journey, however, would be the Holy Land.

For all the passion of his personal determination

to walk where Jesus had walked, John Paul's March 2000 pilgrimage to the Holy Land had a decidedly pastoral and evangelical purpose: to make the world look, intently, at the stuff of its redemption, thereby underscoring that Christianity rested on what English novelist Evelyn Waugh once described, in **Brideshead Revisited**, as "intransigent historical claims." The Great Jubilee of 2000 was not the two thousandth anniversary of a pious fiction; biblical religion had to do with real people, in real places, making real decisions with real consequences in a drama that was embedded in real history. One might accept or reject the Church's claims for the Church's Lord. But one could not dismiss them as rooted in myth. The successor of Peter ought to pray at the places where Peter confessed, and betrayed, and was forgiven by Christ—and was transformed into the man who ended his life in Nero's Circus in Rome. In praying where Peter had prayed, the successor of Peter was reminding the world that the truth of its salvation was revealed, not in anyone's imagination, but in real lives.

On March 20, John Paul II flew to Amman, Jordan, where he was cordially received by King Abdullah. After the arrival ceremonies, the Pope went quickly to Mount Nebo, the site where biblical tradition holds that Moses gazed into the Promised Land he would never enter; how often, in his poet's imagination, had John Paul imagined himself a latter-day Moses as he asked **"Quando me peremet-**

terete di andare?" Two thousand youngsters received their first holy communions the next day as the Pope celebrated an outdoor Mass in an Amman sports complex. John Paul's homily linked Christian faith to the great Old Testament figures of Moses and Elijah, during a liturgy in honor of St. John the Baptist—the prophetic hinge between the Old Testament and the New, in Christian theology. After the Mass, the Pope led a brief prayer service at one of the traditional Jordan River sites of Jesus's baptism by John, before returning to the Jordanian capital for the short flight to Ben-Gurion International Airport outside Tel Aviv.

Public opinion polls taken shortly before the Pope's arrival in Israel suggested that the majority of Israelis were unaware of the sea change in Catholic-Jewish relations that had followed the Second Vatican Council; one poll revealed that 56 percent of Israelis were unaware that the Church condemned anti-Semitism and worked against it across the globe. John Paul II knew at least some of this, and probably intuited more of it. He also had a unique appreciation of the Jewish pain of the twentieth century, having lived it with the friends of his youth in Wadowice and Kraków. Moreover, he was a man fully persuaded of the power of symbols and symbolic action. Within an hour of his arrival in the first sovereign Jewish state in more than 1,900 years, he made manifestly clear that, for all the tortured history of the previous two millennia, something had changed, and changed for the good of both parties. A pope waving a hand in salute to the Israeli flag; a pope listening as the military band at the airport played "Hatikvah," the Zionist anthem; a pope being welcomed as an honored guest by Israel's president and prime minister; a pope reviewing an honor guard composed of the young men and women of the Israel Defense Forces—thirty-five years of interreligious dialogue, reports from official commissions, even John Paul's historic 1986 visit to the Great Synagogue of Rome did not communicate what an hour of ceremony at Ben-Gurion airport communicated. Something fundamental had changed in the relationship between the Catholic Church and the Jewish people—something historic, and good.

On March 22, the Pope went to Bethlehem, controlled by the Palestinian Authority, for a Mass in Manger Square, outside the basilica housing the traditional site of Jesus's birth. In his homily, John Paul spoke of joy to a people who, for more than half a century, had found joy difficult to come by: "The joy announced by the angel" to the shepherds of Bethlehem "is not a thing of the past. It is a joy of today— the eternal today of God's salvation which embraces all time, past, present, and future." To be embraced by that joy, to open one's life to it, was to enter into the depths of the human mystery: "At the dawn of the new millennium, we are called to see more clearly that time has meaning because here Eternity entered history and remains with us forever. . . . Because it is always Christmas in Bethlehem, every day is Christmas in the hearts of Christians."[49] Arrangements had been made for John Paul to spend a private moment in the Grotto of the Nativity, inside the basilica; characteristically, he used his time there to pray the appropriate portion of the Liturgy of the Hours. Clumsy attempts by Palestinian Authority officials to turn the Mass and the Pope's subsequent visit to the Deheisheh refugee camp into political rallies failed to dull the edge of the Pope's evangelical message. Neither did media incomprehension, as when papal spokesman Navarro-Valls was asked the political significance of the Pope kissing a bowl of soil on arriving in Bethlehem. "It would have been very strange of the Pope not to have kissed the earth at the place Christ was born," Navarro-Valls replied.

No one knows precisely where the "Cenacle"—the room in which Jesus instituted the Eucharist and the priesthood at the Last Supper, and the room in which the Holy Spirit descended on the apostles at Pentecost—actually was, but tradition has long identified a large space on Mount Zion near the Cenotaph of King David as the biblical "upper room." In it, on the morning of March 23, John Paul II celebrated Mass with his closest collaborators. Then after meeting the Ashkenazic and Sephardic chief rabbis and talking with Israeli president Ezer Weizman at his official residence, John Paul II was driven to the Holocaust memorial at Yad Vashem—the emotional, and in some respects spiritual, center of the State of Israel.

Weeks of speculation about "how far would the Pope go?" in his remarks at Yad Vashem had preceded this riveting moment, and risked cheapening what the Pope intended to be a moment of solemn remembrance at a place memorializing what was, for most of the world, a universal icon of evil—the murder of the Jews of Europe during World War II. In the intense emotional, psychological, and political atmosphere surrounding the papal pilgrimage, attempts to explain that this was not a game in which someone's loss was someone else's gain were of little avail. In the event, the demeanor and the words of the Pope, at an occasion of the most heart-wrenching solemnity, reduced all talk of "how far" to dust and ashes.

The man who had once told Joaquín Navarro-Valls that he only cried "inside" must have been awash in unseen tears as he walked slowly toward the eternal flame in the Hall of Remembrance and there bent his head in silent prayer: unseen tears in memory of the childhood friends murdered in the gas chambers; unseen tears at the memories of humiliation under the Nazi jackboot in Kraków; tears for the wounds of the survivors; tears at the resistance of those who had treated his own attempts at reconciliation with incomprehension or contempt. Within, and because of, the personal drama of Karol Wojtyła, however, another drama was being played out at Yad Vashem: the dramatic relationship of Christians and Jews over two millennia, which could now never be the same, in light of the iconography of a Bishop of Rome, who shared the memory of the Holocaust, bent in prayer over the eternal flame commemorating the Holocaust's victims.

What could he possibly say? He could speak of silence:

> In this place of memories, the mind and heart and soul feel an extreme need for silence. Silence in which to remember. Silence in which to try to make some sense of the memories which come flooding back. Silence because there are no words strong enough to deplore the terrible tragedy of the **Shoah**. . . .
>
> I have come to Yad Vashem to pay homage to the millions of Jewish people who, stripped of everything, especially of their human dignity, were murdered in the Holocaust. . . . We wish to remember. But we wish to remember for a purpose, namely, to ensure that never again will evil prevail, as it did for the millions of innocent victims of Nazism. . . .
>
> How could man have such utter contempt for man? Because he had reached the point of contempt for God. Only a Godless ideology could plan and carry out the extermination of a whole people. . . .
>
> As Bishop of Rome and Successor of the Apostle Peter, I assure the Jewish people that the Catholic Church, motivated by the Gospel law of truth and

love and by no political considerations, is deeply saddened by the hatred, acts of persecution, and displays of anti-Semitism directed against the Jews by Christians at any time and in any place.[50]

Those present, and those watching on television, felt the weight of history bear down in an almost crushing way as the Pope then walked slowly and in pain across the Hall of Remembrance to meet seven Holocaust survivors. He was not receiving them; he was going to them, honoring their experience by walking with difficulty to take each one by the hand. That simple, human gesture of respect was another papal icon that, combined with the Pope's heartrending words, lifted the entire event into the realm of the epic. Shortly afterward, an Israeli soldier-scholar who had seen a lot in his life called an American friend and said, "I just had to tell you that my wife and I cried throughout the Pope's visit to Yad Vashem. This was wisdom, humaneness, and integrity personified. Nothing was missing. Nothing more needed to be said."

The profound sense of human solidarity that the Pope had evoked for an hour at Yad Vashem was not maintained that evening, at what was supposed to have been a tripartite interreligious meeting at the Notre Dame Center. The Grand Mufti of Jerusalem refused to attend; Yassir Arafat then sent a Palestinian judge, Sheikh Taysir Tamimi. After Ashkenazic chief rabbi Meir Lau created a fracas by asserting that the

Pope had recognized Jerusalem as Israel's "united, eternal capital city" (which the Pope had not done), Sheikh Tamimi shot back by welcoming John Paul "as the guest of the Palestinian people on the land of Palestine, in the city of holy Jerusalem, eternal capital of Palestine"; Tamimi then insisted that there would be no peace until all of "Palestine" was united in one country under "President Yassir Arafat." The meeting dissolved into cacophony; the Pope sat silently, stunned and saddened, holding his hands to his ears against the uproar. After the meeting's chairman, Rabbi Alon Goshen-Gottstein, had achieved something resembling order, John Paul spoke briefly, and with clear intent, about religious conviction as "the enemy of exclusion and discrimination, of hatred and rivalry, of violence and conflict." Sheikh Tamimi then got up and left, explaining in an aside to the Pope that he had a "previous engagement." Hours after John Paul had eloquently mourned the lethal effects of hatred in his address at Yad Vashem, the haters had come out in force to wreck a meeting intended to foster genuine interreligious dialogue.

It was different, happily, the next day, as the Pope went north to Galilee on March 24 and celebrated Mass on the Mount of Beatitudes for 100,000 young people from all over the world. Israeli security was particularly worried about the safety of OLD FRIEND at a site that was impossible to secure, and asked the Pope to wear a bulletproof vest; John Paul declined, as he always did such suggestions. The solemn, tragic memories evoked by Yad Vashem, and the wreckage of the previous evening's interreligious meeting, did not weigh down the Pope, who as always was energized by the young, charging them to be the "joyful witnesses and convinced apostles" in the new century. John Paul then went to pray at Tabgha, the traditional site of the multiplication of the loaves and fishes, before going to Capernaum and the excavations at what was said to be Peter's house—a moment of wonder was etched on John Paul's face as the 263rd successor of Peter prayed at the house of Peter.

On March 25, John Paul was able to celebrate the Solemnity of the Annunciation in the Basilica of the Annunciation in Nazareth, where the savvy and skills of his faithful secretary, Bishop Stanisław Dziwisz, were on display. As the Pope tried to enter the basilica through roiling and boisterous crowds that might have overwhelmed him, Dziwisz fended them off left and right with a rapid distribution of papal rosaries he had had the foresight to bring along. Throughout the pontificate, Mary's **fiat**— "Be it done unto me according to your word" (Luke 1.38)—had been the Pope's favorite example of the essence of Christian discipleship. Now, as he knelt in prayer at the grotto of the Annunciation beneath the modern basilica, it was not difficult to imagine John Paul repeating that **fiat** again, as well as recommitting himself to the Virgin with the phrase he had adopted as his episcopal and papal motto, **Totus Tuus** [Entirely Yours].

John Paul then returned to Jerusalem, where he spent time in prayer at the Garden of Gethsemane before visiting with the Greek Orthodox patriarch, Diodoros I, at the patriarchal residence. Like his brethren at Sinai, the patriarch declined to pray with the Pope. John Paul spontaneously suggested that everyone present say the Lord's Prayer in his or her own language, thereby underscoring the ecumenical commitment that had once led him to think it possible that the breach between Rome and the Christian East could be healed before the Church crossed the threshold of the third millennium. That was not to be. But John Paul's example of charity in Diodoros's residence was another icon of decency in a land riven by historic animosities, where monks from rival Christian communities could and did engage in fistfights at the Holy Sepulcher itself.

The Holy Sepulcher was one of the two focal points of John Paul II's last day in Jerusalem— Sunday, March 26. He had begun the day by creating another visual icon as he walked eighty-six slow steps down the sloping esplanade to the Western Wall, Judaism's holiest site. There, he stood silently for a moment, leaning on his cane, before doing what millions of pious Jews had done for centuries: leaving a prayer-petition in one of the wall's crevices. Written on cream-colored papal note paper, the prayer was constructed as a form of English blank verse by the poet who had become pope, and was signed in Latin:

> God of our fathers,
> you chose Abraham and his descendants
> to bring your Name to the nations;
> we are deeply saddened by the behavior of those
> who in the course of history
> have caused these children of yours to suffer,
> and asking your forgiveness we wish to commit
> ourselves
> to genuine brotherhood
> with the people of the Covenant.
> Amen.
> **—Joannes Paulus PP. II**

The sentiments had been expressed by others before, including at the Day of Pardon at St. Peter's. But these things were now being expressed here, in this singular place, by a man whose entire demeanor gave depth to his words. Prior to the event, there had been a minor flap over whether the Pope should wear his gold pectoral cross when he came to the Western Wall. Wiser Jewish veterans of the interreligious dialogue explained that genuine dialogue meant taking the dialogue partner as he was. Afterward, no such carping was heard: John Paul had come to the Western Wall and prayed as the Bishop of Rome—and that had left an indelible impression.

After having prayed where Jesus had prayed, John Paul celebrated Mass at the Church of the Holy Sepulcher in what was, for him, the climax of the entire pilgrimage. Kneeling at the marble slab over the traditional site of Christ's tomb, he fulfilled the promise he had made in his **Letter Concerning Pilgrimage**, where he had written that, at this holiest of sites, he intended to "immerse myself in prayer, bearing in my heart the whole Church."

He had, in a sense, borne the whole Church and the history of two millennia on his bent back as he walked for seven days where Jesus had walked. The pilgrimage he had longed to make as a younger, more vigorous man took on a richer texture because he had finally come to the Holy Land in his old age— as an old man witnessing to the truths on which he had staked his life, the truths he had deployed to bend the course of history in a more humane direction. John Paul's Holy Land pilgrimage was many things: an irreversible moment in the long and often painful history of Christianity and Judaism, promising a brighter future; a lesson in statesmanship and maturity to the contentious tribes whose ancient animosities had more than once threatened to wreck his visit; an exercise in solidarity and brotherhood. Shortly before the Pope arrived in Jerusalem, senior religious leaders who wished otherwise were worrying aloud that the visit would be a failure. As the Pope's plane took off for Rome on the night of March 26, it was clear to all, except perhaps the haters, that it had been a complete and unmitigated triumph. It was a triumph for the Pope who refused to believe that a pope could not walk where Christ had walked, to be sure. But above all, John Paul would insist, it was a triumph for the truth and love that had been definitively revealed in Jerusalem, the city of "great . . . mystery" where "**the fullness of time became . . . the 'fullness of space.'** "[51]

CHAPTER SIX

The Great Jubilee of 2000

Into the Deep

April 30, 2000	Canonization of Sister Mary Faustyna Kowalska, apostle of divine mercy and the first saint of the new millennium.
May 1, 2000	**Jubilee of Workers.**
May 7, 2000	Ecumenical commemoration of twentieth-century martyrs held in the Roman Colosseum.
May 12–13, 2000	John Paul II in Fátima, Portugal.
May 18, 2000	John Paul II's eightieth birthday; **Jubilee of Priests.**
May 25, 2000	**Jubilee of Scientists.**
May 28, 2000	**Jubilee of the Diocese of Rome.**
June 2, 2000	**Jubilee of Migrants and Itinerants.**
June 4, 2000	**Jubilee of Journalists.**

June 15, 2000	John Paul II hosts lunch in the Vatican for the homeless and the poor.
June 18–25, 2000	Forty-seventh International Eucharistic Congress is held in Rome.
July 9, 2000	**Jubilee in Prisons** celebrated by John Paul II at Regina Coeli prison in Rome.
August 15, 2000	**Jubilee of Youth** opens World Youth Day in Rome.
August 29, 2000	John Paul II declares cloning "morally unacceptable" in address to the Transplantation Society.
September 5, 2000	Congregation for the Doctrine of the Faith issues **Dominus Iesus.**
September 9, 2000	**Jubilee of University Professors.**
September 15, 2000	**Jubilee of Apostolic Nuncios and Papal Representatives.**
September 15–24, 2000	Twentieth International Marian-Mariological Congress.
September 17, 2000	**Jubilee of the Elderly.**
October 8, 2000	**Jubilee of Bishops.**
October 14, 2000	**Jubilee of Families.**
October 18–22, 2000	World Missionary Congress.
October 29, 2000	**Jubilee of the World of Sports.**

November 1, 2000	Mass for the Fiftieth Anniversary of the Dogma of the Assumption of the Blessed Virgin Mary.
November 4, 2000	**Jubilee of Government Leaders and Politicians.**
November 8–10, 2000	John Paul II meets Karekin II, Supreme Patriarch and Catholicos of All Armenians, in the Vatican.
November 12, 2000	**Jubilee of the World of Agriculture.**
November 19, 2000	**Jubilee of Armed Forces and Police.**
November 26, 2000	**Jubilee of the Lay Apostolate.**
December 3, 2000	**Jubilee of the Disabled.**
December 10, 2000	**Jubilee of Catechists.**
December 17, 2000	**Jubilee of the World of Entertainment.**
January 6, 2001	Closing of the Holy Door at St. Peter's Basilica; John Paul II issues apostolic letter, **Novo Millennio Ineunte** [Entering the New Millennium].

On Sunday morning, April 30, 2000, more than 200,000 pilgrims gathered in St. Peter's Square for the canonization of the first saint of the new millennium. The spiritual trajectory of her life had been a striking one, touching several obscure Polish convents, the Index of Forbidden Books, and innumerable Catholic parishes around the world.

Born on August 25, 1905, in the village of Głogowiec near Łódź, Helena Kowalska was the third of ten children born to poor parents who could provide her with only two years of formal education. Unable to enter the convent at seventeen because her family needed the modest income she helped provide, she worked as a housekeeper for two years before making a failed attempt to enter a Warsaw convent. A year later, in 1925, she managed to enter the Sisters of Our Lady of Mercy, having experienced a vision of the suffering Christ. Taking the religious name Maria Faustyna, she completed her novitiate in Kraków and made her final vows in 1933. In the remaining five years of her life, she served her fellow sisters as a doorkeeper, gardener, and cook in convents in Kraków, Płock, and Vilnius (then part of the Polish Second Republic).

On February 22, 1931, in Płock, Sister Mary Faustyna experienced a vision in which Jesus appeared as the merciful savior, with red and white rays of light shining out from his heart; the "King of Divine Mercy" asked her to promote the Second Sunday or Octave of Easter as a celebration of divine mercy and to spread devotion to God's mercy throughout the world. After a psychiatric examination confirmed that Sister Faustyna was not suffering from mental aberrations, Father Michał Sopoćko took the young nun under spiritual direction in 1933, and arranged for a painter to render an image of the vision of Christ Sister Faustyna had seen. Her visions and other extraordinary spiritual experiences (including the hidden stigmata) continued, known only to her religious superiors and her spiritual director, and were recorded in the detailed diary she kept. In 1935, she experienced a vision that laid out the prayer cycle now known as the Chaplet of Divine Mercy. The following year Sister Faustyna fell ill with tuberculosis and spent time in a sanatorium before returning to her convent at Kraków-Łagiewniki, where she died in 1938.

The Łagiewniki convent was close to the Solvay chemical factory where Karol Wojtyła worked from October 1941 until August 1944; the young **robotnik** would sometimes stop at the convent chapel to pray, on his way to or from carrying buckets of lime and doing his clandestine seminary studies. Images of Jesus as the king of divine mercy had begun to appear in Polish churches, but the posthumous course of Sister Faustyna's work took an unexpected turn when, shortly after his election, Pope John XXIII signed a decree prepared by the Holy Office placing the deceased Polish nun's diary on the Index of Forbidden Books. During the Second Vatican Council, Archbishop Karol Wojtyła took up Faustyna's cause with the Roman authorities, convinced that the Divine Mercy devotion had significant pastoral merit and that the condemnation of the diary had been based on a faulty Italian translation of the original Polish. Wojtyła asked one of the readers of his habilitation thesis, Father Ignacy Różycki, to prepare a critical edition of the diary as a first step toward rectifying Faustyna's status with the Holy See. Years of patient work led to the Vatican sanctions being lifted; meanwhile, the Chaplet of Divine Mercy had spread throughout the world, with pastors in a wide variety of circumstances finding it a remarkably effective tool for rekindling Catholic devotional life, which had become decrepit in many countries in the years after Vatican II. Sister Mary Faustyna Kowalska, the apostle of divine mercy, was beatified by John Paul II on April 18, 1993. Now, the Pope wanted to make a point about both the third millennium and its predecessor by canonizing her as the first saint of the Great Jubilee of 2000.

The vast outdoor congregation in St. Peter's Square on April 30, 2000, was living testimony to the spread of the Divine Mercy devotion throughout the Catholic world. The presence of a large number of Polish pilgrims, including prime minister Jerzy Buzek, testified to the Polish character of the gift John Paul II intended to give the world through the canonization of Sister Faustyna: the gift of a renewed sense of God's mercy. The mercy of God, John Paul preached, comes to the world "through the heart of Christ crucified"; the reminder of that great truth came from "this humble daughter of Poland" who had received the vision of the king of divine mercy precisely between the First and Second World Wars. And, as John Paul said, "those who remember, who were witnesses and participants in the events of those years and the horrible suffering they caused for millions of people, know well how necessary was the message of divine mercy."

Thus Sister Faustyna's vision became "the bridge" to the third millennium from the last century of the second millennium: a "gift of special enlightenment that helps us live the Gospel of Easter more intensely, to offer it as a ray of light to the men and women of our time." No one knew what the years of the third millennium would bring, but it was "certain that in addition to new progress there will unfortunately be no lack of painful experiences." All the more need, then, for the "light of divine mercy, which the Lord in a way wished to return to the world through Sister Faustyna's charism," in order to "illumine the way for the men and women of the third millennium." Therefore, the Pope explained, the Second Sunday of Easter would henceforth be known as Divine Mercy Sunday, for John Paul wished to pass to the entire third millennium the message that had been entrusted to Sister Faustyna, now Saint Faustyna.

John Paul concluded his homily by returning to two themes that had been prominent throughout his pontificate. He had spoken frequently about the Law of the Gift—the law of self-giving—built into the human person; the Second Vatican Council's summary of this law, that "man can fully discover his true self only in a sincere giving of himself," had been one of the two most cited Vatican II texts in his magisterium. The Law of the Gift was not, however, easy to live. For "it is not easy to love with a deep love, which lies in the authentic gift of self. This love can only be learned by penetrating the mystery of God's love. Looking at him, being one with his fatherly heart, we are able to look with new eyes at our brothers and sisters, with an attitude of unselfishness and solidarity. All of this is mercy!" And the embrace of that mercy was essential if the third millennium were to be spared the worst experiences of the second:

> It is this love which must inspire humanity today, if it is to face the crisis of the meaning of life, the challenges of the most diverse needs, and, especially, the duty to defend the dignity of every human person. Thus the message of divine mercy is also implicitly **a message about the value of every human being.** Each person is precious in God's eyes; Christ gave his life for each one; to everyone the Father gives his Spirit and offers intimacy.
>
> This consoling message is addressed above all to those who, afflicted by a particularly harsh trial or crushed by the weight of the sins they have committed, have lost confidence in life and are tempted to give in to despair. To them the gentle face of Christ

is offered; those rays from his heart touch them and shine upon them, warm them, show them the way and fill them with hope.[1]

THE WITNESS OF MARTYRS

The canonization of St. Faustyna Kowalska was the first striking moment in the second phase of the Great Jubilee of 2000. The first period of the holy year focused on the history of salvation, with the Church's attention (and much of the world's) riveted on John Paul II's biblical pilgrimage to the places where God had come in search of man. The second period of the jubilee lifted up the imperative of Christian witness in the world. Its dramatic opening came a week after Faustyna's canonization, with the venue shifting from St. Peter's Square to the Roman Colosseum.

The veneration of martyrs lies at the deepest roots of Christian faith, consciousness, and practice. That the martyrs were understood to be crucial actors in the cosmic drama of salvation history is clear from the first century of the Christian era and St. John's vision in the Book of Revelation:

When he opened the fifth seal, I saw under the altar the souls of those who had been slain for the word of

God and for the witness they had borne; they cried out with a loud voice, "O Sovereign Lord, holy and true, how long before thou wilt judge and avenge our blood on those who dwell upon the earth?" Then they were each given a white robe and told to rest a little longer, until the number of their fellow servants and their brethren should be complete, who were to be killed as they themselves had been. [Revelation 6.9–11]

The number of martyrs "to be completed" increased exponentially in the twentieth century. Yet in countries where the practice of Christian faith involved neither pressures nor penalties nor threats, the idea of "martyrdom" was firmly located in the past—"martyrs" were people who had faced lions in the Roman arenas, not people "like us." From the beginning of his pontificate, John Paul II was determined to shake the Church, and especially the Church in the Western world, out of its complacency about the contemporary realities of martyrdom. This was a duty of justice to those who had died. It was also a reminder to the Church in the present that the martyr was the ideal of the Christian disciple, for the martyr had lived the Law of the Gift in the most radical way possible, and to the end. Thus John Paul lifted the tacit ban Pope Paul VI had placed on beatifying and canonizing martyrs from the Cristero uprising in Mexico in the 1920s and the Spanish Civil War; John Paul beatified and canonized those who had suffered death for the faith at Dachau, Auschwitz, Mauthausen, and Buchenwald, as well as martyrs who suffered in Tibet, Papua New Guinea, and Zaire; and he regularly referred to the ecumenism of martyrdom, for in death the martyrs of many Christian confessions had found a unity the Church was still denied in this world.[2]

The Great Jubilee seemed a fitting occasion to underscore the witness of the modern martyrs, which is why John Paul ordered that one of the concrete products of the jubilee year be a revised "Roman Martyrology": the authoritative catalogue of those whom the Church had honored by canonization or beatification. To that end a special commission on "new martyrs" was set up within the Central Committee for the Great Jubilee. Its president, Bishop Michel Hrynchyshyn, was a Canadian Redemptorist of Ukrainian parentage who lived in Paris and served as Apostolic Exarch for Ukrainians of the Byzantine-rite resident in France. The commission was given the formidable task of compiling a historically credible record of the "new martyrs" of our time—formidable, in no small part, because of the frequent anonymity of industrialized murder as committed by communists and Nazis.[3]

"Martyrdom" may not have been a prominent feature of the contemporary Catholic religious imagination in North America and western Europe, but the historical fact of the matter was that the twentieth century, the century of homicidal totalitarian

ideologies, had been the greatest century of martyrdom in two millennia: indeed, more Christians gave
their lives for Christ in the twentieth century than in
the previous nineteen centuries combined.[4] Bishop
Hrynchyshyn estimated that there had been perhaps
twenty-seven million twentieth-century martyrs,
two-thirds of the entire martyrology of the first two
millennia. Their heroic self-sacrifice was honored on
May 7, at a Commemoration of the Witnesses to
the Faith of the Twentieth Century, which was celebrated in the Roman Colosseum. The Commemoration took the form of an ecumenical Liturgy of the
Word, prior to which opening prayers were offered
by John Paul II (in Latin), Greek Orthodox Metropolitan Gennadios (in Greek), and the Rev. Dr.
Ishmael Noko of the Lutheran World Federation (in
English).

In his homily, John Paul immediately struck an ecumenical chord, stressing that "the witness to Christ
borne even to the shedding of blood has become a
common inheritance of Catholics, Orthodox, Anglicans, and Protestants." He then quoted the Russian
Orthodox Metropolitan Benjamin of St. Petersburg
on the eve of his execution in 1922—"The times have
changed and it has become possible to suffer much
for love of Christ"—and the Lutheran pastor Paul
Schneider's charge to his guards at Buchenwald—
"Thus says the Lord: 'I am the Resurrection and the
Life!'" These witnesses and millions of others had
proven that "love is stronger than death" in circum-

stances "where hatred seemed to corrupt the whole of life, leaving no escape from its logic." They had stood firm against "the cult of the false gods of the twentieth century"; pastors had died because, "like the Good Shepherd, they decided to remain with their people, despite intimidation"; women had died "to defend their dignity and purity"; indeed, "on every continent and throughout the entire twentieth century, there have been those who preferred to die rather than betray the mission that was theirs."

Why did the Church honor its contemporary martyrs? For the same reason it had honored its martyrs twenty centuries before: "If we glory in this heritage it is not because of any partisan spirit . . . but in order to make manifest the extraordinary power of God, who has not ceased to act in every time and place." Moreover the Church honored its martyrs by offering pardon, "faithful to the example of the countless witnesses killed even as they prayed for their persecutors." John Paul concluded with a prayer that the example of this "cloud of witnesses which surrounds us" would be the source of a "profound Christian renewal," the "leaven for bringing all Christ's disciples into full communion," and an aid to the Church in the third millennium so that the men and women of the twenty-first century and beyond might "express with no less courage our own love for Christ."[5]

While light rain fell, there were readings from a pan-Christian company of twentieth-century martyrs and confessors, including Tikhon, Patriarch of

Moscow, a martyr-confessor under communism; an Anglican bishop who had died in a Japanese concentration camp; Jolique Rusimbamigera, a seminarian from Burundi who survived massacres there, after praying for those who were killing Hutu and Tutsi seminarians who refused to be separated along tribal lines; W. G. R. Jotcham, a Canadian doctor and a Baptist, who had died while treating Muslim victims of a meningitis epidemic in Nigeria in 1938; Father Christian de Chergé, one of the martyred Trappists of Tibherin in Algeria, killed just four years earlier, in 1996. After each reading, a candle was lit before the Book of the Gospels. In all, 12,692 confessors and martyrs were recognized in eight categories: witnesses to the faith under Soviet totalitarianism; victims of communism in other nations of Europe; confessors under Nazism and fascism; Christians who gave their lives in Asia and Oceania; persecuted Catholics of Spain and Mexico; witnesses to the evangelization of Africa; confessors in the Americas; witnesses to the faith in various other parts of the world. The last category included John Paul II's friend, the Armenian Catholicos Karekin I.

The three-hour service ended with John Paul's prayer that God would continue to cherish all those who had died for the faith and, "in your infinite mercy, their persecutors as well."[6]

MARIAN WITNESS

Marian apparitions had been one of the most striking of Catholic spiritual phenomena in the nineteenth and twentieth centuries. The 1830 apparition
to Catherine Labouré at the convent of the Daughters of Charity on the Rue du Bac in Paris had given
Catholicism one of its most popular "sacramentals,"
the Miraculous Medal; its prescribed invocation, "O
Mary, conceived without sin, pray for us who have
recourse to thee," played a role in creating the conditions in popular piety necessary for the reception of
Pope Pius IX's dogmatic definition of the Immaculate Conception in 1854. The 1858 apparitions to
Bernadette Soubirous outside the village of Lourdes
in the French Pyrenees, during which Mary identified herself to the visionary with the words, "I am
the Immaculate Conception," gave world Catholicism its greatest center of healing, both physical and
spiritual. The 1917 apparitions at Fátima in Portugal, granted to three peasant children, had created a
major world pilgrimage site and were identified in
Catholic popular piety of the pre–Vatican II period
with the upheavals caused by the First World War,
including the rise of Bolshevism in Russia.[7]

John Paul II's Marian piety had long been psycho-
analyzed by the uncomprehending as displaced maternal affection following the death of his mother.[8]
The truth of the matter is that, by his own testi-

mony, Karol Wojtyła had become dissatisfied with the conventional Marian piety of his day by the time he left Wadowice for Kraków and the Jagiellonian University in 1938. It was during the war years that he was introduced to a more theologically sophisticated form of Marian devotion by the lay mystic Jan Tyranowski. In addition to lending Wojtyła books by the classic Spanish Carmelite mystics John of the Cross and Teresa of Ávila, Tyranowski gave the young day laborer and underground theater actor a copy of the seventeenth-century treatise on Marian piety, **True Devotion to Mary,** in which St. Louis Grignion de Montfort explains that all true Marian piety points toward Mary's son, Christ, and through Christ (who is both Son of God and son of Mary), to the Trinity: thus genuine Marian piety is both Christ-centered and Trinitarian. Wojtyła was persuaded, and later adopted the Montfortian slogan **Totus Tuus** [Entirely Yours] as the motto on his episcopal, and later papal, coat of arms.[9]

During his pontificate, John Paul II worked to revive Marian piety and give it a new theological depth—every first Saturday of the month, he led a recitation of the Rosary that was broadcast worldwide on Vatican Radio from the Paul VI Audience Hall—and to deepen the Church's understanding of Mary's role in salvation history and in the life of the Church. He devoted his sixth encyclical, **Redemptoris Mater** [The Mother of the Redeemer] to the subject and declared that the period between Pentecost 1987 and Pentecost 1988 would be celebrated throughout the Church as a special Marian Year. In a striking Christmas address to the Roman Curia in December 1987, the Pope, borrowing from the Swiss theologian Hans Urs von Balthasar, had suggested to some shocked senior churchmen that the "Marian profile" in the Church was prior to, and made sense of, the Church's "Petrine profile." Mary's **fiat,** John Paul said, had set the pattern of Christian discipleship, and the Petrine structure of the Church—its governance by the pope and the bishops—was intended primarily to foster discipleship, and indeed made no sense without discipleship.[10] No small part of John Paul's strategic purpose in deepening the theology of Marian piety was to give the Church materials with which to respond to the more aggressive forms of secular feminism with a positive vision of genuine liberation; thus he issued the apostolic letter **Mulieris Dignitatem** [The Dignity of Women] shortly after the close of the 1987–88 Marian Year.

The most dramatic episode in John Paul II's life of Marian piety came on May 13, 1981. To the Pope, there was nothing accidental about the fact that he had escaped death at the hands of a professional assassin on the day on which the Church liturgically honors Our Lady of Fátima. Mehmet Ali Agca had fired at point-blank range; but as John Paul later put it, "One hand fired, and another guided the bullet."[11] He had gone to Fátima a year later, in May 1982, to give thanks to the Virgin Mary for his life having been spared; one of the bullets from Agca's Browning 9-mm semiautomatic had been placed in the crown of the statue of Our Lady of Fátima. In May 1991, he was back in Fátima for the tenth anniversary of the assassination attempt, and on that occasion gave public thanks to the Blessed Mother for the liberation of east central Europe from communism.

And he would return once again, during the Great Jubilee, spending May 12 and 13 in Fátima. There, he beatified two of the three child-visionaries of the apparitions, Francisco and Jacinta Marto. At the end of the Mass, the Cardinal Secretary of State, Angelo Sodano, offered greetings in the name of all present to the Pope on his impending eightieth birthday, announced that John Paul had decided that it was now time to make public the so-called "third secret" of Fátima (about which there had been enormous, and often lurid, speculation for decades), and then read a statement approved by the Pope:

> [The] text contains a prophetic vision similar to those found in Sacred Scripture, which do not describe photographically the details of future events, but synthesize and compress against a single background facts which extend through time in an unspecified succession and duration. As a result, the text must be interpreted **in a symbolic key.**
>
> The vision of Fátima concerns above all the war waged by atheistic systems against the Church and

Christians, and it describes the immense suffering endured by the witnesses of the faith in the last century of the second millennium. It is an interminable **Way of the Cross** led by the popes of the twentieth century. . . .

The successive events of 1989 led, both in the Soviet Union and in a number of countries of Eastern Europe, to the fall of the communist regimes which promoted atheism. For this, too, His Holiness offers heartfelt thanks to the Most Holy Virgin. In other parts of the world, however, attacks against the Church and against Christians, with the burden of suffering they bring, tragically continue. Even if the events to which the third part of the "secret" of Fátima refer now seem part of the past, Our Lady's call to conversion and penance, issued at the start of the twentieth century, remains timely and urgent today . . . let us thank Our Lady of Fátima for her protection. To her maternal intercession let us entrust the Church of the Third Millennium.[12]

As Cardinal Sodano's announcement indicated, the vision in the third part of the "secret" involved a vast number of twentieth-century martyrdoms, including the shooting of a "bishop dressed in white." That John Paul II would have spiritually identified his own experience of May 13, 1981, with that of the "bishop dressed in white" was quite natural; yet it was also true that the decision to release the so-called "third secret" was intended to dampen down

some of the more dramatic forms of Catholic apocalypticism during the millennium year. In addition
to releasing the texts of the Fátima "secrets" and
the transcript of an interview conducted with the
surviving visionary, the ninety-three-year-old Sister
Maria Lúcia dos Santos, by the secretary of the Congregation for the Doctrine of the Faith, Archbishop
Tarcisio Bertone, S.D.B., in April 2000, the Vatican
also issued a "theological commentary" on the "third
secret" by CDF's prefect, Cardinal Joseph Ratzinger.
Like Sodano, Ratzinger stressed that the visions of
Fátima were not (as so often popularly misunderstood) a cinematic preview of impending events, a
"glimpse into a future which cannot be changed."
Rather, the visions were a call to conversion that
was meant "to bring freedom onto the scene and to
steer freedom in a positive direction." That freedom
should need redemption from its own follies ought
to have been a clear conclusion from the century just
past. Yet that was not the final word, as Ratzinger's
commentary concluded:

The heart open to God, purified by contemplation
of God, is stronger than guns and weapons of every
kind. The **fiat** of Mary, the word of her heart, has
changed the history of the world, because it brought
the Savior into the world—because, thanks to her
yes, God could become man in our world and remains so for all time. The Evil One has power in this
world, as we see and experience continually; he has

power because our freedom lets itself be led away from God. But since God himself took a human heart and has thus steered human freedom toward what is good, the freedom to choose evil no longer has the last word. From that time forth, the word that prevails is this: "In the world you will have tribulation, but take heart: I have overcome the world" [John 16.33]. The message of Fátima invites us to trust in this promise.[13]

The Marian aspect of the Great Jubilee took a scholarly form in September, when the twentieth International Marian-Mariological Congress met in Rome. After several days of papers being presented on various themes related to Mary's place in the history of salvation and in the contemporary life of the Church, the Congress concluded with Mass in St. Peter's Square on September 24. In his homily, John Paul preached on the special relationship of Mary, the Theotokos [Mother of God, or God-Bearer], to the three persons of the Holy Trinity, and concluded with an outline of authentic Marian devotion for the third millennium. Such devotion must be based on Scripture and Tradition; the popular piety arising from it must be rooted in the Church's liturgy; Marian devotion must express itself "**in an effort to imitate the All Holy** in a way of personal perfection"; and it must avoid every form of "**superstition and vain credulousness,**" especially in terms of Marian appearances, which were to be judged by the teaching authority of the Church. Above all, John Paul said, all true devotion to Mary "must **always . . . go back to the source of Mary's greatness,** becoming a ceaseless **Magnificat** of praise to the Father, to the Son, and to the Holy Spirit."[14]

PRIESTLY WITNESS

One of the more intriguing facets of Karol Wojtyła's personality was that this most priestly of priests—a man who had inspired thousands of young men to give their lives to Christ and the Church in the Catholic priesthood—had first intended to live his own Christian life as a layman. In **Gift and Mystery,** the vocational memoir he published in 1996 on the golden jubilee of his ordination, he reflected in a touching way on his struggle to achieve some measure of vocational clarity as a young man. That clarity came, not in a blinding flash, but in a slow process of discernment. At the same time, he was keenly aware of the influential people who had shaped his discernment, including his father (whose example, John Paul wrote, had been his "first seminary") and Jan Tyranowski. He also understood that the experience of the occupation had hammered him into a certain kind of priestly steel, strong yet supple, even as it had deepened in him the conviction that the priest should be a "leaven of fraternity" in a world desperately in need of solidarity.[15]

The priest, John Paul believed, was not somehow "above" the universal call to holiness. On the contrary: the priest was one with his people in living out that call. Yet the priest ought to live the call to holiness in a distinctive way, he wrote in the 1992 post-synodal apostolic exhortation, **Pastores Dabo Vobis** [I Will Give You Shepherds]. For the ordained priest, by reason of his ordination, participated in a unique way in the priesthood of Jesus Christ, becoming an **alter Christus,** a sacramental re-presentation of Christ himself. Ordination, as John Paul explained it, was far more than a matter of the Church's authorizing a man to conduct certain kinds of ecclesiastical business; Holy Orders "configured" a man to Christ in a radical way so that he could make a "total gift of **self to the Church.**"[16]

The specifically priestly form of witness in the Church and in the world was the witness of the Good Shepherd, John Paul taught. That Gospel image also specified the distinctive form of holiness that priests ought to embody, which the Pope called the holiness of "pastoral charity." That, in turn, meant that the spiritual "headship" that the priest exercised in a local Christian community was not the headship of power but of service—the service of one who spends out his life in the care of the sheep.[17]

John Paul II knew that the Catholic priesthood throughout the world was in crisis when he assumed the burden of the papacy. Since the Second Vatican Council, more priests had left the active ministry than at any time since the Reformation in the sixteenth century. The priesthood was aging throughout the Western world, and once full seminaries had been shut or were largely empty. The conventional explanations for this were Latin-rite Catholicism's tradition of priestly celibacy, and the antiauthoritarianism of postsixties Western culture. John Paul thought the problems of the priesthood in the last quarter of the twentieth century had deeper cultural roots. The often unconscious rationalism of late modernity had drained biblical revelation of its drama and often of its credibility, rendering it at best a noble fiction; yet if Christ was not, in truth, the Good Shepherd, why should an intelligent, able man offer himself to such a vocation? Then there was the radical individualism of late modernity, which made close relationships difficult and unleashed, in consequence, a frantic quest for pleasure and instant gratification. Even those young men who were believers were touched by the default atheism of much of Western public culture, which drained life of its mystery and reinforced the culture's tendency to encourage purely pragmatic decisions about life choices. And then there were those confusions of freedom with license and the will to power, both of which uncoupled freedom from truth and thereby rendered the notion of self-sacrifice a form of masochism.[18]

By giving a compelling personal example of priestly holiness, priestly witness, and priestly manliness in Rome and throughout the world, John Paul II had, at the very least, restored the morale of many Catholic priests. Theirs was a witness that the Pope especially wanted the Church to affirm during the Great Jubilee. So the **Jubilee of Priests** was set for May 18, 2000—John Paul's eightieth birthday—and was preceded by three days of celebrations of the priesthood in Rome. The program began on Sunday, May 14, with the solemn celebration of Vespers in the Basilica of St. Mary Major; earlier that day, John Paul II ordained twenty-six new priests on the World Day of Prayer for Vocations. On the morning of May 15, Lauds and Mass were celebrated for the **Jubilee of Priests** in the Basilica of St. John Lateran, followed by a conference in the Paul VI Audience Hall that afternoon on "The Priest: Minister of Hope, Epiphany of God among Men," led by the prefect of the Congregation for the Clergy, the Colombian cardinal Darío Castrillón Hoyos (who had once disguised himself as a milkman in order to confront drug kingpin Pablo Escobar and call him to repentance). On Tuesday, Lauds was celebrated at the Basilica of St. Paul Outside the Walls, followed by testimonies from priests from six continents. That evening, the Slovak cardinal Ján Chryzostom Korec, S.J. (who had spent years in communist prisons and work camps during his days as a clandestinely ordained underground priest and bishop) led a solemn Way of the Cross at the Circus Maximus, recalling the many priests who had suffered for the faith and for their vocations during the previous two millennia.

The greatest of the celebrations of the **Jubilee of Priests** took place on Thursday, May 18, when John Paul II led the largest concelebration of Mass in history, joined in St. Peter's Square by 6,000 priests, 74 cardinals and patriarchs, and 250 bishops. In his homily, the Pope remarked on the paradox that the sacramental gift of the priesthood had been bestowed on "so many frail men," a gift that "never ceases to amaze those who receive it." He looked back with "an intense need to praise and thank God for his immense goodness" in calling them all to the priesthood; and in that need to give thanks, he found himself carried back in memory "to the Upper Room in Jerusalem where, during my recent pilgrimage to the Holy Land, I was able to celebrate Holy Mass . . . in that place where my priesthood and yours arose from the mind and heart of Christ." There, he reminded his brothers in the priesthood, Christ wanted to give his priests a "share in the vocation and mission entrusted to him by the heavenly Father," not for the sake of honor but so that Christ's priests might "bring people into [the] universal mystery of salvation."

He was also thinking, he said, "of the priests who for different reasons no longer exercise their sacred ministry"—of those who had left the practice of the priesthood. They were, the Pope reminded them, still configured to Christ in a special way by "the indelible character of Holy Orders," and so he prayed for them, and invited the whole Church to join him in that prayer, so that these men "may continue to fulfill the commitment to Christian integrity and ecclesial communion."

He closed by challenging the priests present, and priests throughout the world, to give themselves with renewed devotion to their specific "way of holiness," which had been described in the First Letter of St. Peter: "to tend the flock God entrusted to us, not by constraint but willingly, not as domineering over those in our charge, but by setting them an example—a witness that, if necessary, can reach the point of shedding one's blood, as did many of our confrères in the century which has just ended." Then, this priest, bishop, and pope who had been formed in his ministry by the friendship of laypeople closed by asking the people of the Church to pray for the priests of the Church:

Pray for us . . . dear Christian people, who have gathered around us today in faith and joy. You are a royal people, a priestly race, a holy assembly. You are the People of God who, in every part of the earth, share in Christ's priesthood. Accept the gift which we renew today in the service of this, your special dignity. O priestly people, thank God with us for our ministry and sing with us to your Lord and ours: Praise to you, Lord Jesus Christ, for the gift of the priesthood! Grant that the Church of the new millennium may count on the generous work of many holy priests! Amen.[19]

The following day, Maestro Gilbert Levine, who had led a Holocaust Memorial Concert in the Paul VI Audience Hall in 1994, conducted the Philharmonia Orchestra and Chorus in a performance of Haydn's **The Creation** in the same **Aula Paolo VI,** in honor of the Pope's eightieth birthday. It brought to a close, the Pope said afterward, a "day that for me has been one of gratitude to the Lord for the inestimable gift of life and for the numerous graces with which he has wished to enrich my life." And there was yet another birthday present from another great artist, the Polish poet and Nobel laureate, Czesław Miłosz—an "Ode for the Eightieth Birthday of Pope John Paul II":

> We come to you, men of weak faith,
> So that you might fortify us with the example of your life
> And liberate us from anxiety
> About tomorrow and the next year. Your twentieth century
> Was made famous by the names of powerful tyrants
> And by the annihilation of their rapacious states.

You knew it must happen. You taught hope:
For only Christ is the lord and master of history.

Foreigners could not guess from whence came the
hidden strength
Of a novice from Wadowice. The prayers and
prophecies
Of poets, whom money and progress scorned,
Even though they were the equals of kings, waited
for you
So that you, not they, could announce **urbi et
orbi,**
That the centuries are not absurd but a vast order.

Shepherd given us when the gods depart!
In the fog above the cities the Golden Calf shines,
The defenseless crowds race to offer the sacrifice
Of their own children to the bloody screams of
Moloch.
In the air, fear, a lament without words:
Since a desire for faith is not the same as faith.

Then, suddenly, like the clear sound of the bell
for matins,
Your sign of dissent, which is like a miracle.
People ask, not comprehending, how it's possible
That the young of the unbelieving countries
Gather in the public square, shoulder to shoulder,
Waiting for the news from two thousand years ago

And throw themselves at the feet of the Vicar
Who embraced with his love the whole human
tribe.

You are with us and will be with us henceforth.
When the forces of chaos raise their voice
And the owners of truth lock themselves in
churches
And only the doubters remain faithful,
Your portrait in our homes every day reminds us
How much one man can accomplish and how
sainthood works.[20]

A week after the pope's birthday, on May 25, the
heroic witness of which Miłosz wrote was back at
the center of the Great Jubilee, as John Paul II canonized St. Cristóbal Magallanes and his twenty-four
companions, martyrs of modern Mexico during the
Cristero revolt against Mexican anticlericalism in the
late 1920s. Father Magallanes had a special devotion to the evangelization of the indigenous Huichol
people, and before being shot without a trial, forgave his executioners, gave them his few possessions,
and offered them sacramental absolution. He died
on May 21, 1927, praying for the unity of Mexico
and the reconciliation of its people.

FAITH AND REASON, THE EUCHARIST, AND THE YOUNG

At the **Jubilee of Scientists** on May 25, John Paul returned to another theme that had provided a connecting thread throughout his pontificate: the relationship of faith and reason. Citing his 1998 encyclical on that subject, **Fides et Ratio,** the Pope reminded the men and women "of the world of learning and research" that "faith is not afraid of reason," for the two "are like two wings on which the human spirit rises to the contemplation of truth." And to seek the truth was to seek that which bore the imprint of God in man: for God had "placed in the human heart a desire to know the truth—in a word, to know himself—so that, by knowing and loving God, men and women may also come to the fullness of truth about themselves." That was why Christianity was at the foundation of the "scientific culture" of the West: Christian faith in the "knowability" of the world reflected the Christian conviction that the world had been created through the Logos, the Word, the very "reason," of God, which had left an imprint of rationality "in every part of the universe."[21]

To be sure, there had been shadows in the Church's relationship with science, shadows into which John Paul had tried to shed the light of historical research—as in his 1992 recognition that some churchmen of the time had erred in judging Galileo's defense of the Copernican view of the universe incompatible with biblical revelation. Science and theology, John Paul had said then, were "two realms of knowledge" that ought not regard each other as locked in an inevitable confrontation.[22] The Church understood that; the new question was whether science did. Thus the Pope raised a caution flag about a scientific method that, generalized throughout society, accustomed the men and women of late modernity to "a culture of suspicion and doubt." A science that "refused to consider the existence of God or to view man in the mystery of his origin and his end, as if this perspective might call science itself into question," was a science that was, finally, antihumanistic, in that it inevitably "estranged science from man and from the service it is called to offer him." Therefore, he asked those "in the trenches of research and progress" to "let your minds be open to the horizons that faith discloses to you" so that "in constantly exploring the world's mysteries," scientists might be "builders of hope for all humanity."[23]

Late May, June, and early July of the holy year continued the now familiar rhythm of special jubilee celebrations: the **Jubilee of the Diocese of Rome** on May 28, the **Jubilee of Migrants and Itinerants** on June 2, the **Jubilee of Journalists** on June 4. On June 13, the Italian government announced an amnesty for the would-be papal assassin, Mehmet Ali Agca, who was immediately taken to prison in Turkey for crimes committed there. John Paul thanked the Italian government for this jubilee gesture, shortly before sending a jubilee message to prisoners throughout the world on June 24; he then embodied that message of hope by celebrating Mass in Rome's Regina Coeli prison on July 9.[24] On June 15, the Pope hosted a lunch for 200 poor people in the Paul VI Audience Hall and exchanged gifts with them; the guests were chosen by the Sant'Egidio Community, the Caritas organization of the Diocese of Rome, and the "Gift of Mary" guesthouse for the homeless that John Paul II had built in the Vatican and staffed with Mother Teresa's Missionaries of Charity. The lunch, John Paul believed, was a necessary act of hospitality in preparation for the forty-seventh International Eucharistic Congress, which was held in Rome from June 18 through June 25; as usual, the Pope's favorites were the children who scampered throughout the **pranzo,** playing in front of the Pope's table.

The International Eucharistic Congress was intended to underscore the truth that the Church celebrated in each Mass as "the mystery of faith." As John Paul put it succinctly, "Christ—one Lord yesterday, today, and forever—willed to leave his salvific presence in the world and in history to the sacrament of the Eucharist. He willed to make himself the bread that is broken so that every man might be nourished in his own life by his participation in the sacrament of Christ's body and blood."[25] And in this sacrament, he preached in his homily for the closing **Statio Orbis** Mass in St. Peter's Square on June 25, all the people of the Church would find new vigor in their unique apostolic and missionary vocations: the sick would find patience amidst trials; spouses would be strengthened in fidelity to their love; those in consecrated life would find the courage to live their vows; children would learn to be strong and generous; and the young, in whom he reposed such hope, would find the way to take responsibility for the future.

That closing challenge to the young was the bridge to the next epic event of the Great Jubilee, the fifteenth World Youth Day, held in Rome from August 15 through August 20. In a year of spectacular displays of Catholic faith, this was perhaps the most stunning. For by bringing more than two million young people to Rome from every corner of the globe, World Youth Day-2000 became the largest pilgrimage in European history.

The previous seven international celebrations of World Youth Day over which John Paul II had presided had made this dramatic innovation a regular part of the rhythm of global Catholic life. John Paul's own experience as a university chaplain had convinced him that young people would respond to a challenge to lead lives of spiritual and moral heroism. And while it would be naive to suggest that everyone who attended a World Youth Day event became a thoroughly converted Christian, it would also be foolish to ignore just how much these events had already begun to contribute to the new evangelization of which the Pope had spoken so urgently for a decade and a half.

In the first instance, the very experience of a World Youth Day told young people who may have been shaky or nervous in their faith that they were not alone: they had companions "on the way," and those companions were much like them. Intense catechesis of the participants in World Youth Days certainly made a contribution to filling the catechetical gap that had too often followed Vatican II—even as it convinced bishops (who were always the catechists at World Youth Days) that they could in fact speak meaningfully to young people. In the age of the Internet and cell phones, World Youth Days also made it possible for self-organizing networks of young Catholics to form and sustain themselves across geographic barriers that might once have seemed insurmountable. As for the specific genius of World Youth Day-2000, the historically minded had to be impressed by the fact that, after a century of violence, hundreds of thousands of young men and women were marching through Europe as Christian pilgrims rather than as armies.

World Youth Day-2000 was also an integral part of the re-evangelization of Rome, which, for all its self-consciousness as the center of the Catholic world, has also tended over the centuries to wear its Catholicism somewhat lightly, and at times even cynically.

That had begun to turn around with John Paul's relentless efforts to recatechize Rome, which he had undertaken from the beginning of the pontificate; by 2000, the Pope had personally visited almost 300 Roman parishes, celebrating Mass on Sunday and preaching. His vicar for Rome, Cardinal Camillo Ruini, a man with a cast of mind very similar to John Paul's, had launched in the late 1990s a "Mission to the City," which, among other things, distributed innumerable copies of the Gospel of St. Mark throughout Rome's neighborhoods.

Still, it was the witness of the young themselves, in August 2000, that made the biggest difference to Romans who prided themselves on a certain skepticism about public protestations of piety. No one, however jaded, could be cynical at the sight of tens of thousands of young people queuing up politely to pass through the Holy Door of St. Peter's; or standing in lines at the outdoor confessionals set up in the Circus Maximus (which had been transformed into a great, open-air church); or coming in the millions on a stiflingly hot Sunday to the World Youth Day's closing Mass in the suburbs at Tor Vergata. Even the Roman cabdrivers, usually inured to pilgrims, were impressed; as one veteran of the madness that is cab driving in the Eternal City remarked, with a voice full of wonder, the crowds certainly didn't behave like this at rock concerts or soccer games. Even Italy's premier newspaper of the Left, **La Repubblica,** which had not been overly gracious to John Paul II over the years, conceded that "the wall between agnostics and Catholics fell at Tor Vergata."[26]

Housing these vast crowds was, to put it gently, a challenge; the Pope did his bit by hosting fifteen youngsters at the papal summer villa at Castel Gandolfo. One afternoon during their stay, they found themselves at lunch with John Paul, eating tomato fettuccine, roast pork, and zucchini while swapping jokes, stories, and prayers in English, French, Italian, Polish, and Portuguese. The Pope was given a Toronto Maple Leafs jersey by a Canadian youngster, Roger Gudino, which got the pontiff to reminiscing about his own hockey-playing days in Wadowice— a subject unlikely to have come up at any previous papal lunch in the history of the Western world's oldest continuous institution.

Yet those who thought John Paul's magnetism for the young was a form of celebrity worship were brought up short once again when, at the closing Mass at Tor Vergata on August 20, the Pope laid down a demanding challenge to his young followers, who had come from 159 countries. He took his sermon text from Jesus's question to his disciples—"Will you also go away?"—and from Peter's response: "Lord, to whom shall we go? You have the words of eternal life" (John 6.67–68). That was not just a question for an itinerant band of Jews 2,000 years ago, John Paul said. It was a question for today: "it challenges us personally and it demands a decision." And the decision was the most important that anyone could make, for Christ alone was "capable of satisfying the deepest aspirations of the human heart." Why was that the case? Because of the unconditional, radical love of Christ for every human being: "Christ loves us and he loves us forever! **He loves us even when we disappoint him,** when we fail to meet his expectations for us. He never fails to embrace us in his mercy." And that, too, posed a challenge: "How can we not be grateful to this God who has redeemed us? . . . To God who has come to be at our side and who stayed with us to the end?"

From someone else, these might have been dismissed as easy pieties. But those two million young people at Tor Vergata knew, or at least intuited, that here was a man who was not asking them to do anything he had not done himself, to bear any burden he had not borne, to take any chance that he had not taken. Indeed, he had admitted the difficulty of modern belief the night before, in the candlelight vigil that always precedes the closing Mass of World Youth Day: "Is it hard to believe in the third millennium? **Yes! It is hard. There is no need to hide it.**" But they were not alone. The Christ who, at Calvary, had taken all the world's fear, confusion, and doubt on himself, was waiting for them, whether they knew it or not:

It is Jesus in fact you seek when you dream of happiness; he is waiting for you when nothing else satisfies you; he is the beauty to which you are so attracted; it is he who provokes you with that thirst for fullness that will not let you settle for compromise; it is he who urges you to shed the masks of a false life; it is he who reads in your hearts your most genuine choices, the choices that others try to stifle. It is Jesus who stirs in you the desire to do something great with your lives, the will to follow an ideal, the refusal to allow yourselves to be ground down by mediocrity.

Let Christ take over your lives, John Paul concluded, and the world will never be the same: "If you are what you should be, you will set the whole world ablaze!"[27]

THE UNIQUENESS OF CHRIST

The Great Jubilee of 2000, and Pope John Paul II, paused for a break in July of the millennium year. The Pope returned to the two-story chalet he had used previously in Les Combes, in the Italian Alps of the Val d'Aosta, for a summer vacation that lasted from July 10 until July 22. The weather was trying, but mountains had always fired Karol Wojtyła's poetic and spiritual imagination, and the Pope enjoyed looking out a large picture window at the striking scenery. On his last day in Les Combes, the Pope celebrated Mass with the bishop and priests of the Diocese of Aosta, on the liturgical memorial of St. Mary Magdalene. The day's first reading, from 2 Corinthians, spoke of the minister of Christ being compelled by the love of Christ to proclaim that Christ's saving death had been "for all." That same compulsion had inspired Mary Magdalene, in what the Pope called "a race of the heart and the spirit," to travel the long path from sin to conversion to Calvary, and ultimately to the empty tomb—a journey that was paradigmatic for all of Christ's disciples. Thus every Christian believer, but especially those ordained to the apostolate, must find in their personal encounter with the Risen Christ "a new way of living no longer for ourselves, but for him who died and rose for us."[28]

On August 29, John Paul addressed an international congress of the Transplantation Society, then being held in Rome. Describing organ transplants as "a great step forward in science's service to man," so long as organs were donated with "informed consent," the Pope nonetheless proposed that "certain critical issues" required clarification. Foremost among these was the proposal, being bruited in some quarters, to clone human beings as a source of transplantable organs. That, John Paul said, was "morally unacceptable, even when [its] proposed goal is good in itself." The Pope also condemned international organ trafficking, while reiterating the Church's acceptance of xenotransplantation, or the transfer of animal organs to human beings, as long as the recipient was not harmed physically nor psychologically.[29]

Christianity's founding conviction about the unique saving work of Christ was the source of the most controversial episode of the jubilee year: the publication on September 5, 2000, of a Declaration from the Congregation for the Doctrine of the Faith, entitled **Dominus Iesus** [The Lord Jesus], which addressed "The Unicity and Salvific Universality of Jesus Christ and the Church." The language of the subtitle may not have been the most elegant English, but the meaning was plain enough: the Congregation often described in the world media as the Catholic Church's "doctrinal watchdog" (and not infrequently as "the successor to the Inquisition") was underscoring two points that belonged to the deposit of faith and were not subject to change: that Jesus Christ is the one, unique, and universal savior, and that the one Church founded by Christ exists in its fullest and most complete form in the Catholic Church.

Dominus Iesus was written in response to theological speculations that seemed to challenge both of these points. Asian theologians, and Western theologians working in Asia, were trying to develop a theory of salvation that acknowledged some supernatural value in the great Asian religions such as Buddhism and Hinduism, not just natural spiritual or moral value. Ecumenical theologians, by no means confined to Asia, were interpreting two of the Second

Vatican Council's statements—that the one Church of Christ "subsists in" the Catholic Church, and that "elements of sanctification and truth" exist in Christian communities not in full communion with the Catholic Church—to assert a kind of ecclesiological equivalence among Christian communities.[30] The Asian speculations were of interest to Christian communities beyond the boundaries of the Catholic Church, especially those evangelical Protestant communities that insisted on the uniqueness of the salvation wrought by Christ. As for the ecumenical dialogue, at least some of the Catholic Church's bilateral ecumenical dialogue partners took offense at the declaration's statement that "ecclesial communities that have not preserved the valid Episcopate and the integral substance of the Eucharistic mystery"— meaning all Protestants—are not Churches in the proper sense (as the Orthodox Churches, despite their denial of the primacy of the pope, are).

In the general atmosphere of ecumenical and interreligious good feeling surrounding the Great Jubilee of 2000, it was perhaps inevitable that **Dominus Iesus** would be interpreted by some as spoiling the party—perhaps deliberately. The Reverend Ellen Wondra, an Anglican involved in the Catholic-Anglican dialogue, dismissed **Dominus Iesus** as "part of the era of mutual polemics among churches rather than an era of reconciliation and greater communion." A Lutheran ecumenist, Michael Root, took a similar view, suggesting that the declaration put the Catholic-Lutheran dialogue "back where we were thirty years ago."[31] The mainstream media, never given to theological nuance, was even more critical: the **Los Angeles Times** fundamentally misrepresented the teaching of **Dominus Iesus** in a page-one headline, "Vatican Declares Catholicism Sole Path to Salvation," while another newspaper ran a cartoon of John Paul II, with arms raised, under the caption "We're Number One!"

Anyone who took the trouble to read **Dominus Iesus** found in it, not arrogance or aggression, but rather a humble confession of Catholic faith: that there is only one true God, and thus there is only one "economy" of salvation; that if Jesus is Lord— true God and true man—he is Lord of all, not only of those who recognize his lordship; that the God who wishes all to come to the truth and be saved does not deny the grace necessary for salvation to anyone; that all who are saved are saved through the redemption effected by Jesus Christ, whether they have heard of Christ or not; that there is only one Church of Christ (for the Church is the Body of Christ and Christ does not have multiple bodies); that the Catholic Church, which readily recognizes the grace of God at work outside its boundaries, nonetheless understands itself to be the fullest expression in history of the one Church of Christ; and that the Church has an ongoing, never to be abandoned mandate to proclaim Christ through its missionary activity.

Those who expected the Catholic Church to present itself as one consumer option in a supermarket of religious possibilities were thus mistaken. Some (including some Christian ecumenists who had long since abandoned any notion of the ecclesial distinctiveness of their communities) were doubtless disappointed, even angered. But whatever the expectations of those who imagined ecumenism and interreligious dialogue to be a conversation over matters of taste and lifestyle rather than matters of truth, **Dominus Iesus** "fit," if in a challenging way, within the Great Jubilee of 2000. For this was not a jubilee celebrating some generic possibility of salvation, but a holy year lifting up the core Christian conviction that, in the incarnation, life, death, and resurrection of Jesus Christ, the salvation of the world had been achieved in a definitive and unsurpassable way.

In his Angelus remarks on October 1 after the canonization of Saint Augustine Zhao Rong and his 199 Companions (martyrs in China), Saint Katherine Drexel (the Philadelphia heiress who founded a religious order devoted to work with African-Americans and Native Americans), Saint María Josefa del Corazón de Jesús Sancho de Guerra (the first Basque saint), and Saint Josephine Bakhita (a former Sudanese slave), John Paul II tried to end Italian press speculation about a rift between himself and CDF prefect Cardinal Joseph Ratzinger, while meeting the charge of "arrogance" head-on.[32] In words tinged with ecumenical challenge, the Pope said that **Dominus Iesus** had been "approved by me in a special way at the height of the Jubilee Year" in order to "invite all Christians to renew their fidelity to [Christ] . . . to bear unanimous witness that the Son, both today and tomorrow, is 'the way, the truth, and the life' " (John 14.6). To confess Christ as "the only Son through whom we . . . see the Father's face" was not an act of "arrogance that disdains other religions." Rather, it was a joyful—and humbling—acknowledgment that "Christ has revealed himself to us without any merit on our part." Moreover, to have been encountered by Christ was to have undertaken an obligation: "to continue giving what we have received and to communicate to others what we have been given, since the Truth that has been given and the Love which is God belong to all people."

As for the interreligious controversy following **Dominus Iesus,** John Paul was equally firm: to proclaim, with the apostle Peter in Acts 4, that "there is no salvation in anyone else" but Christ "does not deny salvation to non-Christians, but points to its ultimate source in Christ, in whom God and man are united." This should not be an obstacle to genuine interreligious dialogue, just as the Catholic Church's frank statement of its self-understanding as the fullest expression of the one Church of Christ ought not be an impediment to ecumenical dialogue. For **Dominus Iesus** to have clarified these "essential elements" of Catholic faith ought to help make genuine dialogue possible by showing the "bases" of a true conversation; for a "dialogue without foundations," John Paul continued, "would . . . degenerate into empty wordiness." **Dominus Iesus,** despite "so many erroneous interpretations," expressed the "same ecumenical passion" that John Paul himself had stressed in his 1995 encyclical **Ut Unum Sint** [That They May Be One], and the same convictions about the imperative of interreligious tolerance and respect that had motivated his encounters with the world religions throughout his pontificate. Thus the Pope prayed that "this Declaration, which is close to my heart, can . . . finally fulfill its function both of clarification and of openness. May Mary, whom the Lord on the Cross entrusted to us as the mother of all, help us to grow together in our faith in Christ, the Redeemer of mankind, in the hope of salvation offered by Christ to everyone, and in love, which is the sign of God's children."[33]

John Paul II continued to lift up the sanctity of heroic witness to Christ throughout the remaining months of the Great Jubilee. His September 3 beatification of two popes, Pius IX (who reigned from 1846 to 1878) and John XXIII (who had summoned Vatican II), led some of the Pope's Catholic critics to complain that he was trying to take the edge off Pius IX, who had issued the **Syllabus of Errors,** by linking him to "Good Pope John." The charge ignored the fact that John XXIII—whatever he may have thought of Pius's entanglements with nineteenth-century Italian politics and the intellectual ferment of his times—had himself wished to beatify Pius IX, whom he regarded as a man of heroic virtue and pastoral courage. John Paul II, for his part, explained in his beatification homily that for the Church to honor a deceased pope by beatification or canonization is not necessarily to "celebrate the specific historical decisions" a pope may have made, but to acknowledge him as "someone to be imitated **because of his virtues.**" Like everyone else, John Paul reminded the congregation that day, popes live in history and so does sanctity: "**holiness lives in history** and no saint can escape the limits and conditioning that are part of our human nature."[34]

LEAVING THE SHALLOWS, SETTING OFF "INTO THE DEEP"

Every night during the Great Jubilee, a special Vespers service was held in St. Peter's Square for the pilgrims who kept flocking to Rome from all over the world. In the fall and winter of 2000, the vocational jubilee days unfolded with a similar regularity: there were jubilees for university professors (September 9), for papal diplomatic representatives (September 15), for the elderly (September 17), and for bishops (October 8). The **Jubilee of Bishops** was originally intended to be part of a holy year Synod of Bishops, but the Pope was finally persuaded that it would be more prudent to move that meeting, which would consider the bishop's role in the evangelization of the third millennium, to 2001. During the bishops' jubilee, which was the largest gathering of the Catholic episcopate since the Second Vatican Council, John Paul II once again entrusted the world to the Virgin Mary in a public act of consecration in which the 1,500 bishops and 80 cardinals present joined.

History did not stop for the jubilee year, of course; in a preview of more lethal acts to come, the USS **Cole** was attacked by al-Qaeda suicide bombers in the harbor of Aden on October 12, four days before Queen Elizabeth II and the Duke of Edinburgh visited with John Paul II in the Vatican. And still the vocational jubilees continued, with the seemingly indefatigable Pope addressing each one: the **Jubilee of Families** was held on October 14, the **Jubilee of the World of Sports** on October 29, and the **Jubilee of Government Leaders and Politicians** (to whom John Paul gave St. Thomas More as a special patron) on November 4. John Paul then hosted the Armenian Catholicos, Karekin II, for three days (November 8–10) before the special jubilee days began again: farmers (November 12); the armed forces and police (November 19); the lay apostolate (November 26); the disabled (December 3); catechists (December 10); and finally the entertainment world (December 17). At the Sunday Angelus of December 17, the Pope appealed for a worldwide abolition of the death penalty, an appeal rooted in his teaching in the 1995 encyclical on the life issues, **Evangelium Vitae** [The Gospel of Life].[35]

A week after the entertainers had their jubilee day, John Paul began the second Christmas of the Great Jubilee by reminding the congregation at Christmas Midnight Mass in the Vatican basilica that it had been a year since that "unforgettable night . . . when the Holy Door of the Great Jubilee was opened" and "the Door of grace opened wide for all." For twelve months, it had been "as if the Church had never ceased to repeat day after day. . . . '**Today is born our Savior.**'" That proclamation, which was at the center of the jubilee's meaning and message, had an "inexhaustible power to renew" the Church and the world, for the holiness of Christ had "made all time holy: the days, the centuries, the millennia," and had done so "once and for all." At the birth of Christ, time had been turned "into the 'today' of salvation."[36]

That continuous "today" would be lived in many tomorrows. And so at the end of the Great Jubilee of 2000, John Paul II, rather than looking nostalgically back on the past—even the extraordinary immediate past of the jubilee year—determined to point the Church firmly into the future.

The Great Jubilee was solemnly concluded on January 6, 2001, as the Pope, vested in a white cope, knelt in the portal for a moment of prayer, as he had done on December 24, 1999—and then drew closed the two bronze panels of the Holy Door at St. Peter's. A procession led by the Book of the Gospels then left the basilica for the **sagrato,** the esplanade in front of St. Peter's, where John Paul led a concelebrated Mass for the Solemnity of the Epiphany, which was attended by a congregation that completely filled the square and spilled down the Via della Conciliazione. The Pope built his homily around the responsorial psalm in the day's liturgy: "All the peoples of the earth will adore you, O Lord!" That messianic hope, John Paul said, had its first fulfillment when the gentile Magi came to adore the Christ child at Bethlehem, which marked the "beginning of the manifestation of Christ—his 'epiphany' precisely—to those who represented the peoples of the world." That all the peoples of the earth would adore the Lord was also a prophecy "being fulfilled by degrees in the course of time." It was being fulfilled, for example, through the Great Jubilee, during which "countless individuals . . . set out in the footsteps of the Wise Men in search of Jesus . . . the true 'holy Door' [who] makes it possible for us to enter the Father's house and who introduces us into the intimacy of the divine life."

The Holy Door had been closed, but "the Heart of Jesus remains more open than ever," John Paul continued. In gratitude to God for that openness and for allowing all those who participated in the Great Jubilee to experience "the happiness which filled the Wise Men . . . as they [placed] at the Child's feet not only their gifts but their lives," a solemn **Te Deum** would be sung at the end of the day's Mass. Yes, there was much for which to be thankful. But now, the Pope insisted, "it is time to look to the future, for, like the Wise Men, the Church must "start out afresh on a new stage of the journey on which we become proclaimers and heralds." What had been freely received must now be freely given away. That was how the Church would "become in history a true **epiphany** of the merciful and glorious face of Christ the Lord."[37]

At the end of the ceremony John Paul II signed a new apostolic letter, **Novo Millennio Ineunte,** which addressed the entire Church on the themes of its title: "Entering the Third Millennium." Like its 1994 bookend, **Tertio Millennio Adveniente, Novo Millennio Ineunte** was both a lyrical reflection on time and faith and a bold prescription for future pastoral action throughout the world Church.

The Church of the third millennium, John Paul began, could not rest in the shallows of institutional maintenance. Rather, it had to obey Christ's command to his disciples, to "put out into the deep" for a catch (Luke 5.4). That command in its Latin form, **Duc in altum,** was the antiphon woven throughout the Pope's letter, which, while reflecting on many of the major events of the jubilee year, was primarily a challenge to the entire Church "to take up [the] evangelizing mission with fresh enthusiasm."[38] That, indeed, had been one of the primary purposes of both Vatican II and the Great Jubilee: to point the Church into a future that "mirrors **the movement of the Incarnation itself,**" for the impact of that axial moment in history continues down the corridors of time and in every place.[39]

That was why the Church's first duty was the duty of praise—"the point of departure for every genuine response of faith to the revelation of God in Christ." And the Church's praise arises from the Church's continuing experience in history of the profligacy of God's love: "Christianity is grace, it is the wonder of a God who is not satisfied with creating the world and man, but puts himself on the same level as the creature he has made and, after speaking on various occasions and in various ways through his prophets, 'in these last days . . . has spoken to us by a Son'" (Hebrews 1.1–2). Thus the Great Jubilee had been a protracted meditation on the holy face of Christ, who shows us both the countenance of the Father and the truth about our own humanity—and is thus "confessed as the meaning of history and the light of life's journey."[40]

The holy face of Christ, John Paul continued, was what had drawn so many pilgrims to Rome and to the Holy Door that had been one of the jubilee's focal points:

I have often stopped to look at the long queues of pilgrims waiting patiently to go through the Holy

Door. In each of them I tried to imagine the story of a life, made up of joys, worries, sufferings; the story of someone whom Christ had met and who, in dialogue with him, was setting out again on a journey of hope.

As I observed the continuous flow of pilgrimages, I saw them as a kind of **concrete image of the pilgrim Church,** the Church placed, as Saint Augustine says, "amid the persecutions of the world and the consolations of God." . . . Who can measure the marvels of grace wrought in the human heart? It is better to be silent and to adore, trusting humbly in the mysterious workings of God and singing his love without end: **"Misericordias Domini in aeternum cantabo"** [I shall sing the mercy of the Lord forever].[41]

To contemplate the face of Christ—"Christ considered in his historical features and in his mystery"—was not a call to quietism, however: for "in the cause of the Kingdom, there is no time for looking back."[42] Therefore, the postjubilee Church must place itself in the position of those who heard Peter's first sermon and asked, "What must we do?" (Acts 2.37). In answering that question, there was need for neither formula nor program, for "we shall not be saved by a formula but by a person," and "the program already exists": to bring others to Christ, "so that in him we may live the life of the Trinity, and with him transform history until its fulfillment in the heavenly Jerusalem. . . . This program for all times is our program for the Third Millennium."[43]

If there was no "new program" to be announced, there were nonetheless pastoral priorities to be suggested. The first of these was holiness:

[S]ince Baptism is a true entry into the holiness of God through incorporation into Christ and the indwelling of his spirit, it would be a contradiction to settle for a life of mediocrity, marked by a minimalist ethic and a shallow religiosity. To ask catechumens, "Do you wish to receive Baptism?" means at the same time to ask them: "Do you wish to become holy?" It means to set before them the radical nature of the Sermon on the Mount: "Be perfect as your heavenly Father is perfect" [Matthew 5.48].[44]

Holiness, in other words, was the "**standard of ordinary Christian life.**" All were called to it; no one was exempt; no one was permitted to be mediocre. That fact of Christian life led to the second pastoral priority: prayer, the reciprocal conversation with Christ that was "the condition of all true pastoral life." Christian communities ought therefore to be schools of prayer that did not "distract us from our commitment to history" but rather made the Church "capable of shaping history according to God's plan." In that school of prayer, the Christians of the early third millennium ought to recover the spiritual habits of regular Sunday Mass attendance and frequent confession of sins—the latter being a practice that pastors should present "with more confidence, creativity, and perseverance."[45]

From those schools of prayer, the entire Church should set out into the deep on mission and evangelization. Mission, the Pope insisted, "cannot be left to a group of 'specialists' but must involve the responsibility of all the members of the People of God."[46] That responsibility was exercised, in the first instance, by the people of the Church demonstrating by the quality of their own lives that the Church is indeed a "communion of love," a love "which springs from the heart of the Eternal Father and is poured out upon us through the Spirit which Jesus gives us . . . to make us all 'one heart and one soul'" (Acts 4.32). By building this communion of love, "the Church appears as 'sacrament,' as the 'sign and instrument of intimate union with God and of the unity of the human race.'"[47] And, as such, the Church is in a position to add a distinctive voice to the dialogue on the hard questions of the immediate future: the defense of the right to life and other fundamental human rights; the quest for peace; the management of scientific knowledge so that it enhances rather than degrades life.[48] In addressing these and other issues, the "communion of love" that is the Church works best, the Pope wrote, through a charity that "will . . . become a service to culture, politics, the economy, and the family," always building the culture of life on which depend "the destiny of human beings and the future of civilization."[49] At the same time, and toward the same ends, the Church as a communion of love will foster an interreligious dialogue that does not descend into "religious indifferentism" but which bears witness to "the hope that is within us" by "**a profound willingness to listen.**"[50] That principle held true, not only in interreligious dialogue and ecumenism, but for the Christian dialogue with culture and science. Differences were real; genuine tolerance and a willingness to listen led to differences engaged respectfully, not differences ignored.

At the end of the Great Jubilee, John Paul concluded, the Church could not turn from "enthusiasm" to "a dull everyday routine." For if the pilgrimage of the Great Jubilee of 2000 had been a genuine walk with God, then "it will have . . . stretched our legs for the journey still ahead."[51]

Five weeks before he signed **Novo Millennio Ineunte,** John Paul II told a lunch guest that the response to the Great Jubilee had "exceeded my expectations completely."[52] At the end of the meal, the Pope could be found in his private chapel— appropriately enough, for in a true sense he had prayed the entire Church through the Great Jubilee of 2000. His dreams of a celebration of the two thousandth anniversary of the Incarnation had been met with skepticism at first from those to whom he might have normally looked for enthusiastic support. Yet he had persevered, because of his faith and because of his conviction that the Church ought to think of itself, as in apostolic times, as being a mission, not having a mission. That mission was at once evangelical and humanistic: for if Christ was in fact the key to man and to human history, then a deepened encounter with Christ would lead to what he had called at the United Nations in 1995 a "new springtime of the human spirit." That had been the message of the pontificate for twenty-three years; that had been the message of the Great Jubilee of 2000: Christ is the key to the mystery of humanity and its destiny.

Among many other things, the Great Jubilee of 2000 had been a yearlong demonstration of the extraordinary diversity of the Catholic world. There had been national pilgrimages to Rome from Bosnia-Herzegovina, Colombia, the Czech Republic, Estonia, Greece, Guatemala, Hungary, Lithuania, Mexico, Mozambique, the Netherlands, Poland, Romania, Senegal, Slovakia, Slovenia, Switzerland, Uruguay, and Venezuela. There had been diocesan pilgrimages from all over the world, with virtually every Italian diocese celebrating a special jubilee pilgrimage to Rome. In addition to the vocational jubilee days, which underscored the striking plurality of ways in which the Christian life was being lived, other organized pilgrimage groups came from a remarkable diversity of occupations, hobbies, and communities: campers, Cursillo veterans, devotees of St. Rita of Cascia ("the saint of the impossible"), doctors, firemen, Italian municipal police, motorcyclists, the Order of the Holy Sepulcher, pizza makers, Rotary International members, streetcar conductors, teachers in public schools. The Catholic Church's rich diversity of liturgical traditions was marked throughout the year by celebrations of the Mass or Divine Liturgy in the Alexandrine-Ethiopian Rite; the Ambrosian Rite; the Chaldean Rite; the Coptic Rite; the Mozarabic Rite; the Syrian-Antiochene Rite; the Syro-Malabarese Rite (which traces its origins to the work of St. Thomas the apostle in India); and the Syrian-Malankara Rite. The Irish writer James Joyce may or may not have said that the Catholic Church means "here comes everyone," but that was certainly Rome's experience of the Great Jubilee of 2000. Yet amidst that stunning diversity of human experiences and cultures, there was, throughout the year, a clear focus. It had been defined by John Paul II six years before, in **Tertio Millennio Adveniente.** It was given powerful expression in the antiphon within prayer the Pope composed for the jubilee year, in the free-verse style he had used in his literary work and his Christmas and Easter messages **Urbi et Orbi:**

1. Blessed are you, Father,
who, in your infinite love,

gave us your only-begotten Son.

By the power of the Holy Spirit he became incarnate

in the spotless womb of the Virgin Mary
and was born in Bethlehem
two thousand years ago.
He became our companion on life's path
and gave new meaning to our history,
the journey we make together
in toil and suffering,
in faithfulness and love,
towards the new heaven and the new earth
where You, once death has been vanquished,
will be all in all.
**Praise and glory to You, Most Holy Trinity,
you alone are God most high!**

2. By your grace, O Father, may the Jubilee Year
be a time of deep conversion
and of joyful return to you.
May it be a time of reconciliation between people,
and of peace restored among nations,
a time when swords are beaten into ploughshares
and the clash of arms gives way to songs of peace.
Father, grant that we may live this Jubilee Year
docile to the voice of the Spirit,
faithful to the way of Christ,
diligent in listening to your Word
and in approaching the wellsprings of grace.

**Praise and glory to You, Most Holy Trinity,
you alone are God most high!**

3. Father, by the power of the Spirit,
strengthen the Church's commitment
to the new evangelization
and guide our steps along the pathways of the
world,
to proclaim Christ by our lives,
and to direct our earthly pilgrimage
towards the City of heavenly light.
May Christ's followers show forth their love
for the poor and the oppressed;
may they be one with those in need
and abound in works of mercy;
may they be compassionate towards all,
that they themselves may obtain indulgence
and forgiveness from you.
**Praise and glory to You, Most Holy Trinity,
you alone are God most high!**

4. Father, grant that your Son's disciples,
purified in memory
and acknowledging their failings,
may be one, that the world may believe.
May dialogue between the followers
of the great religions prosper,
and may all people discover
the joy of being your children.
May the intercession of Mary,

Mother of your faithful people,
in union with the prayers of the Apostles,
the Christian martyrs,
and the righteous of all nations in every age,
make the Holy Year a time of renewed hope
and of joy in the Spirit
for each of us and for the whole Church.
**Praise and glory to you, Most Holy Trinity,
you alone are God most high!**

5. To you, Almighty Father,
Creator of the universe and of mankind,
through Christ, the Living One,
Lord of time and history,
in the Spirit who makes all things holy,
be praise and honor and glory
now and forever. Amen!

CHAPTER SEVEN

The Turbulence of History

2001–2002

February 21, 2001	John Paul II creates forty-four new cardinals at his eighth ordinary consistory.
March 11, 2001	Beatification of 231 martyrs of the Spanish Civil War.
May 4–9, 2001	Papal jubilee pilgrimage "in the footsteps of St. Paul" to Greece, Syria, and Malta.
June 23–27, 2001	John Paul II in Ukraine.
August 1, 2001	John Paul II's one thousandth general audience.
September 11, 2001	Jihadist terrorism kills thousands in New York, Washington, and Shanksville, Pennsylvania.

September 22–27, 2001	John Paul II in Kazakhstan and Armenia.
September 30–October 27, 2001	Synod of Bishops on the ministry of the bishop in the twenty-first century.
December 16, 2001	John Paul II's three hundredth Roman parish visitation.
January 6, 2002	**Boston Globe** reveals former priest John Geoghan's extensive sexual abuse of minors.
February 11, 2002	Four Catholic dioceses canonically erected in Russia.
April 22–23, 2002	U.S. cardinals meet in Rome to discuss sexual abuse crisis with John Paul II and leaders of the Roman Curia.
May 22–26, 2002	John Paul II in Azerbaijan and Bulgaria.
June 16, 2002	Canonization of Padre Pio of Pietrelcina.
July 23–August 2, 2002	John Paul II in Toronto (World Youth Day-2002), Guatemala City, and Mexico City.
August 16–19, 2002	John Paul II in Poland for consecration of the Shrine of Divine Mercy in Kraków-Łagiewniki.
October 4, 2002	Ecumenical Vespers in St. Peter's for the seventh centenary of the birth of St. Bridget of Sweden.

October 6, 2002	• Canonization of Josemaría Escrivá de Balaguer, founder of Opus Dei.
October 7–13, 2002	• Romanian Orthodox Patriarch Teoctist visits John Paul II in the Vatican.
October 16, 2002	• Beginning the twenty-fifth year of the pontificate, John Paul II issues apostolic letter **Rosarium Virginis Mariae** and adds "Mysteries of Light" to the Rosary.
October 31, 2002	• John Paul II is named honorary citizen of Rome.
November 14, 2002	• John Paul II addresses the Italian parliament.
December 13, 2002	• Cardinal Bernard Law resigns as archbishop of Boston.

Over the twenty-three years of his papacy, Pope John Paul II had come to love the papal summer villa at Castel Gandolfo.

It wasn't always so. At the beginning of the pontificate, the man who was used to kayaking, hiking, and camping on his summer vacations felt a bit confined there, even given the spacious grounds of the villa Pope Pius XI had rebuilt after the Lateran Treaty of 1929 settled the Holy See's differences with the Kingdom of Italy. Never one to take the gilded cage with complete seriousness, John Paul "escaped" from

Castel Gandolfo on occasion, walking into the town of Castelgandolfo. But it eventually seemed better to change Castel Gandolfo, the villa, itself. So John Paul had a swimming pool built near the helicopter pad, in order to get some vigorous exercise during his stays in the Castelli Romani, the hills outside Rome. When some of the traditional managers of popes complained about the cost, the Pope famously replied that the pool cost much less than a new conclave would.

Thus John Paul had formed the habit of staying at Castel Gandolfo for a week or two after the traditional holidays of August, when Rome empties because of the oppressive heat and humidity. In late September 2001, the Pope was heading for two former Soviet republics, Kazakhstan and Armenia; the deferred Synod of Bishops for the jubilee year would finally meet in October; and the Pope was looking forward to the first beatification in history of a married couple, which would take place during the Synod. So it made sense for John Paul, who was already experiencing increased physical difficulties due to his Parkinson's disease, to stay at Castel Gandolfo into the second week of September 2001, preparing for a very busy postjubilee fall.

In midafternoon on September 11, Cardinal Angelo Sodano, the secretary of state of the Holy See, called the papal villa with the news that airplanes had plowed into the World Trade Center in New York and the Pentagon in Washington. Sodano, Stanisław

Dziwisz remembered, "sounded frightened." The Pope had the television turned on; like hundreds of millions of others across a world that suddenly seemed much more dangerous, he saw repeated time and again the images of the Twin Towers crumbling into rubble in lower Manhattan, taking thousands of victims with them. "Filled with suffering," as Dziwisz later recounted, John Paul went straight to the chapel in the papal villa, and shuttled back and forth between the chapel and the television for the next several hours.[1]

On September 12, the Pope returned to Rome by helicopter for the weekly general audience in St. Peter's Square and immediately addressed the horror that was on everyone's mind:

I cannot begin this audience without expressing my profound sorrow at the terrorist attacks which yesterday brought death and destruction to America, causing thousands of victims and injuring countless people. To the President of the United States and to all American citizens I express my heartfelt sorrow. In the face of such unspeakable horror we cannot but be deeply disturbed. I add my voice to the voices raised in these hours to express indignant condemnation, and I strongly reiterate that the ways of violence can never lead to genuine solutions to humanity's problems.

Yesterday was a dark day in the history of humanity, a terrible affront to human dignity. . . . How is it possible to commit acts of such savage cruelty? The human heart has depths from which schemes of unheard-of ferocity sometimes emerge, capable of destroying in a moment the normal daily life of a people. . . .

With deeply felt sympathy I address myself to the beloved people of the United States in this moment of distress and consternation, when the courage of so many men and women of good will is being sorely tested. In a special way I reach out to the families of the dead and the injured, and assure them of my spiritual closeness. I entrust to the mercy of the Most High the helpless victims of this tragedy, for whom I offered Mass this morning, invoking upon them eternal rest. May God give courage to the survivors; may he sustain the rescue-workers and the many volunteers who are presently making an enormous effort to cope with such an immense emergency.[2]

The audience ended unusually, with a special Prayer of the Faithful; the petitions were completed by a poignant prayer that quietly but unmistakably condemned the distorted religious convictions of the 9/11 terrorists: "O almighty and merciful God, you cannot be understood by one who sows discord, you cannot be accepted by one who loves violence: look upon our painful human condition tried by cruel acts of terror and death, comfort your children and open our hearts to hope, so that our time may again know days of serenity and peace. Through Christ our Lord. Amen."

That prayer would go largely unanswered in the remaining years of the pontificate: years in which both the Church and the world were thrust back into the turbulence of history after the relative calm of the Great Jubilee of 2000.

In the period following 9/11, John Paul II would be frustrated time and again in his quest for a world that had learned some lessons from the awfulness of the twentieth century. The hope of a robust inter-religious dialogue would fade under the incapacities of Islamic leaders to come to grips with the lethal pathologies of the complex Muslim world—even as John Paul II bent every effort to underscore the Church's regard for those forms of Islamic piety that sustained lives of devotion and civility. The Holy See would find its fifty-year commitment to the United Nations challenged by the manifest incapacities of that institution to cope with the new world disorder. John Paul II's long-standing affection for the United States—unmistakably clear in his audience of September 12—would be tried by a major policy disagreement over Iraq with an American president who venerated the Pope and whose administration was as supportive of the Holy See's core issues in international organizations as any American government had ever been. Even the Pope's efforts to build bridges within the fractured worlds of Christianity would face new frustrations in the years after the

Great Jubilee. And the horrors of 9/11 would be followed within four months by the revelation of different, but nonetheless odious, crimes committed by Catholic priests in the United States.

Throughout the Great Jubilee of 2000, John Paul II had reminded the Church that sanctity must be lived in history. The disciples of Christ might know that, in the end, God's saving purposes would be vindicated, and that the Kingdom of God would prevail over its enemies. That knowledge provided spiritual ballast within the turbulence of history. It did not diminish the turbulence—for the Pope, or for any other Christian disciple.

Nunc dimittis, Domine?

When Pope John Paul II knelt in the portal of the Holy Door of St. Peter's on Christmas Eve, 1999, observers of a biblical cast of mind could be forgiven for imagining that the seventy-nine-year-old Pope—full of accomplishment but now diminished physically—might be praying, with Simeon in the New Testament, **"Nunc dimittis . . ."**—"Now, Lord, you may dismiss your servant" (Luke 2.29). According to John Paul himself, the Great Jubilee had been the "key" to his pontificate. He had led the Church and the world across the threshold of a new millennium; an enormous task had been accomplished. Might he consider laying down the burden of the papacy after the holy year was completed?

Speculation about this—almost always uninformed—had been rife for years; some of its primary promoters seemed to be those who never thought much of John Paul II in the first place. There were, of course, serious questions involved in the event that a pope became gravely disabled—a possibility that, as May 13, 1981, had made clear, might arise from an assassination attempt as well as from illness. But there were other worst-case scenarios to be considered. Pius XII had given instructions that, were he to be kidnapped by the Nazis and removed from Rome, the Chair of Peter was to be considered vacant so that Hitler would find himself holding Cardinal Pacelli, not Pope Pius XII; the cardinals were to find a safe place to meet in conclave, likely Lisbon, and they were to elect a new pope.[3] In the wake of the 1978 abduction of his old friend Aldo Moro, the former Italian prime minister, Paul VI was concerned about the possibility of the pope being kidnapped, and left instructions that, were he to be impeded from communicating with the Holy See after a kidnapping, the papacy was to be considered vacant and the cardinals were to proceed to an election. These concerns, as well as the question of physical and mental incapacity, were reflected in the revised Code of Canon Law that John Paul II promulgated in 1983. Canon 335 acknowledges the possibility that the Roman See may be vacated by being "completely impeded," as well as by a pope's death. Canon 412, which deals with all dioceses, specifies that "the episcopal see is understood to be impeded if the diocesan bishop is completely prevented from exercising the pastoral office in the diocese by reason of imprisonment, banishment, exile, or incapacity, so that he is unable to communicate, even by letter, with the people of his diocese."

John Paul II, who had spent his entire adult life analyzing and teaching about moral responsibility, was certainly aware of these problems. After consulting quietly with senior churchmen, he came to the conclusion that Paul VI had reached and that both moral common sense and canon law dictated: in the event that he was impeded from the exercise of his papal office, it was the responsibility of the College of Cardinals to declare the See vacant and proceed to the election of a successor. In the case of physical incapacity, this was generally thought, among senior churchmen, to mean a situation in which the pope was reduced to a condition in which it was impossible for him to manifest his will, which was the essence of the exercise of his office.

That was never the case with John Paul II. But what about the **"Nunc dimittis"** scenario? Did the Pope consider resigning after the Great Jubilee?

During the papal Lenten retreat that followed the jubilee Day of Pardon, John Paul added notes to his spiritual **Testament**—a collection of reflections and requests, the first of which were recorded five months after his election, in March 1979. In the March 2000 additions to the **Testament,** the Pope recalled Cardinal Wyszyński's admonition, on the day of his election, that he had been chosen to lead the Church into the third millennium. Well, that had happened. "In accordance with the designs of Providence," John Paul had lived through "the difficult century that is retreating into the past" and had been permitted to lead the Church and the world into a new century and a new millennium. So now, completing his eightieth year, it was time to ask himself **"whether the time has come to say with Simeon of the Bible, 'Nunc dimittis.'"** For a man of the Bible, it was a natural question. God had "miraculously" saved him from death on May 13, 1981, and restored his life. So "ever since that moment," the life of Karol Wojtyła had belonged "ever more" to God. Therefore, what must be done had come into focus:

I hope [God] will help me recognize how long I must continue this service to which he called me on 16 October 1978. I ask him to deign to call me to Himself whenever he wishes: "If we live, we live to the Lord, and if we die, we die to the Lord; so then . . . we are the Lord's" [cf. Romans 14.8]. I hope that as long as I am granted to carry out the Petrine service in the Church, God in His Mercy will grant me the necessary strength for this service.[4]

It was, simply, a matter in God's hands. The **Nunc dimittis** of John Paul II's **Testament** was a prayer of thanksgiving for having been spared in order to bring the Church through the portal of the Great Jubilee; it was not a valedictory. Providence would decide when to end the pontificate. To be sure, there would be questions, perhaps doubts, certainly "dark nights" ahead. That was normal in any Christian life, even a pope's. But the responsibility was clear—to set out with the rest of the Church "into the deep" of the third millennium.

IN THE FOOTSTEPS OF ST. PAUL

On February 21, 2001, Pope John Paul II held his eighth consistory for the creation of new cardinals, raising forty-four churchmen to what earlier generations had called "the sacred purple." Prior to the consistory, there was an unusual amount of turmoil in senior Church circles over the Pope's intention to create Bishop Walter Kasper a cardinal. A distinguished German theologian who sometimes treated crucial questions of the nature of the Church somewhat differently than John Paul II or Cardinal Joseph Ratzinger, Kasper had been brought to Rome as secretary of the Pontifical Council for Promoting Christian Unity, where he was heir apparent to the president of the council, Cardinal Edward Cassidy. The flap over a possible Kasper nomination, coupled with other German ecclesiastical turmoil, as well as the time it was taking for the synod of the Ukrainian Greek Catholic Church to elect a new major-archbishop of L'viv, led to the oddity of the new cardinals being announced over two Sundays, whereas the normal procedure was to announce everyone at once.

The consistory, like the Great Jubilee, displayed the remarkable diversity of the Catholic world. The new cardinals included a considerable number of curialists (including both Sergio Sebastiani and Crescenzio Sepe, the man who replaced Sebastiani as chief staff officer for the Great Jubilee); a large Third World contingent from Argentina, Bolivia, Brazil, Chile, Colombia, Ecuador, Guatemala, India, Ivory Coast, Peru, and South Africa; Europeans from France, Great Britain, Ireland, Lithuania, Poland, Portugal, Spain, and Ukraine; two American residential archbishops (Edward Egan of New York and Theodore McCarrick of Washington); three Germans (Kasper; Karl Lehmann of Mainz, a progressive whose nomination was also protested by some senior churchmen; and Johannes Degenhardt, whom some regarded as a "balance" to the liberal Lehmann); John Paul's longtime trip planner, Roberto Tucci, S.J.; and the most distinguished of American theologians, Avery Dulles, S.J., the first U.S. scholar honored in such a way.[5] The first cardinal named, and thus the "head" of the "Class of 2001," was Giovanni Battista Re, longtime **Sostituto,** or papal chief of staff, who had recently been appointed prefect of the crucial Congregation for Bishops. Two cardinals whose names had been held **in pectore,** or secretly, by the Pope at the 1998 consistory received their red hats publicly in 2001: the Latvian Janis Pujats, and John Paul's old friend and fellow philosopher, the Pole Marian Jaworski, Latin-rite archbishop of L'viv in Ukraine.

The entire College of Cardinals was called back to Rome three months later to discuss the immediate future of the postjubilee Church in light of **Novo Millennio Ineunte.** This sixth extraordinary consistory of the pontificate took place from May 21 to May 23, 2001. With 155 cardinals in attendance, John Paul stressed in his opening remarks the importance of discussing "a number of practical suggestions for the Church's mission of evangelization at the dawn of the new millennium," including "the superlative formation and intelligent assignment of our priests and lay collaborators, because the field of apostolic action before us is vast and complex."[6] Some cardinals seemed to have a different agenda; the meaning of "collegiality" was debated yet again, as were proposals for more synods and changes in the functioning of the Roman Curia. One of the newly created cardinals, Cormac Murphy-O'Connor of Westminster, called for a pan-Christian council of churches to be held in Jerusalem, Compostela, or perhaps even England, in which the Catholic Church would not predetermine the agenda and the Pope would preside only "in love"; Cardinal Christoph Schönborn, O.P., of Vienna remarked to reporters after the meeting that Cardinal Murphy-O'Connor's proposal was an "eschatological dream," a theologically polite way of saying that any such gathering would likely happen only after the return of Christ in glory. Another European cardinal, Belgium's Godfried Danneels, struck some observers and journalists as behaving rather like an American presidential candidate in an early primary election; future conclave politics were also at work in the cardinals' discussions of the relationship between the Church's Roman center and the local Catholic Churches around the world. The newly created Cardinal Dulles made an intervention defending a strong papacy, pointing out how other Christian communities suffered from the lack of such a center of unity and teaching authority.[7]

At the end of the three-day session, it was hard for some observers not to draw the conclusion that the cardinals were, as a body, far more eager to debate bureaucratic change than to ponder the specifics of the new evangelization, out there "in the deep" of the third millennium. For all the talk of "collegiality," it would, once more, be John Paul II who had to take the lead in demonstrating that mission remained the Church's entire raison d'être. He did so in a dramatic way by continuing his jubilee pilgrimage to "the places linked to the history of salvation"—in this case, walking in the footsteps of St. Paul, the great missionary **ad gentes** [to the nations], in Greece, Damascus, and Malta, all of which had been sites of Pauline mission in the Acts of the Apostles.

For the first two decades of the pontificate, John Paul II nurtured the hope that the first rupture in Christianity—between Rome and the Christian East—might be repaired so that the spiritual heirs of Peter and Andrew could once again concelebrate the Eucharist together. As the jubilee year approached, however, it became increasingly clear that history was not yet ready for John Paul's vision of a great reconciliation between Rome and Constantinople at the end of a millennium of division. The Orthodox themselves were extravagantly divided. There was competition between the Ecumenical Patriarchate of Constantinople—a tiny Orthodox island in a Turkish and Islamic sea—and the Patriarchate of Moscow, which imagined itself the "Third Rome." The Orthodox Churches of eastern Europe had been deeply damaged by communism. Perhaps even more to the point, many Orthodox had, over the centuries, internalized a view of Orthodoxy in which the fracture with Rome was an integral part of Orthodox identity. So while the Catholic Church regarded the Orthodox Churches as sister "Churches" (as **Dominus Iesus** had reaffirmed), most Orthodox did not reciprocate—thus the refusal of several Orthodox leaders to join in public prayer with John Paul II.

John Paul's proposal to visit the Areopagus of Athens as part of his jubilee pilgrimage had met with a frosty initial reception in Greek Orthodox circles. The Holy Synod of the Greek Church declared that the Pope could come only if he recanted the historic errors of Rome; the Orthodox monks of Mount Athos, who considered themselves the true guardians of Orthodoxy, laid down a propaganda barrage against the Pope as the leader of a heretical community. The logjam was broken when Greek president Constantinos Stephanopoulos, on a visit to Rome, extended an invitation to John Paul to visit Greece in the Pope's capacity as head of state of Vatican City. This put the Holy Synod in an awkward position, and, after an exchange of letters between the Pope and Archbishop Christodoulos of Athens, an invitation from the Holy Synod was forthcoming, if grudgingly. Christodoulos had to spend weeks trying to calm down his Orthodox brethren; the Athonite monks went on the rhetorical rampage again, denouncing "another of Wojtyła's hegemonic tours." As late as April 2001, the senior Catholic prelate in Greece, Archbishop Nikolaos Foscolos, confessed that he was unsure how the visit would work out, or even if it would happen, because "ecumenism does not exist in Greece." That Archbishop Foscolos was not being overly pessimistic was made clear on April 25 when a large anti-papal demonstration in Athens featured banners denouncing John Paul as a "two-horned heretic." Posters describing the Pope as "the Beast of the Apocalypse" sprouted all over the Greek capital, and one of the demonstration organizers, a Greek Orthodox priest, decried the Pope's "sins against humanity."

When he kissed Greek soil at the Athens airport in the late morning of May 4, John Paul II became the first Bishop of Rome to set foot in Greece since the schism of 1054 had formalized a breach between Rome and Constantinople that had been widening for centuries. Neither President Stephanopoulos nor Archbishop Christodoulos was at the airport to greet John Paul, who went to the presidential palace and praised the Greek Fathers of the Church who had made decisive contributions to the civilization of the West, such as St. Basil and St. John Chrysostom. Through these great teachers, the Pope said, "gradually the Hellenistic world became Christian and Christianity became to a certain extent Greek." After paying that tribute to the Greek contribution to Europe, John Paul went to the residence of Archbishop Christodoulos and seized the initiative by asking God's forgiveness "for the occasions past and present when sons and daughters of the Catholic Church [had] sinned by action or omission against their Orthodox brothers and sisters." The Pope specifically cited the sack of Constantinople by the Fourth Crusade in 1204, which, he said, "fills Catholics with deep regret." Christodoulos, touched, still clung to ancient grievances. Insisting in his remarks that "the Greek and Orthodox people have suffered a great deal at the hands of the West," the archbishop cited Rome's full communion with the Eastern Catholic

Churches as an obstacle to dialogue and complained that the Holy See did not take up the Greek cause with respect to Cyprus.[8]

Still, hardened hearts had been moved: when the Holy Synod met John Paul on the Areopagus that afternoon, they spontaneously applauded him. The Areopagus had long held a special place in John Paul II's religious imagination, for the apostle Paul's attempt to crack the facade of Athenian cynicism there by appealing to the "unknown god" seemed to the Pope an apt metaphor for the Church's mission in post-Christian Europe. During the brief ceremony, John Paul and Christodoulos signed a common "Declaration on the Christian Roots of Europe," which was then read aloud; virtually every sentence in it had been contested prior to the trip between the Holy See and the Greek Orthodox authorities.

On May 5, John Paul celebrated Mass at the Sports Palace in the Athens Olympic Complex and then left for Damascus. At his farewell meeting with Christodoulos, he proposed that each say the Lord's Prayer in his own language, which the Orthodox archbishop was willing to do. During the private encounter, Christodoulos admitted to being "proud of this visit" and conceded that "a new era is opening," according to Joaquín Navarro-Valls.[9] At least some of the Greek press agreed: the newspaper **Kathimerini** claimed that "the ice of twelve centuries has cracked," while the magazine **Etnos** had a large front-page headline, "John Paul II Changes History."[10] It was the future that John Paul wanted to shape; but with the exception of the irreconcilables, such as the monks of Mount Athos, it did seem that the Pope's self-evident humility and generosity of spirit had healed at least a few of history's wounds.

Ancient hatreds were on virulent display when John Paul II arrived in Damascus later on May 5. There, he was greeted by Syrian president Bashar al-Assad with an anti-Israeli and anti-Semitic tirade in which Assad appealed to the blood libel of Jews by denouncing those "who try to kill the principles of all religion with the same mentality with which they betrayed Jesus Christ." The Pope spoke of his hopes for peace and for reconciliation among Jews, Christians, and Muslims. That he did not immediately rebut Assad's calumnies set off an international media tempest. Rabbi Arthur Schneier of New York did not take the bait and simply said that "People know what this man stands for"; Abraham Foxman of the Anti-Defamation League graciously allowed as how John Paul "has earned our patience," even though he spoke of the Pope's "sin of silence."[11] As the Syrian portion of the Pope's visit unfolded, it became clear that the Pope was in fact responding to Assad's butchery of history and Catholic doctrine by laying out a radically different view of the Catholic Church's relations with Judaism and Islam, and of the civility that ought to prevail among people of genuine faith in the God of Abraham.[12]

The ecumenical climate was considerably warmer

in Syria than in Athens, as the Eastern Catholic Churches and the Orthodox Churches in the country enjoyed good relations. Patriarch Ignatius IV Hakim of the Antiochian Orthodox Church went out of his way to make clear that he and his flock, the largest Christian group in Syria, did not share the animosities of their Greek Orthodox brethren: "We have our own Orthodox personality, and our circumstances are different," the patriarch said. (As they certainly were: the various Christian groupings in Syria amounted to about 7 percent of the total population.) During the visit, the patriarch recited the Creed together with the Pope during an ecumenical meeting.[13]

On May 6, John Paul II presided and preached at a Mass attended by 40,000 people and all the bishops of Syria, of whatever Catholic rite, which was held in the Abbassyine stadium outside Damascus. In his homily, he spoke of the importance of Damascus in Christian history, a point he underscored by visiting the traditional site where St. Paul had been lowered through an opening in the city wall to escape his persecutors. Later that day, John Paul became the first pope to set foot in a Muslim house of worship when he came to the Omayyad Grand Mosque for a meeting with Muslim leaders. Presented with a Qur'an, he kissed it. It was a gesture that would be criticized for the duration of his pontificate by some of his most ardent supporters, who could not seem to grasp that, as one close Catholic student of Islam put it, the gesture was a "kiss for Muslims," not a recognition of the Qur'an as divine revelation—a notion the Pope had specifically rejected in his 1994 bestseller, **Crossing the Threshold of Hope.**[14]

In the view of one of the Catholic Church's leading experts on Islam, the German Jesuit Christian Troll, John Paul II's address at the Omayyad Grand Mosque was his "testament concerning his vision of Islam and its relationship to Christianity in a globalized world." The venue itself was deeply suggestive, as the Grand Mosque had formerly been the Cathedral of St. John the Baptist, known to Muslims as Yahya, and includes a traditional site of the tomb of the beheaded prophet whom both Christians and Muslims venerate. Thus it was important, Father Troll wrote, that the papal address in the Grand Mosque began by invoking this shared figure as the exemplar of a common responsibility: "John's life, wholly dedicated to God, was crowned with martyrdom. May his witness enlighten all who venerate his memory so that they—and we, too—may understand that life's great task is to seek God's truth and justice." The Pope then stressed the common Christian and Muslim commitment to prayer. After discussing the importance of places of worship and education where the young could learn the faith of their fathers, John Paul deplored the "misuse of religion itself to promote or justify hatred and violence," which "destroys the image of the Creator in his creatures and should never be considered as the fruit of religious conviction." Thus the Pope's "ardent hope" was that "Muslim and Christian leaders and teachers will present our two great religious communities **as communities in respectful dialogue, never more as communities in conflict.**" Given the realities of the moment, that "ardent hope" was also an unmistakable challenge to the Pope's Muslim hosts.[15]

On May 7, John Paul II prayed for peace in the ruins of a Greek Orthodox church in Quneitra on the Golan Heights before returning to Damascus and a youth meeting at the Greek-Catholic Cathedral in the Syrian capital. Spokesman Navarro-Valls, conscious of the world media storm over President Assad's anti-Israeli remarks (which had been echoed by the Grand Mufti of Syria, Sheikh Ahmad Kaftaro, at the Omayyad Grand Mosque), cautioned reporters against over-interpreting the Quneitra visit: its "sole objective and sole reason was to pray for peace," Navarro said, and "people of goodwill will understand and . . . appreciate this gesture."[16]

After the chilly reception in Greece, which he managed to thaw, and the political histrionics (and worse) in Syria, which he tried to counter by proposing a different vision of the future than that held by either President Assad or Sheikh Kaftaro, it was a relief for an obviously tired Pope to arrive in Malta, which is 98 percent Catholic and has a high rate of Catholic practice. Site of St. Paul's shipwreck in Acts 27–28, the island had been ruled from the sixteenth through the eighteenth centuries by the Catholic equestrian order, the Knights of Malta.[17] Two-thirds of the island's population attended John Paul's beatification of three Maltese natives at an outdoor Mass on May 9.[18]

That celebration marked the end of John Paul II's jubilee biblical pilgrimage. He had overcome an enormous number of political, emotional, and psychological obstacles—as well as his own infirmities—to walk in the footsteps of the great figures of salvation history whose lives had been touched by the God of Abraham, Moses, and Jesus. He had done it to fulfill a desire of his heart. Above all, though, he had done it to remind the Church that Providence worked through, not around, the turbulence of history—and that fidelity to the Church's apostolic mission always meant taking the risk of putting out "into the deep."

Before the Storm

Polish-Ukrainian relations had long exemplified the drama of ethnic and religious history in the borderlands between central and eastern Europe. Latin-rite and deeply patriotic Poles tended to look on Ukrainians as their religious and political inferiors; Ukrainians tended to look on Poles as members of an overbearing landlord class. Karol Wojtyła was a rarity among the Polish clergy of his generation: a Polish patriot who had deep sympathies with Ukrainian national aspirations and who esteemed the Greek Catholic Church of Ukraine (which was Byzantine in liturgy and polity but in full communion with Rome after the 1596 Union of Brest).[19] From the end of the Second World War through the collapse of the Soviet Union, the Ukrainian Greek Catholic Church—or, as the Ukrainians often preferred, the Catholic Church of Kyïv—was the largest illegal religious body in the world and the repository of Ukrainian national identity. Wojtyła's well-known affinity for Ukraine and its struggles explained in no small part the fear in which he was held by Moscow Center and by the Ukrainian KGB, which had close working relations with the Polish SB.[20]

In the aftermath of the Soviet collapse and the rebirth of an independent Ukraine, in which the Ukrainian Greek Catholic Church had emerged from underground and had become a potent religious and cultural force, the Moscow Patriarchate tried to assert its authority over Ukrainian Orthodoxy while assailing the Greek Catholic Church as a usurper in its "canonical territory." The result was that Ukrainian Orthodoxy was split three ways, thus vastly complicating the post-1991 ecumenical efforts of John Paul II and the Holy See. So it was no surprise that, when it was announced that John Paul would make a pastoral pilgrimage to Ukraine in June 2001, elements of Ukrainian Orthodoxy protested bitterly, aided and abetted by the Moscow Patriarchate, whose external affairs department had been trained by the KGB in the old Soviet days. Stories were planted in newspapers and magazines warning that a papal visit to Ukraine could be the ugliest of John Paul's pontificate—and this, despite the invitations the Pope had received from the Ukrainian government and from the country's Greek Catholic and Latin-rite bishops. Patriarch Aleksy II of Moscow—DROZDOV to his erstwhile KGB associates—told an Italian Catholic magazine in April 2001 that John Paul II's visit should be "postponed."[21] Anti-papal demonstrations were organized: not so large as in Greece, but with incense, bearded clergy, and icons, wonderfully apt for television. The demonstrations, in which a group processed daily to the Vatican nunciature in Kyïv and ended their march with a prayer that the Pope would not come, were organized by the faction of Ukrainian Orthodoxy that was loyal to Moscow, by a local political movement that wanted to stitch back together Russia, Belarus, and Ukraine, and by what was left of the Communist Party in Ukraine.

All of this agitation was for naught. One-half of one percent of the population declared itself "adamantly opposed" to the Pope's visit. (When the visit was over, 65 percent of Russians surveyed said that they'd like to have a papal visit, too.)[22] On his arrival at Boryspil International Airport in Kyïv on June 23, John Paul saluted Ukraine as a **"brave and deter-**

mined witness to . . . faith" and marveled at "how much you suffered in order to vindicate, in difficult times, the freedom to profess this faith!" Ever hopeful about warming hearts frozen by centuries-old animosities, the Pope then said that he was sure he would be welcomed "with friendship . . . by those who, although they are not Catholics, have hearts open to dialogue and cooperation." He had come to Ukraine, he said, not to proselytize or sow discord, "but to bear witness to Christ together with all Christians of every Church and Ecclesial Community, and to invite all the sons and daughters of this noble Land to turn their eyes to him who gave his life for the salvation of the world." It was also time, he suggested, to look to the future rather than to the past, so as "not to disappoint the expectations which now fill the hearts of so many, especially the young." The task before them all, he said, was to fulfill the dream of the Ukrainian poet Taras Shevchenko and to see "in the cities and villages of Ukraine the blossoming of a new, authentic humanism," built by men and women who were, in Shevchenko's words, **"enemies . . . no more,"** but rather fellow citizens of a country with a **"clearly European vocation."** [23]

There were to be more moving words and great public spectacles during the five days of John Paul's visit to Ukraine; the address at the Kyїv airport, however, set the tone for a remarkably successful visit. The first thing that Ukrainians noticed was that the Pope spoke far more fluent Ukrainian than their

president, Leonid Kuchma, who had once been a Soviet missile engineer and was clearly more comfortable speaking in Russian. The historically minded
were also struck by the fact that, while the alleged
usurper, the Bishop of Rome, spoke to the people of
Ukraine in their own tongue, no Patriarch of Moscow, asserting his jurisdiction over their religious
lives, had ever done so. As for the politically sensitive, the clear statement that Ukraine was an integral
part of Europe was an important marker: the man
who had come to embody a vision of Europe reinte-
grated across the Cold War divide did not consider
Ukraine to be marginal to the Europe of the twenty-
first century, a place on "the border" (as the very
name "Ukraine" implied etymologically). Ukraine,
for John Paul II, was a participant in a common European culture with deep Christian roots.

The Pope stayed in Kyïv for two days, meeting with representatives of the country's cultural,
political, intellectual, and business communities,
celebrating Mass in both the Latin and Byzantine
rites (whose complex rubrics he had carefully studied and rehearsed), and meeting with the Catholic
bishops of Ukraine and with representatives of the
Pan-Ukrainian Council of Churches and Religious
Organizations. On June 25, the Pope shifted his pilgrimage to the heart of the Greek Catholic world in
western Ukraine, the city of L'viv, which had long
been a part of Poland and known as Lwów. (When,
that is, it was not known as Lemberg, the German

name it had acquired when Galicia, like Kraków, was part of the Austro-Hungarian Empire. Interestingly, in private conversation John Paul II habitually referred to L'viv/Lwów as "Lemberg," and laughed when guests jokingly cautioned against using that terminology in the city itself.) At the Hippodrome racecourse in L'viv, John Paul celebrated a Latin-rite Mass on June 26 and beatified Ukrainian martyrs killed during the Nazi and communist persecutions of the twentieth century; the group included the Pope's episcopal great-grandfather, Archbishop Józef Bilczewski (Bilczewksi had ordained as bishop Archbishop Bolesław Twardowski, who had ordained Archbishop Eugeniusz Baziak a bishop, who had ordained Karol Wojtyła a bishop). John Paul, the Pole with deep Ukrainian sympathies, then made a poignant plea for an end to the mutual suspicions of the past between Latin-rite Ukrainians, often of Polish descent, and Greek Catholic Ukrainians:

> Today, in praising God for the indomitable fidelity to the Gospel of these his Servants, let us feel ourselves gently nudged to recognize the infidelities to the Gospel of not a few Christians of both Polish and Ukrainian origin living in these parts. It is time to leave behind the sorrowful past. The Christians of the two nations must walk together in the name of the one Christ, towards the one Father, guided by the same Holy Spirit, the source and principle of

unity. May pardon given and received spread like a healing balm in every heart.[24]

After his homily, which he preached in Ukrainian, John Paul greeted the foreign pilgrims to the beatification Mass in their own languages—Russian, Belarussian, Slovak, Hungarian, and Romanian.

The next day, June 27, another Mass was celebrated at the Hippodrome, this time in the Byzantine-rite, and more twentieth-century martyrs were beatified, bringing the total over two days to thirty. Cardinal Lubomyr Husar reciprocated the Pope's gestures of reconciliation and forgiveness at the beginning of the Divine Liturgy, asking forgiveness for the sins committed against the Latins by his Ukrainian flock over the centuries. An unexpected participant in the second beatification was Father Ioan Sviridov, an archpriest of the Moscow Patriarchate, who had been so impressed by the Pope's remarks in Kyïv that he felt he had to be present at a moment that would "help [everyone] toward a better mutual understanding."[25] The following day, his last in Ukraine, John Paul II blessed the cornerstone of a new building for the Ukrainian Catholic University, a dream of the great mid-twentieth-century Ukrainian Metropolitan Andrei Sheptyts'kyi, which was being realized under the leadership of a young Ukrainian-American priest with a Harvard doctorate, Father Borys Gudziak.

Four months after the visit, Cardinal Husar was

still amazed at John Paul's success. Despite the recalcitrance of the Moscow Patriarchate and the nervousness of local security officials in Kyïv, the Pope's
remarkable speech at the airport had led to far more
interest in his visit than could have been anticipated;
95 percent of those who had come to see and greet
the Pope along the packed streets of the Ukrainian
capital were "Orthodox or nothing," Husar said. As
for L'viv, the crowds had been ten deep along the
motorcade route, and people had begun gathering at
Husar's residence at 4 A.M. in order to see the Pope
leave the building at 9 A.M. At one point, as they were
driving through L'viv in the Popemobile, John Paul
turned to Husar and said, "I never expected anything
like this. This is a Catholic city." That John Paul had
deliberately deployed a profoundly Slavic set of images in his homilies and speeches in order to preach
peace and reconciliation had had "a very strong impact," Husar thought; months after the Pope left,
people were still talking about his visit. Moreover,
John Paul had made a "very positive impression"
on the Orthodox faithful. Those Orthodox monks
who later went to the sites in Kyïv that the Pope had
visited in order to "reconsecrate holy ground" were,
Husar observed, "fanatics on the fringes." Contrary
to what Patriarch Aleksy II of Moscow had said,
there was, in Husar's view, "no trace whatsoever" of
the Pope having "aggravated" Catholic/Orthodox
relations in Ukraine, except among the fanatics, who
were already aggravated.[26]

John Paul II had come to Ukraine "very humbly, with a walking-stick," and as a "close neighbor . . . who had himself been through the communist era and [knew] what touched our people," Cardinal Husar remarked some time later. "He was one with us and we were one with him." That experience of solidarity and unity, Husar concluded, had allowed John Paul to show how a long-persecuted Church could free itself of the "mentality of the persecuted" and be a force for spiritual and cultural renewal in a deeply wounded society.[27]

After giving the pallium, the symbol of a metropolitan archbishop's jurisdiction, to prelates from twenty-one countries on five continents at the annual Mass in St. Peter's Square for the Solemnity of Sts. Peter and Paul on June 29, John Paul received the bishops of Cuba on their **ad limina** visit before going back to the Italian Alps and the Val d'Aosta for a twelve-day summer vacation that ran from July 9 until July 20. Returning to Castel Gandolfo, he received U.S. president George W. Bush on July 23, showing the American the view of Lake Albano from the papal villa. In his formal remarks, John Paul noted that "America continues to measure herself by the nobility of her founding vision in building a society of liberty, equality, and justice under the law," and recalled that "these same ideals inspired the American people to resist two totalitarian systems based on an atheistic vision of man and society." The "revolution of freedom of which I spoke at the United Nations in 1995," John Paul continued, "must now be completed by a revolution of opportunity, in which all the world's peoples actively contribute to economic prosperity and share in its fruits." After thanking President Bush for America's "commitment" to "the promotion of religious freedom . . . in the international community," the Pope challenged the American people and the president (who would soon make a historic decision on federal funding for embryonic stem cell research) to build a "vibrant culture of life," noting that "a free and virtuous society, which America aspires to be, must reject practices that devalue and violate human life at any stage from conception until natural death." By doing so, John Paul concluded, "America can show the world the path to a truly humane future, in which man is the master, not the product, of his technology."[28]

Nine days later, on August 1, the Pope held the thousandth general audience of his pontificate; a large part of the crowd consisted of youngsters who had come on pilgrimage to Rome, and the Pope asked those among them who were altar servers to consider the possibility that the friendship they were nurturing with Jesus in the liturgy might lead to vocations to the priesthood or the consecrated religious life. On August 30, John Paul hosted the world premiere of a new film adaptation of Henryk Sienkiewicz's novel **Quo Vadis** at the Vatican. He would leave the film criticism to the film critics, he said. What he wanted everyone to remember was the human drama embodied in the Polish Nobel laureate's tale and Jerzy Kawalerowicz's film, set in the turbulence of early Christian life in Rome: "We cannot understand the way the film presents the Church and Christian spirituality if we do not return to the religious events that involved the men and women who, in their enthusiasm for the 'Good News' of Jesus Christ, became his witnesses (martyrs). We must return to the drama which they experienced in their souls, in which they confronted, face to face, human fear and superhuman courage, the desire to live and the willingness to be faithful until death, the sense of solitude before unfeeling hatred and the experience of power that flows from the close, invisible presence of God."[29]

Twelve days later, unfeeling hatred would make its presence felt in lower Manhattan, Washington, and Shanksville, Pennsylvania, as would human fear and superhuman courage.

NEW WORLD DISORDER

In an accident of timing thick with irony and poignancy, the Pope was due to receive the credentials of the new U.S. ambassador to the Holy See, R. James Nicholson, on September 13, 2001—two days after the Twin Towers fell and the Pentagon was attacked by suicidal jihadists bent on mass homicide. The two men met for twenty minutes at Castel Gandolfo, prayed together, and discussed the immediate post-9/11 responsibilities of the U.S. government. Ambassador Nicholson said that the United States had to respond militarily to al-Qaeda and those who supported it, both for its own defense and for that of its allies; the Pope responded that the 9/11 attacks were an assault on "all mankind," and added that the United States was "justified in undertaking defensive action," asking that America also retain its sense of justice as it pursued security in the new world disorder.[30]

John Paul's formal remarks at the credentials ceremony began with a reiteration of his sympathy for the American people "at a moment of immense tragedy for your country," stressing his "participation in the grief of the American people" and his prayers for everyone touched by this act of irrational violence. After expressing his continued admiration for "the rich patrimony of human, religious, and moral values which have historically shaped the American character," he challenged the U.S. government to take the lead in addressing the myriad questions of justice involved in the globalization of the world economy, in trying to find a path to peace in the Middle East, and in defending the right to life of all innocent human beings. At the same time, he challenged the Church in the United States to be "actively present in . . . discerning the shape of your country's future course."[31]

The Pope's strategy in the wake of what quickly became known as "9/11" was driven by several concerns. He understood immediately that the attacks had created a new and very dangerous situation. He was concerned that the West had been culturally weakened since the eruptions of the sixties: postmodernist skepticism, indeed insouciance, about the human capacity to know the truth of anything had left the West unprepared spiritually for a challenge that would test its moral convictions about human rights and the rule of law, he feared.[32] He was determined to condemn irrational violence, especially when committed in the name of God; he was also determined to do nothing that would bolster the jihadists' claim that this was a religious war. He hoped, perhaps against hope, that this might be an occasion for "the international community" to become a concrete political reality rather than an ephemeral ideal. He wanted the Church to be a voice for reason and dialogue in a season of irrationality and cacophony. He wanted Europe to take seriously its commitments to religious freedom for its new Muslim immigrants; yet, as he sometimes put it, the world was "still waiting" for greater reciprocity in questions of religious freedom from Islamic states such as Saudi Arabia. (The Saudis had helped fund the building of a new mosque in Rome—which the Pope had welcomed— but the Kingdom forbade public Christian worship within its national borders.)[33] John Paul was also determined that this new world disorder not disrupt his pastoral priorities, such as his forthcoming visit to a majority-Muslim country, Kazakhstan, and the 2002 World Youth Day, which was scheduled for Toronto. Now, however, his attempts to forge ahead on missions of reconciliation and cultural bridge building ran new risks of being misinterpreted, especially by a European press that quickly recovered from its immediate, post-9/11 spasm of pro-American sentiment and began trying to recruit the Pope to the causes of appeasement and pacifism.

That John Paul's strategic objectives might sometimes be in tension with one another, given certain circumstances, was amply demonstrated by the Pope's pastoral visit to Kazakhstan in formerly Soviet Central Asia, and to Armenia, home of one of the world's oldest Christian communities, from September 22 through September 27, 2001. Kazakhstan was a place close to the Pope's Polish heart, as it had been the destination of many Polish families deported from the Soviet-occupied parts of Poland at the beginning of World War II. In three days of meetings in the city of Astrana with politicians, religious and intellectual leaders, and young people, and in his homilies at two Masses, John Paul stressed the imperatives of peace, civility, and mutual respect among diverse ethnic and religious traditions, in what he termed a "land of encounter and dialogue." Quoting "one of your country's great thinkers, the teacher Abai Kunanbai," he reminded an audience of Kazakh cultural leaders that reason must never give way to passion; as Abai Kunanbai had put it in a poem,

> If the heart no longer aspires to anything, who can unveil its thought?
> . . . If reason abandons itself to desire, it loses all its depth.
> . . . Can a people worthy of this name do without reason?

It was in this context, he said, that he wished to reaffirm "the Catholic Church's respect for Islam, for authentic Islam: the Islam that prays, that is concerned for those in need. Recalling the errors of the past, including the most recent past, all believers ought to unite their efforts to ensure that God is never made the hostage of human ambitions." Terrorism, and the hatred that lay beneath it, was both a profanation of "the name of God" and a disfigurement of "the true image of man."[34]

The thoughts were noble and unexceptionable. Yet with the world expecting imminent U.S. military action in Afghanistan in response to the attacks of 9/11, the European Left and its allies in the European media began interpreting the Pope's admonitions to dialogue and peace as an implicit papal condemnation of the expected American assault on al-Qaeda and the Taliban. Joaquín Navarro-Valls, concerned about this, raised the point with the Pope, saying that once military action started there was a danger that the pontiff would be hijacked by the European media as a symbol of opposition to U.S. policy and action. On his own initiative but as a "matter of conscience," Navarro then gave an interview to Philip Pullella of the Reuters news agency while the two men were together in Astrana. In the interview, Navarro made clear that John Paul's promotion of peace and interreligious reconciliation should not be twisted into a papal case for pacifism in response to 9/11, and that military action to forestall any such attacks in the future was morally justifiable. The cardinal secretary of state, Angelo Sodano, seemingly unaware of what was afoot, was unhappy with Navarro's initiative; the papal spokesman simply told him that something had to be done or the Pope's position would have been compromised. Bishop Stanisław Dziwisz, the papal secretary, asked Navarro what was going on, and quickly understood when the Spaniard explained the reasons for what he had done.[35]

The Pope spent three days in Armenia, where he was warmly welcomed by the Catholicos of the Armenian Apostolic Church, Karekin II, with whom he joined in an ecumenical celebration in the newly consecrated Cathedral of St. Gregory the Illuminator in Yerevan. The two also signed a common declaration that noted the many martyrs among the million and a half victims of the Armenian genocide during World War I. It was a welcome moment of ecumenical warmth in the former Soviet Union, as the winds blowing from the Moscow Patriarchate remained chilly. John Paul's hopes for a visit to Russia were not making progress; the head of "external affairs" for the Russian Orthodox Church, Metropolitan Kirill of Smolensk, had recently declared that all eleven time zones of Russia were "canonical Orthodox territory" within which Catholics should not be permitted to work to convert others, even from atheism.[36] Yet despite the slow but steady decline in John Paul's physical condition, his mind remained both clear and imaginative. In an attempt to break through another ancient barrier of animosity (and perhaps open the door to another great nation he yearned to visit), he had recently sent a letter to a congress marking the four hundredth anniversary of the Jesuit scholar Matteo Ricci's arrival in Beijing, in which the Pope asked God's forgiveness for offenses Christians may have committed against China in the past. As papal spokesman Navarro-Valls noted at the time, this bold stroke was entirely John Paul's idea: "nobody in the [Vatican] bureaucracy would ever have thought of such a thing."[37]

BISHOPS "INTO THE DEEP"

One of the great accomplishments of the Catholic Church since the French Revolution (and perhaps the single greatest accomplishment of modern Holy See diplomacy) often goes unremarked: the lengthy, sometimes delicate, and occasionally contentious process by which the Church regained control over the appointment of its bishops. In the mid-nineteenth century, Pope Pius IX had a free choice of appointment in only a small number of Catholic dioceses in the world, primarily in Australia, Belgium, and the United States. The appointment of bishops elsewhere was heavily influenced, or in some instances controlled, by governments—a concession the Second Vatican Council tried to bring to a definitive end and that was in fact banned by the 1983 Code of Canon Law.[38] By the time of John Paul II's election in 1978, the Holy See exercised a free right of episcopal appointment throughout the world, with the Church's freedom of action being seriously impeded only in Vietnam and China. John Paul appointed thousands of bishops; the gravity with which he took this responsibility could be read from his nominations to the crucial curial post of prefect of the Congregation of Bishops—the Beninese cardinal, Bernardin Gantin, the first African to hold the position; the Brazilian Dominican, Lucas Moreira Neves; and his former **Sostituto,** or chief of staff, Giovanni Battista Re. All were men in whom John Paul reposed great trust.

No one would claim, however, that the system of episcopal appointment was perfect. And at times, the Pope seemed frustrated with the inability of bishops to share his own sense of evangelical urgency and his own commitment to a vibrant Catholic public witness in the world; on one occasion, John Paul told several luncheon guests, who had asked whether a forthcoming compendium of Catholic social doctrine was really necessary, that "it is necessary because the bishops don't know the social doctrine of the Church."[39] Some obviously did, as indeed some shared the Pope's sense of high adventure in setting out "into the deep" of the third millennium. But others clearly did not, and it was to send a jolt of evangelical energy into the world episcopate that John Paul had planned a synod on the role of the bishop in the new century as part of the Great Jubilee of 2000. It just couldn't be done in 2000, however, given everything else that was happening in Rome during the holy year. So the Synod **of** Bishops **on** bishops was deferred a year, and convened in Rome on September 30, 2001.

In his opening homily at St. Peter's, John Paul made unmistakably clear that he expected the bishops of the Church to join with the Bishop of Rome in leaving the shallows of institutional maintenance and setting out into the turbulent "deep" of twenty-first-century history:

Dear Brothers in the Episcopate! Christ repeats to us today: "**Duc in altum—Put out into the deep!**" [Luke 5.4]. Following his invitation, we may reread the triple **munus** entrusted to us in the Church: **munus docendi, sanctificandi et regendi** (the ministry of teaching, sanctifying, and governing). . . .

Duc in docendo! (Lead in teaching.) With the Apostle, we will say: "Preach the world, be urgent in season and out of season, convince, rebuke, and exhort—be unfailing in patience and in teaching" [2 Timothy 4.2].

Duc in sanctificando! (Lead in sanctifying.) The "nets" we are called upon to cast among men are, first of all, the Sacraments, of which we are the principal dispensers, governors, guardians, and promoters. . . . They form a sort of saving "net," which frees from evil and leads to the fullness of life.

Duc in regendo! (Lead in governing.) As Shepherds and true Fathers, assisted by the Priests and other collaborators, we have the task of gathering the family of the faithful and in it fostering charity and brotherly communion.

As arduous and laborious a mission as this may be, we must not lose heart. With Peter and the first disciples, we, too, with great confidence renew our sincere profession of faith: Lord, "**at your word I will lower the nets**" [Luke 5.5]![40]

Four weeks of speeches (technically known as "interventions") and small group discussions followed. There were debates over "effective collegiality" (theological code for ecclesial power sharing between Rome and the world episcopate) and "affective collegiality" (the bishops' mutual support of one another). Some Synod fathers argued that the social doctrine principle of subsidiarity, which held that decision-making should be located at the lowest level possible in a social hierarchy, also applied to the internal governance of the Church; others disagreed, arguing that the purpose of the papal magisterium was to be the ultimate safeguard of the truths of the faith, which are universal and not local. Interesting in themselves, these debates also served as a polite, intellectual facade behind which some bishops pressed for a decentralization of decision-making in the world Church. Thus it seemed noteworthy that the most vigorously applauded intervention of the Synod's first week was given by Cardinal Joseph Ratzinger of the Congregation for the Doctrine of the Faith, who told his brother bishops that if they were exercising the **munus regendi** and defending orthodoxy, the so-called problem of decentralization would "take care of itself." That Ratzinger was applauded suggested, at a minimum, that the Synod fathers were happy to recognize courage, even if some were not prepared to exercise that cardinal virtue as often as Cardinal Ratzinger might have liked.

The Synod was also an occasion for some bishops and cardinals to engage in a bit of discreet politicking in anticipation of the Pope's death. Others took the opportunity to denounce globalization and the free economy in terms that suggested they had not read John Paul's 1991 encyclical, **Centesimus Annus.** Still others voiced the now-familiar complaints about the Curia and the Synod process. After several weeks of interventions that oscillated between serious theological argument and oratorical inventories of discontents, one Synod auditor summarized her view of those narrowly focused on internal Church power issues by saying that she wished they would "stop complaining and act like men." Many, of course, did, and spoke eloquently about the imperative of evangelization in what was becoming, at least in the West, a postreligious culture. Moreover, as John Paul often remarked about these lengthy synodal exercises, what happened outside the Synod Hall, in the informal conversations between bishops, was often as important, and sometimes more so, than what happened inside. For it was often "outside" that the ordained leaders of the Church got to know one another and one another's problems—and gained a new sense of possibility in the process.[41]

One high point of the monthlong assembly came on October 21, World Mission Sunday, when John Paul II fulfilled a long-standing ambition and celebrated history's first beatification of a married couple, Luigi and Maria Beltrame Quattrocchi, three of whose children were present for the Mass in St. Peter's Square. Their lives, the Pope said in his homily, were a shining example of a positive answer to Christ's question: "And when the Son of Man comes, will he find faith on earth?" (Luke 18.8). The beatification of the Quattrocchis had been scheduled to coincide with the twentieth anniversary of one of John Paul's favorite documents in a pontificate replete with magisterium: the apostolic exhortation **Familiaris Consortio** [The Community of the Family], by which he had completed the work of the 1980 Synod of Bishops. With **Familiaris Consortio** doubtless in mind, the Pope noted that Luigi and Maria Beltrame Quattrocchi had lived "**an ordinary life in an extraordinary way,**" showing that heroic virtue was indeed a possibility in the vocation of spouse and parent; through their example, the Church had "distinctive confirmation that the path of holiness lived together as a couple is possible, beautiful, extraordinarily fruitful, and fundamental for the good of the family, the Church, and society." Like the bishops present, the Pope concluded, married couples must "renew your missionary zeal," by making their homes "privileged places for announcing and accepting the Gospel in an atmosphere of prayer and . . . Christian solidarity."[42]

The Synod concluded with Mass in St. Peter's on October 27, and the Pope took as his homily text the responsorial psalm antiphon for the Mass of the day—"Proclaim his salvation to every people." He called the bishops to have, "above all," the "**courage to announce and defend sound doctrine,**" even when it entails suffering, and urged them to be good pastors and fathers to their priests. At the end, John Paul read an honor roll of the twenty-two bishops who had been canonized as saints during the twentieth century, a roster that included two Doctors of the Church (Albert the Great and Robert Bellarmine), the English martyr John Fisher, the Irish martyr Oliver Plunkett, several bishops martyred in Vietnam, and the Bohemian emigré who had become bishop of Philadelphia, John Neumann. From these men, as well as from those martyr-bishops who had been beatified (most recently in Ukraine), "there emerges, as in a mosaic, the face of **Christ the Good Shepherd and Missionary of the Father.**" At the "beginning of a new epoch," the Pope concluded, "we fix our eyes on this living icon . . . so that with ever greater dedication we may be servants of the Gospel, hope of the world."[43]

On October 7, as the Synod was concluding its first week of work, American and British forces had begun the military campaign that would eventually depose the Taliban regime in Afghanistan while uprooting the al-Qaeda terrorist camps that had been welcomed by the radical Islamist government; the Taliban collapsed on December 9. John Paul, continuing to carve his own unique path through the turbulence of late 2001, accelerated the planning for a second meeting of world religious leaders in Assisi, which would be held on January 24, 2002. As the new Afghan government took over in December, the Pope marked another milestone, visiting his three hundredth Roman parish in the course of what was by then a twenty-three-year-long personal effort to re-evangelize his own diocese. It was the Third Sunday of Advent, Gaudete Sunday, a traditional day of rejoicing during a season of penitential preparation for Christmas. The Pope thanked the parish of St. María Josefa of the Heart of Jesus and all the parishes of the city for the great encouragement he had received from being with the people of Rome in their neighborhood churches. At the end of a difficult year in which the lethal face of distorted religious conviction had horrified the civilized world, he reminded his Roman parishioners that the Christ Child, whose birth they would celebrate in a few short days, would "come in the silence, humility, and poverty of the crib, and will bring his joy to all who welcome him with open hearts."[44]

THE LONG LENT OF 2002

On January 6, 2002, the **Boston Globe** reported on its front page that a former priest, John Geoghan, had been credibly accused of molesting more than 130 boys over a period of some thirty years—during which time he had been assigned by officials of the Archdiocese of Boston to three different parishes, after the officials were assured by therapists that Geoghan had been "cured." Thus began one of the darkest periods in the history of the Catholic Church in the United States and a period of prolonged anguish for John Paul II.

Karol Wojtyła had come to the papacy with little direct experience of the U.S. Church, save that which he had gained by two visits to America, primarily spent visiting American Polish communities. Over more than two decades of the pontificate, the Pope had come to the view that the Catholic Church in America, for all its difficulties, was in far stronger condition than the Church in western Europe. He had begun to sense that this was the case during his first pastoral visit to the United States in 1979; his evolving view of American Catholic possibility had been confirmed by the tremendous success of World Youth Day-1993, held in Denver at the Pope's insistence (and despite the considerable skepticism of more than a few U.S. bishops). John Paul was also aware that his encyclicals on social doctrine, on the reform of moral theology, on the imperative of Christian mission, on the life issues, on ecumenism, and on the relationship of faith and reason were closely analyzed and vigorously debated in the United States, not simply in ecclesiastical circles but in national newspapers such as the **Wall Street Journal.** In the wake of the communist crack-up, the Pope had encouraged American scholars to work with Polish colleagues in developing a leadership training program for students from the United States and the new democracies of east central Europe; there was much to be learned in both directions, he believed, and the engaged U.S. Church seemed to him a better model for the newly liberated Church in Poland and throughout the Warsaw Pact than the hard-beset Catholic communities of western Europe, which he believed risked becoming a post-Christian culture. John Paul II knew that nothing was perfect in the Church, this side of the Second Coming; but all things considered, the Church was in rather good shape in the United States.

John Paul's response to the unfolding drama of clerical sexual abuse and episcopal misgovernance in America was influenced by this conviction that the Church in the United States was, relatively speaking, sound. The incapacities of the apostolic nunciature in Washington and the Roman Curia also played a role; the papal apartment did not seem to be fully informed of the scandals as the revelations came into the public eye, day by day and week by week. The fact that the Vatican, historically skeptical about media exaggerations, had not yet begun to grapple with the 24/7 world of instant communications and commentary was another factor. So was the ingrained curial instinct, in the face of grim news, to think that "it can't be as bad as all that"—an attitude that shaped (and blunted) perceptions at the senior levels of both the Congregation for Bishops and the Congregation for the Clergy, to whom the Pope would have looked for counsel and guidance. Yet another factor was John Paul's memory of the ways in which charges of sexual impropriety had been used by the SB and other communist intelligence services to destroy the reputations of priests and bishops. In addition, it must have seemed to him almost impossible, at first, that so many American bishops could have been so malfeasant in the exercise of their office, or so taken in by the assurances of the psychotherapists.

The chronology and details of the crisis of Catholic life in the United States, which was aptly dubbed the "Long Lent of 2002" by Father Richard John Neuhaus, have been put on the public record elsewhere.[45] John Paul's first public comment on what had by then become a firestorm in the United States came in his annual Holy Thursday letter to the priests of the world, in which he acknowledged "the sins of some of our brothers who have betrayed the grace of Ordination in succumbing even to the most grievous forms of the **mysterium iniquitatis** [mystery of evil] at work in the world." Unfortunately, in his presentation of the papal letter to the press, the prefect of the Vatican's Congregation for the Clergy, Cardinal Darío Castrillón Hoyos, dismissed reporters' questions about the crisis in the United States, implied that the Pope had far graver matters to worry about (such as peace in the Middle East), and suggested that the whole affair was an American media circus.[46] This only exacerbated the problem with the press, which could readily see that the Pope had made no such suggestion in his Holy Thursday letter.

The American crisis escalated dramatically on April 8 (the Monday after Divine Mercy Sunday), when the **Boston Globe** reported at length on the case of Paul Shanley, who had made a reputation as a "street priest" in Boston. Shanley, it turned out, had defended sex between men and boys at a 1978 meeting of the North American Man-Boy Love Association, and had committed numerous acts of sexual abuse in the following decades. Yet he had been recommended by the Archdiocese of Boston to the Diocese of San Bernardino, California, in a 1990 official letter stating that the abuser had had no known difficulties during his time as a priest in the Massachusetts capital. Other documents obtained by the newspaper demonstrated that Shanley had received several letters of praise from Boston archdiocesan officials, as recently as 1996, when he had retired. Two days later, the **Globe** editorially called on the archbishop of Boston, Cardinal Bernard Law, to resign his office. The **Globe** had long been unhappy with Law's vigorous public pro-life advocacy, but its editorial call for the prelate's resignation was repeated by a much less anti-Law paper, the **Boston Herald.** On April 13, Cardinal Law arrived secretly in Rome and went immediately to see the Pope. At a meeting in the papal apartment with John Paul and Cardinal Giovanni Battista Re of the Congregation for Bishops, Law offered to resign. But the others, who had yet to be fully informed of the magnitude of the problem because of months of inadequate reporting from the nuncio in Washington, Archbishop Gabriel Montalvo, urged Law to stay and resolve the problems, and promised their full help.

To his credit, Cardinal Law was reflecting the realities of the moment, April 13, 2002; John Paul II, Cardinal Re, and others were, in effect, three months behind and were reacting as they might have done had Law come to Rome in January, when the Geoghan story first broke. The following weekend, John Paul and Bishop Stanisław Dziwisz, his secretary, received a dossier of materials on the U.S. crisis, including commentary from prominent U.S. Catholics who were known to be defenders of the pontificate and who were urging strong leadership to address the twin problems of clerical sexual abuse and episcopal misgovernance. That materials of this sort seemed not to have been sent to the papal apartment before underscored that the Holy See was not dealing with the crisis in real time.

The secret meetings with Cardinal Law, the dossier of press materials, and the tough message delivered to the Pope on April 9 by the president of the U.S. Conference of Catholic Bishops, Bishop Wilton Gregory of Belleville, Illinois, convinced John Paul and his senior colleagues in the Curia that something had to be done, and soon, before the situation spiraled out of control. Thus on April 15, the cardinals of the United States and the senior officials of the U.S. bishops conference were summoned to Rome for an emergency meeting to be held a week later with the Pope, Curia officials, and the American cardinals then resident in Rome. John Paul II addressed the emergency meeting on April 23, making it unmistakably clear that "there is no place in the priesthood or religious life for those who would harm the young." He also spoke of his own distress at the gravity of what had been revealed, acknowledged that people were justifiably concerned at how bishops had handled these cases, and put the entire crisis in its proper religious context:

I have been deeply grieved by the fact that priests and religious, whose vocation it is to help people lead holy lives in the sight of God, have themselves caused such suffering and scandal to the young. Because of the great harm done by some priests and religious, the Church herself is viewed with distrust, and many are offended at the way in which the Church's leaders are perceived to have acted in this matter. The abuse which has caused this crisis is by every standard wrong and rightly considered a crime by society; it is also an appalling sin in the eyes of God. To the victims and their families, wherever they may be, I express my profound sense of solidarity and concern.

John Paul concluded with a call to a "holier priesthood, a holier episcopate, and a holier Church," a call that underscored that this was, at bottom, a crisis of fidelity that could be met only by a deeper, more radical fidelity to the truths of Catholic faith—an important response to those Catholics, especially numerous in the Boston area, who were calling for changes in the moral teaching and governance of the Church in response to the crisis.[47]

Further damage was done by a notably inept press conference at the end of the U.S. cardinals' meeting. Few of the American prelates attended; there was no opening statement; a kind of chaos of questioning ensued. Yet despite that sorry end to the process, several crucial points had finally been clarified by the emergency meeting, if months later than they should have been.

The crisis was real, and it was the Church's crisis, not a fantasy concocted by a hostile press. The crisis had many dimensions—psychological, legal, canonical, and political—but it was, fundamentally, a spiritual crisis, a point John Paul had stressed several times in his address to the cardinals' meeting. The demographics of the crisis—subsequently confirmed by a study commissioned by the U.S. bishops—were better understood: there had been odious cases of genuine "pedophilia" (i.e., sexual abuse of prepubescent children), but the overwhelming majority of the abuse had been a matter of homosexual predation by a small percentage of priests over a period of decades. The linkage between those patterns of abuse and the inadequate episcopal response to them, on the one hand, and a culture of dissent against Catholic moral teaching, on the other, had not been thoroughly evaluated, but the subject had been broached. And it had been made unmistakably clear that bishops had failed in their tasks of oversight and would have to exert far more courageous and dynamic leadership in the future.[48]

Some reporters and commentators may have missed the significance of the Pope's assertion in his Holy Thursday letter to priests that the crisis of sexual abuse and episcopal misgovernance had been a powerful example of the **mysterium iniquitatis**— the mystery of evil—at work in the world. That, however, was how John Paul II experienced the Long Lent of 2002. He had spoken forcefully about the reform of the priesthood, all over the world, for more than twenty-three years. He had convened an international Synod of Bishops to spend a month discussing seminary formation, and had completed its work with a powerful apostolic exhortation, **Pastores Dabo Vobis** [I Will Give You Shepherds], that had become the magna carta of seminary reform, especially in the United States. He had sought out priests to strengthen and encourage them; he had shared his eightieth birthday with priests in a global celebration of priestly goodness, less than two years before. He had urged priests to work closely with the young, and had shown just how that could be done during the half century of his own priestly service. For a man who had lived his priesthood nobly, as a continuing act of self-giving, the revelation that some of his brother priests had deeply harmed the Church's young was a terrible wound.

So was the revelation that bishops, whom he had also summoned to a more courageous exercise of their office, had often been less than wise, less than prudent, and in some cases less than honest or courageous in facing clerical sexual abuse. The irony was that John Paul had bent every effort for more than two decades to get bishops thinking of their ministry more in terms of evangelization and less in terms of institutional maintenance; now it seemed that, in some instances, bishops weren't even capable managers, and their administrative failures had created fresh impediments to the credibility of the new evangelization.

A very long Lent, indeed, and one that, for John Paul, would continue to cast shadows for some time. No one having the slightest acquaintance with Karol Wojtyła could doubt that he had been appalled by what had come to light during the Long Lent. Indeed, throughout the first four months of 2002, the question, "Why doesn't Rome do something about this?" reflected the great confidence that U.S. Catholics had in a pope they had come to revere. That, until late April, the Holy See was not experiencing the crisis in real time was an important reminder that even so strong a pope as John Paul II could not always get the Roman Curia to function as it ought, and that the patterns of clericalism and careerism still present in curial life could cause a pope deep personal grief and impede his evangelical mission.[49]

The Continuing Challenge of Holiness

On January 24, John Paul II left Rome by train for Assisi, where, as in 1986, he would welcome world religious leaders whom he had invited to bear witness to their commitment to peace. The 1986 Assisi meeting had been sharply criticized in some quarters as a form of syncretism, despite the Pope's insistence that the meeting was a matter of "being together to pray," rather than "praying together." The 2002 program was arranged to avoid any confusions. The religious leaders (representing the Catholic Church, the Orthodox Churches, the Anglican Communion, the Reformation communities, Judaism, Islam, Hinduism, Buddhism, traditional African religions, and other faiths) began by giving "testimonials to peace" in Lower St. Francis Square. With an eye clearly focused on the events in New York and Washington more than four months before, John Paul opened the gathering by citing the North African Father of the Church, Cyprian: "Let us pray to the heavenly father. Let us implore him as befits those who weep over the ruins, and who fear what remains standing." After the "testimonials to peace" (during which

Sheikh Muhammad Sayyid Tantawi made a political statement about Vatican "support for the Palestinian people"), the leaders went with their coreligionists to various sites in Assisi to pray for peace; John Paul led the Christians in prayer in the Basilica of St. Francis. After sharing a "fraternal meal," the leaders returned to St. Francis Square where a "common commitment to peace" was read in English, Arabic, and Italian. The leaders then each lit a lamp on a candelabrum, and a sign of peace was exchanged before they visited several other Assisi sites and reboarded the train for Rome.[50]

John Paul II had been a staunch defender of Assisi I in 1986; he had also supported the Assisi I follow-up activities of the Sant'Egidio Community, and he believed Assisi II could be helpful in addressing a world of fraying religious comity. Throughout his pastoral life, Karol Wojtyła had never demanded immediate results, content to plant seeds that might flower at a much later date. The Assisi meetings were expressions of that long-range view.

Of perhaps greater immediate importance for the future of interreligious dialogue, however, was a lengthy document issued by the Pontifical Biblical Commission and released in May 2002: "The Jewish People and Their Sacred Scriptures in the Christian Bible." In an interview with the ZENIT News Service, the Commission's secretary, Father Albert Vanhoye, S.J., put in strikingly unambiguous terms the continuing religious debt that Christianity owes to Judaism and to the Hebrew Bible, the privileged place that Judaism will always hold in genuine interreligious dialogue conducted by the Catholic Church, and the reasons why:

> The divine initiatives of deliverance and salvation, the election of Israel, the Covenant, the Law, prayer and worship, the privileged position of Jerusalem and the Temple—all are elements of Israel's Testament that nourish the spiritual life of Christians. . . . We Christians and Jews are really united. Religiously, we are intensely brothers, as we accept the same divine revelation, with the difference that Christians complete it with the paschal mystery of Jesus, which is a great novelty, but this novelty does not cancel the previous revelation, but rather highlights it. . . . [So] this must be the truly Christian attitude: We must consider Jews as brothers and sisters of Jesus and Mary, and, therefore, elder brothers and sisters, as the Holy Father has said.[51]

These were themes that John Paul II had been stressing for more than two decades. That they could be deeply anchored in scholarly biblical analysis suggested that this way of considering Catholicism's relationship to Judaism was not something idiosyncratic to the biography of Karol Wojtyła, but was securely rooted in the foundations of Catholicism—a crucial point to have made if the third millennium of Catholic-Jewish relations was to continue the progress that had been made at the very end of the second millennium, after centuries of pain and difficulty.

ORTHODOX DIFFICULTIES, ORTHODOX POSSIBILITIES

For a brief moment in early 2002, John Paul's efforts to open a door to Russia seemed to be making some progress. On January 15, 2002, the Russian president, Vladimir Putin, told the Polish newspaper **Gazeta Wyborcza** that he was "willing to invite the Pope at any time," but that the ultimate decision on a papal visit to Russia "unfortunately does not depend on me," but on the leadership of Russian Orthodoxy (a curious formulation, given the pattern of relations between the Russian state and the Russian Church for centuries, as well as the KGB connections of both Putin and Patriarch Aleksy II).[52] In any event, the patriarchate seemed to be thawing ever so slightly in its attitude toward John Paul and the Catholic Church, agreeing on January 17 to send a representative to Assisi II.[53] The following day, Patriarch Aleksy said that Putin's willingness to invite the Pope had been "wise," but its wisdom lay in its focus on "the problems between the two Churches," which consisted primarily in the Vatican's "continuing its proselytizing activity in Russia, Ukraine, and Belarus."[54] The mini-thaw began to refreeze a week later, when Russian Orthodoxy's chief ecumenist, Metropolitan Kirill of Smolensk, insisted that the Catholic Church in Russia has "no future." Kirill conceded that the Pope's pastoral visit to Ukraine "was not a catastrophe" but immediately added that it had not "contributed anything to Catholic-Orthodox relations."[55]

The freeze became virtually arctic three weeks later. Determined to provide for the pastoral care of Catholics across the vast expanses of "all the Russias," John Paul canonically erected four Catholic jurisdictions in that country on February 11, 2002: the archdiocese of the Mother of God at Moscow; the diocese of St. Clement at Saratov; the diocese of St. Joseph at Irkutsk; and the diocese of the Transfiguration at Novosibirsk. The unusual diocesan nomenclature—saints and a biblical event, rather than cities—was an effort to ease the aggravations of a still-hostile Russian Orthodox leadership about what some of its leaders were determined to misperceive as an encroachment into its "canonical territory." Joaquín Navarro-Valls issued a statement describing the acts as a "normal administrative decision" and noting that the decision corresponded "to the same pastoral concern that has led the Russian Orthodox Church to create dioceses and other organizational structures for the faithful who live outside the traditional territory." Thus "Catholics in Russia are [being] given the same organization and pastoral care that is enjoyed by Russian Orthodox who live in the West."

Predictably, the Moscow Patriarchate had a different view, describing the moves as "an unfriendly act." Metropolitan Kirill found the Vatican decision "very alarming" and warned that "to divide people on religious grounds means to weaken the nation."[56] The Orthodox attitude hardened even more when it was announced that, on March 3, John Paul II would make a "virtual" visit to Moscow via a television link to the Catholic cathedral in the Russian capital, during which he would lead a prayer service for Russian young people. Orthodox spokesman Vsevolod Chaplin's response to the news was harsh: "One can only be astonished by the irrational persistence and determination with which the Vatican suggests different methods to mark, even if only symbolically, the Pope's presence in Russia."[57]

What could be plausibly interpreted as retaliation was not long in coming, and in a form that illustrated the continuing linkages between Russian Orthodoxy and the Russian state. On April 5, the Russian visa of an Italian priest who had worked in Moscow for thirteen years was lifted from his passport at Sheremetyevo-2 airport outside the Russian capital. Two weeks later, on April 19, Bishop Jerzy Mazur of the diocese of St. Joseph at Irkutsk was returning to Russia from Poland when he was told by the Border Guard Service at the Moscow airport that his multientry visa was no longer valid, because he was named on a list of those to be denied entry to the country. A Polish Embassy official who went to the airport to find out what was happening was told that the decision to block Bishop Mazur's entry had been made by "higher authorities."[58] The dubiously orthodox linkage between Russian Orthodoxy and Russian nationalism was continuing to prove itself the hardest obstacle both to John Paul's ecumenical efforts with the Moscow Patriarchate and to his desire to bring the icon of the Kazanskaya home to Russia.

Yet the Pope refused to retreat from his ecumenical probes into the more open sectors of Orthodoxy, and scheduled a visit to Bulgaria in May 2002. He took a circuitous route there, however, stopping briefly in the Caucasus at Baku, the capital of Azerbaijan, on May 22–23. Azerbaijan is one of the world's few Shia Muslim countries, and the Pope took the opportunity to plead once again for religious tolerance and peace. As they were getting off the plane in Baku, Joaquín Navarro-Valls (who had been fielding questions from the press about the reasoning behind a papal visit to a country with an infinitesimal Catholic population) said to the Pope, "Holy Father, there are only one hundred twenty-three Catholics in this country." John Paul corrected him: "No, it's one hundred twenty." However many there were, or weren't, they, too, had a right to think that Peter's ministry of strengthening the brethren extended to them. In addition to interreligious contacts and an address to Azeri cultural, political, and religious leaders in which he described holiness as "the fullness of beauty," John Paul celebrated Mass in a sports center, the country's last Catholic church having been destroyed by Stalin in 1937. For the first time in his travels, the Pope spent the night in a hotel, where the manager gave him **ash,** the Azeri national dish, made of rice, meat, cabbage, and grape sauce; press reports indicated that John Paul asked for more.[59]

The Pope's increasing frailty was now more evident on each of his pilgrimages, but he prepared for each pastoral visit as he had for those he had made when he was in vigorous good health—by learning what he could of the local language. So a young Bulgarian priest was recruited to teach Bulgarian to the eighty-two-year-old pontiff.[60] The Pope brought a relic of Blessed John XXIII as a gift to Bulgarian Catholics; a quarter century before his election as pope in 1958, Angelo Roncalli had been apostolic nuncio in Sofia, the Bulgarian capital. While predominantly Orthodox, Bulgaria had a small Byzantine-rite Catholic community, which had suffered terribly under Bulgarian communism. Their exarch, Christo Proikov, told the London-based **Tablet** that "the Pope's visit shows that we are not forgotten. . . . We had no contact with Rome for 50 years, but we stayed faithful. This is measured with the martyrdom of many priests and monks who died for the faith, and the suffering of some who are still living."[61]

John Paul was greeted at the airport by the Bulgarian president, Georgi Parvanov, and bantered with the crowd in his new Bulgarian: "The president is young and that's why he's standing," the Pope told a crowd of some 5,000; "he asked the Pope to sit because the Pope is old."[62] In a conversation later with Parvanov, John Paul told the former communist that he had never taken seriously "the so-called Bulgarian connection" to the 1981 assassination attempt on his life "because of my great esteem and respect for the Bulgarian people." The Bulgarian foreign minister, Solomon Passy, told **The Tablet** that the Pope had "put an end to a big and unjust lie which has stained the name of Bulgaria," a feat that Passy described as Bulgaria's "largest diplomatic success since the Second World War."[63] Close students of the events before, during, and after May 13, 1981, who knew that the "Bulgarian connection" referred to the Bulgarian secret police and their KGB masters, not to the Bulgarian people, understood and appreciated the Pope's willingness to reassure the Bulgarian people of his affection, but were less inclined than foreign minister Passy to declare the case closed.

Ecumenical advance was John Paul's strategic goal in Bulgaria, a country whose Orthodox Church had close ties to the Patriarchate of Moscow. He had previously been to the historically Orthodox countries of Romania, Georgia, and Greece; he had persuaded many of the Orthodox faithful in Ukraine that he was a friend, not an aggressor; he had forged close ties to the Armenian Apostolic Church. Now he was in Bulgaria. Perhaps this slow pilgrimage around the borders of Eastern Christianity in Europe would eventually open the path to Moscow, in a process John Paul described in Sofia as "gradual growth in ecclesial communion." His homily at the May 26 beatification of three Assumptionist priests martyred during Bulgaria's postwar communist period stressed that both Catholic and Orthodox Christians had suffered at the hands of the Stalinist regime, and that "the ecumenism of saints and martyrs . . . is perhaps the most convincing."[64] His witness was not a matter of words alone, however. The Pope impressed Bulgarians by his determination and patience as much as by his familiar words about the Latin and Byzantine dual lungs of a renewed and reunited Europe. One Orthodox archbishop worried aloud about John Paul's frailty: "I think the people around him, they must tell him he has to stop." But as Cardinal Walter Kasper, president of the Pontifical Council for Promoting Christian Unity, nicely put it when asked about the Pope's health, "Suffering is in a sense his profession."[65]

John Paul's obvious physical difficulties—his difficulties walking, the tilt of his head, a sometimes frozen expression on his face, and the trembling in his arm—continued to feed the media rumor mill.

So did some changes in the manner in which he conducted events in Bulgaria (for example, by reading only small portions of his addresses or homilies, with the balance being read by aides). Speculation on the Pope's condition and the prospects for his pontificate were also primed by Vatican "insiders," who more often than not were low-level curial bureaucrats with no access to serious information. Thus after the apostolic visit to Azerbaijan and Bulgaria, a Czech newspaper, **Tyden,** ran a story suggesting that the Pope would step down after an August 2002 trip to Poland. Navarro-Valls denied the rumor, noting that the pontifical schedule remained a full one and that events were being added for 2003. John Paul's old friend Bishop Tadeusz Pieronek lived up to the Polish meaning of his surname ["Little Thunder"] with a more pungent comment on the latest speculations about a papal abdication: John Paul would remove himself from office, the rector of the Pontifical Theological Academy in Kraków said, "when hens grow teeth."[66]

On June 16, three weeks after his return from Bulgaria, John Paul II canonized Catholicism's most famous twentieth-century stigmatic, Padre Pio of Pietrelcina. A Capuchin Franciscan, born Francesco Forgione in 1887, Padre Pio had borne the wounds of Christ in his hands, feet, and side from 1918 until his death fifty years later. John Paul attributed the miraculous cure of an old friend, Dr. Wanda Półtawska, to the intercession of Padre Pio, to whom he had written just prior to the opening of Vatican II, asking prayers for Połtawska when her life seemed in danger from cancer. A decade and a half earlier, the Capuchin's devotion to the priestly ministry of the confessional and his willingness to endure physical suffering had made a lasting impression on Karol Wojtyła during his student days in Rome in 1946–48—when Wojtyła would also have learned about Roman suspicions of Padre Pio and controversies surrounding his ministry.[67] Thus the Pope's homily at the canonization Mass began with a reflection on the famous saying of Jesus, from that day's Gospel reading, that "my yoke is easy and my burden light" (Matthew 11.30):

Jesus's words to his disciples, which we have just heard, help us to understand the most important message of this solemn celebration. Indeed, in a certain sense, we can consider them as a magnificent summary of the whole life of Padre Pio, today proclaimed a saint.

The evangelical image of the "yoke" recalls the many trials that the humble Capuchin of San Giovanni Rotondo had to face. Today we contemplate in him how gentle the "yoke" of Christ is, and how truly light is his burden, when it is borne with faithful love. The life and mission of Padre Pio prove that difficulties and sorrows, if accepted out of love, are transformed into a privileged way of holiness, which opens onto the horizons of a greater good, known only to the Lord.[68]

Yet that yoke and burden included the cross, of which St. Paul had spoken in the day's second reading: "But may I never boast except in the cross of Our Lord Jesus Christ" (Galatians 6.14). That, John Paul said, was the radiance that "shines above all in Padre Pio"—the willingness to "wear the marks of the Cross," which was a reminder to the world that it "needs to rediscover the value of the Cross in order to open the heart to love."[69]

NEW WORLD TRIUMPH

Part of the long shadow cast by the events of September 11, 2001, fell on the planning for World Youth Day-2002, scheduled for Toronto, Canada. Ought the event be postponed until the threat of al-Qaeda had been reduced? Would young people simply refuse to travel, given the threat of hijacking? Would a terrorist organization attempt to disrupt the event itself, or poison the mass-produced food for the pilgrims, or take hostages? All these scenarios, and others, were bruited inside and outside the Vatican. Then there was the Pope's health—suppose he didn't come? Every time John Paul insisted that he would be there without fail, just as unfailingly another spate of rumors that he wouldn't, or couldn't, seemed to start.

On the afternoon of July 23, Pope John Paul II, having declined the use of an electronic cargo lift to get to the ground from the door of the Alitalia 767 on which he had flown from Rome, walked slowly, steadily, and by himself down the stairway that had been rolled up to the jetliner's door. On reaching the tarmac at Toronto's Lester B. Pearson International Airport, he pounded his cane onto the ground three times, as if to say, "You see? I told you I'd be here and you didn't believe me. Well, I'm here."

Toronto in July 2002 was a city whose high culture and media tended toward a certain smugness about their secularist certainties. Over six days, those certainties would be challenged—and if not displaced, then at least shaken. The challenge came primarily from the young people of World Youth Day themselves: pilgrims from forty countries and thirty-eight Canadian cities defied the terrorists, the endless bad news of the Long Lent of 2002, and the skeptics to come to Toronto and be with John Paul II at a World Youth Day whose icons were youthful heroes of the Catholic faith, including Blessed Marcel Callo, a martyr of the Mauthausen concentration camp, and Blessed Gianna Beretta Molla, a wife, mother, and pediatrician who had sacrificed her life for that of her unborn child in 1962.

Perhaps the event's most dramatic moment came on Friday night, July 26, when, according to the now well-established rhythm of World Youth Day, the pilgrims were to participate in the traditional devotion known as the Way of the Cross, replicating Christ's journey to Calvary. At World Youth Day-1997 in Paris, the Way of the Cross had been celebrated in several venues; in Toronto in July 2002, it was one great act of spiritual witness on the part of perhaps half a million people, walking solemnly through the center of the city, beginning at City Hall and continuing up University Avenue to the Ontario Provincial Parliament buildings in Queen's Park. Friday night in Toronto is usually full of buzz; Friday night in Toronto had never been abuzz like this. Both local citizens and the local media were stunned by this public display of religious devotion in which one billion people throughout the world shared through a television feed from the CBC (Canadian Broadcasting Corporation).

The official World Youth Day-2002 souvenir album captured the spiritual electricity of the moment:

Jesus, Mary, the women, the soldiers, Pilate, Simon of Cyrene, the apostles and all the others pass by City Hall, enormous hospitals, corporate headquarters, and the provincial legislature. They walk along streets of concrete and asphalt, along the tree-lined boulevard that is University Avenue with its adjoining parks and tiny gardens, from the fading light of

524 THE END AND THE BEGINNING

sunset to the darkness of night. An immense crowd, hundreds of thousands strong, . . . line[s] the route to watch and wonder and pray. Pilgrims without borders, pilgrims of the night, they come together with Jesus to relive his suffering and death.

Jesus moves through the heart of the city. He carries the Cross past air-conditioned skyscrapers filled with the busy and the powerful. He walks past the sick in the hospitals that line University Avenue. He shares their suffering, the young and old, male and female.

He makes his way, station after station, through the believers and the atheists, the hopeful and the despairing, the rich and the poor, the happy families and the forlorn individuals. He is the object of scrutiny by curious onlookers, excited children, contemplative crowds. He passes through a gathering of nations, languages, and cultures, sowing on his way the question that every Christian must answer: "And you, who do you say that I am?" He is nailed to the cross, then placed in the tomb. The crowd disperses into the night, each person looking for the last station—the station that manifests itself in life's many twists and turns.

Tonight Jesus passes among us on the Way of the Cross—just as he does every day on the streets of the world.[70]

While the young people of World Youth Day were meeting in their catechetical groups, getting acquainted at Exhibition Place, and then giving Toronto an unexpected shock by turning its downtown into a medieval mystery play on Friday night, John Paul II was resting on Strawberry Island in Lake Simcoe, where the general secretary of the event, Father Thomas Rosica, C.S.B., had arranged something akin to the kind of vacation lodgings the Pope had long enjoyed in the Italian mountains. But John Paul was not only resting: he visited the "developmentally delayed adults" at the Huronia Regional Centre; took a boat ride on Lake Simcoe and dispensed rosaries to startled boaters whom he encountered; and hosted a lunch for fourteen young people on Friday afternoon, including Robin Cammarota, five members of whose Bronx parish in New York City had been killed on 9/11. Stories were exchanged over spaghetti, asparagus, salad, and cake; one youngster from Germany, twenty-year-old Anneke Pehlmöller, quickly caught on to Karol Wojtyła's lifelong sweet tooth: "I think the Holy Father really liked the cake." A twenty-six-year-old teacher from China, Shirley Tso, told John Paul that her people "loved him." "They love me?" the Pope responded. "Yes," Ms. Tso assured him, to which the Pope replied, "It is incredible."[71]

So was World Youth Day-2002's last event, the closing Mass at Toronto's Downsview Park, a 664-acre former Canadian military base in the northern part of the sprawling metropolis. The previous night's vigil had been built around World Youth

Day-2002's "salt and light" theme, with the Pope asking the hundreds of thousands of young people present to be his spiritual heirs and to build the civilization of love, as he had tried to do for decades. At the end of the vigil, just before his final blessing, John Paul gave pieces of salt to twelve young people, representing all present. He then returned to the motherhouse of the Sisters of St. Joseph, his Toronto residence, promising to return the next morning for the closing Mass. Then the weather intervened, dramatically.

As 9:30 A.M., the hour for the closing Mass, approached, some 800,000 pilgrims and congregants at Downsview Park were pelted by fierce rains and told not to come near the massive metal cross at the high altar, for fear of lightning strikes. The winds were so strong that tubular, four-story-high television platforms began tilting ominously, and correspondents and commentators were wiping rivers of water off their faces, live and in color. Local weather forecasters warned of the danger of tornadoes at just about the time Mass was scheduled to begin; their concerns were relayed to the papal party by the chief of security. On the helicopter ferrying the Pope to the venue, Stanisław Dziwisz said to John Paul II, "We need an intervention from God." After the helicopter landed safely, the Pope was taken to a temporary sacristy where he was vested for Mass—a time during which he habitually prayed, as a preparation for the liturgy. Dziwisz asked the Pope to pray that

God would clear the weather so that the Mass could go forward and no one would be hurt. John Paul made a great sign of the cross toward the sky, and went back to his prayer.

The worst of the storms passed; the weather began to quiet down; and by the time John Paul began his homily, the sun was shining on the drenched crowds. To Dziwisz, it was all eerily reminiscent of what had happened in Ukraine the year before. During John Paul's address to young people in L'viv, rain began pouring down so heavily that no one could hear what the Pope was saying. So John Paul began singing a Polish children's song, the equivalent of "Rain, rain go away . . ." He finished the song, the rain stopped, the crowd was stunned—and the rain commenced again after the Pope's remarks.[72]

However the resolution of the meteorological drama might be explained, John Paul's final Mass in Toronto was a fitting conclusion to what had been a remarkable week. Vested in the green chasuble Catholic priests wear while celebrating Mass during "Ordinary Time," the Pope reminded his young charges that there were, in fact, no ordinary times for believers: for every life is by definition an extraordinary life, because every life is a life for whom Christ died. "Be the salt of the earth, be the light of the world!" he urged them "Do not be afraid to follow Christ on the royal road of the Cross!" At one point in his homily, John Paul pointed out that "you are young and the Pope is old"—which produced a spontaneous and lengthy chant in reply: "The Pope is young! The Pope is young!"

This being 2002, something had to be said about the Long Lent, and John Paul said it, forthrightly:

> **If you love Jesus, love the Church!** Do not be discouraged by the sins and failings of some of her members. The harm done by some priests and religious to the young and vulnerable **fills us all with a deep sense of sadness and shame.** But think of the vast majority of dedicated and generous priests and religious whose only wish is to serve and do good! . . . At difficult moments in the Church's life, the call to holiness becomes ever more urgent. **And holiness is not a question of age;** it is a matter of **living in the Holy Spirit.**[73]

The night before, a young man named Rémy Perras, who had been chosen to address the Pope on behalf of his generation, spontaneously exclaimed, "You are our father and our grandfather!"[74] His sentiments were not unique, but they left open the question: why did John Paul II affect young people this way? An answer suggested itself at the conclusion of the Pope's homily. The young people at Downsview Park had grown up in a world that constantly pandered to them, in advertising, dress codes, language; here was a man who did not pander, but who challenged. Moreover, he was not asking the young to take up anything other than the cause in which he was so clearly pouring out his life:

> Although I have lived through much darkness, under harsh totalitarian regimes, I have seen enough evidence to be unshakably convinced that no difficulty, no fear is so great that it can completely suffocate **the hope that springs eternal in the hearts of the young.** You are our hope; the young are our hope. Do not let that hope die! Stake your lives on it! **We are not the sum of our weaknesses and failures;** we are the sum of the Father's love for us and our real capacity to become the image of his Son.[75]

At the end of the Mass, John Paul asked the pilgrims present to take out the small wooden crosses they had been given in their knapsacks and to put them on—a kind of commissioning to take the Gospel out into the world. World Youth Day-2002 concluded with the Sunday Angelus, during which the Pope announced that World Youth Day-2005 would be held in Germany, at Cologne. John Paul then thanked the authorities and the planners for their work and extended final greetings to the pilgrims in English, French, Spanish, Portuguese, German, and Polish. His French remarks, quoting one of Augustine's tractates on the Gospel of John, were poignant—and, at the end, put Christ once again at the center of the pilgrim way: "We have been happy together in the light we have shared. We have really enjoyed being together. We have really rejoiced. But as we leave one another, let us not leave Him."[76]

John Paul's route home took him to Guatemala—where he canonized "Brother Pedro" de San José de Betancourt, a seventeenth-century apostle of charity sometimes called the "St. Francis of the Americas"—and to Mexico City. There, before one of the greatest throngs of a pontificate that had already drawn some of the largest crowds in human history, the Pope canonized Juan Diego Cuauhtlatoatzin, the sixteenth-century Indian who had received the impress of the icon of Our Lady of Guadalupe on his mantel, or tilma, in 1531. Juan Diego had been a figure of controversy for decades, and some scholars had denied his existence; six years after his 1990 beatification by John Paul II at the Basilica of Our Lady of Guadalupe in Mexico City, an abbot long associated with the shrine, Father Guillermo Schulenberg, revived the controversy by describing Juan Diego as a fictional character in a myth. A Vatican investigation followed; the report of a group of thirty scholars from different countries, presented to the Holy See's Congregation for the Causes of Saints, took the position that Juan Diego had indeed existed, thus clearing the way for the canonization.

For John Paul, Juan Diego embodied the meeting of two cultures, and the formation of a new national identity, through the power of a universal Gospel that could speak to all:

> **"The Lord looks down from heaven, he sees all the sons of men"** [Psalm 33.13], we recited with the Psalmist, once again confessing our faith in God who makes no distinctions of race or culture. In accepting the Christian message without forgoing his indigenous identity, Juan Diego discovered the profound truth of the new humanity, in which we are all called to be children of God. Thus he facilitated the fruitful meeting of two worlds and became the catalyst for the new Mexican identity, closely united to Our Lady of Guadalupe, whose mestizo face expresses her spiritual motherhood which embraces all Mexicans.[77]

The following day, August 1, John Paul beatified two seventeenth-century Indian lay martyrs, Juan Battista and Jacinto de los Angeles, during a Liturgy of the Word at the Basilica of Guadalupe. Another controversy ensued when the master of papal liturgical ceremonies, Bishop Piero Marini, arranged for the rite to include a traditional Zapotec Indian "blessing" of the Pope, featuring a native woman and a great deal of smoke.

WOODEN SHOES, DIVINE MERCY, AND THE MYSTERIES OF LIGHT

John Paul returned to Castel Gandolfo for a few weeks of relative quiet after his New World travels before leaving on August 16 for a brief visit to Poland. After arriving at the Kraków airport, he went to stay in his old rooms in the archiepiscopal residence at Franciszkańska, 3. The next day, he consecrated the new (and starkly modernist) Basilica of Divine Mercy in the Łagiewniki area of Kraków, a few hundred yards from the convent chapel where the relics of St. Faustyna Kowalska were venerated. He had come to Łagiewniki, he said in his homily, because humanity's need for God's mercy comes "from the depth of hearts filled with suffering, apprehension, and uncertainty, and at the same time yearning for an infallible source of hope." They had all come to Łagiewniki "to look into the eyes of the merciful Jesus, in order to find deep within his gaze the reflection of his inner life, as well as the light of grace which we have already received so often, and which God holds out to us anew each day and every day." He wished **"solemnly to entrust the world to Divine Mercy"** for it was only **"in the mercy of God [that] the world will find peace and mankind will find happiness!"**[78] No one begrudged the native son a few moments of reminiscence before the final blessing:

At the end of this solemn liturgy, I want to say that many of my personal memories are tied to this place. During the Nazi occupation, when I was working in the Solvay factory near here, I used to come here. Even now I recall the street that goes from Borek Fałęcki to Dębniki that I took every day, going to work on the different [shifts] with the wooden shoes on my feet. They're the shoes we used to wear then. How was it possible to imagine that one day the man with the wooden shoes would consecrate the Basilica of the Divine Mercy at Łagiewniki [in] Kraków.[79]

The following day, a Sunday, John Paul II celebrated yet another in his series of colossal outdoor Masses on the Błonia Krakowski, the Kraków Commons, where in June 1979 he had begged his people never to lose touch with the Christian roots of their nation and culture. The holiness that had nurtured those roots was the theme on this occasion, as the Pope beatified four Poles: Sancja Szymkowiak, a sister who had died in 1942 from the hardships of the Nazi occupation; Jan Beyzym, a missionary to the lepers of Madagascar who died there in 1912; Jan Balicki, who had suffered much from both the Nazi occupation and the communist usurpation of Poland's liberties before dying in 1948; and Zygmunt Feliks Feliński, the archbishop of Warsaw in 1862–63, who spent twenty years in Siberian exile before his death in 1895. John Paul returned to Rome on

August 19, having said Mass once again at one of his favorite spots for meditation and reflection during his years as a bishop in Kraków, the Holy Land shrine of Kalwaria Zebrzydowska, which was on the road to his boyhood home, Wadowice.

After presiding and preaching at the September 20 funeral Mass of another twentieth-century confessor, Cardinal Francis Xavier Nguyên van Thuân, whom he described as a man "who lived his whole life under the banner of hope," John Paul led a joint Catholic-Lutheran Vespers service in St. Peter's on October 4, marking the seventh centenary of the birth of St. Bridget of Sweden. Two days later, before a tremendous crowd in St. Peter's Square composed in large part of members of Opus Dei, the Pope canonized Josemaría Escrivá de Balaguer, the founder of "The Work." In his homily, the Pope stressed the ways in which the new saint had helped others to see that "work, and any other activity, carried out with the help of grace, is converted into a means of daily sanctification." St. Josemaría, John Paul continued, had taught a "supernatural vision of life" in which every activity is undertaken in the midst of a "life in which God is always present." What can seem monotonous to us is in fact the way that God comes to us, and the way that "we can cooperate with his plan of salvation." Yet for all his determination to see Christians convert the world through apostolic witness in their daily lives, St. Josemaría had recognized "what is not a paradox but a perennial truth: the fruitfulness of the apostolate lies above all in prayer and in intense and constant sacramental life." Conversation with the Lord was "the secret of holiness and the true success of the saints."[80]

The next day, while more than 100,000 pilgrims remained in Rome after the Escrivá canonization, John Paul II welcomed Romanian Orthodox Patriarch Teoctist to Rome, formally greeting him at the end of an audience for the pilgrims and entrusting Teoctist and his ministry to the pilgrims' prayers. It was, papal spokesman Navarro-Valls remembered, another way to underscore the ecumenical imperative, as was the grand program laid out for the patriarch, which included visits to the Roman major basilicas, lectures at the Pontifical Gregorian University and the Pontifical Institute for Oriental Studies, an evening with the Sant'Egidio Community, and lunch following several hours of meetings with the Pope. The week came to an end with a Mass at St. Peter's on October 13, at which the two octogenarian leaders, eighty-two-year-old John Paul II and eighty-seven-year-old Teoctist, jointly presided over the Liturgy of the Word and preached (John Paul deferring to Teoctist for the first homily), before they recited the Creed together in Romanian. During the Liturgy of the Eucharist, Teoctist returned to the altar for the sign of peace, and then at the end of Mass came back to the altar again to give the final blessing to the congregation after the Pope had given his.[81] In a pontificate of exceptional ecumenical hospitality, an especially warm welcome had been reserved for Patriarch Teoctist, the first Orthodox leader to welcome John Paul to a historically Orthodox country.

Seventy-two hours after Teoctist returned to Bucharest, John Paul II gave the Catholic Church another surprise: five new mysteries of the Rosary, which he described in an apostolic letter, **Rosarium Virginis Mariae,** signed on October 16, 2002, to mark the beginning of the twenty-fifth year of his pontificate. The letter began with the Pope reminding his readers that the Rosary, while an instrument of Marian piety, was "at heart a Christocentric prayer," as each of its fifty-three invocations of Mary centered on the phrase, "And blessed is the fruit of thy womb, Jesus." John Paul then invited the Church to rediscover the power of the Rosary as a prayer containing "all the **depth of the Gospel message in its entirety**"—a kind of "compendium" of the New Testament.[82] It was to underscore that Gospel-centeredness of the Rosary that the Pope proposed as "an addition to the traditional pattern" of reciting the Rosary.

As the Rosary had evolved over the second millennium of Christian history, it had invited meditation on the incarnation, death, and resurrection of Christ, and on the fruits of the resurrection in the early Church, by means of three clusters of five "mysteries": the Joyful Mysteries, dealing with the birth of Christ and his youth; the Sorrowful Mysteries, dealing with the Passion; and the Glorious Mysteries, from the Resurrection through the Descent of the Holy Spirit and on to the Assumption of Mary, first of disciples and pattern for all discipleship, into heaven. What was missing from this schema, John Paul noted, was a "meditation on certain particularly significant moments in [Christ's] public ministry." Thus he proposed, subject to "the freedom of individuals and communities," a fourth set of meditations, the "Mysteries of Light" or Luminous Mysteries, centered on the public life of Jesus: "(1) his Baptism in the Jordan, (2) his self-manifestation at the wedding of Cana, (3) his proclamation of the Kingdom of God, with his call to conversion [as at the Sermon on the Mount], (4) his Transfiguration, and finally (5) his institution of the Eucharist, as the sacramental expression of the Paschal Mystery."[83] Each of these new Luminous Mysteries, John Paul explained, was **"a revelation of the Kingdom now present in the very person of Jesus."** It was true, he noted, that "in these mysteries, apart from the miracle at Cana, **the presence of Mary remains in the background."** Yet it was also true that Mary's instruction to the waiters at the wedding feast—"Do whatever he tells you"—was first made "directly by the Father at the Baptism in the Jordan and echoed by John the Baptist" before being "placed upon Mary's lips at Cana" and becoming her "great, maternal counsel . . . to the Church of every age."[84]

Throughout his pontificate, John Paul II was accused of a kind of rigid traditionalism, especially by an often uncomprehending secular press, but not infrequently within the Church as well. The addition of the Mysteries of Light to one of the most traditional of Catholic devotions underscored the poverty of this characterization. Not only was the Pope "changing the Rosary," as some put it; he was doing so in order to bring into clearer light the radical character of the Incarnation: here, in Jesus and in the Church that is his Mystical Body in history, we can touch the Kingdom of God present among us. Evangelical witness to the truth of the Gospel amidst the turbulence of history was at the heart of Marian piety, as Karol Wojtyła had learned from reading St. Louis Grignion de Montfort during World War II. To remind the Church of that truth at the beginning of the third millennium was the strategic goal of introducing the Mysteries of Light.[85]

To those with a sense of modern Italian history, the Pope's address to the Italian parliament on November 14 was a surprise as great as the alteration of the "traditional pattern" of the Rosary. Modern Italy had been born in a decades-long fit of anticlericalism leading to the occupation and absorption of the Papal States; the effects of that ugliness had lingered in some minds far beyond the resolution of the outstanding issues in the 1929 Lateran Treaty, by which the popes were recognized as sovereigns of a new entity, Vatican City State, and several extraterritorial properties in and around Rome (such as Castel Gandolfo). Roman mayor Walter Veltroni, not wishing to be trumped completely by the national parliament, made John Paul a citizen of Rome on October 31. The Pope (who ended every day by blessing the city from his bedroom window) couldn't resist a joke: "It took me twenty-four years of work to get this," he told the mayor. "St. Paul had it easier."[86]

In his address at the Palazzo Montecitorio to 800 parliamentarians and national political figures, including Prime Minister Silvio Berlusconi and President Carlo Azeglio Ciampi, John Paul stressed a theme that was becoming ever more prominent in his public witness: the importance of Europe remaining in contact with its Christian roots. As he put it to the heirs of the revolution of Garibaldi and Cavour, "Italy's social and cultural identity, and the civilizing mission it has exercised and continues to exercise in Europe and the world, would be most difficult to understand without reference to Christianity, its lifeblood." Some declined to applaud during the forty-five-minute speech. But when it was over, the entire audience gave the Pope a standing ovation, a tribute to his physical courage as well as a gesture of gratitude to the Polish pope who had paid more attention to being a pastor in Rome and Italy than had many of his Italian predecessors.[87]

The year ended with a reminder that the Long Lent in America continued. On December 13, 2002, John Paul II accepted the resignation of Cardinal Bernard Law as archbishop of Boston, finally acceding to the cardinal's judgment that the circumstances made it impossible for him to govern the diocese effectively.

A Boston auxiliary bishop, Richard Lennon, was appointed apostolic administrator until a successor was named. In May 2004, John Paul named Law, who had spent the intervening year and a half out of the public eye, the archpriest of the Basilica of St. Mary Major.

The turbulence of history had displayed itself with a kind of inexorability in the two years following the Great Jubilee of 2000. September 11, the war in Afghanistan, the Long Lent of 2002, continuing ecumenical and interreligious conflict—all of these wore on the Pope at least as heavily as the burden of his illness. Yet John Paul had not failed to keep faith with his own charge to the entire Church at the end of the jubilee year—to leave the safe, shallow waters of institutional maintenance and put out into the deep of history in order to advance the new evangelization. His witness to truth and charity in Greece, Ukraine, the Caucasus, Central Asia, and Bulgaria, as well as the remarkable success of World Youth Day-2002 in Toronto, defined a new phase in the pontificate, one in which the Pope would lead by suffering, and lead through his suffering.

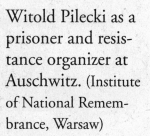

Witold Pilecki as a prisoner and resistance organizer at Auschwitz. (Institute of National Remembrance, Warsaw)

Witold Pilecki, prisoner of Poland's postwar communist regime. (Institute of National Remembrance, Warsaw)

Exhumation of the bodies of Polish officers murdered by the Soviet NKVD at Katyń in 1940. (Institute of National Remembrance, Warsaw)

Father Karol Wojtyła and young friends, June 1952. (Stanisław Rybicki)

Father Karol Wojtyła in Zakopane, April 1953. (Danuta Ciesielska)

Cardinal Karol Wojtyła preaching in defense of human rights during the 1970s. (Archives of the Archdiocese of Katowice)

Confrontation at Gdańsk, 1970. (Institute of National Remembrance, Warsaw)

The men's pilgrimage to Piekary Śląskie, May 27, 1973. (Archives of the Archdiocese of Katowice)

"Be not afraid!": St. Peter's Square, October 22, 1978. *(L'Osservatore Romano)*

Pope John Paul II and Cardinal Stefan Wyszyński, October 23, 1978. *(L'Osservatore Romano)*

Lech Wałęsa and Mieczysław Jagielski sign the Gdańsk Accords, August 31, 1980. (Institute of National Remembrance, Warsaw)

The Three Crosses Monument in Gdańsk, December 1980. (Institute of National Remembrance, Warsaw)

John Paul II celebrates Mass for Solidarity delegation in the papal apartment chapel, January 18, 1981. *(L'Osservatore Romano)*

John Paul II exchanges gifts with Solidarity delegation, January 1981. *(L'Osservatore Romano)*

CHAPTER EIGHT

Darkening Valley

2003–2004

February 7, 2003	John Paul II approves revisions in canon law requested by American bishops in light of sexual abuse crisis.
March 6, 2003	John Paul's poem cycle, **Roman Triptych,** is published in Poland.
March 19, 2003	American-led coalition military forces invade Iraq.
April 17, 2003	John Paul II issues his fourteenth encyclical, **Ecclesia de Eucharistia** [The Church from the Eucharist].
May 3–4, 2003	John Paul II in Spain.
June 5–9, 2003	John Paul's visit to Croatia marks his hundredth pastoral pilgrimage outside Italy.
June 22, 2003	John Paul II in Bosnia-Herzegovina

June 28, 2003	Publication of **Ecclesia in Europa** [The Church in Europe], John Paul's apostolic exhortation completing the 1999 Synod on Europe.
September 11–14, 2003	John Paul II in Slovakia.
October 16, 2003	On the twenty-fifth anniversary of the pontificate, John Paul issues the apostolic exhortation **Pastores Gregis** [Shepherds of the Flock], which completes the work of the 2001 Synod of Bishops.
October 19, 2003	Beatification of Mother Teresa of Calcutta.
October 21, 2003	John Paul II creates thirty-one new cardinals at his ninth ordinary consistory.
March 14, 2004	John Paul II becomes third-longest-serving pope in history, after Peter and Pius IX.
May 16, 2004	John Paul II's last canonization ceremony.
May 18, 2004	**Alzatevi, andiamo!** [Rise, Let Us Be on Our Way!], John Paul's memoir of his life as a bishop, is published.
June 5–6, 2004	John Paul II in Switzerland.
August 14–15, 2004	In Lourdes, John Paul describes himself as "a sick man among the sick."

| August 28, 2004 | Kazanskaya icon is returned to Patriarch Aleksy II in Moscow. |
| October 7, 2004 | John Paul issues **Mane Nobiscum Domine** [Stay with Us, Lord] for the 2004–5 Year of the Eucharist |

On Sunday evening, October 12, 2003, Polish national television staged a two-and-a-half-hour tribute to Poland's most famous son, four days before John Paul II's silver jubilee as Bishop of Rome. The program was anchored from the Sala Clementina of the Apostolic Palace in Rome, with live participation from Kraków, Częstochowa, Warsaw, and the Pope's hometown of Wadowice. The audience in the Sala Clementina consisted of senior members of the Roman Curia and members of the diplomatic corps accredited to the Holy See. For a half hour or so before the live broadcast began, the guests were entertained by a Polish youth choir, whose voices could be heard in the chapel of the papal apartment, the windows of which open into the Clementina.

The five commentators who had been invited to speak from the program's Roman anchor site had been told that the Holy Father, who would not appear during the broadcast, would watch the program in his apartment via a special direct feed. But the

Pope had evidently heard the choir and decided he wanted to go downstairs to thank the youngsters. Thus, twenty minutes or so before airtime, John Paul II was wheeled into the Sala Clementina on a mobile chair, from which he greeted and blessed the choir. He then asked that the Polish anchorman, Piotr Kraśko, and the five commentators be brought to the rear of the Sala Clementina so that he could extend his greetings.

One by one, the six men bent down and shook hands with the man being honored—a man who found it difficult to hold his head upright, whose face seemed a frozen mask, and whose suffering was almost palpable, but who spoke with burning intensity through his eyes. He could say little; but then there was little to say. In the week in which he celebrated his twenty-fifth anniversary as pope, Karol Wojtyła of Wadowice, Kraków, and Rome was continuing his pilgrim's journey through a darkening valley. Those clear, blue eyes spoke of his pain at what his body had done to him. Yet they also spoke silently of suffering borne in faith and of the abandonment of self to the will of God.[1]

His silver jubilee was celebrated as his pilgrim's progress took him into two years of troubles, both personal and public. Among the latter were the war he tried and failed to prevent in Iraq, and his ever more frustrating efforts to convince the newly expanded European Union to acknowledge the Christian roots of European civilization as one important resource for building Europe's future. Yet his anniversary year also saw the return of Karol Wojtyła, poet, and the following year saw another installment of papal memoirs and the completion of a book-length philosophical conversation on the nature of freedom, the concept of "nation," cultural and personal memory, the coexistence of good and evil in the world—and what all this might mean for the twenty-first century. In 2003 and 2004, there was sanctity to be acknowledged publicly—as with the beatification of Mother Teresa of Calcutta and the canonization of the pro-life heroine Gianna Beretta Molla—and there were new cardinals to be created. Determined to "strengthen the brethren" as long as possible, John Paul II continued his pastoral pilgrimages, concentrating now on a Europe he saw drifting ever more into spiritual, cultural, and moral malaise.

Throughout the last two active years of the pontificate, John Paul II tried to answer the question of whether the Church could be led from a wheelchair as well as from a throne. The mode of leadership would be different, to be sure: rather than exercise power the way the world usually understood the term, John Paul would govern by example, and that example would reflect the truth of Christ's admonition to Peter in the twenty-first chapter of John's Gospel, that he would be bound and taken where he did not want to go. Although the binding in this case was not a matter of chains and an inverted cross, but of a broken body that refused to obey the Pope's will, the witness was manifestly Petrine. For as the French journalist André Frossard, a convert from the fashionable atheism of his professional class, had once put it, "This is not a pope from Poland; this is a pope from Galilee."

COSMOS AND CHAOS

On his return from World Youth Day-2002 in Toronto and his brief stops in Guatemala City and Mexico City, John Paul II spent the rest of the summer at Castel Gandolfo. There, he resumed an old and cherished practice he had long thought a part of his past: writing poetry.

For Karol Wojtyła, poetry had always been a way to ponder some of the deepest mysteries of the human condition and to express his questions and answers about those mysteries in a medium that seemed better suited to the material than discursive prose. He had written numerous poems as a teenager and young man; he had written poems during the debates of the Second Vatican Council; he had used poetry as a medium for reflecting on his challenges and experiences as a bishop.[2] On his way to the second conclave of 1978, which would elect him pope, he worked on a poem, "Stanisław," based on the life of his martyred predecessor as bishop of Kraków. In that poem, he said, he had "paid my debt to Kraków," and for almost twenty-four years, that seemed to be it—leaving poetry aside, he recalled nineteen years later, was "not a decision, but a feeling."[3]

Evidently, in the late summer of 2002, he felt that he should take up his poet's pen once again. After he had completed several poems and poem fragments, he asked his old friend, the Kraków poet and journalist Marek Skwarnicki, to come to Rome "to talk about poetry."[4] Skwarnicki came, made editorial suggestions, and John Paul II completed the work in the fall of 2002. The result, which was published on March 6, 2003, by the archdiocesan publishing house in Kraków, was entitled **Roman Triptych.**[5]

As the title suggested, **Roman Triptych** was a three-panel meditation: "The Stream"; "Meditations on the Book of Genesis at the Threshold of the Sistine Chapel"; and "A Hill in the Land of Moriah." As Cardinal Joseph Ratzinger said in presenting the book to the press in Rome, the first panel "mirrors the experience of creation, its beauty and its life," which seems to suggest the existence of a benign Creator. Yet at the conclusion of the first panel's second section, the poet-pope stops short of the act of faith: "Source, where are you?!" he asks. And then he prays—

Let me wet my lips
in spring water
to feel its freshness, its life-giving freshness.[6]

The second panel draws on John Paul's multiple experiences of the Sistine Chapel and Michelangelo's astonishing frescoes, which had come to signify for him a kind of **axis mundi,** the meeting of cosmos and chaos: God bringing the world out of chaos in the ceiling frescoes from Genesis, God bringing the cosmos to completion in the fresco of the Last Judgment over the high altar.[7] Here, Karol Wojtyła had been through the intense human and spiritual drama of two conclaves. He had taken the bold decision to have the frescoes cleaned—a much controverted act at the time. And in April 1994, at its rededication after the completion of the entire cleaning project, he had preached a memorable homily about the Sistine Chapel as the "sanctuary of the theology of the human body," a place where we are brought to recognize both "the beauty of man created by God as male and female" and "**the hope of a world transfigured,** the world inaugurated by the Risen Christ."[8]

Roman Triptych's middle panel, the longest of the three, begins with the answer to the prayer at the end of the first panel, in the form of a meditation on God the Creator and God the Word as "the First to see," the God who "found in everything a trace of his Being, of his own fullness," of the "true and good and beautiful." Perhaps, the poet-pope suggests, this stupendous vision of God creating all that is true, good, and beautiful through his Word could have been said "more simply," as in the first chapters of Genesis; but no, "the Book awaits its illustration.— And rightly. / It awaited its Michelangelo." More than in a book, it is here that we

> look and we see / the Beginning, which came forth from nothingness . . . / It speaks from these walls.

But so, too, does "the End that speaks even more powerfully," for judgment is the common destiny of all humanity. That, the second panel concludes, is why papal elections are held beneath the gaze of the Creator God and Christ the Lord—so that the cardinal-electors "see themselves in the midst of the Beginning and the End / between the Day of Creation and the Day of Judgments," and are thus reminded to look for him whom God "will point . . . / out."

The third panel of the poem cycle was inspired by Abraham and Isaac's journey up Mount Moriah— as Cardinal Ratzinger put it at the press presentation, "the mountain of sacrifice, of self-gift without reservation." In God's call to complete self-giving and God's sparing of the son of Abraham's old age, we recognize a "God who gives himself," Ratzinger said, "who is simultaneously the beginning, way, and final goal." Which is why the poet-pope ends his poem with the injunction, "Remember this place when you go forth from here, this place will await its day"—the day when the Son of God completely empties himself in obedience to the Father, so that all who believe in the Son "should have eternal life."[9]

The reference to a future conclave "after my death" in **Roman Triptych**'s second panel inevitably led to media speculations about an imminent papal succession and a flurry of ill-informed stories about the poem as a valedictory-in-verse from John Paul II. The Pope's poetry was, rather, a "human testament," in Marek Skwarnicki's view: the Pope had some things he wanted to say and some emotions he wanted to express, and he couldn't say or express these things in any way other than this particular way. **Roman Triptych** wasn't a document of the papal magisterium, Skwarnicki told Catholic News Service; rather, "it's a conversation with faithful brothers and sisters, lay and clerical, at the highest levels of spiritual intensity."[10] The triptych also confirmed the extraordinary role that the Sistine Chapel played in John Paul II's religious imagination. In a perceptive review, the American poet and critic Joseph Bottum took Skwarnicki's point deeper, pointing out that **Roman Triptych** was an effort to puzzle out answers to some very difficult questions—questions that might only have occurred to a man like Karol Wojtyła who was poet, philosopher, priest, and mystic:

If God is one, then truth is one—and yet the experience of artistry, reason, and faith are so different, they do not feel one. All mystics reach eventually to the same peak, which may be why each mode of knowing produces, at its highest expression, genuine mystics: there is a mysticism of art, a mysticism of the mind, a mysticism of pure faith—and they are in the end the same. But short of the mystical vision, how can we be sure that the three divided paths will converge at the mountain's top?

Bottum's conclusion was that the Pope's poem did not supply an answer but a pathway: each of the panels, which reflects a different mode of human knowing, takes us "to the edge of something that the verse itself cannot reveal." It is, to use a word much favored by John Paul II, poetry-as-**threshold**: "John Paul II takes us with him to the threshold—of his own impending death, of the mystical vision, of the ultimate unity of human experience, of the final fulfillment of the promise implicit in Genesis." Thus, in the end, "**Roman Triptych** is not so much a poem as a doorway."[11]
As doorway, **Roman Triptych** "fit" within Karol Wojtyła's long-standing interest in restoring the idea that beauty can be a pathway to God. Modern religious thought had grappled with two of the classic transcendentals, truth and goodness, but it had paid relatively little attention to beauty. John Paul's interest in the theology of Hans Urs von Balthasar—the

Swiss thinker who made a bold attempt to read the entirety of Christian doctrine and practice through the prism of **Herrlichkeit,** "the glory of the Lord"— reflected the Pope's conviction that to lose touch with the beautiful was to lose touch with the ultimate source of beauty, which is God himself. In that respect, **Roman Triptych** and its evocation of the beautiful in nature and in the human form was another facet of John Paul's confrontation with modern Western nihilism—this time, in terms of nihilism's corruption of the beautiful in defense of its soured conclusions about the meaninglessness of life. The recovery of beauty, the Pope believed, could lead to the recovery of an authentic humanism, which in turn would open anew the question he posed in the first panel of his poem: "Where are you? . . . Source, where are you?!"[12]

Roman Triptych sold several hundred thousand copies in Poland during the first week of its publication. World translation and publishing rights were handled by the Vatican publishing house, the Libreria Editrice Vaticana; translations—some very poorly done, alas—were available in the major European languages by the summer of 2003.[13]

The Eucharistic Church

John Paul II had underscored his devotion to the Rosary in the 2002 apostolic letter **Rosarium Virginis Mariae.** His first question on awakening from the anesthesia after the operation that saved his life in May 1981 had been, "Have we said Compline yet?"—a striking indication of his dedication to the Liturgy of the Hours, the daily sequence of prayers recommended to the entire Church and formally prescribed for all the ordained and for those in solemn religious vows. Yet the Holy Eucharist—the sacramental celebration of Christ's presence to his people in his body and blood and the sacramental representation of the sacrifice at Calvary—was the epicenter of Karol Wojtyła's spiritual life, and had been for more than six decades.

By 2003, John Paul had celebrated Mass in a greater number and variety of venues than any priest in history. His altars had been overturned kayaks and great stone tables of sacrifice in the major basilicas of the Catholic world. He had summoned congregations in their millions to participate in the central act of the Church's worship, and had somehow created a profound sense of ecclesial communion amidst remarkable human diversity. In his own celebration of Mass, he embodied "Jesus Christ, Priest and Victim," the title of the famous litany recited daily during his brief seminary years in Kraków. John Paul II at the altar was, it seemed, somewhere else, in an intense experience of communion with the Lord, whose body and blood the words of consecration make present under the forms of bread and wine. The Church draws its strength and its evangelical vitality from the Eucharist, he was convinced, because every celebration of the Mass is a spiritual recapitulation of the central events of human history—the Paschal Triduum of Holy Thursday, Good Friday, and Easter Sunday.

As his poet's mind had adopted the form of the three-paneled altarpiece to think through some basic questions of God's relationship to nature, humanity, and history in **Roman Triptych,** so the mind of John Paul, pastor and teacher, adopted the method of a documentary triptych in proposing to the Church the shape of its life "in the deep" of the twenty-first century and the third millennium. The 2001 apostolic letter **Novo Millennio Ineunte** was the center of this pastoral altarpiece. **Rosarium Virginis Mariae** was one flanking panel. The second flanking panel was John Paul's fourteenth encyclical, **Ecclesia de Eucharistia** [The Church from the Eucharist], which was signed and issued on April 17, 2003—Holy Thursday, the day the Church commemorates the institution of the Eucharist and the priesthood at Christ's Last Supper with the apostles.

There was a nice historical symmetry here: Leo XIII, the pope whom John Paul was about to pass in papal longevity, had issued an encyclical on the

Eucharist, **Mirae Caritatis** [Wondrous Love], in 1902, the twenty-fifth year of his pontificate. **Ecclesia de Eucharistia** was likewise given to the Church as a pontificate was completing a quarter century, and in some respects covered ground similar to that mapped by Leo XIII. For as John Paul II emphasized in **Ecclesia de Eucharistia,** the Church's eucharistic doctrine was constant, settled, and unchangeable: in the Holy Eucharist, the bread and wine brought by the people to the altar are transformed substantially into the body and blood of Christ, in obedience to the Lord's command at the Last Supper, "Do this in memory of me"—a command given after he had spoken the words that would be repeated in the act of eucharistic consecration for two millennia: "Take this, all of you, and eat it: this is my body which will be given up for you. . . . Take this, all of you, and drink from it: this is the cup of my blood, the blood of the new and everlasting covenant. It will be shed for you and for all, so that sins may be forgiven."[14]

The solidity of the Church's eucharistic doctrine should encourage, not blunt, what John Paul called our sense of "eucharistic amazement"; an amazement that "in this gift, Jesus Christ entrusted to his Church the perennial making present of the paschal mystery . . . and brought about a mysterious 'oneness in time' between that **Triduum** and the passage of the centuries." Thus the Eucharist, he continued, has a "truly enormous 'capacity' which embraces all of history as the recipient of the grace of the redemption."

It was to "rekindle this Eucharistic 'amazement'" that he had written **Ecclesia de Eucharistia.**[15]

A certain recapturing of the amazement of the Holy Eucharist was, John Paul thought, already under way in the Church through the liturgical reforms of the post–Vatican II period, which had "greatly contributed to a more conscious, active, and fruitful participation" in the celebration of Mass by the laity. Then there was the recovery in some parts of the world Church of eucharistic adoration—silent or vocal prayer in front of Christ eucharistically present in the reserved sacrament. This recovery had revived "an inexhaustible source of holiness," which took more public forms in public eucharistic processions such as those on the Solemnity of the Body and Blood of Christ (Corpus Christi). Such processions had played an important role in Karol Wojtyła's evangelical work in Kraków; they were doing so in many other venues in a new century and millennium.

Yet amidst these signs of intensified eucharistic piety there were also what the Pope called "shadows": the abandonment of eucharistic adoration in some parts of the Church; liturgical abuses of various sorts; an "extremely reductive understanding" of the Eucharist, which took the Eucharist to be "simply a fraternal banquet"; the loss of a sense of connection between the ministries of bishop and priest and the vitality of the Eucharist. Thus the Church needed some reminders about the full doctrine of the Holy

Eucharist in order to regain a sense of eucharistic amazement.

The first reminder was that the Eucharist is a true sacrifice. There is only one sacrifice of the New Covenant, as there is only one passion and one cross. Yet it is precisely that one sacrifice of Christ that is made present throughout history, day after day, at every Mass. To recover and appreciate the truth of the Eucharist as sacrifice is to recover the "universal charity" of the Eucharist, John Paul wrote. By saying that his body is "given for you" and his blood is "poured out for you," the Lord "did not simply state that what he was giving [the apostles] to eat and drink was his body and blood; he also expressed **its sacrificial meaning** and made sacramentally present his sacrifice which would soon be offered on the Cross for the salvation of all." For the Christian, therefore, to participate in the Eucharist is to be brought into the Son's uniquely redemptive gift of himself to the Father—to be brought into the very life of the Holy Trinity.[16]

The Church also needed to regain a sense of the "apostolicity" of the Eucharist, John Paul wrote: to recapture the full meaning of the fact that the Eucharist comes to us from the apostles, to whom it was entrusted by Christ and who in turn passed it down to the Church of all times and places. Thus the local bishop is the primary celebrant of the Eucharist in his diocese, in cooperation with priests whose ordination has conferred on them the power of eucharistic consecration. A deeper sense of the apostolicity of the Eucharist, the Pope continued, explains why full communion with the apostolic community of the Church is required for a true and valid Eucharist and for full participation in the celebration of the Eucharist. There can be no true Eucharist without apostolicity, without connection to the great apostolic chain that traces its origins to the Last Supper. That is why only a bishop or a validly ordained priest, ordained by a bishop whose own orders derive from that apostolic succession, can consecrate the Eucharist. That (and not some defect of hospitality or sensitivity) is why the Church does not admit to the reception of holy communion those who are not linked ecclesiastically to a member of the college of bishops in full communion with the Bishop of Rome, except in exceptional circumstances (primarily having to do with the Orthodox Churches). That is why those Catholics who are in a gravely defective state of communion with their own Church—because of mortal sin, canonically irregular marriage, or persistent public acts of defiance of the teaching authority of the Church—should not present themselves for holy communion. And that is why Catholics should not present themselves for communion in other Christian communities that "lack a valid sacrament of orders."[17]

Rediscovering the "amazement" of the Eucharist also required the Church to reimagine its celebrations of the Mass as a privileged participation in the liturgy of saints and angels around the throne of divine grace. The Church celebrates the Eucharist until the Lord comes again in glory. Thus the Eucharist, John Paul wrote, "is a straining toward that goal, a foretaste of the fullness of joy promised by Christ [cf. John 15.11]," for it is "in the Eucharist that we also receive the pledge of our bodily resurrection at the end of the world . . . [which] comes from the fact that the flesh of the Son of Man, given as food, is his body in its glorious state after the resurrection." Thus, in the reception of holy communion, "we digest, as it were, the 'secret' of the resurrection," which is why the early Church Father Ignatius of Antioch "rightly defined the Eucharistic Bread as 'a medicine of immortality, an antidote to death.'"[18] At Mass, John Paul suggested, those who receive holy communion are time travelers, for the reception of the glorified body of Christ brings us into as close contact as is possible in history with the time-beyond-time, the time of God's Kingdom come in its fullness.

If the Eucharist is, in a sense, trans-temporal, it is also trans-spatial or, in John Paul's preferred word, "cosmic." Reflecting on the wide variety of circumstances and places where he had been privileged to celebrate Mass had given the Pope "a powerful experience of [the] universal and, so to speak, cosmic character" of the Eucharist:

[E]ven when it is celebrated on the humble altar of a country church, the Eucharist is always in some way celebrated **on the altar of the world.** It unites heaven and earth. It embraces and permeates all creation. The Son of God became man in order to restore all creation, in one supreme act of praise, to the One who made it from nothing. He, the Eternal High Priest who by the blood of his Cross entered the eternal sanctuary, thus gives back to the Creator and Father all creation redeemed. He does so through the priestly ministry of the Church, to the glory of the Most Holy Trinity. Truly this is the **mysterium fidei** [mystery of faith] which is accomplished in the Eucharist: the world which came forth from the hands of God the Creator now returns to him redeemed by Christ.[19]

Ecclesia de Eucharistia was the product of a convergence of motivations. Approaching the end of his life and Petrine ministry, John Paul II wanted to bear witness in an authoritative way to the centrality of the Eucharist for the Church. The great hopes of liturgical reform at the time of Vatican II had been partially realized, as John Paul acknowledged in the encyclical; but no one could reasonably say that the evangelical and pastoral jolt the liturgical reform was intended to produce had in fact happened with full intensity. On the contrary: the reform was followed rather rapidly, and surprisingly, by diminished Mass attendance throughout Europe and North America and a deteriorated sense of eucharistic "amazement" (due in part to poor catechesis based on dubious or inadequate Eucharistic theology). The Pope's effort to rekindle a sense of awe and wonder at the gift and mystery of the Eucharist was based on a pastoral strategy he had followed throughout the pontificate: reminding the Church of the fundamental truths of faith, after a season of skepticism about or indifference to those truths, would lead, he believed, to a revival of Catholic practice.

It would be a mistake, however, to think of **Ecclesia de Eucharistia** as primarily remedial, an encyclical aimed at correcting faults.[20] Rather, **Ecclesia de Eucharistia** is best understood in the context of the Great Jubilee of 2000 and what the Pope hoped would be its enduring effects within the world Church. The Eucharist as the recapitulation and making-present of the Paschal Mystery of Christ's passion, death, and resurrection; the Eucharist as a kind of window into Kingdom come in its fullness; the cosmic Eucharist, in which all of creation is caught up in Christ's sacrificial self-gift to the Father—these themes from **Ecclesia de Eucharistia** are very much jubilee themes.

In the sacrament of the Holy Eucharist, John Paul seemed to be saying, we meet in a unique way the God "who has gone before us and leads us on, who himself set out on man's path, a God who does not look down on us from high but who became our traveling companion."[21]

WAR IN IRAQ

John Paul II's opposition to the war in Iraq that began on March 19, 2003, was determined, passionate, thoroughgoing—and, by comparison to that of some of his subordinates, carefully crafted. That opposition was based on a number of convictions and perceptions.

At the beginning of a new millennium, the Pope believed it important to manifest in his own address to world affairs the hope he had expressed during the Great Jubilee of 2000—that humanity had learned from the horrors of the twentieth century that there were better ways to settle problems and assuage grievances than the resort to arms. Like his papal predecessors, John Paul was committed to strengthening legal and political alternatives to war as a means of resolving conflicts, which in practice meant deferring war-making powers to the UN system—although it should be remembered that even when the UN authorized the use of force to reverse the 1990 Iraqi invasion and annexation of Kuwait, the Pope and the Holy See's diplomacy had opposed the use of armed force to the end.[22] Grave concern for the embattled Christian communities in the Middle East, especially in the event of a general Middle Eastern conflagration, was never far from the Pope's mind in the 1990s. And in the wake of 9/11, John Paul remained determined to do everything he could to demonstrate to the world the falsity of the jihadists' claim that the war between Islamist terrorism and the West was a religious war.

Taken together, these convictions, commitments, and perceptions set the foundation for the Pope's steady and increasingly urgent stream of statements in late 2002 and early 2003 in opposition to the use of armed force against the Saddam Hussein regime in Iraq.[23] The Pope was not fooled by Saddam, whom he knew to be a brutal dictator; John Paul would certainly have welcomed regime change in Baghdad as a way to relieve the suffering of the people of Iraq, to stabilize the politics of the volatile Middle East, and to vindicate the viability of the United Nations, which Saddam had defied for a decade. He was committed, however, to promoting such change through nonmilitary means.

John Paul's response to the Iraq crisis of 2002–3 was also shaped by his sense of the boundaries of his own role in addressing an international crisis such as that posed by Saddam Hussein's defiance of UN disarmament resolutions. The **Catechism of the Catholic Church,** which he had authorized, taught that the responsibility for determining when the strict moral conditions for a morally justified use of armed force had been reached "belongs to the prudential judgment of those who have responsibility for the common good."[24] In practice, this meant that the burden of moral judgment fell on statesmen, exercising the virtue of prudence. It was not the Pope's role, in other words, to adjudicate between differing readings of what prudence dictated in a given situation; it was the Pope's task to continue to press for nonmilitary solutions, even—perhaps especially— when such solutions seemed beyond the grasp of practical politics. Moreover, John Paul was aware that for him to declare any given military action "unjust" would place a heavy burden of conscience on Catholic members of the armed forces involved in that action, with potentially grave personal, political, and military consequences. Soldiers as well as statesmen bore the weight of moral responsibility for making judgments about the war in question and the means by which it was conducted. That responsibility could not be outsourced to the Pope; neither would it be usurped by John Paul II, the lifelong teacher of personal moral responsibility.

John Paul's response to the crisis in Iraq was both amplified and distorted in 2002 and 2003 by what often seemed an uncoordinated (and sometimes unintelligible) diplomatic and communications strategy on the part of the Holy See. In the months leading up to war, Archbishop Jean-Louis Tauran, the Frenchman who had served since 1990 as the Holy See's secretary for relations with states (and who was usually referred to as "the Vatican's foreign minister"), took an increasingly stringent line, repeatedly juxtaposing what he termed the "force of law" with a "law of force."[25] Tauran also argued that the only way to legitimate the use of armed force in Iraq, or in any other circumstance, was through the authorization of the United Nations—an authorization that Tauran and the rest of the Vatican senior bureaucracy did not believe had been granted by Security Council Resolution 1441 (which, on November 8, 2002, declared that Iraq was "in material breach" of the cease-fire terms agreed to in 1991, and which gave Iraq "a final opportunity to comply with its disarmament obligations").[26] Later in the debate, Tauran went so far as to say that, absent such an authorization (which would have meant a new, post-1441 Security Council Resolution, something France had sworn to veto), military action against Saddam Hussein would be "a war of aggression and therefore a crime against humanity"—a moral judgment it was difficult to imagine John Paul II, who had personal experience of crimes against humanity, sharing. At the very end, in February 2003, Tauran approved a visit to the Vatican by Tariq Aziz, Iraq's foreign minister, a longtime associate of Saddam Hussein's and a Chaldean Christian. As Massimo Franco, a columnist for **Corriere della Sera,** put it, "The Iraqi's visit was arranged by French-born Father Benjamin, a colorful former pop singer turned priest with long-standing Baghdad connections and an equally long history of anti-Americanism. . . . [The] visit . . . was Saddam's last attempt to save himself and his regime by trying to engage the Pope on his side."[27] How this tacit alignment of the Holy See's diplomacy with the passions of the European Left advanced either the cause of peace or the witness of John Paul II was never clear.[28]

Dramatic statements in the months before the war were also forthcoming on a regular basis from the Holy See's volatile and voluble permanent representative at the United Nations, the Italian archbishop Renato Martino, and from the Vatican's semiofficial newspaper, **L'Osservatore Romano,** which ran bloodcurdling banner headlines such as "The Madness of War." The Jesuit journal, **La Civiltà Cattolica,** whose articles were vetted by the Vatican's Secretariat of State, published a brutally anti-American editorial in its January 18 issue that was, according to Vatican analyst Sandro Magister, an "implacable indictment . . . of Bush's America" for upsetting the world order, delegitimating the United Nations, "wounding" international law, fracturing the alliance between Europe and America, and stirring up jihadist sentiment in the Islamic world, all in pursuit of imperial "dominion."[29]

The commentary from the Vatican bureaucracy, from **L'Osservatore Romano,** and from **La Civiltà Cattolica** seems to have been shaped by casts of mind and judgments that John Paul II cannot simply be assumed to have shared. In those quarters, Samuel Huntington's "clash of civilizations" analysis of the post–Cold War world was read as a prescription for U.S. foreign policy rather than as a description of world realities—a fundamental misunderstanding of Huntington's thesis, which, among other things, was the first global analysis in decades in which a leading secular scholar took culture and religious conviction seriously as factors in world politics.[30] European frustrations over Europe's declining role in world affairs played a role in the more bitter commentary coming from Vatican sources, as did European concerns that the Bush administration's declared policy of preemption in case of imminent threat risked completely disempowering the United Nations—the only forum in which European states still acted as major powers. Various European mythologies about George W. Bush's evangelical religious convictions and general incompetence played a role, as when **L'Osservatore Romano** editorialized that Bush's Iraq policy was gravely deficient in "the intelligence necessary at certain levels"—a charge the Vatican paper could never have imagined leveling at France's Jacques Chirac or Germany's Gerhard Schröder. European fears about the rising tide of immigration into the European Union from the Muslim world and the possibility of further terrorist attacks in Europe were also in play in the Vatican bureaucracy, at the Vatican paper, and at **La Civiltà Cattolica,** which took a consistently sympathetic line toward Islamic and Arab grievances even as it accused the United States of following "the law of the jungle."[31]

Over against this bombast, which reached one low point when Archbishop Martino announced that he had found U.S. secretary of state Colin Powell's explanation of the administration's case against Iraq at the UN Security Council "vague and unconvincing," even though he had neither attended Powell's presentation nor read it, John Paul II's opposition to the war in Iraq reads as both convinced and measured. It reached a rhetorical apogee in the Pope's January 13, 2003, address to the ambassadors accredited to the Holy See, when John Paul asked the "peoples of the earth and their leaders to have the courage to say 'No' . . . No to Death! . . . No to Selfishness! . . . No to War!"[32] There can be no doubt that John Paul believed it his duty to bend every possible effort to find an alternative to war in Iraq. Yet as Sandro Magister wrote months later,

> John Paul II never pronounced the anathemas that his various collaborators were offering to the media. The Pope opposed the war in Iraq but he never condemned it as immoral or contrary to the Christian faith. He never affirmed that it was a "crime against humanity," as Tauran and Martino, on the other hand, repeatedly did. . . .
>
> The Pope's words distinguish themselves for their religious character. The peace that he preaches essentially "comes from God." The passages he dedicates to concrete ways of building peace in the Gulf are rare and extremely measured—and they take the form of a discourse on method, not of precept. One example of his focus on method came on January 13, 2003, in a speech to ambassadors from around the world: "War cannot be decided upon, even

when it is a matter of ensuring the common good, except as the very last option and in accordance with very strict conditions." Another appeal for responsible decision-making came in the Angelus address of March 16: "We know well that peace is not possible at any price. But we all know how great is this responsibility."[33]

In his conclusion, Magister claimed that John Paul II "never exclude[d] war in Iraq from the array of practicable and just decisions."[34] That was arguably an analytic bridge too far, in that the Pope seems always to have believed, even after the war began, that further diplomatic and other nonmilitary pressures might have brought about the necessary policy change, or even regime change, in Iraq. Whether that was a realistic and prudent expectation will long be debated. But Magister is surely right to point out that John Paul never used the word "unjust" to describe a war he deeply opposed—because he believed that judgment had to be made by others, as the **Catechism** said, and because he would not place a burden of conscience on Catholic military personnel in the coalition forces that invaded Iraq on March 19 and deposed the regime in Baghdad on April 9.

Throughout the Iraq crisis of 2003, U.S. ambassador R. James Nicholson worked hard to demonstrate to the Holy See that the American approach to the problem of Iraq was indeed multilateral, not unilateral, as he tried to keep lines of communication open between the Vatican and a U.S. administration that was becoming both confused and aggravated by the rhetoric of Archbishop Tauran, Archbishop Martino, and others. Nicholson later described the situation, and the problems he faced, as he experienced them in late 2002 and early 2003:

> Part of my job was to help overcome what seemed to be a high level of suspicion over the power and influence of the U.S. and its alleged "lust for oil." The feeling, shared by many in Europe, was that America, being the world's leading capitalist country, must necessarily have some profit motive in Iraq. The media's efforts to portray the United States and the Holy See as diametrically opposed on the war continued to intensify, with one Italian Catholic magazine even commissioning a poll asking respondents whether they were "with President Bush for war" or "with the Pope for peace." Notwithstanding such efforts, our positions were never as far apart as the media portrayed. Both the Pope and President Bush believed that war should be the last resort. Both recognized the danger posed by Iraq and called for Iraq to disarm. Both recognized that decisions on war and peace must be made by legitimate civil authorities. The difference we had essentially came down to the question of whether all diplomatic means to achieve Iraqi disarmament had been exhausted before resorting to military action. The United States believed after twelve years

of Iraqi defiance in the face of a strong U.N. consensus that Iraq would never willingly comply with the U.N. The Holy See continued to believe that inspections and dialogue offered a means to meet the international community's concerns—a view the Pope conveyed to President Bush in a late October [2002] communication.[35]

For her part, U.S. national security adviser Condoleezza Rice claimed that she couldn't "understand the Vatican position" given the brutalities and nature of the Saddam Hussein regime, which seemed to make a diplomatic settlement of the problem impossible. When John Paul announced on March 4, 2002, that he was starting a fast in order to ask God's help in preventing war, Ambassador Nicholson said that he, too, would fast for peace, but he also said that he understood Rice's puzzlement, for "unfortunately, the Holy See doesn't mention the crimes against humanity committed by Saddam Hussein. We didn't hear them mentioned after Cardinal Roger Etchegaray's mission to Iraq."[36]

Etchegaray, a veteran diplomatic troubleshooter for John Paul II, was sent to Baghdad in early March 2003 to try to persuade Saddam Hussein to cease and desist. Saddam kept the French cardinal waiting for several days and then offered what Massimo Franco describes as a "tenuous agreement to cooperate" with UN weapons inspectors.[37] The Etchegaray mission was thus a failure. So was a parallel mission to Washington by the former apostolic nuncio to the United States, Cardinal Pio Laghi, who had formed a friendship with Vice President George H. W. Bush during the Reagan administration, when the two lived across Washington's tree-lined Massachusetts Avenue from each other and played tennis together. At the White House on March 5, Cardinal Laghi first met Condoleezza Rice and then President George W. Bush, to whom he gave a letter from John Paul II. Leaving Rome, Laghi, never one to underplay his role, had told **Corriere della Sera** that, while the meeting would be polite, "it won't be a meeting of friends." Ambassador Nicholson described the substance of the meeting in these terms:

> Laghi repeated the Holy See's view that war should be the last resort, and that any decision on military action needed to be taken within the framework of the U.N. The President eloquently outlined his view of both the legality and morality of military action, noting that the U.N. had already provided the needed framework for action with Resolution 1441 and previous resolutions, and that his duty was to protect the American people from the potential risks posed by Saddam's regime.[38]

Still, as Massimo Franco would put it later, "a wall of incomprehension separated the Holy See and Washington." The Vatican's diplomatic bureaucracy, as represented by Laghi, believed that the United

States "risked dragging the entire western world into a conflict with Islam" because the root cause of all Middle Eastern troubles was the Israeli-Palestinian conflict.[39] The Bush administration believed that a post-Saddam, democratic Iraq would be a political-cultural magnet drawing other Arab and Islamic states into a more rational posture in world affairs— and thereby opening a path to resolving the Israeli-Palestinian conflict. The differences in perception were irreconcilable.[40]

On March 17, Secretary of State Colin Powell telephoned Archbishop Jean-Louis Tauran and told him that, if Saddam Hussein and his sons did not leave Iraq immediately, which President Bush had stated was the last option for avoiding war, then military action by the coalition assembled on Iraq's borders would follow. Powell told Tauran that the Bush administration was aware of the Pope's concern and would do everything possible to keep civilian casualties at a minimum. Tauran thanked Powell, noting that the decision on when all diplomatic means had been exhausted rested with the civil authorities, who bore a heavy responsibility for their judgment.[41]

When war began days later, the statement by papal spokesman Joaquín Navarro-Valls was both strong and measured, as befit the combination of determination and self-discipline with which John Paul II had conducted himself throughout the preceding months. Navarro said that the Pope had taken the news of the commencement of hostilities with "deep pain," and then observed that "On the one hand, it is to be regretted that the Iraqi government did not accept the resolutions of the United Nations and the appeal of the Pope himself, as both asked the country to disarm. On the other hand, it is to be deplored that the path of negotiations, according to international law, for a peaceful solution of the Iraqi drama has been broken off."[42] To "deplore" is, of course, stronger than to "regret." Yet Navarro's statement did not comport with the charge, previously laid down by **La Civiltà Cattolica,** that the United States was behaving (or better, misbehaving) according to "the law of the jungle," nor was the language of a "crime against humanity" deployed. What still remained absent from any public commentary by the Holy See was a critique of the role played by France and others in taking pressure off Saddam Hussein at the UN Security Council by preemptively threatening a veto of any measure beyond the disputed Resolution 1441.

The Holy See's nuncio in Baghdad, Archbishop Fernando Filoni, remained at his post as the war took its course. When the conquest of Baghdad brought one phase of the war to its conclusion, the Holy See shifted the focus of its concerns to humanitarian relief for the Iraqi people, UN involvement in Iraqi reconstruction, and the necessity of transferring power as soon as possible to a new Iraqi government.[43] This new phase of the U.S./Holy See conversation was strengthened by a visit to the Vatican on April 9, the day Baghdad fell, by U.S. undersecretary of state John Bolton, who came to discuss the possibilities of U.S./Vatican cooperation in post-Saddam Iraq. Bolton was told of the Holy See's relief that casualties had been kept to a minimum; on April 10, the Vatican stated that the fall of the Saddam Hussein regime offered a "significant opportunity for the people's future" in Iraq and pledged Holy See cooperation in providing the Iraqi people the "necessary assistance through [Catholic] social and charitable institutions."[44]

When it became clear, later in 2003, that Iraq had not been pacified and that various forms of resistance continued, now aided and abetted by jihadist terrorists who saw in Iraq a new battlefield for fighting the Great Satan, the Holy See's diplomatic line began to shift, and the Vatican argued against any premature withdrawal of coalition forces that would leave Iraq to Shia fundamentalism and terrorism. That position solidified further when, on November 12, 2003, nineteen Italian soldiers were killed by a suicide bomber in Nasiriyah, in the southern part of Iraq. Cardinal Camillo Ruini, the Pope's vicar for the diocese of Rome and the president of the Italian Bishops Conference, preached at a memorial service for the fallen, held at the basilica of St. Paul Outside the Walls on November 18, and declared that "we will not run away from the terrorist assassins . . . [but] confront them with courage, energy, and determination." It was, **Corriere della Sera** wrote, an effort to "encourage the involvement of other countries, thus making the pacification of Iraq a truly international effort backed by the United Nations."[45]

That, too, was a vain hope, but Ruini's homily was one more indicator of a change in Vatican perceptions of what was at stake in Iraq, and how the country's problems ought to be addressed. The Italian losses in Nasiriyah prompted **L'Osservatore Romano** to describe the Italian mission in Iraq as a "mission of peace." In October 2003, **La Civiltà Cattolica** began evening out its criticism, charging Islam with having shown a "warlike and conquering face" in history and deploring the "perpetual discrimination" against Christians in Islamic lands. There were also important changes in the bureaucratic cast of characters in the Holy See. In late November 2003, Jean-Louis Tauran, a cardinal since October 21, 2003, became Vatican archivist and librarian and was replaced as "foreign minister" by Archbishop Giovanni Lajolo. Renato Martino, also a cardinal as of October 21, was redeployed to the Pontifical Council for Justice and Peace as its president, and replaced at the United Nations by Archbishop Celestino Migliore, from whom, Sandro Magister wrote, there would be "no more Third World rhetoric and pacifist homilies."[46] Martino was briefly back in the news on December 16, when he complained that U.S. forces had mistreated Saddam Hussein on capturing him in hiding: "I felt pity to see this man destroyed, being treated like a cow as they checked his teeth."[47] By this point, however, few serious observers were paying Cardinal Martino much attention.[48]

John Paul II continued to deplore the resort to war, lamenting in his Christmas Midnight Mass homily that "too much blood is still being shed on earth" while "too many conflicts disturb the peaceful coexistence of nations."[49] His **Urbi et Orbi** blessing on Christmas Day 2003 returned to the theme of peace in a heartfelt prayer:

> Save us from the great evils that rend humanity in these first years of the third millennium. . . .
>
> Save us from the wars and armed conflicts which lay waste whole areas of the world, from the scourge of terrorism and from the many forms of violence which assail the weak and vulnerable. Save us from discouragement as we face the paths to peace, difficult paths indeed, yet possible and therefore necessary—paths that are always and everywhere urgent, especially in the land where you were born, the Prince of Peace.[50]

CRISIS OF FAITH IN EUROPE

The Pope's health oscillated, although it generally moved in a downward direction, throughout 2003. He did not travel outside Italy in the first third of the year, but he was in strong form for Holy Week 2003, presiding over all the ceremonies and preaching in a strong and clear voice. As veteran Vatican correspondent John Allen noted at the time, a pope is never more regularly in the public eye than in the period between Holy Thursday and Easter Sunday; thus from the late 1990s on, John Paul II's performance at the lengthy ceremonies of the Easter Triduum had become "the most-watched annual bellwether of his physical condition." The strength of the Pope's presentations during Holy Week in April 2003 made an impression, as did his delivering greetings in sixty-two languages at the end of the Easter **Urbi et Orbi** message; the last language was Latin, and he sang the greeting in that ancient tongue before joking that "the last language is the first!" As Allen also noted, the Pope was being considerably aided by a new device, a rolling hydraulic wheelchair (or, in the hypersensitive language of the Vatican, a "wheeled throne"). Using the hydraulic chair, the Pope, who was suffering more and more from acute arthritis in his right knee, could be wheeled into place and then hydraulically raised to the altar so that he could celebrate the Eucharist without standing.[51] No one seemed to mind, but the media had found another object to tweak its curiosity. Papal spokesman Navarro-Valls noted that the Pope's infirmities "have become more of an instrument [of evangelization] than a limitation," and recalled that in his 1999 **Letter to the Elderly,** John Paul had written that "despite the limitations that age has imposed upon me, I still feel the zest for life." "With such a spirit," the spokesman concluded, "of what consequence is a chair?"[52]

By Polish custom, November 4, the feast of his patron saint, Charles Borromeo, was more important to Karol Wojtyła than his birthday. Nonetheless, he marked the completion of his eighty-third year on May 18 by canonizing four new saints and remarking in his homily that "there is no age that is an obstacle" to living a fulfilled life. "Grateful for the gift of life," he continued, "today I again entrust to the Virgin my life and the ministry that Providence has called me to fulfill." One of the new saints, Bishop Józef Sebastian Pelczar (who died in 1924), was the founder of the Sisters Servants of the Most Sacred Heart of Jesus, a Polish congregation of religious women, some of whose members looked after the papal household—and who reportedly prepared a special dinner for the occasion.[53]

Before and after his birthday, John Paul II focused his attention on Europe, a continent of increasing concern to him as it seemed to be sinking ever more deeply into a post-Christian cultural and spiritual morass.

All the Pope's international travels in 2003 were within the European Union. The first pastoral visit was his fifth pilgrimage to Spain, on May 3 and 4. Six hundred thousand young people joined the Pope in a vigil of songs and prayers at the Cuatro Vientos air force base on the night of May 3, and one million people came to the Plaza de Colón in the center of Madrid for the May 4 canonization of three nuns and two priests, including Pedro Poveda, one of the 12,000 Spanish priests and religious martyred during the Spanish Civil War. As usual, the meeting with young people produced some banter back and forth. When John Paul asked, "How old is the Pope?" and then answered his own question, "Almost eighty-three years," the crowd picked up the chant from World Youth Day-2002: "The Pope is young! The Pope is young!" "A youth of eighty-three years," John Paul riposted, to more cheers. There was more than banter, however. John Paul challenged the young to be "builders of peace" and to "respond to blind violence and inhuman hate with the fascinating power of life. Defeat animosity with the force of pardon. Stay far from every form of extreme nationalism, racism, and intolerance. Testify with your life that ideas are not imposed but proposed." At the canonization Mass in Madrid, the papal challenge to the crowds was to revitalize European culture through the power of faith: "Do not abandon your Christian roots. Only in this way will you be able to bring to the world and to Europe the cultural richness of your history."[54]

A month later, John Paul made his hundredth pastoral pilgrimage outside Italy, visiting Croatia from June 5 to June 9. It was his third trip to a country still recovering from the ravages of the wars that had wracked the region during and after the dissolution of Yugoslavia—wars that brutally illustrated for John Paul the incapacities of Europe to manage its own house peacefully. Here, the stress was on lay responsibility for the development of society. Christianity, he insisted, could make a crucial difference to Croatia's future: "For there are values—like the dignity of the human person, moral and intellectual integrity, religious freedom, the defense of the family, openness to and respect for life, solidarity, subsidiarity and participation, respect for minorities—which are inscribed in the nature of every human being but which Christianity has the merit of clearly identifying and proclaiming." What was true for Croatia was true for Europe as a whole.[55]

Two weeks later, the Pope was back in the Balkans for a thirteen-hour visit to Banja Luka in the Republika Srpska, the Serbian section of Bosnia-Herzegovina, where the Pope pleaded for reconciliation—taking, as always, the first step himself: "From this city, marked in the course of history by so much suffering and bloodshed, I ask Almighty God to have mercy on the sins committed against humanity, human dignity, and freedom also by children of the Catholic Church, and to foster in all a desire for mutual forgiveness. Only in a climate of true reconciliation will the memory of so many innocent victims and their sacrifice not be in vain, but encourage everyone to build new relationships of fraternity and understanding."[56]

Finally, in September, John Paul spent four days

in Slovakia, his third pastoral pilgrimage to that intensely Catholic country. At the very outset, in his September 11 address at the airport in Bratislava, the Slovak capital, he challenged Slovakia to bring its Christian heritage with it into the European Union, which it would enter on May 1, 2004: "Bring to the construction of Europe's new identity the contribution of your rich Christian tradition!" John Paul urged. "**Do not be satisfied with the sole quest for economic advantage.** . . . Only by building up . . . a society **respectful of human life** in all its expressions . . . will there be guarantees of a future based on solid foundations and rich in goods for all."[57]

CONSTITUTING EUROPE

That theme—that Europe could be itself only if the new European Union were something other than a pragmatic arrangement for mutual economic advantage—would preoccupy John Paul II for the rest of his pontificate. One specific focus of his concerns was the constitutional treaty being developed in 2003 to govern the expanding EU, which would grow to twenty-five member states on May 1, 2004. The Pope's diplomats were primarily concerned with whether the new treaty would recognize the legal personality of the Church and other religious communities and institutions. John Paul II was worried that the treaty might accelerate Europe's secularization by the way its preamble—its declaration of moral purpose—described the roots of contemporary European civilization.[58]

The preamble to the draft constitutional treaty began by defining the sources of twenty-first-century European civilization and modern Europe's commitments to human rights, democracy, and the rule of law as the continent's classical heritage, the Enlightenment, and modern thought: 1,500 years of Christian culture were simply ignored, as if nothing of consequence for what was now "Europe" had happened between Marcus Aurelius and Descartes. John Paul II devoted weeks of his Sunday Angelus addresses in the summer of 2003 to this striking omission, warning that the Christian heritage of Europe "cannot be squandered."[59] On July 13, speaking at Castel Gandolfo, the Pope worried aloud that the continent's loss of Christian memory and identity threatened the very commitments to human rights the constitutional preamble celebrated:

A certain loss of Christian memories [in Europe] is accompanied by a sort of fear in facing the future: a widespread fragmentation of life often goes hand in hand with the spread of individualism and a growing weakness in interpersonal solidarity. We are witnessing, as it were, a loss of hope; at its root is the attempt to make a Godless, Christless anthropology prevail. Paradoxically, the cradle of human rights thus risks losing its foundation, eroded by relativism and utilitarianism.[60]

The government of Poland (largely composed of ex-communists) supported the Pope's campaign for a recognition of Europe's Christian roots in Europe's new constitutional framework, as did the governments of Italy, the Czech Republic, Lithuania, Malta, Portugal, and Spain—although Spain revised its view after the government of José María Aznar was replaced in March 2004 by the radically secularist administration of José Luis Rodríguez Zapatero. But that was all. The head of the constitutional treaty's drafting committee, former French president Valéry Giscard d'Estaing, said that "Europeans live in a purely secular political system, where religion does not play an important role."[61] Incumbent French president Jacques Chirac stated that "France is a lay state and as such she does not have a habit of calling for insertions of a religious character in constitutional texts." That fact, Chirac concluded, would "not allow . . . a religious reference" in the preamble, no matter what John Paul II said—or what the facts of history dictated.[62] Others went further. One British Labour member of the European Parliament declared that any mention of the Christian roots of Europe would "offend those many millions of different faiths or no faith at all."[63] The Swedish tabloid

Aftonbladet, Scandinavia's largest newspaper, wrote in an editorial that mentioning Christian values in the Euro-constitution would be a "huge mistake" as it would "exclude groups and raise new walls."[64] A French Socialist member of the Chamber of Deputies, Olivier Duhamel, claimed that mentioning God or Christianity in the preamble or anywhere else in the Euro-constitution would be "absurd," as doing so would exclude Muslims, atheists, and other non-Christians from the political community of the EU.[65] How, was not specified.

The ferocity of this debate suggested that something more than a combination of historic French **laïcité,** modern European secularism, and a passion for inclusivity was afoot. For as John Paul well knew, if mentioning Christianity's contributions to Europe's contemporary civilization "excluded" Jews, Muslims, and nonbelievers, then mentioning the Enlightenment meant "excluding" Aristotelians, Thomists, and postmodernists such as Jacques Derrida (then demanding that the new EU be "neutral toward worldviews"), all of whom thought that Enlightenment rationality was deeply flawed.[66] The argument, such as it was, was absurd on its face. Something else must be at work.

John Paul II defined that "something" in **Ecclesia in Europa,** the apostolic exhortation he issued on June 28, 2003, to complete the work of the October 1999 Synod on Europe. In addition to offering a penetrating analysis of contemporary Europe's crisis of cultural morale, **Ecclesia in Europa** was John Paul's most developed exposition of the twenty-first-century implications of Catholic social teaching since his 1991 encyclical, **Centesimus Annus.**[67] As such, **Ecclesia in Europa** stands as John Paul's last gift to the world Church of his distinctive reading of the cultural, social, economic, and political signs of the times in the developed world.

Ecclesia in Europa candidly recognized that Europe was on the verge of becoming a post-Christian continent, in that the Gospel must now bring its "message of hope to a Europe that seems to have lost sight of it."[68] After coming safely through the seventy-seven-year trial that began with the guns of August 1914 and ended with the collapse of the Soviet Union in 1991, Europe ought to be experiencing a new springtime of the human spirit, as John Paul had put it to the United Nations in 1995. Yet Europe seemed beset by "grave uncertainties at the levels of culture, anthropology, ethics, and spirituality": Europeans were uncertain about the worth of their own civilizational achievement, about the nature of the human person, about right and wrong, and about the relationship of the true, the good, and the beautiful to twenty-first-century life.[69] A widespread experience of ambiguity, John Paul suggested, helped explain Europe's loss of faith in the future. Thus at this crowning moment of European integration—a process the Catholic Church had vigorously promoted since the end of World War II—Europe's greatest need was not for a new pan-European currency, a transnational budgeting system, continent-wide regulations, or even a new constitutional treaty, important as all those things doubtless were. Rather, "the most urgent matter Europe faces, in both East and West," John Paul wrote, "is a growing need for hope, a hope that will enable us to give meaning to life and history and to continue on our way together."[70]

The signs of Europe's loss of hope were readily at hand, and **Ecclesia in Europa** did not hesitate to describe them sharply:

> A kind of practical agnosticism and religious indifference whereby many Europeans give the impression of living without spiritual roots and somewhat like heirs who have squandered a patrimony entrusted to them by history . . . Fear of the future . . . [An] inner emptiness that grips many people . . . [A] widespread existential fragmentation [in which] a feeling of loneliness is prevalent . . . Weakening of the very concept of the family . . . Selfishness that closes individuals and groups in upon themselves . . . A growing lack of concern for ethics and an obsessive concern for personal interests and privileges [leading to] the diminished number of births.[71]

The latter was perhaps the leading indicator of Europe's loss of hope and fear of the future. For when an entire continent, richer, healthier, and more secure than ever before, stopped producing the future in the most elemental sense—by producing future generations—then something was awry in the realm of the human spirit. That was precisely what was happening in a European Union in which no country had a replacement level birth rate and several countries seemed headed into demographic winter.

The determination to prevent any reference to Europe's Christian roots in the basic document of Europe's political future reflected, even as it compounded and exacerbated, all these problems, the Pope suggested: for "at the root of this loss of hope is an attempt to promote a vision of man apart from God and apart from Christ. . . . Forgetfulness of God has led to the abandonment of man."[72] Ideas had consequences, as ever, and the ideas that John Paul's old friend the French Jesuit Henri de Lubac had bundled together under the rubric "atheist humanism" had had lethal consequences in modern European history: first, by helping underwrite the trauma of 1914–91; then, by depriving Europe of a reason to create the future.[73] The net result was a Europe in which men and women who should have been living vigorously in freedom were in fact being left alone in a guilt-wracked and existentially painful way: "One of the roots of the hopelessness that assails many people today . . . is their inability . . . to allow themselves to be forgiven, an inability often resulting from the isolation of those who, by living as if God did not exist, have no one from whom they can seek forgiveness."[74]

The "shadows" were not the whole reality of Europe, John Paul proposed. The twentieth-century martyrs, and the Christians of many denominations who had played such a key role in the Revolution of 1989, had demonstrated that the Gospel could still inspire men and women to build a "moral and societal life which honors and promotes the dignity and freedom of every person." That freedom had triumphed in 1989 through the victory of spiritual courage over material force was surely a sign of hope, as was the reconciliation of countries that had been bitter enemies for centuries. Even the widespread, if often confused, "desire for spiritual nourishment" evident across the continent bespoke at least the possibility of a recovery of "ethical and spiritual values" in "creative fidelity to the humanist and Christian traditions of our continent."[75]

Making that possibility a reality, however, meant that the Europe of the twenty-first century could not read the history of freedom exclusively through the prism of the French Revolution and 1789, and still less through the prism of the cultural upheavals of 1968. These cataclysms were not, John Paul insisted, the sources of Europe's historic commitment to the public goods the new constitutional treaty celebrated: democracy, human rights, civility and tolerance, the rule of law. Rather, it was from "the biblical conception of man [that] Europe drew the best of its humanistic culture, found inspiration for its artistic and intellectual creations, created systems of law, and, not least, advanced the dignity of the person as the subject of inalienable rights."[76] Moreover, if the historical truth were to be fully told, it was the Church that had given Europe the creative capacity to make this humanistic heritage the center of the world's unfolding history: for it was "the Church, as the bearer of the Gospel, [that] helped spread and consolidate these values which have made European culture universal."[77] Had there been no missionary impulse, European civilization would likely have remained confined to a small peninsula jutting into the Atlantic from the vastness of the Eurasian landmass.

The English author G. K. Chesterton had once observed that the crisis of modernity was one of "virtues gone mad." John Paul seemed to agree, and warned that when "the great values which amply inspired European culture" were "willfully separated from the Gospel," such virtues as tolerance and civility "[lose] their very soul and [pave] the way for any number of aberrations." It was not difficult to imagine the Pope thinking that one of those "aberrations" would be the constitutional enforcement of a rigorous **laïcité,** a European public square bereft of religiously informed ideas, in the very name of civility, tolerance, and pluralism.

As throughout his social magisterium, John Paul II

was at pains in **Ecclesia in Europa** to stress that the Church had no interest in running either European states or the EU. In the apostolic exhortation, there is no hint of nostalgia for the days of the ancien régime, the days of altar-and-throne alliances. Those days were over. And from John Paul's point of view, that was a good thing, for the entanglement with coercive state power had impeded the Church's evangelical mission and had done its part to fracture Western Christendom. No, what the Church now had to offer Europe was a challenge: a challenge to "the moral quality of its civilization." If the Europe of the future were to prosper in a genuinely humane way, it had to be, not simply a free society, but a free and virtuous society—a society in which "the moral structure of freedom" was well understood, such that European culture and society were safeguarded "both from the totalitarian Utopia of 'justice without freedom' and from the Utopia of 'freedom without truth' which goes hand in hand with a false concept of 'tolerance.'" Both those Utopias, John Paul reminded his European readers, "portend errors and horrors for humanity, as the recent history of Europe sadly attests."[78]

To redeem the tears of that "recent history," the new Europe could not be merely a geographical or administrative entity, soldered together politically by the public profession of certain values whose primary claim on Europeans' allegiance was that they "worked." For Europe was and is "primarily a cultural and historical concept," in which Christian truth had been, and would continue to be, essential in helping create societies "capable of integrating peoples and cultures among themselves" in a "new model of unity in diversity." The new EU would be a brittle shell, without substance, if it were to reduce itself to "its merely geographic and economic dimensions." Therefore, John Paul wrote,

Europe needs a religious dimension. If it is to be "new," by analogy with what is said about the "new city" of the Book of Revelation [Revelation 21.2], it must open itself to the workings of God. The hope of building a more just world, a world more worthy of man, cannot prescind from a realization that human effort will be of no avail unless it is accompanied by divine assistance: for "unless the Lord builds the house, those who build it labor in vain" [Psalm 127]. For Europe to be built on solid foundations, there is need to call upon authentic values grounded in the universal moral law written on the heart of every man and woman.[79]

That was the moral law, he had told Croatia, that "Christianity [had] the merit of clearly identifying and proclaiming." And so he ended his appeal to Europe—and beyond Europe, to all postmodern societies in the twenty-first century—with a familiar challenge, to open the doors to God:

Do not be afraid! The Gospel is not against you, but for you. . . . The Gospel of hope does not disappoint! Throughout the vicissitudes of your history, yesterday and today, it is the light that illumines and directs your way; it is the strength which sustains you in trials; it is the prophecy of a new world; it is the sign of a new beginning; it is the invitation to everyone, believers and nonbelievers alike, to blaze new trails leading to a "Europe of the spirit," in order to make the continent a true "common home" filled with the joy of life.[80]

The end of **Ecclesia in Europa** was typically hopeful—but with a sting, even a warning. That the Pope chose the Book of Revelation as the biblical framework for his apostolic exhortation was not accidental. Written in the first century A.D., the Book of Revelation was initially addressed to the "seven Churches" of what is now called Asia Minor. Only one of those local Churches exists today as a living Christian community; the classical European civilization from which the seven Churches grew was eventually displaced. By choosing to highlight the Book of Revelation in **Ecclesia in Europa,** John Paul was suggesting that Europe is not guaranteed a future. Europe must choose to have a future. That would mean choosing to have children. That would mean choosing a firmer foundation for Europe's human rights commitments than pragmatism or utilitarianism. That would mean, above all, a Europe reclaiming the spiritual and moral patrimony of its biblical and Christian heritage, a crucial and irreducible part of Europe being Europe.

DARK NIGHTS

When Cardinal Walter Kasper remarked on suffering being John Paul II's "profession" during the Pope's 2002 pastoral visit to Bulgaria, he was not far off the mark—although "vocation" might have been a more apt term than "profession," for Karol Wojtyła had long understood suffering as part of his (and indeed everyone's) Christian discipleship. He had known physical hardship and pain throughout his life: hunger and cold in Nazi-occupied Poland; having his shoulder broken by a German army truck and being left in a roadside ditch during the war; Agca's bullet wounds, then the pain of infection and physical deterioration caused by the "auxiliary terrorist," the cytomegalovirus, in 1981; a stomach tumor in 1992; a broken shoulder in 1993; a broken femur and an ill-fitted hip joint prosthesis in 1994; an appendectomy in 1996; the merciless Parkinson's disease that was relentlessly wearing him down from the mid-1990s on. Whenever he could, John Paul treated his infirmities with the medicine of humor. After the 1994 hip replacement, when he had learned to walk again with the aid of a cane, he shuffled slowly down the aisle to the presider's table in the Synod Hall before turning to the prelates assembled for a Synod meeting and wisecracking, **"Eppur' si muove"** [Yet it moves]—Galileo's sotto voce comment to his judges about the earth's revolution about the sun. Still, for John Paul II, suffering was no laughing matter, but a reality at the heart of the Christian call to follow Christ.

His suffering as pope was spiritual and moral as well as physical. Each day, the household sisters put prayer requests from around the world into the top of the prie-dieu at which he began his day, praying privately for an hour or ninety minutes before celebrating daily Mass. Thus every day, John Paul took upon himself and brought before his Lord the suffering of the world that came to him in microcosm through those notes—strained marriages, sick children, lost jobs, lethal disease, lost faith—as well as in macrocosm, as his mind's eye surveyed the gravest needs of both the Church and the world during his personal prayer. Those who came to join the morning Mass and heard the Pope groaning on his prie-dieu had, in those moments, some sense of what St. Paul meant when he wrote that, while we do not know how to pray as we ought, "the Spirit himself intercedes for us with sighs too deep for words" (Romans 8.26). Then there was moral suffering: the pain inflicted on the Pope by priests who abandoned their vocations or abused the trust reposed in them by harming the young; the moral pain of his failure to prevent war; the moral suffering imposed on him by those who tried to use him politically, such as Yassir Arafat and Tariq Aziz; the moral horror of late modernity's slaughter of the innocents, in the widespread practice of abortion.

John Paul II knew that "evil" was no abstraction and that the world was an arena of spiritual and moral combat between light and darkness; for him, these were not biblical metaphors, but realities of everyday life. Modern psychiatry and psychology—in which he had long been interested—might explain some facets of the human propensity for wickedness; it could not explain the kind of evil he had encountered in Nazism and communism, or the kind of evil that had produced 9/11. Every Tuesday night, like every other Catholic who prayed the Liturgy of the Hours, John Paul read a brief biblical passage during Compline, the day's last prayer: "Be sober, be watchful. Your adversary the devil prowls around like a roaring lion, seeking someone to devour. Resist him, firm in your faith" (1 Peter 5.8–9a). The presence of the ancient adversary had been all too real to Karol Wojtyła for decades.

So had been the faith through which he had met the mystery of evil and suffering. John Paul II may have displayed a certain stoicism in his personal response to suffering. But he was no Stoic in the philosophical sense; it was in Christian terms that he tried to understand suffering and unite himself to Christ through it. He had shared what he had learned from a lifetime of suffering and reflection upon suffering in a 1984 apostolic letter, **Salvifici Doloris** [Salvific Suffering], which he published a month and a half after meeting with Mehmet Ali Agca in Rebibia prison in Rome.

Suffering, John Paul wrote, "seems to be particularly essential to the nature of man." Animals feel pain; only men and women suffer. That suggested that suffering was, in perhaps a paradoxical way, a signal of transcendence: suffering is, he wrote, "one of those points in which man is in a certain sense 'destined' to go beyond himself."[81]

Suffering could be described psychologically, phenomenologically, clinically; but no description of suffering, however accurate, could get to the mystery of suffering as experienced by human beings. Nor could a rational explanation of suffering get us to the truth that "love is . . . the fullest source of the answer to the question of the meaning of suffering." That required, not an argument, but a demonstration: a demonstration that God had given, in history, "in the cross of Jesus Christ," whose suffering as the incarnate Son of God had had an "incomparable depth and intensity."[82] God's answer to that incomparable suffering, which included humanity's greatest suffering, death, came in the resurrection. Suffering in the world continued after the death and resurrection of Christ. But the suffering Christian could now identify his or her suffering with that of

Christ, and thus enter more closely into the mystery of the redemption, which is also the mystery of human liberation. Thus suffering led to new insights into life lived as vocation.[83]

During the late summer of 2003 and through the celebration of his silver jubilee as pope, John Paul II would draw on everything he had learned about physical, spiritual, and moral suffering from the time of his mother's premature death in 1929 through his eighty-third birthday.

He had hoped to have an operation that summer to relieve the increasingly harsh knee pain he was suffering from acute arthritis. But it was finally decided that it was too dangerous to put a man with advanced Parkinson's disease under general anesthesia, so the surgery was called off, leaving the Pope crippled and in pain. There were changes in the medication regimen for his Parkinson's. It was unusually and unbearably hot at Castel Gandolfo in August 2003, to the point where it made no sense to try to use the pool he had built on the villa grounds; moreover, the villa itself lacked air-conditioning. The Europeans didn't seem to be listening to his pleas not to cut the new EU off from one source of its cultural heritage. His efforts to prevent war in Iraq had failed. Tales of priestly and episcopal infidelity continued to bear down on him. In that season of his discontent, John Paul II might well have lived through something akin to what his closest theological adviser, Joseph Ratzinger, had once written about the meaning of hell as understood by St. John of the Cross, one of John Paul's spiritual masters, and by St. Thérèse of Lisieux, whom the Pope had named a Doctor of the Church:

> For [these] saints, "Hell" is not so much a threat to be hurled at other people but a challenge to oneself. It is a challenge to suffer in the dark night of faith, to experience communion with Christ in solidarity with his descent into the Night. One draws nearer to the Lord's radiance by sharing his darkness. One serves the salvation of the world by leaving one's own salvation behind for the sake of others. In such piety, nothing of the reality of Hell is denied. Hell is so real that it reaches right into the existence of the saints. Hope can take it on, only if one shares in the suffering of the One who came to transform our night by his suffering. . . . Such hope cannot, however, be a self-willed assertion. It must place its petition into the hands of its Lord and leave it there.[84]

The summer produced another disappointment when a quietly discussed papal visit to Mongolia had to be abandoned because of the SARS epidemic. The Catholic population of Mongolia was very small, but that had not stopped the Pope from going to Azerbaijan. The strategic reason for the trip, however, was to create circumstances for a refueling stop in Kazan, where John Paul II could return the Kazanskaya icon to Russia. The government of the People's Republic of China had invited the Pope to stop over in their country during any Mongolian visit, but the invitation was rebuffed by the Holy See on the grounds that since the regime was persecuting the underground Catholic Church in China it was not an auspicious time for a papal visit.[85] Thus John Paul II was frustrated yet again in his efforts to get to Russia and China.

John Paul carried his suffering from Castel Gandolfo into his pastoral visit to Slovakia in September 2003, where at the airport welcoming ceremony, he slumped down on the first day of the pilgrimage and couldn't finish his opening remarks—a stirring call to bring Slovakia's Christian heritage into the European Union. This set off another media frenzy, with networks that had previously deemed the trip uninteresting now rushing correspondents to Bratislava and Rome. Throughout the fall, bizarre and unfounded rumors circulated in the Roman press corps: that the Pope was to undergo dialysis; that he was being treated with a papaya-based wonder drug.[86]

Amidst intensifying global concern about his health, John Paul II's silver jubilee fell on October 16, 2003. Over the previous twenty-five years, he had been seen by more than 250 million people in the course of 700,000 miles of travels around the world (which did not count the tens of thousands of miles he had traveled in Italy). He had welcomed 16.6 million people to his Wednesday general audiences and 570 heads of state to the Vatican. He had canonized 476 saints and beatified 1,314 Servants of God—more than all his papal predecessors combined. He had created some two hundred cardinals. He had issued fourteen encyclicals, fifteen apostolic exhortations, twelve apostolic constitutions, and more than forty apostolic letters and other teaching letters—an exercise of the papal magisterium with which the Church would be grappling for centuries.

The anniversary was marked by several events during which the Pope soldiered on, visibly in pain. At the silver jubilee Mass in St. Peter's Square on October 16, John Paul signed and issued the apostolic exhortation **Pastores Gregis** [Shepherds of the Flock], to complete the work of the 2001 Synod of Bishops on the episcopate in the twenty-first century. The liturgy began with the Litany of the Saints; Cardinal Joseph Ratzinger greeted the Pope on his anniversary on behalf of the vast crowd assembled; the Gospel reading chosen was Christ's description in John 10 of the Good Shepherd who lays down his life for his sheep. In his homily, John Paul said that, twenty-five years before, he had "had a special experience of divine mercy" as he heard "echo in my soul the question addressed to Peter . . . **'Do you love me? Do you love me more than these?'** [John 21.15–16]. Humanly speaking, how could I not have been apprehensive? How could so great a responsibility not burden me? I had to turn to divine mercy in order to answer the question, 'Do you accept?' with confidence."

Every day since, "that same dialogue between Jesus and Peter takes place in my heart." From the beginning of the pontificate, "my thoughts, prayers, and actions were motivated by one desire: to witness that Christ, the Good Shepherd, is present and active in his Church. . . . That is why, from the very first day, I have never ceased to urge people: 'Do not be afraid to welcome Christ and accept his power!'" So, on this silver jubilee, he wished to say it one more time, forcefully: "Open, indeed open wide the doors to Christ! Let him guide you! Trust in his love!" He closed by thanking everyone for upholding him in prayer, and asked that that special form of help continue: "I implore you, dear brothers and sisters, do not stop your great work of love for the Successor of Peter. I ask you once again: help the Pope, whoever wants to serve Christ, to serve man and all humanity!"[87]

The **Gloria, Sanctus**, and **Agnus Dei** of the silver jubilee Mass were taken from the Gregorian **Missa de Angelis**, which young Father Karol Wojtyła had taught to his university students in the choir loft of St. Florian's Church in Kraków, more than fifty years before. As a gift to the cardinals who had come to Rome for the occasion, John Paul II had had prepared boxed replicas of the Bodmer VIII papyrus of the First Letter of Peter—the first papal encyclical, as it were.

On October 19, the silver jubilee celebrations continued with another solemn Mass in St. Peter's Square, during which John Paul II beatified a woman with whom he had shared a remarkable spiritual friendship: Mother Teresa of Calcutta. The last public meeting between the two, who had met numerous times during the pontificate, had taken place a few months before Mother Teresa's 1997 death, when the fragile, Albanian-born nun, herself in precarious health, had insisted on attending the Mass for the Solemnity of Sts. Peter and Paul in St. Peter's Basilica, and was seated in a wheelchair to the right of the altar. At the end of Mass, John Paul II hobbled over to greet her, and, as Mother Teresa's successor, Sister Nirmala, remembered, "Mother with great effort and the support of his [trembling] hand stood up and kissed his ring. . . . The Holy Father bent down and kissed her head."[88] Her death shortly afterward, John Paul II had commented to lunch guests, had "left us all feeling a little orphaned."[89]

St. Peter's Square was filled to overflowing for the beatification Mass, with the vast crowd spilling down the Via della Conciliazione and filling the piazza itself bright with flags: Albania and India, Mother Teresa's native land and her adopted home; Portugal, France, Poland, Argentina, the United States, and others. A large banner from Wadowice congratulated the Polish town's most famous son on his silver anniversary. John Paul made a valiant effort to force his voice to do what he wanted it to do, but after a few phrases, his breathing problems would take over; every time he got through a prayer or a phrase, waves of applause rippled through the great crowd, as if to support and encourage him. At the Canon of the Mass, John Paul began Eucharistic Prayer II, which was then picked up and carried by Cardinal Joseph Ratzinger and the other principal concelebrants. Ratzinger, in his beautifully pronounced, sonorous Latin, led the parts of the Mass between the Great Amen and the **Agnus Dei**. At the end of the ceremony, John Paul got into the Popemobile and did a circuit of the piazza, tilted over but waving to the enormous congregation.

John Paul's homily described Mother Teresa as **"an icon of the Good Samaritan"** who had gone "everywhere to serve Christ in the poorest of the poor." Her beatification on World Mission Sunday "reminds everyone that **the evangelizing mission of the Church passes through charity**, nourished by prayer and listening to God's word." As her spiritual journals had revealed, she, too, had experienced dramatic dark nights of the soul—decades in which God seemed absent from her life. Yet "in her darkest hours she clung even more tenaciously to prayer before the Blessed Sacrament. This harsh spiritual trial led her to **identify herself more and more closely with those whom she served each day**, feeling their pain and, at times, even their rejection. She was fond of repeating that **the greatest poverty is to be unwanted**, to have no one to take care of you."

She had won the Nobel Peace Prize (and had made an impassioned plea for the right to life of the unborn during her acceptance speech). She had befriended Diana, Princess of Wales, and had received the homage of the world's great and good. Still, the truth about Mother Teresa, John Paul concluded, was that she had become "one of the most important figures of our time" and "a tireless benefactor of humanity" because she was "a humble Gospel messenger . . . **in love with God**"—a tiny woman of immense courage who had taken with utmost, life-expending seriousness the Lord's injunction: "Whoever would be first among you must be the servant of all!" (Mark 10.44).[90]

The third and final major event of John Paul II's silver jubilee was a consistory held on October 21, 2003, for the creation of thirty-one new cardinals, one of whose names was reserved **in pectore.** Among the thirty receiving red hats that day were Jean-Louis Tauran and Renato Martino, along with several other curial officials, and five of the Church's most impressive young scholar-bishops: Philippe Barbarin, the archbishop of Lyon; Péter Erdö, the archbishop of Esztergom-Budapest; Marc Ouellet, P.S.S., the archbishop of Québec; George Pell, the archbishop of Sydney; and Angelo Scola, patriarch of Venice. One of the new cardinals, Keith Michael Patrick O'Brien of St. Andrews and Edinburgh, had made several curious comments about priestly celibacy in the past, and was asked to make a public profession of faith in his cathedral before coming to Rome for the consistory; Cardinal O'Brien subsequently became a fierce defender of the Christian conception of marriage and the right to life in Scotland. The longtime theologian of the papal household, Georges Cottier, O.P., became a cardinal, as did three other elderly theologians: Belgium's Gustaaf Joos (whom Karol Wojtyła had first met at the Belgian College in Rome in 1946); the Czech Jesuit ecumenist Tomáš Špidlík; and Poland's Stanisław Nagy.[91] Justin Rigali, archbishop of Philadelphia, was the lone American in the cardinalitial Class of 2003.

John Paul II was visibly exhausted by October 21, and did not impose the red biretta on his new cardinals' heads; rather, they knelt in front of him and he handed them the biretta, which they then placed on their heads themselves. Two of the new cardinals, Gabriel Zubeir Wako of Khartoum and Australia's Pell, were very tall men. On exchanging the kiss of peace with his new brother cardinals, Pio Laghi greeted Pell with the remark, "Ah, the greatest [of the new cardinals]!" "No, Your Eminence," Pell replied, "only the largest." The new cardinals were given their rings at a Mass on October 22, 2003—the twenty-fifth anniversary of John Paul's inaugural Mass and its signature challenge, "Be not afraid!"

By December 2003, John Paul II had bounced back from the physical and emotional difficulties of the late summer and fall, thanks to a combination of a new medication regimen, some physical therapy, and his own determination to carry on. Given a copy of the collected poems of T. S. Eliot by a pre-Christmas dinner guest, John Paul immediately responded, "Eliot. **Murder in the Cathedral**."[92] Asked whether he would write any more poetry, the Pope responded, **"No, e finito!"** [No, that's over!], at which Archbishop Dziwsz (as he had been since September 29) muttered, **"Si, per oggi . . ."** [Yes, for today . . .]. Dziwisz himself was showing signs of wear, which was entirely understandable in someone almost sixty-five years old who was caring constantly for an incapacitated man and likely getting fewer than five hours of sleep a night in the process. Yet the Pope's secretary retained both his utter devotion to the man he had served for four decades and his own good humor.

Those closest to John Paul were increasingly aware that they were witnesses to something quite dramatic: the outpouring of a life in service to God and the world, by a man who was beyond caring what anyone thought about how he looked in his illness. Some might have wished for a different kind of ending; but as Archbishop James M. Harvey, the prefect of the papal household, put it at the end of 2003, "Isn't that a sign of his greatness? That he's willing to submit himself to public humiliation daily out of dedication to the mission?"[93]

Longtime Vatican aides weren't the only ones to understand; some journalists understood, too. Writing shortly before the Pope's silver jubilee, **New York Times** columnist David Brooks commented on the fact that the man "who has had a more profound influence on more people than any other living human being" was never going to win the Nobel Peace Prize. Brooks was right in observing that the Pope didn't care about being passed over time and again by the Norwegian Nobel Committee. But Brooks was even more acute in noting that John Paul II was "too big and complex" for what the world imagined to be one of its highest accolades. His main achievement, Brooks continued, had been "to remind us—Catholics and even us non-Catholics—that you can't pare people down. . . . The Pope is always taking us out of our secular comfort zone and dragging us toward ultimate issues. You can't talk about politics, economics, science, philosophy, or war, he argues, while conveniently averting your eyes from God and ultimate truth."

"When history looks back on our era," David Brooks concluded, "Pope John Paul II will be recognized as the giant of the age, as the one individual who did the most to place . . . freedom at the service of the highest human goals."[94]

THE LONG-DISTANCE PONTIFICATE

Simon, son of John, also known as Peter, a man whose friendship with Jesus of Nazareth brought him from an obscure Galilean fishing village to the center of the world imperium, died according to tradition in either 64 or 67 A.D., crucified upside down in Nero's Circus, which was located in what is now Vatican City, quite near the site of the basilica named for him. But no one really knows how long Peter lived with the power of the keys. The longest pontificate since Peter was that of Pope Pius IX, who was elected on June 16, 1846, and died on February 7, 1878. The cardinal-electors who chose the successor to Pio Nono (or, as the irreverent had it, "Pio No-No") probably imagined that they were taking out an insurance policy against another such lengthy pontificate when they elected sixty-eight-year-old Cardinal Vincenzo Gioacchino Pecci as Pope Leo XIII two weeks later. Leo then proceeded to live the second-longest pontificate in reliably recorded history, expiring at the ripe age of ninety-three on July 20, 1903. During that twenty-five-year reign, Leo XIII created the modern papacy as an office of moral instruction and witness, launching Catholic social doctrine into the deep of the industrial age and its immense social problems, and creating the intellectual framework by which the Catholic Church finally worked its way through to a Catholic theory of religious freedom and the modern constitutional state at the Second Vatican Council.

No pope since Leo XIII had done more to enrich the Church's social thought over the next century than John Paul II, who passed Leo on the roster of papal longevity on March 14, 2004, becoming the second-longest-serving pope in reliably recorded history—or, to pay Peter the deference owed him, the third-longest-serving Bishop of Rome in the two millennia of the Catholic Church's history. According to some stories, Leo XIII began to show signs of intellectual diminishment in the last few years of his pontificate. That could not be said of John Paul II, whose mind remained sharp even as his body continued to betray him throughout 2004.

The year began with an unfortunate flap over comments the Pope was said to have made after viewing in December 2003 a prerelease screening of Mel Gibson's movie **The Passion of the Christ**—that "It is as it was." The comment, which had been made privately, was picked up by those promoting the film (not without encouragement from some in the Vatican), which landed John Paul II, unwittingly, in the middle of the controversy the movie had generated over its alleged anti-Semitic undertones. Conflicting signals from the Holy See Press Office and the papal apartment added to the confusion, which finally dissipated, leaving a bad taste in many mouths.[95]

On January 26, the Sala Clementina of the Apostolic Palace witnessed something it had never seen before: a performance of break dancing, accompanied by music from a boom box, by a Polish troupe that worked with disadvantaged young people in the Pope's homeland. As one report put it, "one dancer . . . planted his head on the inlaid marble floor of the Vatican and spun to loud applause from his group and from Vatican officials." Whatever he might have thought of break dancing, John Paul applauded the performance and commended the troupe's work with the poor.[96] Sixteen days later, on the evening of February 11, the liturgical commemoration of Our Lady of Lourdes, the Pope paid a surprise visit to the Discalced Carmelite nuns then living in the house of contemplative prayer he had established in 1994 in the Vatican, behind the **Governatorato**, the main administration building of Vatican City. After greeting each of the startled sisters personally, John Paul, his two secretaries, and the sisters sang the Latin Marian hymn **Tota Pulchra Est** [Thou Art All-Beautiful], before the Pope was taken back to the Popemobile for the drive back to the Cortile Sesto Quinto and the elevator ride up to the papal apartment on the **terza loggia** of the Apostolic Palace. The surprises were not yet over for the Carmelites, though. A half hour later, their doorbell rang again, and a messenger brought gifts from John Paul to the sisters: chocolates; a cake; a wax bas-relief of St. Teresa Benedicta of the Cross (Edith Stein), the Carmelite martyr of Auschwitz; and a large candle, which was immediately lit and placed in front of the convent's statue of Mary.[97]

John Paul did not begin Lent as usual in 2004, by going to the Basilica of Santa Sabina on the Aventine Hill, the first of Rome's Lenten stational churches, to receive ashes. Instead of going to the Aventine on February 25, Ash Wednesday, the Pope received ashes in the Paul VI Audience Hall of the Vatican, in a ceremony at which those attending the weekly papal general audience were also invited to be marked with the age-old sign of Lenten repentance and penitential resolution. Three days later, John Paul resumed his visitations of Rome's parishes, which had been suspended in the last months of 2003 because of his illness. At this stage of the pontificate, there had to be a change in the normal visitation routine: now, the parishes came to celebrate Mass with the Pope in the Vatican, rather than the Pope going out to celebrate Mass in the parishes. On February 28, the parishes that were present were from the rapidly expanding southern part of Rome: St. Anselm, St. Charles Borromeo, St. John Baptist de la Salle, and St. Mary Star of Evangelization. None had its own facility yet; the Pope urged the congregation, consisting principally of young families, to "make your parishes genuine spiritual buildings, which rest on the cornerstone that is Christ." In his homily, John Paul also asked the parishioners not to forget "the affection that unites me more intensely to you," for this was the portion of the Lord's flock "entrusted, in a special way, to my pastoral care." His homily, like many of his public addresses in this phase of his Parkinson's disease, may have been difficult to hear at some points. But there was no doubt in the Romans' mind of the truth of what the man they called "Pope Wojtyła" said when he told them that "I carry you in my heart."[98] Two weeks later, on March 11, jihadist terrorists exploded ten bombs in and around four Madrid railroad stations, killing 200 Spaniards, wounding 2,000 more, and leaving bloody body parts strewn over station platforms and commuter railway lines. John Paul condemned the "execrable crimes" in his March 14 Angelus address for the Third Sunday of Lent.[99]

Despite fears of further jihadist slaughter in Europe, young people flooded St. Peter's Square on Palm Sunday, April 4, the twentieth anniversary of John Paul II's initiation of diocesan and international world youth days, and the Pope challenged the young people to proclaim Christ crucified to a skeptical world: "Do not be afraid to swim against the tide!"[100] The Pope was able to preside at all the major Holy Week liturgies, although accommodations were made because of his condition; thus on Holy Thursday, it was Cardinal Joseph Ratzinger who conducted the **Mandatum**, the traditional washing of feet in imitation of Christ's act of humility at the Last Supper. John Paul did not walk the evening **Via Crucis** at the Colosseum on Good Friday, but he did offer a brief reflection, praying at the end that the "mystery of the **Way of the Cross** of the Son of God . . . [may] comfort and strengthen us when our own hour arrives."[101] Earlier in the day, the Pope had presided over the Solemn Liturgy of the Lord's Passion in St. Peter's, during which, according to custom, the preacher to the papal household, the Italian Capuchin Raniero Cantalamessa, gave the homily.

At the Great Vigil of Easter on Holy Saturday evening, the Pope both presided and preached in St. Peter's, and did the same the next morning outdoors in the piazza, before giving his **Urbi et Orbi** greetings in sixty-two languages. In the free-form verse that had become customary for the **Urbi et Orbi** message, John Paul prayed in particular that humanity might find the courage and solidarity to

> face the inhuman,
> and unfortunately growing, phenomenon of terrorism,
> which rejects life and brings anguish and uncertainty
> to the daily lives of so many hard-working and peaceful people.
> May your wisdom enlighten men and women of good will
> in the required commitment against this outrage.[102]

The year 2004 was one of those rare years on which the Western and Eastern Christian calendars coincided on the date of Easter, and the Pope concluded the **Urbi et Orbi** with greetings to "the venerable Patriarchs, the Bishops, and the faithful of the Eastern Churches" and prayed to the Risen Lord that "all of us who are baptized may soon come to **relive together on the same day every year** this fundamental feast of our faith. **Surrexit Christus. Alleluia!**"[103]

Heroic Virtue in Defense of Life

On May 16, the Fifth Sunday of Easter, John Paul II led what would be his last canonization ceremony in St. Peter's Square, honoring four religious founders; a Lebanese Maronite monk; and a young Italian wife, mother, and pediatrician, Gianna Beretta Molla, who had become the icon of the pontificate's promotion of the right to life of the unborn.

Born on October 4, 1922, in Magenta, a town in Lombardy, Gianna Beretta was the tenth of thirteen children, five of whom died in infancy or childhood. At age twenty-eight, having earned degrees in medicine and surgery at the University of Pavia, Dr. Beretta opened a clinic in Mesero, near her hometown, before returning to the University of Milan for a specialist's certification in pediatrics in 1952; after that, her medical practice focused on the care of mothers and their young children, the elderly, and the poor. A skier and mountain climber, she was also engaged in Italian Catholic Action, working particularly with very small children. She married another Catholic Action member, Pietro Molla, on September 25, 1955, at the basilica of St. Martin in Magenta. She gave birth to three children—Pierluigi, Mariolina, and Laura—between 1956 and 1959, each time experiencing a difficult pregnancy. Her medical practice and charitable activities continued along with her blossoming family life until September 1961, when, two months into her fourth pregnancy, a fibrous ovarian tumor was discovered that threatened both her life and that of her unborn child. There were three medical options: remove the uterus and the affected ovary, which would spare her life but kill the unborn child; remove the tumor alone and terminate the pregnancy, which would likely result in her being able to bear more children later; or remove the tumor while trying to save the pregnancy, a procedure that posed immediate risks to the mother and promised a dangerous delivery. Dr. Molla told the surgeon to take the third option. Throughout the remaining seven months of her pregnancy, she told both her physicians and her husband that, were it to come to a choice between her life and that of the child, they should choose to save the child. "Do not hesitate. I insist on it. Save the baby."

Gianna Beretta Molla entered St. Gerard's Hospital in Monza on Good Friday, April 20, 1962, where Gianna Emanuela was born the following day. Shortly after the birth, the new mother began to suffer excruciating pain from septic peritonitis, and died a week later, on April 28, 1962, at the age of thirty-nine. Her last words were "Jesus, I love you! Jesus, I love you!" The grave of Gianna Beretta Molla soon became a place of prayer and pilgrimage, and her cause for beatification was recognized by Pope Paul VI in 1973. Beatification followed on April 24, 1994, with Gianna Emanuela, herself a doctor, present.

John Paul II delivered the homily at the canonization Mass in Italian, Spanish, and French, seated in front of the altar on the **sagrato** in front of St. Peter's and leaning his text on the small portable desk he now used on such occasions. "The extreme sacrifice" which Saint Gianna Beretta Molla had "sealed with her life testifies that only those who have the courage to give of themselves totally to God and to others are able to fulfill themselves." It was a theme that Karol Wojtyła had been developing since his 1974 lecture, "The Personal Structure of Self-Determination," given at an international congress on St. Thomas Aquinas: there is a Law of the Gift, or law of self-giving, built into the moral structure of the human person, such that we only come to the fulfillment of ourselves by making our lives into the gift to others that our own life is to each of us.[104] As a young bishop at Vatican II, Karol Wojtyła had seen the Law of the Gift inscribed in the Pastoral Constitution on the Church in the Modern World.[105] Now, before the world Church, he lifted up the example of Gianna Beretta Molla, the last saint he would canonize, as the embodiment of the Law of the Gift lived in its most radical and dramatic form—and did so in the presence of a now frail, ninety-one-year-old Pietro Molla; Gianna's children; a grandchild; her surviving siblings; former patients of the young pediatrician; and Elisabeth Acomparini Arcolino, a young Brazilian mother, whose fourth pregnancy was miraculously saved through what the Congregation for the Causes of Saints concluded was the intercession of Gianna Beretta Molla.

There was a fitting symmetry in the fact that a pro-life witness to radical charity—charity lived to the ultimate degree—would be the last of the 482 saints John Paul II canonized. Yet the Pope's pro-life convictions were sometimes misunderstood as the very opposite of charity—they were mistaken for a form of Catholic misogyny by some, and deplored by others as an example of the impossibility of the Catholic Church's sexual ethic. For John Paul, however, abortion was not a matter of the sixth commandment and its injunction to chastity but of the fifth commandment and the injunction not to do murder. Moreover, as he put it at Mount Sinai in 2000, the truth that had been inscribed on the second tablet of the law, that one must not take innocent human life, had first been inscribed in the human heart, as a moral truth of the human condition that could be known by reason.

John Paul also insisted that the Church's defense of life did not violate any proper understanding of the separation of Church and state, for in defending the right to life of the unborn, the severely handicapped, and the elderly, and in insisting that the state not declare entire classes of human beings outside the protection of the laws, the Church was appealing to moral truths that could be known by any thinking person willing to work through an argument—moral truths that were part of the cultural foundations of democracy. The Catholic defense of the right to life was not some arcane bit of Catholic doctrine, accessible only to the initiate. It was based on first principles of justice that every human being of democratic sensibility should intuitively grasp. As always, however, demonstrations were likely to be more effective than arguments in moving hearts and minds. Thus the canonization of Saint Gianna Beretta Molla put a fitting capstone on John Paul II's quarter-century-long effort to lift up moral heroism in the defense of life through examples drawn from the contemporary world.

A BISHOP REMINISCES

In April 2004, the bishops of the United States began their **ad limina** visits to Rome, as all bishops do in a quinquennial cycle of meetings, organized nationally or regionally. For more than two decades, the **ad limina** schedule put maximum demands on the Pope, who received each bishop individually for a talk that might last from fifteen minutes to a half hour, hosted a group lunch in the papal apartment for the visiting prelates, celebrated Mass with them as a group, and delivered a formal address to them after the Mass. In the postjubilee years of the pontificate, John Paul's declining health dictated that this schedule be reduced. Thus he still met each bishop individually, but more briefly; the lunch was eliminated; Mass might or might not be celebrated together, depending on the Pope's condition; and the papal discourse to the group was not read to them, but was given to the bishops as a kind of personal letter from the Pope. Bishops' reactions to their private sessions with John Paul in 2004 varied, depending on his health, medication cycle, and general level of energy. Some found him relatively robust; others worried that his energies were flagging at long last. Different bishops within the same regional or national group could bring away dramatically different impressions, depending on the day of the week and time of the day they met the Pope. Some bishops were even more concerned with the listlessness they found during their meetings with the Roman Curia (another important part of the **ad limina** process), for, like most bureaucracies in similar situations, the Curia in 2004 was in **fin de régime** mode, with careerists jockeying for endgame position and unwilling to take initiatives that might not sit well with the next pontificate.

The Pope may have been displaying declining energy during **ad limina** visits, but he had more to say to his brother bishops beyond the apostolic exhortation **Pastores Gregis**, which he had signed on the occasion of his silver jubilee. He did so by adding another book to his personal bibliography when, on May 18, 2004, the Italian edition of **Alza-**

tevi, andiamo! [Rise, Let Us Be on Our Way!] was published.[106] In the book's introduction, John Paul explained that his new book, a memoir of his life as a bishop, was a kind of autobiographical complement to **Pastores Gregis**, as **Gift and Mystery**, his 1996 memoir of his priestly vocation, had been a personal complement to **Pastores Dabo Vobis**, the 1992 apostolic exhortation on the priesthood, priestly formation, and seminary reform.[107]

By most critics' lights, the book would have been improved by more stringent editing. As it is, **Alzatevi, andiamo!** rambles, in the voice of a reflective elder telling stories whose meaning he has long pondered. Yet those with the patience to work through it could find much interesting material, some of it surprising.

John Paul began with the story of his having to leave a July 1958 kayaking trip to go to Warsaw at the summons of Cardinal Stefan Wyszyński.[108] There, along with three other priests, he was told of his appointment as a bishop by Pope Pius XII. The bare facts of the incident were already on the public record; now, John Paul added a detail that may have been one of the only public demonstrations that the formidable "Primate of the Millennium" had at least something of a sense of humor. When Wyszyński told him that the Pope had named him auxiliary bishop of Kraków, Wojtyła said, "Your Eminence, I am too young. I'm only thirty-eight." To which the Primate replied, "That is a weakness which can soon be remedied." Wyszyński asked that the young priest not "oppose the will of the Holy Father," Wojtyła accepted, and then the Primate concluded the proceedings with a practical suggestion: "Then let's have lunch."

Wojtyła went from Warsaw to Kraków in order to speak with Archbishop Eugeniusz Baziak about the appointment. Baziak, another stern personality, met him at the door of the episcopal residence and walked him through a waiting room where priests were sitting, saying, **"Habemus papam"** [We have a pope]. "In the light of subsequent events," John Paul wrote, "one might say that these words were prophetic." Baziak, having made his little joke, initially said that the bishop-elect's return to the kayaking trip would not "be appropriate"; but when Wojtyła persisted (after going across the street to pray the Stations of the Cross at the Franciscan basilica), Baziak conceded and then had his second smile of the day: "Please come back in time for the consecration."[109]

Karol Wojtyła's admiration for the heroism of Cardinal Adam Sapieha, the "unbroken prince," was well known; in **Alzatevi, andiamo!** he added to his list of heroic episcopal role models his two co-consecrators in 1958, Bishop Franciszek Jop of Opole (a former Kraków auxiliary who had held the archdiocese together during Stalinist times), and Bishop Bolesław Kaminek of Wrocław, whom the communists forbade from living in his diocese for a period and whom Paul VI had named a cardinal. These men, in addition to Sapieha and Wyszyński, offered him a "heroic spiritual heritage" in which "personal greatness" grew from "faithful witness to Christ and to the Gospel."[110] Wyszyński, the Pope recalled, had defined the type of the bishop-hero, and its distinctive Christian texture, on the day before his own episcopal consecration in 1946: "Being a bishop has something of the Cross about it, which is why the Church places the Cross on the bishop's breast. On the Cross, we have to die to ourselves; without this, there cannot be the fullness of priesthood. To take up one's Cross is not easy, even if it is made of gold and studded with jewels." Later, the Primate would remark that "lack of courage in a bishop is the beginning of disaster" and that "the greatest weakness in an apostle is fear. . . . Fear in an apostle is the principal ally of the enemies of the cause."[111] Courage, John Paul seemed to be reminding his brothers in the episcopate, was not an optional accessory—it was of the essence of the bishop's vocation to speak and defend the truth.

Alzatevi, andiamo! also added to the world's knowledge of Karol Wojtyła's experience of the Second Vatican Council. The author slipped as close as he ever did to a public expression of irony when he wrote of his "Italian colleagues" at Vatican II "who took charge, so to speak, of the Council proceedings," but it was his contacts with African bishops that remained most striking in his memory. John Paul remembered being especially impressed by Archbishop Raymond-Marie Tchidimbo of Conakry in the west African country of Guinea, a man persecuted by his country's communist president and eventually exiled. Other Africans with whom Wojtyła had "cordial and frequent contact" were two future Francophone cardinals, the Senegalese Hyacinthe Thiandoum and Paul Zoungrana of Burkina Faso, then known as Upper Volta. John Paul mentioned, in addition, his Council-based friendships with the Frenchman Gabriel-Marie Garrone, the German bishops Alfred Bengsch and Joseph Höffner, and two eminent theologians: Henri de Lubac, S.J., and Joseph Ratzinger, whom the Pope described as a "great man who is a trusted friend"—a striking break from the usual papal protocol of never commenting on the work of a collaborator.[112]

Finally, **Alzatevi, andiamo!** contained some interesting self-criticism, touching on the author's "reluctance to rebuke others":

Another responsibility that certainly forms part of a pastor's role is admonition. I think that in this regard I did too little. There is always a problem in achieving a balance between authority and service. Maybe I should have been more assertive. I think this is partly a matter of my temperament. Yet it could also be related to the will of Christ, who asked His Apostles not to dominate but to serve.[113]

Critical reaction to **Alzatevi, andiamo!** was luke-warm and the book's sales outside Poland were not particularly strong. For those with the patience to work through its ellipses and side trips, however, and to read carefully between some of its lines, **Alzatevi, andiamo!** was a valuable, and at points touching, window into various aspects of Karol Wojtyła's spiritual life, his work, and his relationships.

SOLDIERING ON

On June 4, John Paul received U.S. president George W. Bush in their first meeting since the Iraq War had begun. The Pope did not mince words about the "unequivocal position of the Holy See" in regard to the "situation of grave unrest in the Middle East, both in Iraq and in the Holy Land," but he also praised the Bush administration's "great commitment . . . to overcoming the increasingly intolerable conditions in various African countries, where the suffering caused by fratricidal conflicts, pandemic diseases, and a degrading poverty can no longer be overlooked," and Bush's own "commitment to the promotion of moral values in American society, particularly with regard to respect for life and the family."[114] The Pope spoke in English, got through all but one paragraph of his text, and while he was sometimes difficult to understand, twice interjected a perfectly clear "God bless America!" into his formal remarks. Bush presented the Pope with the highest civilian award bestowed by the United States, the Medal of Freedom. The debate continued between U.S. and Vatican officials on the first use of force, international law, and the UN's authority, but both sides remained agreed on the necessity for the coalition forces to remain in Iraq until stability was achieved.[115]

The next day, John Paul left for what seemed likely to be a difficult pastoral visit to Switzerland, where forty-one prominent Catholic personalities had signed a public petition asking him to step down as pope. Things turned out better than expected. As the spokesman for the Swiss bishops' conference, Marc Aellen, put it, "at the beginning, for the meeting in the Bern Arena, we did not expect more than 3,000 to 4,000 young people; there were 14,000. On Sunday, we didn't dare to hope for the figure of 40,000—and 70,000 people attended Mass."[116] That was 25,000 more than had attended the closing Mass in Sion, on John Paul's first Swiss visit in 1984. The Pope challenged the outdoor congregation on Sunday to "pass from a **faith of habit** to a **mature faith**, which is expressed in clear, convinced, and courageous personal choices."[117]

Father Michael Sherwin, an American Dominican theologian working in Fribourg, described the

events and the atmosphere, and his surprise, in an
on-site report:

> The Mass on Sunday was the most impressive. There
> is only one word for it: joy, two and a half hours of
> joy. That is not a [word] that one uses often in ref-
> erence to the Swiss, so this made it doubly remark-
> able. People just had a wonderful time together in
> a real spirit of celebration and prayer. And 70,000
> people—the largest religious gathering in Switzer-
> land for over fifty years.
>
> On Saturday night the Pope was virtually unin-
> telligible in each of the three languages he spoke to
> us in, but the youth responded anyway. They es-
> pecially loved seeing him forcefully reject two dif-
> ferent attempts to get him off the stage before he
> was ready to go. During the Mass, he was in much
> better form.[118]

One Catholic news agency wrote of the Pope's
"magic" with the young, which was certainly on
full display in Bern. Still, the fact remained that the
pontificate of John Paul II had had a particularly
rough reception in the German-speaking world,
and most particularly among German theologians.
There were numerous reasons for this, including
the extraordinary sense found among many German Catholic intellectuals that they bore a special
responsibility for the Catholic theological enterprise

in the twenty-first century, as they had in the twentieth. The 1993 encyclical on the reform of moral theology, **Veritatis Splendor** [The Splendor of Truth], had hardened attitudes in the German-speaking intellectual world, as two of its most prominent figures, Josef Fuchs, S.J., and Bernard Häring, C.SS.R., were among those whose moral theological method was rejected in the encyclical, although neither man was named.[119] There were certainly legitimate scholarly issues being contested in these debates, as well as dramatically different readings of the meaning of modernity, but it was difficult not to think that at least some part of the poor reception of the pontificate in Germany, Austria, and the German-speaking parts of Switzerland had to do with certain unexamined (and false) assumptions prevalent in those regions about Poles living outside the mainstream of European intellectual life.

On June 8, John Paul II sent a telegram of condolence to Mrs. Nancy Reagan on the death of former president Ronald Reagan, who had succumbed to Alzheimer's disease on June 5: "I recall with deep gratitude the late president's unwavering commitment to the service of the nation and to the cause of freedom, as well as his abiding faith in the human and spiritual values which ensure a future of solidarity, justice, and peace in our world." The language was that of the Vatican Secretariat of State, but the sentiments of "deep gratitude" were wholly those of John Paul II, who gave a further indication of his

regard for Reagan by sending Cardinal Angelo Sodano, the secretary of state of the Holy See, to President Reagan's funeral as a special papal envoy.[120]

Ecumenical Patriarch Bartholomew I came to
Rome on June 29 for the Solemnity of Sts. Peter and
Paul, in part to mark the fortieth anniversary of the
meeting in Jerusalem in 1964 of Pope Paul VI and
Ecumenical Patriarch Athenagoras. John Paul and
Bartholomew both preached at the Mass in St. Peter's Square, with John Paul deferring to his guest
for the first homily, and Bartholomew speaking cordially of the "Sister Church of Rome." The two men
then signed a "Common Declaration" that took
note of the progress that had been made in ecumenical dialogue over the past forty years; the obstacles
that remained; the necessity of Europe recovering its
Christian roots; the imperative of rejecting terrorism and building a new interreligious dialogue with
Islam; the duty to defend the right to life; and the
preservation of the beauties of the earth against en-
vironmental degradation (the last being a particular
interest of Bartholomew). Five months later, on November 27, 2004, the Patriarch came to Rome for
another ecumenical celebration at which John Paul
returned to the Church of Constantinople relics of
two great Eastern Fathers of the Church, Gregory
Nazianzen and John Chrysostom, which had been
kept in Rome since being taken from Constantinople centuries before. In his message to Bartholomew
for the transfer of the relics, John Paul wrote that

he would "never tire of searching out, steadfastly and with determination . . . communion between Christ's disciples," and signed the message "in the patience of Christ and the charity of God, with fraternal love, **Johannes Paulus II**."[121]

"A SICK MAN AMONG THE SICK"

John Paul spent his summer holidays in the first half of July in Les Combes, in the Italian Alps, where he could sit outdoors and read at the foot of Mont Blanc. It was "an enchanting place," in which the exceptional Alpine scenery made visible the "omnipotent providence" of God, he told local officials on July 17, the day of his departure.[122] What John Paul II could not make visible any longer was his own laughter, as the Parkinson's disease had virtually destroyed his ability to make his face convey what he wanted to convey. Knowing that, for John Paul, the circus clown with bulbous red nose was a kind of archetype of something that always makes for laughter, Joaquín Navarro-Valls, the papal spokesman, had bought a red nose at a novelty store and brought it to the Val d'Aosta. Camera in hand, he then tried to surprise the Pope, who was reading, by putting on the clown's nose, jumping in front of the pontiff, and saying, "Holy Father, look at me!" John Paul managed as much of a laugh as the disease would allow; and here, Navarro remembered later, was "the drama: the face refused to express what was in the heart—laughter."[123]

The Pope spent the rest of July and early August at Castel Gandolfo before leaving on August 14 for what would be his last foreign pilgrimage, to the Marian shrine at Lourdes in the French Pyrenees, where he would celebrate the Solemnity of the Assumption the following day. It was his second visit to Catholicism's premier healing shrine, and he made it the occasion to demonstrate in an unmistakable way his conviction that his physical suffering was part of a providential plan for his Petrine ministry.

Wearing his patriotism and his **laïcité** on different sleeves, as it were, French president Jacques Chirac welcomed the Pope at the airport at Tarbes and praised Bernadette Soubirous, the visionary of Lourdes, as "a source of comfort and inspiration for Catholics the world over," but studiously declined to mention the apparitions of the Virgin that Bernadette had received or the miraculous cures that had made Lourdes world-famous. John Paul was not about to let Chirac's commitment to secularism in the European public square go completely unremarked. In his formal reply to Chirac's words of welcome, the Pope said that "the Catholic Church wishes to offer society a specific contribution towards the building of a world in which the great ideals of liberty, equality, and fraternity can form the basis of social life."

The key word was "specific," for Chirac had long insisted that the Church had something to say in the public arena only insofar as what it said reflected "universal values."

The Pope drove into Lourdes through flag-waving crowds whose enthusiasm seemed to hearten him. At the Grotto of Massabielle, he was lifted to a prie-dieu for a moment of prayer, but then seemed to fall back; caught by his aides, he was then pulled into a chair, wet-eyed—whether from pain or emotion, no one knew. But the planned service quickly resumed, with the Pope drinking a glass of Lourdes water and handing the basilica's rector, Father Raymond Zambelli, a golden rose as a gift to the Virgin. Cardinal Roger Etchegaray read the Pope's prayer for him, which began with a greeting to the sick: "I share a time of life marked by physical suffering, yet not for that reason any less fruitful in God's wondrous plan."

The Pope returned to the grotto Saturday afternoon for the daily recitation of the Rosary, which he began by saying that, "when kneeling here before the Grotto of Massabielle, I feel with emotion that I have arrived at the end of my pilgrimage." In a voice cracking under the strain of his effort, John Paul then compared the Grotto to the cave of Mount Horeb, where the prophet Elijah had listened for the "still small voice" of God (1 Kings 19.12), and noted that Lourdes had become a "unique school of prayer" where one could come to Mary and learn "an attitude of docility and openness to the Word of God."[124]

The Mass for the Solemnity of the Assumption on Sunday morning, held outdoors in temperatures close to 90 degrees Fahrenheit, was marked, as British correspondent Austen Ivereigh put it, by "the Pope's frailty and dogged determination."[125] Some 300,000 people were present to mark the Assumption and the 150th anniversary of Pope Pius IX's dogmatic definition of the Immaculate Conception. Two thousand **malades** were present in wheelchairs, cared for by the volunteers who make Lourdes a global synonym for loving care—a place where, as a longtime Lourdes confessor put it, "It's the sick people who are real; it's the rest of us who are unreal."[126] Fourteen cardinals, 120 bishops, and over 1,000 priests concelebrated the Mass with John Paul. During his homily, the Pope began to gasp for breath and whispered to an aide in Polish, "Help me." He was brought a glass of water and then whispered, once more in Polish, "I **must** finish!" Which he did, the crowd applauding and encouraging him. The homily concluded with a plea to respect life "from conception to its natural end," and to recognize that life was a sacred gift of which "no one can presume to be master."[127]

John Paul II's 104th and last pastoral pilgrimage outside Italy ended on the afternoon of August 15, when the Pope returned one last time to the Grotto, where he prayed for eight minutes, his eyes focused on the statue of the Virgin who had told Bernadette Soubirous, "I am the Immaculate Conception."

At Lourdes, John Paul II described himself as "a sick man among the sick." That was certainly true, but something else transpired at Lourdes on two hot summer days in August 2004. Vatican reporter John Allen caught it nicely: at Lourdes, John Paul II somehow completed "his transformation from 'the supreme pastor of the Catholic Church,' to quote the formula in the Code of Canon Law, into a living symbol of human suffering, in effect, an icon of Christ on the cross."[128] He remained the pastor, of course. But now his pastorate would be defined by his witness to the power of redemptive suffering. There was in fact an essential theological and spiritual clarification being played out here, and French cardinal Jean-Marie Lustiger summed it up well:

> The Pope, in his weakness, is living more than ever the role assigned him of being the Vicar of Christ on earth, participating in the suffering of our Redeemer. Many times we have the idea that the head of the Church is like a super-manager of a great international company, a man of action who makes decisions and is judged on the basis of his effectiveness. But for believers the most effective action, the mystery of salvation, happens when Christ is on the cross and can't do or decide anything other than to accept the will of the Father.[129]

Or, as John Allen concluded his report on Lourdes, "One simply can't watch the Pope these days and not think about the final things, about the meaning and purpose of life. That, indeed, is a legacy."[130]

No Disposable Human Beings

The remainder of 2004 had something of the character of an anticlimax after the high drama of Lourdes, albeit an anticlimax in which a failing but determined Pope still took significant initiatives.

It was now abundantly clear—and in fact had been for some time—that the recalcitrant Patriarch Aleksy II of Moscow would never concede to a papal visit to Russia. So John Paul II characteristically went the extra mile himself, and dispatched Cardinal Walter Kasper, president of the Pontifical Council for Promoting Christian Unity, on a mission to return the Kazanskaya icon to its homeland. The icon had come into the Pope's possession after a lengthy global peregrination following the Russian Revolution, and at one point was lodged in Fátima; for several years, John Paul had kept the priceless Kazanskaya and its heavily jeweled frame in the papal chapel in the Apostolic Palace, or in the chapel in Castel Gandolfo when he was in residence there.[131] Now that Aleksy had made it impossible for the Pope to fulfill his desire to bring the Kazanskaya home to Russia as an expression of his respect for Russian Orthodoxy, the time had come to send the icon home—but with a message.

Kasper gave the Kazanskaya to Aleksy in an August 28 ceremony at the Kremlin's Cathedral of the Dormition (the Orthodox term for what Catholicism calls the Assumption) and delivered a formal message from the Pope, in which John Paul wrote that "during the long years of her pilgrimage the Mother of God in her sacred icon . . . has gathered about her the Orthodox faithful and their Catholic brethren from other parts of the world."[132] Thus the Kazanskaya had become a symbol of the Christian unity that Russian Orthodoxy had so bitterly resisted within Russia since 1991. Cardinal Kasper's remarks to Aleksy underscored the Pope's affection for those who had deemed him an aggressor, and asked that Rome and Moscow work together in rebuilding the Christian foundations of European civilization:

I would like to end with the words that Pope John Paul II spoke at the Vatican last Wednesday, solemnly bidding farewell to this icon: "May the ancient image of the Mother of God tell His Holiness Aleksy II and the Holy Synod of the Russian Orthodox Church of the Successor of Peter's affection for them and for all the faithful entrusted to their care. May it speak of his esteem for the great spiritual tradition of which the Holy Russian Church is custodian. May it speak of the desire and firm determination of the Pope of Rome to progress with them on the journey of reciprocal knowledge and reconciliation, to hasten the day of that full unity of believers for which the Lord Jesus ardently prayed. . . ."

Your Holiness, I return the Icon of the Mother of God of Kazan to your hands. May the Most Holy Mother of God be the mother of her people and their refuge in all danger and need; may she be the mother of Europe and of all humanity; may she be the mother of peace in the world; the mother of the church and of full unity between East and West; may she be our common mother, our advocate, our helper, and sustain us on our pilgrimage towards a future that we hope will be reconciled and peaceful. Holy Mary, intercede for us![133]

Joaquín Navarro-Valls described the return of the Kazanskaya as a historic moment that marked a "new beginning," and noted that the Kasper delegation had been given a "very cordial welcome" in Moscow.[134] The hospitality was certainly appreciated; the further truth of the matter was that all honor in the affair of the Kazanskaya and her return to Russia belonged to John Paul II. He had borne abuse and bitter criticism from Russian churchmen whose own performance under communism had been less than honorable; he had never once raised the point of comparison between their behavior and his, when both had been confronted by the greatest persecutor of Christians in history. He had asked only that he be allowed to provide for the pastoral care of Catholics in Russia, as the Moscow Patriarchate was welcome to provide pastoral care for its people in historically Catholic lands—and had been deemed an aggressive "proselytizer" for doing so. His efforts throughout the pontificate to build a bridge to Orthodoxy's largest Church had run aground on ancient Russian animosities toward Poles and on the Patriarchate of Moscow's theologically dubious identification of Russian Orthodoxy with Russian ethnicity and Russian nationalism. The return of the Kazanskaya was the last, dramatic clarification of who had behaved in a manner befitting a Christian in these controversies, and who had not.

On October 3, John Paul II celebrated what would turn out to be his final beatification ceremony in St. Peter's Square; among the five new **beati** were Anne Catherine Emmerick, a German stigmatic and mystic, and the last Austro-Hungarian emperor, Karl (or Charles) of Austria, who died in exile on Madeira in 1922 and whom John Paul had once called (when greeting his widow, Zita) "my father's sovereign." The day before the beatification Mass, the Pope received the Prix du Courage Politique from the French journal **Politique Internationale** in cooperation with the Foreign Policy Association of the Sorbonne and the French Catholic television channel, KTO. John Paul used the occasion to plead for an end to the "trading in human lives" that was displayed in hostage taking, especially in Iraq.

The principal papal document of the last half of 2004 was the apostolic letter **Mane Nobiscum Domine** [Stay with Us, Lord], which John Paul II signed on October 7 to reflect on a Year of the Eucharist that would be celebrated between October 2004 and October 2005. The title was beyond poignant, in that the Gospel story of the two disciples who asked the Risen Christ to "stay with us" on the road to Emmaus that first Easter did so because "it is toward evening and the day is now far spent" (Luke 24.29)—as it surely was for Karol Wojtyła. The Year of the Eucharist was to have two bookends: an October 2004 International Eucharistic Congress in Guadalajara, Mexico, and a Synod of Bishops on "The Eucharist: Source and Summit of the Life and Mission of the Church," which would be held in October 2005. The Pope addressed the Eucharistic Congress via a live television hookup from the high altar of St. Peter's on Sunday, October 17, concluding with a moving and manifestly personal prayer:

Mane nobiscum, Domine! Like the two disciples in the Gospel, we implore you, Lord Jesus, stay with us!

Divine Wayfarer, expert in our ways and reader of our hearts, do not leave us prisoners in the evening shadows.

Sustain us in our weariness, forgive ours sins, and

direct our steps on the path of goodness. Bless the children, the young people, the elderly, families, and the sick in particular. . . .

In the Eucharist, you made yourself the "medicine of immortality": give us the taste for a full life that will help us journey on as trusting and joyful pilgrims on this earth, our gaze fixed on the goal of life without end.

Stay with us, Lord! Stay with us! Amen.[135]

Mane Nobiscum Domine ended with a plea to the world Church to respond in solidarity to "the many forms of poverty present in our world": hunger, disease, loneliness, unemployment, the struggles of immigrants. Christian concern for those in need had, from biblical times on, been a distinguishing hallmark of the followers of Christ; "this will be the criterion," John Paul wrote, "by which the authenticity of our Eucharistic celebrations is judged."[136]

The Pope was well enough to enjoy company at lunch and dinner, taking the trouble to write Christmas greetings by hand, if laboriously, to the family of a guest who came to see him shortly before the holiday. Presented with a book of photographs of U.S. national parks as a Christmas gift, John Paul immediately recognized Rocky Mountain National Park outside Denver, which he had visited during World Youth Day-1993, and couldn't resist a fraternal jibe at the American prelates who had warned that the World Youth Day format would never work in the

United States: "Denver!" he said. "The bishops said it couldn't be done. I proved them wrong!"[137]

Throughout 2004, John Paul II's determination to carry on with his mission despite increasing incapacity, and in a condition the world often regarded as embarrassing, demonstrated in action what he had taught so firmly throughout his life: there are no disposable human beings. There was nothing of ego, vanity, or stubbornness in his commitment to see his pontificate through to his death. This was the way of discipleship, and a pope was, before all else, a Christian disciple. He enjoyed Christmas, as he always did, singing Polish Christmas carols over the phone with his old **Środowisko** kayaking companions, who had gathered around a phone in Kraków for this annual rite. Within a few weeks, however, the joyful mysteries of the Christmas season would give way to the sorrowful mysteries, as Karol Wojtyła set out on the final pathway of his disciple's life—the way of the cross.

CHAPTER NINE

The Last Encyclical

January–April 2005

February 1, 2005	Suffering from breathing difficulties, Pope John Paul II is taken to the Policlinico Gemelli.
February 7, 2005	**Memory and Identity**, John Paul II's last book, is published.
February 9, 2005	John Paul celebrates Ash Wednesday Mass in the Gemelli.
February 10, 2005	John Paul II returns to the Vatican from the Gemelli through crowds of cheering Romans.
February 24, 2005	John Paul is taken back to the Gemelli and receives a tracheotomy.
March 13, 2005	John Paul II returns to the Vatican.

March 20, 2005	Unable to speak, the Pope blesses the Palm Sunday congregation in St. Peter's Square.
March 25, 2005	John Paul participates in the **Via Crucis** at the Roman Colosseum through a television in the chapel of the papal apartment.
March 27, 2005	John Paul II attempts to speak to Easter crowds in St. Peter's Square but manages only a silent blessing.
March 31, 2005	John Paul falls into septic shock.
April 1, 2005	John Paul concelebrates Mass for the last time and receives visitors.
April 2, 2005	Pope John Paul II dies at 9:37 P.M.
April 8, 2005	Pope John Paul II is interred in the Vatican grottos.

The Stations of the Cross played an important role in Karol Wojtyła's spiritual life for more than seventy-five years. As a boy, he had seen Christ's passion dramatically reenacted at Kalwaria Zebrzy-dowska, the Holy Land shrine near his hometown of Wadowice, shortly after his mother's death. As a priest and bishop, he prayed the fourteen stations every Friday; during Lent, he prayed them every day. As pope, he had a set of ceramic stations installed in the roof garden atop the Apostolic Palace so that he could pray outdoors, in privacy, when the weather was clement. And, of course, he had led the annual **Via Crucis** at the Roman Colosseum on the evening of Good Friday for a quarter century.

On Good Friday 2005, his health rapidly failing, Pope John Paul II once again led the Church through its walk with Christ from the tribunal of Pontius Pilate to Calvary, the cross, and the tomb—albeit at a distance and in a different way.

The ceremony at the Colosseum was led by Cardinal Joseph Ratzinger, dean of the College of Cardinals, who had written the meditations for each station at the Pope's request. Ratzinger's brief reflections, insightful and eloquent, linked the **Via Crucis** to the Year of the Eucharist the Catholic Church was celebrating throughout the world; they would later be published in booklet form. Yet what struck the Church and the world most powerfully as Good Friday drew to a close on the night of March 25, 2005, was the witness of the man who was not there: John Paul II.

He could barely whisper. But as Cardinal Ratzinger led the solemn procession through the ruins of antiquity, John Paul II prayed the **Via Crucis** while watching the ceremony at the Colosseum on a television set that had been placed in the chapel of the papal apartment. A television camera at the door of the chapel showed the world John Paul's prayer. He was seated, and grasped in his arms a large crucifix, as he prayed through the fourteen stations with the congregation near the Roman Forum. Those watching at the Colosseum and on television could see only John Paul's back; his face was never shown. Contrary to press speculations, however, he was not hiding his pain or the ravages of weeks of illness. Rather, he was doing what he had always done, which was not to say, "Look at me," but rather, "Look to Christ."

The last two months of the life of Pope John Paul II were in some respects the most dramatic in a life already replete with drama. As papal chief of staff Leonardo Sandri (who became the Pope's voice to the Church and the world when John Paul's own voice failed) put it, those last two months were also an eloquent summary of the years of his pontificate since the Great Jubilee of 2000: "His sense of his own weakness paralleled his sense of the power of God at work in him and in the Church. The Cross was a means of joy in his last years, even amidst deep frustration. His silences, punctuated by those vigilant and expressive eyes, were times of meditation."[1]

Pope John Paul II died a priest's death and his dying was his last great teaching moment. His suffering and the manner of his dying led the Church and the world, as Catholic priests must, into a deeper experience of the mystery of the passion, death, and resurrection of Christ. The priest and bishop who could sometimes be found prostrate on the floor of a chapel, his arms extended in imitation of the crucified Christ, died as he had lived—embracing Christ crucified—in the sure conviction that death was the threshold of eternal life. These were things he had taught for decades. His last and perhaps most powerful lesson was the lesson he taught with his silent suffering and his holy death—his last encyclical.

A CHEERFUL MAN

By January 2005, Joaquín Navarro-Valls had been the press spokesman of the Holy See for twenty years, a friend and confidant of the Pope who occasionally used him on informal diplomatic missions. Some measure of John Paul's confidence in the Spaniard who had begun his professional life as a psychiatrist before switching to journalism can be found in the Pope's response to Navarro on the three occasions when the papal **portavoce** asked to be relieved of his duties. Each time, John Paul would say to those in the meeting, "This is a very important question Dr. Navarro has put on the table. We must reflect on it carefully. Come back in five years and tell me what you think."[2]

Navarro experienced the last years of John Paul II, and believed the Pope experienced them, as a time of "great peace." There were frustrations, to be sure; there were questions, as always; there was the dark night of the summer of 2003. But having completed the Great Jubilee of 2000, John Paul II was a man fundamentally at peace—**un'uomo allegro**, Navarro said, a cheerful man. This was not the cheerfulness of a child, the spokesman noted. It was the cheerfulness or serenity that came from a conscious Christian decision to live that way: a decision rooted in the conviction that the end of the story, for John Paul himself and for the world, is a happy one, "because of the infinite mercy of God." That was why the humor and the laughter remained intact until the end, even when the laughter could not be expressed physically.

John Paul's serenity at the end of his life also grew from the intersection of his philosophical realism and his faith, Navarro believed. Like others trapped in a body that would no longer obey them, the Pope might have thought, "It would be nice if I weren't sick, if I could move more easily." But that was not his situation, and it was false to pretend or wish otherwise. Therefore what seems to be an obstacle or a stumbling block must in fact, and in the light of faith, be an opportunity—to live out what he had taught the Church in **Novo Millennio Ineunte**, that the completion of the Great Jubilee was both end and beginning. In the light of that conviction, coupled with his determination to promote cultures that cherished life under all circumstances, the Pope believed his physical deterioration should not be hidden. Some found it embarrassing when John Paul drooled a bit in public because of his inability to control his facial muscles; the Pope, for his part, was determined to live his mission to the end, even at the cost of embarrassment. Thus when, in the last years, the Vatican television producers asked Navarro whether they should arrange the camera angles to avoid showing John Paul's trembling hand, Navarro, knowing the Pope's mind, said they should simply use their best professional judgment and not worry if the world saw the effects of John Paul's Parkinson's disease.[3]

Cardinal Jean-Marie Lustiger's experience of the last years of John Paul II was similar to Navarro's. As he understood the Pope's mind, the question never was "Do **I** stay or do **I** go?" The **Nunc dimittis** of the Great Jubilee, as written in John Paul's **Testament**, was a thanksgiving, not a request for a leave of absence and not a valedictory. No, the question for John Paul, Lustiger believed, was "How do I fulfill **God's** will?" As John Paul knew, the disciple could not ask for anything else than to share the Master's passion—and in doing so, to summon from the world's sometimes cold heart the warmth of compassion for all those who suffer. John Paul II had lived "at the heart of humanity's problems" for a quarter century, Lustiger recalled—longer than any other major figure of his time. The way in which he bore that burden through his own pain and fatigue, the cardinal suggested, revealed a "deeper way" to relate to the world's pain than was possible in the days of John Paul Superstar, important as the great events of that part of his pontificate had been. And since no one in the world was immune from suffering, the serenity with which he bore his share of the common human lot was, for the world, a "great testimony to the universal relevance of Christ's message." For the Church, it was yet another invitation to embrace the "everyday sanctity" that had been the key to John Paul II's pastoral program.[4]

He stayed close to his friends as long as possible, continuing the pastoral strategy of accompaniment he had pioneered as a young university chaplain in Kraków. His **Środowisko**—the network of lay friends that had begun forming in 1948 at St. Florian's—remained a significant part of his life. In August 2000, amidst all the other activity of the holy year, three generations of **Środowisko** came to Castel Gandolfo for a visit. The children of Father Wojtyła's original young charges brought a kayak into the papal villa's courtyard, and thus the reunion was dubbed "Dry Kayaks at Castel Gandolfo." The original plan was to meet for a half hour. In the event, the reunion lasted three hours. Stanisław Dziwisz tried to get the Pope to bed, but when Danuta Rybicka asked the Pope, "Whom would you like to meet, **Wujek**?" John Paul replied, "All of them." Dziwisz said, "But Holy Father, they need to sleep";

the Pope waved him away. So everyone received a personal greeting and at the end they sang the song that had once closed each day on a kayaking trip. Dziwisz then said, "Thank you, and good night." At which point John Paul replied, "I have to say good night to everyone"—and did so, with more than one hundred people. As Mrs. Rybicka remembered, when the Pope finally shuffled off into the villa, the third generation of **Środowisko**, the small grandchildren of the original hikers and kayakers, followed him in a straggly line, "like the Good Shepherd and the sheep." Four years later, John Paul was still saying, "That was beautiful," while the director of Castel Gandolfo told the Poles that he'd never seen anything like it in his decades of service at the papal summer residence.

Three years after the "dry kayaks," Krzysztof Rybicki, a veteran **Środowisko** member, was struck with cancer. The Pope called him for a long conversation prior to major surgery on January 6, 2003; and when Rybicki had to return to the hospital in early March, John Paul called him on the dying man's cell phone: "Krzysiu, do you remember how we used to sing carols together? We can sing together even now." And they did. Krzysztof Rybicki's widow, Maria, took her children and grandchildren to see the Pope at Christmas 2003; when the dinner conversation one night turned to a vacation trip they had made in 1957, John Paul II, the man who cherished the memory of his friendships, described the trip in great detail, as if it had been a recent excursion, not something that had happened forty-six years before.

Stanisław and Danuta Rybicki, two more of the original members of what became **Środowisko**, met **Wujek** for the last time in January 2005, bringing along their granddaughter, Mela Rybicka, who was studying Hungarian philology. John Paul greeted the family and then said to Mela, "Praised be Jesus Christ!"—in Hungarian. During their conversation, the Pope had Mela sit next to him and started querying her: "Tell me what the kids are interested in today."[5]

That same month, Cardinal Camillo Ruini, the Pope's vicar for the Diocese of Rome, came to see the Pope on business and John Paul asked, "When are we going to visit the parishes?" Archbishop Dziwisz replied, "Holy Father, the cardinal visits the parishes now." At which the Pope said, whimsically but jokingly, "But **I'm** the Bishop of Rome. . . ." It was, Cardinal Ruini remembered, another indication of how "terribly important" it was for John Paul II to be able to celebrate Mass with the people of his diocese.[6] At the end of the pontificate, of the 336 parishes of the Diocese of Rome, there were only 16 he had not visited in person or invited to Mass in the Vatican.

On January 24, 2005, John Paul received a Spanish bishop on an **ad limina** visit. At the end of their conversation, the Spaniard began to get emotional and said something to the effect of "Your Holiness, this is probably the last time we will be seeing each other." To which the indomitable John Paul II replied, "Why, what's the matter? Are you sick?"[7]

THINKING THE TWENTIETH CENTURY

In the summer of 1993, during his weeks at Castel Gandolfo, John Paul II had a lengthy series of conversations with the Polish philosophers Józef Tischner and Krzysztof Michalski, who with the Pope's encouragement had launched the Vienna-based **Institut für die Wissenschaften vom Menschen** [Institute for Human Sciences] in 1981.[8] The conversations, which were taped, began with questions probing the Pope's understanding of the meaning of the two twentieth-century totalitarian systems and their fall, but the discussion soon ranged widely over the modern and postmodern political and cultural landscape. The tapes were transcribed, with the thought that the conversations might eventually make a book.

After a lengthy and sporadic editorial process that further broadened the analytic lens beyond Nazism and communism, **Memory and Identity: Personal Reflections**, was published in February 2005 and strongly reflected the Pope's concerns in the early to mid-1990s about the postcommunist situation in central and eastern Europe.[9] Yet the book also returned to perennial issues in Karol Wojtyła's intellectual work, and in that respect was the final movement in the unfinished symphony of Wojtyła's philosophy.

During his years of teaching at the Catholic University of Lublin, Wojtyła had come to the view that the deficiencies of Enlightenment ethical theory were one root of the crisis of Western thought and culture. Putting moral theory on a firmer philosophical base was thus at the center of the intellectual project of Wojtyła and three other Lublin philosophers—Father Tadeusz Styczeń, S.D.S., Father Andrzej Szostek, M.I.C., and Dr. Wojciech Chudy. As the title of Chudy's habilitation thesis put it, modern philosophy had been caught in the "trap of reflection," thinking about thinking-about-thinking, rather than thinking through to the truth of things. This was a particularly urgent problem for philosophical ethics, which needed a secure foundation in the aftermath of the chasm caused by David Hume. As philosophical realists, the Lublin quartet was determined to get to the moral truth of things through a careful analysis of things as they are. "Oughts," they were convinced, could indeed be discerned from a penetrating analysis of "is"—as when a careful study of the dynamics of human personhood discloses certain basic human rights that must be respected.

Memory and Identity also revisited Wojtyła's critique of both Kantian and utilitarian ethics as insufficient to provide a secure cultural foundation for the exercise of freedom. Freedom, John Paul insists, is both a gift and a task; thus freedom rightly understood is not willfulness, nor should free men and women be content with aiming for the greatest good of the greatest number. Rather, freedom is a gift (from God, believers contend) that is to be used to seek what we can know, objectively, to be good. That concept of freedom can be defended philosophically, John Paul argued. It is further illuminated, though, by the gift of faith, which helps us to see that God has given humanity a "particular mission: to accomplish the truth about ourselves and our world . . . [in order to] be able to structure the visible world according to truth, correctly using it to serve our purposes, without abusing it."[10]

Memory and Identity also took up questions about the future of Europe. John Paul was at particular pains to emphasize that "Europe" is only Europe because of its evangelization:

Why do we begin our discussion of Europe by speaking of evangelization? Perhaps the simplest answer is that it was evangelization which formed Europe, giving birth to the civilization of its peoples and their cultures. As the faith spread throughout the continent, it favored the formation of individual European peoples, sowing the seeds of cultures different in character, but linked together by a patrimony of common values derived from the Gospel. In this way the pluralism of national cultures developed upon a platform of values shared throughout the continent.[11]

This was not to "devalue the influence of the ancient world" of Greece and Rome. Rather, it was to recognize how the Church had "absorbed and transformed the older cultural patrimony." The result of that transformation was "the Christian universalism of the Middle Ages," during which Europe's evangelization "seemed not only complete, but mature: not just in terms of philosophical and theological thought, but also in sacred art and architecture, in social solidarity (guilds, confraternities, hospitals)."[12] That universalism was overturned by the Reformation, the wars of religion, and the Enlightenment. And yet even the Enlightenment could not, and did not, invent "Europe" anew; its "positive fruits," including "the ideals of liberty, equality, and fraternity," were based on "values which are rooted in the Gospel." By the same token, the Enlightenment compelled the Church to a "profound rediscovery of the truths contained in the Gospel," which was accomplished by modern Catholic social doctrine from Leo XIII on.

The recovery of its moral culture would be essential if the Europe of the future were to avoid the lethal errors of the Europe of the twentieth century, in which, as John Paul reminded his conversation

partners, Hitler had come to power through democratic means (which, to be sure, he promptly abro-
gated, albeit with the consent of a "regularly elected
parliament"[13]). Poland, he believed, had something
important to share with a Europe recovering from its
twentieth-century wounds: the experience of a nation that had survived the totalitarian flail by moral
and cultural conviction; the experience of a country that had not experienced the wars of religion in
the sixteenth century; the experience of a country in
which the state did not claim to be king of its citizens' consciences.[14]

Memory and Identity was a powerful reminder
that, for John Paul II, "philosophy . . . leads you
to theology and Christology," as the Italian scholar
Rocco Buttiglione once put it.[15] The proper "starting point" for understanding the human person, the
Pope insisted, must always be creatureliness: "man's
creation in the image and likeness of God." It is ultimately futile to try to understand the human world,
its strivings, and its passions by reference only to
"other visible creatures," because such an approach
neglects what is most distinctive about the human
being: our being created according to "the divine
Prototype, the Word made flesh, the eternal Son
of the Father." And so the "primary and definitive
source" for getting to the truth "inside" the human
person was, is, and always will be the Holy Trinity,
that communion of self-giving love and receptivity
in which the Law of the Gift is eternal reality.[16] As

in other writings, John Paul II was proposing that men and women raise, not lower, their sights. It is ultimately by looking up, not down and not simply around, that human beings come to know the full truth about our origins, nature, and destiny.

History, he concluded, is not only horizontal; history has a vertical dimension, because "it is not only we who write our history—God writes it with us," and "the deepest meaning of history goes beyond history and finds its full explanation in Christ, the God-man." We are embedded in time, and thus in memory. Yet "Christian hope projects itself beyond the limits of time. . . . Humanity is called to advance beyond death, even beyond time, towards the definitive onset of eternity alongside the glorious Christ in the communion of the Trinity. 'Their hope is full of immortality' [Wisdom 3.4]." In the time beyond time, memory and identity, purified, are one with the eternal.

Some critics found **Memory and Identity** excessively Polish; John Paul II, they argued, was suggesting that there was some special providential design at work in Poland's history and national identity. It was a familiar complaint and echoed other such criticisms throughout the pontificate, criticisms that sometimes reflected cultural and ethnic stereotypes, and sometimes emerged from uncritical assumptions about modernity and its ways. Against such critics, Father Richard John Neuhaus, one of John Paul's premier interpreters in the United States, described the book as "provocatively wise," in an essay published shortly after the Pope's death:

> Against the airy abstractions of secular modernity, John Paul displayed a way of being in the world that is formed by keeping faith with the memories, sufferings, and aspirations of a particular people. He was that rare thing: a whole man. The many dimensions of his interests, energies, gifts, and inspirations were all of a piece. He refused modernity's imperious demand to choose between the universal and the particular, the world and his place in the world. Critics referred to him as the "Polish pope," implying that he was parochial. Far from apologizing for who he was, he invited others to be the best of who they are. It was as a son of Poland that he was a father to the world.[17]

"I THINK THEY'RE FINALLY BEGINNING TO UNDERSTAND HIM"

According to Stanisław Dziwisz, the suffering John Paul II endured during the last period of his life was not only physical, terrible as that was, but also spiritual: the suffering of a man compelled to suspend or even eliminate "activities that were part of his mission as universal shepherd." Cardinal Joseph Ratzinger understood. In John Paul's life, the dean of the College of Cardinals said, "the word 'cross' is not just a word."[18]

Karol Józef Wojtyła, Pope John Paul II, began to walk the way to Calvary for the last time on Sunday, January 30, 2005. The Pope had difficulty breathing during the Sunday Angelus address from the papal apartment window and, at first, it was thought that he had contracted the flu. But the situation worsened and quickly deteriorated into what the doctors described as "acute laryngotracheitis aggravated by a laryngospasm"—in lay language, a throat infection that was causing spasms that made breathing very difficult. On January 31, the Holy See Press Office announced that the day's audiences had been suspended. By dinnertime on February 1, the Pope was finding it harder and harder to breathe, and the decision was made to take him immediately to the Policlinico Gemelli, where a special tenth-floor suite was always available in case he needed it. Archbishop Leonardo Sandri, the **Sostituto** of the Secretariat of State, or papal chief of staff, met the struggling Pope in the Cortile Sesto Quinto at about 10 P.M., as John Paul was being led to an ambulance, and asked, "Holy Father, bless me." Gasping for breath, John Paul couldn't say the words of a blessing, but blessed Sandri silently.[19]

The international media erupted in a frenzy of speculation about the Pope's imminent death, but John Paul's condition seemed to improve over the next few days at the Gemelli, which, given his frequent stays there, he jokingly referred to as "Vatican III" ("Vatican I" being the Apostolic Palace and "Vatican II" being Castel Gandolfo). He returned to a modified official schedule, working from his hospital suite, and on February 5 received Cardinal Ratzinger for their weekly meeting to discuss the business of the Congregation for the Doctrine of the Faith. Ratzinger later recalled the way in which John Paul conducted his office from the hospital:

> The Pope suffered visibly, but he was fully conscious and very much present. I had simply gone for a working meeting, because I needed him to make a few decisions. In spite of his suffering, the Holy Father paid close attention to what I was saying. He explained his decisions to me in a few words, gave me his blessing, and addressed his parting words to me in German, assuring me of his friendship and trust.[20]

John Paul appeared at his hospital room window for the Angelus on Sunday, February 6; his message was read for him by Archbishop Sandri, with the Pope managing to articulate parts of the Angelus prayer and the sign of the cross. A flap ensued when some in the media suggested that what had seemed to be the Pope's voice was in fact a tape recording. Joaquín Navarro-Valls denied the rumor that night, but the very fact that it spread so rapidly was an indication that at least some in the media were determined to follow their own story line—"the Pope is dying and the Vatican won't admit it"—rather than the facts at hand. The abdication scenario, which seemed to have been at least temporarily buried, was resurrected the following day by some ill-conceived comments from the cardinal secretary of state, Angelo Sodano, who in off-the-cuff remarks to the press on February 7, said, when asked about the possibility of a papal resignation, "If there is a man who loves the Church more than anybody else, who is guided by the Holy Spirit, if there is a man who has marvelous wisdom, that's him. We must have great faith in the Pope. He knows what to do."[21] The cardinal's remarks were promptly, and not surprisingly, interpreted as meaning that resignation or abdication was on the menu of possibilities, which it manifestly was not.

Two days after this unnecessary controversy, John Paul II presided over a concelebrated Mass of Ash Wednesday and received ashes from Archbishop Dziwisz, who nonetheless recalled that he felt "extremely happy" at how well the Pope seemed to be recovering. The doctors evidently agreed, for John Paul returned to the Vatican the next night. Gemelli patients lined the Pope's path applauding as he left; the Pope waved, climbed into the Popemobile, and was escorted during the five-mile trip back home to "Vatican I" by a motorcade and security guards on foot. The Romans by the thousands lined the streets between the Gemelli and the Vatican, and another crowd was waiting in St. Peter's Square to welcome him back. Prior to the motorcade, Navarro-Valls told the press that the "acute laryngeal tracheitis" had been cured and that all the tests that had been administered, including a CAT scan, were negative.[22]

The Pope was back in the papal apartment window on Sunday, February 13, for the weekly Angelus, his message being read by Archbishop Sandri; John Paul managed a wave, a blessing, and a few brief words before giving way to the **Sostituto**. The Papal Lenten retreat began that day, preached by Bishop Renato Corti of Novara in the Italian Piedmont, on the theme "The Church at the Service of the New and Everlasting Covenant"; it had been almost three decades since Karol Wojtyła had preached the papal and curial retreat on the theme "Sign of Contradiction." As per the usual custom during the retreat, audiences were suspended.[23] Prior to the retreat, important papal business continued: John Paul accepted the resignation of the archbishop of Paris, Cardinal Jean-Marie Lustiger, appointing Archbishop André Vingt-Trois of Tours as Lustiger's successor.[24] On the day after the retreat began, the Pope sent a message of condolence to Portuguese bishop Albino Mamede Cleto of Coimbra on the death of Sister Lúcia dos Santos, the last of the Fátima visionaries, who had died on February 13 at age ninety-seven. "Sister Lúcia," the Pope wrote, "bequeaths to us an example of great fidelity to the Lord and joyous attachment to his divine will. . . . I have always felt supported by the daily gift of her prayers, especially during the most difficult moments of trial and suffering. May the Lord reward her for her great and hidden service to the Church."[25]

John Paul managed to lead the praying of the Angelus and to deliver his own Angelus message on Sunday, February 20, looking relatively robust to the crowds in St. Peter's Square. The day before, he had resumed holding audiences, receiving the seventy-seven-year-old Emmanuel III Delly, Patriarch of Babylon of the Chaldeans, whose people continued to suffer persecution from Islamist terrorists in Iraq; and Bishop Renato Corti, whom he thanked for preaching the Lenten retreat. Yet the Pope's breathing difficulties continued, as the stiffening of his chest muscles due to the Parkinson's disease made it difficult for him to inhale. Another crisis struck on Wednesday evening, February 23. At dinner that evening, as Stanisław Dziwisz recalled later, "the Pope's body was convulsed by a new crisis; he was almost asphyxiating." Cardinal Marian Jaworski, Karol Wojtyła's old housemate and fellow philosopher, now the Latin-rite archbishop of L'viv in Ukraine, was a dinner guest that evening and immediately gave his old friend the Sacrament of the Sick, anointing him in the papal apartment.[26]

The Pope returned to the Gemelli the following day, where his personal physician, Dr. Renato Buzzonetti, decided that a tracheotomy had to be performed to allow the Pope to breathe more easily and to avoid another episode of near suffocation. John Paul asked whether the operation couldn't be postponed until the summer holidays; the reaction from Buzzonetti and the other physicians, Archbishop Dziwisz recalled, immediately persuaded the Pope that a delay until the summer was not an option. Dr. Buzzonetti assured John Paul that "it will be a simple operation." True to form, the Pope parried back, "Simple for whom?" The tracheotomy was performed successfully, but it was only afterward, Dziwisz remembered, that John Paul "concretely realized" what the doctors had meant when they had told him that the operation would render him mute for a time. The Pope signaled to Dziwisz that he wanted something on which to write, and then scrawled, "What have they done to me?! But . . . **totus tuus**"—chagrin combined with yet another sign of Karol Wojtyła's determination to bend his will to God's under the protection of the Virgin Mary.[27]

During his two and a half weeks at the Gemelli—his second hospitalization in a month—John Paul II continued to rely on Archbishop Sandri as his voice, with Sandri leading the Angelus and delivering the Pope's Angelus message in St. Peter's Square on February 27 and March 6, while the Pope offered a blessing from the window of his hospital suite. Sandri led the Angelus from the Gemelli on March 13, with the Pope managing a few remarks to the crowd gathered there and to those who could see him via television on large screens in St. Peter's Square.[28] The **Sostituto** remembered being "powerfully impressed" by the Pope's "humility in having me read his words. I blessed the people in his name, and I saw John Paul II humbly making the sign of the cross as he received what amounted to his own blessing through me."[29]

John Paul began daily business meetings in his hospital suite less than a week after the tracheotomy, meeting with Sandri, Secretary of State Sodano, Cardinal Ratzinger, and Cardinal Crescenzio Sepe, prefect of the Congregation for the Evangelization of Peoples.[30] The Pope concelebrated Mass with Archbishop Dziwisz and others every day; at noon on March 9, shortly after the Mass was completed, John Paul, wearing the purple chasuble of the Lenten season, gave an impromptu blessing to the hundreds who were waiting outside the Gemelli in an ongoing and spontaneous prayer vigil.[31] Two days later, on March 11, John Paul concelebrated Mass with Cardinal Polycarp Pengo and Bishop Severine Niwemugizi of Tanzania, who were in Rome for the **ad limina** visit; his visitors were in tears, moved by the Pope's continuing breathing difficulties, his determination, and his composure.[32]

At the Angelus on March 13, John Paul II thanked the media for their "presence and attention," because of which "the faithful in every part of the world can feel that I am closer and can accompany me with their affection and prayers."[33] That evening, the

Pope was driven back to the Vatican, through another throng of cheering Romans, some in ranks ten deep along the streets. The backs of his hands were deeply discolored from the injections and intravenous lines, Archbishop Sandri remembered, and the Pope was "trembling with the chill." Yet that physical disfigurement and weakness was, Sandri said, "the Gospel of the silent mystery of his friendship with God for the salvation of the world—his silent Mass with God."[34]

Three close observers of the pontificate—the Polish ambassador to the Holy See, Hanna Suchocka, the Canadian writer Raymond de Souza, and the physicist Piotr Malecki, Karol Wojtyła's first altar boy at St. Florian's Church in Kraków and a **Środowisko** veteran—caught something of the extraordinary reaction to John Paul's courage in suffering in several well-chosen phrases. This was, Ambassador Suchocka said, "his **via crucis,**" and if some parts of the media could not quite grasp that or understand it, the people who came to the Gemelli and who cheered the frail Pope on his way back to the Vatican had an inkling of it, and wanted to share in it and support him. At the same time, Father de Souza wrote, this was not a deathwatch, but a "lifewatch," in which the Church was being invited to "live this moment together with her chief shepherd." The "reflection, contemplation, and prayer" that John Paul's struggles to continue his mission elicited from the people of the Church were not "something to pass

the time until the Church can get back to work—
they **are** the work of the Church." Dr. Malecki's
comment was succinct and to the point: "I think
they're finally beginning to understand him."[35]

THE FINAL STATIONS

John Paul had come back to the Vatican to die, for
it was now as clear as such things could be that the
end was at hand—and he wanted to die in what had
become his home, as close as possible to the bones of
Peter. For the first time in twenty-six years, John Paul
was unable to lead the Church's Holy Week liturgies
in person. Cardinal Camillo Ruini, the papal vicar
for Rome, took the Palm Sunday Mass in St. Peter's
Square, Cardinal Giovanni Battista Re celebrated
the Chrism Mass on Holy Thursday, and Cardinal
Alfonso López Trujillo celebrated the Mass of the
Lord's Supper in St. Peter's that evening. Cardinal
James Francis Stafford presided at the Good Friday
commemoration of the Lord's Passion in St. Peter's,
and Cardinal Joseph Ratzinger led the Way of the
Cross that evening at the Colosseum and presided
at the Great Vigil of Easter in the Vatican basilica
on Holy Saturday night. Cardinal Angelo Sodano
took the outdoor Easter Sunday Mass in St. Peter's
Square. At each of the major Holy Week liturgies,

a message from the Pope was read by the cardinal presiding.

On Palm Sunday, the Pope had appeared in the window of the papal apartment after the Mass had concluded, and used an olive branch to bless the crowd in the square; once again, Archbishop Sandri was the "voice" of the Pope's Angelus message. Now, John Paul badly wanted to speak to the Easter throng in the square on March 27 and to give the **Urbi et Orbi** blessing. But it was not to be. He had practiced speaking for days beforehand, but when the moment came, nothing would come out. Stanisław Dziwisz recalled the drama of the moment:

[T]he Pope stood motionless in the window, as if frozen. He must have been overwhelmed by a combination of emotion and pain. In any case, he couldn't give the blessing. He whispered, "My voice is gone." Then, still silent, he made the sign of the cross three times, waved to the crowd, and gestured that he wanted to withdraw.

He was deeply shaken and saddened. He also seemed exhausted by his unsuccessful attempt to speak. The people in the square were full of emotion; they were applauding him and calling out his name, but he felt the whole weight of the powerlessness and suffering he had displayed. He looked into my eyes and said, "Maybe it would be better for me to die if I can't fulfill the mission that has been entrusted to me." Before I could answer, he added, "Thy will be done. . . . **Totus tuus.**"[36]

John Paul tried again, when 5,000 youngsters from Milan came to the square on Wednesday, March 30—the day it was announced that the Pope had been given a nasal feeding tube. Dziwisz tried to convince him to simply give his blessing, "but he wanted to say something, even if it was just a word, to thank the kids." So he indicated that the microphone should be brought closer. But, once again, he couldn't get a word out. This time, Dziwisz recalled, "he didn't even show the impatience that he had displayed at Easter. By this point, he knew. He was ready."[37]

The twelfth station of the **Via Crucis** of Pope John Paul II, the station at Calvary, began at 11 A.M. on March 31. While he was preparing to concelebrate Mass in the papal apartment's chapel, "his body was jolted as if something had exploded inside him," as Archbishop Dziwisz put it later.[38] Septic shock, caused by a urinary tract infection, had set in; the Pope's temperature was 104 degrees and his cardiovascular system was in collapse. Dziwisz reminded Dr. Buzzonetti of the Pope's desire to die in the Vatican, so John Paul was taken to his room, where, in his bed, he could look on images of the suffering Christ and of the Black Madonna, Our Lady of Częstochowa, as well as the small photographs of his parents that had long been there. Mass was said at the Pope's bedside in the evening, and John Paul managed to raise his hand at the words of consecration over the bread and wine, and to strike his breast at the **Agnus Dei.** He received holy communion at 7:17 P.M. and was once again given the Sacrament of the Sick by Cardinal Marian Jaworski. The household sisters, his secretaries, the doctors and nurses all came to the bedside to kiss the Pope's hand, and John Paul managed to whisper each one's name. The day ended with a holy hour of reflection and prayer, at the Pope's request; it concluded with the household sisters singing.[39]

Friday, April 1, was a "day of prayer," Dziwisz recalled. The Pope concelebrated Mass and prayed both the Stations of the Cross and the hours of the Divine Office from his bed; passages from the Bible were read to him by his old friend Father Tadeusz Styczeń. He could "say only a few syllables, and even that was difficult," according to Dziwisz.[40] Senior churchmen came to say good-bye, and the Pope insisted on thanking Francesco, the man responsible for cleaning his apartment. At an evening Mass for the Diocese of Rome at St. John Lateran, Cardinal Ruini told the crowds that the end was near, and that the Pope could "already see and touch the Lord."[41]

On April 2, John Paul managed to bless icon crowns that would be placed on the image of Our Lady of Częstochowa in the Vatican grotto and others that would be sent to the Jasna Góra monastery in Częstochowa itself. After he had tried for some time to say something, those in his immediate papal family finally understood that he had a message for the young people who were keeping vigil in the square outside his window: "I have sought you out. Now you have come to me. I thank you." Father Styczeń read aloud to him from the Gospel of St. John—something he had done for himself, a chapter each day, during his graduate student days in Rome; Styczeń got through the ninth chapter before the end.[42]

Sister Tobiana, who had worked with John Paul for decades, heard his last words. The Pope was looking at her, so she came to the bedside and leaned over, placing her ear near his mouth. In the weakest of voices, he made his last request: "Let me go to the Father's house."

At about 7 P.M., John Paul II slipped into a coma, and, according to Polish custom, a small candle was lit and placed in the window of the bedroom. Two hours later, Archbishop Dziwisz felt "a kind of imperative command inside me" and began to celebrate Mass for the Vigil of Divine Mercy Sunday, the Octave of Easter, with Cardinal Jaworski, Archbishop Stanisław Ryłko (a Cracovian priest who was president of the Pontifical Council for the Laity), Father Styczeń, and the junior secretary, Msgr. Mieczysław Mokrzycki. The appointed Gospel reading for the day seemed especially appropriate—the appearance of the Risen Christ to the apostles on the first Easter night, and the greeting, "Peace be with you" (John 20.19). Dziwisz was able to give the Pope a few drops of the blood of Christ as Viaticum, the "food for the journey."

At 9:37 P.M., the monitor display showed that the heart of John Paul II had stopped beating. Dr. Buzzonetti leaned over the Pope and then said to those present, "He's gone home to the Lord." Karol Wojtyła's earthly pilgrimage was complete. The concelebrants and the Polish sisters, "as if we had all agreed beforehand," spontaneously sang the Church's ancient hymn of thanksgiving, the **Te Deum**, while crying "tears of grief and joy at the same time."[43]

Archbishop Sandri, having been called by Archbishop Dziwisz, came into the bedroom a few minutes after the Pope died, while the electrocardiogram was still running, to confirm the death. As Sandri later recalled, Sister Tobiana was kneeling beside the bed with her hand nestling the Pope's head; John Paul's arms were outstretched in the form of the cross, and his face was "utterly peaceful." Cardinal Ratzinger, Cardinal Sodano, Cardinal Ruini, Cardinal Eduardo Martínez Somalo (the Camerlengo, or chamberlain, of the Church), and Archbishop James Harvey (the prefect of the papal household) came in next. Sandri, who was to make the worldwide public announcement in St. Peter's Square, "didn't know what to say" and was "upset and confused" in finding his way through the Apostolic Palace, whose halls he knew as well as anyone. When he arrived in the square, however, "the words just came out: 'our beloved Holy Father has gone home to the Father's house.'"[44]

Cardinal Ruini, as vicar, formally announced to the people of Rome the death of their bishop on the evening of April 2: "Let us thank God for having given us a Pastor after his own heart, a witness to Jesus Christ in his life and with his words." May the Blessed Virgin Mary, Ruini concluded, "clasp him in her Mother's arms and protect the people of Rome."[45]

The body of John Paul II remained in the chapel of the papal apartment overnight, in the presence of the eucharistic Christ and watched over by the Black Madonna, whose icon the Pope had affixed to the apse wall of the chapel shortly after his election.

OBITS AND ARGUMENTS

On Sunday, April 3, the late Pope's body was taken to the Sala Clementina of the Apostolic Palace, after the death had been officially certified and the death certificate prepared and signed. In the Clementina, the Pope lay on a bier, vested in the red chasuble worn on the feasts of apostles, with the white wool pallium of his office as a metropolitan archbishop around his neck and a rosary clutched in his hands; nestled in his left arm was the silver crozier-crucifix he had adopted from Paul VI and used throughout the pontificate in an extraordinary diversity of venues. In death, he remained himself, wearing the brownish red loafers he had always preferred to formal papal slippers, causing no end of grief to the self-appointed custodians of papal sartorial propriety. The marks of so many needles were visible on the bruises on the backs of his hands, but the face that had often seemed frozen in recent years was now natural in repose.

Among those with striking reactions to the death of John Paul II were two men whose ideas of world politics were dramatically different from the late Pope's, but who nonetheless held him in considerable esteem. Henry Kissinger suggested that John Paul had likely had a greater impact on the twentieth century than any other man—a remarkable judgment from a scholar and diplomat who had lived a very different spiritual and political life than Karol Wojtyła. Kissinger's longtime rival, Zbigniew Brzeziński, who had briefed the Pope in Polish during the Solidarity crisis of December 1980 (and had heard the Pope ask Stanisław Dziwisz in a stage whisper, "Do I have a private telephone number?"), believed that John Paul had connected his Petrine ministry to a spiritual hunger that was global in character.

The British historian Timothy Garton Ash, a self-described "agnostic liberal" and one of the first Anglophone historians of Solidarity, argued that John Paul II had been "the first world leader"—someone whose rhetorical skills, personal witness, and courage had led to things happening in what the world often referred to as "the real world." But it was the American columnist Charles Krauthammer, whose great-great-grandfather had been chief rabbi of Kraków, who wrote perhaps the finest appreciation of John Paul II's public accomplishment, and how his life had answered one of the great questions of the late modern world:

> It was Stalin who gave us the most famous formulation of that cynical . . . philosophy known as "realism"—the idea that all that ultimately matters in the relations among nations is power. "The Pope? How many divisions does he have?"
>
> Stalin could only have said that because he never met John Paul II. We have just lost the man whose life was the ultimate refutation of "realism." Within ten years of his elevation to the papacy, John Paul had given his answer to Stalin and to the ages: More than you have. More than you can imagine . . .
>
> Under the benign and deeply humane vision of this Pope, the power of faith led to the liberation of half a continent. . . . We mourn him for restoring strength to the Western idea of the free human

spirit at a moment of deepest doubt and despair. And for seeing us through to today's great moment of possibility for both faith and freedom.[46]

The editors of the **New York Times**, whose predecessors in 1979 had declared that the Pope's Nine Days would have no effect on the politics of east central Europe, continued to miss the mark, arguing in an obituary editorial that John Paul was someone who had "used the tools of modernity to struggle against the modern world," a leader who had had an impact on his time "even as he railed" against it.[47] Britain's leading left-wing daily, the **Guardian**, had a similar reading of Wojtyła's papacy: he had been a "doctrinaire, authoritarian pontiff."[48] Commentators long opposed to John Paul II took their last shots. The **Guardian**'s Polly Toynbee, describing the Vatican as "a potent force for cruelty and hypocrisy," charged that John Paul had "caused the death of millions of Catholics and others in areas dominated by Catholic missionaries, in Africa and right across the world," and suggested that "genuflecting before this corpse is scarcely different than parading before Lenin."[49] The **Boston Globe**'s James Carroll told one American network that John Paul had "faithfully tried to preserve [a] medieval, absolutist notion of pope-centered Catholicism with everything going out from the Vatican," while Marco Politi of **La Repubblica** wrote in the London **Tablet** than an "intransigent" Wojtyła had "always had a problem with modernity," displayed in his "systematic de-monization of the twentieth century."[50] The popular American historian Thomas Cahill took this line of analysis the furthest in a **New York Times** op-ed column, suggesting that John Paul II may, "in time, be credited with destroying his Church."[51] In none of these indictments was an alternative possibility considered: that John Paul II, who had regularly applauded the great accomplishments of twentieth-century science and who had persistently supported the emergence of a global political culture in favor of human rights and democracy, was a modern man who had a very different understanding of modernity's possibilities, difficulties, anxieties, and dangers.

The **Washington Post** had been critical of the Pope's stands on several issues, including population policy, but its obituary editorial nonetheless praised John Paul for his contributions to a more humane and noble conception of the human future. The late pontiff, the **Post** wrote, "will be seen by most . . . as a remarkable witness, to use a favorite term—witness to a vision characterized by humaneness, honesty, and integrity throughout his reign and his life."[52] The London **Daily Telegraph**, for its part, editorialized that John Paul II had "raised the papacy to a political and social influence it had not enjoyed since the Middle Ages."[53] The **Wall Street Journal**, which for years had published lengthy, serious commentaries on John Paul's teaching, did not "expect the secularists who dominate our intelligen-

tsia ever to understand how a man rooted in orthodox Christianity could ever reconcile himself with
modernity, much less establish himself on the van-
guard of world history." But, as the **Journal**'s obituary editorial, posted online immediately after the
Pope's death, concluded, "Many years ago, when the
same question was put to France's Cardinal Lustiger
by a reporter, he gave the answer. 'You're confusing a
modern man with an American liberal,' the cardinal
replied. It was a confusion that Pope John Paul II,
may he rest in peace, never made."[54a]

The man who had embodied much of the trials
and triumphs of the second half of the twentieth
century had become a reference point for many of
the contemporary world's most hotly contested debates—debates over the nature of freedom, love, and
the family; passionate arguments over the moral law
and its relationship to civil and criminal law; debates
over God's ways with the world he created and the
nature of religious truth. The legacy of John Paul II
would continue to be debated in the world's press in
the week following the Pope's death: the debate was
sometimes informed and sometimes ignorant; sometimes clearly sympathetic, and at other times just as
clearly hostile. For the moment, however, millions
whose lives he had touched decided that they had to
come to Rome to say good-bye in person.

SANTO SUBITO!

The **Ordo Exsequiarum Romani Pontificis** [The Funeral Rites of the Roman Pontiff] had been revised by the master of pontifical liturgical ceremonies, Piero Marini, and approved by John Paul II in 2000. It began with a brief ceremony in the Sala Clementina on the evening of April 3, when the Pope's body was brought from the papal apartment and laid on a bier, while the Cardinal Camerlengo, Eduardo Martínez Somalo, led the rite **De recognitione mortis** [On the reception of the dead] in the presence of senior churchmen and Italian state officials. Officials of the Roman Curia, friends of the late Pope, and journalists who regularly worked in the Vatican were invited to pay their respects during the next day. Then, at 5 P.M. on April 4, a solemn procession accompanied the body through the Apostolic Palace, into St. Peter's Square, and from there to the basilica itself, where John Paul II lay in state until the funeral Mass, which the College of Cardinals had decided to celebrate on Friday morning, April 8. Archbishop Marini and the producers of CTV, the Vatican television channel, had artfully arranged cameras throughout the procession route, so that both the vast throng in the square and viewers throughout the world could share in the last earthly journey of the well-traveled John Paul II.

The procession began in the Sala Clementina,

where Martínez Somalo, now joined by dozens of cardinals from around the world, chanted an antiphon drawn from Christ's words to Martha on the death of her brother Lazarus—"I am the resurrection and the life. . . ." After the Pope's body was blessed with holy water, the **Sediarii** lifted the bier to their shoulders and the great procession began. Descending the Scala Nobile and passing through the Sala Ducale and the Sala Regia, the procession was accompanied by the chanting of Psalm 23, Psalm 51, Psalm 63, and Psalm 130, as well as by the three great New Testament canticles, the **Benedictus**, the **Magnificat**, and the **Nunc dimittis**. Then, as the procession descended the Sala Regia and exited the Apostolic Palace through the Portone di Bronzo, the famous "bronze doors," the Litany of the Saints was intoned, as the Church Militant prayed that the Church Triumphant might comfort those in mourning and receive Karol Wojtyła into their company in heaven.

When the body had been placed on the bier in front of the high altar and Bernini's great bronze baldachino inside the basilica, the familiar chant "Come to his aid, saints of God" was sung, followed by the reading of a passage from Christ's high priestly prayer in the Johannine account of the Last Supper. Cardinal Martínez Somalo then invited prayer for the Church throughout the world, before the recitation of the Lord's Prayer and the closing petition: "Eternal rest grant unto him, O Lord. Let perpetual light shine upon him. May he rest in peace. Amen."

By Tuesday morning, April 5, the area around Vatican City known as the Borgo was completely filled with hundreds of thousands of pilgrims and remained that way for three days, while the traditional **Novemdiales**, the daily Masses for a deceased pope, were celebrated by various senior churchmen. The crowds impressed virtually every observer by their patience, kindness to one another, and good humor as they waited in line for twelve hours or more before having a brief moment of prayer in front of the papal bier. Estimates that as many as three million people came to the city during the week were bruited, thus effectively doubling Rome's population. They had come for many reasons, of course, but perhaps the two most common motivations were they felt the need to pay a personal tribute of respect to John Paul II, and an equally palpable desire to share with others, and thus perhaps begin to heal, the feeling of emptiness that had descended over many, many people on the Pope's death. Vatican stamps and coins issued during a papal interregnum bear the Latin inscription SEDE VACANTE [WHILE THE SEE IS VACANT]. On this occasion, that vacancy was felt deeply. And for many, the answer to that sense of vacancy was to seek comfort and courage in community. Yet for all the sense of loss, the prevailing spirit in the Borgo, among the crowds that wound their way through the narrow streets, a crowd that was remarkably managed by the local authorities, seemed to be one of gratitude—gratitude for a life beautifully lived; gratitude that the man who had suffered so long and so nobly was now, as so many believed, where he had always wanted to be—in "the house of the Father."

Some called it the "first spontaneous World Youth Day," as a large percentage of the pilgrims flooding Rome seemed to be young people. They were among the many participants in another moving moment, on the night before the funeral Mass. Along the Via della Conciliazione, the broad avenue that runs from St. Peter's Square to the Tiber, are a mélange of buildings housing bookstores, pharmacies, banks, the Columbus Hotel, the church of Santa Maria in Traspontina, and souvenir shops. On the night of April 7, in doorways on either side of the Conciliazione, were priests, wearing the stole of their office, hearing the confessions of those who were going to remain in the street overnight in order to be close to the basilica for the funeral Mass on Friday morning—and who wanted to prepare themselves sacramentally to say a final farewell to John Paul II, who had constantly urged Catholics to return to the practice of sacramental confession.

Somehow, 800,000 people—300,000 in St. Peter's Square and the Via della Conciliazione, and another half million in the streets of the Borgo—managed to wedge themselves into the areas immediately adjacent to the basilica for the funeral Mass. Millions of others were at different venues in Rome where large-screen televisions had been erected: the Circus Maximus, the Colosseum, the Piazza del Popolo and the Piazza Risorgimento, Tor Vergata (where World Youth Day-2000 had concluded), and the three other patriarchal basilicas—St. John Lateran, St. Mary Major, and St. Paul Outside the Walls. On the **sagrato** in front of St. Peter's were world political leaders, representatives of other Christian communities and other world religions—and several dozen members of Karol Wojtyła's **Środowisko**, who had flown in from Kraków the day before, stayed in parks overnight, and were still in their outdoor apparel (which seemed entirely appropriate). The vagaries of alphabetical seating according to the French names of countries put the American president, George W. Bush, next to the French president, Jacques Chirac, and led to Syrian president Bashar al-Assad being seated near Israeli president Moshe Katzav.[55] King Juan Carlos and Queen Sofía of Spain were accompanied by their secularist prime minister, José Luis Rodríguez Zapatero; Great Britain was represented by Prince Charles (who had to defer his wedding for a day) and by Prime Minister Tony Blair and his wife, Cherie. Ecumenical Patriarch Bartholomew of Constantinople was in the first row of Christian leaders, while the Patriarchate of Moscow was content to send Metropolitan Kirill of Smolensk, its chief ecumenical officer. Teoctist of Romania and forty other Orthodox leaders were present, including Christodoulos of Athens, whom John Paul had finally gotten to agree to pray with him in 2000. Karekin II,

Catholicos of the Armenian Apostolic Church, was there to mourn the man his predecessor, Karekin I, had regarded as a spiritual brother—a sentiment reciprocated by John Paul II. In addition to dozens of other Christian leaders, the Roman Jewish community was represented by its chief rabbi, Dr. Riccardo Di Segni, and by Di Segni's predecessor, Rabbi Elio Toaff, who had become a friend of the late Pope's in the course of planning John Paul's historic 1986 visit to the Great Synagogue of Rome.

The body of John Paul II had been transferred to a cypress casket; its closing, out of sight of the crowds and the television cameras, began the funeral rites on the morning of April 8. The senior churchmen present signed the **rogito,** a legal document summarizing John Paul II's life and work, while the choir sang "My soul thirsts for God, the living God; when shall I enter and see the face of God?" The **rogito** was then sealed in a metal tube and put inside the casket, along with a small bag of coins minted during the pontificate. Archbishop Dziwisz and Archbishop Marini placed a white silk cloth, a reminder of the white robe of the newly baptized, over John Paul's face, and the casket was closed while the choir sang Psalm 42: "Like the deer that yearns for running streams, so my soul is yearning for you, my God."

The **Sediarii** then lifted the casket to their shoulders and carried it through the basilica to the **sagrato,** where the entire College of Cardinals was assembled to concelebrate the funeral Mass. The casket was laid on a rug spread on the pavement in front of the altar, and Marini placed an open Book of the Gospels on the cypress lid. Throughout the Mass, a gentle breeze riffled its pages.

As dean of the College of Cardinals, Cardinal Joseph Ratzinger was principal celebrant of the funeral Mass; the principal concelebrants were the senior cardinals in each "order" of cardinals—Cardinal Angelo Sodano for the cardinal bishops, Cardinal Stephen Kim Sou-hwan for the cardinal priests, and Cardinal Jorge Arturo Medina Estévez for the cardinal deacons—as well as the senior Eastern-rite cardinal, the Lebanese Nasrallah Pierre Sfeir.[56] Ratzinger's homily, delivered in Italian, built on the Gospel text of the funeral Mass, from John 21, where the Risen Christ asks Peter three times whether he loves him, and Peter replies, three times, that he does. It was a text that had long shaped John Paul II's concept of the papacy, as he sought to live the superabundant love—"Do you love me **more** than the rest of these?"—demanded of the prince of the apostles. Ratzinger applied that question, and the Lord's subsequent prophecy that Peter would be led where he did not choose to go, in an eloquent summary of the twenty-six and a half years of the papacy of Karol Wojtyła:

In the very first years of his pontificate, still young and full of energy, the Holy Father went to the very ends of the earth, guided by Christ. But afterwards, he increasingly entered into the communion of Christ's sufferings; increasingly, he understood the truth of the words "Someone else will fasten a belt around you." And in this very communion with the suffering Lord, tirelessly and with renewed intensity, he proclaimed the Gospel, the mystery of that love which goes to the end. . . .

After speaking of how the mystery of divine mercy, as revealed in the cross and resurrection, had found its "purest reflection" in Mary, whom Karol Wojtyła had taken into his home and who had shown him how to conform himself to her son, Ratzinger ended his homily with a memorable coda:

> None of us can ever forget how, in that last Easter Sunday of his life, the Holy Father, marked by suffering, came once more to the window of the Apostolic Palace and one last time gave his blessing **urbi et orbi**. We can be sure that our beloved Pope is standing today at the window of the Father's house, that he sees us and blesses us. Yes, bless us, Holy Father. We entrust your dear soul to the Mother of God, your Mother, who guided you each day and who will guide you now to the glory of her Son, our Lord Jesus Christ. Amen.

In the first centuries of the Church, what would later be called the canonization of saints took place by popular acclamation. On March 12, 604, at the funeral of Pope Gregory I, the assembly went one step further, spontaneously chanting **"Magnus, Magnus!"** [Great, Great!], such that Gregory I was subsequently known as Pope St. Gregory the Great. It hadn't happened again for 1,401 years—until April 8, 2005, when, after the distribution of holy communion had been completed at John Paul's funeral Mass, cries of **"Il Grande!"** [The Great!], **"Magnus!,"** **"Magno!"** [Great!], and **"Santo Subito!"** [A Saint Immediately!] erupted throughout the square and down the Via della Conciliazione, and at such volume that they could be heard atop the Janiculum Hill, overlooking Vatican City. The congregation was declaring its belief that Cardinal Ratzinger had been right, that John Paul II was truly in the Father's house, and that future generations should recognize him as "John Paul the Great." The chants went on for several minutes, while Ratzinger waited patiently to begin the Mass's concluding rites.

After intercessory prayers by the Church of Rome (led by Cardinal Ruini) and the Oriental Churches (led by the Eastern-rite Catholic prelates present), Cardinal Ratzinger blessed the casket with holy water and incensed it once more, while the congregation sang, in Latin, the words of Job: **Et in carne mea videbo Deum, Salvatorem meum** [And in my flesh I shall see God, my Savior]. At the very end, clergy and congregation together sang the venerable farewell hymn: "May the angels lead you to Paradise, may the martyrs welcome you at your arrival, and may they lead you into holy Jerusalem. May the choirs of angels welcome you, and like Lazarus, who was a poor man on earth, may you enjoy eternal rest in heaven." The **Sediarii** then lifted the casket to their shoulders for the procession back into the basilica. As they turned at the top of the steps so that John Paul II in his coffin faced the congregation and Rome for the last time, another round of **"Santo Subito!"** and **"Magnus!"** broke out, as did many tears.

Down in the Vatican grottoes, the last of the funeral rites were completed privately. Two red bands were placed around the cypress casket and sealed with wax. The cypress casket was then placed inside a zinc coffin, on the top of which were a cross, John Paul II's name and dates, and his coat of arms. The zinc casket was then placed inside a walnut casket, after which the zinc casket was soldered shut. The walnut lid, also bearing a cross, the Pope's name and dates, and his coat of arms, was then affixed with screws, and the triple casket was lowered into a marble-lined grave cut into the grotto floor, where Pope John XXIII had lain before his body was translated to a glass casket in the basilica after his beatification. Cardinal Ratzinger and Archbishop Dziwisz blessed the triple casket with holy water, and a marble slab was lowered on top of the tomb. It would later bear a simple inscription:

Ioannes Paulus PP. II
16-X-1978 * 2-IV-2005

Below the inscription was the Chi-Ro, the ancient Greek symbol of Christ, who had called Karol Wojtyła, Pope John Paul II, to love him "more than the rest of these."[57]

AFTERWORDS

The days after the funeral Mass were full of rain, as if Rome were crying for **lo straniero** [the foreigner], **il Polacco** [the Pole], who had won the Romans' hearts as few others of their bishops ever had, and who had become, quite literally, **il Papa**, a father of both challenge and love. The Pope who had brought the world to Rome during the Great Jubilee of 2000 had brought together for his funeral one of the greatest assemblies of world leaders in history—and certainly the greatest at a religious service. More than 6,000 journalists described the death and burial of John Paul II in billions of words and images. The funeral itself was seen on television by some two billion people, the largest broadcast audience ever. As NBC News anchor Brian Williams put it, the remarkable farewell from both Church and world was "the human event of a generation."

As Cardinal Francis Arinze said later, John Paul II
had continued to the end of his life the pastoral strategy of accompaniment he had pioneered as a young
priest: "He didn't hide it. He wasn't embarrassed by
being in a wheelchair. . . . With John Paul II, we
knew and understood his situation, at his invitation.
He invited us into his suffering. And this made a difference to people. Suppose you were sick and confined to a wheelchair: you now saw the Pope in a
wheelchair and you thought, 'I'm not alone, there is
someone with me.' "[58]

Leonardo Sandri, the Pope's voice in his last weeks,
believed that the **Via Crucis** of John Paul II had further deepened the Pope's already rich spiritual life:
there was "more reliance on God as a way to live
his papacy; the losing battle with his body paralleled
the victory of God in his own life and the life of the
Church."[59]

The man who would succeed him as Bishop of
Rome, Pope Benedict XVI, told a group of priests
three years after John Paul's death of how touched he
had been by the humility and patience with which
John Paul II "accepted what was practically the destruction of his body and [his] growing inability
to speak," such that "he who had been a master of
words . . . **showed** us the profound truth that the
Lord redeemed us with his cross, with the passion,
as an extreme act of his love." Thus John Paul had
shown that "suffering accepted for love of Christ, for
love of God and others, is a redeeming force, a force

of love, and no less powerful than the great deeds he accomplished in the first part of the pontificate."[60]

He had become the "sign of contradiction" of which he had preached to Pope Paul VI and the Roman Curia in 1976. In emptying himself of himself, he had struck a chord that resonated in billions of human hearts. And he had done so as a disciple of Jesus Christ. He knew, with T. S. Eliot, that "in my end is my beginning."[61] He had defined and lived his life as a Christian disciple. He had met his end as a Christian disciple. And that end marked a new beginning for Karol Józef Wojtyła, Pope John Paul II—the disciple who had gone home to the Father's house.

PART THREE

METANOIA

A Disciple's Life Explored

CHAPTER TEN

From Inside

The interior lives of great men are often cloaked in mystery.

More books have been written about Abraham Lincoln than about any historical figure other than Jesus; yet there is still disagreement over Lincoln's relationship to the God of the Bible, whom he cited to such powerful effect in his Second Inaugural Address. During a secret August 1941 meeting with Franklin D. Roosevelt in Placentia Bay, Newfoundland, Winston Churchill choked with emotion while singing "Onward, Christian Soldiers" at church parade aboard HMS **Prince of Wales;** yet Churchill's relationship to biblical religion remains murky, although it was likely as distant as Lincoln's, if not more so. Ronald Reagan's inscrutability drove at least one of his biographers to distraction.[1]

At the opposite end of the scale of the admirable and the odious, who would pretend to understand fully the demons that drove Hitler, Stalin, and Mao, not to mention less consequential but no less reprehensible characters such as Dzerzhínskii, Yagoda, Himmler, Heydrich, Eichmann, and the rest of the twentieth-century rogues' gallery of mass murderers? Psychiatry might shed some light on these lethally warped personalities, but even the most secular mind will likely concede that, at bottom, there is a **mysterium iniquitatis** at work here, a deep-rooted and unfathomable wickedness that our science can neither touch nor measure.

Getting to the inside of consequential lives has its fascinations, but it is not essential to understanding the public accomplishments of most public men. That Churchill ranks as one of the few men in history who can be called saviors of civilizations as well as of countries is not much in dispute, save among cranks; yet even if we could identify precisely the spiritual or philosophical sources of the courage with which he summoned Britons to their finest hour, little more about that epic accomplishment would be explained. Grasping in detail the hatreds and passions that drove Lenin is not essential to grasping the essential fact about Lenin's public life: that he successfully created the world's first totalitarian regime and then secured his achievement with singular ruthlessness. In both instances, the admirable and the odious, the public man and what he did are large enough, striking enough, and complex enough to fill the horizon of our curiosity.

The same cannot be said, however, for the life of Karol Wojtyła, Pope John Paul II. In an author's introduction to **Our God's Brother**, the play he wrote about the man he later canonized as St. Albert Chmielowski, Wojtyła observed that there is a "line inaccessible to history" that runs between our understanding of any human being and the person we are trying to understand. For every human being is a mystery, except when we stand before God—the point at which, as St. Paul told the Corinthians, we shall know ourselves, even as we are fully known (**cf.** 1 Corinthians 13.12b). In more direct and personal terms, Pope John Paul II once applied this truth to himself when he observed, of certain attempts to tell the story of his life, "They try to understand me from outside. But I can only be understood from inside."[2]

Grasping as much as we can of the person and accomplishment of Karol Wojtyła means beginning from the premise that the outside of Wojtyła's life— the public accomplishment—was the by-product of the inside: his interior life, the life of the human spirit (and, he would say, the work of the Holy Spirit within him). There are many ways to characterize that interior life: as the life of a radically converted Christian disciple; as the life of a man who combined poetic sensibility and philosophical rigor; as the life of a solitary and frequently orphaned man whose personality was nourished by long and deep friendships; as the life of a celibate who mastered the arts of fatherhood; as the life of a mystic and contemplative who was compelled, by what he believed to be God's design, to be a man of action. He was all of those things. The thread that wove those facets of Karol Wojtyła's life into a single tapestry is perhaps best captured by a term from biblical Greek: **metanoia**, which is usually translated as "conversion." Karol Wojtyła's life was a life of ongoing metanoia.

Conversion was at the heart of the preaching of Jesus. In Mark's Gospel, Christ's first recorded words are a call to conversion: "The time is fulfilled and the kingdom of God is at hand; repent and believe in the gospel" (Mark 1.15). Metanoia, as the Catholic Church understands it, is a complete turning to God that begins with the "first conversion" sacramentally effected by baptism. Metanoia is essentially a lifelong project, however, in which the Christian disciple grows into the new life of grace intellectually, morally, psychologically, and affectively.[3] Intellectual metanoia is that process by which we abandon our empiricist blinders and come to understand that the world of sensory perception is not all the world there is; that, as Guy Crouchback puts it to a skeptical army chaplain in Evelyn Waugh's **Men at Arms**, "the supernatural is the real." Moral conversion is the process by which we grow into our freedom, freely choosing what is truly good as a matter of moral habit.[4] Affective conversion means emptying ourselves of dehumanizing passions and ordering our emotional lives and our imaginations toward the truly good and beautiful, who is God. Each of these processes can be discerned in the life of John Paul II; in each of these conversions Karol Wojtyła grew in the grace of his baptism, in which he was first given the gifts of faith, hope, and love.

The paradox of metanoia, which was manifest in the life of Karol Wojtyła, is that all this emptying of self leads to the richest imaginable human experience: a life unembittered by irony or stultified by boredom, a life of both serenity and adventure. Moreover, for the Christian, the pilgrimage of metanoia is not a solitary or solipsistic one, for the journey is walked in and through the Church, which is both a communion of disciples and the Body of Christ alive in history. Even Christian hermits live the journey of metanoia with and through the Church of which they are members, for to be a member of the Church is to be a member of the Body of Christ, which is different from any other "membership" in which we freely engage. To live that pilgrimage of metanoia as a pastor is to live a special responsibility for the journey of others; to live it as the universal pastor of the Church is a responsibility of a different order of magnitude.

FAITH, HOPE, AND LOVE

If we are to understand John Paul II's life as one of ongoing metanoia, a useful place to begin exploring that life's "inside" is to read the life of Karol Wojtyła—the man, the priest, the bishop, the pope—through the prism of the three theological virtues: faith, hope, and love. As the Catholic Church understands them, the theological virtues are not like muscles—native capacities that can be developed by natural training. Rather, the theological virtues of faith, hope, and love are gifts from God that animate our natural capacities—"the pledge of the action of the Holy Spirit in the faculties of the human being," as the **Catechism of the Catholic Church** puts it.[5]

Faith

Karol Wojtyła's faith was supernaturally given him when he was baptized in the Church of the Presentation of the Blessed Virgin Mary in Wadowice on June 20, 1920; it was first nurtured by his parents, and especially by his father. From the Captain, Karol Wojtyła, Sr., the son learned that manliness and piety are not antinomies, but rather complements; or as John Paul II would write of his father forty-five years after the Captain's death, "**his example was in a way my first seminary**, a kind of domestic seminary."[6] If one is looking for a source of John Paul's remarkable equanimity and resilience in situations ranging from international crises to grave personal illness, one need look no further than the example of his father, whose devotion to his son, whose prayer, and whose manly acceptance of suffering taught deep if unspoken lessons about Christian realism: facts submitted to without tears; duties accepted without complaint.

The early lessons in faith that shaped the interior life of Pope John Paul II are embodied in Kalwaria Zebrzydowska, the vast, wooded Holy Land shrine between Kraków and Wadowice that he first visited as a boy, and that he continued to frequent until a few years before his death. In its design, Kalwaria is both Christ-centered and Marian: its two principal trails, the Path of Our Lord and the Path of Our Lady, intersect at the chapel of the Assumption of Mary: the first fruits in heaven of Mary's Son's victory over death. Walking the paths of Kalwaria thus taught young Karol Wojtyła a basic lesson in faith: Christ is the center of the life of faith, and a sure path to Christ is found through a proper devotion to the Mother of God. The lesson stayed with him throughout his life. For Karol Wojtyła to adopt the Marian motto **Totus Tuus** [Entirely Yours] as his episcopal and papal motto for almost forty-seven years was a distinctively Marian way of making that most basic of Christian acts of faith, that "Jesus is Lord."

Kalwaria's very name, evoking as it does the place

of Jesus's crucifixion, taught another lesson: the spiritual life of the Christian is always cruciform, for, as the Lord himself said, "If any man would come after me, let him deny himself and take up his cross and follow me" (Matthew 16.24). Karol Wojtyła's introduction to this aspect of the spiritual life was deepened by his encounter with the classic Carmelite mystics John of the Cross and Teresa of Ávila during the Second World War. Reading the Carmelites with Jan Tyranowski amidst the terrors of war and Nazi occupation left a permanent impress on Wojtyła's soul, manifest in his regular practice of making the Stations of the Cross—and, most memorably, in his embrace of the cross on the last Good Friday of his life.

In its most dramatic form, the embrace of the cross and metanoia into Christ lead to martyrdom—and this was the third facet of Karol Wojtyła's interior life that was nourished at Kalwaria Zebrzydowska. Four of the Franciscan priests who lived in the monastery at Kalwaria died in concentration camps during World War II, three at Dachau and one at Auschwitz; all were arrested for giving refuge to a professor from Kraków's Jagiellonian University. Their sacrifice is remembered on a plaque on one of the exterior walls of the basilica at Kalwaria, a place Wojtyła knew well from his regular visits to the shrine during his Cracovian years as a priest and bishop. Thus it is not unlikely that a central feature of Wojtyła's life of faith—his conviction that the ideal of the Christian life is that of the martyr[7]—drew at least in part on his experience of Kalwaria Zebrzydowska.

Throughout his life, John Paul II's faith was nourished by prayer. His spiritual life had its daily rhythms: Mass; the Liturgy of the Hours (which he once described as "very important, **very** important"[8]); periods of meditation, Scripture reading, and other spiritual reading; adoration of the Blessed Sacrament; recitation of the Rosary (or, as Stanisław Dziwisz once observed puckishly, "**Many** Rosaries . . ."[9]). At the same time, his prayer spilled over into just about every other facet of his life. He never made a decision without praying over it—sometimes, for a considerable period of time.[10] Walking between meetings in the Apostolic Palace, he prayed. Preparing to celebrate Mass in the far corners of the world, he disappeared into prayer while his aides wrestled with the liturgical details of the moment. The same habit continued during his vacations. The physicist Jerzy Janik, John Paul's old friend and partner in skiing and hiking in the mountains of Poland, remembered years later that being outdoors with Karol Wojtyła was a time of jokes, songs, and serious discussions. Yet, as Janik recalled, "what was [also] characteristic of such a day was that, after some hours of walking and hiking in the mountains, he would gradually withdraw to the back of the group and contemplate for two hours or so. It was almost difficult to notice . . . but everyone felt that we should not disturb him; that was his private time with God."[11]

The man who succeeded him as Bishop of Rome, Joseph Ratzinger, once described Karol Wojtyła's immersion in God as the source of energy animating John Paul's spiritual and intellectual life and his pastoral work:

> [H]is personal meditation, his personal dialogue with God, is decisive for his life. He is a man of God, and his philosophy and theology are essentially born in his dialogue with God. The deepest source of what he says is that, every day, he is, for an hour, alone with his Lord and speaking . . . about all the problems of the world. But he is also seeking the face of God, and this is very important. In his meditations he is in personal contact with the Lord and thus directed to sanctity and sanctification. Before the literary sources, before his experiences of life, this dialogue with God is the central element in his spiritual and intellectual life.
>
> But it's clear that the dialogue with God is also living from the dialogue with man. All his intellectual reflections helped him to be more intensive in his dialogue with God and in his pastoral experience, because dialogue is not an isolated and individual phenomenon, it is always with the Lord, for others: for the sanctification not only of his own person but to do the work of sanctification with the Lord in the world.[12]

That lifelong dialogue of faith, which continued through Wojtyła's dark nights, sheds light on two facets of his personality that puzzled some who tried to get to him from the "outside": his seeming inscrutability, and his lack of concern for closure. Another old friend, the art historian Jacek Woźniakowski, felt that, even after decades of conversation, he "never had the feeling of getting to the bottom, so to say, of [Wojtyła's] thoughts and attitudes. There was something he kept for himself. . . . With some people, you have the feeling, which may be misleading, of coming to the bottom. But with Wojtyła you did not have that feeling."[13] Which was, Woźniakowski understood, the way of all mystics—for the experiences of the genuine mystic are, by definition, indescribable, at least in discursive terms (which perhaps also explains Wojtyła's affinity for such mystical poets as John of the Cross). Thus John Paul II was not so much "inscrutable," in the psychological sense of having built up formidable interior defenses; he was, rather, a man whose deepest human and spiritual experiences took place in a realm beyond words, which he could only begin to describe through such vehicles as his poetry. Or, one suspects, in those groans that often accompanied his private prayer.

His immersion in God was also the true explanation for John Paul II's seeming lack of interest in getting closure on a project or initiative, according to Jacek Woźniakowski. That, Woźniakowski remembered, was his way in Kraków—sometimes, perhaps, to the discomfort of his colleagues in the management of the archdiocese. It was also his way in Rome, as in his ecumenical and interreligious initiatives—and this was certainly to the discomfort of the traditional managers of popes. Some read this as a flaw in his composition as an administrator, which perhaps it was, at least from one angle of vision. But Woźniakowski believed that the deeper truth of John Paul II's willingness to live with incompleteness was his faith: "there is a path you tread," Woźniakowski once put it, "and you leave the rest in God's hands."[14]

Hope

In October 1995, speaking from the green marble rostrum of the United Nations General Assembly, Pope John Paul II described himself as a "witness to hope" at the end of a century of fear:

It is one of the great paradoxes of our time that man, who began the period we call "modernity" with a self-confident assertion of his "coming of age" and "autonomy," approaches the end of the twentieth century fearful of himself, fearful of what he might be capable of, fearful for the future. . . .

In order to ensure that the new millennium now approaching will witness a new flourishing of the human spirit, mediated through an authentic culture of freedom, men and women must learn to conquer fear. **We must learn not to be afraid**, we must rediscover a spirit of hope and a spirit of trust . . . [and] regain sight of that transcendent horizon of possibility to which the soul of man aspires.[15]

Coming from other public figures, such sentiments might have been taken as inspiring, or perhaps illusory, optimism. The key to grasping the hope that animated John Paul II, however, is to understand that Karol Wojtyła was not an optimist (or a pessimist, for that matter). Optimism and pessimism are matters of optics, of how one sees things—and the optics can change with the observer's mood. John Paul II lived beyond optimism and pessimism, in a world of Christian realism infused with Christian hope. Christian realism requires seeing things as they are; or, as he put it in that same UN address, "hope is not empty optimism springing from a naive confidence that the future will necessarily be better than the past."[16] Yet Christian realism has an open-ended, not crabbed, quality about it, because it is enlivened by Christian hope.

All of which is to say that the hope of John Paul II was built, not on optics, but on the far sturdier foundation of Christian faith. His hope, he told the assembled leaders of the world in the UN General Assembly hall, was "centered on Jesus Christ," whose "Death and Resurrection . . . fully revealed

God's love and his care for all creation." Christ-
centered hope, the source of which is God's presence in "the radiant humanity of Christ," fills the
Christian with a hope that reaches every human person, John Paul concluded, in an echo of Vatican II's
Pastoral Constitution on the Church in the Modern
World: "nothing genuinely human fails to touch the
hearts of Christians." It was to proclaim that Christ-
centered hope in the world, recognizing the God-
given dignity of every human being, that the Bishop
of Rome, a "witness to hope," came to the UN to
speak to the world of power, of a power different
from and greater than the power the world typically
recognized.[17]

John Paul II's hope animated his conviction that
sanctity was within the reach of every baptized person who was willing to open himself or herself to the
grace of God. Thus this hope was one of the sources
of the extraordinary numbers of beatifications and
canonizations over which he presided, a sometimes
criticized aspect of the pontificate. Roman bureaucrats occasionally said, tartly or slyly, that these beatifications and canonizations were a matter of the
Pope's "wanting to take a new blessed in his pocket"
on his travels. John Paul's deeper intention, however,
was to rekindle around the world a vibrant Christian
hope in the possibility of sanctity, for his faith had
taught him that the gifts of the Holy Spirit were not
exhausted in that Upper Room in Jerusalem on the
first Christian Pentecost.

The hope that grew from Karol Wojtyła's faith also accounts for several other dimensions of his personality. It helps explain his intense interest in the person who was in front of him at any given moment—here was someone called to sanctity, someone for whom the Son of God had become incarnate, suffered, and died. It helps account for his conviction that life itself was sanctifying, especially that part of life that engaged the moral relationships between people (as his friend and fellow philosopher Karol Tarnowski once put it).[18] That hope was another source of his remarkable calm amidst adversity, as well as of his willingness to let situations and decisions mature. Because his hope was grounded in an Easter faith that taught him that God's purposes would, ultimately, be vindicated, he did not demand instant results from history: his hope informed the humility by which he was content to sow the seed, in the confidence that others would reap the harvest.

Karol Wojtyła's hope also sheds light on his life-long disregard of possessions and material comfort. As his hope was centered elsewhere, he was liberated from acquisitiveness, even as he was grateful for the generosity of the people of the Church that made it possible for him to live his ministerial life without regard for income.

In the wake of his death, it was far too soon to judge whether that hope for a "springtime of the human spirit" of which John Paul II spoke to the United Nations as well as his hope for a parallel "springtime of evangelization" in the life of the Catholic Church were shaped by too sanguine a reading of the possibilities present in the riptides of early twenty-first-century history. No man is an infallible judge of the future, though, and if John Paul's hope led him to imagine possibilities incapable of actualization at the world's turn into the third millennium, it must also be remembered that that same hope led him to discern possibilities for liberation in the contest with communism that others quite simply missed.

In a season of fear, John Paul challenged the Church and the world to courage with his signature antiphon, "Be not afraid!" In a moment of foreshortened horizons, he dared to challenge the world to hope. Both the courage and the hope were, in the life of Karol Wojtyła, built on faith. He was a man of hope, not because of a psychological tick or an invincible naïveté, but because the virtue of hope infused into him at his baptism grew throughout a life of metanoia, which was not without its moments of darkness.

Love

While references to St. Paul's famous delineation of the characteristics of Christian love in 1 Corinthians 13 are not frequent in the preaching and writing of Karol Wojtyła, his interior life does seem to have been shaped by the "more excellent way" with which the apostle introduces his hymn to **caritas**. The spiritual director of Archbishop Sapieha's underground seminary, Stanisław Smoleński, once described Wojtyła as a man who "loved easily," and from an early age.[19] As the Catholic Church understands it, **caritas** is the greatest of the theological virtues, and is both "the source and the goal" of the Christian practice of faith and hope.[20] Examining the ways in which Karol Wojtyła exercised the virtue of Christian charity thus sheds light on many other aspects of his personality and his interior life.

High-energy individuals are often thought to be working out some psychological crotchet or meeting some inner "need." Love, however, was the engine of Wojtyła's astonishing energy, manifest in the relentless giving of himself that characterized his priesthood, his episcopacy, and his Petrine service as Bishop of Rome. Christian love is "harsh and dreadful," according to Dorothy Day, cofounder of the Catholic Worker movement, because Christian love is unsparing; it demands everything of those who would practice it. John Paul II demonstrated what the immolation of self might mean in his embodiment of crucified love in the last months of his life. Yet Wojtyła's personal pilgrimage also suggests that the other side of this "harsh and dreadful" love is joy—for, as Joaquín Navarro insisted, he was, to the end, **un'uomo allegro**, a cheerful man. No small part of that cheerfulness came from expending himself in the proclamation and demonstration of the "more excellent way."

Caritas was also at the root of one of John Paul II's most striking personal characteristics: his insatiable curiosity. To the end of his life, he always wanted to know what was happening—intellectually, culturally, ecclesiastically, and in the personal lives of his friends and those with whom he came into conversation. Again, this could be read psychologically as the turbulence of a restless mind. But to those who experienced the force of Wojtyła's curiosity, it seemed something else entirely: a curiosity born of his commitment to introducing others to the "more excellent way," or to deepening the experience of **caritas** for those already embarked on the journey of Christian faith. He had the good pastor's memory for difficulties and problems; years after being asked to pray for someone, he would spontaneously ask, "How is——?" Thus he continued to exercise a personal pastoral charity amidst all the other demands of his papal office.

The power of his love was notably displayed in his conversation in prison with Mehmet Ali Agca, the man who had tried to kill him. Agca had no serious religious formation and was deeply superstitious; someone had told him that he had shot the Pope on the feast day of Our Lady of Fátima; the veteran Turkish assassin was convinced that the "Goddess of

Fátima" was very angry with him and was going to express that anger in a dramatic (and, for Agca, unpleasant) way. John Paul patiently explained that this was no "goddess," but the Mother of Jesus, honored by Muslims, and that she, too, forgave him for what he had done. At the other end of the spectrum of his public life, it was also **caritas** that informed John Paul II's passionate defense of the most defenseless of human beings: the unborn, the elderly, the severely handicapped. His **caritas** taught him that, as all lived within the ambit of divine love, all ought to belong within the human community of common care and protection. To narrow the boundaries of that community was wrong as a matter of justice, John Paul II believed; it was also a defect of love—and injustice wedded to a lack of charity would, he was persuaded, yield very unfortunate public consequences.

The character of John Paul II's love is perhaps best described as "paternal": through his love, he exercised forms of spiritual paternity that touched human lives in an astonishing variety of milieu. Here, his curiosity, his pastoral skill, and the instinct for fatherhood he had learned from his own father, the Captain, and from the unbroken prince, Cardinal Sapieha, intersected. As Stefan Sawicki, who knew Wojtyła at the Catholic University of Lublin, once put it, Wojtyła was "enormously interested in another man, not in the sense of prying into his personal life or in terms of trying to direct him; rather, he tried to accompany someone in their problems; he was open to revealing the humanity of another."[21] Karol Tarnowski put the same characteristic in a slightly different way: Wojtyła had the "faculty of entering into others' experiences, even when he had not had the same experiences." In another personality, not formed by **caritas**, this could have led to manipulation and dominance. Because he had been formed in **caritas**, which led him to respect the freedom of others, Wojtyła "never pressed."[22] Indeed, as Tarnowski recalled, Wojtyła the confessor "did not order or dictate; the stress was always on personal responsibility—'you can decide because you are capable of understanding the truth.'" Because the distinctive form of his **caritas** as a pastor was paternal, he "didn't treat [adults] like children."[23] As his friend and fellow philosopher Józef Tischner once put it, it was all a matter of "meeting someone wisely": meeting someone with the respect for another's freedom that comes from the liberating experience of the love of God.[24]

Wojtyła's concept of spiritual paternity was also shaped by his meditation on St. Joseph, the foster father of Jesus, about whom he wrote the 1989 apostolic exhortation **Redemptoris Custos** [Guardian of the Redeemer]. More than a decade later, in **Alzatevi, andiamo!**, John Paul II returned to the largely unknown figure of Joseph while making a striking theological observation about what the "guardian" had contributed to the human formation of Christ, and to the Christian understanding of God:

We know that Jesus addressed God with the word "**Abba**"—a loving, familiar word that would have been used by children in first-century Palestine when speaking to their fathers. Most probably Jesus, like other children, used this same word when speaking to Saint Joseph. Can any more be said about the mystery of human fatherhood? Jesus himself, as a man, experienced the fatherhood of God through the father-son relationship with Saint Joseph. This filial encounter with Joseph then fed into Our Lord's revelation of the paternal name of God. . . . Christ in his divinity had his own experience of divine fatherhood and sonship within the Most Holy Trinity. In his humanity, he experienced sonship thanks to Saint Joseph.[25]

From the point of view of Karol Wojtyła's Trinitarian faith, then, paternity was the source of all that is. He put that conviction most concisely in concluding his 1964 essay, "Reflections on Fatherhood":

And in the end . . . everything else will turn out to be unimportant and inessential, except for this: father, child, love.

And then, looking at the simplest things, all of us

will say: could we have not learned this long ago? Has this not always been embedded at the bottom of everything that is?[26]

Paternal love played itself out in history in what Karol Wojtyła came to understand as a cosmic drama, inside which the drama of each human life was enacted. While John Paul II clearly respected the work of the Swiss theologian Hans Urs von Balthasar, with its stress on drama as the "form" of the Christian life, John Paul came to his understanding of the drama of **caritas** by a route different from that of Balthasar. As Wojtyła's former student Stanisław Grygiel put it, Balthasar's understanding of drama as the "form" or gestalt of life came from reading dramatic literature. Wojtyła's convictions about the dramatic structure of the human condition came from his life experiences (the deaths of his mother, brother, and father; the deaths and deportations of his friends during the war; the fate of his Jewish classmates); from his work in the theater; and from his pastoral experience with the drama of human love in others' lives.[27] Spiritual paternity thus came to mean, for him, accompanying another in the dramatic gap between the person I am today and the person my human and Christian destiny calls me to be.

The cosmic drama of divine love being played out in the human quest for a true and pure love could only be lived in freedom: this was one angle from which John Paul II saw the world and its story, and because he saw things that way, he was determined to be an agent of freedom, of authentic human liberation, for others. That dramatic optic on history and humanity also bred in him a deep respect for others who understood the springs of moral tension in the human drama, even if, like Václav Havel (a man John Paul II much admired), they were not believers in the sense of conventional Christian piety.[28] He brought an understanding of the universality of the human drama to the Office of Peter; that office gave his instinct for paternity a wider geography, as it were. That John Paul could "connect" with people in an extraordinary diversity of cultural settings tells us something about the depth of that paternal instinct within him. That he took upon himself the burden of others' pain in microcosm, in the daily prayer that was shaped by requests for his prayers from around the world, tells us something about the strength that came from his **caritas**, and his willingness to make himself vulnerable to others' suffering.

A Richness of Character

Faith, hope, and love combined in Karol Wojtyła to form an exceptionally attractive human character and personality.

Contrary to the ill-informed (and in some instances, malicious) charges of some critics, he retained his intellectual curiosity throughout his life; in his ninth decade, he may have been the only man who ever read the French philosopher of dialogue, Emmanuel Levinas, for enjoyment.[29] At the same time, he was an avid sportsman and, until his body failed him, he was not simply an observer: the man who had hiked, swam, skied, and kayaked all over Poland surreptitiously escaped from the Vatican to ski, once surprising Italian president Alessandro Pertini on the slopes of the Adamello Mountains (Pertini: "Compliments, Your Holiness, I must confess that I am amazed to see you move so skillfully in the snow." John Paul II: "Mr. President, I am a son of the mountains.")[30]

He was a man of disciplined personal habits, who cared little for food (except dessert) and lived in as simple a manner as possible within the renaissance grandeur of the Apostolic Palace. His discipline was also psychological. He was, if not indifferent to criticism, then at least emotionally immune to the slings and arrows of often critical commentary that whizzed past his head daily. Polish prime minister Hanna Suchocka, meeting John Paul in 1992, noted that she shared with the Pope the burden of being constantly criticized; the Pope waved the comment away, saying, "You should see what they say about me," and then offered his sympathy and personal support.[31] That same personal discipline was also a barrier against succumbing to the calculations that politicians and statesmen ordinarily make. No one, least of all John Paul II, would claim that his every decision as pope was correct. But it seems clear that his decision-making was also strikingly disinterested, with no concern for whatever trouble or criticism he might be bringing upon himself. In this respect, he was quite different from a predecessor he admired, Paul VI, who felt criticism keenly and thus worried constantly over his decisions.[32]

Karol Wojtyła cherished and nurtured his friendships while remaining a man of somewhat courtly manners; he rarely used the familiar form of the Polish personal pronoun, even with men and women he had known for decades. He was faithful to friends, even if their demands on him became burdensome, or, as with his former colleagues at **Tygodnik Powszechny**, their views veered off onto a track different from his own.[33] Part of his gift for friendship (as for paternity) was his marked ability as a listener—as a young priest, according to veteran **Środowisko** member Stanisław Rybicki, he had "mastered the art of listening."[34] There were rituals to his friendships, as there are in all friendships; within the circle of **Środowisko**, some folk songs and ballads were understood to be **Wujek's** only, and he sang them in all their verses with gusto. Every Christmas season, a phone call would be arranged with John Paul II at one end and a large gathering of several generations of **Środowisko** on the other—and, as they had done during the old days in Kraków, they sang Christmas carols together, for a considerable period of time. (Wojtyła had a remarkable memory for lyrics, and by the account of some very sober-minded academics and professionals, knew virtually every traditional Polish carol down to the last verse.) His personal favorites among Polish patriotic anthems were "Red Flowers on Monte Cassino" and "Legionowa," the latter dating back to the heady first days of Polish independence in 1918.[35]

Wojtyła's sense of humor, frequently displayed among clerical colleagues and **Środowisko** members alike during his Kraków years, remained robust during his papacy—and on more than one occasion turned on the papacy itself. Jerzy Stuhr, a distinguished Polish actor and later rector of the Kraków Academy for the Dramatic Arts, once found himself in Rome and was invited to dinner at the papal apartment. John Paul asked him about his present work and Stuhr replied that he was playing in a production of Adam Mickiewicz's **Forefathers' Eve**, arguably the most famous drama in the history of Polish literature. John Paul said that it was a very important play indeed, and what part did Stuhr take? Stuhr, a bit embarrassed, said he regretted to report that he was playing Satan. To which John Paul replied, "Well, we don't get to choose our roles, do we?"[36]

John Paul's humor was not mean, but he could enjoy making the occasional jab that didn't quite draw blood. At one of the first of the Castel Gandolfo humanities seminars he occasionally hosted during the summer months, the participants included the German theologian Johann Baptist Metz, sometimes considered the intellectual inspiration of liberation theology and a man firmly on the port side of Catholic intellectual life. On the seminar's last day, several dozen distinguished scholars were shuffling around while lining up for a group picture, with no one wanting to look as if he was jockeying for position closer to the Pope. John Paul spotted Metz, and said in a loud voice, "You, Metz, a little closer to the Pope!" Everyone laughed, including Metz, who did as he was told.[37]

Another German Catholic personality came within range of the skirmishing fire of John Paul's humor a bit later. In the aftermath of the Banco Ambrosiano scandal of the 1980s, in which the Vatican bank, the Institute for the Works of Religion, was deeply involved, the Pope summoned a group of fifteen cardinals, all presumably knowledgeable about finance, to the Vatican to sort through the mess. After a morning listening to a sorry tale of incompetence, perfidy, and bureaucratic self-preservation, John Paul decided that it was time for lunch and walked with the cardinals to the meal. Spotting the German Joachim Meisner, and remembering that Germans had often referred to shoddy goods or general incompetence during the 1970s as **polnische Wirtschaft** [Polish business], he walked up to Meisner and said, in German, "So, Eminence, do you think we have some **polnische Wirtschaft** in the

Vatican finances?" Meisner was speechless. Others, seeing the laughter in the Pope's eyes, asked the German what John Paul had said; Meisner replied that "it can't be translated."[38]

John Paul was quite capable of turning his humor upon himself, too. In 1994, a lunch guest at Castel Gandolfo, Father Richard John Neuhaus, told the Pope that he was "ahead of history." "So that is why I broke my leg?" John Paul replied. Another New Yorker, Cardinal John O'Connor, remembered being amazed that he, a man who grew up in a Philadelphia row house, could find himself talking quite naturally with a pope. Once, at the end of a conversation, the cardinal archbishop of New York (who could be very wry) said to the Bishop of Rome, "You know, I'll never get anywhere in this Church because I was never a bishop's secretary." "Neither was I," said John Paul II.[39] Late one evening at Castel Gandolfo, after dining with guests, an obviously tired John Paul was presented with the day's official documents, which required his signature. He sighed, took up his Mont Blanc pen, and began to sign vellum sheets to heads of state, ambassadors, and so forth, looking up to say at one point, "**Povero Papa!**" [Poor Pope!]. He then laughed and went back to work.[40]

He was also comfortable with his own fallibility. On September 27, 1997, John Paul was scheduled to give the closing address at an Italian National Eucharistic Congress in Bologna—and Bob Dylan was slated to perform before the Pope spoke. Dylan came on stage, sang several popular songs, concluded with "Blowin' in the Wind," and left. John Paul scrapped his prepared text, picked up where Dylan had left off, and began speaking about the wind of the Holy Spirit blowing through the Church today. Three days later, after a rapid-fire Latin grace-before-meals, the Pope fixed a lunch guest with a sharp stare and asked, "Who ees Bob DEE-lahn?"[41]

PRUDENCE, JUSTICE, COURAGE, MODERATION

Freedom, John Paul II taught for decades, is not a matter of doing what we like, but of freely choosing what is truly good. Thus growth in the interior life and in the practice of Christian faith is a growth into a deeper, nobler freedom that seeks "whatever is true, whatever is honorable, whatever is just, whatever is pure, whatever is lovely, whatever is gracious" (Philippians 4.8). Freedom, rightly understood, is exercised through what the Catholic Church calls the "cardinal virtues": prudence, or right judgment; justice; courage (often called "fortitude"); and moderation, or "temperance." The cardinal virtues were known to pagan antiquity and analyzed by Plato in **The Republic**, but in the Christian understanding of them, they have a goal that pre-Christian Greek philosophers could not conceive: as St. Gregory of

Nyssa put it in his treatise on the beatitudes, "The goal of a virtuous life is to become like God." Progress toward this goal comes about through a deepening, not an abandonment, of our humanity, even as growth in the practice of the cardinal virtues takes both human effort and (the Church would insist) the aid of God's grace.[42] The story of Karol Wojtyła's Christian journey can thus be read "from the inside" through the prism of the cardinal virtues as well as through the matrix of the theological virtues.

Prudence

Thomas Aquinas followed Aristotle in defining the virtue of prudence as "right reason in action"; the Hebrew Bible puts it more graphically—"The prudent man looks where he is going" (Proverbs 14.15). The medievals called prudence **auriga virtutum**, the charioteer of the virtues, for it is this capacity for right judgment—for applying principle and moral judgment to particular cases and actions—that guides the practice of the other virtues in true measure, without either timidity or fanaticism.

Prudence in true ecclesiastical leadership (and indeed in any form of human leadership) includes several other notable characteristics, including the ability to see around corners (i.e., to see possibilities where others see only obstacles) and to see into hearts (i.e., to discern character). No priest, bishop, or pope, no matter how much he has given himself over to the will of God or how much he has been trained in the demanding school of the virtues, ever exercises the virtue of prudence with complete success. Pope Paul VI, for example, made the prudential judgments that the Cold War would last for the foreseeable future and that the **Ostpolitik** devised by Agostino Casaroli was necessary for the survival of the Catholic Church in communist-dominated east central Europe; both of those exercises of prudence turned out to be mistaken, as history subsequently demonstrated.

Similarly, it would be fatuous, or hagiographical, to suggest that every prudential judgment Karol Wojtyła made as archbishop of Kraków or Bishop of Rome was infallibly "prudent," in the sense of being accurate in its reading of circumstances and personalities and effective in achieving the desired ends. He appointed bishops who, in retrospect, should not have been appointed (although this was at least as much a failure of some of his nuncios and of the Vatican's Congregation for Bishops as it was a personal failure). During his papacy, he seemed to think that certain political situations (e.g., the Middle East) and certain ecclesiastical situations (e.g., the deterioration of the Society of Jesus) were more pliable and open to change than they turned out to be. John Paul II could be deceived, as in the case of the founder of the Legionaries of Christ, Marcial Maciel, whom the Pope supported for decades; it was revealed after the Pope's death that Maciel had long led a double life of moral dissolution.

Karol Wojtyła's profound disinclination to humiliate, or make a spectacle of, someone else; his intense dislike of gossip; his occasional tendency to project his own virtues onto others; and his determination to find something good in another's actions or words—these characteristics of his personality (which were shaped by his experience of "humiliation at the hands of evil" during World War II and were clearly evident to both students and faculty colleagues during his early teaching days at the Catholic University of Lublin) could and did lead him, as bishop and pope, to misjudgments about personalities, including clergy and senior members of the hierarchy who ought to have been disciplined or compelled to retire.[43] He was aware of these psychological and spiritual predispositions, and confessed aloud in **Alzatevi, andiamo!** that he had likely been too lax, in Kraków, in his exercise of the episcopal **munus regendi**: the responsibilities of ecclesiastical governance that include the responsibility to admonish and, if necessary, discipline wayward clergymen.[44] Those same predispositions shaped his response to the crisis of clergy sexual abuse and episcopal misgovernance in the United States that came to light during the Long Lent of 2002, as they did his response to other demonstrations of episcopal irresponsibility in other countries.

Thus the life of John Paul II, for all its accomplishment and despite the richness of his spiritual life, demonstrates the ancient truth that no pope exercises infallible prudential judgment about men and circumstances. The question in judging Karol Wojtyła as a man of prudence must not be whether he got everything right, which was clearly not the case, or even whether he got the majority of his prudential judgments right, which is a question incapable of being given an answer. The question is whether his failures in prudential judgment were a function of deeper personal faults (weakness, negligence, culpable gullibility, willful ignorance) or whether the faults that were manifest in his failures of judgment were, in fact, expressions of John Paul II's virtues—and particularly (in terms of the **munus regendi** and his mode of governance) the expression of his **caritas**. The latter seems far more likely the case. Historians centuries from now will recognize, as the observant did in the years immediately following his death, that not all his judgments and actions were correct. Yet throughout his life, it was clearly his intention to act prudently, that is, to bring his best judgment to bear on a personality or a situation without fear and without seeking favor.

Moreover, if the exercise of prudence by senior churchmen involves the ability to read what Vatican II called "the signs of the times," and in doing so to discern possibilities and opportunities for evangelical action, then Karol Wojtyła exercised the virtue of prudence in a truly heroic way for decades.

To the intense aggravation of Poland's communist masters, he proved a wily, disciplined, and determined foe. The Ark Church was finally built. The Corpus Christi procession was allowed off Wawel hill and became the occasion to defend the human rights of all Poles. The restive Catholic intelligentsia maintained (sometimes grudging) support for the church-state policies of the Primate, Cardinal Wyszyński. And Wojtyła resolutely refused to let a millimeter of distance show between himself and Wyszyński in the Church's ongoing chess match with Polish communism. This was prudence in action.

The same virtue—prudence as discernment of the "signs of the times"—was evident in some of his signature accomplishments as pope. He saw, and pursued, possibilities in central and eastern Europe that were invisible to the Vatican diplomats of the **Ostpolitik**. He refused to believe that Latin America could only be governed by authoritarians (of either the Left or the Right), and he patiently sowed the seeds of democratization on the world's most Catholic continent. He brushed aside the skepticism of senior churchmen who believed it impossible to reach the modern and postmodern young, created World Youth Day, and drew tens of millions of young people into an encounter with the "more excellent way." Similarly, he took no heed of the counsels of despair or skepticism coming from bishops who thought catechisms either impossible to write or hopelessly passé, and saw to the production of the **Catechism**

of the Catholic Church—which revitalized catechetics in some parts of the Church while providing ordinary Catholics with a ready reference point with which to challenge teaching and preaching that misrepresented the truth of Catholic faith. He took the risk of supporting renewal movements and new Catholic communities, his prudential judgment being informed by his confidence in the ongoing role of the Holy Spirit in the Church. He was open to new insights about how twenty-first-century economies were likely to function, and thus redirected the Church's social doctrine in **Centesimus Annus**. He saw nothing imprudent in a pope writing in his own voice for a world audience, and thereby produced an international bestseller, **Crossing the Threshold of Hope**, that brought the Catholic Church into conversation with men and women who would never consider reading an encyclical, a catechism, or the Bible. Perhaps most dramatically, he insisted that there was nothing imprudent, but in fact something evangelically imperative, in the Church confessing to God the sins and errors of the sons and daughters of the Church over two millennia so that the message of the Church might be heard more clearly in the third millennium. He was criticized for all these decisions; his critics turned out to have been less well formed in the cardinal virtue of prudence.

Justice

The **Catechism of the Catholic Church** defines the cardinal virtue of justice as "the moral virtue that consists in the constant and firm will to give their due to God and neighbor."[45] Karol Wojtyła's determination to give God his due was evident very early in his life: the drama of his vocational discernment was the drama of a just man who, despite his own prior plans and preferences, sought to render under God what was God's in his life—which turned out to be his entire life. Put another way, Karol Józef Wojtyła emulated one of his heavenly patrons, St. Joseph, by living from his early twenties on as if God, not he, were in charge of his life. He was not falsely humble and knew himself to be a man of considerable talent. But he wore that knowledge very lightly indeed, and over the course of his life stripped himself of ego so that he might be even more just in rendering to God what was God's.

As to giving his neighbor his or her due, Wojtyła's great capacity for friendship, and the time and energy he invested in others, testified to his determination to live justly in his relationships with others. Everyone who ever worked for, or with, him remarked on his probity, his fairness, and his seemingly inexhaustible capacity to let others have their say. He was a man of his word who kept his promises to the end, even when doing so cost him aggravation, even personal pain. In this respect, he was a true son of his father, whose granitelike integrity and manly piety were a great paternal lesson in justice.

As with prudence, Karol Wojtyła's faults in this sphere were the defects of his virtues. He could be too trusting of those in whom he had reposed confidence, or to whom he had entrusted positions of responsibility. His determination to be fair sometimes led him to misread the urgency of situations requiring immediate discipline. His loathing for communist injustice (displayed, for example, in the use of sexual innuendo to destroy a man's reputation), his determination never to behave like that, and his difficulty in comprehending how men could so betray the grace and gift of the priesthood and the episcopate were factors in what seemed to some to be his slow reaction to the Long Lent of 2002 in the United States, and to charges of clerical sexual misconduct elsewhere; yet it should also be noted that, when presented with clear evidence of priestly or episcopal malfeasance, he acted.

Karol Wojtyła was also a man committed to the cause of justice in society. Unlike others who had endured lethal injustice in their youth, he did not become a cynic about politics, but held firmly to the belief that the exercise of political power could be bent to the norms of social justice. His approach to questions of the right ordering of society was informed by the social doctrine of the Church, but it was just as profoundly shaped by his pastoral experience. When discussing postcommunist Poland with

prime minister Hanna Suchocka in the years immediately following the "shock therapy" that had been
applied to the moribund Polish economy, his first
concerns were not about systems, but about people:
"How are people handling the transition [to a market
economy]?" he asked. "How do you find the social
element in the free market system? What happens to
the people who can't fit in?" Thus, for John Paul II,
"solidarity was a value," a manifestation of justice,
"not just a movement."[46]

Courage

Yugoslavian dissident Milovan Djilas, who remained
committed to the idea of communism but broke
with Tito over the latter's brutal authoritarianism,
was much impressed by John Paul II; and what most
impressed him, he once said, was Karol Wojtyła's
utter fearlessness.

Yet Karol Wojtyła did not live without fear; still
less did he deny fear. Rather, he lived beyond fear,
and his courage was an expression (in his human
virtues) of his faith. Because he believed that all the
world's fear had been taken by the Son to the cross
and offered to the Father in an act of perfect obedience, and because he also believed that the Father
had given his answer to that radical act of self-giving
love by raising the Son from the dead, he believed
that the disciples of the Son could face fear and then

live courageously beyond its stifling grasp. That was how he lived under Nazi occupation. That was how he lived under communism. That was the courage with which he faced down his own fears of the burdens of the papacy, when the call came to him on October 16, 1978. And those convictions about the cross and resurrection were the source of the fearlessness with which he faced down both a Sandinista mob and General Wojciech Jaruzelski in the space of four dramatic months in 1983.

Wojtyła's courage was the source of several of his other notable personal characteristics, including his remarkable patience with people and with situations: if God were truly in charge of history, as he believed, then he ought to prudently and courageously wait in patience for a person or a situation to mature. His courage also informed the serenity with which he accepted physical suffering, which was increasingly his lot in the last decade of his life. Those who were with him at the Policlinico Gemelli in February and March 2005 uniformly commented on his remarkable patience with his wrecked body; that patience was not stoic, but Christian, and it was the fruit of the kind of fearlessness that led him to embrace, mutely, the crucifix on the last Good Friday of his life.

His courage also expressed itself in his willingness to bear spiritual and mental suffering as an inescapable part of his vocation. He lived through dark nights, including the hard summer and fall of 2003.

Months like that, however, were the most dramatic manifestations of the spiritual suffering that is part and parcel of being the successor of Peter who, like Peter himself, is inevitably bound and led where he does not want to go (as the Risen Christ warned Peter in John 21.18). That forbidding land where a pope may not want to go, but must, includes a terrain marked by quotidian human suffering, of which John Paul was daily aware from the prayer petitions the household sisters put into the prie-dieu where he spent his solitary hour or ninety minutes with the Lord, every morning; but it also includes the even harsher terrain of evil writ large—knowledge of the world's wickedness, news of which floods the Vatican daily; knowledge of the Evil One at work in the Church, news of which also inexorably finds its way to the papal apartment. No one who has not borne the burden of knowledge the papacy brings a man can fully understand how crushing that burden must be; novelist Morris West once wrote that "the man who wore the Fisherman's ring . . . carried . . . the sins of the world like a leaden cope on his shoulders."[47] West might just as well have added the sins of the Church's sons and daughters. The grace with which John Paul wore that invisible, leaden cope is perhaps the greatest testimony to his courage—and to the source of that courage in his embrace of the drama of Calvary as it replayed itself in his own life.

Moderation

In early 1995, John Paul II replied to a letter in which a correspondent had suggested that the "hermeneutics of suspicion" informing so much contemporary biblical exegesis, history, biography, and theology—the methodological assumption that things can't be what they seem to be, or have been thought to be—seemed to be receding a bit. While noting that this analysis struck him as "more optimistic than [what] one usually reads," the Pope went on to observe that, in the currents of history (including the history of ideas), "it is the 'turning point' that is the most important, as when a train enters a switch where an inch decides its future direction."[48] It was the observation of a temperate man: a man who had mastered his passions, found a "balance in the use of created goods," and kept "desires within the limits of what is honorable" (as the **Catechism of the Catholic Church** puts it, explaining the cardinal virtue of temperance).[49] John Paul II did not demand the impossible, but he was willing to test and stretch the limits of what others considered possible.

In the more conventional meaning of the virtue of temperance or moderation, Karol Wojtyła was a man of temperate habits and lifestyle. He worked very hard, and his work was both steady and productive; even in his seventies, the hours he put into a day's work would have staggered younger men. Yet he also knew how to pace himself, both when working and in taking breaks from work, and he had the good (and temperate) sense to take holidays in order to renew himself physically as well as spiritually. His asceticism was obvious, in that he cared nothing for material things, but it was never oppressive and it was never imposed on others. He lived a life of evangelical poverty, often gave away what was given to him as a priest and bishop, and conducted his papacy with as much material simplicity as circumstances permitted. He practiced various forms of spiritual discipline, including forms of physical mortification; in his later years, the constant rhythm of his prayer and meditation were the principle expressions of his balanced spiritual life.

His temperance was also evident in his modesty and his obedience. He had absolutely no interest in ecclesiastical honors or preferment. By all accounts he was an obedient son, seminarian, and priest. He bent his own will to that of Archbishop Baziak in the matter of his habilitation thesis, as he bent his will to that of Cardinal Wyszyński and Pope Pius XII in accepting his nomination as auxiliary bishop of Kraków. He raised up other men of quality, such as Bishop Jan Pietraszko (one of his auxiliary bishops), whom a less temperate and less just superior might have regarded as a rival and thus a threat. As his challenging sermon on the death of John Paul I indicated, he had no desire to be pope, knowing as he did that the papacy demanded of a man an even more complete emptying of self; he accepted his election in obedience to what he believed to be the will of God, manifest through the decision of the College of Cardinals.[50]

Karol Wojtyła's moderation was also displayed in his manner of governance. He did not evade his own responsibilities, but throughout his years as archbishop of Kraków he led a genuinely collaborative effort, in which the opinions and concerns of priests and laity were regularly sought. To the aggravation of some of his Cracovian associates, he was exceptionally patient in building a consensus among the relevant leaders of the archdiocese before initiating a new pastoral initiative. He tried to apply the same model of collaborative discernment and governance to his responsibilities as pope, making extensive use of both the Synod of Bishops and the College of Cardinals for thrashing out problems and seeking collaborative solutions. It may be doubted whether the results of these collaborative efforts in Rome were as measurable as they had been in Kraków. But if the results were not what he might have wished, it was not for a lack of effort on the part of John Paul II—who was also prepared to take the lead when it became clear (as with the planning for the Great Jubilee of 2000) that others simply lacked the vision to see the possibilities he saw.

The Crux of the Drama

Gaudium et Spes, the Pastoral Constitution on the Church in the Modern World, is thought to be the most positive of Vatican II's analyses of the human condition, brimful of optimism about the possibilities that humanity's coming of age have set before the world of politics, economics, science, and culture. Yet at the very beginning of the pastoral constitution's discussion of the ways in which human creativity shapes the world and history, the Council saw fit to insert a striking caution:

> The whole of man's history has been the story of arduous combat with the powers of evil, stretching, so our Lord tells us, from the very dawn of history until the last day. Finding himself in the midst of the battlefield, man has to struggle to do what is right, and it is at great cost to himself, and aided by God's grace, that he succeeds in achieving his own inner integrity.[51]

Karol Wojtyła was a combatant on that battlefield for decades, and his experiences in spiritual warfare undoubtedly shaped his interior life—even as the richness of that interior life helped him cope with challenges from the powers of evil that could be as great as the other challenges of the office to which he ultimately rose. For as John Paul II wrote in the

1995 encyclical **Evangelium Vitae** [The Gospel of Life], **"life is always at the center of a great struggle** between good and evil, light and darkness" in which "the powers of evil" conduct an ongoing and "insidious opposition" to all that is good, true, and beautiful.[52]

In reckoning with this dimension of Karol Wojtyła's interior life, it is important to grasp that, for him, "powers of evil" was not a metaphor drawn from the allegedly primitive world of biblical religion to express what would now be analyzed in scientific or psychiatric terms. He did not understand the evil he experienced, and rejected, in the anti-Semitism of the late 1930s as merely a matter of the accumulated prejudices of centuries; it was a work of the Evil One, determined to undermine the covenant and to distort the history of salvation.[53] The same was true of the evil at work in a man like Hans Frank, the thuggish bureaucrat who ruled the Nazi-occupied rump of Poland from Wawel Castle, or the evil at work in Polish communism that led to the murder of heroes such as Witold Pilecki and Jerzy Popiełuszko. To miss the dimension of spiritual warfare in the human struggle with good and evil, he was convinced, was to miss the depth of the drama being played out.

During the Great Jubilee of 2000, the power of the Evil One displayed itself before the Pope and a shocked Stanisław Dziwisz during the September 6 papal general audience. Dziwisz, as he later recounted, had once thought that what tradition referred to as demonic possession was really a psychiatric matter; but his experiences with John Paul II convinced him otherwise, and none more so than the Pope's encounter with a nineteen-year-old Italian girl who began shouting uncontrollably after John Paul had given his blessing at the end of the September 6, 2000, general audience. The police were unable to control the young woman, who also screamed curses at Bishop Gianni Danzi, then an official of the government of Vatican City. Danzi informed Dziwisz, who arranged for the Pope to see the girl in a private area after John Paul had completed his Popemobile **giro,** or drive around St. Peter's Square. John Paul II prayed with her for a half hour and promised that he would offer his Mass for her the following day so that she would be freed of her possession. Dziwisz later said he was convinced that "Satan was at work" in the young woman, whose demeanor "changed completely" at the Pope's promise of a Mass offered for her healing; before that, Dziwisz recalled, "you could see Hell destroying someone."[54]

News sources at the time referred to at least two other exorcisms attributed to John Paul II. One, at the beginning of the pontificate, was performed at the request of Father Candido Amantini, a Roman exorcist. The other, in March 1982, was witnessed by the prefect of the papal household, Bishop Jacques Martin, and involved a young woman named Francesca who later returned to the Vatican to thank

John Paul.[55] However one judges the various factors at work in these cases—and it is striking that some who were once skeptical of the very idea of demonic possession changed their minds after witnessing these dramatic encounters with the "powers of evil"—it seems clear that Karol Wojtyła, the man who had sworn to follow the Curé of Ars, St. John Vianney, and make himself as a priest into a "prisoner of the confessional," was a man through whom the divine grace of spiritual healing worked for decades, both sacramentally (in his administration of absolution) and in sometimes more dramatic circumstances.

He was a vessel of healing power in other ways, too. Without presuming to make the judgment, which only the Church can make, that John Paul II was the occasion of miraculous cures during his life, one can only note that there were, as Stanisław Dziwisz once put it, "lots of these things," in the sense of reported cures and healings.[56] After John Paul's second pilgrimage to Mexico in May 1990, Javier Lozano Barragán, the bishop of Zacatecas, sent the Vatican documentation on the cure of a young man during the Pope's visit. The same could happen after papal audiences: a pastor from Trent came once with his sister, who had cervical cancer, and returned weeks later to report that the cancer had disappeared; a man walking with crutches and wearing the icon of divine mercy was blessed by the Pope and returned two weeks later without the crutches, walking quite normally. Childless couples would write the Pope, asking for his prayer that they might conceive a child; pregnancies would follow. When approached directly by a sick person asking his help, Dziwisz recalled, John Paul II would always draw the petitioner into the orbit of his own interior life, saying, "We will pray **together** for this intention."[57]

As the Catholic Church understands these things, these two delicate matters—reported exorcisms and reported cures by John Paul II during his lifetime—were related. The power of the Evil One, the **Catechism of the Catholic Church**, teaches, "is . . . not infinite. [Satan] is only a creature, powerful from the fact that he is pure spirit, but still a creature. He cannot prevent the building up of God's reign."[58] Karol Wojtyła believed that. He also believed that the problem of evil, which has vexed believers and unbelievers alike for millennia, comes into clear focus only by contemplating the face of Christ, the conqueror of evil who reveals the superabundance of God's grace, a grace that can thwart the designs of the Evil One and shake his grip on fragile human souls.[59] That grace often works through secondary human instruments; the mature believer opens himself or herself to the workings of that grace so that it might touch the lives of others, gently or dramatically. Whether becoming such a vessel of grace involves what tradition calls extraordinary spiritual gifts is a judgment for the Church, not the individual, to make. What is important in life is to hold oneself open to the effects of the redemption working through the earthen vessels of our humanity.

In its discussion of the "scandal" of evil, the **Catechism** issued by John Paul II notes, with emphasis, that **"there is not a single aspect of the Christian message that is not in part an answer to the question of evil."**[60] A man of Christian joy and hope, convinced that humanity had the capacity, under grace, to construct a better future, Karol Wojtyła nonetheless spent more than eighty years wrestling with the problem of evil, and with the Evil One. Perhaps the densest theological reflection in his voluminous magisterium, the 1986 encyclical on the Holy Spirit, **Dominum et Vivificantem** [Lord and Giver of Life], discusses at some length what the Gospel of John describes as "the sin of the world" (John 1.29)—the fact that the human condition, marked by original sin and by the effects of millennia of human sinfulness, is always shaped by falsehood and by **"the rejection of the gift and the love"** by which God created the world and the human family.[61] The Holy Spirit "convicts" the world of this sin, John Paul writes; the Church, which is born from the outpouring of the Spirit's spiritual gifts, must constantly point the world and humanity toward the "Lamb of God who takes away the sin of the world," as John the Baptist put it.

Thus the interior life of Karol Wojtyła, Pope John Paul II, once again displays itself as cruciform. That interior life was built on the foundation of the conviction that it is on the cross, where the Lamb of God takes upon himself the sin of the world, that the world's redemption is achieved and the answer to the problem of evil is given: for the cross is the necessary passover toward the resurrection, which is God's final and definitive answer to the scandal of evil. The young boy who had walked the trails of Kalwaria Zebrzydowska with his father grew into the priest and bishop who, on the last Good Friday of his life, embraced the crucified Christ as his own life was ebbing away. It was all of a piece. Karol Wojtyła was a man of Easter, who fully understood that Easter comes after Good Friday, that eternal life is promised to those who make their lives into a gift to others here and now, and that such radical self-giving—such metanoia—is only possible through the grace of God in Christ.

CHAPTER ELEVEN

The Measure of a Pontificate

When Karol Józef Wojtyła was elected to the Chair of Peter on October 16, 1978, there were serious questions as to whether any man could successfully carry out the Petrine ministry under the conditions of late modernity.

At his election to the papacy fifteen years before, Giovanni Battista Montini seemed perfectly prepared to be a successful pope: he was an Italian of deep piety and a good family, learned and gifted in languages, with broad cultural interests and the appropriate political contacts and sensibilities, a man who had enjoyed a successful career in both the Roman Curia and a major Italian diocese. Yet it hadn't worked out that way; not at all. The contentiousness of post–Vatican II Catholicism turned the papacy into a decade-and-a-half-long crucifixion for Paul VI; the Church suffered accordingly from what struck many as a deficit of evangelical energy and vigorous leadership in the Holy See. No one doubted Pope Paul's personal holiness, his integrity, or his deep love for the Church. But in the mid-1970s things seemed adrift and the question inevitably arose among thoughtful Catholics: Can **anyone** do this anymore?

It was an unexpected question. For in one of the great surprises of modern history, the papacy inherited by Paul VI in 1963 had made a dramatic recovery from its historic nadir, at least insofar as the second millennium of Christian history goes. In 1799, Pius VI, kidnapped by the armies of revolutionary France the year before, died far from Rome, a prisoner in the citadel at Valence; at his death, historian J. N. D. Kelly notes, "many assumed that the destruction of the Holy See had at last been accomplished."[1] Seventy years later, that verdict seemed decisively confirmed when the new Kingdom of Italy conquered Rome, put an end to the Papal States (which the popes had governed since the mid-eighth century), and reduced the pope to being **il prigioniero del Vaticano** [the prisoner of the Vatican], as Pius IX described himself.

Yet in the paradoxes of history the loss of the Papal States liberated Pius IX's successors for a new role: the pope as universal moral teacher and witness. The outlines of this evangelical form of papacy were defined by Pius IX's immediate successor, Leo XIII, who initiated an internal intellectual reform of the Church while engaging the new politics and economics of modernity through the novelty of what came to be called Catholic social doctrine. The path to a revival of papal influence was neither straight nor easy: Leo's second successor, Benedict XV, who virtually bankrupted the Holy See providing aid to refugees and prisoners of war during World War I, was denied a role in the postwar deliberations at Versailles by the victorious Great Powers. But Benedict's successor, Pius XI, was a fierce foe of both fascist and communist totalitarianism and a man to be reckoned with in the politics of Europe. So was his successor, Pius XII. In his brief pontificate, Pius XII's successor, John XXIII, became a kind of universal paterfamilias, beloved by millions for his pastoral charity, ecumenical goodwill, and interreligious openness. The papacy, it seemed, had made a remarkable comeback. And if popes no longer ruled substantial territories as sovereigns among the sovereigns of Europe, the popes of the mid-twentieth century had nonetheless carved out a new territory within which to exercise considerable sway—the consciences of men and women, where the power of argument and persuasion was key.

Then came the pontificate of Paul VI, during which the Catholic Church seemed to tear itself apart in a bitter theological and disciplinary civil war—the last thing John XXIII, who believed that Vatican II could ignite a new Pentecost, expected from his Council. Curiously, though, the future Pope Paul VI worried that an ecclesiastical implosion was possible and perhaps even likely, given the amount of dry tinder at hand: on the night of January 25, 1959, hours after John XXIII had stunned the Church and the world by announcing his intention to summon history's twenty-first ecumenical council, Montini telephoned a friend and said, of John XXIII and his plans, "This holy old boy doesn't know what a hornet's nest he's stirring up."[2] The instinct was prescient; no doubt Paul VI had many occasions to remember it as he strove to bring the Council to a successful end after John XXIII's death in 1963, and then see to its proper implementation. Yet while Paul VI steered the sometimes balky Council to its conclusion, his efforts to implement Vatican II while maintaining the integrity of doctrine and the unity of the Church were frequently frustrated. Thus by 1978, the Catholic Church was fractious and embittered, adrift in Rome and in turmoil throughout the world.

At a moment, then, when the papacy seemed to be in its deepest crisis since Pius VI's death in exile, the College of Cardinals, shocked by the wholly unanticipated death of Pope John Paul I after a thirty-three-day pontificate, turned to a man who had not followed a conventional pre-papal career path but who came to the Office of Peter as one called from a far country—not unlike Peter himself. Yet for all the surprise registered at the election of the first non-Italian pope in 455 years and the first Slavic pope ever, Karol Wojtyła brought to the papacy certain qualities that ought to have suggested the possibility of a pontificate of great consequence.

He had inherited a heroic concept of the bishop's office from the unbroken prince, Adam Stefan Sapieha. He came to Rome after twenty years of experience as a successful diocesan bishop in Kraków, where he had led the kind of imaginative and unifying implementation of Vatican II that had eluded so many of his brother bishops around the world. He had a well-honed intelligence, firmly grounded in the realism of Aristotle and Aquinas, and was thus convinced that human beings could grasp the truth of things, including the moral truth of things; he had also engaged for a quarter century in an open, robust dialogue with some of the most adventurous intellectual currents in contemporary culture. He had shown himself a formidable foe of communism, but not in defense of the old European social order; rather, he preached a different and challenging form of human liberation. He insisted on maintaining close contact with lay friends during his episcopate and thus knew the lives of the men and women of modernity from the inside. He had developed into a compelling public personality, bringing to his defense of human rights some of the skills he had learned from two of his early masters in the arts of the theater, Mieczysław Kotlarczyk and Juliusz Osterwa; yet even as he was testing Kotlarczyk's convictions about the power of the "living word" of truth to cut through the static of communist lies, he was refining his public rhetoric so that it touched the hearts and minds of ordinary men and women.

Perhaps most important, he brought to his pontificate a profound conviction that the trajectory of his life was being guided by divine providence: that, as he often put it, if the Holy Spirit had seen fit to call the archbishop of Kraków to be the Bishop of Rome, then that **must** mean that there had been something in the experience of Kraków—and the experience of Karol Wojtyła as its archbishop—that would be of use to the universal Church.

He came to the papacy an outsider. And despite the warmth with which he would be adopted by the people of Rome and the people of Italy, he remained something of an outsider to the end, at least in terms of the ways of the Vatican and the traditional managers of popes. He died in a glow of virtually universal admiration and affection, and his death was felt keenly by many of those, from Italy and around the world, with whom he had worked closely. Yet almost all those at his deathbed were Poles, fellow exiles, keeping vigil with the man who had come from a far country and who would be buried in his adopted land, rather than at home.

For all that difference of career path and culture, Karol Wojtyła, Pope John Paul II, created the most consequential pontificate in centuries—one whose impress will be felt on both the Church and the world for centuries to come. It was not a pontificate without flaws, for no pontificate ever is and none ever could be. But that John Paul's was a pontificate of exceptional consequence, not even his harshest critics can deny.

THE RECORD

The accomplishments of Pope John Paul II—as well as those accomplishments that eluded him—cannot be properly assessed statistically. Nonetheless the statistics do convey something of the magnitude of his effort and the breadth of his reach into the worlds-within-worlds of humanity.

The pontificate unfolded over 9,665 days, making John Paul the second-longest-serving pope in recorded history after Pius IX (and the third-longest-serving pope after Peter, whose tenure is remembered by tradition as encompassing either thirty-four or thirty-seven years).

In the course of fulfilling the Petrine mandate to "strengthen your brethren," Pope John Paul II went on pilgrimage to 129 different countries on 104 apostolic voyages, traveling 1,247,613 kilometers (approximately 750,000 miles), the equivalent of circumnavigating the globe more than thirty times or traveling more than three times between the Earth and the Moon. The Pope was outside of Rome for 822 days (or 8.7 percent) of the pontificate, during which he visited 1,022 cities and delivered 3,288 prepared discourses. In addition, John Paul made 146 visits within Italy itself, not counting 748 visits within the Diocese of Rome or to Castel Gandolfo, in the course of which he met with all but 16 of Rome's 336 parishes.

Determined to remain a priest and bishop, John Paul baptized 1,501 new Christians during his pontificate and personally ordained hundreds of new priests and bishops.

His magisterium, collected in the **Insegnamenti di Giovanni Paolo II**, fills 56 large folio volumes and covers almost a dozen linear feet of library shelf space: 14 encyclicals, 15 apostolic exhortations, 12 apostolic constitutions, 45 apostolic letters, and thousands of other letters, messages, speeches, homilies, audience addresses, and addresses at the weekly Angelus or Regina Coeli. John Paul held 1,164 general audiences, attended by 17,665,800 people from around the world, in addition to some 1,600 meetings with heads of state, heads of government, and other political figures.

John Paul II beatified 1,338 Servants of God (including 1,032 martyrs) in 147 beatification ceremonies, while canonizing 482 new saints (of whom 402 were martyrs) in 51 canonization Masses; previous popes had canonized 302 saints since Pope Sixtus V regularized the process in 1588.

He had far more extensive and regular contact with his brother bishops than did any of his papal predecessors. He received thousands of bishops individually during their quinquennial **ad limina** visits to Rome and for years devoted as much as 40 percent of his public schedule to these meetings. He presided over six ordinary general assemblies, one extraordinary general assembly, and seven special assemblies of the Synod of Bishops, in addition to a "particular synod" to address the challenges facing the Church in the Netherlands—thus devoting, in the aggregate, at least a year of his pontificate to the world's bishops gathered in synod. He held nine ordinary consistories during which he created 231 new cardinals, and summoned six plenary assemblies (or extraordinary consistories) of the College of Cardinals to seek advice and make pastoral plans for the future.

Keenly aware of the rhythms of time and the importance of anniversaries in the Church's life, John Paul II led nine "dedicated years" during the twenty-six and a half years of his pontificate: the Holy Year of the Redemption in 1983–84, the Marian Year in 1987–88, the Year of the Family in 1993–94, the three Trinitarian years of preparation for the Great Jubilee of 2000, the Great Jubilee itself, the Year of the Rosary in 2002–3, and the Year of the Eucharist, which began on October 17, 2004, and concluded six months after the Pope's death.

And then there were the international World Youth Days. John Paul II presided over nine of them: in Rome (1985 and 2000), Buenos Aires (1987), Santiago de Compostela (1989), Częstochowa (1991), Denver (1993), Manila (1995), Paris (1997), and Toronto (2002). Total attendance at these signature events of the pontificate was in the tens of millions, with the closing Mass in Manila in 1995 drawing what was then reported to be the largest crowd in history, some five million people—a record Mexico City claimed to have topped during the papal visit of 2002.[3]

Whatever the precise numbers, it seems beyond dispute that Karol Wojtyła was seen in person by more human beings than any man in history; given the multiplier effects of the world communications revolution, it was a very remote and isolated part of the world that had not encountered Pope John Paul II, in person or through the media, between 1978 and 2005. That the most visible man in the history of the world should have been a man living in late modernity was not a surprise. That the most visible man in history was one who understood himself primarily as a Christian disciple and evangelist—that was one of the great surprises of late modernity, and suggested that more was going on in the modern world and the postmodern world than those worlds typically imagined.

ENDURING ACCOMPLISHMENT

The full measure of a pontificate and its achievements can come only with the passage of centuries. At the death of Pius V in 1572, no one knew whether his efforts to implement the Council of Trent would succeed, such that he would be remembered as a great reforming pope rather than another would-be reformer who failed. As things turned out, his work left an impress on the Church for centuries. In that respect, the full measure of the accomplishments of Pope John Paul II—and of the things he failed to accomplish—can only be taken in centuries to come. Yet the universal outpouring of sympathy and gratitude at his death suggested that large parts of the world had already rendered a verdict: this was a great man and a great pope, whose greatness came from his ability to summon men and women to a nobler vision of their own possibilities, under the grace of God. Years after his death, people around the world talked of having met him, having seen him, having been touched by him physically or spiritually. His place was secure in the hearts of perhaps billions of human beings; his memory would be cherished for generations.

But what of his achievement as pope? Even conceding the impenetrability of the future, it seemed in the aftermath of his death that he had indeed left a considerable legacy of accomplishment.

The Evangelical Papacy

John Paul II recast the Office of Peter for the twenty-first century and the third millennium of Christian history by sharpening its evangelical edge and giving the papal **munus docendi**, or teaching office, a genuinely global reach.

He did this through a classic Catholic method of reform: knowing that all true reform in the Church is a return to the form, or essential constitution, given to the Church by Christ, John Paul retrieved elements of the Office of Peter that had become muted over time and made those elements the materials for a renewal of the papal mission. The retrieval looked back to the New Testament, where Peter is a witness to the resurrection, the Church's first great preacher, the apostle who makes the initial outreach to the Gentiles, and a focal point of the Church's unity; the renewal involved bringing these elements of the Petrine office to the world through a deliberate and disciplined exploitation of the possibilities created by modern communications and transportation.[4]

As Peter had gone from his native Capernaum to Jerusalem, and thence to Antioch and Rome, Karol Wojtyła, called from Kraków to Rome, went from Rome quite literally to the ends of the earth, witnessing to God's love for humanity displayed in the life, death, and resurrection of Jesus Christ—and revitalizing the papacy as an office of evangelical consequence in the process.

The Young. Some of the most dramatic effects of this evangelical form of papacy were evident in John Paul II's impact on the young. In 1978, very few senior churchmen believed that Catholicism could reach the restless and affluent young adults of the developed world. On the basis of thirty years of pastoral experience with young people, Karol Wojtyła believed that, notwithstanding obvious cultural differences, there was a universality to the human experience of adolescence and young adulthood—a universality summed up, as he often put it, in the quest for a pure love. Put the challenge of that quest before the youth of the world, he was convinced, and they would respond.

The response he drew (which confounded all expectations, except perhaps his own) was often misunderstood as a matter of celebrity fever among impressionable youngsters. There was no doubt an element of that involved, but there was much more. In a world that pandered to the young in advertising, modes of dress and language, and lifestyle, John Paul II did not pander. His challenge to live a life of heroic virtue stirred young hearts and minds in a way that few of his associates anticipated. The challenge was credible, however, because of the life of the man who issued it. The young have very good instincts for hypocrisy and respond accordingly; and it was manifestly clear at World Youth Days and in other venues that John Paul II did not ask of his young followers anything that he had not asked of himself. The integrity of his own life—particularly his ability to live through suffering without becoming embittered and cynical—was immensely attractive across the spectrum of the world's youth. In a world often bereft of paternity, he lived the strong love and challenge of genuine fatherhood, and the youth of the world responded.

Divine Mercy. One of the Pope's favorite metaphors for the Church's situation at the turn into the third millennium of its history was the apostle Paul's attempt to catechize the cynics of ancient Athens on the Areopagus, by appealing to the Athenians' putative reverence for "an unknown god" (see Acts 17.16–34). And on the Areopagus of the late modern world, as the Pope put it in the 1990 encyclical, **Redemptoris Missio** [The Mission of the Redeemer], "the Church proposes; she imposes nothing."[5] Over the course of twenty-six and a half years of papal teaching, John Paul II proposed many truths to the world. One of the foremost among them, in his view, was the message of divine mercy.

This emphasis was sometimes thought an idiosyncracy of Karol Wojtyła's Polish, and specifically Cracovian, roots. In fact, here was another example of Wojtyła's conviction that the Church's experience in Kraków had something to offer the universal Church. For Wojtyła brought to the papacy a profound understanding of the guilt and anxiety that lay over the late twentieth century like a thick fog: the psychic and spiritual by-products of the slaughters of World Wars I and II, the mass murders of the Gulag, the Holocaust, the Ukrainian terror famine, Mao's Great Leap Forward, and so on. To whom could that guilt be confessed, and thus expiated? Who could relieve the anxiety of a world cracking under the pressure of the knowledge that it had the capacity to destroy itself—and just might be wicked enough to do so?

The divine mercy, manifest in God the Father of mercies, was thus an element of the Christian kerygma, or proclamation, that was of consequence far beyond Kraków and Poland. To proclaim the compassion of the Father who welcomes home his prodigal children and restores to them the dignity they have squandered was to meet a universal human need, after a century in which humanity had turned its creations upon itself and turned the world into a slaughterhouse in the process. That was why John Paul II, the evangelical pope, made divine mercy one of the focal points of his teaching: in the 1980 encyclical, **Dives in Misericordia** [Rich in Mercy]; in lifting up the healing riches of sacramental confession and penitential practice in the 1984 post-synodal apostolic exhortation, **Reconciliatio et Paenitentia** [Reconciliation and Penance]; in beatifying Sister Faustyna in 1993 and making her the first saint of the new millennium in 2000; and by decreeing that the Octave of Easter should be celebrated throughout the Church as Divine Mercy Sunday. That the Divine Mercy devotion outlined by Saint Faustyna Kowalska became, during the pontificate of John Paul II, a means for the recovery of devotional life in Catholic parishes throughout the world suggested that John Paul II's pastoral intuitions about the imperative of the Church's preaching God's mercy at the turn into a new millennium were squarely on target.

Italy. The evangelical tenor of John Paul II's papacy had a marked effect on the Church's position in Italy. No pope in centuries put more time and effort into living out his titles as Bishop of Rome and Primate of Italy than the pope who had come to Rome from the Slav lands in central Europe. Those efforts bore fruit over time, as the Catholic Church in Italy got itself out of a defensive crouch, with its every initiative being defined "against" the political Left and secular culture, and engaged in a more robust, Gospel-centered proposal to Italian hearts and minds, and to Italian culture. At the same time, John Paul changed Italian high culture's view of the Church, which had been reactively dismissive and anticlerical for decades.[6]

These effects could not have been predicted on October 16, 1978; in fact, much of the Italian Church deeply resented the "loss" of the papacy, which remained Italy's premier claim to some prominence in the world. Attitudes changed, however, as Italians saw their primate expend enormous energies in bringing what he would come to call "the new evangelization" directly and personally to them. One turning point came in 1985, when the Pope held a national meeting with the Church of Italy at the shrine of Loreto. There, John Paul challenged Italian Catholicism to recognize that it was no longer possible to transmit the faith by cultural osmosis. The Church had to reimagine itself as robustly evangelical and culturally assertive, engage modernity without surrendering to it, and confront the default secularism of Italian high culture with a nobler vision of the modern world and its possibilities.

This culture-first approach to the Church's public role was difficult to grasp for many Italian bishops, who imagined that the drift toward secularism was inevitable, that the Church could not change the inexorable tides of history, and that political accommodation to an ascendant Italian Left was imperative. A pope from a "fighting Church" (as Cardinal Camillo Ruini once described Wojtyła's background) was in a strong position to challenge such premature surrender, and to do so, not by evoking the alleged glories of the ancien régime (about which Karol Wojtyła was very skeptical), but by invoking the abiding power of the Gospel to change lives, and thus change cultures and societies. Over time, this approach showed itself capable of rallying Catholics (whose practice of their faith increased in Italy during John Paul's pontificate) and attracting the interest of secular intellectuals such as Giuliano Ferrara and Marcello Pera: men who understood that the question of the dignity of the human person had moved to the center of the post–Cold War debate, and that the Catholic Church was the premier institutional barrier to the triumph of a soul-withering and dehumanizing utilitarianism.[7]

Global Witness. John Paul's culture-first approach to public affairs, which was rooted in both his understanding of the dynamics of history and his concept of the evangelical papacy, reshaped world politics on at least two occasions—beyond, of course, his impact on what became the Revolution of 1989 in central and eastern Europe.

The first was in 1994, when the Pope almost singlehandedly derailed the plans of the Clinton administration and the U.S. government to have abortion on demand declared a universal human right, akin to religious freedom and freedom of the press, at the Cairo World Conference on Population and Development. John Paul went over the heads of the world's leaders to make a direct appeal to the peoples of the world to resist any such declaration, using the megaphone of the papacy to bring to light what the Clinton administration and its allies in the United

Nations population control bureaucracy preferred to keep hidden. That public witness, as well as some adroit Holy See diplomacy at Cairo, frustrated what seemed to be a certain victory for the pro-abortion forces.[8]

Then there was the Fourth World Conference on Women, held in Beijing in September 1995, where the forces that had been defeated at Cairo attempted a comeback. John Paul II once again took to the world stage, using more than a dozen audience addresses and a **Letter to Women** to lay out a distinctive feminism that did not reduce women to simulacra of men. He also broke all precedent by naming Harvard law professor Mary Ann Glendon, an expert on comparative family law and international human rights law, as head of the Vatican delegation to the conference. The results at Beijing were mixed, but the population controllers' effort to get abortion defined as a universal human right was thwarted, even as the Vatican delegation—whose most visible members were highly accomplished professional woman and mothers—proposed ways of supporting women's struggle for equality and opportunity that addressed the concerns of most of the world's women (and especially women in the developing world), rather than what was proposed in the ideological feminism of the conference's UN sponsors.[9] Once again in the pontificate of John Paul II, evangelical witness had trumped conventional diplomatic practice, and with notable results.

Vatican II: Keys to a New Pentecost

When John Paul II assumed the papacy in 1978, the Second Vatican Council, which had concluded less than thirteen years before, seemed almost a dead letter. One faction in the Church, appealing to a "spirit of Vatican II," made little reference to the Council's actual documents while arguing that the Council marked a deliberate rupture with a Catholic past too beholden to tradition. Yet another faction thought the Council a terrible mistake, best forgotten quickly in order to effect what some frankly called a "Catholic restoration." The four years of Vatican II had been a decisive personal and theological experience for Karol Wojtyła; neither rupture, leading to revolution, nor retrenchment, leading to the restoration of a mythical Catholic golden age, struck him as an appropriate response to what had seemed, during the heady Council years of 1962–65, the most important Catholic event since the sixteenth-century Council of Trent. Thus Wojtyła came to the papacy determined to make the full implementation of Vatican II his program, a commitment he announced at the outset of his pontificate.

The Second Vatican Council was unique in that, unlike previous councils, it did not provide keys to its own interpretation—canons, creeds, anathemas, and so forth. Thus the crux of the problem of the full implementation of Vatican II lay in a basic question of interpretation: Was the Council indeed a moment of rupture, after which virtually any innovation was conceivable, or were its reforms to be understood in light of the Church's two millennia of tradition? That question was given a decisive answer at the Extraordinary Assembly of the Synod of Bishops that John Paul II summoned in 1985: the Second Vatican Council was to be understood in terms of continuity—that is, reform through retrieval and renewal.[10] To underscore that answer, the Extraordinary Synod commissioned the **Catechism of the Catholic Church**, in which the approach to Christian faith and practice outlined at Vatican II was located within the full theological and spiritual tradition of the Catholic Church. Published in 1992, the **Catechism** was also an important statement to make on the edge of the third millennium (a threshold never far from the Pope's mind); for at the end of 2,000 years of Christian history, it was necessary for the Church to demonstrate that it could still give a coherent, comprehensive, compelling account of its faith, its hope, and its love. That was part of what it meant to be a Church that proposes, rather than imposes.

The Eastern Catholic Churches. The full implementation of Vatican II required addressing vexing questions of the relations among the various component parts of the Church. One of those questions involved the position of the Eastern Catholic Churches, Byzantine in liturgy and polity but in full communion with the Bishop of Rome. Curial officials tended to see the Catholic Churches of the East as exotic curiosities (and rather second-class curiosities at that); papal diplomats and ecumenists dealing with the Orthodox Churches found the Eastern Catholic Churches an embarrassment at best and a continuing source of conflict at worst. By sharp contrast, Karol Wojtyła brought to the papacy a deep respect for these distinctive Catholic communities, including the most turbulent of them, the Greek Catholic Church in Ukraine. John Paul II's steadfast support for the independence of the Greek Catholics of Ukraine throughout his pontificate was an expression of his respect for the courage shown for decades by a bitterly persecuted local church. It also reflected his determination to implement Vatican II fully, and thus treat the Eastern Catholic Churches in such a way as to make clear, to Catholics and Orthodox alike (but perhaps especially to Catholics), that these communities were fully members of the one, holy, catholic, and apostolic Church, and that their liturgical and governmental traditions were fully a part of the global Catholic reality.

Africa. A similar, Council-driven vision of the breadth or catholicity of the Catholic Church was one source of John Paul II's determination to keep Africa before the eyes of the Church and the world during his pontificate. After the Cold War, the world's great powers lost interest in Africa, which itself suffered under corrupt and often despotic leadership. John Paul refused to let Africa be written out of the script of twenty-first-century history. He was convinced by his experience of the new churches of Africa that they had a freshness of evangelical fervor that could help revitalize the Church in parts of the world where Christianity had become stale from centuries of familiarity. And by his frequent travels to Africa, where he became a beloved figure—"Baba" [the old man]—he tried to refocus the world's attention on a continent most of the rest of the world tried to ignore. And then there were his colleagues in the Vatican. The two regional synods for Africa that he held were efforts to get the center of the world Church in Rome to pay more attention to Africa and to senior African churchmen, and to take these new churches seriously as embodiments of the possibilities of Christian mission at the turn of the millennium.[11]

The Laity. John Paul II constantly lifted up the distinctive mission of lay Catholics in the world, which he understood to be another mandate of Vatican II. Here, too, confusions followed the Council, as Vatican II's reaffirmation that all the baptized shared in various ways in the priestly mission of Christ had come to be understood by some as flattening out the differences between those who exercised the ministry of the ordained priesthood and those who shared in the common priesthood of the baptized. The net result, especially in the Western world, had been a drift toward a laicized clergy and a clericalized laity, with the Council's primary intention—to empower the laity to be evangelists in the worlds of politics, economics, culture, the professions, and family life—being lost somewhere along the way.

To restore that sense of the distinctive lay apostolate as a mission to sanctify the modern Mars Hills where the hierarchical Church was invisible or ineffective, John Paul summoned an international Synod of Bishops in 1987; that synod led to the post-synodal apostolic exhortation of December 30, 1988, **Christifideles Laici** [Christ's Faithful Lay People], and the Pope's dynamic vision of the laity as the principal agents of the new evangelization in family, business, professional, political, and cultural life.[12] That same intent to implement the Council's teaching that the laity **are** the Church in "the world" undergirded John Paul II's steady and strong support for Opus Dei, his beatification and canonization of Opus Dei's founder, Josemaría Escrivá and his friendship with Escrivá's successor, Alvaro del Portillo, at whose bier the Pope came to pray on the day after Portillo's death in 1994.[13] For John Paul, Escrivá and Opus Dei had anticipated the Council's theology of the laity by decades, and thus deserved support as one effective means of promoting the lay vocation in the world.

Consecrated Life. The full implementation of Vatican II was also one of the motive forces at work in John Paul II's efforts to reform and revitalize consecrated life in the Church—the life of radical witness to Christ through perpetual vows of poverty,

chastity, and obedience. Communities of consecrated life (often called "religious communities")
had been in crisis ever since the Council; both men's
and women's communities had suffered steep losses
from resignations while concurrently finding it difficult to recruit new members.[14] Like the leaders of
those religious communities that were not dying, the
Pope believed that this distress had much to do with
the abandonment of a distinctive manner of life; it
was to revitalize the Church's sense of the adventure
of consecrated life and its distinctive character that
John Paul dedicated the 1994 international Synod
of Bishops, which he completed with the 1996 apostolic exhortation, **Vita Consecrata** [The Consecrated Life]. Years later, the effects of these initiatives
could be seen in the theological work of American
religious women who blended the teaching of **Vita
Consecrata** with other facets of the magisterium of
John Paul II (including his theology of the body)
to propose a dramatically reformed vision of consecrated life—and whose thought emerged from communities that were growing, rather than dying.[15]

The Priesthood. Many Council commentators
(and not a few priests) believed that the priesthood
had been given short shrift at Vatican II.[16] However
one assessed that criticism, the blunt fact in 1978
was that the Catholic priesthood was in crisis: it
had suffered the greatest number of defections since
the Reformation; once full seminaries were virtually empty; priests were confused and demoralized.

John Paul II's love for the priesthood and for priests, and his determination to implement Vatican II, led to a number of initiatives aimed at strengthening the world presbyterate, including his annual Holy Thursday letter to all the priests of the world and his regular meetings with priests and seminarians during his travels, which culminated in his inviting the priests of the world to share his eightieth birthday with him during the Great Jubilee of 2000. The alleged "gap" in the Council's teaching was filled by the post-synodal apostolic exhortation **Pastores Dabo Vobis** [I Will Give You Shepherds], which the Pope issued in 1992 to complete the work of the 1990 international Synod of Bishops. While aimed at a practical reform of the Church's seminaries, **Pastores Dabo Vobis** also included a rich theology of the priesthood, stressing that the ordained priesthood was a continuation of the mediating priesthood of Jesus Christ himself.[17]

John Paul's efforts to revitalize the priesthood produced measurable results during the pontificate. By the early 1990s, it was a rare seminary in which the majority of students did not say that a primary inspiration for their priestly vocation was John Paul II; as Cardinal William Baum once put it, John Paul had become "the greatest vocation director the Church has ever had."[18] Throughout the developed world, men once again saw the priesthood as a compelling vocation amidst a plethora of opportunities for personal fulfillment. In the developing world, men saw in John Paul II a priestly agent of genuine human liberation and a bold evangelist, and responded by giving their lives to the Church. In both instances, the Pope's witness had at least as great an impact as his teaching. The man who wrote on his golden jubilee about the "gift and mystery" of the priesthood had demonstrated with his own life that a celibate under a vow of obedience to his ecclesiastical superiors could lead an immensely rich human life, one worth the sacrifice of a family and the loss of personal independence that the Catholic priesthood entails.

Sanctity for All. The Dogmatic Constitution on the Church is generally regarded as the theological centerpiece of Vatican II's teaching; one of its signature themes is the universal call to holiness.[19] John Paul II worked to give effect to this teaching by two of the defining initiatives of the pontificate: his canonizations and beatifications, and his support for renewal movements and new Catholic communities. The 1983 reform of the beatification and canonization process that the Pope mandated with the apostolic constitution **Divinus Perfectionis Magister** [The Divine Teacher of Perfection] was intended to bring the tools of modern historical scholarship to bear on the Church's assessment of candidates for beatification and canonization; it also accelerated the process, so that the Church could be inspired by more contemporary witnesses to the workings of grace in history. Sanctity, John Paul II believed, was in fact all around us, for God is not grudging in his gifts; the processes by which the Church recognizes sanctity should recognize that.[20]

Sanctity, moreover, was essential if the Second Vatican Council's implementation was to be the occasion for a new Pentecost, a new burst of evangelical energy, in the world Church. Thus where other senior churchmen saw confusion and potential trouble in many of the renewal movements and new Catholic communities that came to prominence after Vatican II, John Paul II saw possibilities. If it was true theologically that all true reform in the Church had to refer back to the Church's originating form, it was also true historically that reform in the Church usually came from outside the normal structures of parochial and diocesan life: as it had in the Counter-Reformation, and as it had in the face of the secularist assault in the nineteenth century. The task of ecclesiastical leadership was to discern true from false charisms in the Church; those responsible for such discernments, the Pope believed, should be open and generous, understanding that it took new movements and communities time to find their proper place within the unity of the Church's communion. Here, as elsewhere, was compelling evidence that those who charged John Paul II with a penchant for authoritarianism and centralization were ill informed.

The New Evangelization. John Paul II's authoritative interpretation of the Second Vatican Council was intended, as he understood the Council to have been intended, to prepare the Church for a springtime of evangelization at the beginning of the third millennium of its history. The notion of a "kerygmatic" Church, or Church of proclamation, had been developed by mid-twentieth-century European theologians, whose influence on the documents of Vatican II was decisive and measurable. As Avery Dulles pointed out, the First Vatican Council used the word "gospel" (in Latin, **evangelium**) only once, and then as a synonym for the four canonical Gospels of the New Testament; by sharp contrast, the Second Vatican Council spoke of "the gospel" 157 times, of the imperative to "evangelize" 18 times, and of "evangelization" 31 times. It was John Paul II, however, who put the "new evangelization" at the center of Catholic self-understanding in what Dulles described as a "remarkable shift" in Catholic life and thought:

For centuries, evangelization had been a poor stepchild. Even when the term was used, evangelization was treated as a secondary matter, the special vocation of a few priests and religious. And even these specialists were more concerned with gaining new adherents for the Church than with proclaiming the good news of Jesus Christ. Today we seem to be witnessing the birth of a new Catholicism that, without loss of its institutional, sacramental, and social dimensions, is authentically evangelical.[21]

John Paul II's new evangelization was both Christocentric and mission oriented: all the baptized were called to the task of evangelization, which required every baptized Catholic to develop a personal relationship with Jesus Christ as Lord and Savior and to commit themselves to being instruments by which others came to know Christ. Thus the new evangelization belonged to the entire Church, not just to religious professionals in the clergy and consecrated life. Moreover, the new evangelization was global in scope: it involved deepening the faith where the Church was strong; the re-evangelization of those parts of an older Christendom that had become lax in their belief, piety, and witness; the first evangelization of places where the Gospel had never been successfully planted, especially in Asia; and Christian witness in the worlds of economics, culture, politics, and the mass media.[22]

Thus the Church, to be true to the heritage of Vatican II, must put out into the deep of proclamation and witness: its "first and highest priority" must be to "proclaim the good news concerning Jesus Christ as a joyful message to all the world."[23] That proclamation is the precondition to everything else the Church does in the world, and for the world; that proclamation is what the Church is **for**. John

Paul II's understanding of the Council as the platform from which to launch a new evangelization on the model of the Acts of the Apostles seemed likely, at his death, to shape Catholic self-consciousness and Catholic practice for the foreseeable future—not least because the most vibrant parts of the world Church were those that took John Paul's teaching on the new evangelization to heart.

Legislation. The new codes of canon law promulgated by John Paul II were efforts to translate the Council's teaching on the Church into juridic norms. The 1983 **Codex Iuris Canonici** for the Latin-rite Church was explicitly structured to reflect the ecclesiology of Vatican II; it embodied John Paul's idea of canon law as juridic theology, not legal positivism. The 1990 Code of Canons of the Eastern Churches was another facet of John Paul II's effort to integrate the Church's Eastern "lung" into the life and practice of the universal Church. Both codes helped provide legal keys to the proper interpretation of the Second Vatican Council while recasting the Catholic understanding of canon law as an instrument in service to the Church as a communion of disciples called to proclaim the Gospel.

The Centrality of Christ. The two most frequently cited Vatican II texts in John Paul II's magisterium were from the Pastoral Constitution on the Church in the Modern World: **Gaudium et Spes** 22 and **Gaudium et Spes** 24. According to the first, Christ, by revealing "the mystery of the Father and his love," also "reveals man to himself and brings to light his most high calling"; the second teaches that "man can full discover his true self only in a sincere giving of himself." Faithful to his December 1959 letter to the Council's Ante-Preparatory Commission, Karol Wojtyła explicated the Second Vatican Council for forty years as the Council dedicated to unveiling a true humanism and a genuine human liberation: the liberating humanism that comes from conversion to Christ, who reveals both the truth about God and the truth about human beings.

This, Wojtyła was convinced, was the primordial key to the proper interpretation of Vatican II. The rest of his magisterium of conciliar interpretation revolved around it, as his pontificate sought to embody Christian humanism in action.

"1989"

John Paul II's pivotal role in the events leading to "1989" and the collapse of European communism is now broadly acknowledged by historians.[24] How, though, should that role be understood within the larger landscape of his pontificate and its evangelical objectives?

The Dynamics of History. From his youthful immersion in Polish history and literature, Karol Wojtyła came to a distinctive view of history that had parallels in other Slavic thinkers such as Vladi-

mir Soloviev and Aleksandr Solzhenitsyn. His nation, Poland, had survived when the Polish state was
erased from the map of Europe in 1795: it survived
through its language, its literature, and its religious
faith—in a word, through its culture. The lesson?
That culture, not political power, economic power,
or other forms of material power, is the most dynamic force in history, over the long haul. And at
the heart of culture is cult—what men and women
cherish, honor, and worship; what men and women
are willing to stake their lives, and their children's
lives, on.

Wojtyła thus brought to the papacy a different
understanding of the dynamics of history than that
typically found in London, Paris, Berlin, Washington, Moscow, Beijing, or certain circles in the Vatican. Culture is the key to history, and thus the key to
political change. Change or reform a culture—give
it new energy by helping it recapture and re-express
the truths about the human condition that it embodied—and you had an Archimedean lever with
which to move the world. That is what John Paul
did in the Nine Days of June 1979: by giving back
to the people of Poland their authentic history and
culture, and thus their true identity, he gave them
tools of resistance that communism could not match
or counter.

At the same time, his accomplishment in 1979 and
throughout the 1980s taught the rest of the world a
lesson about two of modernity's great fallacies: the

Jacobin fallacy, set loose in the French revolution, according to which history is driven by the quest for power, understood as my capacity to impose my will on you; and the Marxist fallacy, according to which history is the exhaust fumes of impersonal economic forces. In challenging these two fallacies, both conceptually and in effective action, John Paul II gave the West the opportunity to recover one of the salient truths inscribed in its cultural foundations: politics is an extension of ethics; politics is a realm of "ought" as well as "is"; politics, even world politics, takes place within the ambit of moral judgment. That was no minor lesson for Karol Wojtyła to have taught, and embodied, in the second half of a twentieth century that had run knee-deep in blood because the world had forgotten it.

True Liberation. John Paul II's role in "1989" also challenged the Marxist-Leninist domination of the global vocabulary of "liberation." The first and most urgent liberation, the Pope insisted, was liberation into the moral truth about the human person— a truth that could be known by reason as well as revelation. Every other truth about liberation from oppression, and about life lived in freedom, flowed from that central truth about the inalienable dignity and inestimable value of every human life. Politics and economics that were built on the foundation of that understanding could lead to genuine human flourishing; politics and economics that ignored the truth about man would create new shackles, all the more dangerous in the twenty-first century because they would be more subtle than the shackles of the totalitarians.

The atheistic humanism analyzed by John Paul II's friend Henri de Lubac, S.J., taught that the God of the Bible was the enemy of human freedom—a notion with considerable cultural traction beyond the borders of the communist world.[25] The role of the Polish pope in "1989" demonstrated on a twentieth-century global stage the truth of what had been first revealed in the Exodus, 1,300 years before the Christian era: the God of Abraham comes into the world and into history as a liberator, and his commandments are a moral code intended to keep liberated men and women from reverting to the habits of slaves.

That moral code, as John Paul said at Mount Sinai in 2000, had been inscribed on human hearts before being engraved on tablets of stone. And this, too, was one of the lessons of John Paul's "1989": there is a universal moral law that can be known by reason; all are accountable to that moral law by reason of their humanity; that accountability is the moral foundation of human equality. That was the message John Paul took to the United Nations in 1995: the Pope's distinctive role throughout the 1980s gave him the moral authority to stand before the world and defend the universality of human rights at a moment when the very notion of human rights was being decried by postmodernists, Islamists, east Asian autocrats, and the world's remaining communists as a Western imperial imposition. It was that same role in the events leading up to "1989" that gave weight to the Pope's suggestion that the universal moral law could be a grammar by which the world turned cacophony into conversation. The weight came from the fact that he had embodied the truth he proposed in his own public witness and in his diplomacy, by defending and promoting the rights of all, not simply the rights of the Church and its members.

Europe Restored. For John Paul II, "1989" also marked the end of the artificial division of Europe into two warring camps, separated by vastly different claims about the nature of the human person, human community, human history, and human destiny, and physically separated by the Iron Curtain. When the Wall and all it represented came down, thanks in no small part to John Paul's inspiration and leadership, Europe had a chance to be itself again after a century of division and bloodletting. What Europe would make of that chance was not something the Pope could determine, but that he was one of those most responsible for a whole Europe recovering control of its own destiny, few serious students of contemporary history could doubt.

A New Model? Finally, "1989" for John Paul II suggested the possibility that modernity's usual method of effecting large-scale social change—mass slaughter—was not the only option. Communism had fallen for many reasons; the power of aroused consciences, which created new forms of nonviolent political power, was among those reasons. Might this template be applied to other, seemingly intractable situations? It was not to be, as the first Gulf War and Europe's inability to manage the deconstruction of Yugoslavia soon demonstrated. That was John Paul's hope, however, and the hope was a noble one.

The Free and Virtuous Society and the Priority of Culture

The social magisterium of John Paul II, and particularly the encyclical **Centesimus Annus**, pointed the century-long tradition of Catholic social doctrine firmly into the twenty-first century, absent any whiff of nostalgia for the premodern social, political, and economic order and with a clear vision of the dangers that awaited democratic polities and free economies that cut themselves loose from sturdy moral-cultural moorings.[26]

John Paul's social teaching stressed the priority of culture in building and sustaining the free and virtuous society. He insisted that democratic politics and market economies were not machines that could run by themselves; rather, both democracy and the market required a vibrant public moral culture to discipline and direct the tremendous human energies let loose by freedom. Thus the goal was to build and sustain not simply free societies, but free and virtuous societies; the two adjectives were always linked in his mind, as he was convinced that freedom and virtue were linked in the moral order.

John Paul II's social doctrine described the free and virtuous society as composed of three interlocking parts: a democratic polity, a free or market-centered economy, and a robust public moral culture. The third component part, he insisted, was the key to the proper functioning of the political and economic sectors. It took a certain kind of people, possessing certain virtues, to make democracy and the market work so that human beings were ennobled by their participation in free political and economic life. Here was an important challenge to the political science functionalists and economic libertarians who taught that the only thing that mattered was getting the machinery of governance, or of productivity and exchange, properly designed and built. Moreover, the Pope wedded this teaching about the priority of moral culture to a realistic and empirically sensitive grasp of postindustrial economic life and a sober but hopeful analysis of democracy.

In the encyclical **Centesimus Annus**, in which he taught that the wealth of nations resided primarily in human creativity and entrepreneurial skills, John Paul II sought to cure Catholic social doctrine of the curious materialism that had often characterized it. He also aimed to recenter the Catholic discussion on aiding the poor, giving primary attention to the inclusion of the poor in the networks of productivity and exchange where wealth was created and shared, rather than to schemes of wealth redistribution. Thus with **Centesimus Annus**, the Catholic Church's social doctrine abandoned the quest for a "Catholic third way" that was somehow between or beyond capitalism and socialism. John Paul's encyclical, looking at the empirical facts, recognized the economic truths on which market economies were built, but also insisted that those truths were not the only truths relevant to economic life: there were moral truths that ought to guide markets, moral truths that could be embodied in legal regulation of economic activity. As always, recognition of the truth about the dignity of the human person was the key to the ultimate success of any human activity. Thus John Paul II's affirmation of free economies was not fundamentally a question of their relative superiority in terms of economic efficiency; it was based on the conclusion that markets allowed for the exercise of human creativity and responsibility in the economic world.[27]

That same conviction about the dignity of the human person and its relationship to social structures applied to democratic politics as well as market economies. Karol Wojtyła had a remarkably keen grasp of the problems and prospects of twenty-first-century democracy, informed by a Burkean sense that the health of society's "little platoons"—its voluntary associations, beginning with the family—was crucial in securing a sound democratic polity. As the pontificate moved through the 1990s, however, John Paul frequently expressed his concern that democracies that declared wrongs to be rights were in grave peril of becoming "tyrant states," as he put it in the 1995 encyclical **Evangelium Vitae** [The Gospel of Life].[28] Here, the experience of Weimar Germany loomed large in his historical imagination: a beautifully constructed democratic system that eventually produced a tyrant state, because its moral and cultural foundations were insufficiently strong.

John Paul II's social magisterium also accelerated the process by which the Catholic Church reevaluated its concept of the state and of political authority. Although the Church had once thought of political authority, and particularly royal authority, as reflecting divine authority, John Paul's concept of the state seemed, at times, to reduce the state to a set of limited and defined legal and political tasks (or, as Russell Hittinger put it, John Paul II "de-ontologized" the state). At the same time, the Pope insisted that the modern constitutional state, born from a commitment to protect basic human rights, hold fast to this promise, particularly in its approach to the life issues of abortion and euthanasia. This tension between Catholic thinking about the state as a set of discrete and constitutionally circumscribed tasks, on the one hand, and the state as an entity required by its nature to uphold certain fundamental moral truths about the human person, on the other, is a legacy of the social teaching of John Paul II certain to provoke serious thought, and perhaps controversy, in the future.[29]

The Ecumenical Imperative

Considerable ecumenical ardor had been ignited by the Second Vatican Council. The participation of Orthodox, Anglican, and Protestant observers at all four sessions of Vatican II, and the solicitude shown them by Cardinal Augustin Bea's Secretariat for Christian Unity; the historic meeting in Jerusalem in 1964 between Pope Paul VI and Ecumenical Patriarch Athenagoras of Constantinople; the Council's 1964 Decree on Ecumenism, with its statement that all who believe in Christ and have been baptized are in a real but imperfect communion with the Catholic Church, albeit in different degrees; the Council's affirmation of a hierarchy of truths within the deposit of faith, which seemed to suggest that some differences ought no longer be regarded as church dividing; the mutual lifting of the excommunications of 1054 by the Pope and Ecumenical Patriarch on the day before the Council ended; the post-conciliar institutionalization of the Catholic Church's ecumenical commitment in a new organ of the Roman Curia, which continued the work of Bea's conciliar Secretariat—all this seemed to presage an ecumenical golden age as the warmth of the Council rapidly melted the deep freeze of centuries.[30] Yet within a decade of the Council's conclusion, ecumenical enthusiasm had waned, as it became clear that substantive doctrinal issues dividing the component parts of what had once been Christendom remained, and in some cases were becoming more aggravated.

Ecumenism was not a pastoral priority in Poland, given the country's religious demographics, but Karol Wojtyła, faithful to the Council's ecumenical mandate, did what he could to foster new patterns of dialogue with his Protestant and Orthodox neighbors in Kraków. Yet despite his lack of extensive pre-papal ecumenical experience, John Paul II expended more effort on the quest for Christian unity than any pope since the formalization of the East/West fracture in 1054 and the subsequent disintegration of Western Christian unity in the sixteenth century.

By the Pope's instructions, every papal pilgrimage included an ecumenical meeting, which was often accompanied by an ecumenical prayer service or Liturgy of the Word. John Paul hosted hundreds of Christian leaders at the Vatican over more than a quarter century, inviting Orthodox hierarchs, Anglicans, and Lutherans to share with him in leading worship, and in some cases preaching, in St. Peter's. He participated in several prayer vigils at the Vatican basilica sponsored by the ecumenical monastery at Taizé in France, visited Taizé in 1986, and became a friend of Taizé's founder, Brother Roger Schutz.[31] He concluded formal Christological agreements with the heads of the Assyrian Church of the East, the

Armenian Apostolic Church, the Coptic Orthodox Church, and the Syrian Orthodox Church, while acknowledging a common faith in Christ when meeting with the patriarch of the Ethiopian Orthodox Church and the patriarch of the Malankara Orthodox Syrian Church; these agreements and affirmations healed doctrinal breaches that sometimes went back fifteen centuries.[32] The Joint Declaration on the Doctrine of Justification signed by the Holy See and the leaders of the Lutheran World Federation on October 31, 1999—Reformation Sunday in the Lutheran liturgical calendar—had a difficult gestation, but notwithstanding those difficulties, the declaration's theological achievement was no small one, as the official statement of the Holy See and the LWF made clear: "The teaching of the Lutheran Church presented in this Declaration does not fall under the condemnations of the Council of Trent. The condemnations of the Lutheran Confessions do not apply to the teachings of the Roman Catholic Church presented in this Declaration." What had originally precipitated the crisis of 1517 and the subsequent division of Western Christianity—the doctrine of justification—was no longer to be regarded as a church-dividing issue.[33]

Orthodoxy. Ecumenism **ad orientem** was a priority for John Paul II, who hoped that the breach between Rome and Constantinople could be closed so that Catholicism and Orthodoxy could cross the threshold of the third millennium in full communion, reunited at the eucharistic table of the Lord. The Pope made his commitment to this dramatic goal clear in his first visit to the Ecumenical Patriarchate in November 1979, telling the Ecumenical Patriarch Dimitrios I that he hoped the day was "very near" when they could concelebrate the Eucharist together. Dimitrios came to Rome in December 1987 for an extensive round of engagements, including Solemn Vespers at the Basilica of St. Mary Major and a Mass in St. Peter's on December 5. On both occasions, the services were described as being celebrated "with the participation of the Ecumenical Patriarch Dimitrios I," and while it was not concelebration, Dimitrios preached in the Vatican basilica before John Paul's homily and jointly blessed the congregation with the Pope at the end of Mass. The same courtesies were extended to Dimitrios's successor, Bartholomew I, on his several visits to Rome, as they were to the leader of Romanian Orthodoxy, Teoctist, in 2002. Every year the Pope sent a senior Vatican delegation to Istanbul to participate in the Ecumenical Patriarchate's celebration of the patronal feast of St. Andrew; Orthodox representatives were always prominent guests at the annual Roman celebration of the patronal feast of Sts. Peter and Paul, save when they declined to attend.[34]

An Unprecedented Offer. John Paul II's **Ut Unum Sint** [That They May Be One], issued in 1995, was the first encyclical ever devoted exclusively to the ecumenical imperative. In this groundbreaking exercise of the papal magisterium, John Paul first addressed the Catholic Church: the ecumenical commitment made at Vatican II was irreversible, he taught his fellow Catholics, and the quest for Christian unity ought to be reignited, both internationally and in the local churches. He then focused on the situation **ad orientem**. Despite the Orthodox opposition he had faced throughout the 1990s, John Paul continued to press in **Ut Unum Sint** for a full communion between Rome and Constantinople based on the experience of the first millennium, in which the See of Peter was acknowledged as the final reference point on matters of doctrine but the popes made no jurisdictional claims in the East. As for Western Christianity, the encyclical could not be so bold in addressing the fractures of the sixteenth century, given the doctrinal chaos in much of the Anglican and Protestant worlds in the latter decades of the twentieth century. Nonetheless, John Paul asked Orthodox, Anglican, and Protestant leaders alike to help him find a way of exercising the papal primacy that could serve all Christians in the future: "Could not the real but imperfect communion" already existing among Christian communities set the foundation on which Anglican, Catholic, Orthodox, and Protestant theologians and leaders could explore together a Petrine ministry that served everyone's needs, he asked?[35] John Paul's offer was perfectly serious. Few of those to whom the offer was made were prepared to take it up seriously, however.

Difficulties. That pattern had been evident throughout the pontificate. The Anglican–Roman Catholic dialogue foundered in the mid-1980s when it became increasingly evident that what had often been assumed to be the case—namely, that the two communities believed the same things about the Eucharist and the sacramental priesthood—could no longer be assumed. The Anglican Communion's acceptance of the ordination of women and the explanations offered for it, which were primarily sociological rather than theological, also suggested that the two communities had moved in radically different directions in their understanding of the nature of the Church and its relationship to the authority of apostolic tradition (a chasm that was also widening between Anglicanism and Orthodoxy).[36] The same split was evident in the 1990s and the first decade of the twenty-first century on questions of biblical morality, especially the immorality of homosexual acts. Similar questions bedeviled the Lutheran-Catholic dialogue despite the Joint Declaration on the Doctrine of Justification. The precipitating issue of the Lutheran reformation might have been theologically resolved, but other church-dividing questions of ecclesiology, the sacraments, and Christian morality had emerged to create new and grave divisions, in the light of which discussions of a pan-Christian Petrine ministry were not likely to be very fruitful.

John Paul's initiatives with Orthodoxy ran into a different set of obstacles. One was psychological:

over a millennium of division, the tacit affirmation that "I am not in communion with the Bishop of Rome" had come to seem an essential part of Orthodox self-identity for many Orthodox believers. In most cases, that default instinct was more likely a matter of ecclesial culture than of considered theological reflection. Yet something akin to that instinct seemed to have been suggested by Ecumenical Patriarch Bartholomew I's 1998 statement at Georgetown University, in which the ecumenically attuned Bartholomew (who had studied for the doctorate in Rome) stated bluntly that the "divergence" between Rome and Constantinople, which he believed had increased over the centuries, was not simply "a problem of organizational structures [or] jurisdictional arrangements," but involved "ontologically different" experiences of being the Church. But if Catholicism and Orthodoxy were "ontologically different"—meaning essentially different—then John Paul II's proposal for a return to the status quo ante 1054 was a dead letter.

The problem of closing the breach of 1054 was made immensely more complicated by the ecumenical obstreperousness of the Patriarchate of Moscow, which posed severe difficulties for both Rome and Constantinople. These difficulties were themselves exacerbated by the deep linkages between the Russian Orthodox leadership and Soviet—later, Russian—state power, which were in turn made more complex by the intersection of Russian imperial ambition and the Moscow Patriarchate's conception of itself as the "third Rome," in succession to the Rome of Peter and Paul and to the Constantinople of Andrew and John Chrysostom. Then there was the unhappy fact that many of the Russian Orthodox clergy who wanted to free their community from the corrupting embrace of the Russian state regarded "ecumenism" as a term of opprobrium, for the KGB had used Russian Orthodox agents and informants in its successful efforts to achieve influence at the World Council of Churches, which resulted in the WCC's virtual abandonment of persecuted Christians within the Soviet Union.

Thus history, and history's effects on both theology and ecclesial psychology, conspired to frustrate many of John Paul II's ecumenical initiatives in both the Christian East and the Christian West. Yet **Ut Unum Sint** remains part of the patrimony of the Catholic Church, an unavoidable reminder of the ecumenical imperative that ultimately derives from the will of Christ that his Church should be one. And despite John Paul's ecumenical frustrations and failures, Methodist theologian Geoffrey Wainwright, who long cochaired the joint Methodist–Roman Catholic international dialogue, considered John Paul II a "great evangelist" and a "great ecumenist," who had "offered Christ to millions . . . [who] heard him gladly . . . and countless numbers responded." Then there was John Paul's personal example of ecumenical commitment, which Wainwright thought was at least as important as his evangelical preaching, his ecumenical meetings, and his magisterium:

> The last time I saw Pope John Paul was in November 2004 . . . at a . . . symposium organized by the Pontifical Council for Promoting Christian Unity to mark the 40th anniversary of the Second Vatican Council's decree on ecumenism, **Unitatis Redintegratio**. The Pope presided over a special service of Vespers in St. Peter's. When he was wheeled in, he looked radiant; and the thought struck me from the Apostle Paul in 2 Corinthians 12.8–10: this was "strength perfected in weakness."[37]

Evangelical Appreciations. The greatest ecumenical surprise of the pontificate was the enthusiastic embrace of John Paul II by American evangelical Protestants, who saw in the man their grandfathers might have described as the "Whore of Babylon" a premier exponent of the truth of Christian faith and a stalwart defender of the right to life. That embrace led Billy Graham to describe John Paul II, at his death, as "the greatest Christian leader of our time," and, in the United States at least, gave birth to a new, theologically sophisticated intellectual dialogue that operated under the title "Evangelicals and Catholics Together."[38] A key participant in those new conversations, Baptist scholar Timothy George, predicted an interesting future for these two traditions of Christian faith, whose relations had been characterized by a "tortuous history of conflict and mutual condemnation":

> [Evangelicals and Catholics] will discover that we are comrades in a struggle, not a struggle against one another, and not really a struggle against those outside the Christian faith who reject the light of divine grace because they have fallen in love with the darkness which surrounds them. No, our conflict is with the evil that loiters in the noonday, and slithers through the midnight hour. Against such principalities and powers, John Paul II, our common teacher, [called] us to recognize the splendor of truth and the fullness of life, that luminous presence the New Testament calls the glory of God in the face of Jesus Christ.[39]

Whether American evangelical appreciation of John Paul II and for a robust Catholic defense of classic Christian orthodoxy would shape ecumenical relations in Latin America, Africa, and Asia, where evangelical, fundamentalist, and pentecostalist Protestantism was growing exponentially at the turn into the third millennium, seemed likely to be a key question in twenty-first-century global religious life.[40] The answer to that question was by no means certain at John Paul II's death. What was certain, however, was that the question would not have been posed at all, absent the evangelical witness of John

Paul II and its dramatic effects in reconfiguring the world ecumenical context.

Catholicism and Judaism: Covenants in Conversation

As a papal diplomat, Angelo Giuseppe Roncalli worked clandestinely to save Jews from the Holocaust; as pope, John XXIII (who greeted one Jewish delegation with the exclamation, "I am Joseph, your brother!") had his car stopped so that he could bless the Jews of Rome as they left their synagogue after Sabbath worship. As a young man, Karol Wojtyła, who joined a resistance movement whose components included a section dedicated to Jewish rescue, lost friends to the Holocaust; as pope, John Paul II visited and spoke in the Great Synagogue of Rome, met Jewish delegations on virtually all of his papal pilgrimages, established diplomatic relations with the State of Israel, and oversaw the publication of several documents crucial for the future of Jewish-Catholic dialogue. John XXIII's human warmth created a new sense of possibility in an ancient and often painful relationship. John Paul II created an entirely new era in Jewish-Catholic relations, making possible the reconvening of a conversation that had broken down more than nineteen centuries before.

Wojtyła's palpable respect for Judaism and its role in the world gave him a unique capacity to accelerate the pace of the Jewish-Catholic dialogue into previously uncharted territory—a journey paved by several crucial gestures rich in both symbolism and impact.

The first was his visit to the Great Synagogue of Rome on April 13, 1986, which was the Pope's personal initiative.[41] There, he reiterated the Church's condemnation of the sin of anti-Semitism, the Second Vatican Council's rejection of the collective charge of deicide against the Jews, and the Catholic Church's determination to contest the notion that there was theological justification for discrimination against Jews and Judaism. The Jewish people, he affirmed, had been called by God "with an irrevocable calling." And despite the pain of history, Catholics now understood (as they should have understood all along) that Catholicism and Judaism were inextricably entangled, locked into a unique relationship by the will of God: as John Paul put it, "the Jewish religion is not 'extrinsic' to us, but in a certain sense is 'intrinsic' to our own religion," so that, "with Judaism . . . we have a relationship which we do not have with any other religion." Jews were, for Catholics, "elder brothers."[42]

To have come to those understandings after centuries of strife was remarkable; to some, it was enough. But it was not enough for John Paul II, the first Bishop of Rome to enter the Great Synagogue of Rome. The people who shared a "common heritage drawn from the Law and the Prophets," he continued, had to deepen their "collaboration in favor of man," bearing witness together to the moral truths about the human person inscribed both on human hearts and on the tablets of the Mosaic covenant. Beyond that, however, Jews and Catholics ought to ponder the mystery of divine election, which they both experienced. It was time to reconvene the theological conversation that had been abruptly adjourned during the First Jewish War in approximately A.D. 70, at the "parting of the ways" between what became Christianity and what became rabbinic Judaism.[43]

The second initiative of John Paul II that set the foundations for a dramatically reconfigured Jewish-Catholic dialogue was the establishment of diplomatic relations between the Holy See and the State of Israel. As the negotiating record makes clear, the 1993 Fundamental Agreement between the two parties that made possible diplomatic exchange at the ambassadorial level would not have happened absent John Paul's insistence that it happen, given the diplomatic caution prevailing in the Vatican Secretariat of State and the resistance of the Latin Patriarchate of Jerusalem.[44] The Pope insisted on seeing the agreement through for several reasons. It was an important diplomatic analogue to the turning of the page he had described at the Great Synagogue of Rome; absent the Holy See's formal diplomatic recognition of the Jewish state, John Paul knew, many Jews, however mistakenly, would continue to believe that the existence of the State of Israel constituted a theological problem for the Catholic Church.[45] It was important in clearing the political path for a papal pilgrimage to the Holy Land. It might give the Holy See a greater purchase in discussions about peace in the Middle East. But beyond all such prudential calculations, the Fundamental Agreement was, for John Paul, simply the right thing to do: right for the Catholic Church, right for Catholic-Jewish relations, right for the State of Israel, and right for the pursuit of peace in the Middle East. Despite the slow pace of follow-on negotiations between the Holy See and Israel, few could doubt at the time of John Paul's death that he had been right about what was right.

The third and fourth symbolic moments at which John Paul II accelerated the Jewish-Catholic dialogue occurred during his Great Jubilee Holy Land pilgrimage. In his stunning and stark address at Yad Vashem, the head of the Catholic Church made unmistakably clear that he shared the ongoing pain inflicted on Jews and Judaism by the Holocaust. In his prayer at the Western Wall of the Temple, he asked God's forgiveness for the sins committed against Jews by Christians over the centuries and recommitted the Church to resist any future attempts to harm the people who carried God's covenant with Abraham through history.

In his determination to reconvene the theological conversation between Catholicism and Judaism

after nineteen centuries, John Paul II was, arguably, far ahead of his time—save in North America,
where the secure position of the Jewish community
made it possible for precisely such a new, in-depth
theological encounter to take place. Those conversations produced one important result in September 2000, when 170 Jewish religious leaders and
scholars in North America signed and issued **Dabru
Emet** [Speak the Truth], which boldly tried to fit
Christians and Christianity into an Orthodox Jewish understanding of God's abiding covenant with
the Jewish people. Picking up one of John Paul's key
points (and challenging many of their Jewish brethren), the signatories of **Dabru Emet** declared that
"a new religious dialogue with Christians will not
weaken Jewish practice or accelerate Jewish assimi-
lation." **Dabru Emet** had its Jewish critics, but the
very fact of its existence suggested that John Paul II's
initiatives in the sphere of Jewish-Catholic relations had indeed broken new ground, despite the
nervousness of some Jews and the reticence of some
Catholics accustomed to the familiar grooves of the
post-conciliar Jewish-Catholic dialogue.[46]

Science and the World Religions: Dialogues in Truth

As both philosopher and theologian, Karol Wojtyła
was convinced that any genuine dialogue between

religious communities, between believers and unbelievers, or between the Catholic Church and the
worlds of science and philosophy, had to aim at the
clarification of truth. In John Paul's mind, tolerance did not mean ignoring differences in an effort
to achieve a temporary bonhomie; rather, genuine
tolerance meant engaging differences with a full
recognition of the difference that differences can
make, but also within a bond of civility and mutual respect. Contrary to the conventional wisdom
of secular modernity and postmodernity, according
to which a man's doubts equip him for tolerance, civility, and dialogue, John Paul II was able to engage
differences on the basis of his own profound Christian faith. For according to that faith, the **Logos**, the
Word through whom God had created the world,
had left the imprint of God's own reason in the creation, such that all human beings are drawn toward
the truth. Men and women needed the nourishment
of truth as much as they needed the nourishment
provided by food and water, John Paul was convinced; he also knew that that attraction to the truth
was blunted by the facts of sin (including pride and
fear) and by the accumulated prejudices of centuries
and millennia. Yet the attraction to truth—including moral truth—remained, and it was on that basis
that he sought to engage other world religions and
the world of science.

Getting Beyond Galileo. Karol Wojtyła brought
to the papacy an acute sense of the difficulties the

Church had had in engaging scientific modernity and an intuition that the materialist and positivist assumptions shaping the contemporary scientific worldview were fraying. A new dialogue was possible, as physics and astronomy encountered phenomena for which their own analytic methods could not account, and as some philosophically adventurous scientists began to speculate about the reasons that the universe seemed perfectly adapted to mathematical analysis and modeling. But before that new dialogue could be fully engaged, John Paul knew, the debris of the past had to be cleared away.

That was why he established a study commission in 1981 to reexamine the entire Galileo case, which had become a powerful cultural myth underwriting hostile secularism's conviction that biblical religion and science were simply incompatible. The commission's 1992 report recognized that Galileo's clerical judges had erred by identifying the truth of Catholic faith with an unsustainable cosmology. Accepting the report, John Paul II urged both scientists and theologians to move beyond "a tragic mutual incomprehension" based on the false notion of "a fundamental opposition between science and faith." Truth could not contradict truth. If that seemed to be the case, then a mistake had been made somewhere along the analytic line. The Christian humanism the Catholic Church proposed to the world recognized that there were different modes of knowing the truth; respecting that diversity, the Church recognized science as a "realm of knowledge" with its own proper canons of inquiry. The question now was whether science was willing to make the same affirmation about theology. If so, then science and theology could mutually reinforce each other's quest for the truth about the great mysteries of the human condition, including the mystery of every individual human life.[47]

The resolution of the Galileo affair caused little controversy; such was not the case with John Paul II's October 22, 1996, message on evolution to the Pontifical Academy of Sciences. The message described "the theory of evolution" as "more than a hypothesis," even as it went on to note that "we should speak of several theories of evolution," some of which were admittedly "materialist" and "reductionist." Those "theories of evolution which, in accordance with the philosophies inspiring them, consider the [human] spirit as emerging from the forces of living matter or as a mere epiphenomenon of this matter" were, the message insisted, both "incompatible with the truth about man" and unable to "ground the dignity of the human person." Yet the message did not go on to note that those were precisely the dominant theories of evolution among evolutionary scientists, nor were those defective theories examined critically in any depth. Those lacunae, plus the message's lack of attention to what some scientists regarded as deep gaps in the evolutionary record, plus the affirmation that evolution is "more than a hypothesis," raised questions that continued to be debated heatedly during the remainder of the pontificate and beyond.[48]

The Hard Road of Interreligious Dialogue. Controversy also dogged several of John Paul II's efforts at interreligious dialogue. The October 27, 1986, World Day of Prayer for Peace, which the Pope hosted in Assisi, was criticized within the Curia and throughout some parts of the world Church from the moment John Paul II announced the initiative on January 25, 1986.[49] Some feared sending a signal of religious indifferentism by having leaders from dozens of world religions appearing together on the same platform. Others charged that the event hinted (and perhaps more than hinted) at religious syncretism; how, they asked, could the Pope pray with men and women who prayed to a different deity, or to many deities? John Paul's patient explanation that this was not a matter of praying together but of being together to pray did not satisfy the critics, so the Pope devoted virtually his entire Christmas address to the Roman Curia in December 1986 to a defense of the Assisi initiative, which he portrayed as a "visible illustration, a factual lesson, a catechesis intelligible to all of what the duty of ecumenism and the duty of interreligious dialogue recommended and promoted by the Second Vatican Council presupposed and signified."[50]

Similar criticism followed John Paul's kiss of a Qur'an during his visit to the Omayyad Grand

Mosque in Damascus in 2001; the critics could not seem to grasp that this was a gesture of respect for Muslims, not a papal endorsement of the Qur'an as divine revelation. John Paul II had a very clear view of the gulf in theological sensibility between Christianity and Islam, and what that gulf meant in terms of the two religions' views of the just society. His analysis of the essential difference between the two, in **Crossing the Threshold of Hope**, was rather more stringent than what his successor, Pope Benedict XVI, would say in his famous Regensburg Lecture of September 2006. In John Paul's view,

> Whoever knows the Old and New Testaments, and then reads the Qur'an, clearly sees the **process by which it completely reduces Divine Revelation**. It is impossible not to note the movement away from what God said about Himself, first in the Old Testament through the Prophets, and then finally in the New Testament through His Son. In Islam all the richness of God's self-revelation, which constitutes the heritage of the Old and New Testaments, has definitely been set aside.
>
> Some of the most beautiful names in the human language are given to the God of the Qur'an, but He is ultimately a God outside of the world, a God who is **only Majesty, never Emmanuel**, God-with-us. **Islam is not a religion of redemption**. There is no room for the Cross and the Resurrection. Jesus is mentioned, but only as a prophet who prepares for

the last prophet, Muhammad. There is also mention of Mary, His Virgin Mother, but the tragedy
of redemption is completely absent. For this reason
not only the theology but also the anthropology of
Islam is very distant from Christianity.[51]

John Paul II's approach to interreligious dialogue
reflected both his personality and his convictions.
He reached out to those of different religious beliefs
from the font of his profound respect for persons.
That outreach was shaped, however, by three convictions: that there is only one truth; that all truths,
from whatever source, tend toward the Truth, who is
God; and that the God who is Truth revealed himself
in a definitive way in his Son, Jesus Christ. The third
conviction did not preclude, but in fact demanded,
forms of dialogue based on the first two convictions.
The same personality characteristics and the same
convictions undergirded the Pope's dialogue with
science, with secular philosophy, and with the arts.
He could engage differences civilly, and he was prepared to build out from the points of tangency that
existed between different philosophical positions or
different religious traditions—as when, in 1985, he
addressed a stadium full of Muslim young people
in Casablanca, at the invitation of King Hassan II,
acknowledging the facts of difference but appealing
for cooperation on the basis of faith in the one God
of Abraham and submission to the one universal
moral law.

Solidarity Extended: The Life Issues

In the aftermath of the Revolution of 1989 and the Soviet crack-up of 1991, others may have believed, at least temporarily, that the end of history—the definitive and final form of human social, political, and economic organization—had been realized with the triumph of democratic politics and market economics over communism. John Paul II quickly and presciently scouted the terrain of the postcommunist contest for the human future where, as he knew and the world soon discovered, new challenges to freedom rightly understood quickly emerged. Some of the most urgent challenges involved the life issues of abortion and euthanasia, and related questions of the management of the biotechnological revolution ignited by humanity's new genetic knowledge.[52]

In the face of widespread efforts to portray the Catholic Church's defense of the right to life of the unborn as yet another example of Catholicism's impossible sexual ethic, or Catholic misogyny, or both, John Paul II insisted for more than a quarter century that abortion was a matter of the fifth commandment's injunction not to kill the innocent, not the sixth commandment's admonition to chastity.[53] Abortion, in other words, was a justice issue, not an issue of sexual morality. Moreover, abortion was a **social** justice issue, for states that claimed the right to declare entire classes of human beings outside the boundaries of legal protection were states in which no one's right to life was secure. If the state could declare the unborn, whom embryology texts recognized as members of the human family, susceptible to unpenalized lethal violence, then why not the inconvenient or burdensome elderly, or the radically handicapped, or indeed any other class of human beings whose fundamental right to life the majority did not wish to endorse?[54]

Then there was the question of what had (and had not) been learned from modern history, and the question of freedom's debasement into sheer willfulness. Hadn't the late twentieth century learned anything from the experience of immediate predecessor generations, in which the notion of "life unworthy of life" [**Lebensunwertes Leben**] had contributed to the self-destruction of democracy and to mass slaughter? As John Paul wrote in **Evangelium Vitae**, "To claim the right to abortion, infanticide, and euthanasia, and to recognize that right in law, means to attribute to human freedom a **perverse and evil significance**: that of an **absolute power over others and against others**."[55]

Democracy could only sustain itself over time, the Pope argued, if the machinery of self-governance rested on the foundation of a "culture of life," for only a culture that cherished life as a radical gift could sustain a "culture of human rights." The individualism and subjectivism underwriting the pro-abortion movement (and its analogue, the euthanasia movement) were incompatible with democratic self-governance, John Paul insisted, for individualism and subjectivism run amok would inevitably erode the experience of social solidarity that is crucial to democracy. Moreover, a radical ideology of "choice" violated the rationally knowable moral norm according to which no human being is to be instrumentalized, used for the convenience of another, or disposed of.[56]

If the great public contest of the mid-twentieth century had been between freedom and totalitarian political power, the great public issue of the late twentieth century and the early twenty-first for John Paul II was the clash between the "culture of life" and the "culture of death," as he described the contending forces in **Evangelium Vitae**.[57] In addition to the ongoing debates over abortion and euthanasia, that clash also shaped the debate over the future of biotechnology. In 1987, the Congregation for the Doctrine of the Faith issued **Donum Vitae** [The Gift of Life], an instruction approved by John Paul II, which warned against deploying humanity's new genetic knowledge and biotechnological skills to turn human begetting into human manufacture. Those issues were of concern to the Pope throughout the pontificate, even as the public debate expanded to include questions of "perfecting" humanity in what some scientists unblushingly called the "immortality project."[58]

John Paul II's vigorous pro-life teaching and activism were extensions of his commitment to the principle of solidarity as a building block of the free and virtuous society. Having lived in an environment where human beings were murdered with impunity behind a facade of legality, Karol Wojtyła knew the dangers of taking the first step down the slippery slope of allowing the state to determine which members of the human community deserve the protection of the laws. The moral resources that had given birth to Solidarity against overwhelming odds could, he was convinced, build a culture of life that took cross-generational solidarity as a hallmark of respect for the dignity of the human person and built strong barriers against abortion and euthanasia. His critics and opponents, from the Italians who voted in favor of permissive abortion laws shortly after Mehmet Ali Agca's assassination attempt to Catholic members of the United States Congress who supported the pro-abortion agenda, could not seem to grasp the link between Solidarity and the pro-life cause—between the quest for freedom against the communist culture of the lie, and the defense of life against the culture of death. For John Paul II, it was all one contest—a struggle for the defense of human dignity, a struggle to grasp and live the true meaning of freedom as self-gift. The Pope had at least as many defeats as victories on the life issues. His pro-life witness, however, was consistent, persistent, thoughtful, and passionate, and it helped keep alive a set of questions that many in the world of power wished would disappear.

A Legacy of Ideas

That John Paul II remained a working intellectual throughout more than a quarter century as Bishop of Rome reflected both his unique personality and his conception of the papal office. From the time he began an active episcopal ministry as auxiliary bishop of Kraków in 1958, this man of ideas and arguments had had few opportunities to lead an orderly intellectual life; his poetry, his philosophical essays, and books such as **Love and Responsibility**, **Sources of Renewal**, **Sign of Contradiction**, and **Person and Act** were all written in the interstices of his pastoral work. Yet, as a diocesan bishop, he liked to have a significant intellectual project in hand, not least as a way to bring some order into the fragmentation of his busy program as a bishop. That pattern continued throughout his even more demanding pontificate, during which he produced several book-length collections of audience addresses (including the catecheses that were eventually gathered together into his Theology of the Body), an international bestseller in **Crossing the Threshold of Hope**, two books of memoirs, and **Memory and Identity**, the extended philosophical reflection published shortly before his death. Thinking and writing—and thinking through writing—had been essential parts of Karol Wojtyła, the man, since the Second World War; thinking and writing—and thinking through writing—remained an essential facet of the life of Karol Wojtyła the pope.

The intellectual legacy of the pontificate of John Paul II will shape the pastoral life and mission of the Catholic Church for centuries. At the same time, the Pope's intellectual legacy belongs to the world, for John Paul addressed some of the most pressing questions of world culture at the end of the twentieth century and the beginning of the twenty-first: the nature, goals, and limits of freedom; the structural and moral requirements of the free society; the meaning of human sexuality; the relationships between religious conviction and scientific knowledge, and between faith and reason; the very capacity of the human person to know anything with certainty.

In Defense of Reason. The Pope's address to this last issue may well be his most enduring contribution to world culture—and, from a certain point of view, the most unexpected. It would have been a great surprise to Voltaire and other proponents of Enlightenment rationalism to learn that, two centuries after they had sworn to rid the world of the bewitchments of priestcraft in the name of reason, the Catholic Church was the world's premier institutional defender of the prerogatives of reason—and that the defense was being led by a Polish priest, himself a philosopher of international repute. Yet that is one major part of the intellectual legacy of John Paul II, who throughout his pontificate insisted that human reason could get to the truth of things as they are—and in doing so, could teach us what is right and what is wrong, what is noble and what is base, what is snare and delusion and what is truly liberating.

At a moment in the history of civilization in which the claims of reason were under assault from sundry religious and/or political fanaticisms and from philosophy itself, the head of the Catholic Church stood at the rostrum of the General Assembly of the United Nations in October 1995 to defend the human capacity to know, through the exercise of reason, those moral truths of the human condition we call "human rights," and to make that knowing the basis of a genuinely cross-cultural conversation. Three years later, in the encyclical **Fides et Ratio** [Faith and Reason], John Paul II reaffirmed philosophical reason's capacity to grasp the truth, while simultaneously arguing that the human journey to the full truth of things can be completed only by faith—for just as faith seeks understanding (and thus theology needs philosophy), so our understanding of the human condition is enriched by faith, which grasps those truths that can be apprehended only in love.[59]

As Avery Dulles put it a year before John Paul's death, John Paul II, the pastor, patiently and persistently insisted that "faith, by sharpening the inner eye of the mind, enables reason to rise above itself and in no sense diminishes it"; thus faith, by "reinforcing reason," enables reason to "transcend its normal limits."[60] Yet John Paul the philosopher would always insist that human beings can get to the moral truth of things and reach conclusions in which we can have real confidence by "arguing rigorously from rational criteria."[61] **Fides et Ratio** was thus a signal contribution to world culture at a moment in which the detachment of faith from reason had led to the Taliban, al-Qaeda, and lethal violence on a mass scale, while a loss of faith in reason had left the West intellectually paralyzed in the face of mortal threats to its core political commitments: civility, tolerance, human rights, democratic decision-making, and the rule of law.

Giving an Account. Another enduring artifact embodying the intellectual legacy of John Paul II will be the **Catechism of the Catholic Church,** which the Pope understood as both a fruit of the Second Vatican Council and a proposal to the world of the third millennium. As the catechism commissioned by the Council of Trent had shaped Catholic thought, mission, and piety during the second half of the second millennium, so, John Paul believed, the 1992 **Catechism of the Catholic Church** could provide a sturdy intellectual framework for Catholic life in the third millennium, by drawing together in one comprehensive presentation of Catholic faith the Council's twin theological commitments: to a recovery of the basic sources of Christian wisdom in the Bible and the Fathers of the Church (**ressourcement,** as the theologians of the mid-twentieth century put it), and to a fruitful encounter with contemporary intellectual culture (**aggiornamento,** or "updating," in John XXIII's famous description). At the same time, the **Catechism** was an extended offer to the world: here is what the Catholic Church believes; this is how the Catholic Church prays; this is how the Catholic Church thinks we should live in a truly humane way. In a season of skepticism about the capacity of religious believers to give an account of their beliefs and practices, the **Catechism** was a humble yet confident confession that the Catholic Church still believed itself capable of putting the pieces of the human drama together in a coherent and compelling way: the drama of every human life, and the drama of history. Giving that kind of comprehensive account of Christian faith and life was important in itself, and for the life of the Church. It was also, John Paul was convinced, a duty the Church owed the world—the duty to make the Christian proposal in a thorough way so that the world might have the opportunity to believe.

Closely allied to the **Catechism** in the intellectual legacy of John Paul II was the 1993 encyclical **Veritatis Splendor** [The Splendor of Truth].[62] It, too, was addressed to both the Church and the world. Within the Church, John Paul criticized forms of moral theology that, in his considered judgment, emptied the moral life of its drama by weakening our sense of the moral consequences of specific choices and acts. At the same time, **Veritatis Splendor** tried to restore to Catholic moral theology the centrality of virtue and the virtues, after centuries in which rules (either stringent or lax) had been the focal point of theological argument.[63] In doing so, **Veritatis Splendor** built a bridge to those schools of contemporary moral philosophy intent on recovering virtue ethics as a guide through the brambles of moral choice. At the same time, the Pope's insistence in the intra-Catholic discussion that certain acts were "intrinsically evil"—that is, always and everywhere wrong, no matter what combination of motivations and intended consequences is in play—was an important proposal to the postmodern West, where skepticism about the human capacity to know the moral truth of anything had eroded commitments to basic human rights, and had created a public moral culture in which the mantra of "choice" tended to drown out arguments about the rightness or wrongness of things.

Body Language and Papal Feminism. Karol Wojtyła came to the papacy convinced that the classic Catholic sexual ethic was true—and that its presentation to the Church and the world in the post-conciliar period left much to be desired. The Church's seeming incapacity to speak moral truth to the power of the sexual revolution was a serious pastoral problem, as he knew from extensive pastoral experience. That incapacity was also a grave defect in the Church's response to contemporary culture, which badly needed moral ballasting amidst the storms of an upheaval that promised sexual fulfillment yet seemed to deliver a good measure of dissatisfaction and suffering. Wojtyła brought to the conclave that elected him pope in 1978 the first sketches of a new approach to sexual ethics on which he had been working in Kraków; those sketches were developed, amplified, and expanded in four clusters of general audience addresses between September 1979 and November 1984 that would come to be known as John Paul II's Theology of the Body.[64]

The Galileo crisis had challenged the credibility of the Catholic Church's grasp of the truth of the cosmos. The sexual revolution challenged the Church's credibility in some of the most sensitive dimensions of the human microcosm. John Paul II was determined not to reprise the errors of the past in confronting the new moral and cultural challenges symbolized by (and in some respects created by) the invention of the oral contraceptive—a scientific development that, with atomic fission and the breaking of the genetic code, dramatically changed the human world of the late twentieth century and beyond. A new situation required a new account of ancient truths; that is what John Paul proposed in the Theology of the Body, a work of theological adventure that took our human embodiedness as male and female with utmost seriousness and sought to find in sexual differentiation and complementarity an ethic of interpersonal communion capable of expressing the nobility of human love. At the same time, the Pope pushed the Catholic sacramental imagination—the conviction that the extraordinary lies just on the far side of the ordinary, through which the extraordinary manifests itself—to new heights through his teaching that the self-giving love of sexual communion within the bond of marriage is an icon of the interior life of God the Holy Trinity. To the advocates of the sexual revolution, John Paul's dramatic combination of body language and God-talk offered a bold challenge: Who takes human sexuality more seriously? Those who imagine sexual love as another contact sport? Or those who think of it as revelatory of the interior life of God? To Catholic moral theologians obsessed with rules—either rigid and strict or flexible and lax—the Theology of the Body proposed a reading of the drama of human moral choosing in matters of the heart that revitalized an ethics of virtue and happiness, or beatitude.

The striking reception of the Theology of the Body among younger Catholic intellectuals in the last decade or so of John Paul's pontificate suggested that the old battles between "progressive" and "conservative" moral theologians were fading into irrelevance. Five years after the Pope's death, that process seemed likely to be extended by a global network of theological centers, the John Paul II Institutes for the Study of Marriage and Family, centered at the Pontifical Lateran University in Rome and with outreach on every continent. In addition to the scholarly analysis of the Theology of the Body, these institutes were engaged in helping prepare a responsible secondary literature by which the complexities and subtleties of John Paul's thought could be brought in accessible form to a more general pastoral audience by bishops, priests, deacons, and pastoral counselors. Parish- and diocesan-based marriage preparation programs were already one venue in which such materials were widely deployed.

The Theology of the Body also contained some of the seeds of John Paul II's distinctive papal femi- nism, another facet of his intellectual legacy likely to be under discussion in the Church and in world cul- ture for a long time. John Paul's feminism had four focal points: the defense of the legal and political equality of women in civil society; the explication of a distinctive "feminine genius," manifest in women's uniquely maternal embodiment of the Law of the Gift; the critique of theories of priestly ordination that regarded Holy Orders as a question of power rather than of iconography; and the Pope's theology of Mary as the primary model of Christian disciple- ship.[65] The last, into which the first three were in- corporated, was brought to a finely sharpened point of development during the 1987–88 Marian Year in the encyclical **Redemptoris Mater** [The Mother of Redeemer] and the apostolic letter **Mulieris Digni- tatem** [The Dignity of Women], but with perhaps special force in John Paul's 1987 Christmas address to the Roman Curia.

Speaking to men who understood themselves to be working at the center of the world Catholic reality in Rome, the Pope reminded his curial collaborators that the Petrine Church of authority and jurisdiction they embodied, like the Pauline Church of proclamation and evangelization and the Johannine Church of contemplation and prayer, takes its purpose and meaning from the prior and even more fundamental Marian Church: the Church formed in the image of a woman, Mary, whose assent to Gabriel's message in Luke 1.38 was the first act of Christian discipleship, in that it made possible the incarnation of the Son of God. In fact, John Paul told the Roman Curia, their work had no other purpose "except to form the Church in line with the ideal of sanctity already programmed and prefigured in Mary."

These various images of the Church drawn from the great New Testament figures—Peter, Paul, John, and Mary—were mutually reinforcing and complementary. But the Marian image or "profile," as John Paul termed it, was "pre-eminent," not only in time but in its meaning for every Christian's vocation to discipleship. Authority and power in the Church—even the awesome sacramental power to bind and loose sins—were always in service to the deepest realities of the Church: discipleship and sanctity, lived in communion with Mary's son, Jesus, and with the fellowship of believers throughout the world. Thus John Paul made his own, and then gave to the world

Church, the teaching of the Swiss theologian Hans Urs von Balthasar, who had once written that "Mary is 'Queen of the Apostles' without any pretensions to apostolic power: she has other and greater powers."[66]

In his 1987 Christmas address to the Curia, John Paul II deployed his distinctive, Marian feminism to fill out Vatican II's theology of the Church as communion, to explain the Council's abandonment of a monarchical model of the Church, and to set one of the theological foundations for understanding the Catholic Church's conviction that it could ordain only men to the ministerial priesthood. In 1999, John Paul lifted up striking examples of sanctity among great women of the Church, naming St. Bridget of Sweden, St. Catherine of Siena, and St. Teresa Benedicta of the Cross (Edith Stein) as co-patrons of Europe with St. Benedict and Sts. Cyril and Methodius.[67] None of this resolved the Church's debate over the meaning of the feminist revolution for Catholic life. Thanks to John Paul's papal feminism, however, the Catholic discussion had been located in its properly theological context and the world had been offered a model of the feminine genius that did not turn women into imitation men. Thus both theology and public policy seemed likely to be touched by John Paul's Marian feminism for the foreseeable future.

The Restoration of Christian Humanism. Speaking to leaders of American Catholic higher education in New Orleans in 1987, John Paul II noted that "religious faith itself calls for intellectual inquiry, and the confidence that there can be no contradiction between faith and reason is a distinctive feature of the Catholic humanistic tradition as it has existed in the past and as it exists in our own day."[68] The entire intellectual project of John Paul II, which grew, of course, from the pre-papal intellectual project of Karol Wojtyła, was in some sense summed up here. As the rescue of the Western humanistic tradition from its decay into skepticism and nihilism had seemed to him a fitting task for Vatican II, so the re-presentation of Christian doctrine through the prism of a thoroughly humanistic Christian analysis of the human person seemed to him a useful, and perhaps imperative, papal contribution to the Church and the world on the threshold of the third millennium—and at the end of a century in which false ideas of who and what human beings are had made an abattoir of history. Thus, toward the end of the Pope's life, the American theologian and cardinal Avery Dulles suggested that the heart of John Paul II's message, and the key to unlocking his uniqueness as an intellectual, was to be found in his steady focus on the mystery of the human person, his philosophical analysis of the Law of the Gift or law of self-giving inscribed in the human heart, and his explication of the entire doctrinal heritage of the Church through the prism of his Christian personalism.

Personalism was thus the ground on which John Paul could insist that "Christianity is not an opinion" or a set of propositions, but rather "Christianity is Christ! It is a Person!" Personalism shaped John Paul's presentation of the Kingdom of God as an encounter with the person of Jesus of Nazareth, the image of the invisible God. As for the Church itself, it was a privileged embodiment in history of the **communio personarum,** the communion of persons, that is both a longing of the human heart and a sign of the interior life of God the Holy Trinity. Thus, for John Paul, the Trinity is the first "model of the Church," precisely in its personalist dynamism. So, too, with the Church's sacraments, which for John Paul II were encounters with "the risen Jesus [who] accompanies us on our way and enables us to recognize him, as the disciples of Emmaus did, 'in the breaking of the bread' [Luke 24.35]." Christian personalism shaped John Paul II's theology of the priesthood, which stressed the ordained priest's sacramental ministry at the altar and in the confessional as a ministry conducted **in persona Christi,** "in the person of Christ." A personalist conviction about the human yearning for truth and the human capacity for genuine dialogue underwrote John Paul's ecumenism, his approach to interreligious affairs, and his lifelong conversations with the sciences and the humanities. Personalism and the development of Christian humanism shaped the Pope's teaching on Catholic higher education, which "enables people to rise to the full measure of their humanity, created in the image of God and renewed in Christ and his spirit," as John Paul put it in the 1990 apostolic constitution on Catholic higher learning, **Ex Corde Ecclesiae** [From the Heart of the Church]. Christian personalism was also evident in John Paul II's social doctrine: from his teaching in the encyclical **Laborem Exercens** on work as humanity's participation in God's ongoing creativity, to his proclamation of solidarity as the most authentic of human stances toward society, and on to his defense of the human right of economic initiative, his critique of the initiative-stultifying welfare state, and his teaching in **Centesimus Annus** on human creativity, imagination, and skill as the sources of the wealth of nations.[69] Christian personalism and the development of a humanism capable of sustaining nobility in the twenty-first century were also, and obviously, at the root of John Paul II's papal feminism, his sexual ethics, and his defense of the prerogatives of reason.

The Christian personalism of John Paul II was not, Dulles concluded, without its tensions with earlier explications of the Church's faith. Could a "rigorous and convincing proof" of God's existence be "erected on a personalist foundation"? Dulles asked. And if so, was that kind of proof preferable to the traditional philosophical arguments for the reality of God? How does Christian personalism, with its stress of Christ's lordship as a lordship of humility and service, understand Christ the King,

Christ the lawmaker, Christ the judge of the living and the dead? How does Christian personalism account for the traditional, penal aspects of Purgatory and for the possibility that some men and women may be lost for eternity? How could John Paul's personalist ethics (in which the Pope spoke "far more of the human person than of human nature") be integrated with classic understandings of the natural moral law? Could a personalist ethic account for the morality or immorality of acts in themselves? Does Christian personalism and its stress on dialogue as an expression of human dignity risk blunting the Church's voice when the condemnation of injustice is required? Did John Paul's personalism run into intellectual difficulties when questions of state power—such as the state's authority to execute a capital sentence, or the state's capacity to wage a just war, or the international community's moral obligation to "humanitarian intervention" in cases of genocide—were engaged?[70]

In the final analysis, Dulles concluded, John Paul's intellectual legacy was built on the foundations of his twin commitments to Christ and to human freedom. The Pope avoided "threatening words" because he believed that "fear . . . diminishes the scope of freedom and makes only a poor Christian." Preferring to hold up "the more perfect motives of hope, trust, and love" as the grounds for belief, for living a righteous life, and for sustaining free and virtuous societies, John Paul bent his intellectual project to the service of the call with which he began his pontificate: "Be not afraid!"[71]

Lives Transformed

There was something entirely appropriate about the fact that several dozen members of Karol Wojtyła's **Środowisko** were seated directly behind the heads of state and government at John Paul II's funeral Mass. The liturgy of the funeral Mass made clear that the man in whose memory the powers of the world were gathered was a Christian disciple; the presence of **Środowisko** was a vivid reminder that one striking characteristic of Karol Wojtyła's discipleship during the almost fifty-nine years of his priesthood, the forty-six years of his episcopacy, and the twenty-six years of his papacy was his capacity to inspire others to new depths of faith—faith in God, faith in Christ, faith in the Church, and faith in themselves.

The archbishop of Glasgow, Thomas Winning, described this Wojtyła effect with humility and precision when speaking to a full house at St. Andrew's Cathedral in 2001: "I'm grateful to John Paul II," Winning said, "not so much because he made me a cardinal, but because he made me a better Christian."[72] Karol Wojtyła could make men and women better Christians because he had a marked capacity to get inside others' lives—not to manipulate them but to offer them, out of the font of his own discipleship, the possibility of encountering the "more excellent way" of Christian love. He had first displayed that gift in his early priesthood at St. Florian's in Kraków, when this unknown young cleric of provincial background drew the respect, affection, and loyalty of some very demanding members of the Kraków Catholic intelligentsia. He had been a magnet for the conversion, the metanoia, of others in his roles as university professor and diocesan bishop. One of the remarkable things about his papacy was that he continued to touch the interior lives of others from what had previously seemed the virtually unapproachable distance of the papal throne.

Three and a half years before his own death in 2000, New York's Cardinal John J. O'Connor, no mean personality in his own right, marveled at John Paul II's capacity to exude "presence" and to shape the world's conversation through that personal and spiritual trait. And by "presence," O'Connor meant "not just physical presence—I mean that the world knows it has a pope. It's [the] very powerful, radiating presence . . . of a man who is listened to whether heeded or not; a man whose positions and potential positions are of concern to governments all over the world." John Paul II's "presence," O'Connor continued, created an "influence that goes beyond the quantifiable. Even the people who reject what he has to say, or the governments that reject what he has to say, are moved by it, restricted by it. They know that limits have been set, boundaries have been set."

Yet even more important, in Cardinal O'Connor's judgment, was John Paul II's magnetism in the microcosm of intimate personal contact: "He has this almost hypnotic effect on people. Every individual he meets feels at that moment that he or she is the only person in the world. . . . [That reflects] his sense of the sacredness of the human person, but . . . it [also] . . . springs from his philosophical position. He watches; he listens; he looks—it's almost as if he's reflecting on the whole phenomenon" of the individual before him.[73]

Massimo D'Alema, a secular man of the Italian political Left, came to appreciate John Paul II from a dramatically different political and theological position than that of Cardinal Winning or Cardinal O'Connor. Yet he, too, was struck by John Paul's powerful impact on individuals, in this case individuals who might never have previously imagined paying attention to a pope. As D'Alema put it in 1997,

I think the personality of [John Paul II] has a relevance that goes beyond the borders and the imprints of the Catholic Church. . . . [John Paul] has highlighted a spiritual dimension that is not only Catholic but that cuts across the different religions. From this perspective I don't think that to read or understand the Pope you have to proceed from inside the Catholic faith. I think the Pope is looked on as a leading figure by other cultures as well, not just by Catholicism. His influence is greater than the influence of the Church. It's not always been like that; there have been popes who have had less influence than the Catholic Church. But in the case of John Paul II we have a universality that moves beyond the borders of the Catholic Church.[74]

The universal appeal of John Paul II was widely commented on at his death. Yet contrary to the expectations of secular modernity and its suspicions about the cramping effects of particular commitments, John Paul II's universality, as Massimo D'Alema described it, grew from a very intense and specific particularity: Karol Wojtyła's Christian faith. Willing to acknowledge the genuine truths that others had discovered in their own journeys through life, he nevertheless engaged those other truths through the prism of Catholic faith, which he understood to be the truth of the world and which he wished to share with others. His Christian faith was neither cloying nor aggressive; but neither was it hidden or muted. In a season of Christian timidity, John Paul II's unapologetic Christian witness explained no small part of his transformative impact on individuals from an extraordinarily wide variety of backgrounds.

Baylor University professor Francis Beckwith found his way back into the Catholic Church of his youth through the example of John Paul II; Beckwith and his wife were particularly impressed by the Pope's way of "living the truth of Christ's Lordship and the intrinsic dignity of the human person," and by John Paul's "defense of a culture of life [which] revealed an understanding of political liberty and the intrinsic value of the human person that had a philosophical power that was [also] deeply biblical." As an intellectual, Beckwith was also struck by the Pope's teaching on the nature of higher education, which "persuasively offered an understanding of what it means for a university to think of its theological beliefs as knowledge: that, for example, the Apostles Creed is just as normative for theology as the periodic table is for chemistry." In a world skeptical of its grasp on any truth, John Paul had shown that "faith and reason are like two eyes, each of which can function well, but on its own incompletely; when they work together, they provide [us] with a richer and more complete vision of the world."[75]

The transformative impact of John Paul II on Francis Beckwith took place in the robustly if confusedly religious culture of the United States. The late Pope's dramatic influence on the life of Nina Sophie Heereman, a bright and beautiful young German lawyer, unfolded at the intersection of the arid secularity dominant in contemporary European high culture and what Baroness Heereman experienced as the empty Catholicism in which she grew up: "Catholicism hollowed out . . . a shell with no serious sin and therefore no state of grace [and] no encounter with Christ." Struggling with the meaning and import of a powerful experience with the eucharistic Christ at World Youth Day-1997 in Paris, Nina Heereman attended the Pentecost 1998 meeting of Catholic renewal movements and new Catholic communities in Rome. There, on seeing the Pope, a thought occurred: "Suppose John Paul II had said 'No'? What a disaster that would have been for the world. . . . So I thought I'd better say 'Yes'"—"yes" to the invitation to a deep personal relationship with Christ that she had first sensed in Paris. In Nina Heereman's case, it was the challenge of the Christian life as embodied by John Paul II—a life of heroism built on friendship with Jesus Christ—that broke open everything else and gave focus to her personal, religious, and vocational yearning. As she once put it, if you accept that the truth of Christian faith and life will "set you free, then you want to learn everything you can about it." So Nina Heereman dedicated her life to the new evangelization as a consecrated laywoman in the world.[76]

Sister Mary Karol Widomska, O.P., a Dominican nun of the Congregation of St. Cecilia in Nashville, Tennessee, discovered her religious vocation and took her religious name from the man who had written and spoken for decades about the importance of consecrated religious life, both for the Church and for the salvation of the world. As she put it, "My decision to enter religious life was supposed to be a gift to John Paul II . . . I was getting ready to [enter] the Nashville Dominicans as a direct answer to his frequent messages, talks, or letters on the splendor of the encounter with Christ in religious life. I heard those talks [and] read the letters, but the witness of his life given totally and unconditionally to the Son of God drew me even more to desire that same commitment. . . . In this constant gift of self to Christ, in this constant spending of himself, he seemed to gain a new vigor and his life . . . spoke of the exhilarating joy and freedom of such a total commitment."[77]

It was John Paul II's analysis of the dark underside of late modernity and its misconception of freedom that began to make sense of the carnage Nicholas Fernandez saw in the concrete jungle as a New York City police officer—and that subsequently redirected Fernandez's life plans: "I came across concrete examples of what Pope John Paul II called the 'culture of death'—suicides, homicides and domestic situations" to which Fernandez could offer "no external solution" as a policeman. "There needs to be a change of heart on the inside, and that's where a priest is needed." So Nicholas Fernandez left the police force and entered the New York archdiocesan seminary at Dunwoodie to prepare for a different life than what he might have imagined for himself, absent the thought and inspiration of John Paul II.[78]

Such stories could be multiplied over and over again, in a kaleidoscope of human experiences: the story of actor Cary Elwes, who came to a new appreciation of the Catholic faith in which he had been reared by getting "inside" Karol Wojtyła while playing him in a film; the story of actress Sophia Loren, who told the office investigating the possible beatification of the late Pope that "I jealously keep the memory of John Paul II in my heart," and who "went to the tomb of John Paul II in the Vatican to pay homage to him and to pray, in order to show my great admiration and devotion."[79] Then there was one of Fidel Castro's sisters who, on meeting John Paul II privately during the papal pilgrimage to Cuba in January 1998, told John Paul that she had "dreamed about embracing the Pope"—who replied, "Well, why not now?" and drew the sister of the Cuban dictator into a hug, at which point she began sobbing like a child.[80]

Václav Havel, welcoming John Paul II to the free Czechoslovakia that had emerged out of the choking smog of communist lies, confessed that he was not sure he knew what a "miracle" was—but that he knew he had witnessed something miraculous as he, the former jailed dissident playwright, welcomed to his liberated country a fellow dramatist, the Pope, who had himself been the target of communist hatred and fear. That same sense of the miraculous might be suggested by the fact that there are schools and seminaries named for a son of Wadowice in such diverse venues as Campbell's Bay, Québec; Hendersonville, Tennessee; and Lome, Togo; or that, in the years after his death, letters from all over the world arrived at the office in charge of investigating his possible beatification, addressed simply to "Pope John Paul II, Heaven"; or that a man like Henry Kissinger could describe Karol Wojtyła, at the Pope's death, as the singular embodiment of the trials, tragedies, and triumphs of humanity in the second half of the twentieth century. None of this was expected on October 16, 1978, when the man "from a far country" presented himself to the Church and the world from the loggia of St. Peter's.

Men and women who have bent the course of history in unexpected directions are rarely the best witnesses to the source of their accomplishment. Yet here, too, John Paul II might be granted something of an exception. For, if asked, he surely would have said that his influence on others, and on history, reflected the grace of God at work in his life. The simplicity, and profundity, of that conviction within him is the best explanation of his impact on the lives of others—and through others, on history and on the human future.

THE CONTEXTS OF A LIFE

As those whose lives he touched came to recognize, Karol Wojtyła was a human singularity, a kind of once-in-a-lifetime personality. John Paul II, for his part, did not think of himself that way. Rather, he thought of his papacy as an expression of the Catholic Church and the Catholic priesthood in the distinctive circumstances of the mid-twentieth century.

Thus in marking the accomplishment of Pope John Paul II, the historian does no disservice to the man or his memory by acknowledging the contexts that produced the conditions for the possibility of Pope John Paul II.

There was, at the beginning, the Polish context. The modern historical experience of the Polish nation and its struggle for freedom was the wellspring from which Karol Wojtyła drew his understanding of the dynamics of history, which he then deployed to change the history of the world. The Polish context of his life and accomplishment was also informed by the unique twentieth-century experience of the Catholic Church in Poland. Considered a backwater (and often a reactionary backwater) by many in the North Atlantic world, Polish Catholicism was in fact a fighting Church that had important lessons to teach the world Church—lessons about self-sacrifice and martyrdom, which shaped Wojtyła's thinking about the Law of the Gift inscribed in the human heart; lessons about a heroic exercise of the offices of priest and bishop, which left a profound imprint on his own ministry; lessons about the liberating power of popular piety and its capacity to coexist with authentic Catholic reform, which shaped John Paul II's interpretation of the Second Vatican Council.

Then there was the mid-twentieth-century Catholic theological context. Many of the signature themes and initiatives of the pontificate of John Paul II were drawn from the renewal of Catholic theology that took place, primarily in continental Europe, in the decades prior to the Second Vatican Council. John Paul II's teaching that the Church **is** a mission, and his concept of the "new evangelization," reflected, even as it stretched and developed, the kerygmatic theology pioneered by Josef A. Jungmann, S.J., in Innsbruck in the pre–World War II years.[81] John Paul's ecumenical initiatives would have been difficult to imagine, and impossible to execute, absent the intellectual foundations of Catholic ecumenism laid by theologians such as Yves Congar, O.P., by the teaching of the Second Vatican Council, and by the personal efforts of Pope John XXIII, Cardinal Augustin Bea, S.J., and Pope Paul VI.[82] John Paul's II social doctrine assumed, even as it extended, the thinking of theologians dating back to Augustine, Aquinas, and Suárez; the thought of such modern exponents of Catholic social theory as Wilhelm Emmanuel von Ketteler, Heinrich Pesch, Oswald von Nell-Breuning, S.J., Jacques Maritain, and John Courtney Murray, S.J.; and the social magisterium of Popes Leo XIII and Pius XI. The twentieth-century renewal of Catholic biblical studies and the mid-twentieth-century liturgical movement, both of which were ratified at Vatican II, had obvious impacts on the teaching and ministry of John Paul II, as did the speculative theological work of such preeminent twentieth-century Catholic thinkers as Henri de Lubac, S.J., and Hans Urs von Balthasar. Karol Wojtyła, in other words, was a great learner as well as a great teacher, and his teaching was, in some respects, the culmination of processes that had been at work in Catholic intellectual life for over a century.

Finally, there was the personal context. Karol Wojtyła was a man of conversation and a leader who thought through his decisions with the help of others. Yet he was also a man who trusted his own instincts because those instincts had been refined by prayer. Thus some of the signature accomplishments of John Paul II—World Youth Days and the revitalization of youth ministry; the revivification of the priesthood and the consecrated life; the open dialogue with science—reflected the distinctive pastoral experience of Karol Wojtyła, priest and bishop, whose confidence in the providential guidance of his life led him to think that there was something of use in his pre-papal experience for the exercise of the Office of Peter. Similarly, the dynamic synthesis of twentieth-century Catholic thought expressed in his magisterium and his papal ministry was distinctively his. The understanding of the third millennium as a privileged moment of grace in which the Church could reexperience itself as a communion of disciples called to a new evangelization of the world; the personalist Christology according to which Jesus Christ reveals both the face of the merciful Father and the truth about our humanity; the notion of a Law of the Gift, built into the structure of moral choice and action, as the royal road to human fulfillment; solidarity as the key to living freedom nobly in free and virtuous societies; the revelatory iconography of our embodiedness and complementarity as male and female—these signature themes of the pontificate reflected a uniquely Wojtyłan synthesis of Catholic thought and practice, and a crucial set of keys for interpreting the event at which the twentieth-century Catholic renewal reached its dramatic watershed, the Second Vatican Council.

These three contexts—the Polish, the theological-historical, and the personal—often intersected. Wojtyła brought a distinctively Polish and intensely personal devotion to the Blessed Virgin Mary to the papacy; he refined his thinking about Mary's unique role in salvation history with the aid of Balthasar's theology; he then deployed that thinking to propose a profound shift in the self-understanding of the entire Church. Because of the distinctive circumstances of the Church in Poland under communism, Wojtyła had not been embroiled in the theological controversies of the post–Vatican II period; he was himself a world-class intellectual, however, with particular competence in philosophical anthropology and ethics, and thus he could bring the best of pre- and post-conciliar theology to bear in his papal magisterium; in seminal documents such as his inaugural encyclical, **Redemptor Hominis;** his encyclical on the moral life, **Veritatis Splendor;** and his Theology of the Body. He was a man who had fought a distinctive kind of fight at the barricades of freedom's cause; thus his criticism of deficiencies in the theologies of liberation did not arise from any fondness for the ancien régime, but from his commitment to the truth of Catholic faith and his development of a more profound theory of human liberation through the Polish struggle for religious freedom, his philosophical work, and his reading of the Second Vatican Council's teaching on the Church in the modern world (which he had helped formulate in 1964–65).

The connecting thread that bound these three contexts together in the singularity of Pope John Paul II was the Christian radicalism of Karol Wojtyła: the depth and intensity of his belief in the liberating power of Christ's love was the deepest taproot of his papal accomplishment, because it was the deepest wellspring of his life and his thought.

FRUSTRATIONS, FLAWS, FAILURES

The pontificate of John Paul II was subject to intense criticism from late 1979, when the Congregation for the Doctrine of the Faith declared that Swiss dissident Hans Küng "could not be considered a Catholic theologian," until the Pope's death on April 2, 2005.[83] The criticism came from all points along the spectrum of Catholic and secular opinion, but by conventional reckoning, the criticism from inside the Catholic Church tended to cluster into two categories: a liberal or progressivist critique, and a conservative or restorationist critique.

The progressivist critique, which readily found a platform in the global media, was influenced by an interpretation of Vatican II that held that the Council marked a decisive break with Catholic tradition and the beginnings of a new, modernity-friendly form of Catholicism.[84] According to this line of critique, John Paul II conducted an authoritarian pontificate that betrayed, retarded, or at the very least diminished the achievements of Vatican II. In more than a few instances, this alleged betrayal was thought to be a by-product of the Pope's Polish background. For some in the progressivist camp, the principal manifestations of John Paul's "authoritarian style" were the Pope's alleged centralization of power and his degradation of the Council's teaching on the common responsibility of the world episcopate for the Church's governance.[85] For others, John Paul's alleged authoritarianism displayed itself chiefly in what was regarded as a campaign of repression against speculative theologians and progressive bishops. Still others charged that the pontificate abandoned the "spirit of Vatican II" in what they described as John Paul II's misogyny; this was not infrequently regarded as a function of the Pope's defense of classic Catholic sexual ethics, which many Catholic progressives considered indefensible.

The conservative or restorationist critique came

from those who hoped that John Paul II would restore a Catholic golden age, which they imagined to have reached something of an apogee in the pontificate of Pius XII. It is important to note that the restorationist critique was not identical with the position of the French archbishop Marcel Lefebvre and his followers in the Society of St. Pius X, whose skepticism about Vatican II's teachings on religious freedom, on church and state, and on Christianity's relationship to Judaism bordered on, when it did lapse over into, radical rejection of the Council.[86] Rather, restorationist Catholics criticized John Paul II for not acting more vigorously as a papal disciplinarian. On this view, a pope from a disciplined Church like Polish Catholicism ought to have brought order out of the ecclesiastical chaos the restorationists perceived as having followed the Council (whose basic teachings they accepted, if sometimes grudgingly). Restorationists argued that John Paul II's commitment to dialogue within the Church jeopardized the Council's legitimate achievements, continued the trivialization of the liturgy, failed to reverse a collapse of catechetics, intensified a breakdown of discipline in the clergy and among women's religious orders, and reinforced the tendency of bishops to think of themselves as discussion-group moderators rather than as authoritative teachers of the truth of Catholic faith and guardians of the integrity of the sacraments.[87]

While both of these critiques are worth engaging in light of the enduring achievements of John Paul II's papacy outlined above, they are, in the final analysis, unsatisfactory as analytic frameworks for identifying and understanding the undoubted frustrations, flaws, and failures of the pontificate.

Both the progressivist and the restorationist critiques share an assumption with the global media: all tend to assume a model of the papacy in which the pope is understood as someone akin to a local governor, prime minister, or president—that is, someone who can change "policy" as he wills (and if policy doesn't change, the unacceptable status quo must reflect a defect of the leader's intelligence or will). This is to misunderstand both the nature of the papacy and the relationship between the stable and dynamic elements in the Church, however. The papacy does not create "policy" in matters of doctrine or morality the way political leaders create social welfare policy, education policy, health care policy, and so forth. Rather, the pope is the guardian and, in communion with the College of Bishops, the authoritative interpreter of what classic theology called the deposit of faith. Moreover, what is fixed and stable in the Catholic Church (like the canon of Scripture, the creeds, the sacraments, the Church's structure of authority, and certain moral teachings) exists in order to foster a dynamism and a creativity that are faithful to the Church's one supreme rule of faith, the living Christ.[88] Thus the creativity with which John Paul II sought to proclaim the truth of Catholic faith through the prism of his Christian personalism was a creativity within boundaries. Those boundaries were set by the Catholic tradition, not by the imagination or will of Karol Wojtyła.

A more apt framework for grasping and understanding the frustrations and flaws in the pontificate of John Paul II, and wherein John Paul failed, comes from inside the Catholic tradition itself.

According to the Church's doctrine, all baptized Christians are empowered by the Holy Spirit to grasp the truth and proclaim it, to worship God truly, and to serve others. Thus every baptized Christian exercises three missions, which Catholic theology refers to as the **munus docendi** (the mission to teach), the **munus sanctificandi** (the mission to sanctify), and the **munus regendi** (the mission of governance, or servant leadership). These three **munera,** or missions, are a reflection in each Christian's life of the triple mission of Christ himself, into whose Mystical Body the baptized are incorporated. According to the Catholic doctrine of Holy Orders, the bishops of the Church exercise the fullness of these three missions of Christ as priest, prophet, and king. The Office of Peter, as Catholics understand it, is a gift of Christ to the Church for the sake of the Church's unity in truth, in worship, and in service. Thus the frustrations, the flaws, and the failures of any pontificate can be thematically organized and analyzed through the prism of this tripartite scheme.

Munus Docendi: **The Mission to Teach**

The pontificate of John Paul II was one of the great teaching pontificates in history, in both the breadth and depth of the Pope's magisterium. John Paul's exercise of the **munus docendi** in the broadest sense of the term was not without its frustrations, its misapprehensions, and its insufficiencies, however.

Europe. At the Spanish shrine of Santiago de Compostela, one of the great pilgrimage destinations in medieval Christendom, John Paul II challenged Europe during World Youth Day-1989 to rediscover itself as a "beacon of civilization and a force for progress in the world" as it crossed the threshold of its impending post–Cold War reunification.[89] During the 2003–4 debate over the new constitutional treaty to govern the expanded European Union, the Pope passionately urged the people and the leaders of Europe to reject a constitutional abandonment of the Christian roots of European civilization, which he regarded as crucial to Europe's capacity to be a protagonist of freedom in the twenty-first century. Both pleas fell on deaf ears, in the main. A Europe committed to the pursuit of what Jean-Louis Tauran, John Paul II's longtime "foreign minister," once described as "happiness without constraints" was not prepared to listen to John Paul's teaching on the law of self-giving as the key to authentic human liberation, or to see in the Pope's teaching on solidarity the remedy for its culture of solitary individualism.[90]

Hostility to John Paul II's understanding of true freedom, to his interpretation of the teaching of the Second Vatican Council, and to his method of papal governance was most pronounced and widespread in German-speaking Europe: Germany, Austria, and the Germanic cantons of Switzerland. In Germany itself, the pontificate's difficult reception was due to several factors, not least of which was John Paul's Polishness.[91] Ethnic stereotypes and resentments die hard, and in the case of the German Church, which was typically led by theologians convinced that German theology had a special, leading role to play in post-conciliar Catholic life (as it had in shaping Vatican II), the idea that a Polish intellectual might have a deeper grasp of the Council's teaching and a firmer grip on the dynamics of modern and postmodern Western culture did not go down easily.[92] In many cases, it did not go down at all. And despite a certain sympathy in German Catholic circles for John Paul II's human warmth, and for his ecumenical and interreligious initiatives, the Pope's magisterium was ill received, and in some instances flatly rejected, in German-speaking Catholicism, except among a scattering of intellectuals, a few bishops, and the younger members of various renewal movements and new Catholic communities.[93] Whether this would change in the decades after John Paul's death, such that German-speaking Catholicism would actually engage the magisterium of Karol Wojtyła rather than peremptorily dismissing it, could not be predicted. According to Cardinal Joachim Meisner of Cologne, if change came, it might come because German-speaking Catholicism discovered that its twentieth-century martyrs—many of whom had been beatified by John Paul II—and not its intellectual accomplishments were its greatest modern heritage and its noblest gift to the Catholic future.[94]

Toward the end of the pontificate, some German Catholic leaders were reconsidering their situation. One of them, Cardinal Karl Lehmann of Mainz, Germany, sensed the possibility of new intuitions among his countrymen: that it was impossible for human beings to "live with the silence," and that solitary individuals incapable of making and living "permanent commitments" were dooming themselves to serial unhappiness and their nations to demographic oblivion.[95] Whether this latter intuition would open up the possibility of the German-speaking world reconsidering Karol Wojtyła's Law of the Gift remained, at the Pope's death, an open and urgent question for the German Church and for German society.

The frustrations of John Paul's exercise of the **munus docendi** in Europe were paralleled by some modest successes. John Paul II's challenge to Italian Catholicism to redefine itself in more culturally assertive terms led to a modest but nonetheless real revival of Catholic practice in Italy, and a new evangelical self-confidence among at least some members of the Italian episcopate.[96] Moreover, John Paul's articulate and passionate defense of the right to life over more than a quarter century reshaped the public debate, such that certain key right-to-life positions were successfully defended in an Italian national referendum conducted shortly after the Pope's death.

Despite the election of an aggressively secular government led by José Luis Rodríguez Zapatero in 2004, the Spanish Church, according to Madrid archbishop Antonio María Rouco Varela, had rediscovered "the rich meaning of 'evangelization' as a matter of both urgency and hope"—and had displayed a willingness to live out that rediscovery in large-scale public opposition to the Zapatero government's redefinitions of the family. Cardinal Rouco Varela attributed both accomplishments to the teaching and witness of John Paul II, whose Spanish strategy mirrored his culture-first understanding of the dynamics of history: John Paul challenged Spanish Catholics to stop acquiescing in the secularists' proclamation of Catholic marginality, and called Catholics to recover their national cultural memory—and through that recovery, to develop a new Catholic will to build a genuinely humanistic future on the foundations of what was noble in Spain's Catholic past.[97] Nonetheless, the pace of Catholic reform in Spain remained slow, and the Zapatero government was reelected three years after the Pope's death.

Thanks to John Paul, similar stirrings of a new Catholic self-consciousness were also discernible in France. According to Cardinal Jean-Marie Lustiger, the archbishop of Paris from 1981 until 2005, John Paul II was already a keen student of the French Catholic scene at the time of his election to the papacy. That is, the Pope knew that the ecclesiastical civil war between Lefebvrists and progressivists that had crippled French Catholicism since the Second Vatican Council was, as Lustiger put it, a "quarrel from the nineteenth century, and that's finished." France in the last quarter of the twentieth century was not a Catholic society riven by two rival parties, rooted in two bitterly opposed understandings of French history since 1789. Rather, it was a "pagan society," in which the first task of Christians was to rediscover the mystery of divine election. Prior to John Paul II's teaching and witness, Lustiger argued, even practicing French Catholics were evangelically complacent and imagined that "faith . . . coincided with culture and society": which meant that Catholics were "not used to [giving] testimony." Then came John Paul II, who was "ready to give to Christian self-consciousness a renewal of the sense of God's call, of God's gracious gift." The result, the cardinal concluded, was that the Pope had "made it easier for people to be witnesses." At the same time, John Paul II's analysis of the tensions and contradictions within contemporary European high culture challenged the "conformism to certain Marxist orthodoxies" that had long characterized French intellectual life; the Pope did this by embodying "a humanistic and realistic, rather than political, opposition to communism" and by his ability to speak in ways that displayed a philosopher's familiarity with the various currents at work in twentieth-century European thought.[98] Lustiger's own intellectual and pastoral witness during his twenty-four years as archbishop of the French capital were no small part of whatever transformations were under way in French Catholicism during the pontificate of John Paul II; but Lustiger would not have had the platform from which to make the witness he did if John Paul had not had the courage to appoint the son of emigré Polish Jews as bishop of Orleans and then archbishop of Paris.[99]

Poland's reception of the pontificate was, obviously, unique, and was shaped by the powerful emotional bond between the Polish people and the native son whose election to the papacy seemed to redeem Poland's terrible sacrifices during the twentieth century. The tremendous crowds that came out for every one of John Paul's Polish pilgrimages; seminaries filled to overflowing and abundant religious vocations; a high level of Catholic practice for a decade and a half after the Revolution of 1989—all of these measurable factors confounded the expectations of those who thought Poland would follow the path of Ireland, Spain, and Portugal into rapid secularization after a delayed encounter with modernity, and bore witness both to the firm grip John Paul II had on the loyalties of his fellow countrymen and to their determination to keep faith with him. In the wake of

John Paul's death, the challenge for Polish Catholicism was to look forward, not back; to grapple with and absorb the magisterium of John Paul II, as well as bask in the spiritual glow of his Polishness and his sanctity; and to find a public voice that mirrored the late Pope's ability to engage society and culture through the arts of reason and persuasion. Five years after John Paul's death, there was serious debate in Polish Catholicism as to the degree to which these challenges were being met—a debate that was itself a reflection of the Pope's continuing influence.

Thus the European reception of the teaching of John Paul II was decidedly mixed. Without precluding the possibility of dramatic change over the long haul, however, it must be conceded that John Paul's extensive efforts to re-evangelize Europe and lead it out of the twenty-first-century version of John Bunyan's Slough of Despond achieved only modest short-term results. One of the causes of Europe's crisis of civilizational morale, the Pope believed, was western European Catholicism's acquiescence in its own cultural marginalization, to which the Church had become too accustomed; thus his extensive efforts to shake European Catholicism out of the doldrums, by appealing to both its mind and its heart. To the end, John Paul II remained a man of the long view and a man of hope. But within a few years of John Paul's death, Europe's unprecedentedly low birth rates had become an unmistakable empirical fact, as the continent's demographic self-destruction cast a long shadow over its cultural, fiscal, and political future. At least some of those aware of the gravity of the situation understood, with the late Pope, that one of the roots of this crisis was Europe's postmodern insouciance about the human capacity to know the truth of things—an insouciance that John Paul II had bent every effort to shake, but without transformative success.

The Anglosphere. The European Anglosphere in Great Britain and Ireland, and its offshore expression in English-speaking Canada, may have been less vociferously resistant to John Paul II's exercise of the **munus docendi** than were its German cousins. Still, it cannot be said that John Paul's ideas were as thoroughly engaged and debated in these parts of the English-speaking world as they were in the United States. Nor did the reception of John Paul's magisterium in the European Anglosphere and in Canada lead to the kind of institutional renewal that was visible in the U.S. Church in the latter years of the pontificate: in the episcopate, the priesthood, religious life, seminaries, Catholic intellectual life, and some Catholic institutions of higher education. As elsewhere, John Paul II was taken seriously by Catholic renewal movements and new Catholic communities in England, Wales, Scotland, Ireland, and Canada, and by some of the younger members of the clergy and hierarchy; there was even evidence that John Paul's teaching had had an effect on some bishops who were previously inclined to share in the progressivist critique of the Pope's magisterium. In the last period of the pontificate, for example, Cardinal Cormac Murphy-O'Connor of Westminster tried to bring the teaching of **Veritatis Splendor** to bear in a United Kingdom where, in the cardinal's view, "we have no idea today of absolute moral norms," particularly in reference to issues posed by the new biotechnologies.[100] But, as a general proposition, the reception of John Paul II's teaching in the Anglosphere outside the United States reflected the stance of the London-based **Tablet,** which, while open to occasional defenses of the Pope's magisterium, far more frequently reflected the fixed positions of the progressivist critics of the pontificate, especially on questions of morality. As for Ireland, neither the witness nor the teaching of John Paul II could slow its rapid transformation into one of the most thoroughly (and, in media terms, aggressively) secularist countries in Europe—a transformation later intensified by revelations of the sexual abuse of the young in Irish Catholic institutions and the cover-up of abuse by Irish bishops, which came to light a half decade after John Paul's death.[101]

In the farther reaches of the Anglosphere, John Paul II's teaching had as difficult a reception in New Zealand as it did in the United Kindgom. The exception in the Antipodes was Australia, where, in the last eighteen years of the pontificate, Cardinal George Pell led a powerful movement in support of vibrant Catholic orthodoxy that drew explicitly on John Paul's teaching to change dramatically the reference points in the Australian Catholic debate, which were once as monolithically shaped by the progressivist critique of the pontificate as were those in Germany.[102]

Ecumenical Logjams and Interreligious Impossibilities. The ecumenical and interreligious frustrations and failures of the pontificate of John Paul II cannot be fairly laid to deficiencies in the Pope's exercise of the **munus docendi,** despite charges to the contrary from progressivist critics (who sometimes seemed to imagine Christian ecumenism as a negotiation in which both sides bargained over nonessentials in order to arrive at mutually agreeable compromises) and restorationist critics (who misread aspects of the Pope's Assisi initiatives and his expressions of respect for Muslim piety). On the other hand, John Paul's readings of the ecumenical signs of the times and the nature of certain interreligious conflicts were not flawless.

Orthodoxy was not prepared for a restoration of full communion between Constantinople and Rome on the basis of a return to the status quo ante 1054, as John Paul seemed to propose in the 1995 encyclical **Ut Unum Sint.** That unpreparedness likely reflected a historical fact that was not reckoned with in the encyclical's analysis: that the mutual excommunications between Rome and Constantinople in 1054 were the culmination of a drifting apart between Eastern and Western Christianity that had been under way for centuries, and that had been shaped by powerful linguistic, philosophical, and political forces. The events of 1054, in other words, did not take place in a historical vacuum; the status quo ante 1054 to which John Paul proposed a return was far shakier and more roiled than the Pope seemed prepared to acknowledge. That fact of history continued to shape Orthodox ecumenical attitudes and approaches a millennium later.

As for the post-Reformation fractures within Western Christianity, the theological and doctrinal confusions of liberal Protestantism in the last decades of the twentieth century made any achievement of full communion unlikely in the extreme, it being impossible to achieve a consensus on faith and practice with Christian communities that were unable to define their doctrinal and moral borders—communities that were also willing to change those borders without significant reference to apostolic tradition. None of this was, of course, John Paul II's fault, but it was a source of disappointment nonetheless, particularly in terms of the Anglican and Lutheran dialogues. As for the new ecumenism that ran along various (and usually informal) axes of discussion between Catholics and evangelical Protestants, it was not altogether clear that John Paul II completely grasped the considerable differences between those American evangelical Protestants who embraced aspects of his magisterium and who eagerly entered into serious theological dialogue with Catholics, and those Pentecostalist "sects" of whose proselytism in Latin America his Curia frequently complained. Nor was the Pope willing to acknowledge, at least publicly, that one reason that Latin American evangelicalism was making serious inroads into formerly Catholic countries was because it inculcated moral habits of sobriety, male financial responsibility, and male marital fidelity that Latin American Catholicism had failed for centuries to teach effectively.[103] On the other hand, John Paul's insistence that the 1997 Synod be styled the "Synod for America" rather than "for the Americas" (which reflected a concern that the component parts of the New World open themselves to mutual enrichment) suggested a papal recognition of the possibility that the new Catholic-Evangelical ecumenism in the United States might have salutary effects in reshaping ecumenical relations in Central and South America—a recognition the Pope expressed in private conversation.[104]

John Paul's most significant achievements in inter-religious dialogue were in the field of Catholic-Jewish relations; the solidity of those accomplishments was evident during certain difficult moments in the first years of the pontificate of Benedict XVI—another pope with a profound sense of Jewish election, and of the divinely mandated entanglement of Christians and Jews. One might ask, however, whether the theological adventure for which John Paul II called at the Great Synagogue of Rome and elsewhere—an adventure in which faithful Jews and faithful Catholics reconvened the conversation about election, covenant, and messianic expectation that had broken off about A.D. 70—was heard in Jewish religious and intellectual circles beyond a few North American enclaves. As important as civility and good manners are, it would mark something of a failure of John Paul II's teaching on Jews and Judaism if the Christian-Jewish dialogue of the twenty-first century devolved into an ongoing negotiation about the meaning of civility and good manners in the public square.

In the wake of the events of September 11, 2001, John Paul II made significant efforts to ensure that the Catholic Church did not tacitly or overtly reinforce Osama bin Laden's claim that his war against the West, and that of his fellow jihadists, was a religious war. This was important, for it underscored the falsity of the jihadists' argument while keeping open lines of communication that might otherwise have been shut down. Yet it was not clear, in the last three and a half years of the pontificate, that John Paul had grappled conceptually with the intra-Islamic causes of the Islamic civil war that had spilled out of the Islamic world to engage virtually all humanity, often violently. Nor was it clear that the Pope had reckoned in detail with the meaning of the new Islamic demographics of Europe, or with aggressive Islamist political and legal claims in Europe, for the European future.[105] These insufficiencies were not the result of any papal misunderstanding of the theological flaws of Islam from a Christian point of view, which the Pope had clearly identified in **Crossing the Threshold of Hope.** Rather, they may have reflected the difficulties of John Paul's personal situation in the last several years of the pontificate, in which his energies were being consumed by his valiant efforts to sustain as much of his ministry as possible. (The Holy See's approach to these post-9/11 and European questions was also, and undoubtedly, shaped by the determination to be nonconfrontational that dominated thinking about Catholic-Islamic relations in the Pontifical Council for Interreligious Dialogue.)[106]

Catholic International Relations Theory and the Just War Tradition. A soldier's son who honored the soldier's vocation, John Paul II nevertheless displayed little interest in exercising the **munus docendi** to facilitate the intellectual development of the Church's moral theory of just and limited war, which, as it had evolved since the fourth century, constituted an entire way of thinking about international relations.[107] At the end of the pontificate, the Holy See enjoyed full diplomatic relations with over 170 states; under John Paul's leadership, the Holy See had shown itself on occasion an effective international "player"; the Pope's teaching on the universality of human rights was a significant factor in shaping the rights debate globally, as his personal intervention had been decisive in a number of events over the previous quarter century; yet John Paul II made no serious or sus-

tained attempt to revive the intellectual tradition
once known as Catholic International Relations
Theory.[108] Nor did he effect significant change in
the analytic default positions in the Section for Relations with States of the Vatican Secretariat of State
(the papal "foreign ministry") and the Pontifical
Council for Justice and Peace. There, the ingrained
institutional instincts remained far more reflective
of the default positions found in western European
chancelleries than of John Paul II's thought about
the cultural dynamics of history.[109]

This failure to develop and inculcate a different
and distinctively Catholic way of thinking about the
moral exigencies of world politics in the relevant offices of the Roman Curia was of little account in
those instances in which John Paul took the conceptual and operational lead—as in his 1979 and 1995
speeches to the United Nations, his 1978–79 initiative in avoiding a war between Argentina and Chile
over the Beagle Channel, his witness and diplomacy
in the years leading up to "1989," his support for
the 1993 Fundamental Agreement with Israel, his
public campaigns prior to the 1994 Cairo International Conference on Population and Development
and the 1995 Beijing World Conference on Women,
and his 2003–4 appeals for a non-Christophobic
European Constitutional Treaty.[110] But the Pope's
disinclination to initiate, and then institutionalize,
a reform of the default positions in the Vatican foreign ministry and at Justice and Peace left the Holy

See ill equipped to play the role of moral counselor effectively in the roiling worlds of twenty-first-century global politics. This was a loss for both the Church and the world, as new and grave problems at the intersection of morality and world politics were being raised by history at precisely the moment when the papacy enjoyed unparalleled global moral authority and a unique capacity to shape the terms of global moral argument.

Thus, in the years immediately following John Paul II's death, the default positions in those Vatican offices responsible for the Holy See's international engagement tended to remain where they had been at the end of the pontificate of Pope Paul VI: a fulsome embrace of international organizations as inherently superior to the bilateral politics of nations; a willingness to appease authoritarians (in this case, Islamic authoritarians), rather than boldly defend religious freedom and other fundamental human rights; a functional pacifism that, while holding on to the theoretical husk of the just war tradition, seemed unable to imagine the just and limited use of armed force in the defense of justice and freedom and that effectively assigned moral **competence de guerre** to the United Nations; an unwillingness to face the facts of global ideological challenge (Islamist, rather than communist); a disinclination to name Third World corruption for what it was, and a concomitant instinct to blame all Third World conflicts on injustices of underdevelopment caused by the developed world; and a lavish use of the language of "human rights" to describe virtually every conceivable social good.

These curious gaps in a pontificate that did not hesitate to address virtually every other grave moral issue on the human agenda at the end of the twentieth century and the beginning of the twenty-first may well have reflected an over-reading of the meaning of "1989" by John Paul II, and by his diplomats and his Justice and Peace bureaucracy. That "1989" contained important lessons for achieving progress in international relations (as John Paul insisted), few could deny. But for the Pope's diplomats and his Pontifical Council for Justice and Peace, the vindication of nonviolent resistance in the Revolution of 1989 tended to become an intellectual crutch: rather than thinking through the morality of world politics (including the morality of the use of limited armed force) in the post–Cold War world, it was simpler (and more in keeping with western European instincts) to universalize the experience of "1989" and imagine that there were, in reality, political and diplomatic solutions to virtually every conflict in the world; one had only to try hard enough to find them. Thus the Holy See was left conceptually adrift when men like Saddam Hussein, the butchers of Bosnia and Kosovo, and Osama bin Laden took center stage and tried to bend history to their wills.[111]

During the pontificate of John Paul II, the Roman pontifical universities, once incubators of new ideas

for the Roman Curia, did not take seriously the necessity of reconceptualizing the just war tradition to
meet the moral and political challenges of the post–
Cold War world that quickly followed the collapse of
communism. Rather, those intellectual centers, like
the Pontifical Council for Justice and Peace (which
they influenced, and which influenced them), tended
to interpret John Paul II's Assisi meetings of world
religious leaders, and especially the 1986 meeting, as
occasions on which the Church tacitly bade farewell
to the just war tradition as the normative Catholic
way of thinking about morality and world politics—
and did so in the name of "dialogue." That is not
what John Paul II intended by the Assisi meetings,
to be sure. But it was what many in Rome learned.
And it must be conceded that John Paul's inattention
to developing and explicating the Church's thinking about the morality of international politics (as
he had, for example, developed and explicated the
Church's sexual ethic) played its part in that diminishment of intellectual vigor.[112] Thus the irony of
this facet of the pontificate: the most diplomatically
and politically consequential pontificate in modern
history, led by a pope whose magisterium developed
Catholic thought in a host of fields, did little to advance the Church's thinking about the distinctive
moral problems of the politics of nations.

Temptations, and Some Topics Unaddressed.
Creative thinkers who extend the boundaries of
thought and culture risk the vulgarization of their

thought, often by their disciples. That is one risk that John Paul II's Theology of the Body faced in the last years of his pontificate and the years immediately following his death. Still, with John Paul II Institutes for marriage and family studies at work on every continent, that risk, while real, seemed less threatening to the truths involved in the Theology of the Body than did the vulgarization of Catholic thinking about "1989." There was another difference, though. Enthusiasts for the Theology of the Body were so eager to bring this fresh way of thinking to the Church and the world that they sometimes vulgarized it in the name of making it more accessible; moreover, they did so in the face of fierce resistance from the forces unleashed by the sexual revolution. Those who inappropriately universalized "1989" and made it into an all-purpose template for the moral analysis of world politics seemed to do so, at least in part, to avoid thinking through some hard questions, and their defense of Catholic functional pacifism drew the plaudits of postmodern progressive opinion in Europe and North America. In both instances, however, hard work was going to be required to secure the intellectual legacy of John Paul II.

The Pope's creative exercise of the **munus docendi** in developing his distinctive papal feminism was, like the Theology of the Body, sure to be the subject of discussion for a long time. Catholic feminist defenders of John Paul II's magisterium sometimes wondered, though, when the Pope was going to develop a theology of masculinity; or as one such feminist, a philosopher, once put it, "Tell the Pope that we're not the problem, men are"—by which she meant that John Paul ought to address, in a systematic way, the abandonment of responsibility that many men had readily indulged as a result of the feminist revolution.[113] John Paul's 1980 encyclical on God the Father, **Dives in Misericordia** [Rich in Mercy], might be considered the beginning of the contemporary papal magisterium's reflection on the Christian understanding of paternity, which was then developed further in the 1989 apostolic exhortation on St. Joseph, **Redemptoris Custos** [Guardian of the Redeemer]. In developing a theory of true Christian masculinity, there is also material to work with in John Paul's analysis of the meaning built into our human complementarity as male and female "in the beginning," which he discussed in the Theology of the Body. But far more work is needed to develop a reflection on maleness and the "masculine genius" that can match the insight and depth found in John Paul II's thinking on femaleness and the "feminine genius."

As indicated above, John Paul II's social doctrine included a more constrained view of the state and its role in the human drama than that articulated by any of his papal predecessors from Leo XIII through Paul VI—a view that was in some tension with traditional Catholic understandings of the nature and sources of state authority, and that raises questions about the claims John Paul II made about the modern state's human rights responsibilities. While this papal reduction in what might be called the metaphysical cash value of the state made considerable sense in light of the twentieth century's experience of state power, as a reflection of the Pope's culture-first theory of the free and virtuous society, and as an implication of his Christian personalism, intellectual work is going to have to be done to fit the twenty-first-century state into the social doctrine of the Church as developed by John Paul II—and to do so without giving tacit aid and comfort to those who imagine the democratic state to be devoid of substantive moral commitments.

This is, in fact, a major issue for the development of all post–Vatican II Catholic social thought, for the tensions suggested here antedate the magisterium of John Paul II. The Council disenthroned the state in its Declaration on Religious Freedom, which declared governments incompetent in theological questions. How, then, are we to understand the origins and nature of the modern, limited, constitutional state's **moral** competence and responsibility? From whence derives the modern state's moral responsibility to defend fundamental human rights, including the right to life? The beginnings of an answer to these questions might be found in the teaching of **Centesimus Annus** on the moral foundations of democracy, in John Paul II's 1995 UN address and its teaching on natural law as a universal moral grammar, and in the Pope's criticisms of thin theories of democracy in **Ecclesia in Europa.** Much work remains to be done, however, to ensure that the sturdiness of John Paul II's vision of the tripartite free and virtuous society does not dissipate.

Munus Sanctificandi: **The Mission to Sanctify**

John Paul II was elected pope at a time of some turmoil in Catholic sacramental theology, a time also marked by a dramatic decline in Catholic sacramental life throughout much of the world. John Paul addressed various late-twentieth-century problems of Catholic eucharistic theology in the 1980 apostolic letter **Dominicae Cenae** [The Lord's Supper] and the 2003 encyclical **Ecclesia de Eucharistia** [The Church from the Eucharist], both of which, like the 1992 **Catechism of the Catholic Church,** affirmed the Church's classic understanding of the Mass as both sacrament and sacrifice. John Paul also addressed a certain weakening of the Church's eucharistic self-consciousness and its effects on the priesthood in the 1992 apostolic exhortation, **Pastores Dabo Vobis** [I Will Give You Shepherds], as well as in his 1996 memoir **Gift and Mystery.** The decline in the practice of auricular confession in post–Vatican II Catholicism was addressed by the Pope in his 1984 apostolic exhortation, **Reconcili-**

atio et Paenitentia [Reconciliation and Penance]; there, John Paul characteristically reframed the entire issue of sacramental confession in personalist terms, describing the relationship between the sacrament of penance or reconciliation and the human drama of freedom.[114] John Paul II also strove to revitalize Catholicism spiritually through his teaching on consecrated religious life, through his promotion of the Divine Mercy devotion, and by his 2002 reform of the Rosary.

These exercises of the papal **munus docendi** to strengthen the Church's mission to sanctify the Church and the world were complemented by John Paul's beatifications and canonizations. John Paul II was determined to provide examples of sanctity for the people of the Church to emulate, and by doing so in a global fashion, to demonstrate the universality of the Holy Spirit's sanctifying gifts. The Pope also believed that the Church's invocation of those whom he beatified and canonized opened new channels of grace in the late twentieth and early twenty-first centuries. Thus the extensive roster of Christian heroes whom John Paul raised to the honors of the altar ought to be considered an aspect of his exercise of the papal **munus sanctificandi,** the mission to sanctify the Church and the world.

So, too, should the continuous personal example he gave of a deep and life-shaping Catholic piety, embodied during his travels, in his Masses, and in his ecumenical prayer-services, as well as in his personal pastoral work in Rome: his parish visitations, his hearing confessions in St. Peter's every Good Friday, his baptisms, his priestly and episcopal ordinations, his monthly recitation of the Rosary on Vatican Radio, and his weekly recitation of the Sunday Angelus (during the year) and Regina Coeli (during the Easter season). That his last hope was to be able to give his blessing vocally from the window of the papal apartment at Easter 2005 was powerful testimony to the seriousness with which Karol Wojtyła took his priestly and episcopal responsibility to be a vessel of God's sanctifying grace.

The Liturgy. Criticism of John Paul's exercise of the **munus sanctificandi,** especially in the last half of the pontificate, centered on what critics perceived as a lack of papal attention to the continuing trials and tribulations of post–Vatican II Catholic liturgical life. Some critics charged that those problems were exacerbated by innovations in papal liturgies created by the longtime master of pontifical liturgical ceremonies, Piero Marini; the use of a ritual of Hindu origin involving smudge pots during the 2003 beatification Mass for Mother Teresa of Calcutta was perhaps the most dramatic (and most criticized) example.[115]

John Paul II was undoubtedly aware that there were liturgical abuses throughout the Catholic world. These were addressed at length in a 2004 instruction from the Holy See's Congregation for Divine Worship and the Discipline of the Sacraments,

Redemptionis Sacramentum [The Sacrament of Redemption]. Critics replied that it was too little too late, and that absent strict enforcement from the Vatican, the world's bishops would prefer to maintain peace within their dioceses rather than enforce a measure of liturgical discipline. In this regard, at least, the critics were often right.

Karol Wojtyła's reverence for the liturgy and convictions about the truth of Catholic sacramental doctrine were obvious; thus the question of why, as pope, he did not do more to correct liturgical abuses throughout the world Church is not easy to answer, perhaps because there are no easy answers. Wojtyła had had a positive experience of post–Vatican II liturgical reform in Poland, where many of the abuses that beset the Church in western Europe, North America, and parts of the Third World were unknown. On assuming the papacy, he seemed to think problems of liturgical abuse were at bottom theological, and he set out to address those. Yet the fact remains that the Holy See under John Paul II's leadership seemed reluctant to enforce liturgical discipline throughout the world Church except in the most egregious cases of abuse.

Did this constitute a default in John Paul's exercise of the **munus sanctificandi** (and the **munus regendi,** or mission of governance), as conservative and traditionalist critics suggested? The Pope was aware that liturgical issues were extremely neuralgic throughout the Church, and he may have deter-

mined that a long-term approach to a reform of the
liturgical reform, rooted in a deeper understanding
of the mystery of Christian worship as our participation in the divine liturgy of heaven, was required
for both the unity of the Church and the eventual
vindication of the Second Vatican Council.[116] John
Paul II's respect for the legitimate prerogatives of
local bishops was also a factor in his approach to liturgical abuse and reform. It was not the pope's job,
as he understood it, to conduct a global liturgical
policing operation; preserving the integrity of the
sacraments and the liturgy was first and foremost the
responsibility of the local bishop, and it was neither
possible nor desirable for the pope to monitor the
liturgical disciplinary zeal of every bishop in the
world. Here, the inability of national conferences
of bishops to discipline their own members loomed
large. The same problem beset the question of faithful and appropriate translations of the liturgy from
Latin into vernacular languages, which was particularly difficult in the English-speaking world. It was
the U.S. bishops' conference, not the papacy or the
Vatican, that was the most significant obstacle to the
reform of the English translation of the Church's liturgical books.[117]

Then there was John Paul's respect for other cultures and his commitment to honor those cultures
as he could—aspects of his personalist approach to
the exercise of the papacy that shaped papal liturgies
throughout the world and in Rome, sometimes in

ways that seemed to critics to push the boundaries of inculturation beyond the appropriate. A more subtle, and perhaps more telling, critique of the use of local customs in pontifical liturgies came from those who argued that, while it may have been appropriate (and effective, in terms of the **munus sanctificandi**) to incorporate local rituals into the Pope's Mass while he was visiting other countries, it was inappropriate to do so during pontifical liturgies in Rome, which ought to embody the Roman rite as a common heritage of the entire world Church.

Throughout the more than twenty-six years of his pontificate, Pope John Paul II exercised a kind of universal priesthood, which enlivened the papal mission to sanctify in an unprecedentedly global way. Cardinal John O'Connor's observation that, with John Paul II, the world knew it had a pope could be amplified in this respect: the world knew it had a pope who was a priest, a mediator between God and humanity, and an instrument of God's grace. The critics' charge that John Paul II was inattentive to restoring discipline in Catholic liturgical life will be debated for decades, and perhaps centuries; it was not without interest that John Paul's papal successor, Benedict XVI, took a similar tack in terms of pastoral discipline in the first years of his pontificate, while concurrently displaying in his papal liturgies a more classic approach than that of Piero Marini. What cannot be gainsaid is the world's appreciation of John Paul II as a man of sanctity who poured out his life offering the possibility and the means of sanctification to others—which is surely at the heart of the papal **munus sanctificandi.**

Munus Regendi: **The Mission to Govern**

According to Catholic doctrine and canon law, the plenitude of legislative, executive, and judicial authority in the Church resides in the Office of Peter. Nonetheless, popes are not absolute monarchs. Their authority to teach is bounded by Scripture and the Church's authoritative tradition; their authority to sanctify is governed by the Church's sacramental system, itself one of the stable and unchangeable elements of Catholic life and practice.[118] As for the exercise of the papal **munus regendi**—the mission to govern—the last pope whose mode of leadership resembled what authors of fiction (and some reporters) imagine to be typical papal authoritarianism was Pope Pius XI. And it is certainly true that Achille Ratti, who came to the Office of Peter in 1922 after a few brief months as a cardinal, was not a man to be crossed, being the last pope to compel a cardinal—the Frenchman, Louis Billot—to renounce the red hat. Yet Pius XI leaned heavily on his cardinal secretaries of state, Pietro Gasparri and Eugenio Pacelli, in his diplomacy, and on Catholic intellectuals such as the German Jesuit Oswald von Nell-Breuning and the American Jesuit John LaFarge in the formulation of his magisterium.[119]

As these examples suggest, the exercise of the papal **munus regendi** is determined by a complex of factors: a given pope's personal gifts and dispositions; the quality of the counselors he chooses and the subordinates he appoints to implement his decisions; the breadth, depth, and timeliness of the flow of information; and the insightfulness of the analysis that reaches the papal apartment from papal nuncios, from the Curia, and from informal sources of information. The **munus regendi** is also shaped by a pope's sense of deference to the authority of local bishops and superiors of religious communities, by his willingness to risk division, and by his capacity to absorb criticism for unpopular decisions. In several of these respects, the pontificate of John Paul II set new standards of excellence in the exercise of the **munus regendi.**

No pope in modern papal history ever sought such a wide-ranging flow of information and opinion as did John Paul II. His determination to speak the truth as he had come to understand it was a striking facet of his papal personality, as were his courage and his equanimity in the face of uncomprehending or simply mean-spirited criticism. He grasped the importance of the world media in communicating his message and hired a papal spokesman of singular competence in the annals of that position; yet unlike most public figures of his time, John Paul II refused to craft his message to satisfy either his ecclesiastical critics or his journalistic critics (who were often aided and abetted by his ecclesiastical critics). He was willing to follow his instincts when it came to men and positions, making such bold episcopal appointments as Jean-Marie Lustiger to Paris, John J. O'Connor to New York, Francis E. George, O.M.I., to Chicago, Norberto Rivera Carrera to Mexico City, Jorge Mario Bergoglio, S.J., to Buenos Aires, Marc Ouellet, P.S.S., to Québec, George Pell to Melbourne and later Sydney, and Camillo Ruini to the Vicariate of Rome and the presidency of the Italian bishops' conference. Joseph Ratzinger's immediate predecessors as prefect of the Congregation for the Doctrine of the Faith—a post he held under John Paul II for more than twenty-three years—were able men, but they were hardly world-class theologians, as Ratzinger was; would other popes have been as comfortable with a prefect who was not only a more accomplished theologian than the Pope but who spoke his mind in a series of books that were debated throughout the Catholic world? Further, at the border between the **munus regendi** and the **munus docendi,** John Paul was willing to seek the counsel of others in the formulation of his magisterium and to entertain suggested corrections and changes, as he did in formulating **Centesimus Annus, Veritatis Splendor, Ordinatio Sacerdotalis, Tertio Millen-**

nio Adveniente, Evangelium Vitae, and **Fides et Ratio.**

Karol Wojtyła was not a man who naturally savored the roles of administrator and manager. Yet as archbishop of Kraków and Bishop of Rome he invested considerable energies in the administration of large institutions, sacrificing no small part of his intellectual life to what he understood to be responsibilities laid on him by the Church and, ultimately, by God. And if the mark of the successful administrator of large enterprises is the ability to set and achieve large goals, then Wojtyła's was, in the main, an effective exercise of the papal **munus regendi.**[120] Those who argued during the latter years of the pontificate that John Paul should be given " 'A' for 'prophet,' 'A' for 'priest,' and 'D' for 'king' " (as the saying often went) seemed to imagine the possibility of a new Pius XI. But that was not going to happen during the papacy of John Paul II: for (good) reasons of character and personality; because of the constraints on the exercise of the **munus regendi** inherent in the post-conciliar Church and in the Vatican itself; and because of John Paul II's sense of priorities, which reflected both his prayer and his knowledge of his own strengths and weaknesses.

Nonetheless, John Paul's mission of governance experienced its share of flaws, frustrations, and failures.

The Curia. Acutely aware of the trauma his election had caused in a still Italianate Curia, John Paul II tried to assuage curial anxieties during his pontificate while nudging the Curia toward a more evangelical concept of its functions. His respect for Paul VI was likely a factor in his unwillingness to wrestle with what some considered the deepest flaw in Pope Paul's post-conciliar curial reform: the substitution of the Secretariat of State for the Congregation for the Doctrine of the Faith as the supreme office of the Roman Curia—a momentous change that gave a bureaucracy staffed largely by diplomats operational precedence, not only over the Church's chief doctrinal and theological agency, but over every other curial office, for under Pope Paul's system all business of whatever sort was filtered through to the pope by the Secretariat of State. Further difficulties were caused by many of the "pontifical councils" Paul VI had created to give a place in the Church's central administration to some of Vatican II's key concerns—ecumenism, interreligious dialogue, international justice and peace; these councils had long ceased to be the in-house research centers they were originally intended to be and had become mini-Vaticans in their own right, churning out numerous documents and statements and creating confusion over who, in fact, spoke for the Holy See and the Catholic Church. Both of these issues went unaddressed by John Paul II. Their resolution, and the more general question of strengthening the competence of the Roman Curia (including its ability to absorb the vastly increased information flows created by the Internet), was of significant concern to some of the most influential cardinals during the conclave of 2005, who expected John Paul II's successor to address them decisively.

The latter years of the pontificate also saw something of a reversal of John Paul's prior practice of internationalizing the Roman Curia. That process had been begun by Paul VI, but it was accelerated by John Paul II, who appointed Beninese and Brazilian prefects of the Congregation for Bishops, a German prefect of the Congregation for the Doctrine of the Faith, a Slovak prefect of the Congregation for the Evangelization of Peoples, American and Polish prefects of the Congregation for Catholic Education, Chilean and Nigerian prefects of the Congregation for Divine Worship, a Belgian head of the Synod of Bishops, an American prefect of the papal household, and a Spanish papal spokesman, among many other examples. By the end of the pontificate, though, this pattern seemed to have been, if not reversed, then at least modifed, under the influence of John Paul's cardinal secretary of state from 1991 through 2005, Angelo Sodano. And in the latter years of John Paul II, the work process in the Curia often reverted to its pre-1978 habits and pace, which, among other things, did the Pope no good service during the Long Lent of 2002.

John Paul II knew that his strengths lay in teaching, witnessing, and exercising the **munus sanctifi-**

candi throughout the world; it would have been out of character for him to attempt a wholesale reform (much less a radical redesign) of the Roman Curia. Whether he might have deputed someone to do that for him is an interesting question, although it seems unlikely, given John Paul's sense of himself as a Polish outsider in the Vatican. The structural problems of the central administration of the Catholic Church—which, in the main, John Paul II successfully bent to his purposes for more than two decades—were not ones he was prepared to tackle. Some future pope would surely have to do so.

The Theologians and the Universities. Despite the intellectual creativity John Paul II exhibited throughout his pontificate, the charge that he was repressive and authoritarian in matters of speculative Catholic theology followed him for a quarter century. The charge first took hold in the press and in progressivist Catholic circles after the 1979 Vatican decision to withdraw Hans Küng's license as a professor of Catholic theology at the University of Tübingen; it achieved the status of an unchallengeable truism in certain circles when, in 1986, the American moral theologian Charles Curran lost his ecclesiastical license as a teacher of Catholic theology at the Catholic University of America, from whose faculty he was subsequently dismissed. Neither man's priestly faculties were suspended; Küng continued to teach at Tübingen as a professor of ecumenical theology and Curran quickly found a senior faculty position at Southern Methodist University in Dallas; both men continued to publish and were widely quoted for years in the global press; Küng even became an occasional counselor to the annual gathering of the global business and political elite at Davos, Switzerland.

If this was repression, it was of a very mild sort. Moreover, both Küng and Curran candidly admitted that they did not believe to be true, and would not teach as true, what the Catholic Church believed and taught to be true. In Küng's case, the issue was the doctrine of papal infallibility, even as defined in quite narrow terms by the First Vatican Council.[121] Curran argued that the Church's teaching on sexual morality was in error across a wide range of issues.[122] That John Paul II should be accused of an abuse of the **munus regendi** by withdrawing the license to teach Catholic theology of men who had made clear their dissent from settled Catholic doctrine seemed to many, including Catholic thinkers on the port side of the Church, an unwarranted charge.

Yet it stuck, and it persisted. Six weeks before John Paul II's death, the **National Catholic Reporter,** a progressivist U.S. weekly, published a roster of some twenty-three "theologians and others disciplined by the Vatican during the papacy of John Paul II." The disciplinary actions varied across the cases cited. As for the issues at stake, they included, in addition to the infallibility doctrine and the Church's sexual ethic, the truth of Christ's resurrection; the virgin birth,

Christ's work as redeemer, and other central questions of Christology; the structure of the Church; the nature of salvation and its relationship to political struggle; original sin; pantheistic interpretations of God's presence in creation; abortion; refusal to accept the legitimate orders of ecclesiastical superiors to leave political office; and malfeasance in episcopal governance.[123] Some of those disciplined left the priesthood, their religious orders, and, in a few cases, the Catholic Church. One, the French archbishop Marcel Lefebvre (who incurred excommunication by his illicit ordination of four bishops in 1988) came from outside the orbit of progressivist Catholicism, which was itself instructive: the only formal schism after Vatican II came from the extreme right (to use the conventional taxonomy), which suggested that most dissidents at the other end of the Catholic spectrum understood that their relevance to the future of the Catholic debate required them to remain formally inside the Catholic Church. This undoubtedly reflected a sincere love for the Church on the part of some dissenters; it also reflected a shrewd judgment that the world press would lose interest in Catholic dissidents who were no longer Catholic (as several of those on the **National Catholic Reporter** list, including the Brazilian Leonardo Boff and the American Matthew Fox, discovered).

The pontificate of John Paul II stretched the boundaries of Catholic thought in several respects. Like every other pope, however, John Paul was bound to teach that certain boundaries existed, as he was obliged to enforce those boundaries when they were egregiously breached on core questions of doctrine. Yet for all the charges of repression leveled against John Paul II, the fact remained that, at the end of the pontificate, scholars deeply critical of his magisterium remained firmly in control of many theological faculties throughout the world, including theological faculties in Rome. In the always controversial field of moral theology, the influence of the critics of John Paul II may have been declining, as a younger generation of Catholic moral theologians, shaped by John Paul II's Theology of the Body, took seriously the possibility denied by many of their theological elders—that the Church may in fact have been teaching the truth about sexual ethics. Five years after John Paul's death, however, anyone interested in a tenured position on the theology faculty of any number of prestigious Catholic universities in the United States would have been ill advised to defend, during the hiring interview, John Paul II's teaching on the intrinsically immoral nature of homosexual acts or the inadmissability of women to Holy Orders.

As in other aspects of his exercise of the **munus regendi,** John Paul II chose a strategy of encouraging what was new, challenging, and vibrantly orthodox in Catholic intellectual life, rather than conducting a war of repression against dissent. In the case of the Roman pontifical institutions, John Paul encouraged the work of new foundations such as the Pontifical University of the Holy Cross and the Pontifical Athenaeum Regina Apostolorum—both of which quickly established themselves as first-class intellectual centers—rather than trying to compel the Pontifical Gregorian University to bring its teaching of fundamental moral theology into closer congruence with **Veritatis Splendor,** or trying to force the Pontifical Urban University (where many future leaders of the Third World Church study) to align its teaching on Christian mission and the new evangelization more closely to **Redemptoris Missio.**

The long-term effects of this strategy will reveal themselves over the course of the twenty-first century, and beyond. It may have been mistaken. That the most intellectually consequential pontificate in centuries, led by a man with a deep reverence for university life, did not undertake a serious reform of the content and method of instruction at the older pontifical universities in Rome will strike some as a lost opportunity, and others as a failure in the **munus regendi.** Yet however the strategy is judged, it closely paralleled the strategy John Paul chose in his exercise of the papal teaching office, or **munus docendi**: to make compelling arguments for the truth of Catholic faith, often deploying new methods of analysis, rather than issuing a string of condemnations.

In any case, it seems far-fetched to conclude that John Paul's exercise of the **munus regendi** in the face of theological dissent was repressive and authoritarian—unless one believes that those who make plain their disagreement with what the Catholic Church teaches to be true have some unchallengeable claim to be considered teachers of Catholic theology.

The World Episcopate, Collegiality, and the Synod of Bishops. John Paul II appointed more Catholic bishops than any previous pope, and by a considerable degree. The seriousness with which he took this aspect of the papal **munus regendi** was evident in the quality of the men whom he appointed as prefects of the Congregation for Bishops, which vets candidates for the episcopate and presents them to the pope: the Beninese cardinal, Bernardin Gantin, the Brazilian Dominican, Lucas Moreira Neves, and Giovanni Battista Re, the Italian curialist who served for almost eleven years as **Sostituto** of the Secretariat of State, or papal chief of staff. At times, John Paul II displayed dissatisfaction with the way the appointment process functioned. In 1984, he rejected the **terna,** or list of three candidates, for archbishop of New York that had come to him from the Congregation for Bishops on the advice of the apostolic delegate in Washington; it seemed to him to reflect a self-satisfied approach to Catholic life in America, then dominant in the leadership of the U.S. bishops conference, that he was determined to change. So he took the advice of Moreira Neves (the second-ranking official of the Congregation for Bishops at the time), rejected the status quo–oriented **terna** for

New York, and surprised the entire Catholic world by appointing John J. O'Connor, who had only been bishop of Scranton for some eight months, as what John Paul liked to call "archbishop of the capital of the world." In the main, however, John Paul accepted the nomination process as it typically functioned, while trying to strengthen it by putting men in whom he reposed confidence in charge at the Congregation for Bishops.

John Paul II was strikingly successful in many of his episcopal appointments over twenty-six years. Yet there were also mistakes, some of them serious, and at the end of the pontificate it was difficult to say that the world episcopate as a whole reflected John Paul II's dynamic, courageous, intellectually sophisticated, and spiritually profound model of episcopal leadership. It would be absurd, of course, to expect the nomination process to have identified a virtually unlimited supply of men with the exceptional personal gifts of Karol Wojtyła. Yet the criteria by which candidates for the episcopate were initially vetted by apostolic delegates or nuncios were not significantly changed in order to reflect the evangelically assertive idea of the bishop's office for which the Second Vatican Council called, and which John Paul II embodied. Consultations by papal representatives on potential nominees for the episcopate often took place within a narrow, dominantly clerical, and sometimes exclusively episcopal sphere. And while it was appropriate that priests being considered as bishops should be unimpeachably orthodox, a man's demonstrated ability to make the Church's proposal in a compelling and effective way did not seem to weigh as heavily as it might in the consideration of candidates: as late as the last half decade of the pontificate, the standard questionnaire by which candidates were first vetted asked about a man's orthodoxy, but not about his talent in convincing others of the truth of Catholic faith, his success in bringing others into the Church, or his boldness in advancing the Church's social doctrine publicly.[124]

At the end of the pontificate, and throughout the world Church, thoughtful Catholics who would have given their lives for John Paul II and who esteemed both the man and his teaching nonetheless believed that one of the Catholic Church's most serious problems was the quality of its episcopal leadership—and this despite the Pope's obvious accomplishments in reshaping parts of the world Catholic episcopate and his sponsorship of an impressive **Directory for the Pastoral Ministry of Bishops,** published in 2004. Debate on why that should have been the case would continue long after the Pope's death, with the thoroughgoing reform of the criteria and process for selecting bishops—a reform that John Paul II did not effect—occupying a prominent place in the discussion.[125]

Critics of the pontificate from the Church's progressivist wing argued that the "centralizing" tendencies they detected in John Paul II's exercise of the **munus regendi** demeaned the role of national conferences of bishops, which had been mandated by the Second Vatican Council.[126] This charge seems overwrought. In fact, John Paul's typical response when a bishop raised a difficult pastoral problem during an **ad limina** visit was, "Have you discussed this with the conference? What can the conference do to help?"

The Pope's experience of a unified and courageous national bishops' conference in Poland may have colored his judgment about the inherent capacities of these institutions in the post–Vatican II Church. The Polish situation was, in many respects, unique; throughout the rest of the world Church, and especially in the developed world, some national conferences came to be controlled by their staffs, while concurrently exhibiting the negative qualities of old-fashioned men's clubs in which criticism of fellow members was beyond the pale. Thus the more realistic critique of John Paul II's relationship to national conferences of bishops is that the Pope put too much confidence in the capacity of these bodies to address key local problems forthrightly and effectively. That commitment to collegiality betrayed him on several occasions, not least when the failures of the U.S. bishops conference to address significant problems of clerical sexual abuse (about which the American prelates had been warned years before the Long Lent of 2002) burst into public view and suddenly had to be addressed in Rome. Similar incapacities marked many local bishops conferences dealing with dissident theologians and women religious, and in a few cases with fellow bishops of dubious orthodoxy. In many of these instances, national episcopal conference failures left the Vatican—and the Pope—with the unavoidable task of taking needed disciplinary action, and thus absorbing the inevitable, and sometimes harsh, criticism for enforcing the Church's doctrinal and moral boundaries. Thus a strong case can be made that the failures of national bishops conferences to exercise the **munus regendi** effectively within their own spheres of authority were of far greater moment during the pontificate than any alleged centralizing by John Paul II.

The modus operandi of the Synod of Bishops under John Paul II was also criticized throughout the pontificate (including, in private, by the Pope himself). The general secretary of the Synod once defended its tortuous procedures on the grounds that the Synod (which was created by Paul VI as an institutional expression of Vatican II's teaching on episcopal collegiality) could not be understood on a sociological or political model. The Synod, Cardinal Jan Schotte insisted, was "not a 'legislature' over-against or beside the papal 'executive.'" Majority rule concepts did not apply, for the Synod was, "more and deeper," a matter of "listening to Christ and the Spirit," and thus a body that "cannot be understood in terms of its procedures."[127] The theology of the Synod here was true enough; but the cardinal's defense of the

Synod process did not address the question of why "listening to Christ and the Spirit" necessarily involved weeks of listening in the Synod assembly to ten-minute speeches arranged in no particular order with no follow-on debate, discussion being largely restricted to smaller language groups that formulated various theses for the Pope's consideration.

Some Synod veterans respected John Paul II's patience with the clumsy body's lengthy deliberations (the Pope attended every Synod session in person), but found the process too diffuse and deficient in setting priorities. Cardinal Francis George of Chicago, however, thought that while the process could never yield more than a minimum consensus, given the substantial number of bishops involved, that was no bad thing: a minimum consensus, in addition to being an achievement in itself, left room for further reflection on the subject at hand.[128] This was a striking observation, considering that the 1985 Extraordinary Synod had achieved "minimum consensus" on two crucial points—that Vatican II was to be interpreted as a Council in continuity with the Church's tradition, and that the key to the Council's teaching was the concept of the Church as a **communio** or "communion" of disciples. Defenders of the Synod also remarked on the importance of its informal moments, during which the leaders of the world episcopate got to know one another (and one another's problems) better.

Still, the fact remained that the most notable products of the Synod of Bishops during the pontificate of John Paul II were the Pope's own post-synodal apostolic exhortations. **Pastores Dabo Vobis,** to take one example, reshaped seminary life throughout the world Church. That result was far more the product of the apostolic exhortation than the Synod process, but Synod defenders could argue that, absent the process, the post-synodal document would have lacked the weight the Synod gave it.

Corruptions. The corruptions in the priesthood brought to public attention during the pontificate of John Paul II cannot in any fairness be blamed on John Paul II, who taught and exemplified an upright and heroic idea of priestly ministry for almost sixty years, and who inspired thousands, and perhaps tens of thousands, of priests to live in fidelity to their vocation—thus putting in place the medium- and long-term solution to the problem of abusive clergy. The corruptions manifest in clergy sexual abuse in the United States, Canada, and Ireland, which caused such scandal in the last years of the pontificate, did illustrate, however, the limits of even the most compelling papal example and the imperatives of a more thorough reform of the world episcopate; so did the problems of clerical concubinage that afflicted the Church in Africa and some parts of Latin America. For in virtually all of these instances, individual crimes became public scandals because of failures of leadership on the part of local bishops.

Throughout the pontificate, however, John

Paul II's exercise of the **munus regendi** with regard to religious orders of both men and women was a subject of legitimate criticism. Karol Wojtyła had long believed and taught that consecrated life was a kind of spiritual energy core for the entire Church; a man formed by these convictions would never deliberately countenance corruption in religious communities living under vows of poverty, chastity, and obedience, as some suggested he did. Yet a pontificate that worked very hard to reform the diocesan priesthood did not expend a similarly serious effort on addressing the corruptions of doctrinal dissent and lifestyle that beset numerous religious communities of both men and women.

One particularly notable failure here was John Paul's effort to instigate a reform of the Society of Jesus, which he took under a form of papal receivership in 1981 in an attempt to apply shock therapy to one of Catholicism's elite religious communities.[129] The intervention did not work as John Paul had hoped. And while the Jesuits in the last decade and a half of the pontificate attracted aspirants whose vocations were formed in part by the witness of John Paul II, the Society as a whole (which was sometimes beset by strange interpretations of poverty, chastity, and obedience) remained one of Catholicism's premier centers of theological dissent on issues ranging from the unique status of Christ as universal redeemer to grave questions of sexual morality.[130]

Similar troubles weakened once vibrant American communities of religious women throughout the pontificate, to the point where a new body, the Council of Major Superiors of Women Religious, was established in 1992 by leaders of communities dedicated to the vision of religious life that John Paul II would lay out in detail in **Vita Consecrata.** The new Council was explicitly intended as an alternative to the long-established Leadership Conference of Women Religious [LCWR], which was dominated throughout the pontificate by communities whose understanding of religious life was quite different from that of John Paul II, and who in some cases considered themselves post-Christian.[131] Modest efforts were made to engage the LCWR congregations in an examination of their positions on issues including the ordination of women, homosexuality, and lifestyle. A commission led by San Francisco archbishop John R. Quinn was appointed by the Pope in 1983 and eventually produced an anodyne document entitled "Essential Elements in Church Teaching on Religious Life," which many members of the LCWR repudiated.[132] The Congregation for the Doctrine of the Faith issued a warning to the LCWR in 2001, but during the last years of the pontificate, the LCWR continued to defend and live its understanding of religious life as one of "loyal dissent."[133]

There seemed to be little interest at the Congregation for Religious, the relevant Vatican office, in coming to grips with a situation that to some observers seemed one of de facto schism, or at the very least, psychological schism; the same reticence characterized the attitude of most American bishops and of their episcopal conference.[134] Attention would almost certainly have been paid, however, had firm instructions to do so come from the papal apartment. Here, as in so many other cases, John Paul II chose to affirm and support what was growing and healthy in the Church, leaving dissent to die of its own implausibility. Thus disciplinary actions were taken only when American sisters publicly challenged the truth of Catholic teaching on abortion and homosexuality, or refused to leave public office when instructed to do so.

John Paul's strategy worked, in the sense that the communities of women religious that were attracting new members in the United States were those who took **Vita Consecrata** seriously, while the LCWR communities were dying demographically. This difficult situation may well have been inevitable, given post–Vatican II dynamics in American women's religious communities that intersected with the more ideologically hardened forms of feminism. It is also true that primary responsibility for addressing these problems lay, first, with local bishops and the U.S. bishops conference, and then with the Congregation for Religious in Rome; it was not up to the Pope to act as an apostolic visitor assessing the orthodoxy and probity of life in American women's religious communities. Yet the fact remains that the doctrinal and lifestyle troubles that had fallen upon communities of American sisters were known in Rome and little effective action was taken to address the problems. On this front, the papal **munus regendi** was not, to put it gently, assertive.[135]

The most dramatic questions about John Paul's exercise of the **munus regendi** in relationship to consecrated religious life emerged with full force only after his death, when the Holy See took action against Father Marcial Maciel, founder of the Legionaries of Christ, a community of religious men, and Regnum Christi, a lay Catholic renewal movement. In 2006, the Holy See "invited" Father Maciel to retire to a "life of prayer and penitence, renouncing any form of public ministry."[136] The invitation, a de facto order, followed an investigation by the Congregation for the Doctrine of the Faith into charges that Maciel had sexually abused seminarians and had further abused the sacrament of penance to conceal his sexual abuse; it is unlikely that Maciel would have been sent into what amounted to ecclesiastical house arrest had the CDF not found those charges credible. After Maciel's death in 2008, reports that he had fathered at least one child out of wedlock, whom he supported with funds raised for the Legionaries of Christ, appeared in the international press and were confirmed by the superiors of the Legion.[137] An apostolic visitation of the Legion was ordered by Pope Benedict XVI in 2009.

John Paul II was deceived and betrayed by Marcial

Maciel, a master deceiver who successfully deceived many others. No one who knew Karol Wojtyła could possibly believe that the Pope, informed of Maciel's sordid double life, would have continued to support him, the Legionaries of Christ, and Regnum Christi—as John Paul had done for decades.[138] John Paul II was, in fact, badly deceived. He may well have been ill served by associates and subordinates who ought to have been more alert to the implications of the cult of personality that surrounded Maciel in both the Legion and Regnum Christi. The reasons that those associates and subordinates were skeptical of the charges that had quietly swirled around Maciel for years—charges that came to public light when those alleging previous abuse by Maciel filed complaints with the Holy See in 1998—will be investigated and debated for decades. The results are not likely to be edifying, in some cases.

The reasons that John Paul II gave his support to the Legionaries of Christ and Regnum Christi are clear: both the religious congregation and the lay movement embodied a vibrant orthodoxy that, as even their critics admit, produced many admirable religious vocations and lay activists. Legionary efforts in seminary formation were also of great interest to John Paul, who encouraged the Legion to pursue this work around the world and in Rome. It was this confidence in the good fruits that had been produced by the Legion and Regnum Christi that led John Paul to what may have been his gravest error in exercising the **munus regendi** with respect to the Legion: his approval of the constitutions of the Legionaries of Christ, according to which every member of the Legion vowed to refrain from criticizing a superior and to report to superiors anyone in the Legion who did. The constitutions had been under review in the Congregation for Religious for decades; according to Maciel, the Pope broke the logjam (which involved the Legion's rules on assignment of personnel and its practice of maintaining a "centralized economy" headquartered in Rome) and facilitated the approval of the governing statutes of the Legion by a personal intervention in 1983.[139] In the wake of revelations about Maciel's double life, it seems likely that the constitutions' proscription against criticism of superiors, and the "centralized economy," helped facilitate Maciel's sexual and financial corruption. But real clarity about the process by which the Legion's constitutions were approved may be difficult to reach, given Maciel's protean skills at prevarication and deception.

After the public revelations in 2009 of Marcial Maciel's extensive perfidy, critics of the pontificate did not hesitate to point out John Paul II's lengthy record of support for Maciel and the institutes he founded; genuine concern for the victims of Maciel's crimes was at work here, as well as genuine concern for the Church. Nonetheless, and despite the negative implications for the evaluation of John Paul's reputation that some of these critics quickly drew, it was noteworthy that Benedict XVI and others who sought to save the good that John Paul II saw in the Legionaries of Christ and Regnum Christi did so with John Paul's teaching on the priesthood and the lay vocation in the world in mind, recognizing that what was at work in this scandalous affair was deception in the service of the **mysterium iniquitatis.**[140]

The Last Years. During the last years of the pontificate, critics of the Pope's exercise of the **munus regendi** sometimes suggested that Karol Wojtyła's personal drama was impeding Pope John Paul II's governance of the Church. The Roman Curia did revert to its accustomed languid pace at the end of the pontificate; whether this would have been the case had the cardinal secretary of state been a more forceful figure than Angelo Sodano is an open question. Throughout the pontificate, John Paul had declined the role of curial micromanager and was certainly not going to take it up at the end of his life. More vigorous leadership from senior curial officials, led by Cardinal Sodano, might have helped dispel the **fin de régime** atmosphere that characterized parts of the Vatican apparatus in the last years of the papacy of John Paul II.

Critics also worried that the Pope's longtime secretary and confidant, Archbishop Stanisław Dziwisz, had become, toward the end, a kind of vice-pope, a position for which there is no room in the Church. Archbishop Dziwisz was indeed the gatekeeper to John Paul II, but that was a role he had played since

October 1978, and as he knew Karol Wojtyła's mind well, he kept the papal apartment door open to an extraordinarily wide range of contacts, until it became physically impossible for the Pope to conduct meetings beyond those absolutely essential for the functioning of his office—which John Paul did until the very end. Dziwisz was as susceptible to misreading personalities as any man and no doubt made his share of mistakes in trusting those he ought not have trusted, including Marcial Maciel. The criticism that, in functioning as the link between an increasingly disabled Pope and the Curia, Dziwisz was acting on his own judgment rather than executing the Pope's will was, however, rarely if ever heard—and with reason.

The lot of a papal secretary after his master's death is not, typically, a happy one, as the secretaries of Pius XII, John XXIII, and Paul VI quickly learned. That Stanisław Dziwisz retained the affection and respect of those senior churchmen with whom he had worked—and to whom he had had to say no on many occasions—testifies to the fact that his loyalty to John Paul II was well understood, as was his commitment to executing what he believed to be the Pope's will, not his own.

Did the **munus regendi** suffer in the last years of John Paul II because of his increasing physical debilitation? In some respects, yes. But that was often the result of incapacity and weakness on the part of the Pope's subordinates, who ought to have had, when circumstances demanded it, the courage to lead according to the pattern he had set. In any event, the powerful evangelical witness John Paul gave in his last encyclical—his patient suffering and his holy death—was of such magnitude as to render the defects in the **munus regendi** over the past years of the pontificate of far less immediate consequence.

The Unavoidable Dilemma. Shortly before John Paul II's death, the distinguished German theologian Hermann Josef Pottmeyer wrote an intriguing essay defending John Paul II as an underappreciated reformer. John Paul's exercise of the **munus regendi,** Pottmeyer argued, was an impressive, if not always successful, effort to hold together the twin imperatives of spiritual reform (centered on the notion of the Church as a communion of radically converted disciples) and shared responsibility (manifest in various forms of consultation and common deliberation within the Church, from the local parish council to the Synod of Bishops). Reflecting on John Paul's reiteration of these two imperatives in the 2001 apostolic letter, **Novo Millennio Ineunte,** Pottmeyer offered an analysis of the unavoidable dilemma in which John Paul II found himself in the course of exercising the **munus regendi.** The German theologian's observations are worthy of consideration by anyone attempting a serious appraisal of John Paul II's successes and failures in governing the Catholic Church:

By laying out his view of the mutual relationship between spiritual and structural reform, the Pope indicates a dilemma which all demands for structural reform, no matter how well founded, must confront. The dilemma is this. Without conversion to the **communio** mentality which the Pope describes, all forms of consultation and shared responsibility remain empty shells which can easily be manipulated to obtain goals that do not promote the Church's welfare. At the same time, without such forms, the many gifts bestowed by God on the Church will remain either ineffective or of limited effect—which would also be a disservice to the Church's welfare and to its mission. That is why the Pope demands from the Church's pastors and faithful alike **both** spiritual and structural reform. . . . We cannot have reform of either kind without the other. This is a tremendous challenge to the Church. That the Pope does not consider this challenge hopeless is rooted in his remarkably strong faith that the Holy Spirit is at work in the Church and in each of us. In this, the Pope differs from many of his associates, and indeed from many of us.[141]

THE CHRISTIAN DISCIPLE AS PROPHET OF A NEW HUMANISM

The communications revolution of the late twentieth century and its effects on the human attention span have not been kind to large-scale public figures. One after another, men and women who were long accustomed to dominating the public square lost the public's attention and were tuned out—and, in some cases, turned out. The exception to this law of declining public affection was Karol Wojtyła, Pope John Paul II. Unlike the men and women of the world of power with whom he dealt, John Paul's ability to capture the public imagination—which had begun at his election and during his epic first pilgrimage to Poland—increased in the last dozen years of his pontificate and peaked during the period of his greatest physical decline. In the first half of the pontificate, John Paul II shared the global stage with other large personalities whose impact on history was considerable. After the publication of **Crossing the Threshold of Hope** in 1994, John Paul II held the world's attention, and indeed became an ever greater focus of interest and concern, in a way that no other figure of his time managed.

Why?

It surely had something to do with his remarkable ability to embody paternity in a world yearning for the combination of manly strength and compassion that is true fatherhood lived well. Then there was his palpable respect for others, especially those others who did not share his convictions and commitments, which offered a model of genuine human encounter amidst intolerance and fanaticism. Many of the men and women of late modernity sensed a human and spiritual hollowness in their lives, and found in John Paul II a thoroughly modern man who could put contemporary searchers in touch with ancient spiritual and moral truths.

A further reason for Karol Wojtyła's unique capacity to hold the world's attention for more than a quarter century may lie in his singular intuition into the central problem of the late twentieth and early twenty-first centuries: a world striving for freedom had not learned to live freedom nobly because it had lost touch with the nobility of the human person, which consists in our ability to know, choose, and adhere to the truth.

Wojtyła's 1959 letter to the Vatican commission preparing the agenda for the Second Vatican Council was arguably the pivot on which his life turned, defining his public vocation and giving him the lever by which he moved history. In that letter, he located the deepest wound of modernity in a defective humanism that had left the world morally adrift and had created a global charnel house in which great hopes had been burnt to ashes. Life had become fragmented and atomized. The alienation experienced by the men and women of late modernity was far deeper and more complex than the alienation analyzed by Karl Marx: men and women had become alienated from their own interiority, having lost sight of a transcendent spiritual and moral horizon against which to live their lives. This deeper alienation had profound public consequences. Like his friend Henri de Lubac, Wojtyła was convinced that defective humanisms had created a situation in which men and women could only organize the world against each other.[142] Ultramundane humanism inevitably became inhuman humanism.

In the face of this crisis, Karol Wojtyła believed that the Catholic Church should bend its global mission toward the recovery, defense, and promotion of the inalienable dignity and value of every human person. That conviction was at the center of everything he proposed to the world during the twenty-six and a half years of his pontificate, both in his teaching and in his living. It was the focus of his anthropology and his ethics, including his sexual ethics. It informed his defense of the family and his development of a new Christian feminism. It shaped his social doctrine, including his defense of universal human rights, his philosophy of freedom, and his theory of democracy. It was at the foundation of his idea of culture as the chief dynamic of history. It enlivened his thinking and teaching about the Church itself. It defined the way he lived, and it defined the way he died.

In the Lenten retreat he preached before Pope

Paul VI and the Roman Curia in 1976, Karol Wojtyła told the assembled leaders of the Catholic Church that they were "in the front line in a lively battle for the dignity of man."[143] When he assumed the supreme pastoral leadership of the Church as Pope John Paul II, he took command of the battle, called the Church out of the trenches, and spent two and a half decades leading Catholicism in a forth-right engagement with the principal ideas contesting for the future of humanity: first, communism; later, pragmatism and utilitarianism, hedonism, secular-ism, and Islamism. In each instance, the struggle was for the dignity of the human person.

For Karol Wojtyła, of course, the truth about the human person was ultimately revealed in Jesus Christ, in whom we discover the truth about the merciful Father and the truth about ourselves. What was so striking about the accomplishment of John Paul II was that this unshakable and distinctively Christian conviction set the platform on which he became a universal figure, a reference point for uni-versal moral truths. Because he truly believed that Jesus Christ is the answer to the question that is every human life, and because he further believed that that question deserved the utmost respect, he could engage those who did not know Christ, who were hostile to Christ, or who had simply become bored with the claims of religion.

He was sometimes called a prophet, because he seemed to have seen possibilities in history—such as the imminence of the communist crack-up—that escaped others. He was indeed a prophet. But the nature of his prophetic charism, which included a penetrating insight into historical circumstances and possibilities, had to do, not with clairvoyance, but with faith: faith in the dignity of the human person; faith in the human capacity to choose the good freely; faith, ultimately, in Christ. Karol Wojtyła, Pope John Paul II, became the prophet of a new and genuine humanism—and changed the world—because he was a disciple: a radically converted Christian whose unshakable faith in Christ gave birth to a world-changing hope for a new springtime of the human spirit.

NOTES

Prologue

1. See George Weigel, **Witness to Hope: The Biography of Pope John Paul II** (New York: HarperCollins, 1999).

2. Sapieha came from the Polish-Lithuanian nobility and was thus known as the "prince-archbishop."

3. **Środowisko** doesn't translate very well. One possibility is "Environment." Wojtyła always preferred the more humanistic "Milieu."

4. For an explanation of why **Person and Act** is preferable to the more familiar English-language title of Wojtyła's work (**The Acting Person**), see Weigel, **Witness to Hope,** pp. 172–78.

5. Author's conversation with Pope John Paul II, March 20, 1997.

Chapter One

1. The story of Witold Pilecki and his persecution by Polish communists was not publicly revealed until the collapse of communism in 1989. Pilecki and others falsely condemned were legally rehabilitated by Poland's first postcommunist government on October 1, 1990. In 1995, Witold Pilecki was posthumously awarded the

Order of **Polonia Restituta.** A Polish Foundation, **Fundacja Paradis Judaeorum**, now works to have May 25, the day Pilecki was shot, declared a European Union holiday, "The Day of the Heroes of the Struggle with Totalitarianism."

An extensive literature on Pilecki now exists, and his remarkable Auschwitz report is available online. For links, see the entry "Witold Pilecki" at http://en.wikipedia.org.wiki/Witold Pilecki; a brief article with details on Pilecki's resistance activities may be found at http://www.polishresistance-ak.org/14%20Article.htm. See also Kamil Tchorek, "Double life of Witold Pilecki, the Auschwitz volunteer who uncovered Holocaust secrets," **Sunday Times,** March 29, 2009.

2. See Richard Pipes, ed., **The Unknown Lenin: From the Secret Archive** (New Haven, CT: Yale University Press, 1996), pp. 95–115.

3. On these three points, see Andrzej Paczkowski, **The Spring Will Be Ours: Poland and the Poles from Occupation to Freedom,** trans. Jane Cave (University Park: Pennsylvania State University Press, 2003), pp. vii–viii.

4. On Poland being "completely changed" by World War II, see ibid., p. ix.

5. Ibid., p. 38.

6. Norman Davies reviews the arguments in **Rising '44: The Battle for Warsaw** (New York: Viking, 2003), pp. 619ff.

7. On this point, see Jan Nowak, **Courier from Warsaw** (Detroit: Wayne State University Press, 1982), pp. 450–52.

8. See Paczkowski, **The Spring Will Be Ours,** pp. 161–62.

9. Quoted in Christopher Andrew and Vasili Mitrokhin, **The Sword and the Shield: The Mitrokhin Archive and the Secret History of the KGB** (New York: Basic Books, 2001), p. 3.

10. See George Weigel, **The Final Revolution: The Resistance Church and the Collapse of Communism** (New York: Oxford University Press, 1992), pp. 4–12.

11. See Pope John Paul II, **Gift and Mystery: On the Fiftieth Anniversary of My Priestly Ordination** (New York: Doubleday, 1996), pp. 34–36.

12. See Marek Lasota, **Donos na Wojtyłę: Karol Wojtyła w teczkach bezpiecki** (Kraków: Znak, 2006), chapter 1. See also Jan. M. Małecki, **A History of Kraków for Everyone** (Kraków: Wydawnictwo Literackie, 2008), p. 252.

13. For a detailed account of Karol Wojtyła's wartime years, see Weigel, **Witness to Hope,** chapter 2.

14. See Paczkowski, **The Spring Will Be Ours,** p. 186.

15. Małecki, **A History of Kraków for Everyone,** p. 253.

16. The idiocy was neatly illustrated by a Soviet delegate to a cultural congress in Wrocław in 1948, who said that "If hyenas knew how to use a fountain-pen and jackals could type, they would write like T. S. Eliot" [cited in Paczkowski, **The Spring Will Be Ours,** p. 258].

17. Ibid., p. 228.

18. Ibid, p. 231.

19. Ibid.

20. Ibid., p. 237.

21. Lasota, **Donos na Wojtyłę,** chapter 1.

22. Paczkowski, **The Spring Will Be Ours,** p. 192.

23. Author's interview with T. David Curp, July 13, 2008. For further detail on some of these activities in the "recovered territories," see Curp, **A Clean Sweep? The Politics of Ethnic Cleansing in Western Poland, 1945–1960** (Rochester, NY: University of Rochester Press, 2006).

24. See Paczkowski, **The Spring Will Be Ours,** p. 251.

25. Author's interview with Kazimierz Wóycicki, June 10, 1991.

26. The full text may be found in **Conscience and Captivity: Religion in Eastern Europe,** ed. Janice Broun (Washington, DC: Ethics and Public Policy Center, 1988), pp. 330–32.

27. See ibid., pp. 333–34. Poland's Catholic Church has long been accused of an untoward involvement in political affairs. Yet the 1953 bishops' statement ended on a note that affirmed the institutional separation of Church and state and defended social pluralism:

> We are conscious of the special tasks and duties of the Catholic priest toward his country, and that is why we have often reminded our priests of them. . . . But we also demand, emphatically, that our priests should not be torn away from their religious duties; that they should not be drawn into political affairs which are alien to their vocations; that political pressure aimed at using them as instruments in the struggle

of the State against the Church should be stopped [a clear reference to the work of the secret police]; and that they should not be forced to break the oath by which they pledged loyalty to the Church and their bishops. In short, in accord with the principle of the separation of Church and State, as guaranteed in our Constitution, the State must abstain from intruding in the religious, spiritual, and internal affairs of the Church. [Ibid.]

28. See Weigel, **The Final Revolution,** pp. 110–11.

29. For more on Father Karol Wojtyła's work as curate in Niegowić, see Weigel, **Witness to Hope,** pp. 91–93.

30. For further detail on this phase of Karol Wojtyła's life and ministry, see ibid., chapter 3.

31. **Our God's Brother** was rejected by the Catholic literary monthly **Znak** and would not be published until 1979, when **Tygodnik Powszechny** ran the play in its entirety in its Christmas issue.

Karol Wojtyła's literary work in this period is discussed in more detail in ibid., chapter 3.

32. See Lasota, **Donos na Wojtyłę,** chapter 2. Wojtyła had to resign from UNIA because its strict command structure and its equally strict rules of wartime confidentiality about personalities and operations were incompatible with a seminarian's obligations to obey and speak freely to his religious superiors.

33. See Małecki, **A History of Kraków for Everyone,** pp. 254–55.

34. For a more detailed analysis of Wojtyła's work on Scheler, see Weigel, **Witness to Hope,** chapter 4.

35. Author's interview with Stefan Swieżawski, April 7, 1997.

36. The Lublin Committee's formal name was the Polish Committee of National Liberation, **Polski Komitet Wyzwolenia Narodowego.** While technically a coalition of various political factions, the Lublin Committee was for all practical purposes an instrument of Soviet state power.

37. Author's interview with Stefan Swieżawski, April 7, 1997.

38. For a more complete discussion of Wojtyła's development as a philosopher and his work at KUL, see Weigel, **Witness to Hope,** chapter 4.

39. For a developed discussion of the Law of the Gift from a later period of Wojtyła's intellectual life, see Karol Wojtyła, "The Personal Structure of Self-Determination," in Wojtyła, **Person and Community: Selected Essays,** trans. Theresa Sandok, O.F.M. (New York: Peter Lang, 1993), pp. 188–95.

40. See Karol Wojtyła, **Love and Responsibility,** trans. H. T. Willetts (San Francisco: Ignatius Press, 1993).

41. For a more complete discussion of Wojtyła's exposition of Catholic sexual ethics, see Weigel, **Witness to Hope,** chapter 4.

42. See Małecki, **A History of Kraków for Everyone,** p. 267.

43. See Paczkowski, **The Spring Will Be Ours,** p. 267.

44. On these points, see Lasota, **Donos na Wojtyłę,** chapters 1 and 4.

45. See ibid., chapter 2.

46. Paczkowski, **The Spring Will Be Ours,** p. 286.

47. Ibid., p. 293.

Chapter Two

1. Adam Boniecki, M.I.C., **The Making of the Pope of the Millennium: Kalendarium of the Life of Karol Wojtyła,** trans. Irina and Thaddeus Mirecki et alia (Stockbridge, MA: Marian Press, 2000), p. 754 [hereinafter **Kalendarium**].

2. Ibid., p. 755.

3. For a more detailed portrait of the Great Novena, see Weigel, **The Final Revolution,** pp. 111–19.

4. See Andrzej Grajewski, "Security Services of the Polish People's Republic Against the Vatican in 1956–1978," in **NKVD/KGB Activities and Its Cooperation with Other Secret Services in Central and Eastern Europe 1945–1989,** ed. Alexandra Grúňová (Bratislava: Nation's Memory Institute, 2008); hereinafter Grajewski, "Security Services."

5. See Lasota, **Donos na Wojtyłę,** chapter 2.

6. Ibid.

7. See ibid., pp. 83–84; trans. by Paula Olearnik.

8. See ibid., chapters 2 and 5.

9. See ibid., chapter 3.

10. Andrew and Mitrokhin, **The Sword and the Shield,** p. 487.

11. Ibid.

12. Agostino Casaroli, **The Martyrdom of Patience: The Holy See and the Communist Countries (1963–1989),** trans. Marco Bagnarol, I.M.C. (Toronto: Ave Maria Centre of Peace, 2007), p. 7.

13. Ibid., p. 14.

It is worth noting that the beginnings of the Black Legend of Pius XII's alleged affinity for fascism and alleged indifference to Jewish suffering during World War II—which originated in Radio Moscow broadcasts in June 1945 and set in place the outline of the anti-Pius case that would intensify in the 1960s with the production of Rolf Hochhuth's play, **The Deputy**—antedate this period of high anticommunist Vatican rhetoric. Part of Moscow's strategy for the Stalinization of its new imperium in east central Europe was the destruction of the Catholic Church's reputation, which it believed could be advanced by an all-out assault on Pius XII, then at the height of his international authority. (See Sandro Magister, "Pius XII: A Book and an Essay Shed Light on the Black Legend," available at http://chiesa.espresso.re-pubblica.it/articolo/1337848?eng-y; see also Robert A. Graham, S.J., **The Vatican and Communism During World War II** [San Francisco: Ignatius Press, 1996].)

14. Casaroli, **The Martyrdom of Patience,** p. 20.

15. Ibid., pp. 36–37.

16. Ibid., p. xxi.

17. Author's interview with Cardinal Franz König, December 11, 1997.

18. Author's interview with Cardinal Agostino Casaroli, February 14, 1997.

19. Author's interview with Jan Nowak, May 13, 1998.

Nowak, the longtime director of Radio Free Europe's Polish service and a close observer of the Catholic contest with communism behind the Iron Curtain, believed that Casaroli's view of the dynamics of the underground Church in the communist bloc was mistaken, despite the fact that there were occasional liturgical and canonical aberrations in those countries.

20. For a detailed portrait of these Hungarian intelligence efforts, see Stefano Bottoni, "A Special Relationship: Hungarian Intelligence and the Vatican, 1961–1978," in Alexandra Grúňová, ed., **NKVD/KGB Activities,** pp. 147–76.

21. See John Koehler, **Spies in the Vatican: The Soviet Union's Cold War Against the Catholic Church** (New York: Pegasus Books, 2009), p. 11.

22. Grajewski, "Security Services," p. 185.

23. For an extensive discussion of Wojtyła's work at Vatican II, see Weigel, **Witness to Hope,** chapter 5.

24. Grajewski, "Security Services," pp. 177–82.

25. Cited in Lasota, **Donos na Wojtyłę,** chapter 5.

26. Author's interview with Rev. Msgr. Andrzej Bardecki, July 11, 1996. For more detail on Wojtyła's appointment as archbishop of Kraków, see Weigel, **Witness to Hope,** chapter 6.

27. Institute of National Remembrance [hereinafter IPN], document 0648/38.

28. Author's interview with Andrzej Grajewski, July 15, 2007.

29. See Weigel, **Witness to Hope,** p. 186.

30. Grajewski, "Security Services," pp. 185–86.

31. Ibid., p. 186, with reference to IPN document 0445/12, vol. 1, file 3.

32. Boniecki, **Kalendarium,** pp. 258–60.

33. Paczkowski, **The Spring Will Be Ours,** pp. 309–10.

34. Author's interview with Cardinal Agostino Casaroli, February 14, 1997.

35. Andrzej Micewski, **Cardinal Wyszyński: A Biography** (San Diego: Harcourt Brace Jovanovich, 1984), p. 266.

36. Author's interview with Cardinal Agostino Casaroli, February 14, 1997.

37. On Maliński's identity as DELTA, see Marek Lasota, "Zawartość dokumentacji tajnego współpracownika o ps. 'Delta,'" in **Kościół katolicki w czasach komunistycznej dyktatury: Między bohaterstwem a agentur,** eds. Ryszarda Terleckiego and Fr. Jana Szczepaniaka (Kraków: Wydział Historii Kościoła Papieskiej Akademii Teologicznej, 2007).

38. Lasota, **Donos na Wojtyłę,** pp. 239–43.

39. Cardinal Wyszyński's worries on this front would seem to have been justified, given Casaroli's standard diplomatic modus operandi. Thus in 1975, Casaroli made clear to Cardinal Alfred Bengsch of Berlin that, during his forthcoming trip to Berlin, he, Casaroli, would be an "official guest of the government" and that any meetings with Casaroli's fellow churchmen would be of a strictly private character—an admonition duly reported to the Stasi's religious affairs department by a mole in Bengsch's office. [See Koehler, **Spies in the Vatican,** p. 139, citing an official Stasi record.]

40. Andrew and Mitrokhin, **The Sword and the Shield,** pp. 499–500, quoting from official records copied by Mitrokhin.

41. See ibid., pp. 6ff.

42. See Benjamin Weiser, **A Secret Life: The Polish Officer, His Covert Mission, and the Price He Paid to Save His Country** (New York: Public Affairs, 2004),

chapter 1. Kukliński's revulsion at the crushing of the Prague Spring was intensified by the Security Services' lethal attack on striking Polish workers in Gdańsk in 1970.

43. See Leszek Kołakowski, **Main Currents of Marxism,** 3 vols. (New York: Oxford University Press, 1981).

44. Paczkowski, **The Spring Will Be Ours,** p. 330.

45. Andrew and Mitrokhin, **The Sword and the Shield,** p. 500.

46. Wojtyła's work as archbishop of Kraków is described in detail in Weigel, **Witness to Hope,** chapter 6.

47. Paczkowski, **The Spring Will Be Ours,** pp. 352, 353.

48. Ibid., pp. 368–69.

49. Ibid., p. 372.

50. Straszewski had long been familiar with the internal dynamics and tensions within Polish Catholicism, as one of his interlocutors was Mieczysław Albert Krąpiec, O.P., the distinguished philosopher at the Catholic University of Lublin, who had talked with Straszewski for years.

51. See Lasota, **Donos na Wojtyłę,** pp. 28–29.

52. See Koehler, **Spies in the Vatican,** pp. 23, 41, 45–51. In the conversation with the South Vietnamese foreign minister (in 1973), Paul VI displayed a remarkable naïveté about Vietnamese communist intentions.

53. See Grajewski, "Security Services," pp. 187–89.

54. Author's interview with Bishop Stanisław Smoleński, April 9, 1997.

55. On Wojtyła and the Corpus Christi procession, see Weigel, **Witness to Hope,** pp. 191–92.

56. Boniecki, **Kalendarium,** p. 539.

57. Ibid., p. 596.

58. Ibid., p. 654.

59. Ibid., p. 708.

60. Ibid., p. 820.

61. Author's conversations with Archbishop Damian Zimoń, May 24–25, 2008.

62. Jacek Purchla developed this theme at a conference held at the Kraków Academy of Music on November 5, 2008.

63. Stanisław Dziwisz, **A Life with Karol: My Forty-Year Friendship with the Man Who Became Pope,** trans. Adrian J. Walker (New York: Doubleday, 2008), p. 33.

64. Author's interview with Henryk Woźniakowski, April 10, 1997.

65. Andrew and Mitrokhin, **The Sword and the Shield,** p. 509.

66. Author's interview with Father Andrzej Bardecki, July 11, 1996.

67. Cited in Thomas A. Sancton, "He Dared to Hope," **Time,** January 4, 1982.

68. Author's conversation with Stanisław Rybicki, November 8, 2008.

69. Author's interview with Dominik Duka, O.P., March 21, 1998.

70. Andrew and Mitrokhin, **The Sword and the Shield,** pp. 500–501.

71. Author's interviews with Cardinal Achille Silvestrini, March 12, 2008, and November 20, 2008; no such concern is evident in Casaroli's memoirs, either.

72. Andrew and Mitrokhin, **The Sword and the Shield,** p. 503; Bottoni, "A Special Relationship."

73. Lasota, **Donos na Wojtyłę,** chapter 1.

74. Ibid., chapter 9.

75. Author's interview with Bohdan Cywiński, November 14, 1998.

76. Paczkowski, **The Spring Will Be Ours,** pp. 391–92.

77. See Peter Raina, **Arcybiskup Dąbrowski— rozmowy vatykańskie** (Warsaw: Instytut Wydawniczy Pax, 2001), pp. 190–93.

78. Author's interview with Cardinal Stanisław Dziwisz, December 2, 2008.

79. Author's conversation with members of **Środowisko,** November 8, 2008.

Chapter Three

1. On immediate KGB reactions to the election of John Paul II, see Andrew and Mitrokhin, **The Sword and the Shield,** pp. 510–12.

2. Agostino Casaroli was hardly unaware of the criticism of the **Ostpolitik** he had engineered; yet he continued to be unaware, it seems, of the fact that Soviet-bloc intelligence had penetrated what he must have imagined to have been sacrosanct Vatican conversations. Thus Hungarian intelligence reported to Budapest that, at a meeting of Holy See diplomatic representatives in Frascati in early 1974, Casaroli challenged the characterization of the **Ostpolitik** as "ideological compromise" with communism; he then conceded its "disappointing results" while arguing that it should continue because

"so long as we dialogue, East-European Christians are not at risk" [cited in Bottoni, "A Special Relationship," p. 173].

3. Author's interview with Cardinal William Baum, September 2, 2008.

4. Author's interview with Cardinal Franz König, December 11, 1997.

5. See Andrew and Mitrokhin, **The Sword and the Shield,** p. 490; the report on ADAMANT/Nikodim's last words is from the author's interview with historian Bohdan Bociurkiw, August 10, 1996.

6. Ibid., p. 494.

7. Paczkowski, **The Spring Will Be Ours,** p. 393. For details of the election of John Paul II and the reaction in Poland and elsewhere, see Weigel, **Witness to Hope,** chapter 7.

8. Cited in ibid., pp. 508–9.

9. Author's interview with Jerzy Turowicz, July 19, 1996.

10. Author's interview with Irina Ilovayskaya Alberti, April 13, 1998.

11. Ibid.

12. Koehler, **Spies in the Vatican,** p. 61.

13. Author's interview with Msgr. Andrzej Bardecki, July 11, 1996.

14. An English translation of the entire homily may be found in **Origins** 8:20 (November 2, 1978). The original Italian text is in **Insegnamenti di Giovanni Paolo II, 1978.** I have modified the NC News Service translation for greater accuracy.

15. Author's interviews with Cardinal Achille Silvestrini, March 12, 2008, and November 20, 2008.

16. For further details on the first weeks of John Paul II's pontificate, see Weigel, **Witness to Hope,** chapter 8.

An early CIA analysis of the probable impact of John Paul II's election on the politics of central and eastern Europe displayed a surprisingly accurate view of Wojtyła's likely capacity to reinvigorate Church-based resistance to communism in Ukraine and Lithuania, although overstating the likely effect of John Paul II on what was then the Byelorussian Soviet Socialist Republic. [See Koehler, **Spies in the Vatican,** pp. 59–60.]

17. See Andrew and Mitrokhin, **The Sword and the Shield,** p. 512.

18. Author's interview with Andrzej Grajewski, July 14, 2009. See also Andrzej Grajewski, "About the Plague," **Gość Niedzielny,** October 18, 2009, for more on the SB's modus operandi in Rome.

19. The Stasi document in question, logged as 6847/78, was obtained from the German archives by Dr. Andrzej Grajewski and provided to the author. It was translated from the German by John Rock, S.J., Szymon Malecki, and the author.

20. Author's conversation with Pope John Paul II and Archbishop Stanisław Dziwisz, December 16, 1998.

21. See Weigel, **Witness to Hope,** pp. 298–99.

22. See Christopher Andrew and Vasili Mitrokhin, **The World Was Going Our Way: The KGB and the Battle for the Third World** (New York: Basic Books, 2005), pp. xxvi; 24; 33ff. (on Cuba as the "bridgehead"); pp. 117ff. (on the Sandinistas in Nicaragua); and pp. 127ff. (on El Salvador).

23. Dziwisz, **A Life with Karol,** p. 75.

24. The Stasi document in question, "Information 241/79," was obtained from the German archives by Dr. Andrzej Grajewski and provided to the author. It was translated from the German by John Rock, S.J., Szymon Malecki, and the author.

The "IM" may have been LICHTBLICK (Father Eugen Brammertz, O.S.B., who worked in the Vatican Secretariat of State and on the German edition of **L'Osservatore Romano** and who had been a Stasi informant for years) or LICHTBLICK's former student, ANTONIUS (Dr. Alfons Waschbüsch, another Stasi informant who worked for the German Catholic news agency in Rome).

25. Benelli, who was almost elected pope at the second conclave of 1978, seems to have been a bête noire to both the Stasi and the KGB, who regarded him as an anticommunist hard-liner.

26. The Stasi document in question, "Information 228/79," was obtained from the German archives by Dr. Andrzej Grajewski and provided to the author. It was translated from the German by John Rock, S.J., Szymon Malecki, and the author.

27. See Koehler, **Spies in the Vatican,** pp. 67–68.

28. For more on the strategy behind John Paul II's appointment of Casaroli and Silvestrini, see Weigel, **Witness to Hope,** pp. 299–300.

29. The Stasi document in question, "Information 316/79," was obtained from the German archives by Dr. Andrzej Grajewski and provided to the author. It was translated from the German by John Rock, S.J., Szymon Malecki, and the author.

30. Author's interview with Cardinal Stanisław Dziwisz, December 2, 2008.

31. See Weigel, **Witness to Hope,** p. 301, for a fuller account of this bizarre episode.

32. See Lasota, **Donos na Wojtyłę,** chapters 9 and 10.

33. See Koehler, **Spies in the Vatican,** p. 213.

34. Andrzej Grajewski, "Operacja papież," **W prost,** No. 43/2008 (1348).

Brammertz was a prolific mole. The extant summaries of his voluminous reports run to over 200 pages; each was classified "A," for "reliable," and variously graded as being of "medium value" or "very valuable" in utility. It seems virtually certain that all of the LICHTBLICK materials were shared with the KGB. Brammertz's work included a 1984 report on Opus Dei as an instrument of John Paul II's anticommunist activism and was likely intended as support for an anti–Opus Dei disinformation campaign, given its discussion of Opus Dei's "economic criminality," which allegedly included arms running and narcotics trafficking—standard smears in Stasiland. [See Koehler, **Spies in the Vatican,** pp. 157–59.]

35. Dziwisz, **A Life with Karol,** p. 118.

36. For a detailed analysis of John Paul II's first papal pilgrimage to Poland, see Weigel, **Witness to Hope,** pp. 300–323.

37. One particularly busy Stasi spy during the Nine Days, STEPHAN, acidly reported to his East Berlin masters that Polish president Jabłonski's farewell to John Paul II had been "a **Bruderschaftskuss** [brotherhood kiss]" [cited in Koehler, **Spies in the Vatican,** p. 84].

38. Polish composer Henryk Gorecki protested

Gierek's refusal to allow the Pope into the Silesian city of Katowice, and lost his job at the State Higher School of Music in Katowice as a result.

39. Adam Michnik, "A Lesson in Dignity," in Michnik, **Letters from Prison and Other Essays** (Berkeley: University of California Press, 1987), p. 160.

40. Author's interview with Jan Nowak, May 13, 1998.

41. Casaroli, **The Martyrdom of Patience,** p. 340.

42. Quoted in "Information 228/79" (cf. note 26).

43. Paczkowski, **The Spring Will Be Ours,** p. 399.

44. Ibid., pp. 401–2.

45. Andrew and Mitrokhin, **The Sword and the Shield,** p. 513.

46. For an analysis of John Paul II's 1979 UN address, see Weigel, **Witness to Hope,** pp. 327–28, 346–50.

47. A photocopy of the decree and supporting documents, in the original Russian, was given to the author by Dr. Andrzej Grajewski, who had obtained the materials from Dr. Andrzej Paczkowski. The translations are by Ashley Morrow.

48. Author's interviews with Andrzej Grajewski, May 8, 2008, and November 7, 2008.

49. **Sprawozdanie z rozmów przeprowadzonych z Papieżem Janem Pawłem II, z kardynałem Agostino Casaroli, prałatem Lewandowskim I innymi osobami w Watykanie w dniach 18-21.III.1980 r.** [Report on Conversations Carried out with Pope John Paul II, Cardinal Agostino Casaroli, Msgr. Lewandowski, and Others in the Vatican between 18 and 21 March 1980], from the Archives of the Polish Foreign Ministry, AMSZ

D.IV Wat-0-22; original Polish document translated by Paula Olearnik.

50. Antoni Dudek, "The Carnival," in **The Road to Independence: Solidarność 1980–2005,** trans. Robert Strybel (Warsaw: Oficyna Wydawnicza Volumen/ Komisja Krajowa NSZZ 'Solidarność,' 2005), p. 15 [hereinafter: Dudek, "The Carnival"].

51. John Paul II, **Address to the Fiftieth General Assembly of the United Nations Organization,** October 5, 1995, 2.

52. Cited in Timothy Garton Ash, **The Polish Revolution: Solidarity** (Sevenoaks, Kent: Hodder and Stoughton, 1985), p. 331.

53. Details here are taken from Dudek, "The Carnival," pp. 17–27.

54. On the strike bulletin name and logo, see Roman Laba, **The Roots of Solidarity: A Political Sociology of Poland's Working-Class Democratization** (Princeton, NJ: Princeton University Press, 1991), pp. 132–33.

55. Dudek, "The Carnival," p. 29; for Wojtyła on "solidarity," see Weigel, **Witness to Hope,** pp. 175–76.

56. Andrew and Mitrokhin, **The Sword and the Shield,** pp. 517–18.

57. Ibid., pp. 518–19.

58. Author's interview with Tadeusz Mazowiecki, April 7, 1997.

59. Author's interviews with Cardinal Achille Silvestrini, March 12, 2008, and November 20, 2008.

60. Author's conversation with Hanna Gronkiewicz-Walz, December 5, 2008.

61. Paczkowski, **The Spring Will Be Ours,** pp. 416–17.

62. Cited in Sancton, "He Dared to Hope," p. 11.

63. Andrew and Mitrokhin, **The Sword and the Shield,** p. 520.

64. Ibid.

65. Paczkowski, **The Spring Will Be Ours,** pp. 418–19.

66. See Weigel, **Witness to Hope,** pp. 405–6.

67. The full text of the letter, which was written in French, is available in English translation in ibid., pp. 406–7.

68. Author's interviews with Cardinal Achille Silvestrini, March 12, 2008, and November 20, 2008; author's interview with Cardinal Stanisław Dziwisz, December 2, 2008.

69. See Lasota, **Donos na Wojtyłę,** epilogue.

70. Polish Ministry of Foreign Affairs, "Code Message No. 260/1/70 from Rome, 9 January 1980." This document was obtained from the foreign ministry archives by Dr. Andrzej Grajewski, who shared it with the author. The translation from the Polish was done by Paula Olearnik.

71. Twenty-eight years later, reflecting on this period, Cardinal Silvestrini conceded that he and Casaroli believed that a "certain caution, a certain prudence" was required in dealing with an unknown quantity like Solidarity. But, as Silvestrini put it, with a rueful smile, the Pope had the initiative on this front and, in any event, "**Il Papa aveva meno** . . . [The Pope had less (prudence) . . .]." Author's interview with Cardinal Achille Silvestrini, November 20, 2008.

72. John Koehler, Claire Sterling, and Paul Henze all report that a veteran KGB operative, Luigi Scricciolo,

who worked for an Italian labor federation, kept Moscow Center and the Soviet Politburo informed of the Pope's discussion with the Wałęsa delegation, to which Scricciolo had attached himself as a guide. [See Koehler, **Spies in the Vatican,** p. 92.]

73. Author's interview with Tadeusz Mazowiecki, April 7, 1997. John Paul II's homily: "Mass for the Polish Delegation . . ." **L'Osservatore Romano/English Weekly Edition,** February 9, 1981, p. 23.

74. Martin Anderson and Annelise Anderson, **Reagan's Secret War: The Untold Story of His Fight to Save the World from Nuclear Disaster** (New York: Crown, 2009), pp. 74–75.

75. The "holy alliance" myth was aggressively promoted by Carl Bernstein and Marco Politi in **His Holiness: John Paul II and the Hidden History of Our Time** (New York: Doubleday, 1996), an unreliable study of John Paul II on this and a host of other important points.

76. On these aspects of Reagan, see Anderson and Anderson, **Reagan's Secret War,** pp. 49–50, 52, 63–65, and 75.

77. See ibid., p. 48, for the effects of John Hinckley's assassination attempt on Reagan's sense of vocational purpose.

78. See Paczkowski, **The Spring Will Be Ours,** pp. 420ff.

79. Dudek, "The Carnival," p. 49.

80. Carl Bernstein and Marco Politi took the Soviet disinformation bait in **His Holiness,** pp. 277–78; John Paul II and Stanisław Dziwisz confirmed to the author, in a conversation on December 16, 1998, that the Pope

had never met with the Soviet ambassador to Italy to discuss Solidarity, or anything else. On the Pakistan bomb plot, see Andrew and Mitrokhin, **The World Was Going Our Way,** p. 358.

81. Andrew and Mitrokhin, **The Sword and the Shield,** p. 521.

82. Dudek, "The Carnival," p. 55.

83. Quoted in Andrew and Mitrokhin, **The Sword and the Shield,** p. 522.

84. Dudek, "The Carnival," p. 59.

85. Cited in ibid.

86. Polish Ministry of Foreign Affairs, "Code Message No. 161/II/1423 from Rome, 3 April 1981." This document was obtained from the foreign ministry archives by Dr. Andrzej Grajewski, who shared it with the author. The translation from the Polish was done by Paula Olearnik.

87. Ibid. This document provides one of the clearest windows into the cast of mind of the veterans of the Vatican **Ostpolitik,** who seemed to share conventional European and liberal American concerns of the time about irresponsible Reaganite rhetoric and a bilateral, action/reaction cycle "arms race" that was, in fact, heavily weighted in early 1981 in favor of the USSR. It is possible, of course, that Silvestrini was simply telling Szablewski what he thought the Pole wanted to hear; possible, but very unlikely, given other evidence about the fundamental conceptual framework of the Casaroli/Silvestrini **Ostpolitik.**

88. Polish Ministry of Foreign Affairs, "Code Message No. 1340/II/1855 from Rome, 7 May 1981." This doc-

ument was obtained from the foreign ministry archives by Dr. Andrzej Grajewski, who shared it with the author. The translation from the Polish was done by Paula Olearnik.

89. For a detailed account of the assassination attempt and its immediate aftermath, see Weigel, **Witness to Hope,** pp. 397–98, 411–16.

90. Author's interview with Gabriel Turowski, June 10, 1997.

Two American pilgrims, Anne Odre and Rose Hull, were hit by ricochets or missed shots from Agca's fusillade.

91. Http://www.reagan.utexas.edu/archives/speeches/1981/51381b.htm.

92. See Thomas Joscelyn, "Crime of the Century: How the Media Elite and the CIA Failed to Investigate the 1981 Papal Assassination Attempt," **Weekly Standard,** April 7, 2005.

Post–Cold War revelations suggested that the KGB had designs on getting as "close to [John Paul II]" as possible from the first months of the pontificate. One KGB officer defected to the United States in 1980 after hearing discussions of possible anti–John Paul II measures. [See Koehler, **Spies in the Vatican,** pp. 57–64.]

93. Among the refinements of prevarication in Operation **Papst** was a forged letter, leaked to the European press, in which conservative Bavarian Christian Democratic leader Franz-Josef Strauss was implicated in the papal assassination plot via alleged links to Turkish right-wing parties. Never reluctant to try killing two birds with one stone, the Stasi aimed this piece of dis-

---

926   NOTES

information at undermining a major West German political figure while continuing to provide cover for the Bulgarians.

The Stasi was also involved in what may have been another effort to cover Agca's links to Soviet-bloc intelligence agencies. In 1983, Emanuela Orlandi, the daughter of an Italian worker in the Vatican, was kidnapped. Subsequent letters to the Italian press claiming to be from her captors and suggesting that the Grey Wolves had captured her in order to trade her for Mehmet Ali Agca were in fact written by Stasi officers, acting again on behalf of their Bulgarian colleagues. Emanuela Orlandi was never found.

Information on Operation **Papst** comes from the author's July 2007 and November 2008 interviews with Dr. Andrzej Grajewski and from Grajewski's article, "Operacja papież," No. 43/2008.

94. For the "second agony," see Weigel, **Witness to Hope,** pp. 415–16.

95. When Glemp received the cardinal's red hat in 1982, reports on his conversations with John Paul II were filed by a Hungarian intelligence operative and shared by Budapest with the Stasi and the KGB; the report speculated that Cardinal Casaroli had been impelled to adopt "the hard line of the Pope." [See Koehler, **Spies in the Vatican,** p. 205.]

96. Andrew and Mitrokhin, **The Sword and the Shield,** p. 523.

97. Ibid., p. 524.

98. See Paczkowski, **The Spring Will Be Ours,** p. 434.

99. Dudek, "The Carnival," p. 63.

100. Andrew and Mitrokhin, **The Sword and the Shield,** p. 526.

101. Cited in Weigel, **Witness to Hope,** p. 419. For more on the first Solidarity Congress and its relationship to John Paul II's first social encyclical, **Laborem Exercens,** see ibid., pp. 418–21.

102. Paczkowski, **The Spring Will Be Ours,** p. 436.

103. Dudek, "The Carnival," p. 67.

104. Paczkowski, **The Spring Will Be Ours,** p. 439.

105. Andrew and Mitrokhin, **The Sword and the Shield,** p. 528.

106. Paczkowski, **The Spring Will Be Ours,** p. 441; Dudek, "The Carnival," p. 73.

107. Operational details on the impending martial law crackdown had been given to the U.S. Central Intelligence Agency in mid-September 1981 by Colonel Ryszard Kukliński, who, with his family, was subsequently exfiltrated to the West some weeks before martial law was imposed. Rumors that Kukliński's cover had been blown from inside the Vatican circulated in some circles for years afterward.

108. Cited in Paczkowski, **The Spring Will Be Ours,** p. 443.

109. Cited in ibid., p. 444.

110. Ibid., p. 447.

111. On Glemp as "a second Khomeini": Andrew and Mitrokhin, **The Sword and the Shield,** p. 530. Glemp's remarks on December 13, 1981, are cited in Paczkowski, **The Spring Will Be Ours,** p. 451.

112. Paczkowski, **The Spring Will Be Ours,** p. 452.

113. Andrew and Mitrokhin, **The Sword and the Shield,** p. 534.

114. Cited in Thomas Swick, "Laughter in Red," **Weekly Standard,** October 26, 2009, p. 31.

115. See Weigel, **Witness to Hope,** pp. 432ff.

116. Dziwisz, **A Life with Karol,** pp. 143–44.

117. Http://www.reagan.utexas.edu/archives/speeches/1981/121481b.htm.

118. Author's interview with Bohdan Cywiński, November 14, 1998. Jonathan Kwitny created the myth of a John Paul II/Cywiński "conspiracy" to aid Solidarity in his **Man of the Century** (New York: Henry Holt, 1997), pp. 418ff. Cywiński flatly denied that any such "conspiracy" had taken place.

119. Author's interviews with Bohdan Cywiński, November 14, 1998; and Jan Nowak, May 13, 1998.

Nowak, who was in close contact with the Reagan administration during this period, had an interesting analysis of Jaruzelski's position and intentions during the imposition of martial law, stating that Jaruzelski had asked for a small number of Soviet troops to come in after WRON had imposed martial law: this would have provided him cover ("You see? I had to do it or they would have invaded.") and would have deflected criticism. The Soviets, knowing what game he was playing, refused. Jaruzelski was also not sure, Nowak suggested, that he would be successful on the night of December 12–13 and wanted backup in case his initial plans did not succeed. In addition, Nowak argued, Jaruzelski was terrified of occupation strikes and sit-down strikes in 500 factories, which would instantly have become 500 fortresses—a concern that perhaps explains, although it certainly does not justify, the lethal brutality at the **Wujek** mine on December 16.

120. These excerpts are taken from the "Minutes of the President's Working Lunch with Agostino Cardinal Casaroli, Secret, The Map Room, The White House, December 15, 1981, 12:45–2:15 p.m.," in Executive Secretariat, NSC: Subject File: Records, 1981–1985. Memorandums of Conversation—President Reagan (December 1981) (1)(2). Box 49, Ronald Reagan Presidential Library. A full copy of this now-declassified document was generously provided to the author by Martin Anderson and Annelise Anderson.

121. Polish Ministry of Foreign Affairs, "Code Message No. 3240/IV from New York on 18 December 1981." This document was obtained from the foreign ministry archives by Dr. Andrzej Grajewski, who shared it with the author. The translation from the Polish was done by Paula Olearnik.

122. See Koehler, **Spies in the Vatican,** p. 197.

123. See ibid., p. 200.

124. Author's interview with Zbigniew Brzeziński, February 7, 1997.

Chapter Four

1. Author's interview with Cardinal Jean-Marie Lustiger, October 24, 1996.

2. See Anderson and Anderson, **Reagan's Secret War,** pp. 90–91 and p. 408, note 23.

3. Author's interview with Jan Nowak, May 13, 1998. Ryszard Kukliński died in 2004, his two sons having predeceased him under strange circumstances during their exile in the United States. The Polish officer's career remained controversial in Poland until his death, with some insisting that he was a traitor who had betrayed his

officer's oath; among those arguing this were, perhaps not surprisingly, Wojciech Jaruzelski and Czesław Kiszczak. John Paul II had a dramatically different view, and quietly passed the word to friends in the Polish Church that Kukliński should be regarded as a Polish patriot and hero. [Jaruzelski's and Kiszczak's views are noted in Weiser, **A Secret Life,** pp. 308–10. John Paul II's role in arranging a warm welcome for Kukliński on the latter's return to Poland for a 1998 visit was related to the author by Radek Sikorski in a conversation on November 11, 1998.]

4. Václav Havel et al., **The Power of the Powerless: Citizens Against the State in Central-Eastern Europe** (Armonk, NY: M.E. Sharpe, 1985), pp. 23–96.

5. Paczkowski, **The Spring Will Be Ours,** p. 470.

6. Author's interview with Andrzej Grajewski, May 26, 2008.

7. Paczkowski, **The Spring Will Be Ours,** p. 458.

8. Henryk Głębocki, "The Underground," in Strybel, trans., **The Road to Independence,** p. 111.

9. For a description of the wide-ranging program at the Maximilian Kolbe Church in Nowa Huta, see Weigel, **The Final Revolution,** pp. 151–52.

10. On the concept of "moral extraterritoriality," see ibid.

11. Author's interview with Jacek Woźniakowski, November 5, 1998.

The story of how Woźniakowski got to Rome reveals something of the temper of those times. Woźniakowski had been teaching in Toulouse in the fall of 1981, but happened to be back in Poland when martial law was imposed, the French academic semester having ended.

Thinking that he'd never get a passport to return to France, and wanting to remain in Kraków in any event, given the circumstances, he prepared to see the martial law through with his family and friends. An SB official involved in passports tracked Woźniakowski down and asked him, on the street one day, "Why aren't you in France? You'll give a bad impression if you don't fulfill your commitment. Come to my office tomorrow and I'll give you and your wife passports." As the only plane out of Warsaw was to Rome, they took that—which was fine with Woźniakowski, who knew that the Pope would be eager for firsthand information. They asked the wife of a French diplomat in Warsaw to get their passports stamped with visas at the Italian Embassy in the Polish capital; she got the job done and the passports delivered to the Woźniakowskis shortly before the plane took off. Thus did the SB's determination to maintain a facade of "normality" in Poland lead to John Paul II getting his "first decent report" on what had been happening in his homeland.

12. Ibid.

Some years later, Woźniakowski mentioned the Pope's approval of the Brussels operation to Wałęsa, who replied, "That's interesting; I have a report to the contrary"—which was likely another example of SB or KGB disinformation.

13. Author's interview with Tadeusz Mazowiecki, April 7, 1997.

14. Http://www.reagan.utexas.edu/archives.speeches/1982/60782a.htm.

15. Głębocki, "The Underground," pp. 91–93, 99.

16. Ibid., p. 101.

17. Ibid., p. 99.

18. Cited in Paczkowski, **The Spring Will Be Ours,** p. 461.

19. Ibid., p. 460.

20. See Andrew and Mitrokhin, **The Sword and the Shield,** p. 213; Anderson and Anderson, **Reagan's Secret War,** p. 136.

21. For Dobrynin, see Andrew and Mitrokhin, **The Sword and the Shield**, p. 213.

22. Memorandum to the author from Andrzej Grajewski. Przemyśl was created an archdiocese in 1992; Archbishop Ignacy Tokarczuk, who retired in 1993, was a native of L'viv, the once predominantly Polish city incorporated into the Ukrainian Soviet Socialist Republic after World War II, and the diocese of Przemyśl was located on the Polish-Soviet (Ukrainian) border. Thus Tokarczuk was perceived as a particular threat by the SB and the Ukrainian KGB.

23. On TRIANGOLO: memorandum to the author from Andrzej Grajewski; Lasota, **Donos na Wojtyłę,** chapter 6.

24. Kotowski's reports doubtless intersected with material coming to the KGB from other sources, including the ever busy Hungarian intelligence service in Rome. In mid-1982, Hungarian agents in Rome reported that Cardinal Casaroli and other curialists were opposed to what became Poland II, on two grounds: first, that a papal visit risked exacerbating church-state tensions throughout the Soviet bloc, and, second, because a papal visit in the context of martial law (which John Paul II seemed likely to criticize, either overtly or subtly) seemed to contradict the Pope's strictures against

clerical involvement in politics. If the second alleged motive for caution was in fact reflective of curial views, then those who held it betrayed a striking ignorance of the difference between John Paul II's concerns over clerical partisan politics in the context of the various theologies of liberation and the Pope's insistence that the Church's leaders had a responsibility to defend basic human rights—even if in doing so they were accused of being partisans. [On the Hungarian-based report, see Koehler, **Spies in the Vatican,** p. 20.]

25. Kowalczyk was "registered" by PIETRO as an "information contact" in November 1982 and given the code name CAPPINO. The debate over Kowalczyk's interaction with the SB became sharp in Poland in early 2009, not least because Kowalczyk had served as the Holy See's nuncio to his homeland since 1989. Archbishop Kowalczyk's probity in his interactions with PIETRO was defended in an article, "Lustrowanie nuncjusza," by Andrzej Grajewski, in **Gość Niedzielny,** January 18, 2009, pp. 26–28. The case was also discussed in the Polish daily **Rzeczpospolita** on January 20, 2009 (Sławomir Cenckiewicz, "Współpracownicy wywiadu PRL"), and February 5, 2009 (Sławomir Cenckiewicz, "Opowie ci officera 'Pietro'").

26. The information on Kotowski's operations in Rome was given to the author by Andrzej Grajewski in an interview on July 14, 2009, shortly after Dr. Grajewski had had an extensive conversation with Dr. Kotowski.

27. For a more detailed account of John Paul II's 1983 pilgrimage to Central America, see Weigel, **Witness to Hope,** pp. 438–39, 451–59. On KGB and Cuban in-

telligence operations in Central America, see Andrew and Mitrokhin, **The World Was Going Our Way,** pp. 115–36.

28. Author's interview with Andrzej Grajewski, July 14, 2009.

29. Stefan Olszowski, "URGENT NOTE from a conversation with Archbishop Luigi Poggi, chairman of the Committee for Working Relations between the Apostolic See and the Government of the Polish People's Republic, on March 17, 1983." This document was obtained from the Polish foreign ministry archives by Dr. Andrzej Grajewski and given to the author. The translation from the Polish was done by Paula Olearnik.

30. It is possible that Poggi pushed back and that Olszowski failed to report it, but that seems unlikely, given the general tenor of Poggi's approach, which was further illustrated the next day.

31. "Notes from a conversation with Archbishop Poggi from the Office of Religious Affairs—18.III.83." This document was obtained from the Polish foreign ministry archives by Dr. Andrzej Grajewski and given to the author. The translation from the Polish was done by Paula Olearnik.

32. "Code Message No. 1256/II/2095 from Rome, April 25, 1983." This document was obtained from the Polish foreign ministry archives by Dr. Andrzej Grajewski and given to the author. The translation from the Polish was done by Paula Olearnik.

33. Cited in ibid.

34. Andrew and Mitrokhin, **The Sword and the Shield,** p. 538.

35. Ibid., pp. 538–39.

36. Author's conversations in Katowice, May 2008.

37. Dziwisz, **A Life with Karol,** p. 151.

38. Author's interview with Father Robert Tucci, S.J., September 25, 1997.

39. Author's interview with Bohdan Cywiński, November 14, 1998.

40. For a detailed account of Poland II, see Weigel, **Witness to Hope,** pp. 459–64. Stanisław Dziwisz provides telling details in **A Life with Karol,** pp. 150–56. See also Timothy Garton Ash, "The Pope in Poland," in Garton Ash, **The Uses of Adversity: Essays on the Fate of Central Europe** (New York: Vintage Books, 1990).

41. Cited in Paczkowski, **The Spring Will Be Ours,** p. 474.

42. Dziwisz, **A Life with Karol,** p. 151.

43. Ibid., p. 150.

44. Andrew and Mitrokhin, **The Sword and the Shield,** p. 549.

45. Author's interview with Cardinal Stanisław Dziwisz, December 2, 2008.

46. Ibid.

L'Osservatore Romano may not have understood, but the Stasi did. Its agents had been busy during Poland II, which, according to Stasi analysis, had been one long "display of anti-socialist manifestations." An East German spy reported that John Paul had made a "veiled attack against the Soviet Union," the evidence for which, ironically enough, was the Pope's defense of Polish sovereignty. Of perhaps more concern in both East Berlin and Moscow, however, was what the Stasi analysts regarded as the weakness of Poland's communist leadership in the face of what the Stasi described as a relentless papal assault. The Polish comrades had "suffered defeats" and had shown themselves "inconsistent in important questions," backing off under the pressure of "Church demands." The entire pilgrimage, the analysis concluded, had been "an encouragement of counter-revolutionary forces in their hostile anti-state activities"; worse still, Poland II aligned the Pope "with the political line of U.S. imperialism vis-à-vis Poland and the increasing attacks of the reactionaries against socialism." The Stasi's analysis was based in part on a lengthy report on John Paul II's remarks to the Polish bishops during their meeting at Częstochowa on June 19, where, according to the analysts, the Pope "laid out the long-range aims of the Vatican's battle against the socialist order and support of the counter-revolution." [See Koehler, **Spies in the Vatican,** pp. 216–21.]

47. Andrew and Mitrokhin, **The Sword and the Shield,** p. 540.

48. Ibid., p. 541.

49. Głębocki, "The Underground," p. 121.

50. See Koehler, **Spies in the Vatican,** pp. 225–28. The report of this meeting contained at least one bizarre target assignment: operatives were to do what they could to impede the work of professors at the Pontifical Gregorian University, "in which the policies of the Roman Curia vis-à-vis the socialist states are formulated." In fact, the general cast of mind in the Gregorian faculty at that period would have been broadly sympathetic to the pre–John Paul II **Ostpolitik** and highly critical of John Paul's critique of the theologies of liberation.

51. See ibid., p. 233. This LICHTBLICK report

would have raised a few eyebrows at the U.S. bishops conference, whose staff was then in the forefront of efforts to impede Reagan administration policies on nuclear weapons and on Central America.

52. See Głębocki, "The Underground," p. 125.

53. Cited in Antonin Lewek, "New Sanctuary of Poles: The Grave of Martyr-Father Jerzy Popiełuszko," (Warsaw, 1986); pamphlet obtained by the author at the St. Stanisław Kostka Church in Warsaw.

54. Michael Kaufman, **Mad Dreams, Saving Graces—Poland: A Nation in Conspiracy** (New York: Random House, 1989), p. 141.

55. These details are taken from Weigel, **The Final Revolution,** pp. 148–51.

56. John Paul II expressed his concern for Father Popiełuszko at his general audience on October 24, 1984, and in his Angelus remarks on October 28, and deplored his murder at the general audience of October 31 and the Angelus of November 1.

57. The "Litany of Our Lord Jesus Christ, Priest and Victim," was a staple of the devotional life of Kraków seminarians during Wojtyła's years of preparation for the priesthood. John Paul II reproduced it as an appendix to his vocational memoir, **Gift and Mystery.**

58. Cited in Anderson and Anderson, **Reagan's Secret War,** p. 207.

59. Author's conversation with Pope John Paul II, December 13, 1997.

60. See Broun, ed., **Conscience and Captivity,** pp. 93–94.

61. Author's interview with Andrzej Grajewski, May 26, 2008. In his memoir, **The Martyrdom of Patience,**

Cardinal Casaroli conceded that the **Ostpolitik** had met its most intransigent resistance from the Husak regime in Czechoslovakia.

62. Author's interview with Pavel Bratinka, October 23, 1991.

63. Author's interviews with Václav Vaško, October 22, 1991, and Father Václav Malý, October 25, 1991.

64. For a more detailed discussion of the evolution of the resistance Church in Czechoslovakia, including comments on John Paul II's role by leading Catholic dissidents, see Weigel, **The Final Revolution,** pp. 174–85.

65. Author's interviews with Irina Alberti, April 13, 1998, and April 16, 1998. John Paul II met Sakharov himself in 1989, encouraging him to remain active in democratic reform politics in the Soviet Union. See Weigel, **Witness to Hope,** pp. 569–71.

66. See Koehler, **Spies in the Vatican,** pp. 244–46. Given the report's warnings about any unwarranted distribution that might compromise its source, it seems likely that the Stasi analysis was based on information from LICHTBLICK (the German Benedictine Eugen Brammertz) or his former student, ANTONIUS (Dr. Alfons Waschbüsch).

67. E-mail to the author from General Edward Rowny, U.S. Army (Ret.), April 5, 2005.

68. Author's interview with Andreas Widmer, January 28, 2009.

69. "Report on the Visit of Wojciech Jaruzelski, Chairman of the State Council of the Polish People's Republic, to the Vatican, January 13, 1987," archives of the Polish Ministry of Foreign Affairs, Department IV, No. D IV Wat.0.22-1-87, archived March 23, 1987.

This document was obtained from the Polish foreign ministry archives by Dr. Andrzej Grajewski and given to the author. The translation from the Polish was done by Paula Olearnik.

70. Author's interview with Archbishop Tadeusz Gocłowski, C.M., December 4, 2008.

71. Ibid.

72. The citation was from the Pastoral Constitution on the Church in the Modern World [**Gaudium et Spes**], no. 31.

73. Details are taken from Weigel, **Witness to Hope,** pp. 543–48.

74. Ibid., p. 548. On Polish communist complaints about John Paul II's "tone," see Koehler, **Spies in the Vatican,** pp. 253–54.

75. Author's interview with Andrzej Grajewski, July 14, 2009. Kotowski told Grajewski that he had done this both for "reasons of state" and because "the people needed it."

76. Author's conversation with Piotr and Teresa Malecki, Stanisław and Danuta Rybicki, Maria Rybicka, Karol Tarnowski, and Danuta Ciesielska, November 8, 2008.

77. Memorandum to the author from Andrzej Grajewski.

78. On the 1988 discussion and the work of the Round Table, see Paczkowski, **The Spring Will Be Ours,** pp. 491–505.

79. On the Velvet Revolution, see Weigel, **Witness to Hope,** pp. 605–7.

80. Author's interviews with Irina Alberti, April 13, 1998, and April 16, 1998.

81. The viciousness and brutality with which the KGB attacked Orthodoxy was one of the reasons that Vasili Mitrokhin began creating his archive. See Andrew and Mitrokhin, "The Penetration and Persecution of the Soviet Church," in **The Sword and the Shield,** pp. 486–507.

82. See Bohdan R. Bociurkiw, **The Ukrainian Greek Catholic Church and the Soviet State, 1939–1950** (Edmonton: Canadian Institute of Ukrainian Studies Press, 1996), pp. 148–88.

83. According to Irina Alberti, one of John Paul II's private diplomatic agents in Russia, the diplomats and ecumenical officers of the Roman Curia were normally acquiescent and accommodating to the demands of their Russian Orthodox interlocutors, on the strategic grounds that the dialogue had to be maintained and that, if humiliation and accommodation were the price, so be it. Thus these men were "surprised," according to Mrs. Alberti, when Patriarch Pimen flatly refused to have the Pope in Russia in 1988. [Author's interviews with Irina Alberti, April 13, 1998, and April 16, 1998.]

84. For a detailed account of the Moscow meeting of Casaroli and Gorbachev, see Weigel, **Witness to Hope,** pp. 571–76.

The 1974 "Furov Report" was a KGB document categorizing the Orthodox hierarchy into three classes. Pimen was in category "A," men whose characteristics the report described in these terms: the "A" bishops affirm both in words and deed not only loyalty but also patriotism towards the socialist society; strictly observe the laws on cults, and educate the parish clergy and believers in the same spirit; realistically understand that our state is not interested in proclaiming the role of religion and church in society; and, realizing this, do not display any particular activeness in extending the influence of Orthodoxy among the population [Andrew and Mitrokhin, **The Sword and the Shield,** p. 490].

Patriarch Pimen's successor, Patriarch Aleksy II, was also in the Furov "A" category, and was known to the KGB as DROZDOV [ibid., p. 499].

85. Author's interview with Joaquín Navarro-Valls, February 18, 1998. For the text of John Paul II's letter to Gorbachev and the text of the Soviet leader's response, see Weigel, **Witness to Hope,** pp. 573–75.

86. Author's interview with Joaquín Navarro-Valls, December 17, 1998.

A memorandum of conversation of this meeting, likely dictated by Mikhail Gorbachev afterward, is available at http://www.gwu.edu/~nsarchive/NSAEBB/NSAEBB298/index.htm.

87. Zbigniew Brzeziński, **Power and Principle: Memoirs of the National Security Adviser 1977–1981** (New York: Farrar, Straus and Giroux, 1983), p. 461.

88. Author's conversation with Henry Kissinger, September 4, 2007.

89. "Havel: Sharing a Miracle," **L'Osservatore Romano** [English Weekly Edition], April 30, 1990, p. 4.

90. Author's interview with Joaquín Navarro-Valls, January 20, 1997.

91. Ibid.

92. Author's interview with Cardinal Miloslav Vlk, December 5, 1997.

93. Author's interview with Jan Nowak, May 13, 1998.

94. Author's interview with Bohdan Bociurkiw, August 10, 1996.

95. Author's interview with Cardinal Agostino Casaroli, February 14, 1997.

96. "Us and them, all the time" was Stanisław Dziwisz's description of the situation during one of the author's conversations with Pope John Paul II, who agreed, saying "**Si, eranno loro e noi** [Yes, it was them and us]." John Paul then elaborated the point: "The communists tried to be accepted, not just as a political authority, but as a moral authority, as an expression of the Polish nation. But the Church became that expression, especially in Cardinal Wyszyński. The communists tried to pretend that we did not exist; but this was impossible." [Author's conversation with Pope John Paul II, September 10, 1996.]

97. See Weigel, **The Final Revolution,** pp. 26–30.

98. Henry Kissinger, **Years of Renewal** (New York: Simon & Schuster, 1999), p. 635.

99. "The Polish Pope in Poland," **New York Times,** June 5, 1979.

100. John Lewis Gaddis, **The Cold War: A New History** (New York: Penguin Press, 2005), p. 193.

101. Ibid., pp. 195–96.

102. Ibid.

103. A particularly apt capturing of this facet of Reagan's personality and policy may be found in Anderson and Anderson, **Reagan's Secret War.**

Reagan and John Paul II shared, as well, the same disdain for liberal bromides about the nature of and purposes of communism, which no doubt helps explain, at least in part, the boundless liberal animus against them during the 1980s.

104. For more on John Paul II and Mikhail Gorbachev, see Weigel, **Witness to Hope,** pp. 604–5.

105. Gaddis, **The Cold War,** p. 257.

106. Andrew and Mitrokhin, **The Sword and the Shield,** p. 542.

107. Cardinal Agostino Casaroli: "Ostpolitik: Chipping Away at Marxism's Crumbling House," **L'Osservatore Romano** [English Weekly Edition], June 18, 1990, pp. 6–7.

Chapter Five

1. Pope John Paul II, **Letter Concerning Pilgrimage to the Places Linked to the History of Salvation,** 11.

2. The curial cardinals who had heard Cardinal Karol Wojtyła preach the Lenten retreat for Pope Paul VI and the Roman Curia in March 1976 should not have been surprised by this facet of John Paul II's vision, as, during that retreat, he had described the next quarter century as a "New Advent" for a Church en route to its third millennium. See Karol Wojtyła, **Sign of Contradiction** (New York: Seabury, 1979), p. 206. One of John Paul II's closest collaborators, Cardinal Stanisław Ryłko, stresses that the Great Jubilee was "both the focal point and the center of the pontificate. Everything aimed at this, and everything in a sense revolved around it." [Author's interview with Cardinal Stanisław Ryłko, December 15, 2007.]

3. John Paul II's address to the cardinals, with its characteristic italicized emphases, may be found in

L'Osservatore Romano [English Weekly Edition], June 22, 1994, pp. 6–8. For a more complete account of the 1994 consistory, the fifth extraordinary consistory of the pontificate, see Weigel, **Witness to Hope,** pp. 741–43.

4. John Paul II, **Tertio Millennio Adveniente,** 6 [emphasis in original].

5. Ibid., 10 [emphases in original].

6. Ibid., 4.

7. Ibid., 23 [emphasis in original].

8. Author's interview with Bishop Rino Fisichella, March 13, 2008.

9. For a more detailed analysis of **Tertio Millennio Adveniente,** see Weigel, **Witness to Hope,** pp. 743–46.

10. In a break with tradition that rattled the Roman Curia and the Holy See's Permanent Representative to the United Nations, Archbishop Renato Martino, John Paul II appointed Professor Glendon the head of the Vatican delegation to the 1995 UN-sponsored Beijing World Conference on Women.

11. Sepe had previously served in the third-ranking post in the Secretariat of State and as secretary of the Congregation for the Clergy. Sebastiani was named president of the Prefecture for the Economic Affairs of the Holy See, with the American cardinal Edmund Szoka (who had reformed the Vatican's budgeting and auditing procedures in the wake of the Banco Ambrosiano scandal of the early 1980s) being moved from the Prefecture to the **Governatorato** of Vatican City to make room for Sebastiani; some of Szoka's reforms did not survive the change of leadership at the Prefecture for Economic Affairs.

12. According to the Central Committee, "The sym-

bol [i.e., logo] of the Jubilee represents the centrality of the Christian message. In the blue field in circular form is inserted the cross, which sustains humanity gathered in the five continents, represented by as many doves. The blue field symbolizes the mystery of the Incarnation of the Son of God, who became Man through the work of the Holy Spirit in the womb of the Virgin Mary. The light which radiates from the center of the cross indicates Christ, the Light of the world, the only Savior of mankind, 'yesterday, today, and always.' The intertwinement of the doves signifies the unity and brotherhood that the children of God are longing for. The vividness and harmony of the colors want to recall joy and peace as desirable gifts of the celebration of the Jubilee." However noble the sentiments, critics wondered why a Church whose message had inspired Michelangelo, Raphael, and Bernini had approved a design that was more evocative of Disney World than of the **mysterium incarnationis.**

The Diocese of Rome held an architectural competition to build a "Millennium Church" in the parish of St. Sylvester, located in the suburban neighborhood of Tor Tre Teste. The competition was won by an American, Richard Meier, who, as one fellow architect put it, was "known for his sophisticated neo-Corbusian essays in white panels and gridded glass." What was intended to be a church for the future turned out to have been a trip into the past, "the tradition of mid-20th-century modernism." [Duncan G. Stroik, "Modernism Triumphs in the Eternal City," **Catholic World Report,** August–September 1996, pp. 58–61.]

13. "St. Peter's Facade Is 'the Restoration of the Cen-

tury,'" ZENIT News Service, September 28, 1999. The restoration brought out the pastels remaining from the original facade as designed by Carlo Maderno.

14. The first of the regional Synods was the Special Assembly of the Synod of Bishops for America, which met from November 16 through December 12, 1997; that it was styled the "Synod for America," and not "for the Americas," was a reflection of John Paul's conviction that, as the entire New World was once the subject of a great evangelization from Europe, so North, Central, and South America ought to consider various possibilities of engaging together in the new evangelization for which the Pope had called in the 1990 encyclical, **Redemptoris Missio.** Less than five months later, the Special Assembly for Asia met in Rome, from April 19 through May 14, 1998. The Synod Special Assembly for Oceania then met from November 22 through December 12, 1998. The sequence was completed by the Special Assembly for Europe, which met from October 1 through October 23, 1999.

Each of these synods was completed by a post-synodal apostolic exhortation, in which John Paul took the proposals of the Synod fathers and synthesized them along with his own reflections on the distinct evangelical imperative in each region of the world. **Ecclesia in America** [The Church in America] was issued on January 22, 1999; the Pope went to Mexico City for the signing ceremony and concluded a whirlwind visit to the western hemisphere with a brief stop in St. Louis, Missouri (where he was given a St. Louis Blues ice hockey jersey with "John Paul II" on the back). John Paul signed **Ecclesia in Asia** [The Church in Asia] in New Delhi, the capital of India, on November 6, 1999; it was his last pastoral voyage outside Italy before the Great Jubilee, and he concluded it with a brief visit to the former Soviet republic of Georgia on his way back to Rome. **Ecclesia in Oceania** [The Church in Oceania] was not completed until after the jubilee year, and was issued on November 22, 2001. **Ecclesia in Europa** [The Church in Europe] was issued on June 28, 2003, and is discussed in detail in Chapter Eight.

15. John Paul II, **Mysterium Incarnationis,** 1, 6.

16. Ibid., 10. The theology of the indulgence tradition, which rests on the Church's belief in a "communion of saints" that transcends time, is explained in the **Catechism of the Catholic Church,** 1471–79.

17. See ibid., 7–13.

18. Harvey had been named prefect of the papal household in 1998, with Dziwisz as his **Aggiunto,** or deputy, in order to coordinate the papal schedule during the Great Jubilee more efficiently. Harvey and Dziwisz were named bishops as part of this rearrangement of the management of the papal schedule. This led to complaints that the papal master of ceremonies, Piero Marini, was not being similarly promoted, so Marini, too, was named a bishop—which seemed to many a theological and liturgical oddity.

19. John Paul II, **Tertio Millennio Adveniente,** 33.

20. Bishop Marini, who had ordered the "cope of many colors" John Paul had worn to open the Holy Door, had ordered a similarly dramatic chasuble of the same color scheme for the Pope to wear at the Mass. The papal apartment wisely vetoed its use, substituting a more traditional white chasuble. The "cope of many

colors" was also noticeably absent on Christmas Day (when John Paul II gave the traditional blessing **Urbi et Orbi** [To the City and the World] from the central loggia of St. Peter's) and from the papal openings of the holy doors of the three other patriarchal basilicas in the weeks ahead.

21. John Paul II, **Homily for the Opening of the Great Jubilee of the Year 2000, Midnight Mass, 24 December 1999.**

22. John Paul II, **Urbi et Orbi, 25 December 1999.**

23. John Paul II, **Homily at the Opening of the Holy Door at the Basilica of St. John Lateran, 25 December 1999.**

24. John Paul II, **Homily for the Celebration of First Vespers of the Solemnity of Mary, Mother of God, and "Te Deum" for the End of the Year, 31 December 1999.**

25. Central Committee of the Great Jubilee of 2000, **Il Grande Giubileo dell'Anno 2000: Diario di un evento di fede** (Vatican City, 2001), p. 17 [hereinafter, **Diario**]; author's translation.

26. John Paul II, **Homily at the Celebration of Second Vespers of the Solemnity of Mary, Mother of God, 1 January 2000.**

27. John Paul II, **Message for the Celebration of the World Day of Peace, January 1, 2000,** 5, 7, 9, 11, 17, 18.

28. Author's conversation with Pope John Paul II, January 4, 2000.

29. The participants included representatives of the Ecumenical Patriarchate of Constantinople, the Greek Orthodox Patriarchate of Alexandria, the Greek Or-

thodox Patriarchate of Antioch, the Greek Orthodox Patriarchate of Jerusalem, the Patriarchate of Moscow, the Patriarchate of Serbia, the Orthodox Patriarchate of Romania, the Orthodox Church of Greece, the Orthodox Church of Poland, the Orthodox Church of Albania, the Orthodox Church of Finland, the Coptic Orthodox Patriarchate of Alexandria, the Syrian Orthodox Patriarchate of Antioch, the Armenian Apostolic Church, the Catholicosate of Cilicia (Armenian Apostolic Church), the Assyrian Church of the East, the Anglican Communion, the Old Catholic Church (Union of Utrecht), the Lutheran World Federation, the World Methodist Council, the Disciples of Christ, the Pentecostal Church, and the Ecumenical Council of Churches. [**Diario,** p. 18.]

30. John Paul II, **Homily for the Opening of the Holy Door at St. Paul Outside the Walls and the Week of Prayer for Christian Unity, 18 January 2000.**

31. Jonathan Luxmoore, "Pope Weeps as He Watches Polish Film," **The Universe,** January 30, 2000.

32. John Paul also addressed here a problem that would preoccupy him throughout the remaining years of his pontificate: the attempt to erect secularism as the official creed of the world's democracies, thus driving religiously informed moral argument out of public life:

> Life takes shape in our daily choices. And political leaders, since they have the role of administering the **res publica,** can by their personal choices and their programs of action guide whole societies either towards life or towards death. For this reason believers, and the faithful of the Catholic

Church in particular, consider it their duty to take an active part in the public life of the societies to which they belong. Their faith, their hope and their charity represent additional and irreplaceable energies to ensure that not only will there be unfailing concern for others, a sense of responsibility and the defense of fundamental rights, but also to ensure that there is a perception that our world and our personal and collective history are invested with a Presence. I therefore insist that believers be granted a place in public life because I am convinced that their faith and their witness can reassure our contemporaries, who are often anxious and disoriented, and can ensure that despite failures, violence and fear, neither evil nor death will have the last word. [John Paul II, **Address at the Exchange of Greetings with the Diplomatic Corps, 10 January 2000.**]

33. **Diario,** pp. 26–44.

34. John Paul II, **Letter Concerning Pilgrimage to the Places Linked to the History of Salvation,** 5.

35. The day after Navarro's announcement, Archbishop Jean-Louis Tauran, the papal "foreign minister," said that the visit had been "indefinitely postponed" rather than "canceled": a nice diplomatic technicality (in that no formal invitation had ever been extended by the Iraqi government) that held open the possibility of something happening in the future. Yet the fact re-

mained that it was the Iraqi regime that was responsible for the "indefinite postponement."

In March 2000, the Italian newspaper **Avvenire,** which had good Vatican sources, ran a story stating that the Baghdad government's position had "compromised" the "spiritual nature" of the Pope's pilgrimage, thus making it impossible for the Pope to come to Ur. Two days later, the Iraqi ambassador to the Holy See wrote a stiff letter to **Avvenire,** blaming the Pope's inability to come to Ur on British and American violations of Iraqi sovereignty. Few were persuaded. [ZENIT News Service, March 3, 2000; March 6, 2000.]

36. For John Paul's homily, see **L'Osservatore Romano** [English Weekly Edition], March 1, 2000, p. 11.

37. See ibid., p. 5.

38. See ibid., pp. 6–7.

39. Ibid., pp. 1–2 [emphasis in original].

40. For an appreciative evaluation of John Paul's pre-2000 acts of contrition for the sins of the Church's children, see Mary Ann Glendon, "Contrition in the Age of Spin Control," **First Things,** November 1997, pp. 10–12.

41. John Paul II, **Tertio Millennio Adveniente,** 33 [emphases in original].

42. The task of preparing a study on the various questions involved was given to a subcommission of the ITC, chaired by Msgr. Bruno Forte and including Rev. Christopher Begg, Rev. Sebastian Karotemprel, S.D.B., Msgr. Roland Minnerath, Rev. Thomas Norris, Rev. Rafael Salazar Cardenas, M.Sp.S., and Msgr. Anton Strukelj. The ITC discussed the work of the subcommission in

its 1998 and 1999 plenary sessions, then voted its approval of **Memory and Reconciliation: The Church and the Faults of the Past.** Cardinal Ratzinger then approved the document for publication.

43. International Theological Commission, **Memory and Reconciliation: The Church and the Faults of the Past,** p. 27.

44. The Pope's homily may be found in **L'Osservatore Romano** [English Weekly Edition], March 15, 2000, pp. 1–2 [emphases in original].

45. "The Pope's Apology," **New York Times,** March 14, 2000. In addition to confusing the Pope's request for God's forgiveness with the kind of "apologies" then being offered by U.S. president Bill Clinton (for slavery) and British prime minister Tony Blair (for colonialism), the **Times'** editorial smacked of hypocrisy (or, at the very least, a remarkable lack of self-awareness), as the paper had never seen fit to ask God's forgiveness, or its readers', for its grotesque misrepresentations of Stalin's regime in the 1930s, or its romanticized rendering of the Castro revolution in Cuba in the 1960s.

46. Cited in http://chiesa.espresso.repubblica.it/articolo/173182?eng=y.

47. Author's conversation with Pope John Paul II, January 16, 1997.

48. For an account of the negotiations resulting in the Fundamental Agreement between the Holy See and the State of Israel, and John Paul II's crucial role in them, see Weigel, **Witness to Hope,** pp. 697–713.

49. See **L'Osservatore Romano** [English Weekly Edition], March 29, 2000, p. 5.

50. John Paul II, **Speech at Yad Vashem, 23 March 2000.**

51. John Paul II, **General Audience Address, 29 March 2000.**

Chapter Six

1. John Paul II, **Homily at the Mass for the Canonization of Sister Mary Faustyna Kowalska, 30 April 2000** [emphasis in original].

2. Paul VI, ever the cautious diplomat, did not want beatifications or canonizations of the Mexican and Spanish civil war martyrs to exacerbate the Church's situation in officially secularist Mexico or to suggest some sort of benediction on the government of Francisco Franco. John Paul II took a more evangelical approach to these questions, believing that the beatifications and canonizations of the twentieth-century martyrs of Mexico and Spain were essential elements of the new evangelization in those two historically Catholic countries.

3. The revised "Roman Martyrology" was published in October 2001. A second edition of the revision, including information on those canonized and beatified between 2001 and June 2004, was published in December 2004.

4. See Robert Royal, **The Catholic Martyrs of the Twentieth Century: A Comprehensive World History** (New York: Crossroad, 2000).

5. John Paul II, **Homily for the Ecumenical Commemoration of the Witnesses to the Faith in the Twentieth Century, 7 May 2000.**

6. See **Diario,** pp. 150–53.

7. For an overview and analysis of these phenomena,

see Sandra L. Zimdars-Swartz, **Encountering Mary: Visions of Mary from La Salette to Medjugorje** (New York: Avon Books, 1991). In **Lourdes: Body and Spirit in the Secular Age** (New York: Penguin, 2008), Ruth Harris locates the cult of Lourdes within the spiritual yearnings of a society governed by an anticlerical and exclusively male elite.

8. Tad Szulc was particularly flat-footed on this; see Szulc, **Pope John Paul II: The Biography** (New York: Scribner, 1995), pp. 66, 77.

9. John Paul II, **Gift and Mystery,** pp. 27–31. On Jan Tyranowski's enduring influence on Wojtyła, see Weigel, **Witness to Hope,** pp. 58–62.

10. See Weigel, **Witness to Hope,** pp. 576–78.

11. André Frossard and Pope John Paul II, **Be Not Afraid!** (New York: St. Martin's Press, 1984), p. 251.

12. "Announcement made by Cardinal Angelo Sodano, Secretary of State," in Congregation for the Doctrine of the Faith, **The Message of Fatima** [emphasis in original].

13. Joseph Cardinal Ratzinger, "Theological Commentary," in ibid.

The CDF statement also noted that the "solemn and universal act of consecration" by which John Paul II had entrusted the world to Mary on March 25, 1984, had been "personally confirmed" by Sister Lúcia as corresponding to what the Virgin of Fátima had requested, and thus "any further discussion or request is without basis"—a conclusion denied by some Fátima devotees, who continued throughout the pontificate to insist, against Sister Lúcia's own testimony, that John Paul II had not done what Mary had asked.

14. John Paul II, **Homily at the Closing of the 20th International Marian-Mariological Congress**, 24 **September 2000** [emphases in original].

15. John Paul II, **Gift and Mystery,** p. 100.

16. John Paul II, **Pastores Dabo Vobis,** 12, 23 [emphasis in original].

17. Ibid., 21.

18. On these four points, see "Editor's Introduction" to **Pastores Dabo Vobis,** in **The Post-Synodal Apostolic Exhortations of John Paul II,** ed. J. Michael Miller, C.S.B. (Huntington, IN: Our Sunday Visitor Publishing Division, 1998).

19. John Paul II, **Homily for the Jubilee of Priests, 18 May 2000**.

20. Czesław Miłosz, "Ode for the Eightieth Birthday of Pope John Paul II," in Miłosz, **New and Collected Poems, 1931–2001** (New York: Ecco/HarperCollins, 2003), pp. 709–10.

21. John Paul II, **Address to the Jubilee of Scientists, 25 May 2000**.

22. John Paul II, "Lessons of the Galileo Case," **Origins** 22:22 (November 12, 1992), pp. 369–74.

23. John Paul II, **Address to the Jubilee of Scientists, 25 May 2000**.

24. For John Paul, the release of Agca from Italian imprisonment completed the forgiveness he had freely offered Agca the day after he was shot. It was not clear to some observers, however, that trading the relative comforts of an Italian prison for a Turkish lockup made for an improvement in Agca's situation.

25. John Paul II, **Homily for the Solemnity of Corpus Christi, 22 June 2000**.

26. See ZENIT News Service, August 22, 2000.

27. See **L'Osservatore Romano** [English Weekly Edition], August 23, 2000, pp. 1–3 [emphases in original].

28. John Paul II, **Homily at Mass with the Bishops and Priests of the Diocese of Aosta, 22 July 2000.**

29. John Paul II, **Address to the 18th International Congress of the Transplantation Society, 29 August 2000.** In the course of defending the "dead donor rule" in organ transplantation, John Paul discussed the "neurological criterion" as the means of "ascertaining death" and concluded that "the criterion adopted in more recent times for ascertaining the fact of death, namely the **complete** and **irreversible** cessation of all brain activity, if rigorously applied, does not seem to conflict with the essential elements of a sound anthropology" [ibid., 5]. This conclusion intersected with, and in some respects intensified, a debate already under way in international scientific and philosophical circles. For critiques of the "neurological criterion" from various perspectives, see Finis Vitae: **Is Brain Death Still Life?,** ed. Roberto de Mattei (Rome: Consiglio Nazionale delle Ricerche, 2006). In the United States, the President's Council on Bioethics addressed the subject in a December 2008 white paper, "Controversies in the Determination of Death," the conclusions of which were parallel to those of John Paul II. The "personal statements" appended to the white paper by Gilbert Meilaender and Edmund Pellegrino offer a convenient summary of the state of the debate as of late 2009.

30. These two conciliar statements are found in **Lumen Gentium** [The Dogmatic Constitution on the

Church], 8. The Latin formulation **subsistit in** [subsists in] had been substituted in **Lumen Gentium** for the flat statement that the one Church of Christ "is" [**est**] the Catholic Church. An ocean of ink had been expended in the three and a half decades since the Council on parsing the meaning of **subsistit** and its difference, if any, from **est.**

31. Jerry Filteau, "U.S. Dialogue Partners Are Troubled by New Vatican Text," **Catholic Review,** October 5, 2000, p. 12.

32. The canonization of the Chinese martyrs was bitterly criticized by the communist government in Beijing, which claimed that the martyrs had been Western imperialist agents (since some had come to China from Spain, France, Italy, Belgium, and the Netherlands) or had "bullied" the Chinese people. Papal spokesman Navarro-Valls replied that the Holy See was "profoundly saddened" by such incomprehension on the part of the Chinese government, for the canonization had "no political motivation" and John Paul II's respect for Chinese civilization was well known. [Sarah Delaney, "China Scolds Vatican Over Sainthoods," **Washington Post,** September 27, 2000; "Beijing Steps Up Accusations Against Vatican Over Martyrs," ZENIT News Service, September 26, 2000.]

33. John Paul II, **Angelus, 1 October 2000.**

34. John Paul II, **Homily for the Beatification of Pius IX, John XXIII, Tommaso Reggio, William Chaminade, and Columba Marmion, 3 September 2000** [emphases in original]. Abbot Marmion, a native of Ireland who spent most of his religious life in France at the Abbey of Maredsous, had a marked influence on

Karol Wojtyła's theology and spirituality of the priesthood. Chaminade was the founder of the Marianists. Reggio was a priest-journalist who became Archbishop of Genoa in the late nineteenth century.

35. "Pope Calls for Worldwide Abolition of Death Penalty," ZENIT News Service, December 12, 2000.

36. John Paul II, **Homily at Midnight Mass, 24 December 2000** [emphasis in original].

37. John Paul II, **Homily for the Solemnity of the Epiphany and the Closing of the Holy Door, 6 January 2001.**

Prior to the Holy Door of St. Peter's being completely sealed on the inside with masonry, a bronze urn was placed with it, containing twenty-three silver coins from each year of the pontificate of John Paul II and seventeen bronze coins corresponding to the years since the jubilee of 1983; a parchment scroll attesting to the opening and closing of the Holy Door in the Great Jubilee of 2000; and the keys of the Holy Door. The holy doors of the other patriarchal basilicas were solemnly closed over the next three weeks. [**Diario,** p. 344.]

38. John Paul II, **Novo Millennio Ineunte,** 2.

39. Ibid., 3 [emphasis in original].

40. Ibid., 4, 15.

41. Ibid., 8 [emphasis in original].

42. Ibid., 15.

43. Ibid., 29.

44. Ibid., 31.

45. Ibid., 37 [emphasis in original].

46. Ibid., 40.

47. Ibid., 42, citing **Lumen Gentium,** 1.

48. See ibid., 51.

49. Ibid.

50. Ibid., 56 [emphasis in original].

51. Ibid., 59.

52. Author's conversation with Pope John Paul II, November 29, 2000.

Chapter Seven

1. Dziwisz, **A Life with Karol,** pp. 243–44.

2. John Paul II, **General Audience, 12 September 2001.**

3. Pius XII's concerns were not unfounded; see Dan Kurzman, **A Special Mission: Hitler's Secret Plot to Seize the Vatican and Kidnap Pope Pius XII** (New York: Da Capo Press, 2007).

4. John Paul II, **Testament, 12–18 March 2000,** 2 [emphasis in original].

5. Cardinal Dulles, who in his old age bore an uncanny resemblance to Abraham Lincoln, was the last of the new cardinals to receive his red hat. As the American Jesuit knelt before him, John Paul placed the biretta on Dulles's head, the new cardinal bent down to kiss the Pope's ring, and the newly imposed biretta fell into the Pope's lap. John Paul reimposed the biretta, Cardinal Dulles bent down yet again to kiss the Pope's ring, and the biretta fell into the papal lap once more. John Paul was still capable of grinning at this stage of his Parkinson's disease, and did so as he and Cardinal Dulles put the uncooperative biretta back where it belonged. The next day, when the Pope gave the new cardinals their rings—which were of the same design John Paul had

used throughout the pontificate—Cardinal Dulles got the loudest and most sustained round of applause from the large crowd in St. Peter's Square.

6. John Paul II, **Remarks at the Sixth Extraordinary Consistory, 21 May 2001.**

7. See John L. Allen, Jr., "Cardinals Debate Church's Future," **National Catholic Reporter,** June 1, 2001.

8. See "Focus on Unity," **Catholic World Report,** June 2001, for these and other details of John Paul's Greek pilgrimage.

9. "Pope and Orthodox Primate Did Pray Together, After All," ZENIT News Service, May 6, 2001.

10. Cited in "A Pilgrimage that May Change Church History," ZENIT News Service, May 10, 2001.

11. Clyde Haberman, "Welcome, Man of Peace. Let's Go Hate My Enemy," **New York Times Week in Review,** May 13, 2001.

12. While many Jewish leaders understood the situation, the Catholic Left in the United States took the occasion to criticize the Pope, with the editor of **Commonweal,** Margaret O'Brien Steinfels, averring that "a lot of people have been hurt and shocked, including a lot of Catholics" [ibid.].

13. See "Focus on Unity," **Catholic World Report,** June 2001.

14. Author's interview with Father Samir Khalil Samir, S.J., March 8, 2008. The Pope discussed Islam in **Crossing the Threshold of Hope** (New York: Alfred A. Knopf, 1994), pp. 91–94.

15. Christian W. Troll, S.J., "John Paul II and Islam," unpublished paper for a conference at St. Mary's Uni-

versity College in London on "The Theological Legacy of Pope John Paul II," March 25–26, 2008; paper provided to the author by Father Troll; emphases in John Paul II's text are in the original.

16. Cited in "Focus on Unity," **Catholic World Report,** June 2001.

17. The Knights' headquarters had subsequently moved to the Aventine Hill in Rome; the Order's Grand Master is the only man in the Catholic Church, other than cardinals, who is addressed as "Your Eminence."

18. See "Focus on Unity," **Catholic World Report,** June 2001.

19. On the Union of Brest, see Borys A. Gudziak, **Crisis and Reform: The Kyivan Metropolitanate, the Patriarchate of Constantinople, and the Genesis of the Union of Brest** (Cambridge, MA: Harvard University Press, 1998).

20. On the forced "incorporation" of the Greek Catholics of Ukraine into Russian Orthodoxy, see Bociurkiw, **The Ukrainian Greek Catholic Church and the Soviet State,** pp. 148–88.

21. "In Interview, Moscow Patriarch Alexis Asks Pope to Postpone Ukraine Trip," **National Catholic Register,** April 23–28, 2001, p. 5.

Born in Tallinn in independent Estonia in 1929, Aleksy Mikhailovich Ridiger, who would become Aleksy II, was admitted to the Leningrad Theological Seminary in 1947, ordained a priest in 1950, took monastic vows in 1961, and was ordained bishop of Tallinn and Estonia (then a Soviet "republic") later that year. He was chancellor of the Patriarchate of Moscow from

1964 until 1986. Such a career in Russian Orthodoxy in those years was inconceivable without the approbation of the KGB.

22. See Andriy Chirovsky, "Letter from Ukraine," **First Things** (October 2001), pp. 15–18.

23. John Paul II, **Address at Kyïv International Airport, 23 June 2001** [emphases in original].

24. John Paul II, **Homily at Eucharistic Celebration in the Latin Rite and Beatifications, Lviv, 26 June 2001**.

25. "Next Stop Moscow?" **Catholic World Report,** August/September 2001, pp. 34–37.

26. Author's interview with Cardinal Lubomyr Husar, October 19, 2001. Asked for his explanation of the Orthodox hostility toward the Pope and the Catholic Church, the cardinal replied, "They are very much afraid of something." There was indeed something to be feared about corruptions from Western culture, Cardinal Husar added, "but there is also a deeper insecurity."

27. Antoine Arjakovsky, **Conversations with Lubomyr Cardinal Husar: Towards a Post-Confessional Christianity** (L'viv: Ukrainian Catholic University Press, 2007), pp. 32, 40.

28. John Paul II, **Address to the President of the United States of America, H. E. George Walker Bush, 23 July 2001.**

29. John Paul II, **Address at the World Premiere of the New Polish Version of the Film "Quo Vadis," 30 August 2001.**

30. Massimo Franco, **Parallel Empires: The Vatican and the United States—Two Centuries of Alliance and Conflict,** trans. Roland Flamini (New York: Dou-

bleday, 2008), p. 127; R. James Nicholson, **The United States and the Holy See: The Long Road** (Rome: Trenta Giorni Società Cooperativa, 2004), pp. 82–83.

Nicholson notes that, "On the basis of the Pope's recognition that the September 11 attacks would justify a response, the Holy See's Secretary for Relations with States, Jean-Louis Tauran, at that time Archbishop, gave public backing to U.S. actions to track down the perpetrators when he affirmed in an October 2001 interview that everybody recognizes that the United States government, like any other government, has the right to legitimate defense 'because it has the duty to guarantee the safety of its citizens'" [ibid., p. 83].

31. John Paul II, **Address to the New Ambassador of the United States of America to the Holy See, 13 September 2001.**

32. Author's interview with Cardinal Camillo Ruini, March 17, 2008; author's conversation with Pope John Paul II, November 3, 2001.

33. Author's interview with Cardinal Francis Arinze, March 18, 2008.

34. John Paul II, **Address to Meeting with Representatives of the World of Culture, 24 September 2001.**

35. E-mail to the author from Philip Pullella, May 27, 2009; Philip Pullella, "Vatican Says Would Understand U.S. Self-defense Move," Reuters, September 24, 2001; author's interview with Joaquín Navarro-Valls, October 26, 2001.

36. Author's interview with Joaquín Navarro-Valls, October 26, 2001.

37. Ibid.

38. See **Christus Dominus** [Decree on the Pastoral

Office of Bishops in the Church], 20. Canon 377.1 states, "For the future, no rights or privileges of election, appointment, presentation or designation of bishops are conceded to civil authorities."

39. Author's conversation with Pope John Paul II, January 4, 2000.

40. John Paul II, **Homily at the Inauguration of the 10th Ordinary General Assembly of the Synod of Bishops, 30 September 2001** [emphases in original].

41. One source of amusement during the speech making in the Synod Hall was the newly created German cardinal Karl Lehmann, who snored through some of the proceedings in a rather dramatic way. One American cardinal noted, "Lehmann sits behind me and snores. I don't mind him sleeping; everyone does. But he snores!" The Pope was clearly amused by all this; at lunch on the fifth day of the Synod, the Synod general secretary, Cardinal Jan Schotte, told the Pope that "Cardinal Lehmann has made twelve interventions already." [Author's conversations with Cardinal Francis George, O.M.I., and Archbishop George Pell, October 2001.]

42. John Paul II, **Homily for the Beatification of the Servants of God Luigi Beltrame Quattrocchi and Maria Corsini, Married Couple, 21 October 2001** [emphases in original].

During the course of the Beltrame Quattrocchi beatification process, the Congregation for the Causes of Saints insisted that two miracles were required to complete the cause. The cause's postulator, Archbishop Giuseppe Mani, raised the point over lunch with John Paul II: "If they want two miracles, then don't beatify a couple but two people. In that case, everything that we have done [to advance the cause of a married couple] is useless." The Pope said nothing, but a month later, the Congregation decided that one miracle was sufficient for the completion of the beatification cause. It may be assumed that John Paul took Archbishop Mani's point and convinced the authorities of the Congregation of it. [See Giuseppe Mani, "A Bishop for the Family," **Totus Tuus** 4/2006, pp. 2–3.]

43. John Paul II, **Homily for the Conclusion of the Synod of Bishops, 27 October 2001** [emphases in original].

44. John Paul II, **Homily at Pastoral Visit to the Roman Parish of St. María Josefa of the Heart of Jesus, 16 December 2001.**

45. For an account of the Boston situation, see Philip Lawler, **The Faithful Departed: The Collapse of Boston's Catholic Culture** (New York: Encounter Books, 2008). For an overview of the crisis, see George Weigel, **The Courage To Be Catholic: Crisis, Reform, and the Future of the Church** (New York: Basic Books, 2002; revised paperback, 2003). Throughout the Long Lent, Richard John Neuhaus provided insightful running commentary in the "Public Square" section of the journal **First Things.**

For the **Boston Globe**'s account of its reporting during 2002, see **Betrayal: The Crisis in the Catholic Church** (New York: Little, Brown, 2002). Nicholas Cafardi, a civil and canon lawyer, offers another analysis of the crisis prior to the U.S. bishops' adoption of new clergy personnel guidelines in **Before Dallas: The U.S. Bishops' Response to Clergy Sexual Abuse of Children** (New York: Paulist Press, 2008).

46. Cardinal Castrillón's implied view—that this was a secularist, anticlericalist media conspiracy against the Church—seems to have been shared by more than a few senior Latin American churchmen, which was another factor impeding a prompt and effective response to the crisis from the Holy See.

47. John Paul II, **Address to the Cardinals of the United States, 23 April 2002.**

48. For more on the Roman response to the American crisis of 2002, see Weigel, **The Courage To Be Catholic,** pp. 117–46. On the failures of bishops, see ibid., pp. 87–115.

49. The American crisis had one Polish parallel, in that the Pope accepted the resignation of Archbishop Juliusz Paetz of Poznań on March 28, 2002. The resignation followed months of back-channel controversy in both Poland and Rome, and the occasional news story, over allegations that the former Vatican official, who had been archbishop since 1996, had made inappropriate sexual advances to seminarians in his archdiocese. Paetz denied the allegations; the acceptance of his resignation suggests that the Pope was finally persuaded that something was gravely awry.

50. John Tagliabue, "Pope Denounces Violence in Religion's Name," **New York Times,** January 25, 2002; "Pope's Program for Day of Prayer for Peace," ZENIT News Service, January 7, 2002.

51. "Rediscovering the Contribution of Jewish Scriptures," ZENIT News Service, February 6, 2002.

Cardinal Joseph Ratzinger concluded his preface to the document by addressing an ongoing point of neuralgia in Christian-Jewish relations:

The question of how Jews are presented in the New Testament is dealt with in the second part of the Document; the "anti-Jewish" texts there are methodically analyzed for an understanding of them. Here, I want only to underline an aspect which seems to me to be particularly important. The Document shows that the reproofs addressed to Jews in the New Testament are neither more frequent nor more virulent than the accusations against Israel in the Law and the Prophets, at the heart of the Old Testament itself. . . . They belong to the prophetic language of the Old Testament and are, therefore, to be interpreted in the same way as the prophetic messages: they warn against contemporary aberrations, but are essentially of a temporary nature and always open to new possibilities of salvation. [**The Jewish People and Their Sacred Scriptures in the Christian Bible** (Rome: Libreria Editrice Vaticana, 2002), p. 12.]

52. "Putin Willing to Invite Pope to Moscow 'at Any Time,'" ZENIT News Service, January 15, 2002.

53. "Moscow Patriarchate to Join in Assisi Day of Prayer," ZENIT News Service, January 17, 2002.

54. "Moscow Patriarch Describes Putin's Invitation to Pope as 'Wise,'" ZENIT News Service, January 18, 2002.

55. "Moscow Patriarchate Lays Down Conditions for Papal Visit," ZENIT News Service, January 25, 2002.

56. Sharon LaFrontiere, "Rift Grows as Russian Orthodox Church Rebukes Vatican," **Washington Post,** February 14, 2002.

57. "Visit Will Be Virtual but Orthodox Ire Is Real," ZENIT News Service, March 1, 2002.

58. SEIA Newsletter on the Eastern Churches and Ecumenism, n. 79, April 29, 2002.

59. "Pope Brings Solace to the Heart of Former Soviet Republics," **The Tablet,** June 1, 2002, p. 25.

60. Cardinal Francis George, O.M.I., of Chicago met the Bulgarian priest at breakfast in the Domus Sanctae Marthae, the Vatican guesthouse, during the U.S. cardinals' meeting with the Pope and the Roman Curia in April 2002 [**Catholic New World,** May 12, 2002].

61. "Pope Brings Solace to the Heart of Former Soviet Republics," **The Tablet,** June 1, 2002, p. 25.

62. "Never Ceased to Love You, Pope Tells Bulgarians," ZENIT News Service, May 23, 2002.

63. "Pope Brings Solace to the Heart of Former Soviet Republics," **The Tablet,** June 1, 2002, p. 26.

64. John Paul II, **Homily at Eucharistic Celebration and Beatifications,** May 26, 2002.

65. Quoted in "Pope Brings Solace to the Heart of Former Soviet Republics," **The Tablet,** June 1, 2002, p. 27.

66. "Endurance Test," **Catholic World Report,** July 2002, p. 25.

67. Stories that Padre Pio, in an exercise of his extraordinary spiritual gifts, had predicted to Wojtyła his election as pope when the young priest had gone to San Giovanni Rotondo during his studies at the Angelicum continued throughout the pontificate. Asked once about

his experience of Padre Pio as confessor, John Paul II replied that the Capuchin had been a "very simple confessor, clear and brief"—a description that did not seem to substantiate the stories. [Author's conversation with Pope John Paul II, December 13, 1997.]

68. John Paul II, **Homily for the Canonization of St. Pio of Pietrelcina, Capuchin Priest, 16 June 2002**.

69. Ibid.

70. **World Youth Day 2002—The Official Souvenir Album** (Ottawa: Novalis, 2002), p. 111.

71. Tim Drake, "John Paul's Toronto Triumph," **National Catholic Register,** August 4–10, 2002, p. 7; "Papal Lunch: Spaghetti and a Beatles Singalong," ZENIT News Service, July 28, 2002.

72. Author's interview with Cardinal Stanisław Dziwisz, December 2, 2009.

Twenty-five hundred World Youth Day-2002 patients were treated for hypothermia on Saturday night and Sunday morning by a mobile medical center set up at Downsview, but only forty-four had to be taken to hospital emergency rooms. [Prithi Yelaja, "Nasty Weather Keeps Medics Hopping," **Toronto Sun,** July 29, 2002.]

73. John Paul II, **Homily for 17th World Youth Day, 28 July 2002** [emphases in original].

74. **World Youth Day 2002—The Official Souvenir Album,** p. 134.

75. John Paul II, **Homily for 17th World Youth Day, 28 July 2002** [emphases in original].

76. John Paul II, **Angelus, 28 July 2002.**

World Youth Day-2002 gave a jolt of spiritual energy to those parts of the Canadian Church that were willing to be energized. Yet there was little immediate pastoral follow-up by the Canadian bishops conference, which seemed far more concerned with figuring out how to retire the (admittedly considerable) World Youth Day-2002 debt than with seizing the opportunities presented by the largest religious event in Canadian history.

77. John Paul II, **Homily for the Canonization of Juan Diego Cuauhtlatoatzin, 31 July 2002** [emphasis in original].

78. John Paul II, **Homily for the Dedication of the Shrine of Divine Mercy, 17 August 2002** [emphases in original].

79. Ibid.

80. John Paul II, **Homily for the Canonization of St. Josemaría Escrivá de Balaguer, 6 October 2002.**

81. SEIA Newsletter on the Eastern Churches and Ecumenism, n. 85, October 31, 2002; author's interview with Joaquín Navarro-Valls, November 13, 2008.

82. John Paul II, **Rosarium Virginis Mariae,** 1 [emphasis in original].

83. Ibid., 19, 21 [emphases in original].

84. Ibid., 21 [emphasis in original].

85. That the effects of the Long Lent continued to cast a long shadow was evident in the commentary from Dallas journalist Rod Dreher, who confessed himself "chagrined that in the face of this horrible child abuse scandal rocking the Church in America, and the collapse of episcopal authority, liturgy, catechesis, and Catholic identity in the United States and Europe, that the Holy Father would busy himself with thinking up new mysteries of the rosary for us to pray. I'd rather he cleared up the mystery of why Rome won't **act** to clean up this catastrophe. Holy Father, help us! We don't need new

documents, new devotions; we need **action** to restore holiness and integrity to the Church in America." Cited in **catholic eye** 201, October 24, 2002.

Dreher's view was likely shaped in part by the sordid situation of the Church in the Diocese of Dallas, one of the epicenters of scandal. But, like so many commentators, he seems to have missed that it was precisely by a call to renewed fidelity that John Paul believed the scandal time of the U.S. Church could be most effectively addressed.

86. Quoted in **catholic eye** 201 (October 31, 2002), p. 1. On John Paul II closing each day by blessing his adopted city, see Dziwisz, **A Life with Karol,** p. 89.

87. John Paul II, **Address to the Italian Parliament, 14 November 2002.**

Chapter Eight

1. The five commentators taken to meet the Pope were Cardinal Angelo Sodano, the secretary of state of the Holy See; Cardinal Roger Etchegaray, the former chairman of the Central Committee of the Great Jubilee of 2000; Cardinal Achille Silvestrini, the former Vatican "foreign minister"; Professor Rocco Buttiglione, a distinguished Italian philosopher and parliamentarian; and the author.

2. On Wojtyła as poet, see Weigel, **Witness to Hope,** pp. 117–19, 155–57, 218–19, 248–49.

3. Author's conversation with Pope John Paul II, March 20, 1997.

4. Author's interview with Marek Skwarnicki, July 17, 2003.

5. John Paul II, **Roman Triptych: Meditations,** trans.

Jerzy Peterkiewicz (Washington, DC: USCCB Publishing, 2003).

6. See ibid.

In this section of his commentary, Cardinal Ratzinger wrote that John Paul's evocation of nature and the possibility of a path to God through nature in "The Stream" reminded him of something Karol Wojtyła had said when he preached the Lenten retreat for Pope Paul VI and the Roman Curia in 1976: "He related the case of a physicist with whom he had carried on a long discussion, and at the end of it had said to him, 'from the point of view of my science and its method, I'm an atheist.' However, in a letter, the same man wrote, 'Every time I find myself before the majesty of nature, of the mountains, I feel that HE exists.'"

The physicist in question was Marian Mięsowicz, known throughout the world of physics for the "Mięsowicz coefficients" and for his studies of liquid crystals. Mięsowicz was the father of Teresa Malecka and Maria Rybicka, longtime members of Karol Wojtyła's **Środowisko,** the group of lay friends that had first formed around him when he was a student chaplain in Kraków. [Author's conversation with Piotr and Teresa Malecki, September 10, 1997.]

7. Dr. Alicja Baluch of the Institute of Philology at the Polish Academy of Pedagogy in Kraków suggested the notion of the Sistine Chapel as a kind of Wojtyłan **axis mundi** at a conference in Kraków on November 4, 2008.

8. Cited in Weigel, **Witness to Hope,** p. 714 [emphasis in original].

9. Citations from the triptych and from Cardinal

Ratzinger's commentary are taken from John Paul II, **Roman Triptych.**

10. "Poems a Window on Pope's Inner Life, Polish Editor Says," **National Catholic Register,** March 9–15, 2003.

11. Joseph Bottum, "The Threshold of Verse," **First Things** 143 (May 2004), pp. 44–47.

12. For more on John Paul II and beauty, see George Weigel, "Touching the Truth," **The Tablet,** December 20, 2008.

13. Poetry is, of course, notoriously difficult (some would say, impossible) to translate. Still, Poles with a good knowledge of English believed that the English translation of **Roman Triptych** by Jerzy Peterkiewicz exhibited many of the same defects as Peterkiewicz's previous translations of Wojtyła's poetry. The book's U.S. rights were given to the publishing office of the U.S Conference of Catholic Bishops, which produced a handsome book that was nonetheless replete with errors and embarrassments: the cover showed the Pope walking along a mountain stream, which captured the imagery from the first part of the **Triptych** but rather misguided the reader as to the contents of the rest of the poem; the dust jacket suggested that the book was "the spiritual last testament" of the Pope, which was nonsense; the coat of arms of the Pontifical North American College was used instead of the Pope's coat of arms in the author biography on the back dust jacket panel—which also was mistaken in its orthography of Polish names; and the blurb from Nobel laureate Czesław Miłosz had that eminent man of letters speaking ungrammatically.

14. John Paul II, **Ecclesia de Eucharistia,** 2, citing

the relevant texts in the Gospels of Matthew, Mark, and Luke and Paul's first letter to the Corinthians.

15. Ibid., 5, 6.

16. Ibid., 12.

17. See ibid., 27, 29, 35, 37, 46. See also Raymond J. de Souza, "Eucharist Encyclical Provides New Ways to Discover Holy Communion," **National Catholic Register,** May 4–10, 2003, p. 4.

While **Ecclesia de Eucharistia** does not specify particular cases in which a Catholic's defective communion with the Church ought to preclude reception of holy communion, this section of the encyclical clearly bore on the debate throughout the Catholic world about the reception of communion by politicians who regularly promote abortion.

18. Ibid., 18; see also ibid., 19–20 for the "eschatological tension kindled by the Eucharist" and the ways in which that tension "spurs us on our journey through history and plants a seed of living hope in our daily commitment to the work before us."

19. Ibid., 8 [emphasis in original].

20. The remedy was supplied on March 25, 2004, when the Congregation for Divine Worship and the Discipline of the Sacraments issued, with John Paul's approval, the Instruction **Redemptionis Sacramentum** [The Sacrament of Redemption], which prescribed corrections to various liturgical abuses. The corrections were to be enforced by local bishops. Some were.

21. John Paul II, **Letter Concerning Pilgrimage to the Places Linked to the History of Salvation,** 10.

For a thorough discussion of John Paul II's eucharistic theology and its impact on his ecclesiology, see Avery

Cardinal Dulles, S.J., "A Eucharistic Church: The Vision of John Paul II," in Dulles, **Church and Society: The Lawrence J. McGinley Lectures, 1988–2007** (New York: Fordham University Press, 2008), pp. 443–54.

22. On John Paul II and the Gulf War, see Weigel, **Witness to Hope,** pp. 619–24.

On September 22, 2002, Cardinal Joseph Ratzinger, who acknowledged that political questions were not his field of competence, nonetheless told the Italian Catholic newspaper **Avvenire** that, in his view, the United Nations had sole competence to authorize the use of armed force and noted that "the concept of a 'preventive war' does not appear in the **Catechism of the Catholic Church.**" ["Cardinal Ratzinger Says Unilateral Attack on Iraq Not Justified," ZENIT News Service, September 22, 2002.]

Throughout these debates, Vatican officials consistently misstated U.S. policy as one of considering "preventive" war, when in fact the term used by the Bush administration was "preemption." "Preemption" was not, however, the term of choice within the just war tradition, in which the question at issue was the justified first use of armed force, which was certainly considered possible by classic just war theologians such as Augustine and Thomas Aquinas. On this point, see Gregory M. Reichberg, "Is There a 'Presumption against War' in Aquinas's Ethics?" in **Ethics, Nationalism, and Just War: Medieval and Contemporary Perspectives,** eds. Henrik Syse and Gregory M. Reichberg (Washington, DC: Catholic University of America Press, 2007), pp. 72–97. See also George Weigel, **Against the Grain:**

Christianity and Democracy, War and Peace (New York: Crossroad, 2008), pp. 241–44.

23. The Pope's chief statements against war and in favor of a nonmilitary solution to the problems of Iraq's defiance of the UN came in his homily of January 1, 2003, the Angelus address of that same day, his speech to the ambassadors accredited to the Holy See on January 13, 2003, his Angelus addresses of February 9, February 23, March 2, March 9, and March 16, and the general audience address of March 19, 2003. The relevant texts may be found on the Vatican Web site; Sandro Magister excerpted the key passages in "War in the Gulf: What the Pope Really Said," **Chiesa,** March 20, 2003.

24. **Catechism of the Catholic Church,** 2309.

25. See, for example, "Vatican Extols 'Force of Law, Not the Law of Force,'" ZENIT News Service, February 28, 2003. It was never clear precisely what this radical dichotomy meant, as law is never self-enforcing, either within or among states. Moreover, and by the Holy See's own tacit admission, armed force sometimes was justified to enforce international legal norms, as in Afghanistan or, earlier, in the Balkans. "Law of force" seemed more a trope from the European political Left than a concept from the just war tradition aimed at clarifying the moral situation facing world leaders.

26. From an international legal point of view, disagreement over the meaning of Resolution 1441 was the gravamen of the UN debate immediately prior to the commencement of hostilities in Iraq on March 19, 2003, as it was within the British government and between the United States and certain officials of the Holy See.

The debate over 1441 is engaged from various perspectives in **The Price of Peace: Just War in the Twenty-First Century,** eds. Charles Reed and David Ryall (Cambridge, UK: Cambridge University Press, 2007).

27. Massimo Franco, **Parallel Empires,** pp. 130–31.

28. The Holy See's secretary of state, Cardinal Angelo Sodano, was not as strident as some of his colleagues, and consistently warned against interpreting the Vatican's position as pacifism. In a remarkable interview on January 29, 2003, however, he shed light on the political and diplomatic cast of mind at work in the Secretariat of State, in an interview with a group of journalists:

> Some think the Church's representatives are "idealists." We are, but we're also realists.
>
> Is irritating a billion Muslims worth it? This is the question. This is the question I put to some of my American friends: is it advisable? Won't you have the hostility of the whole population for decades?
>
> Without getting bogged down in the question of whether or not the war is moral, I think the question of advantage is worth asking.
>
> We know how to start wars, but not how they will end. I ask the Americans: are you sure you will emerge well from it? Doesn't the experience of Vietnam urge you to be prudent? We see that war isn't even over in Afghanistan. Things are not going well at all. But that's exactly why it's necessary to insist on asking whether or not this war is advantageous.

> We are against the war. Whether the war
> is or is not preventive is not worth talking
> about much; these are ambiguous terms.
> It's certainly not defensive. In the interest of
> harmony with the Muslim world, we must
> ask what is the best way to approach the
> crisis in Iraq. [Sandro Magister, "Iraq: The
> Purely Political Reasons for the Church's
> 'No' to War," **Chiesa,** January 30, 2003.]

The notion of the Catholic Church's second-ranking official warning against "getting bogged down in the question of whether or not the war is moral" was striking, and suggested that the cast of mind embodied by the old **Ostpolitik** of Cardinal Agostino Casaroli was alive and well in certain offices in the Vatican.

29. Sandro Magister, "With the Pope or with Bush? 'Studi Cattolici' Stands with Both," **Chiesa,** July 29, 2003.

30. See Samuel P. Huntington, **The Clash of Civilizations and the Remaking of World Order** (New York: Simon & Schuster, 1998).

31. Cited in Magister, "With the Pope or with Bush?"

32. John Paul II, **Address to the Diplomatic Corps, 13 January 2003.**

33. Magister, "With the Pope or with Bush?"

34. Ibid.

35. Nicholson, **The United States and the Holy See,** pp. 88–89.

The Pope's October 21 letter to President Bush framed the current Middle Eastern conflict in terms of the Secretariat of State's convictions about the centrality of the Israeli/Palestinian conflict, reiterated the Holy

See's conviction that every diplomatic and international legal remedy must be exhausted before armed force was used to resolve conflicts, and underscored the Vatican's standing fear that any military action in the Middle East would inflame the entire region. The Pope concluded: "Convinced that violence is not the only response and that war is not inevitable, I pray that God will inspire you and all concerned to find the appropriate means to build a lasting peace based upon justice and the rule of law. I assure you of my prayers to Almighty God for you in the fulfillment of your demanding responsibilities."

36. Cited in Franco, **Parallel Empires,** pp. 133–34.

37. Ibid., p. 131.

38. Nicholson, **The United States and the Holy See,** p. 95.

39. Cited in Franco, **Parallel Empires,** p. 140.

40. Ambassador Nicholson recalls that the **New York Times** described the Vatican as a "station of the cross of diplomacy" in the months before the war began, and particularly during the debate over a post-1441 Security Council Resolution:

> In the space of two weeks, the Pope received Iraqi Deputy Prime Minister Tariq Aziz, German Foreign Minister Joschka Fischer, United Nations Secretary General Kofi Annan, British Prime Minister Tony Blair, and Spanish Prime Minister José María Aznar. The Pope's visitors brought different perspectives to Vatican City; but regardless of which side of the debate they represented, the Pope's message was clear

and consistent: first, all parties have an obligation to commit themselves to peace and reconciliation; second, all parties have a responsibility to collaborate with the international community and conform to justice, inspired by international law and ethical principles; finally, special attention and consideration must be given to the humanitarian situation of the Iraqi people.

The Aziz visit presented an opportunity to convey to one of Saddam's inner circle the determination of the international community to see Iraq disarm. In a meeting I held with Archbishop Tauran prior to Aziz's visit, it was clear to me that the Holy See intended to use the meeting to send a clear message to Iraq on the importance of complying with U.N. resolutions. In Aziz's subsequent meetings with the Pope and his senior officials, the Holy See told him directly that time was running out and that it needed to make concrete commitments to disarm in order to avert war. Unfortunately, the Pope's message fell on deaf ears. [Nicholson, **The United States and the Holy See,** pp. 93–94.]

41. Ibid., pp. 96–97.
42. Cited in ibid., p. 97.
43. Franco, **Parallel Empires,** p. 144.
44. Cited in ibid., p. 98.
45. Franco, **Parallel Empires,** pp. 144–45.
In an April 2004 interview with the Italian daily **Il**

Giornale, the apostolic nuncio in Iraq, Archbishop Fernando Filoni, warned that the situation in Iraq was getting out of control and urged that the United States "Have the Courage to Transfer Power Immediately." ["Papal Nuncio Gives Grim Report from Iraq," CWNews.com, April 15, 2004.] A rapid transfer of power in Iraq was urged by one faction within the Bush administration, which did not prevail.

46. See Sandro Magister, "Iraq: The Church Goes on a Mission of Peace," **Chiesa,** November 28, 2003.

47. Jason Horowitz, "Vatican Official Says U.S. Treated Hussein 'Like a Cow,'" **New York Times,** December 16, 2003.

48. On May 23, Archbishop Martino, not yet a cardinal, spoke at the Pontifical Gregorian University in Rome and said that "freedom and the restoration of law have never been achieved by force or war." ["Reconsider Tools of International Law," Vatican Information Service, May 23, 2003.] It was a curious claim, in itself— but perhaps even more odd coming from a man whose country had been saved from fascism by American, British, and Polish soldiers.

49. John Paul II, **Homily at Midnight Mass, Christmas, 24 December 2003.**

50. John Paul II, **Urbi et Orbi Message, Christmas 2003.**

51. John L. Allen, Jr., "The Word from Rome," **National Catholic Reporter,** April 25, 2003.

52. "John Paul II Doesn't Know the Meaning of 'Weekend,'" ZENIT News Service, May 30, 2003.

53. "Pope Asks for Prayers to Continue to Fulfill Mission," ZENIT News Service, May 18, 2003.

54. "'A Youth of 83' Enthuses Spain's Youth," **The Tablet,** May 10, 2003, pp. 38–39.

55. John Paul II, **Address at the Welcoming Ceremony, International Airport Adrija Riviera Kvarner of Rijeka/Krk, 5 June 2003** [emphasis in original].

56. John Paul II, **Homily, Mass and Beatification of the Servant of God Ivan Merz, 22 June 2003.**

57. John Paul II, **Address at the International Airport of Bratislava, 11 September 2003** [emphases in original].

58. John Paul's concerns were shared by the distinguished international constitutional legal scholar Joseph H. H. Weiler, himself an Orthodox Jew; see Weiler, **Un'Europa cristiana: Un saggio esplorativo** (Milano: Biblioteca Universale Rizzoli, 2003).

59. John Paul II, **Angelus, 20 July 2003.**

60. John Paul II, **Angelus, 13 July 2003.**

61. Cited in "Unholy Row on God's Place in E.U. Constitution," **Christian Century,** April 5, 2003.

62. Cited in "France Says No to Christianity in Constitution," eurobserver.com, September 14, 2003.

63. Cited in "Unholy Row."

64. Cited in www.religioustolerance.org/const.eu.htm.

65. Ibid.

66. Cited in Gerald Owen, "Habermas + Derrida: Modernism a Beneficiary of War in Iraq," **National Post,** August 2, 2003.

The German philosopher Jürgen Habermas, who had joined Derrida in appealing for a Europe "neutral between worldviews," later modified his position after a public debate with Cardinal Joseph Ratzinger in January 2004. See Ratzinger and Habermas, **Dialectics of**

Secularization: On Reason and Religion, trans. Brian McNeil, C.R.V. (San Francisco: Ignatius Press, 2006).

67. On **Centesimus Annus,** see Weigel, **Witness to Hope,** pp. 612–19. On Leo XIII and the beginnings of modern Catholic social doctrine, see Russell Hittinger, "Commentary on Leo XIII," in eds. John Witte, Jr., and Frank S. Alexander, **The Teachings of Modern Roman Catholicism on Law, Politics, and Human Nature** (New York: Columbia University Press, 2007), pp. 39–75.

68. John Paul II, **Ecclesia in Europa,** 2.

69. Ibid., 3.

70. Ibid., 4.

71. Ibid., 7–8.

72. Ibid., 9.

73. See Henri de Lubac, S.J., **The Drama of Atheist Humanism** (San Francisco: Ignatius Press, 1995).

74. John Paul II, **Ecclesia in Europe,** 76.

75. Ibid., 67.

76. Ibid., 25.

77. Ibid., 25. John Paul might well have added that, had there been no Christian culture in Europe, Europe would not have had the cultural and moral resources to summon the will to defend itself against successive waves of Islamic invasion.

78. Ibid., 98–99.

79. Ibid., 116.

80. Ibid., 121.

81. John Paul II, **Salvifici Doloris,** 3, 2.

82. Ibid., 18.

83. See ibid., 26.

For a more thorough discussion of **Salvifici Doloris,**

see George Weigel, **The Truth of Catholicism: Ten Controversies Explored** (New York: HarperCollins, 2001), pp. 112–26.

84. Joseph Ratzinger, **Eschatology: Death and Eternal Life,** 2nd ed., trans. Aidan Nichols, O.P., Michael Waldstein (Washington, DC: Catholic University of America Press, 2009), pp. 217–18.

85. Author's conversation with Archbishop Celestino Migliore, May 21, 2003.

86. See John L. Allen, Jr., "The Word from Rome," **National Catholic Reporter,** January 2, 2004.

The papaya story was floated in the Times of London on March 13, 2003, by its Rome correspondent, Richard Owen—throughout the pontificate, a notably unreliable source of serious information and analysis. [See Richard Owen, "Papaya Gives the Pope Some Extra Zest," **The Times,** March 13, 2003.]

87. John Paul II, **Homily for the XXV Anniversary of the Pontificate, 16 October 2003** [emphasis in original].

88. Memorandum to the author from Sister Mary Nirmala, M.C., June 27, 2008.

In this same memorandum, Sister Nirmala recounted a remarkable story about Mother Teresa and John Paul II:

> I remember meeting Holy Father around 10th Sept. 1989, after Mass in his private chapel in the Vatican. I had just arrived from Calcutta where Mother was very sick in the hospital. I was praying desperately to Jesus and Our Lady for Mother's recovery. On the 8th Sept., the birthday of Our Lady, I was assured by Jesus during Holy Communion

in the church of Mt. St. Mary of Bandra in Bombay that Our Lady will do everything possible to make Mother alright. Then on the 9th Sept. at St. Peter's Basilica I was telling St. Peter what Jesus had assured me, but in case by mistake Mother would come to the gate of heaven, please to send her back to earth to continue working for the Church, as he had done at the beginning of our Society when in her delirium [from another illness] Mother found herself at the gate of heaven, telling her that there were no slums in heaven. And I felt strongly that St. Peter would hear my prayer.

Now that I was right in front of the Holy Father who was the present Peter, I told Holy Father that Mother was sick. I asked for his prayer for Mother and also asked him to tell Mother not to go to heaven yet, but continue working for the Church on earth. For I knew that Mother would obey Holy Father.

Around 14th or 15th Sept. when I was in New York I got the news that Mother's condition had become worse and it was a question of life and death.

Soon after I was told that Holy Father was informed and Holy Father had sent [a] message to Mother assuring her of his prayer for her recovery and telling her that the Church and the world needed her witness.

. . . Mother responded to his message

and recovered and lived for eight years more fighting with a few more acute medical conditions. [Ibid.]

89. Author's conversation with Pope John Paul II, September 30, 1997.

90. John Paul II, **Homily for the Beatification of Mother Teresa of Calcutta, 19 October 2003** [emphases in original].

The master of pontifical liturgical ceremonies, Bishop Piero Marini, inserted into the beatification liturgy a ritual of Hindu origin known as **ārati,** featuring burning materials soaked in ghee, during which a song of praise to God was sung in Tamil. The appearance of what seemed to be smudge pots at a papal liturgy in Rome was a puzzlement to many.

91. Nagy had been the chaplain to university scientists in Kraków for many years. His nomination as cardinal, John Paul later wrote, was in part "a way of showing my appreciation for Polish science." [John Paul II, **Rise, Let Us Be on Our Way!** (New York: Warner Books, 2004), p. 88.]

Špidlík was an expert in Eastern Christianity who had preached the papal Lenten retreat in 1995 and had been responsible for conceiving one of John Paul II's most dramatic artistic innovations in the Vatican, the redecoration of the **Redemptoris Mater** chapel in the Apostolic Palace with frescoes and mosaics in a modern Byzantine style. The funds for the redecoration came from the purse given John Paul by the College of Cardinals in 1996 on the golden jubilee of his priestly ordination. The redecorated chapel, striking in itself but even more so in its location within a building dominated by Renaissance art, was rededicated by John Paul II on

November 14, 1999. See **La Capella "Redemptoris Mater" del Papa Giovanni Paolo II** (Vatican City: Libreria Editrice Vaticana, 1999); and Sandro Magister, "Spidlik and Caffarra, an Odd Couple Sprung from the Pope's Mind," **Chiesa,** May 1, 2004.

92. Author's conversation with Pope John Paul II, December 15, 2003.

93. Author's conversation with Archbishop James M. Harvey, December 15, 2003.

94. David Brooks, "Bigger Than the Nobel," **New York Times,** October 11, 2003.

95. See Sandro Magister, "Vatican Intrigues: 'The Passion,' the Pope, and the Phantom Review," **Chiesa,** February 6, 2004.

96. "Break Dancers Perform for the Pope," **The Age** (online edition), January 26, 2004; "Pope Greets Dance Crew at Holy Mass-ive," **Daily Mirror,** January 27, 2004.

97. "Pope's Surprise Visit to Contemplative Nuns at Vatican: Carmelites Were Having Dinner When Doorbell Rang," ZENIT News Service, March 2, 2004.

98. "Pope Resumes Meetings with Roman Parishes," ZENIT News Service, March 1, 2004.

99. John Paul II, **Angelus, 14 March 2004**.

100. John Paul II, **Homily for Palm Sunday, 4 April 2004.**

101. Cited in **L'Osservatore Romano** [English Weekly Edition], April 14, 2004, p. 4.

102. Cited in ibid., p. 6.

103. Cited in ibid., p. 7 [emphasis in original].

104. Karol Wojtyła, "The Personal Structure of Self-Determination," in Wojtyła, **Person and Community,** pp. 187–95.

105. See **Gaudium et Spes** [Pastoral Constitution on the Church in the Modern World], 24.

106. The book's title came from the fourteenth chapter of Mark's Gospel, from the scene in the Garden of Gethsemane when Jesus rouses his sleeping disciples to go with him to meet his fate.

107. John Paul II, **Rise, Let Us Be on Our Way!,** pp. vii–viii.

108. The American edition of **Alzatevi, andiamo!** mistranslated this as a "canoeing" excursion, an error that would have caused both the Pope and his fellow kayakers to grimace.

109. Ibid., pp. 9–11.

110. Ibid., p. 30.

111. Ibid., pp. 189–90.

112. Ibid., pp. 164–66.

There was nothing surprising or unconventional in John Paul's suggestions to his brother bishops about the proper exercise of their office, with perhaps one notable exception: his counsel that a bishop should take particular concern to "establish personal contacts with the academic world and its leading figures . . . not only within his own Catholic academic institutions, but . . . with the whole university world: reading, meeting others, discussing, informing himself about their activities" [ibid., p. 89]. That such contacts were not habitual among many bishops was obvious to anyone familiar with the Catholic Church; that they ought to be was the settled conviction of the man who, before becoming a world-changing pope, had been one of the Church's most effective and successful diocesan bishops.

113. Ibid., pp. 49–50.

114. John Paul II, **Address to the Honorable George W. Bush, 4 June 2004.**

115. See John L. Allen, Jr., "The Word from Rome," **National Catholic Reporter,** June 4, 2004.

116. "Swiss Marvel at John Paul II's 'Magic' with Youth," ZENIT News Service, June 7, 2004.

117. John Paul II, **Homily at Almend Esplanade in Bern, 6 June 2004** [emphases in original].

118. E-mail to the author from Michael Sherwin, O.P., June 10, 2004.

119. On **Veritatis Splendor** and its reception, see Weigel, **Witness to Hope,** pp. 686–95 and notes.

120. "Pope Hails Reagan's 'Commitment to the Cause of Freedom,'" ZENIT News Service, June 8, 2004.

121. "Message of the Holy Father for Transferral of Relics," **L'Osservatore Romano** [English Weekly Edition], December 1, 2004, p. 3.

122. John Paul II, "Farewell Address to Citizens of Introd, 17 July [2004]," **L'Osservatore Romano** [English Weekly Edition], July 21, 2004, p. 12.

123. Author's interview with Joaquín Navarro-Valls, November 13, 2008.

124. The details of the Pope's visit to Lourdes are taken from Austen Ivereigh, "Pope in Lourdes Speaks of 'the End of My Pilgrimage,'" **The Tablet,** August 21, 2004, p. 25.

125. Ibid.

126. Cited in John L. Allen, Jr., "The Word from Rome," **National Catholic Reporter,** August 20, 2004.

127. Cited in Ivereigh, "Pope in Lourdes."

128. Allen, "The Word from Rome," **National Catholic Reporter,** August 20, 2004.

129. Cited in ibid.

130. Ibid.

131. There was an element of historical curiosity in the Kazanskaya housed in the papal chapel at Castel Gandolfo: one wall of the chapel is covered by a fresco, commissioned by Pope Pius XI, of the 1920 "Miracle on the Vistula," in which Polish arms defeated the Red Army and thrust Bolshevism back into Russia. John Paul II was not a man to think in ironic terms, but others could not help thinking that the irony was further compounded by the fact that the icon was being returned to the man once known to the KGB as DROZDOV.

132. "Icon of Kazan Is Symbol of Christian Unity, Says Pope," ZENIT News Service, August 29, 2004.

133. The full text of Cardinal Kasper's remarks may be found in **L'Osservatore Romano** [English Weekly Edition], September 1, 2004, p. 2.

134. "'Historical' Return of Icon of Kazan to Orthodox Church," ZENIT News Service, August 29, 2004.

135. John Paul II, **Address on the Opening of the Year of the Eucharist, 17 October 2004.**

136. John Paul II, **Mane Nobiscum Domine,** 28.

137. Author's conversation with Pope John Paul II, December 15, 2004.

Chapter Nine

1. Author's interview with Cardinal Leonardo Sandri, March 15, 2008.

2. Author's interview with Joaquín Navarro-Valls, November 13, 2008.

3. Ibid.

4. Author's interview with Cardinal Jean-Marie Lustiger, December 9, 2006.

5. Author's conversation with Stanisław Rybicki, Danuta Rybicka, Maria Rybicka, Karol Tarnowski, Danuta Ciesielska, Piotr Malecki, and Teresa Malecka, November 8, 2008.

6. Author's interview with Cardinal Camillo Ruini, November 19, 2008.

7. E-mail to the author from the Very Rev. Joseph Augustine DiNoia, O.P., February 23, 2005.

8. On the original idea behind the founding of Institut für die Wissenschaften vom Menschen [IWM], see Weigel, **Witness to Hope,** pp. 466–67.

Over time, IWM became far more a reflection of the main currents of European intellectual life than the challenge to those currents that John Paul II imagined it would be at the outset.

9. John Paul II, **Memory and Identity: Personal Reflections** (London: Weidenfeld and Nicolson, 2005).

10. Ibid., pp. 91–92.

11. Ibid., p. 104.

12. Ibid., p. 108.

13. Ibid., p. 151.

14. Ibid., p. 155.

15. Author's interview with Rocco Buttiglione, January 21, 1997.

16. John Paul II, **Memory and Identity,** p. 125.

17. Richard John Neuhaus, "The New Europes," **First Things** (October 2005); Richard John Neuhaus, **American Babylon: Notes of a Christian Exile** (New York: Basic Books, 2009), p. 30.

18. Dziwisz, **A Life with Karol,** p. 248.

19. Ibid., p. 253; author's interview with Cardinal Leonardo Sandri, March 15, 2008.

20. Cited in Renato Buzzonetti, "The Days of Suffering and Hope," in Stanisław Dziwisz, Czeslaw Drazek, S.J., Renato Buzzonetti, and Angelo Comastri, **Let Me Go to the Father's House: John Paul II's Strength in Weakness** (Boston: Pauline Books and Media, 2006), pp. 68–69.

21. Cited in John L. Allen, Jr., "The Word from Rome," **National Catholic Reporter,** February 11, 2005. Allen's fact-based, calm, and measured reporting during the media firestorm of John Paul's last illness confirmed many in the judgment that Allen was the best Anglophone Vatican reporter ever.

22. Dziwisz, **A Life with Karol,** p. 253; Bruce Johnston, "Pope Sweeps Back to Vatican 'Impatient to Work Again,'" **Daily Telegraph,** February 11, 2005.

23. **L'Osservatore Romano** [English Weekly Edition], February 16, 2005, p. 1.

24. Lustiger had been one of the boldest of John Paul's episcopal appointments: a son of Polish-Jewish parents and convert to Catholicism as archbishop of Paris was not something any other pope would have considered possible. (See Weigel, **Witness to Hope,** pp. 388–90.) Archbishop Vingt-Trois's unusual surname ["Twenty-Three"] derived from the fact that he was a foundling: asked, as a child, what surname he wished to take, he simply took the last two digits of the number of his case. (Author's interview with Archbishop André Vingt-Trois, December 9, 2006.)

25. John Paul II, "A Life Given to Christ at the Ser-

vice of the Church," **L'Osservatore Romano** [English Weekly Edition], February 23, 2005, p. 1.

26. See Dziwisz, **A Life with Karol,** pp. 253–54.

27. Ibid., p. 254.

28. February 27 was another moment of drama: Reporters, producers, and news personalities started arriving one after the other, some manifestly disgruntled to have been pulled away from the glittering red carpets of the Oscars to the damp, muddy knoll outside the Gemelli.

Ominous weather and bleak predictions were the backdrop for Sunday morning's broadcasts. As the television presenters schooled their features into a properly concerned expression and prepared to somberly announce that the Pope would miss the Angelus for the first time in 26 years, sunlight appeared for the first time in days.

And with the sun came the Pope. Weak, hand at his throat, he appeared at his window and blessed all those gathered below.

The visible shock of the assembled journalists was worth a thousand words. Seasoned journalists, world-weary and jaded, suddenly found themselves slack-jawed in utter amazement.

One television producer, unable to conceal her admiration, shook her head and exclaimed aloud, "This guy's a [expletive] superhero! Mike Tyson, eat your heart out!" [Elizabeth Lev, "Wowing the World-weary . . . A Pope Appears—and Jaws Drop," ZENIT News Service, March 3, 2005.]

29. Author's interview with Cardinal Leonardo Sandri, March 15, 2008.

30. "John Paul II Keeping Busy at the Hospital," ZENIT News Service, March 3, 2005.

31. "Pope Gives Impromptu Blessing from Hospital Window," Catholic News Agency, March 9, 2005.

32. See **L'Osservatore Romano** [English Weekly Edition], March 16, 2005, p. 3.

33. Cited in ibid., p. 1.

34. Author's interview with Cardinal Leonardo Sandri, March 15, 2008.

35. Author's conversation with Hanna Suchocka, March 9, 2005; Raymond J. de Souza, "To His Last Breath, a Public Pontiff," **National Post,** February 26, 2005; author's conversation with Piotr Malecki, March 27, 2005.

36. Dziwisz, **A Life with Karol,** p. 255.

37. Ibid., pp. 255–56.

38. Ibid., p. 256.

39. Dziwisz et al., **Let Me Go the Father's House,** pp. 72–73.

40. Dziwisz, **A Life with Karol,** p. 256.

41. Cited in Camillo Ruini, **Alla Sequela di Cristo: Giovanni Paolo II, il Servo dei Servi di Dio** (Siena: Edizione Cantagalli, 2007), p. 36 [author's translation].

42. Dziwisz, **A Life with Karol,** 257–58.

43. Ibid., pp. 258–59; Dziwisz et al., **Let Me Go to the Father's House,** pp. 74–75. According to "Vatican norms," Buzzonetti let the electrocardiogram run for

twenty minutes after the heartbeat stopped, to verify the Pope's death [Buzzonetti, "The Days of Suffering and Hope," p. 75].

44. Author's interview with Cardinal Leonardo Sandri, March 15, 2008.

45. Cited in **L'Osservatore Romano** [English Weekly Edition], p. 5.

46. Charles Krauthammer, "Pope John Paul II," **Washington Post,** April 3, 2005.

47. "Pope John Paul II, Keeper of the Flock for a Quarter of a Century," **New York Times,** April 3, 2005.

48. Cited in Mark Steyn, "Why Progressive Westerners Never Understood John Paul II," **Daily Telegraph,** April 5, 2005.

49. Polly Toynbee, "Not in My Name," **The Guardian,** April 8, 2005. The refreshing note in Ms. Toynbee's screed was the deprecatory remark about Lenin, such remarks not being a staple at her newspaper.

50. Carroll was cited in Virginia Heffernan, "Pope John Paul Appraised as Pope, Not Rock Star," **New York Times,** April 5, 2005; Marco Politi, "A Man Ill at Ease in His Own Century," **The Tablet,** April 9, 2005.

51. Thomas Cahill, "The Price of Infallibility," **New York Times,** April 5, 2005.

52. "Pope John Paul II," **Washington Post,** April 3, 2005.

53. **Daily Telegraph,** April 4, 2005.

54. "The Very Modern Papacy of John Paul II," **Wall Street Journal,** April 2, 2005.

55. True to form, French secularists protested the decision by French prime minister Jean-Pierre Raffarin to lower flags to half-mast in tribute to John Paul II, with

one socialist senator saying that "the French Republic should not descend to such a level." ["French Secular Politicians Criticize Flag Tribute to Pope," **Wall Street Journal Online,** April 4, 2005.]

56. Virtually all cardinals of the Catholic Church are ordained bishops, save for some of those elderly theologians whom popes have honored in recent decades. The three "orders" of cardinals reflect the days long past when the cardinals were in fact the active clergy of Rome and its surrounding areas, but the titles "cardinal bishop," "cardinal priest," and "cardinal deacon" are honorific today. The "cardinal bishops" are the titular bishops of the seven "suburbicarian" dioceses surrounding Rome, which are in fact governed by auxiliary bishops: Ostia, Velletri-Segni, Porto and Santa Rufina, Frascati (Tusculum), Palestrina, Albano, and Sabina; there are only six cardinal bishops, however, for the dean of the College of Cardinals is cardinal bishop of Ostia as well as of his previous suburbicarian diocese. The "cardinal priests," who are usually residential archbishops or bishops from around the world, are titular pastors of Roman parishes, as are the "cardinal deacons," who are generally members of the Roman Curia or elderly theologians. All cardinals receive a "title," which is the name of the Roman church of which they are titular pastor, at the time of the appointment; the cardinal bishops give up these titles when named to the suburbicarian sees.

57. For further details of the funeral Mass of John Paul II and the week preceding it, see George Weigel, **God's Choice: Pope Benedict XVI and the Future of the Catholic Church** (New York: HarperCollins, 2005), pp. 75–103.

58. Author's interview with Cardinal Francis Arinze, December 17, 2007.

59. Author's interview with Cardinal Leonardo Sandri, March 15, 2008.

60. Pope Benedict XVI, "Meeting with Clergy," **Origins** 38:13 (September 4, 2008), p. 207 [emphasis added].

61. T. S. Eliot, "Four Quartets," in Eliot, **Collected Poems 1909–1962** (New York: Harcourt Brace & Company, 1963), p. 190.

Chapter Ten

1. See Edmund Morris, **Dutch: A Memoir of Ronald Reagan** (New York: Random House, 1999).

2. See Weigel, **Witness to Hope,** pp. 7ff.

3. The German theologian Karl Rahner, S.J., argued that the completion of the lifelong process of metanoia is in fact the Christian meaning of death: it is at the point of death that we can make a complete, radical, and unreserved gift of ourselves to God (an offering that can be made in an anticipatory way prior to the moment of death, but which would be impossible were the "immortality project" of certain twenty-first-century bioethicists to reach fulfillment). See Karl Rahner, S.J., **The Theology of Death: Quaestiones Disputatae 2** (New York: Herder and Herder, 1961), chapter 1.

4. See Weigel, **The Truth of Catholicism,** pp. 72–91.

5. **Catechism of the Catholic Church**, 1813.

6. Pope John Paul II, **Gift and Mystery,** p. 20 [emphasis in original]. For more on Karol Wojtyła's education in faith, see Weigel, **Witness to Hope,** chapters 1 and 2.

7. Author's interview with Rocco Buttiglione, January 21, 1997.

8. Author's conversation with Pope John Paul II, October 23, 1998.

9. Ibid.

10. As he did, for example, prior to the appointment of Jean-Marie Lustiger as archbishop of Paris; Lustiger, reluctant to accept the nomination, was told by Stanisław Dziwisz, "You are the fruit of the prayer of the Pope." See Weigel, **Witness to Hope,** pp. 388–90.

11. Author's interview with Jerzy Janik, July 17, 1996.

12. Author's interview with Cardinal Joseph Ratzinger, September 12, 1996.

13. Author's interview with Jacek Woźniakowski, April 11, 1997.

14. Ibid.

15. John Paul II, **Address to the Fiftieth General Assembly of the United Nations Organization,** October 5, 1995, 16 [emphasis in original].

16. Ibid., 17.

17. Ibid.

18. Author's interview with Karol Tarnowski, April 12, 1997.

19. Author's interview with Bishop Stanisław Smoleński, April 7, 1997.

20. **Catechism of the Catholic Church,** 1827.

21. Author's interview with Stefan Sawicki, April 15, 1997.

22. Author's interview with Karol Tarnowski, April 12, 1997.

23. Author's interview with Karol Tarnowski, November 5, 1998.

24. Author's interview with Józef Tischner, April 23, 1997.

25. John Paul II, **Rise, Let Us Be on Our Way!,** pp. 139–40.

26. "Reflections on Fatherhood," in Karol Wojtyła, **The Collected Plays and Writings on Theater,** trans. Bolesław Taborski (Berkeley: University of California Press, 1987), p. 368.

27. Author's interview with Stanisław Grygiel, February 20, 1997.

28. Author's conversation with Pope John Paul II, December 13, 1997.

29. Throughout the pontificate, the dissident Swiss theologian Hans Küng was both ill informed and malicious in his criticism of John Paul II, and not least of the Pope's intellectual openness. See "Hans Küng," in Fergus Kerr, **Twentieth Century Catholic Theologians** (Oxford: Blackwell Publishing, 2007), pp. 146–47, n. 5, for one among many examples.

30. See Franco Bucarelli, "God's Athlete," **Columbia,** November 2007, p. 19.

31. Author's interview with Hanna Suchocka, November 11, 2008.

John Paul's first question, on greeting the prime minister, was "Are your parents still alive?" to which Suchocka had to answer, "No." Having been orphaned himself, Suchocka believed, John Paul wanted to know what other people's parents' reaction had been to their children's rise to unexpected eminence. Thus the first thing on John Paul II's mind when meeting the prime minister of Poland was not public policy, but the person in front of him.

32. Author's interview with Cardinal Franz König, December 11, 1997.

33. Author's conversation with Pope John Paul II, March 20, 1997.

John Paul II retained his deep affection for the veteran editor of **Tygodnik Powszechny,** Jerzy Turowicz, until "Pan Jerzy's" death in January 1999, even as the Pope wondered about the newspaper's seeming fondness for theological currents of thought that cut across the grain of his own theological sensibility and magisterium.

34. Author's interview with Stanisław Rybicki, April 9, 1997.

35. Author's interview with Piotr and Teresa Malecki, Stanisław and Danuta Rybicki, Karol Tarnowski, and Danuta Ciesielska, November 8, 2008.

36. Author's conversation with Father Maciej Zięba, O.P., December 4, 2008.

37. Author's interview with Józef Tischner, April 23, 1997.

38. Author's interview with Cardinal Joachim Meisner, October 17, 2001.

39. Author's conversation with Pope John Paul II, September 25, 1994; author's interview with Cardinal John J. O'Connor, November 8, 1996.

40. Author's conversation with Pope John Paul II, September 24, 1999.

41. Author's conversation with Pope John Paul II, September 30, 1997.

42. Plato identified the four cardinal virtues as prudence, justice, courage (fortitude), and temperance in **The Republic** IV, 427. The **Catechism of the Catholic Church** discusses the cardinal virtues in 1803–5.

43. Author's interview with Jerzy Gałkowski, April 14, 1997.

44. See John Paul II, **Rise, Let Us Be on Our Way,** pp. 49–50.

45. **Catechism of the Catholic Church,** 1807.

46. Author's interview with Hanna Suchocka, November 11, 2008.

47. Morris West, **The Devil's Advocate** (Chicago: Loyola Classics, 2005), p. 25.

48. Letter to the author from Pope John Paul II, January 2, 1995.

49. **Catechism of the Catholic Church,** 1809.

50. For an account of this remarkable sermon, see Weigel, **Witness to Hope,** pp. 250–51.

51. **Gaudium et Spes,** 37.

52. John Paul II, **Evangelium Vitae,** 104.

53. See John Paul II, **Dominum et Vivificantem,** 27.

54. Author's interview with Cardinal Stanisław Dziwisz, December 2, 2008; "John Paul II Helps Possessed Woman in Vatican," ZENIT News Service, September 10, 2000.

55. "John Paul II Helps Possessed Woman in Vatican," ZENIT News Service, September 10, 2000.

56. Author's interview with Cardinal Stanisław Dziwisz, December 2, 2008.

57. Ibid.

58. **Catechism of the Catholic Church,** 395.

59. See ibid., 385.

60. Ibid., 309 [emphasis in original].

61. John Paul II, **Dominum et Vivificantem,** 35.

Chapter Eleven

1. J. N. D. Kelly, **The Oxford Dictionary of Popes** (New York: Oxford University Press, 1986), p. 302.

2. Cited in Antonio Fappani and Franco Molinari, **Giovanni Battista Montini Giovane** (Turin: Marietti, 1979), p. 171.

3. The 1985 World Youth Day in Rome took place prior to the Pope's decision to make these events a regular part of the rhythm of the Church's life, such that some count Buenos Aires-1987 as the first international World Youth Day, strictly speaking.

4. For an ecumenical study of the many roles of Peter in the early Church, see **Peter in the New Testament,** eds. Raymond E. Brown, Karl P. Donfried, and John Reumann (Minneapolis: Augsburg, 1973).

5. John Paul II, **Redemptoris Missio,** 39.

6. Author's conversations with Vittorio Sozzi and Roberto Presilla, February 27, 2002.

7. Author's interview with Cardinal Camillo Ruini, March 17, 2008. See also Marcello Pera, "Relativism, Christianity, and the West," and "Letter to Joseph Ratzinger," in Joseph Ratzinger and Marcello Pera, **Without Roots: The West, Relativism, Christianity, Islam,** trans. Michael F. Moore (New York: Basic Books, 2006).

8. The story of this confrontation is told in detail in Weigel, **Witness to Hope,** pp. 715–27.

9. See ibid., pp. 766–71, for a detailed account of the drama at Beijing.

10. On the Extraordinary Synod, see ibid., pp. 487–90, 502–5.

11. Author's interview with Archbishop John Onai-

yekan, November 30, 2001; author's interview with Cardinal Francis Arinze, December 17, 2007.

12. The Synod on the Laity and **Christifideles Laici** are discussed in Weigel, **Witness to Hope,** pp. 552–55.

13. Author's conversation with Father Alberto Garbin, December 17, 2008.

14. See, for example, Ann Carey, **Sisters in Crisis: The Tragic Unraveling of Women's Religious Communities** (Huntington, IN: Our Sunday Visitor Publishing Division, 1997).

15. See, for example, Council of Major Superiors of Women Religious, **The Foundations of Religious Life: Revisiting the Vision** (Notre Dame, IN: Ave Maria Press, 2009).

16. Despite the Council's decree on priestly formation, the serious theological work at the Council, these commentators argued, had centered on the episcopate (discussion of which dominated the preparation of the Dogmatic Constitution on the Church), while the Council's practical effect within the ordained ministry had been to restore the diaconate as a permanent office in the Church.

17. On **Pastores Dabo Vobis,** see Weigel, **Witness to Hope,** pp. 656–57.

18. Author's interview with Cardinal William W. Baum, November 5, 1996.

19. See **Lumen Gentium,** 39–42.

20. For more on the changes wrought by **Divinus Perfectionis Magister,** see Weigel, **Witness to Hope,** pp. 448–49.

21. Avery Cardinal Dulles, S.J., "John Paul II and the

New Evangelization," in Dulles, **Church and Society,** p. 97.

22. See ibid., pp. 92–96, with the appropriate references in John Paul II's magisterium.

23. Ibid., p. 100.

24. See, for example, Gaddis, **The Cold War.**

25. See de Lubac, **The Drama of Atheist Humanism.**

26. On **Centesimus Annus,** see Weigel, **Witness to Hope,** pp. 612–19.

27. Author's interview with Father Robert Gahl, December 12, 2008.

28. John Paul II, **Evangelium Vitae,** 20.

29. On these questions, see Russell Hittinger, "Introduction to Modern Catholicism," in eds. Witte and Alexander, **The Teachings of Modern Roman Catholicism on Law, Politics, and Human Nature,** pp. 1–38; at p. 21, Hittinger notes "a steady deterioration of any ontological density to the state" in twentieth-century Catholic thought.

On Vatican II's acceleration of the shift from an ontologically "thick" Catholic theory of the state to a thinner notion of the limited, constitutional state and its relationship to the question of religious freedom, see John Courtney Murray, S.J., "The Issue of Church and State at Vatican Council II," **Theological Studies** 27:4 (December 1966).

One controversial facet of this new approach to the state involved John Paul II's teaching on capital punishment. For a review of the debate, see Avery Cardinal Dulles, S.J., "The Death Penalty: A Right-to-Life Issue?" in Dulles, **Church and Society,** pp. 332–47.

As the debate over John Paul II's social doctrine unfolds, it may be hoped that it is not distorted by efforts to portray Karol Wojtyła as beholden to a Marxist analysis of modern social and economic life, a theme advanced doggedly over the years by Jonathan Luxmoore and Jolanta Babiuch in the pages of the London **Tablet.** Their misreading of the sources of Wojtyła's social thought rests in part on a misunderstanding of **Catholic Social Ethics,** a text adopted by Wojtyła from Father Jan Piwowarczyk during Wojtyła's seminary teaching days in Kraków—a text that Wojtyła did not regard as his own—and by a more fundamental failure to recognize that Thomas Aquinas had analyzed questions of distributive justice seven centuries before Karl Marx.

30. On the origins and work of Bea's Secretariat for Christian Unity, see Jerome-Michael Vereb, C.P., **"Because He was a German!" The Origins of Roman Catholic Engagement in the Ecumenical Movement** (Grand Rapids, MI: Eerdmans, 2006). On "real but imperfect" communion, see Vatican II's Decree on Ecumenism, **Unitatis Redintegratio** [The Restoration of Unity], 3. On the "hierarchy of truths," see **Unitatis Redintegratio,** 11. For a description of the scene at the Phanar in Istanbul at the lifting of the mutual excommunications of 1054, see Lawrence Cardinal Shehan, **A Blessing of Years** (Notre Dame, IN: University of Notre Dame Press, 1982), pp. 203–5.

31. See Weigel, **Witness to Hope,** p. 525.

32. Author's interview with Ronald G. Roberson, C.S.P., March 3, 1997.

33. On the difficulties in bringing the Joint Declaration to a successful conclusion, see Weigel, **Witness to Hope,** pp. 826–28.

34. For more on John Paul II's ecumenical initiatives with Orthodoxy and their reception within the complex Orthodox world, see Weigel, **Witness to Hope,** pp. 358–60, 555–57, 651–52, 672–73, 764, 821–22.

35. For a more comprehensive discussion of **Ut Unum Sint,** see ibid., pp. 760–66.

36. On the 1985–86 crisis in Anglican-Catholic relations, see ibid., pp. 518–22.

In 1980, John Paul II created the "Pastoral Provision" by which married Anglican priests and bishops could be received into the full communion of the Catholic Church and be ordained as priests; unmarried former Anglican clergy could also be ordained as Catholic bishops. The Pastoral Provision also permitted the formation of parishes that retained elements of Anglican liturgy. The Pastoral Provision is under the authority of the Congregation for the Doctrine of the Faith. According to former Anglican bishop Jeffrey Steenson, John Paul II urged Cardinal Joseph Ratzinger, prefect of CDF, to "be generous with the Anglicans." [Author's interview with Jeffrey Steenson, December 15, 2008.] See www.pastoralprovision.org for a history of this initiative.

37. Geoffrey Wainwright, "A Methodist Tribute to Pope John Paul II," **Pro Ecclesia** XIV:3 (Summer 2005), pp. 265–67.

38. As of November 2009, "Evangelicals and Catholics Together" had published seven common statements: on Christian political responsibility ("Evangelicals and Catholics Together: The Christian Mission in the Third Millennium," **First Things** 43 [May 1994], pp. 15–22); on salvation by faith ("The Gift of Salvation," **First**

Things 79 [January 1998], pp. 20–23); on Scripture and tradition ("Your Word Is Truth," **First Things** 125 [August/September 2002], pp. 38–42); on the nature of the Church ("The Communion of Saints," **First Things** 131 [March 2003], pp. 36–42); on prayer and mission ("The Call to Holiness," **First Things** 151 [March 2005], pp. 23–26); on the defense of life ("That They May Have Life," **First Things** 166 [October 2006], pp. 18–25); and on Mary in the economy of salvation and in Christian piety ("Do Whatever He Tells You," **First Things** 197 [November 2009], pp. 49–59).

39. Timothy George, "John Paul II: An Appreciation," **Pro Ecclesia** XIV:3 (Summer 2005), p. 270.

40. See David Martin, **Tongues of Fire: The Explosion of Protestantism in Latin America** (Oxford: Wiley-Blackwell, 1993).

41. Author's interview with Bishop Pierre Duprey, M.Afr., January 15, 1997.

42. This theme of the "elder brothers" echoed the 1848 "Manifesto" of the great Polish Romantic poet and playwright Adam Mickiewicz, a philo-Semite. In an interesting historical coincidence, Mickiewicz's "Manifesto" was written in Rome. [Author's interview with Jerzy Kluger, March 15, 1997.]

43. For more on John Paul II's visit to the Great Synagogue of Rome, see Weigel, **Witness to Hope,** pp. 482–85.

44. For an account of this negotiation, see ibid., pp. 697–713.

45. This was not simply a mistaken popular view. It was held by the Israeli scholar and diplomat Sergio Minerbi, who continued to insist until the ink was dry

on the Fundamental Agreement that any such accord was impossible for Catholic theological reasons; see Minerbi, **The Vatican and Zionism: Conflict in the Holy Land 1895–1925** (New York: Oxford University Press, 1990). After John Paul's death, Minerbi argued in an unpersuasive and indeed nasty article that the Pope's initiatives toward Jews and Judaism masked certain classic, if muted, anti-Semitic attitudes (including the deicide charge, which Minerbi bizarrely attributed to John Paul's encyclical on the Holy Spirit, **Dominum et Vivificantem**); see Minerbi, "Pope John Paul II and the Jews: An Evaluation," **Jewish Political Studies Review** 18:1–2 (Spring 2006).

46. The full text of **Dabru Emet** may be found in **First Things** 107 (November 2000), pp. 39–41. The document is summarized in Weigel, **The Truth of Catholicism,** pp. 137–43.

47. John Paul II, "Lessons of the Galileo Case," **Origins** 22:22 (November 12, 1992), pp. 369–74. John Paul's initiative in the reexamination of the Galileo affair is described in more detail in Weigel, **Witness to Hope,** pp. 629–31.

48. The papal message is available at http://www .newadvent.org/library/docs_jp02tc.htm.

49. Assisi I was motivated in part by the Pope's concern about a global nuclear war. John Paul believed that many politicians were "too feeble" to take the lead in the pursuit of peace; thus, as he once put it, "We have to do something with prayer, because prayer can do what politicians can't do." [Author's interview with Msgr. Vincenzo Paglia, December 7, 1997.]

50. John Paul II, **Discorso alla Curia Romana per**

gli Auguri di Natale, 22 December 1986, 7 [author's translation].

Even curial progressives such as Cardinal Roger Etchegaray were opposed to official follow-up activities modeled on Assisi I, so John Paul gave responsibility for the project's continuation to the Sant'Egidio Community. [Author's interview with Msgr. Vincenzo Paglia, December 7, 1997.]

51. John Paul II, **Crossing the Threshold of Hope,** pp. 92–93 [emphases in original].

52. For an overview of the range of issues John Paul II engaged in these fields, see **Live the Truth: The Moral Legacy of John Paul II in Catholic Health Care,** ed. Edward J. Furton (Philadelphia: National Catholic Bioethics Center, 2006).

53. These charges were frequently leveled before the 1994 Cairo International Conference on Population and Development; see Weigel, **Witness to Hope,** pp. 718–19.

54. That the developing human being in the womb was, in fact, a human being was scientifically indisputable, as many leading embryology texts made clear. See, for example, Keith L. Moore and T. V. N. Persaud, **The Developing Human,** 7th ed. (New York: W. B. Saunders, 2003), p. 16.

55. John Paul II, **Evangelium Vitae,** 20 [emphases in original].

56. See ibid., 18–19.

57. See ibid., 28.

58. See Leon Kass, "L'Chaim and Its Limits: Why Not Immortality?" **First Things** (May 2001).

59. On this point, see Avery Cardinal Dulles, S.J.,

"Can Philosophy Be Christian? The New State of the Question," in Dulles, **Church and Society,** pp. 291–305.

60. Avery Cardinal Dulles, S.J., "The Rebirth of Apologetics," in ibid., p. 430.

61. Dulles, "Can Philosophy Be Christian?" p. 296.

62. For a fuller treatment of **Veritatis Splendor** and the reactions to it, see Weigel, **Witness to Hope,** pp. 686–95, and notes.

63. On this point, see Servais Pinckaers, O.P., **The Sources of Christian Ethics,** trans. from the 3rd ed. by Sr. Mary Thomas Noble, O.P. (Washington, DC: Catholic University of America Press, 1995).

64. For a brief synopsis of the Theology of the Body, see ibid., pp. 333–43. For a reliable and scholarly one-volume translation with extensive notes and an informative introduction, see John Paul II, **Man and Woman He Created Them: A Theology of the Body,** trans. and ed. Michael Waldstein (Boston: Pauline Books and Media, 2006).

65. On John Paul II's feminism, see Weigel, **Witness to Hope,** pp. 578–81; on the controversy over the possibility of ordaining women to the ministerial priesthood, see ibid., 727–34.

66. John Paul II, "Annual Address to the Roman Curia," **L'Osservatore Romano** [English Weekly Edition], January 11, 1988, pp. 6–8. See also Hans Urs von Balthasar, **The Office of Peter and the Structure of the Church** (San Francisco: Ignatius Press, 1986); and two essays by Avery Cardinal Dulles, S.J., "Priesthood and Gender" and "Mary at the Dawn of the New Millennium," in Dulles, **Church and Society.**

67. John Paul II, **Spes Aedificandi** (Apostolic Letter Issued **Motu Proprio** Proclaiming Saint Bridget of Sweden, Saint Catherine of Siena, and Saint Teresa Benedicta of the Cross Co-Patronesses of Europe).

68. Cited in Avery Cardinal Dulles, S.J., "University Theology as a Service to the Church," in Dulles, **Church and Society,** p. 11.

69. On these points, and for the relevant citations, see Avery Cardinal Dulles, S.J., "John Paul II and the Mystery of the Human Person," in Dulles, **Church and Society,** pp. 414–29.

70. The American cardinal's summary judgment of John Paul II's distinctive Christian personalism and his attempt to read the corpus of Christian doctrine through that prism is worth a reflection:

> Personalism has its clearest application in the realm of privacy and one-to-one relations. It is crucial in individual self-realization and in marriage and family life—themes on which John Paul II [wrote] luminously. More remarkably, he . . . found ways of extending personalism to deal with political and economic issues, drawing on his conceptions of human action, personal participation, and free initiative. Although personalism cannot be an adequate tool for handling the larger issues of law and order, war and peace, John Paul II . . . injected important new considerations into the fields of business, jurisprudence, political science, and international relations.
> Theologically, likewise, the Pope [was]

a personalist. He [wrote] movingly of the desire for God inscribed in the human heart. He [dwelt] joyfully on the one-to-one relation between the individual and Jesus Christ, mediated through the Scriptures, the sacraments, and the Church. His concentration on God's amazing love and mercy [was] a welcome antidote to pessimistic preachers who have portrayed God as a demanding master and a rigorous judge. But, as John Paul . . . surely [recognized], God's love cannot be played off against his justice. The Pope [knew] well that the love of God cannot exist without his call to obedience to God's commandments and that persons who reject God's love must reckon with his justice. [Ibid., p. 427.]

On John Paul II's personalism and questions of jurisprudence, see George Weigel, "John Paul II and the Law: Some Preliminary Reflections," **Ave Maria Law Review** 5:2 (2007), pp. 361–66, and the articles following.

71. Ibid.

John Paul II's successor as pope, Joseph Ratzinger, once offered an interesting reflection on Karol Wojtyła's intellectual method in a conversation with the author:

The principal theme of the Holy Father, when he was professor and also when he was pope, has been anthropology.

In the confrontation with Marxism the main problem was not so much physics—demonstrating God from physics, or from the natural sciences—the real problem was the problem of man: the human being. Because the question really is [the question of] our vocation: what are we to do to build history? The problem of Marxism did not come from natural sciences but from an anthropological/historical vision of what man is, and how man will be redeemed. [How one thinks about] the philosophy of history also [determines one's] philosophy of redemption. With a materialistic idea of history, liberation . . . will be realized in a natural redemption of human beings, once oppressed by economic powers, but [now] freed by a correct understanding and application of the mechanisms of history.

The Holy Father had seen [that] the [real] problem, consequently, is "What is man and how does he function in history? What is the Christian answer about human existence?" [And he believed that] the Christian vision of history was a better response than that given by Marxism. But even before the Marxist reality after the war, his study of philosophy was always centered on and guided by this anthropological interest. [And] it is clear that in his vision of man and history—and the parallel of man and history—the question of God is the decisive question. For liberal thinking, in a quite different way from Marxism, development as such is governing history and is decisive for man. For the Holy Father, the absence of God is decisive, and the only true anthropology is the anthropology of God and man.

And so Christology is the center of his anthropology. But I would underline that this is not a positivistic Christology, [the kind of] theological positivism . . . we have in so many theologians. Rather, Christology finds its centrality [against] the background of the philosophical question "What is man?" The Holy Father's open personal dialogue with all his friends (beginning in the war and continuing when he was a priest) was perhaps the personal background of his philosophical and theological thinking. He is a person very interested in his own existence—who am I, myself?—but [also] a person substantially interested in all human beings, in man. It was for him a very priestly vocation to help persons to be [truly] human. . . . His personal charism, his love for man, implies his philosophical interest. The philosophical interest in him is not purely academic or intellectual. His philosophical work is a concretization of his personal charism as priest, his personal passion for human beings. He simply likes dialogue, he likes young people: but all of this is a passion for man. So his philosophical reflection is a necessary consequence of what he is in his deepest heart.

His study of mystics was a study of man, a study of human existence. And human existence in St. John of the Cross can be understood as a theological reality in the [human] openness to God.

For me, his first encyclical, **Redemptor Hominis,** is really a synthesis of his thinking. Here we can meet this passion for anthropology as not [merely] intellectual, but as a total passion for man—and also the perfect identification between philosophical and rational interests [on the one hand] with faith and the work of a priest and of a theologian [on the other]. This is a key text for understanding the Holy Father as a spiritual and intellectual figure. But [the] spirituality and intellectuality are [really] one thing, as in John of the Cross mystical contemplation and anthropological/philosophical reflection are not two things but essentially one thing.

After his study of the New Scholasticism, it was interesting for him to find the phenomenological philosophy of the Twenties. Because here, even if he is in a critical distance from Scheler, he found the possibility of a synthesis between metaphysics and anthropology and between phenomenology (what is appearing) and a metaphysical concept of man. Also this synthesis of anthropology as metaphysical anthropology [coupled with] the phenomenological taking account of what is really the concrete realization of human existence is very significant for him.

We could say that all this is more concretely developed in his different teachings. It was perhaps not foreseen, but what finally [happened] is that **Redemptor Hominis** became the first part of a Trinitarian presentation. And even if that was not his first intention in writing **Redemptor Hominis,** it was a natural development. To [move] to a Trinitarian vision of God, history, and man is an expression of his way of thinking: beginning with anthropology and searching for an answer to what is human existence, he comes to God—to the Trinitarian God of love (in **Dives in Misericordia** and **Dominum et Vivificantem**)—and returns from this to man, because his Trinitarian vision is not purely speculative but makes us understand how God is God-in-history. In the deepest mystery of the Trinitarian existence, we are also [encountering] the concrete possibilities that God, who is himself relation and dialogue, can create history, can be present in history. [Author's interview with Cardinal Joseph Ratzinger, September 12, 1996.]

72. Cardinal Winning made his remarks at the conclusion of the author's lecture on the achievement of Pope John Paul II, St. Andrew's Cathedral, Glasgow, March 9, 2001.

73. Author's interview with Cardinal John J. O'Connor, November 8, 1996.

74. Author's interview with Massimo D'Alema, December 10, 1997.

75. E-mail to the author from Francis J. Beckwith, January 8, 2009. See also Francis J. Beckwith, "Vatican Bible School: What John Paul II Can Teach Evangelicals," **Touchstone,** June 2005 (also available at http://www.touchstonemag.com/archives/article.php?id=18-05-019v).

76. Author's interview with Nina Sophie Heereman, November 21, 2008. See also Nina Heereman, "We Loved Him!" **Inside the Vatican,** August–September 2005.

77. Letter to the author from Sister Mary Karol Widomska, O.P.

78. "Father Finest," **New York Post,** November 13, 2008, cited in **catholic eye** 274 (November 25, 2008), p. 4.

79. E-mail to the author from Cary Elwes, September 7, 2009; "Loren Wants Pope John Paul II Beatified: Report," Agence France Presse, April 1, 2009.

80. Author's interview with Joaquín Navarro-Valls, December 16, 1998.

81. On this point, see Avery Cardinal Dulles, S.J., "John Paul II and the New Evangelization," in Dulles, **Church and Society,** pp. 87–90.

82. John Paul II created Father Congar a cardinal in 1994, the year before the French theologian's death.

83. On the Küng affair, see Weigel, **Witness to Hope,** pp. 356–57.

84. While international in scope, this interpretation of

the Council received its most extensive scholarly treatment from the "Bologna School" of Catholic historians; its principal work was the five-volume study **History of Vatican II,** eds. Giuseppe Alberigo and Joseph A. Komonchak (Maryknoll, NY: Orbis Books, 1995–2006).

See also Sandro Magister, "The Council of Bologna: The Rise and Fall of a Dream of Church Reform," available at http://chiesa.espresso.repubblica.it/articolo.38108?eng=y.

85. For an American example, see John R. Quinn, "Considering the Papacy," **Origins** 26 (July 18, 1996), pp. 119–27. A more politically deft, but essentially similar, critique came from Cardinal Joseph Bernardin, in his essay launching the Catholic Common Ground Project; see "Called to Be Catholic: Church in a Time of Peril," **Origins** 26 (August 29, 1996), pp. 165–70. For a critique of the Quinn and Bernardin critiques, see Avery Cardinal Dulles, S.J., "The Travails of Dialogue," in Dulles, **Church and Society,** pp. 221–33.

86. On John Paul II's handling of the Lefebvrists and the schism that resulted from Archbishop Lefebvre's defiance of the Pope, see Weigel, **Witness to Hope,** pp. 562–64. The Lefebvrist schism would continue to bedevil Pope Benedict XVI, who, as Cardinal Joseph Ratzinger, was John Paul's principal agent in attempting to reconcile to the teaching of Vatican II the ultimately unreconcilable French prelate. The key issue in all this, it should be stressed, was not the Council's liturgical reforms (which the Lefebvrists intensely disliked) but the Council's teaching on religious freedom (which many Lefebvrists, including Marcel Lefebvre himself, regarded as inauthentically Catholic).

87. For a more complete discussion of both the progressive and restorationist critiques of the first twenty years of the pontificate of John Paul II, see Weigel, **Witness to Hope,** pp. 850–58.

88. On this point, see Hans Urs von Balthasar, **In the Fullness of Faith: On the Centrality of the Distinctively Catholic** (San Francisco: Ignatius Press, 1988), p. 105.

89. Author's interview with Archbishop Jean-Louis Tauran, November 14, 1997.

90. Author's interview with Archbishop Jean-Louis Tauran, March 18, 1997; author's interview with Cardinal Antonio María Rouco Varela, October 20, 2001.

91. The roots of German skepticism about John Paul II, including its ethnic dimension, were analyzed for the author by two German-speaking prelates, Cardinal Walter Kasper (in an interview on February 19, 2002) and Cardinal Joachim Meisner (in an interview on October 17, 2001).

92. Author's interview with Cardinal Walter Kasper, February 19, 2002.

93. Perhaps the most dramatic instance of this rejection came in the wake of **Veritatis Splendor.** See the essay by Josef Fuchs, S.J., in **Understanding "Veritatis Splendor,"** ed. John Wilkins (London: SPCK, 1994); and the essays in **Moraltheologie im Abseits? Antwort auf die Enzyklika "Veritatis Splendor,"** ed. Dieter Mieth (Freiburg/Basel/Vienna: Herder, 1994). See also the author's introduction to **Zeuge der Hofnung: Johannes Paul II—Eine Biographie** (Paderborn: Ferdinand Schöningh, 2002), pp. xiii–xx.

94. Author's interview with Cardinal Joachim Meisner, October 17, 2001.

95. Author's interview with Cardinal Karl Lehmann, October 24, 2001.

96. Whether this new approach would long survive the retirement of Cardinal Camillo Ruini as Vicar of Rome and president of the Italian Bishops Conference [CEI] was an open question, five years after the John Paul II's death. Ruini was John Paul's indispensable deputy for Italian affairs, and created the **Progetto culturale** [Cultural Project] at the CEI as a means for engaging the wider Italian society and culture with the truths of reason and faith. The **Progetto culturale** (with Ruini as its head) remained in place after Ruini's retirement from the Vicariate of Rome and the presidency of the CEI in 2008, and with the support of Benedict XVI. But other forces in Italian Catholic life, including those more comfortable with the pre–John Paul II/pre-Ruini status quo, were asserting themselves in late 2009. See Sandro Magister, "Make or Break: The Italian Bishops at the Final Tally," at http://chiesa.espresso.repubblica.it/articolo/1340096?eng=y.

97. Author's interview with Cardinal Antonio María Rouco Varela, October 20, 2001.

98. Author's interview with Cardinal Jean-Marie Lustiger, October 24, 1996.

99. The story of Lustiger's appointment, arguably the boldest of John Paul II's pontificate, is told in Weigel, **Witness to Hope,** pp. 388–90.

100. Author's interview with Cardinal Cormac Murphy-O'Connor, March 8, 2001.

101. The revelations of clergy sexual abuse in Ireland

were seized upon by the Irish media as evidence for their charge that the Catholic Church had long been awash in hypocrisy in its teaching on sexual morality.

102. See Tess Livingstone, **George Pell: Defender of the Faith Down Under** (San Francisco: Ignatius Press, 2005).

103. On this point, see Amy L. Sherman, **The Soul of Development: Biblical Christianity and Economic Transformation in Guatemala** (New York: Oxford University Press, 1997).

104. On this point, see Richard John Neuhaus, **Appointment in Rome: The Church in America Awakening** (New York: Crossroad, 1999), pp. 123–26.

105. Author's interview with Cardinal Camillo Ruini, March 17, 2008.

106. Author's interview with Archbishop Michael Fitzgerald, M.Afr., April 9, 2002.

107. On this point, see George Weigel, Tranquillitas Ordinis: **The Present Failure and Future Promise of American Catholic Thought on War and Peace** (New York: Oxford University Press, 1987), "Part One: The Heritage."

108. For a review of the centuries-long development of classic Catholic International Relations Theory, see John Eppstein, **The Catholic Tradition of the Law of Nations** (Washington, DC: Carnegie Endowment for International Peace, 1935).

109. On the default positions in the "foreign ministry" of the Secretariat of State, see George Weigel, "Thinking World Politics—a Catholic Optic," in Weigel, **Against the Grain: Christianity and Democracy, War and Peace,** pp. 176–99.

110. On John Paul II's intervention during the Beagle Channel crisis of 1978–79, see Weigel, **Witness to Hope,** pp. 272–73, 378.

111. The Italian philosopher and politician Rocco Buttiglione was a longtime interlocutor of John Paul II, and remembered that, in 1990–91, the Pope had asked in private conversation about the applicability of the lessons of "1989" to the Iraqi invasion and occupation of Kuwait. Was Saddam Hussein more powerful than communism? the Pope wondered. [Author's conversation with Rocco Buttiglione, October 31, 2008.] One reply might have been that Saddam wasn't more powerful, in military terms or in his capacity to wreak havoc in the world; but he was more irrational, and more ruthless, than the communist leaders who eventually gave way in 1989. Saddam Hussein's ruthlessness and taste for mass murder far more resembled Stalin's than any communist leader with whom the forces of freedom in "1989" had to contend.

112. In 1992, for example, John Paul had proposed a "duty" of "humanitarian intervention" in cases of actual or impending genocide in an address to the UN's Food and Agricultural Organization in Rome—a not unimportant subject on the world's agenda, as the collapse of Yugoslavia and the torment of Rwanda would soon demonstrate. Yet the address said nothing about on whom this duty fell or about how it was to be met; little or nothing was done during the pontificate, in either the Vatican "foreign ministry" or the Pontifical Council for Justice and Peace, to flesh out the Pope's idea and engage the world's leaders in a serious examination of an urgent problem.

113. Author's conversation with Jean Kitschel, Joyce Little, and Mary Catherine Sommers, September 18, 1998.

114. See Weigel, **Witness to Hope,** pp. 473–74.

115. As a young priest, Piero Marini had been deeply involved in the implementation of Vatican II's Constitution on the Sacred Liturgy led by the Italian liturgist Annibale Bugnini. Marini described some of that work in **A Challenging Reform: Realizing the Vision of the Liturgical Renewal 1963–1975** (Collegeville, MN: Liturgical Press, 2007), which made clear that Marini understood the Council as having mandated a rather dramatic break in the development of the Roman rite— a position sharply criticized by, among others, Cardinal Joseph Ratzinger in **The Spirit of the Liturgy** (San Francisco: Ignatius Press, 2000).

116. On this point, see Ratzinger, **The Spirit of the Liturgy,** pp. 22–23.

On becoming pope, Benedict XVI quickly discovered, at the Synod of October 2005, that many bishops were reluctant to engage in the reform of the liturgy of which Joseph Ratzinger had long been a principal theological protagonist.

117. The Pope tried to accelerate the reform of English-language liturgical translations through the creation in 2002 of the Vox Clara Committee, which worked under the aegis of the Congregation for Divine Worship and the Discipline of the Sacraments. See John L. Allen, Jr., "'Vox Clara' Commission to Monitor English Translations; Vatican Congregation Creates Body to Clear Logjam in Review of Liturgical Texts," **National Catholic Reporter,** April 5, 2002.

118. During the final phases of debate over Vatican II's Dogmatic Constitution on the Church, Pope Paul VI proposed that the document include the affirmation that the pope is "accountable to the Lord alone." This formulation was rejected by the Council's Theological Commission, which pointed out that "the Roman Pontiff is also bound to revelation itself, to the fundamental structure of the Church, to the sacraments, to the definitions of earlier Councils, and other obligations too numerous to mention." [Cited in Patrick Granfield, **The Limitations of the Papacy: Authority and Autonomy in the Church** (New York: Crossroad, 1987), pp. 62–63. See also the discussion in Weigel, **Witness to Hope,** pp. 263–64.

119. Gasparri negotiated the 1929 Lateran Treaty that created Vatican City State; Pacelli had a major role in writing Pius XI's 1937 denunciation of Nazism, **Mit Brennender Sorge** [With Burning Concern]; von Nell-Breuning drafted Pius's 1931 social encyclical, **Quadragesimo Anno,** which cemented the principle of subsidiarity into the foundations of modern Catholic social doctrine; LaFarge, at the Pope's request, drafted an encyclical condemning racism and affirming the unity of the human race, which was left unfinished and unpublished at Pius XI's death in early 1939.

120. This point was made by, among others, Thomas J. Reese, S.J., in **Inside the Vatican** (Cambridge, MA: Harvard University Press, 1996), pp. 192–201.

121. See Hans Küng, **Infallible? An Unresolved Enquiry,** new expanded edition (New York: Continuum, 1994). See also Küng, **My Struggle for Freedom: Memoirs** (Grand Rapids, MI: William B. Eerdmans Publish-

ing Co., 2003); in his memoirs, Küng set a new low in false and tasteless criticism of Karol Wojtyła, suggesting that the future pope had attended the Angelicum in 1946–48 because he was not sufficiently well-informed theologically to be admitted to the Pontifical Gregorian University.

122. See Charles E. Curran, **Loyal Dissent: Memoir of a Catholic Theologian** (Washington, DC: Georgetown University Press, 2006).

123. "Theological Disputes—The List," **National Catholic Reporter,** February 25, 2005. See also http://natcath.org/NCR_Online/archives2/2005a/022505/022505h.php.

124. For more on this set of problems, see Weigel, **The Courage To Be Catholic,** pp. 202–9.

125. Cardinal Avery Dulles, S.J., one of the most astute students of John Paul's teaching and pastoral accomplishment, shared these concerns; his specific question, in a 2003 essay, addressed the American situation, but clearly touched on an issue of concern throughout the world Church:

> According to the job description in the official directories, the bishop ought to be a man of high culture, firm in faith, solid in orthodoxy, a paragon of holiness, graciously winning in personality, able to assess the talents and weaknesses of others, skilled at managing large corporations and conducting fiscal policy, eloquent in the pulpit, fearless under criticism, indefatigable, and always self-possessed. Do we have in the United States a sufficient supply of

priests with all these qualities? Many of the candidates being elevated to the episcopate, it would seem, are men of ordinary abilities, kind and hardworking, but incapable of measuring up to the almost superhuman responsibilities of the office. They run the risk of being morally, psychologically, and spiritually crushed under the burdens. As a prime structural problem, therefore, I would single out for special attention [in considering true and false reform in the Church] the episcopal office. What can be done to restore the priestly and pastoral ministry of bishops to its position of primacy? [Dulles, "True and False Reform in the Church," in Dulles, **Church and Society,** p. 411.]

126. In addition to the articles by Archbishop John Quinn and Cardinal Joseph Bernardin cited at note 85 above, see Rembert G. Weakland, O.S.B., **A Pilgrim in a Pilgrim Church: Memoirs of a Catholic Archbishop** (Grand Rapids, MI: William B. Eerdmans Publishing Co., 2009).

127. Author's interview with Cardinal Jan Schotte, C.I.C.M., March 14, 1997.

128. Author's conversation with Cardinal Francis E. George, O.M.I., October 20, 2001.

According to another authoritative source, a Francophone discussion group during the 2001 Synod spent most of its time debating whether John Paul II should resign, rather than considering the topic at hand—the bishop's ministry in the twenty-first-century Church.

129. The papal intervention and its immediate after-math are described in Weigel, **Witness to Hope,** pp. 425–30, 468–70.

130. For an overview of the Jesuit situation in the last years of the pontificate, see Paul Shaughnessy, S.J., "Are the Jesuits Catholic?" **Weekly Standard,** June 3, 2002. Shaughnessy's article is a review of Peter McDonough and Eugene C. Bianchi's **Passionate Uncertainty: Inside the American Jesuits** (Berkeley: University of California Press, 2002). Shaughnessy cites the McDonough and Bianchi book to illustrate not untypical U.S. Jesuit attitudes toward John Paul II:

> One of the signal services of **Passionate Uncertainty** is that it lets us hear influential Jesuits—those who shape policy—speak their minds frankly, in words unsoftened by the public relations personnel in their fund-raising offices. "I am appalled by the direction of the present papacy," says a university administrator. "I am scandalized by Rome's intransigent refusal to re-examine its doctrines regarding gender and sex. . . . Frankly, I think the Church is being governed by thugs." "The Church as we have known it is dying," a retreat master insists. "I hope and pray that the Society of Jesus will help facilitate the death and resurrection." An academic gloats, "The Society has not sold its soul to the 'Restoration' of John Paul II." Another Jesuit scholar, a Church historian, ranks John Paul II as "probably the worst pope of all times"—

adding, "He's not one of the worst popes; he's the worst. Don't misquote me." The respondents made it clear that their contempt for the Pope is based almost entirely on his . . . unwillingness to imitate their own adaptability in the matter of doctrine.

Shaughnessy goes on to note the deep tensions (to put it gently) at work here:

As do all priests, the speakers above took a solemn oath swearing that they "firmly embrace and accept and everything concerning the doctrine of faith and morals" proposed by the Church. It must not be assumed that they fail to see the discrepancy. Their willed imbecility derives not from a lack of brainpower or ingenuity but from a deliberate decision to ignore the clash of commitments and to suppress insurgent attempts to throw light on what, for tactical reasons, is better left in darkness.

For an exploration of the formation process that helped produce this situation, see Joseph M. Becker, S.J., **The Re-Formed Jesuits: A History of Changes in Jesuit Formation During the Decade 1965–1975,** 2 vols. (San Francisco: Ignatius Press, 1992, 1997).

John Paul II's decision to require Father Robert Drinan, S.J., to terminate his career in the U.S. Congress was one source of U.S. Jesuit animosity toward the Pope. The history of this affair is discussed by James Hitchcock in "The Strange Political Career of Father Drinan," **Catholic World Report,** July 1996.

131. This latter point was made at the 2007 assembly of the Leadership Conference of Women Religious, whose keynote speaker, Sister Laurie Brink, O.P., noted that some religious communities, in the course of their "sojourning," had "grown beyond the bounds of institutional religion. . . . Religious titles, institutional limitations, ecclesiastical authorities no longer fit [such a] congregation, which in most respects is post-Christian." Sister Laurie then went on to ask, "Who's to say that the movement beyond Christ is not, in reality, a movement into the very heart of God?" [Cited in Ann Carey, "Post-Christian Sisters," **Catholic World Report,** July 2009, p. 22. Carey's article offers a useful overview of the evolution of the LCWR and many of its affiliated congregations during the pontificate of John Paul II.]

132. See Carey, **Sisters in Crisis,** p. 62.

133. See ibid., for details. The formal name of what is often referred to as the "Congregation for Religious" is the Congregation for Institutes of Consecrated Life and Societies of Apostolic Life.

134. On this point, see George Weigel, "Sisters on a Different Mountaintop," **Denver Catholic Register,** April 1, 2009.

135. There were many reasons, not excluding pusillanimity, why most bishops in the United States preferred to keep the drama of American women's religious life at a distance. One serious reason was money: for while the communities represented in the LCWR were decreasing in numbers, becoming ever older while failing to attract new members, they also controlled considerable financial assets, which many bishops did not want to

see jeopardized in canonical and civil legal contests over who would eventually inherit what was clearly the patrimony of the Church.

A conspicuous exception to the general laissez-faire stance of the American episcopate toward communities of women religious was Cardinal James A. Hickey, archbishop of Washington, D.C., from 1980 until 2000, who played an important role in supporting the formation of the Council of Major Superiors of Women Religious and having it recognized by the Holy See.

136. Cited in Sandro Magister, "End of the Line for the Founder of the Legionaries of Christ," http://chiesa .espressonline.repubblica.it/articolo/58361?eng=y.

137. See Sandro Magister, "The Legion Is in Disarray. Betrayed by its Founder," http://chiesa.espressonline .repubblica.it/articolo/215098?eng=y.

138. On November 30, 2004, John Paul II greeted Maciel at an audience in the Vatican attended by thousands of Legionary priests, Legionary seminarians, and Regnum Christi members. Four days earlier, the Pope had given care of the Pontifical Institute of Notre Dame of Jerusalem to the Legionaries of Christ. Throughout the pontificate, Legionary seminarians were called to assist in papal liturgies, and it was widely believed that the Holy See had helped facilitate the construction of the Legion-run Pontifical Athenaeum Regina Apostolorum in Rome by working with Italian authorities to clear certain legal hurdles.

139. Author's interview with Father Marcial Maciel Degollado, L.C., February 19, 1998.

140. See Sandro Magister, "The Legionaries' Last Stand. An Exclusive Interview with Fr. Thomas Berg,"

http://chiesa.espressonline.repubblica.it/articolo/ 1339296?eng=y; see also George Weigel, "Saving What Can Be Saved," **First Things** Web edition, February 2, 2009.

Marcial Maciel frequently gave monetary gifts to prominent Catholic figures, and like many others (including visiting bishops and heads of Catholic organizations), he sometimes directed gifts of cash to the papal apartment. As John Paul II died with virtually no worldly goods, no plausible charge can be made that he personally benefited from Maciel's "generosity."

Falling prey to Maciel's deceptions constituted an objective failure in John Paul's governance of the Church. But this failure was neither willful (he knew something was awry and did nothing about it), nor venal (he was "bought"), nor malicious (he knew of Maciel's perfidies and didn't care), and thus does not call into question John Paul II's heroic virtue.

141. Hermann Josef Pottmeyer, "The Pope as Church Critic? John Paul II's Little Noticed Impulses Toward Church Reform" (trans. John Jay Hughes), **Pro Ecclesia** XTV:3 (Summer 2005), p. 286.

142. See de Lubac, **The Drama of Atheist Humanism,** p. 14.

143. Karol Wojtyła, **Sign of Contradiction** (New York: Seabury, 1979), p. 124.

BIBLIOGRAPHY

I. Works by Karol Wojtyła/Pope John Paul II

WORKS BY KAROL WOJTYŁA

The Acting Person. Dordrecht: D. Reidel Publishing Company, 1979.

The Collected Plays and Writings on Theater. Translated with introductions by Bolesław Taborski. Berkeley: University of California Press, 1987.

Discorsi al Popolo di Dio. Edited by Flavio Felice. Soveria Mannelli: Rubbettino Editore, 2006.

Faith According to St. John of the Cross. San Francisco: Ignatius Press, 1981.

I miei amici. Rome: CSEO biblioteca, 1979.

Love and Responsibility. San Francisco: Ignatius Press, 1993.

Metafisica della Persona: Tutte le opere filosofiche e saggi intergrativi. Edited by Giovanni Reale and Tadeusz Styczeń. Milan: Bompiani Il Pensiero Occidentale, 2003.

Osoba i czyn: oraz inne studia antropologiczne. Edited by Tadeusz Styczeń, Wojciech Chudy, Jerzy W. Gałkowski, Adam Rodziński, and Andrzej Szostek. Lublin: KUL Press, 1994.

Person and Community: Selected Essays. New York: Peter Lang, 1993.

Poezje i dramaty. Kraków: Znak, 1979; revised edition, 1998.

Poezje-: Poems. Translated by Jerzy Peterkiewicz. Kraków: Wydawnictwo Literackie, 1998.

Sign of Contradiction. New York: Seabury, 1979.

Sources of Renewal: The Implementation of Vatican II. San Francisco: Harper & Row, 1980.

The Way to Christ: Spiritual Exercises. New York: HarperCollins, 1994.

The Word Made Flesh: The Meaning of the Christmas Season. New York: HarperCollins, 1994.

Wykłady lubelskie. Edited by Tadeusz Styczeń, Jerzy W. Gałkowski, Adam Rodziński, and Andrzej Szostek. Lublin: KUL Press, 1986.

Zagadnienie podmiotu moralności. Edited by Tadeusz Styczeń, Jerzy W. Gałkowski, Adam Rodziński, and Andrzej Szostek. Lublin: KUL Press, 1991.

WORKS BY POPE JOHN PAUL II

Ad Limina **Addresses: The Addresses of His Holiness Pope John Paul II to the Bishops of the United States During Their** Ad Limina **Visits, March 5–December 9, 1988.** Washington, DC: United States Catholic Conference, 1989.

The Church: Mystery, Sacrament, Community. Boston: Pauline Books and Media, 1998.

Crossing the Threshold of Hope. New York: Alfred A. Knopf, 1994.

Curriculum Philosophicum [unpublished autobiographical memorandum provided to the author].

The Encyclicals of John Paul II. Edited with introductions by J. Michael Miller, C.S.B. Huntington, IN: Our Sunday Visitor Publishing Division, 2001.

Gift and Mystery: On the Fiftieth Anniversary of My Priestly Ordination. New York: Doubleday, 1996.

God, Father and Creator. Boston: Pauline Books and Media, 1996.

The Holy See at the Service of Peace: Pope John Paul II Addresses to the Diplomatic Corps (1978–1988). Vatican City: Pontifical Council for Justice and Peace, 1988.

Insegnamenti di Giovanni Paolo II. 56 vols. Vatican City: Libreria Editrice Vaticana, 1978–2005.

Jesus, Son and Savior. Boston: Pauline Books and Media, 1996.

John Paul II for Peace in the Middle East. Vatican City: Libreria Editrice Vaticana, 1991.

John Paul II Speaks to Youth at World Youth Day. San Francisco/Washington, DC: Ignatius Press/Catholic News Service, 1993.

Letters to My Brother Priests: Holy Thursday (1979–1994). Edited by James P. Socias. Princeton, NJ/Chicago: Scepter Publishers/Midwest Theological Forum, 1994.

Man and Woman He Created Them: A Theology of the Body. Translated with an introduction and index by Michael Waldstein. Boston: Pauline Books and Media, 2006.

Memory and Identity: Personal Reflections. London: Weidenfeld and Nicolson, 2005.

Le Mie Preghiere. Rome: Grandi Tascabili Economici Newton, 1995.

The Post-Synodal Apostolic Exhortations of John Paul II. Edited with introductions by J. Michael Miller, C.S.B. Huntington, IN: Our Sunday Visitor Publishing Division, 1998.

Prayers and Devotions. Edited by Peter Canisius Johannes Van Lierde. New York: Viking, 1994.

Priesthood in the Third Millennium: Addresses of Pope John Paul II, 1993. Princeton, NJ/Chicago: Scepter Publishers/Midwest Theological Forum, 1994.

Rise, Let Us Be on Our Way! New York: Warner Books, 2004.

Roman Triptych: Meditations. Washington, DC: USCCB Publishing, 2003.

The Spirit, Giver of Life and Love. Boston: Pauline Books and Media, 1996.

Spiritual Pilgrimage: Texts on Jews and Judaism 1979–1995. Edited by Eugene J. Fisher and Leon Klenicki. New York: Crossroad, 1995.

Theotókos: Woman, Mother, Disciple. Boston: Pauline Books and Media, 2000.

DOCUMENTS OF THE PAPAL MAGISTERIUM

Encyclicals
Redemptor Hominis (1979).
Dives in Misericordia (1980).
Laborem Exercens (1981).
Slavorum Apostoli (1985).
Dominum et Vivificantem (1986).
Redemptoris Mater (1987).
Sollicitudo Rei Socialis (1987).

Redemptoris Missio (1990).
Centesimus Annus (1991).
Veritatis Splendor (1993).
Evangelium Vitae (1995).
Ut Unum Sint (1995).
Fides et Ratio (1998).
Ecclesia de Eucharistia (2003).

Post-Synodal Apostolic Exhortations
Catechesi Tradendae (1979).
Familiaris Consortio (1981).
Reconciliatio et Paenitentia (1984).
Christifideles Laici (1988).
Pastores Dabo Vobis (1992).
Ecclesia in Africa (1995).
Vita Consecrata (1996).
Ecclesia in America (1999).
Ecclesia in Asia (1999).
Ecclesia in Oceania (2001).
Ecclesia in Europa (2003).
Pastores Gregis (2003).

Apostolic Constitutions
Sapientia Christiana (1979).
Sacrae Disciplinae Leges (1983).
Divinus Perfectionis Magister (1983).
Pastor Bonus (1988).
Ex Corde Ecclesiae (1990).
Sacri Canones (1990).
Fidei Depositum (1992).
Universi Dominici Gregis (1996).

Apostolic Letters
Dominicae Cenae (1980).
Egregiae Virtutis (1980).
Salvifici Doloris (1984).
Redemptionis Anno (1984).
To the Youth of the World (1985).
Euntes in Mundum (1988).
Ecclesia Dei (1988).
Mulieris Dignitatem (1988).
On the Fiftieth Anniversary of the Beginning of the Second World War (1989).
Ordinatio Sacerdotalis (1994).
Tertio Millennio Adveniente (1994).
Orientale Lumen (1995).
For the Fourth Centenary of the Union of Brest (1995).
Ad Tuendam Fidem (1998).
Dies Domini (1998).
Apostolos Suos (1998).
Mysterium Incarnationis (1998).
Spes Aedificandi (1999).
E Sancti Thomae Mori (2000).
Novo Millennio Ineunte (2001).
Rosarium Virginis Mariae (2002).
Mane Nobiscum Domine (2004).

Letters and Messages
For the Sixth Centenary of the Death of St. Catherine of Siena (1980).
To Leonid Brezhnev (1980).
For the Fifth Centenary of the Birth of Martin Luther (1983).

To Mikhail Gorbachev (1988).

To George Bush and Saddam Hussein (1991).

Letter to Families (1994).

Letter to Children (1994).

Letter to Women (1995).

Letter to Artists (1999).

Letter to the Elderly (1999).

II. Studies of Karol Wojtyła/Pope John Paul II

Accatoli, Luigi. **When a Pope Asks Forgiveness: The Mea Culpa's of John Paul II.** Boston: Pauline Books and Media, 1998.

Beigel, Gerard. **Faith and Social Justice in the Teaching of Pope John Paul II.** New York: Peter Lang, 1997.

Bernstein, Carl, and Marco Politi. **His Holiness: John Paul II and the Hidden History of Our Time.** New York: Doubleday, 1996.

Biffi, Franco. **The "Social Gospel" of Pope John Paul II: A Guide to the Encyclicals on Human Work and the Authentic Development of Peoples.** Rome: Pontifical Lateran University, 1989.

Blazynski, George. **Pope John Paul II: A Man from Kraków.** London: Sphere, 1979.

Boniecki, Adam, M.I.C. **The Making of the Pope of the Millennium: Kalendarium of the Life of Karol Wojtyła.** Stockbridge, MA: Marian Press, 2000.

Bujak, Adam, and Michał Rożek. **Wojtyła.** Wrocław: Wydawnictwo Dolnośląskie, 1997.

Buttiglione, Rocco. **Karol Wojtyła: The Thought of the Man Who Became Pope John Paul II.** Grand Rapids, MI: Eerdmans, 1997.

Coyne, George, S.J., Robert John Russell, and William

R. Stoeger, S.J., eds. **John Paul II on Science and Religion: Reflections on the New View from Rome.** Rome: Vatican Observatory Publications, 1990.

Craig, Mary. **Man from a Far Country: A Portrait of Pope John Paul II.** London: Hodder and Stoughton, 1979.

Dulles, Avery, S.J. **The Splendor of Faith: The Theological Vision of Pope John Paul II.** New York: Crossroad, 1999.

Filipiak, Maria, and Andrzej Szostek, M.I.C., eds. **Obecność: Karol Wojtyła w Katolickim Uniwersytecie Lubelskim.** Lublin: Redakcja Wydawnictwo KUL, 1989.

Frossard, André, and Pope John Paul II. **Be Not Afraid!** New York: St. Martin's Press, 1984.

Henze, Paul B. **The Plot to Kill the Pope.** New York: Charles Scribner's Sons, 1983; revised paperback edition with a new postscript, 1985.

Hitchcock, James. **The Pope and the Jesuits: John Paul II and the New Order in the Society of Jesus.** New York: National Committee of Catholic Laymen, 1984.

Hütter, Reinhard, and Theodor Dieter, eds. **Ecumenical Ventures in Ethics: Protestants Engage Pope John Paul II's Moral Encyclicals.** Grand Rapids, MI: Eerdmans, 1998.

Jan Paweł II: Dzień Po Dniu—Ilustrowane Kalendarium Wielkiego Pontyfikatu 1978–2005. 2 vols. Kraków: Biały Kruk, 2005.

John Paul the Great: Maker of the Post-Conciliar Church. Edited by William Oddie. San Francisco: Ignatius Press, 2005.

Karol Wojtyła 1952–1954: Wiara, Droga, Przyjaźń. Bielsko-Biała: Animamedia, 2006.

Kupczak, Jarosław, O.P. **Destined for Liberty: The Human Person in the Philosophy of Karol Wojtyła/John Paul II.** Washington, DC: Catholic University of America Press, 2000.

Kwitny, Jonathan. **Man of the Century: The Life and Times of Pope John Paul II.** New York: Henry Holt, 1997.

Lasota, Marek. **Donos na Wojtyłę: Karol Wojtyła w teczkach bezpieki.** Kraków: Wydawnictwo Znak, 2006.

Lawler, Ronald D., O.F.M. Cap. **The Christian Personalism of John Paul II.** Chicago: Franciscan Herald Press, 1982.

Mary: God's Yes to Man, John Paul's Encyclical Redemptoris Mater. Introduction by Cardinal Joseph Ratzinger, commentary by Hans Urs von Balthasar. San Francisco: Ignatius Press, 1988.

McDermott, John M., S.J., ed. **The Thought of Pope John Paul II.** Rome: Editrice Pontificia Università Gregoriana, 1993.

Il mondo di Giovanni Paolo II: tutti i viaggi internazionale del Papa, 1978–1996. Milan: Mondadori, 1996.

Parker, Michael. **Priest of the World's Destiny: John Paul II.** Milford, OH: Faith Publishing Co., 1995.

Pontifical Council for the Laity. **Il Papa e i Movimenti.** Milano: Edizioni San Paolo, 1998.

Poynter Institute. **Pope John Paul II, May 18, 1920–April 2, 2005—A Collection of Newspaper Front Pages.** Kansas City, MO: Andrews McMeel Publishing, 2005.

Ratzinger, Joseph. **The Legacy of John Paul II: Images and Memories.** San Francisco: Ignatius Press, 2005.

———. **John Paul II: My Beloved Predecessor.** Boston: Pauline Books and Media, 2007.

Rok 27: W Drodze do Domu Ojca—Fotokronika. Kraków: Biały Kruk, 2005.

Ruini, Camillo. **Alla Sequela di Cristo: Giovanni Paolo II, il Servo dei Servi di Dio.** Siena: Edizione Cantagalli, 2007.

Savage, Deborah. **The Subjective Dimension of Human Work: The Conversion of the Acting Person According to Karol Wojtyła/John Paul II and Bernard Lonergan.** New York: Peter Lang, 2008.

Schall, James V., S.J. **The Church, the State and Society in the Thought of John Paul II.** Chicago: Franciscan Herald Press, 1982.

Schmitz, Kenneth L. **At the Center of the Human Drama: The Philosophical Anthropology of Karol Wojtyła/Pope John Paul II.** Washington, DC: CUA Press, 1993.

Smith, Timothy L., ed. **Faith and Reason.** South Bend, IN: St. Augustine's Press, 2001.

Sterling, Claire. **The Time of the Assassins: Anatomy of an Investigation.** New York: Holt, Rinehart, and Winston, 1983.

Szulc, Tad. **Pope John Paul II: The Biography.** New York: Scribner, 1995.

Weigel, George. **Witness to Hope: The Biography of Pope John Paul II.** New York: HarperCollins, 1999.

———. **The Cube and the Cathedral: Europe, America, and Politics Without God.** New York: Basic Books, 2005.

Wierzbianski, Bolesław, ed. **The Shepherd for All People.** New York: Bicentennial Publishing Corporation, 1993.

Wildes, Kevin, S.J., and Alan C. Mitchell, eds. **Choosing Life: A Dialogue on** Evangelium Vitae. Washington, DC: Georgetown University Press, 1997.

Williams, George Huntston. **The Mind of John Paul II: Origins of His Thought and Action.** New York: Seabury, 1981.

Zapis drogi: Wspomnienia "Środowiska" o nieznanym duszpasterstwie księdza Karola Wojtyły. Kraków: Wydawnictwo św. Stanisława, 2005.

Zięba, Maciej, O.P. **The Surprising Pope: Understanding the Thought of John Paul II.** Translated by Karolina Weening. Lanham, MD: Lexington Books, 2000.

III. Other Church Documents

THE SECOND VATICAN COUNCIL

Sacrosanctum Concilium [Constitution on the Sacred Liturgy, 1963].

Lumen Gentium [Dogmatic Constitution on the Church, 1964].

Orientalium Ecclesiarum [Decree on the Eastern Catholic Churches, 1964].

Unitatis Redintegratio [Decree on Ecumenism, 1964].

Christus Dominus [Decree on the Pastoral Office of Bishops in the Church, 1965].

Nostra Aetate [Declaration on the Relation of the Church to Non-Christian Religions, 1965].

Dei Verbum [Dogmatic Constitution on Divine Revelation, 1965].

Dignitatis Humanae [Declaration on Religious Freedom, 1965].

Gaudium et Spes [Pastoral Constitution on the Church in the Modern World, 1965].

CODES OF CANON LAW

Code of Canon Law Annotated. 2nd ed., revised and updated of the 6th Spanish language edition. Woodridge, IL: Midwest Theological Forum, 2004.

Code of Canons of the Eastern Catholic Churches. Washington, DC: Canon Law Society of America, 1996.

SYNODAL AND CONGREGATIONAL DOCUMENTS

Instruction on Certain Aspects of the "Theology of Liberation." Congregation for the Doctrine of the Faith, 1984.

Notes on the Correct Way to Present the Jews and Judaism in Preaching and Catechesis in the Roman Catholic Church. Commission for Religious Relations with the Jews, 1985.

Instruction on Christian Freedom and Liberation. Congregation for the Doctrine of the Faith, 1986.

Donum Vitae. Congregation for the Doctrine of the Faith, 1987.

We Remember: A Reflection on the Shoah. Commission for Religious Relations with the Jews, 1998.

Movements in the Church. Pontifical Council for the Laity, 1999.

The Ecclesial Movements in the Pastoral Concern of the Bishops. Pontifical Council for the Laity, 2000.

The Jewish People and Their Sacred Scriptures in the Christian Bible. Pontifical Biblical Commission, 2002.

IV. The Papacy: General Background

Bunson, Matthew. **The Pope Encyclopedia: An A to Z of the Holy See.** New York: Crown Trade Paperbacks, 1995.

Collins, Roger. **Keepers of the Keys of Heaven: A History of the Papacy.** New York: Basic Books, 2009.

Duffy, Eamon. **Saints and Sinners: A History of the Popes.** New Haven, CT: Yale University Press, 1997.

Granfield, Patrick. **The Limitations of the Papacy: Authority and Autonomy in the Church.** New York: Crossroad, 1987.

Hughes, John Jay. **Pontiffs: Popes Who Shaped History.** Huntington, IN: Our Sunday Visitor Publishing Division, 1994.

Jedin, Hubert, ed. **History of the Church.** 10 vols. New York: Crossroad, 1986–89.

Jung-Inglessis, E. M. **The Holy Year in Rome: Past and Present.** Vatican City: Libreria Editrice Vaticana, 1997.

Kelly, J. N. D. **The Oxford Dictionary of Popes.** New York: Oxford University Press, 1986.

Martin, Jacques. **Heraldry in the Vatican.** Gerrards Cross, Buckinghamshire: Van Duren, 1987.

Miller, J. Michael, C.S.B. **The Shepherd and the Rock: Origins, Development, and Mission of the Papacy.** Huntington, IN: Our Sunday Visitor Publishing Division, 1995.

V. The Catholic Church and the Papacy in the Twentieth Century

Alberigo, Giuseppe, and Joseph A. Komonchak, eds. **History of Vatican II.** 5 vols. Maryknoll, NY: Orbis Books, 1995–2006.

Alvarez, David. **Spies in the Vatican: Espionage and Intrigue from Napoleon to the Holocaust.** Lawrence, KS: University Press of Kansas, 2002.

Barberini, Giovanni. **L'Ostpolitik della Santa Sede: Un Dialogo Lungo e Faticoso**. Bologna: Società editrice il Mulino, 2007.

Called to Holiness and Communion: Vatican II on the Church. Edited by Steven Boguslawski, O.P., and Robert Fastiggi. Scranton, PA: University of Scranton Press, 2009.

Casaroli, Agostino. **The Martyrdom of Patience: The Holy See and the Communist Countries 1963–1989.** Toronto: Ave Maria Centre of Peace, 2007.

——. **La Politica del Dialogo: Le Carte Casaroli sull'Ostpolitik Vaticana.** Edited by Giovanni Barberini. Bologna: Società editrice il Mulino, 2008.

Fappani, Antonio, and Franco Molinari. **Giovanni Battista Montini Giovane: Documenti inediti a testimonianze.** Turin: Marietti, 1979.

Fesquet, Henri. **The Drama of Vatican II.** New York: Random House, 1967.

Franco, Massimo. **Parallel Empires: The Vatican and the United States—Two Centuries of Alliance and Conflict.** Translated by Roland Flamini. New York: Doubleday, 2008.

Graham, Robert A., S.J. **The Vatican and Communism**

During World War II: What Really Happened? San Francisco: Ignatius Press, 1996.

Granfield, Patrick. **The Papacy in Transition.** New York: Doubleday, 1980.

Greeley, Andrew M. **The Making of the Popes 1978: The Politics of Intrigue in the Vatican.** Kansas City, MO: Andrews and McMeel, 1979.

Hebblethwaite, Peter. **Paul VI: The First Modern Pope.** New York: Paulist Press, 1993.

Herbstrith, Waltraud. **Edith Stein: A Biography.** San Francisco: Harper & Row, 1985.

Koehler, John. **Spies in the Vatican: The Soviet Union's Cold War Against the Catholic Church.** New York: Pegasus Books, 2009.

Küng, Hans. **The Council: Reform and Reunion.** Garden City, NY: Doubleday Image Books, 1965.

Latourelle, Rene, ed. **Vatican II: Assessment and Perspectives—Twenty-Five Years After (1962–1987)** 3 vols. Mahwah, NJ: Paulist Press, 1989.

McDowell, Bart. **Inside the Vatican.** Washington, DC: National Geographic Society, 1991.

Minerbi, Sergio I. **The Vatican and Zionism.** New York: Oxford University Press, 1990.

Nicholson, R. James. **The United States and the Holy See: The Long Road.** Rome: Trenta Giorni Società Cooperativa, 2004.

Pontificio Comitato di Scienza Storiche. **Pio XII: L'Uomo e il Pontificato 1876–1958.** Rome: Libreria Editrice Vaticana, 2008.

Reese, Thomas, J., S.J. **Inside the Vatican.** Cambridge, MA: Harvard University Press, 1996.

Rhodes, Anthony. **The Vatican in the Age of the Dictators 1922–1945.** New York: Holt, Rinehart and Winston, 1973.

Riccardi, Andrea. **Il Potere del Papa da Pio XII a Giovanni Paolo II.** Rome: Editori Laterza, 1993.

Roberson, Ronald G., C.S.P. **The Eastern Christian Churches: A Brief Survey.** 6th ed. Rome: Edizioni "Orientalia Christiana," 1999.

Santini, Alceste. **Agostino Casaroli: Uomo del dialogo.** Milano: Edizioni San Paolo, 1993.

Stehle, Hansjakob. **Eastern Politics of the Vatican 1917–1979.** Athens, OH: Ohio University Press, 1981.

Stein, Edith. **Life in a Jewish Family 1891–1916: An Autobiography.** Washington, DC: ICS Publications, 1986.

———. **Self-Portrait in Letters 1916–1942.** Washington, DC: ICS Publications, 1993.

The Teachings of Modern Roman Catholicism on Law, Politics, and Human Nature. Edited by John Witte, Jr., and Frank S. Alexander. New York: Columbia University Press, 2007.

Vereb, Jerome-Michael, C.P. **"Because He was a German!" Cardinal Bea and the Origins of Roman Catholic Engagement in the Ecumenical Movement.** Grand Rapids, MI: Eerdmans, 2006.

Wiltgen, Ralph M., S.V.D. **The Rhine Flows into the Tiber: The Hidden Council.** New York: Hawthorn Books, 1967.

VI. Issues in Contemporary Catholicism

Balthasar, Hans Urs von. **The Office of Peter and the Structure of the Church.** San Francisco: Ignatius Press, 1986.

——. **Dare We Hope "That All Men Be Saved"?—With a Short Discourse on Hell.** San Francisco: Ignatius Press, 1988.

——. **In the Fullness of Faith: On the Centrality of the Distinctively Catholic.** San Francisco: Ignatius Press, 1988.

Bartoszewski, Władysław T. **The Convent at Auschwitz.** New York: George Braziller, Inc., 1991.

Becker, Joseph M., S.J. **The Re-Formed Jesuits: A History of Changes in Jesuit Formation During the Decade 1965–1975.** 2 vols. San Francisco: Ignatius Press, 1992, 1997.

Berger, Peter L., and Richard John Neuhaus, eds. **Against the World for the World: The Hartford Appeal and the Future of American Religion.** New York: Seabury Press, 1976.

Carey, Ann. **Sisters in Crisis.** Huntington, IN: Our Sunday Visitor Publishing Division, 1997.

Curran, Charles. **Faithful Dissent.** Kansas City, MO: Sheed and Ward, 1986.

——. **Toward an American Catholic Moral Theology.** Notre Dame, IN: University of Notre Dame Press, 1987.

De Lubac, Henri, S.J. **At the Service of the Church.** San Francisco: Ignatius Press, 1993.

——. **The Drama of Atheist Humanism.** San Francisco: Ignatius Press, 1995.

————. **Theology in History.** San Francisco: Ignatius Press, 1996.

Neuhaus, Richard John. **The Catholic Moment: The Paradox of the Church in the Postmodern World.** San Francisco: Harper & Row, 1987; revised paperback edition, 1990.

————. **Doing Well and Doing Good: The Challenge to the Christian Capitalist.** New York: Doubleday, 1992.

————. **Appointment in Rome: The Church in America Awakening.** New York: Crossroad, 1999.

Novak, David. **Jewish-Christian Dialogue: A Jewish Justification.** New York: Oxford University Press, 1989.

Oakes, Edward T., S.J. **Pattern of Redemption: The Theology of Hans Urs von Balthasar.** New York: Continuum, 1994.

Oliver, Robert W. **The Vocation of the Laity to Evangelization: An Ecclesiological Inquiry into the Synod on the Laity (1987),** Christifideles laici **(1989), and Documents of the NCCB (1987–1996).** Rome: Editrice Pontificia Università Gregoriana, 1997.

Pasotti, Ezekiel. **The Neocatechumenal Way According to Paul VI and John Paul II.** Middleborough, UK: St. Paul's, 1996.

Pinckaers, Servais, O.P. **The Sources of Christian Ethics.** Washington, DC: Catholic University of America Press, 1995.

————. **Morality: The Catholic View.** Translated by Michael Sherwin, O.P. South Bend, IN: St. Augustine's Press, 2001.

————. **The Pinckaers Reader: Renewing Thomistic**

Moral Theology. Edited by John Berkman and Craig Steven Titus. Washington, DC: Catholic University of America Press, 2005.

Ratzinger, Joseph. **Principles of Catholic Theology: Building Stones for a Fundamental Theology.** San Francisco: Ignatius Press, 1987.

———. **Milestones: Memoirs 1927–1977.** San Francisco: Ignatius Press, 1998.

———. **Eschatology: Death and Eternal Life,** 2nd ed. Translated by Aidan Nichols, O.P., and Michael Waldstein. Washington, DC: Catholic University of America Press, 2007.

Ratzinger, Joseph, and Jürgen Habermas. **Dialectics of Secularization: On Reason and Religion.** San Francisco: Ignatius Press, 2006.

Ratzinger, Joseph, and Vittorio Messori. **The Ratzinger Report: An Exclusive Interview on the State of the Church.** San Francisco: Ignatius Press, 1995.

Ratzinger, Joseph, and Marcello Pera. **Without Roots: The West, Relativism, Christianity, Islam.** New York: Basic Books, 2006.

Ratzinger, Joseph, and Peter Seewald. **Salt of the Earth: The Church at the End of the Millennium.** San Francisco: Ignatius Press, 1997.

———. **God and the World: Believing and Living in Our Time.** San Francisco: Ignatius Press, 2000.

Smith, Janet E. "Humanae Vitae": **A Generation Later.** Washington, DC: Catholic University of America Press, 1991.

Weigel, George. **The Courage To Be Catholic: Crisis, Reform, and the Future of the Church.** New York: Basic Books, 2002.

————. **Against the Grain: Christianity and Democracy, War and Peace.** New York: Crossroad, 2008.

Woodward, Kenneth L. **Making Saints: How the Catholic Church Determines Who Becomes a Saint, Who Doesn't, and Why.** New York: Simon and Schuster, 1996.

VII. The Catholic Church in Central and Eastern Europe, the Cold War, and the Revolution of 1989

Anderson, Martin, and Annelise Anderson. **Reagan's Secret War: The Untold Story of His Fight to Save the World from Nuclear Disaster.** New York: Crown, 2009.

Andrew, Christopher, and Vasili Mitrokhin. **The Sword and the Shield: The Mitrokhin Archive and the Secret History of the KGB.** New York: Basic Books, 2001.

————. **The World Was Going Our Way: The KGB and the Battle for the Third World.** New York: Basic Books, 2005.

Baran, Zbigniew, and William Brand. **Cracow: Dialogue of Traditions.** Kraków: Znak, 1991.

Between East and West: Writings from "Kultura." Edited by Robert Kostrzewa. New York: Hill and Wang, 1990.

Biskup Herbert Bednorz—życie i posługa czwartego biskupa katowickiego. Katowice: Księgarnia św. Jacka, 2008.

Bociurkiw, Bohdan R. **The Ukrainian Greek Catholic Church and the Soviet State, 1939–1950.** Edmonton: Canadian Institute of Ukrainian Studies Press, 1996.

Bourdeaux, Michael. **The Gospel's Triumph over Communism.** Minneapolis: Bethany House Publishers, 1991.

Broun, Janice, ed. **Conscience and Captivity: Religion in Eastern Europe.** Washington, DC: Ethics and Public Policy Center, 1988.

A Carnival Under Sentence: Solidarność 1980–1981. Warsaw: KARTA Centre/City of Warsaw Museum of History, 2006.

Chronicle of the Catholic Church in Lithuania. (Multiple issues, 1979–1988).

Courtois, Stéphane, et al. **The Black Book of Communism: Crimes, Terror, Repression.** Cambridge, MA: Harvard University Press, 1999.

Curp, T. David. **A Clean Sweep? The Politics of Ethnic Cleansing in Western Poland, 1945–1960.** Rochester, NY: University of Rochester Press, 2006.

Davies, Norman. **God's Playground: A History of Poland.** 2 vols. New York: Columbia University Press, 1982.

———. **Heart of Europe: A Short History of Poland.** Oxford: Oxford University Press, 1984.

———. **Rising '44: The Battle for Warsaw.** New York: Viking, 2003.

———. **White Eagle, Red Star: The Polish-Soviet War 1919–1920 and the "Miracle on the Vistula."** London: Pimlico, 2003.

Garton Ash, Timothy. **The Polish Revolution: Solidarity.** Sevenoaks, UK: Hodder and Stoughton, 1985.

————. **The Uses of Adversity: Essays on the Fate of Central Europe.** New York: Vintage Books, 1990.

————. **We the People: The Revolution of '89 Witnessed in Warsaw, Budapest, Berlin and Prague.** Cambridge, England: Granta Books, 1990.

Gorbachev, Mikhail. **Memoirs.** New York: Doubleday, 1995.

Gromyko, Andrei. **Memoirs.** London: Hutchinson, 1989.

Gudziak, Borys A. **Crisis and Reform: The Kyivan Metropolitanate, the Patriarchate of Constantinople, and the Genesis of the Union of Brest.** Cambridge, MA: Harvard University Press, 1998.

Havel, Václav. **Open Letters: Selected Writings, 1965–1990.** New York: Alfred A. Knopf, 1991.

————. **Summer Meditations.** New York: Alfred A. Knopf, 1992.

Havel, Václav et al. **The Power of the Powerless: Citizens Against the State in Central-Eastern Europe.** Armonk, NY: M.E. Sharpe, 1985.

Kaufman, Michael. **Mad Dreams, Saving Graces— Poland: A Nation in Conspiracy.** New York: Random House, 1989.

Kowalska, Faustyna. **Diary of Blessed Sister M. Faustyna Kowalska.** Stockbridge, MA: Marian Press, 1996.

Krčméry, Silvester. **In Prisons and Labour Camps.** Bratislava: Milada Cechova, 1995.

Kubik, Jan. **The Power of Symbols Against the Symbols of Power: The Rise of Solidarity and the Fall of State Socialism in Poland.** University Park, PA: Pennsylvania State University Press, 1994.

Lewek, Antonin. "New Sanctuary of Poles: The Grave of Martyr-Father Jerzy Popiełuszko." Warsaw: St. Stanisław Kostka Church, 1986 (pamphlet).

Markowski, Stanisław. **The Cathedral at Wawel.** Kraków: Postscriptum, 1993.

Micewski, Andrzej. **Cardinal Wyszyński: A Biography.** San Diego: Harcourt Brace Jovanovich, 1984.

Michałowska, Danuta, ed. **" . . . trzeb da wiadectwo": 50-lecie powstania Teatru Rapsodycznego w Krakowie.** Kraków: ArsNova, 1991.

Michnik, Adam. **Letters from Prison and Other Essays.** Berkeley: University of California Press, 1987.

———. **The Church and the Left.** Chicago: University of Chicago Press, 1993.

Mikloško, Frantisek. **You Can't Destroy Them: Catholic Church in Slovakia, 1943–89.** (unpublished manuscript, 1992).

Miłosz, Czesław. **The History of Polish Literature.** 2nd ed. Berkeley: University of California Press, 1983.

Mindszenty, Joseph. **Memoirs.** New York: Macmillan, 1974.

Nagorski, Andrew. **The Birth of Freedom: Shaping Lives and Societies in the New Eastern Europe.** New York: Simon & Schuster, 1993.

NKVD/KGB Activities and Its Cooperation with Other Secret Services in Central and Eastern Europe 1945–1989. Edited by Alexander Grúňová. Bratislava: Nation's Memory Institute, 2008.

Nowak, Jan. **Courier from Warsaw.** Detroit: Wayne State University Press, 1982.

Paczkowski, Andrzej. **The Spring Will Be Ours: Poland and the Poles from Occupation to Freedom.**

Translated by Jane Cave. University Park: Pennsylvania State University Press, 2003.

Pelikan, Jaroslav. **Confessor Between East and West: A Portrait of Ukrainian Cardinal Josyf Slipyj.** Grand Rapids, MI: Eerdmans, 1990.

Pipes, Richard, ed. **The Unknown Lenin: From the Secret Archive.** New Haven, CT: Yale University Press, 1996.

The Road to Independence: Solidarność 1980–2005. Translated by Robert Strybel. Warsaw: Oficyna Wydawnicza Volumen, 2005.

Sakharov, Andrei. **Moscow and Beyond: 1986–1989.** New York: Vintage Books, 1992.

Sikorska, Grazyna. **A Martyr for the Truth: Jerzy Popiełuszko.** Grand Rapids, MI: Eerdmans, 1985.

Il Sinodo Pastorale dell'Archidiocesi di Cracovia 1972–1979. Vatican City: Libreria Editrice Vaticana, 1985.

Solidarnośći upadek komunizmu/Solidarity and the Fall of Communism. Gdańsk: Europejskie Centrum Solidarnośći, 2009.

Szajkowski, Bogdan. **Next to God . . . Poland: Politics and Religion in Contemporary Poland.** New York: St. Martin's Press, 1983.

Tischner, Józef. **The Spirit of Solidarity.** San Francisco: Harper & Row, 1984.

Volkogonov, Dmitri. **Autopsy for an Empire: The Seven Leaders Who Built the Soviet Regime.** New York: Free Press, 1998.

Wałęsa, Lech. **A Way of Hope: An Autobiography.** New York: Henry Holt, 1987.

———. **The Struggle and the Triumph.** New York: Arcade Publishing, 1991.

Watt, Richard M. **Bitter Glory: Poland and Its Fate 1918–1939.** New York: Simon & Schuster, 1979.

Weigel, George. **The Final Revolution: The Resistance Church and the Collapse of Communism.** New York: Oxford University Press, 1992.

Weiser, Benjamin. **A Secret Life: The Polish Officer, His Covert Mission, and the Price He Paid to Save His Country.** New York: Public Affairs, 2004.

ACKNOWLEDGMENTS

It is a pleasure to recognize those whose knowledge, cooperation, and counsel helped bring this amplification and completion of the biography of Pope John Paul II to the public.

In Rome: Here, the first word of thanks must go to Pope John Paul II. Shortly before his death, I told him that I would finish the task I had begun in 1995; this book is the fulfillment of that promise. As he had been during the preparation of **Witness to Hope,** the late Pope was unfailingly gracious as I chronicled the last years of his pontificate and probed his mind on a host of issues, dilemmas, and crises. At no time during this process did John Paul II try to bend my analysis or judgment in a certain direction. As it had been with **Witness to Hope,** so it was with **The End and the Beginning:** in the Pope's view, this work was my responsibility, and I was free to make the judgments that seemed appropriate to me. In the last years of the pontificate, we spent dozens of hours together over meals and in other settings, in the Vatican and at Castel Gandolfo, such that I was able to experience firsthand the remarkable witness he gave through his suffering and death. I treasure the memory of our conversations, and to honor his own unflinching integrity, I have tried to be as honest as possible in chronicling his late years and assessing his legacy.

Cardinal Stanisław Dziwisz, now archbishop of Kraków, was always gracious and helpful in arranging my visits with John Paul II; during our discussions, I often benefited from his insights, which were considerable (and occasionally pungent). Stanisław Dziwisz's self-sacrifice on behalf of the man he served for almost four decades drew widespread and well-deserved respect, and I am happy to add my own words of thanks to him for his cooperation and friendship over many years.

The prefect of the papal household, Archbishop James M. Harvey, was a constant source of insight, wise counsel, and good company, for which I am deeply grateful.

The faculty, staff, and students of the Pontifical North American College helped make the many days I spent as their guest very pleasant indeed. Some who were particularly helpful are acknowledged below individually, but to all on the Gianicolo—**Ad multos annos!**

During the drama of April 2005 I was a guest in Rome of the Religious Sisters of Mercy of Alma, Michigan, to whom I am most grateful for their generous hospitality. Special words of thanks must go to

Mother Mary Quentin Sheridan, R.S.M., and Sister Mary Christine Cremin, R.S.M.

Rome is indeed the crossroads of the Catholic world, and I should like to thank the following individuals for their cooperation in the preparation of this work, during their and my time in Rome over the past decade (ecclesiastical titles are current as of late 2009): Sister Rebecca Able, O.S.B., John L. Allen, Jr., Cardinal Francis Arinze, Cardinal William Baum, Alejandro Bermudez, Rocco Buttiglione, Cardinal Edward Cassidy, Cardinal Darío Castrillón Hoyos, Archbishop Claudio Celli, Msgr. James Checchio, Cardinal Juan Luis Cipriani Thorne, Bishop James Conley, Cardinal Desmond Connell, Roberto de Mattei, Archbishop Joseph Augustine Di Noia, O.P., Jean Duchesne, Bishop Brian Farrell, L.C., Archbishop Rino Fisichella, Archbishop Michael Fitzgerald, M.Afr., Father Kevin Flannery, S.J., Msgr. Anthony Frontiero, Msgr. Thomas Fucinaro, Father Robert Gahl, Father Daniel Gallagher, Father Alberto Garbin, Cardinal Francis E. George, O.M.I., Father Richard Gill, L.C., Ambassador Mary Ann Glendon, Nina Sophie Heereman, Cardinal Lubomir Husar, M.S.U., Gregory Jewell, Cardinal Walter Kasper, Father Mark Knestout, Father Uwe Michael Lang, Cardinal Karl Lehmann, Elizabeth Lev, Sandro Magister, Archbishop Dominique Mamberti, Father Paul Mankowski, S.J., Marta Brancatisano Manzi, Cardinal Joachim Meisner,

Father Krzystof Mięsożerny, Archbishop J. Michael Miller, C.S.B., Msgr. Christopher Nalty, Joaquín Navarro-Valls, Ambassador James Nicholson, Suzanne Nicholson, Virginia Coda Nunziante, Father Paul O'Callaghan, Msgr. Sławomir Oder, Cardinal Marc Ouellet, P.S.S., Cardinal George Pell, Marcello Pera, Father Thomas Powers, Roberto Presilla, Father Joseph Previtali, Philip Pulella, David Quinn, Archbishop Malcolm Ranjith, Ambassador Francis Rooney, Kathleen Rooney, Cardinal Antonio María Rouco Varela, Cardinal Camillo Ruini, Cardinal Stanisław Ryłko, Father Samir Khalil Samir, S.J., Cardinal Leonardo Sandri, Father Martin Schlag, Cardinal Achille Silvestrini, Msgr. K. Bartholomew Smith, Vittorio Sozzi, Cardinal James Francis Stafford, Father Jeffrey Steenson, Ambassador Hanna Suchocka, John Thavis, Bishop Daniel Thomas, Father Richard Tomasek, S.J., Father Christian Troll, S.J., Michael Waldstein, Father John Wauck, Msgr. Peter Wells, and Father Thomas D. Williams, L.C.

Prior to his election as Pope Benedict XVI, Cardinal Joseph Ratzinger was kind enough to continue the conversations that had proven so helpful to me in preparing **Witness to Hope,** and that were equally helpful in conceiving **The End and the Beginning.**

In Poland: I have now spent, all told, more than two and a half years of my life in Poland, where I have always found a cordial welcome. In the preparation of this volume, special thanks must go to the surviving members of the first generation of Karol

Wojtyła's **Środowisko,** who shared decades of reminiscences with me, as well as the books they assembled to create a public record of a remarkable set of friendships. Piotr Malecki and Teresa Malecka were unfailingly helpful in arranging for me to meet with **Wujek**'s friends, among whom I must thank in particular Danuta Ciesielska (widow of the Servant of God Jerzy Ciesielski), Stanisław Rybicki, Danuta Rybicka, Maria Rybicka, and Karol Tarnowski.

Part One of this book—the retelling of the story of Karol Wojtyła's forty-four-year contest with communism—was made possible in part by the scholarly courtesy and insight of Andrzej Grajewski, who generously shared with me many of the fruits of his research at the Institute of National Remembrance in Warsaw and in the Stasi files in Berlin. I am also grateful to Dr. Grajewski for his measured and careful reading of these and other sensitive materials, and I trust that my approach to the interpretation of these documents meets the high standards he has established in his own work.

I am also grateful to the following for their help in, or about, Poland: Paweł Adamowicz, Anne Applebaum, Alicja Baluch, T. David Curp, Rafał Dutkiewicz, Msgr. Marek Gancarczyk, Archbishop Tadeusz Gocłowski, C.M., Jarosław Gowin, Hanna Gronkiewicz-Walz, Stanisław Grygiel, Father Tomasz Jaklewicz, Elżbieta Kot, Father Jarosław Kupczak, O.P., Cardinal Franciszek Macharski, Paweł Malecki, Wiktor Micherdziński, Zbigniew Minda,

Jacek Popiel, Jacek Puchla, Bishop Tadeusz Rakoczy, Stanisław Rodziński, Radek Sikorski, Father Adam Sulikowski, O.P., Father Robert Woźniak, Henryk Woźniakowski, Father Maciej Zięba, O.P., and Archbishop Damian Zimoń. Thanks, too, to the members of the Polish Province of the Order of Preachers who, in addition to the Dominicans named here, offered hospitality and fellowship on many occasions.

In the United States: My thanks to Annelise Anderson and Martin Anderson, Joe and Lori Anderson, Joseph Bottum, Don J. Briel, Fred and Peggy Clark, the late Cardinal Avery Dulles, S.J., Scott Faley, Peter Flanigan, Russell Hittinger, Jim and Claudia Holman, Leon R. Kass, Henry Kissinger, Charles Krauthammer, Hugh McDonald, Jon Meacham, Archbishop Celestino Migliore, Bishop William F. Murphy, Father Jay Scott Newman, Robert Niehaus, Michael Novak, the late Jan Nowak-Jeziora ski, Archbishop Edwin O'Brien, Robert and Lydia Odle, Edmund Pellegrino, James Piereson, Father Ronald Roberson, C.S.P., William E. Simon, Jr., and the board and staff of the William E. Simon Foundation, John and Cindy Sites, Janet Smith, Father David Toups, Andreas Widmer, Robert Louis Wilken, and Archbishop Donald Wuerl for various insights, answers, courtesies, and support. I remain grateful as well to the priests and people of St. Jane Frances de Chantal parish in Bethesda, Maryland, with whom I pray and by whom I am nourished; Msgr. Donald S. Essex has been pastor and friend throughout both **Witness to Hope** and **The End and the Beginning.**

Elsewhere: I am grateful for various forms of assistance received from Father Iwan Dacko, Father Raymond J. de Souza, Theresa Krystiniak Gerson, Father Borys Gudziak, Walter Hooper, Daniel Johnson, Cardinal Cormac Murphy-O'Connor, Archbishop Vincent Nichols, Archbishop John Onaiyekan, Mario Paredes, Archbishop Ioan Robu, Father Thomas Rosica, C.S.B., Cardinal Christoph Schönborn, O.P., Anthony Sivers, Archbishop Beniamino Stella, Jack Valero, and Archbishop Rowan Williams.

It was my privilege to work with NBC News Specials during the years covered by this book; I am particularly grateful for our time together during the funeral of Pope John Paul II in April 2005 and the election of his successor. My thanks go to Joe Alicastro, Philip Alongi, Subrata De, Clare Duffy, M. L. Flynn, Jean Harper, Christine Jansing, Margie Lehrman, Mark Lukasiewicz, Jim Maceda, Keith Miller, Mimi Mouakad, Elena Nachmanoff, Michele Neubert, Beth O'Connell, Marjorie Weeke, Stephen Weeke, and Brian Williams.

Father Wojciech Kania, Magdalena Koc, Szymon Malecki, Ashley Morrow, Paula Olearnik, and Father John Rock, S.J., were most helpful with translations from German, Polish, and Russian.

Father Richard John Neuhaus, who did not live to see this book either completed or published, was, until his death in January 2009, a steady source of insight into the accomplishment of Pope John Paul II.

M. Edward Whelan III and my colleagues at the Ethics and Public Policy Center are as supportive a group of colleagues as could be imagined. My assistants during the years covered by this book, Carrie Gress Stibora and Stephen White, were especially helpful.

Loretta Barrett, my literary agent, has believed in this project since 1995, and I am grateful for her wise counsel and support. Bill Barry and Steve Rubin brought me to Doubleday, and I thank both of them for their confidence in my work. It has been a pleasure to work with Trace Murphy; Gary Jansen's superb editorial skills are accompanied by great good humor. Special thanks to Tricia Wygal, Maggie Carr, and Maureen Clark for their superb production editing, copyediting, and proofreading skills.

I owe an enormous debt of gratitude to my wife, Joan, and to my children, Gwyneth, Monica, and Stephen, for the patience, love, and stamina they have all displayed during the fifteen years I worked on the biography of Pope John Paul II—a debt that came to include my son-in-law, Robert Susil, and Robert and Gwyneth's son, William, when they entered the family circle. Robert died on February 5, 2010, after a heroic battle with cancer during which he conducted himself with the kind of grace and courage displayed by John Paul II in his own protracted suffering. It is a privilege to dedicate **The**

End and the Beginning to the memory of a Christian gentleman, a brilliant young scientist, a model husband and father, and a beloved son-in-law: Robert Charles Susil.

Neither **The End and the Beginning** nor **Witness to Hope** is an authorized biography: no one in the Vatican, or indeed anywhere else, had vetting rights, nor would I have granted any. In both volumes, this telling of the story of Pope John Paul II has been made possible by the cooperation of many, many people; I hope their assistance has made my rendering of events as authoritative as possible. The final responsibility for the narrative, analysis, and judgments in both books is, however, mine alone.

G.W.
April 4, 2010
Easter Sunday

INDEX

About the Author

GEORGE WEIGEL, Distinguished Senior Fellow of Washington's Ethics and Public Policy Center, is one of the world's leading authorities on the Catholic Church. The Vatican analyst for NBC News, Weigel is the author of fifteen books, including the New York Times bestseller **Witness to Hope: The Biography of Pope John Paul II**. His work has been translated into more than a dozen languages.

For more information on the author, visit www.eppc.org.